THE GLOBAL STRUCTURE OF FINANCIAL MARKETS

Financial markets have been revolutionized by megaspeed transmission technology and the integration of regional economic blocs. The global village has become a reality as markets are connected across nations by the invisible hand of worldwide trade.

The Global Structure of Financial Markets uses the original research of experienced contributors to explore these recent changes. Areas discussed include Latin America, Europe, the USA, Mexico and India. The book updates issues including:

- Risk and its minimization
- Business enterprise on world markets
- Capital flows and capital flight
- Offshore markets
- Central bank intervention

This new research sharpens ongoing debates and offers insights into the untouched areas of less-developed and just-emerging economies. The book's rare theoretical and empirical depth will make it invaluable to scholars, policy-makers and market analysts.

Dilip K. Ghosh is Professor of Finance at Suffolk University and editor of *The International Journal of Finance*. He is also the author of ten books on finance.

Edgar Ortiz is Professor of Finance at Universidad Nacional Autonoma de Mexico. He is on the board of several academic journals, including the *International Journal of Finance*. He is President of the International Society for the Intercommunication of New Ideas.

ROUTLEDGE STUDIES IN INTERNATIONAL BUSINESS AND THE WORLD ECONOMY

THE GLOBAL STRUCTURE OF FINANCIAL MARKETS

An overview

Edited by Dilip K. Ghosh
and Edgar Ortiz

London and New York

First published 1997
by Routledge
11 New Fetter Lane, London EC4P 4EE

Simultaneously published in the USA and Canada
by Routledge
29 West 35th Street, New York, NY 10001

Typeset in Times by
J&L Composition Ltd, Filey, North Yorkshire

Printed and bound in Great Britain by
Mackays of Chatham PLC, Chatham, Kent

British Library Cataloguing in Publication Data
A catalogue record for this book is available from the British Library

Library of Congress Cataloguing in Publication Data
The global structure of financial markets: an overview/edited by
Dilip K. Ghosh and Edgar Ortiz.
p. cm.
Includes bibliographical references and index.
1. International finance. 2. Captial market.
I. Ghosh, Dilip Kumar. II. Ortiz, Edgar.
HG3881.G5764 1997
332′.042–dc20 96–17468
CIP

ISBN 0–415–13549–4

CONTENTS

CONTENTS

FIGURES

TABLES

TABLES

TABLES

CONTRIBUTORS

P. Avgoustinos University of Dundee
Alejandra Cabello Universidad Nacional Autonoma de Mexico
Paola Caselli Bank of Italy
Arjun Chatrath University of Portland
Andrea Cividini Bank of Italy
Krishnan Dandapani Florida International University
Maria E. deBoyrie Florida International University
Vincent Dropsey California State University, Fullerton
Karen Duhala Florida International University
Ahmad Etebari University of New Hampshire
Gauri L. Ghai Florida International University
Dilip K. Ghosh Suffolk University, Boston, Massachusetts
Fausto Hernández-Trillo Universidad de las Americas, Puebla, Mexico
Susan Hine Colorado State University
Fred R. Kaen University of New Hampshire
Ramakrishnan S. Koundinya University of Massachusetts, Dartmouth
Alfred Lewis State University of New York at Binghamton
A.A. Lonie University of Dundee
A.G. Malliaris Loyola University of Chicago
Mary E. Malliaris Loyola University of Chicago
Gulser Meric Rowan College
Ilhan Meric Rider University
John Olienyk Colorado State University
Edgar Ortiz Universidad Nacional Autonoma de Mexico
Simon J. Pak Florida International University
Ali M. Parhizgari Florida International University
D.M. Power University of Dundee
Arun J. Prakash Florida International University
Sanjay Ramchander Coppin State College
Harri Ramcharran University of Akron
M. Raquibuz Zaman Ithaca College
Mariano Rojas Universidad de las Americas, Puebla, Mexico

Robert Rollinat Universite de Paris X-Nanterre
Steve Schrepferman California Polytechnic State University
C.D. Sinclair University of Dundee
Luc Soenen California Polytechnic State University
Frank Song Cleveland State University
Fahri M. Unsal Ithaca College
Jorge Urrutia Loyola University of Chicago
Benu Varman-Schneider Christian-Albrechts-Universitat Zu Kiel and
The International Finance Division, The World Bank
William W. Welch Florida International University
John S. Zdanowicz Florida International University

PREFACE

The world is indeed a global village. Technology, telecommunication, and financial transactions, among other things, have brought different people and different nations closer to each other. With such unifying factors the global structure of financial markets has evolved with continuum of change and growth. It is hard as a result to cope with this new and changing market morphology. Just about two years ago we did a book titled *The Changing Environment of International Financial Markets: Issues and Analysis*, and in it we attempted to capture the changing nature of international markets, focusing on different aspects and issues theoretically as well as empirically. We covered various issues on foreign exchange markets, international interest rates, covered interest arbitrage under generalized and imperfect market situations, analyzed balance of payments and international reserves, international lending, foreign debt, political risk analysis, and so on. But, while we were completing that work, we recognized that a lot more remained to be done. A serious and concentrated focus then led us to look for the materials that we must cover in the next project. After many hours of discussions and consultations with several friends and peers in different parts of our world, we decided to examine the global structure of financial markets. This book is the end result of our search and endeavor.

In this book, we have primarily brought out, beyond our introductory overview of this market structure, four sections of analytical and empirical studies. These studies comprise the following areas of research: global capital markets, global foreign exchange markets, global banking issues, and capital flows in the global framework. In Chapter 1, we present our analytical adumbration of global financial markets, and set the stage for other studies. Next, the environment of the emerging capital markets and the globalization of business are discussed. Risk is always the major concern for any business enterprise, local or global. Ever since the pioneering work of William Sharpe, beta has been the measure of systematic risk. Here an attempt is made to measure such risk by estimating global beta. Can there be perverse effect of globalization? An answer to this question is given with reference to Latin American financial markets. A specific Latin

American equity market – Mexican stock market in this context – is then highlighted and the effects of deregulation are studied. An investigation of the benefits from diversification and currency hedging in Latin American financial environment then follows. Next we attempt to ascertain the degree of co-movements of stock markets under the external shocks of market crash; thus such co-movements are studied before and after the 1987 market collapse. Like the market crash of 1987, the Gulf War a few years later, as many feared, created reverberations in the marketplace. How the external shocks emanating from the oil-region war affected market structures, and the link between equity and oil markets are examined in Chapter 8.

Part II – which is an examination of foreign exchange markets – begins with a theoretical analysis of naked and covered speculation in agiotage. In the macrostructure of foreign exchange markets, the unusual relation between currency depreciation and current account deficits is put to further scrutiny. Consistent estimate of exchange-rate pass-through for major European countries is examined. The behavior of exchange rates since the inception of the Bretton Woods System, and the various theories on exchange rates, are discussed here. Forward and futures markets, immunization of currency risk, and purchasing power parity in a new context are discussed and debated.

Global banking issues and ideas are also investigated. Studies on contestable markets in the context of the new environment created with the North American Free Trade Agreements, international transmission of bank lending and borrowing rates, effects of central bank policies with respect to interest rate manipulation and the impact of intervention on stock returns during ERM crisis, and the changing degree of domination by American banks in the global market are then covered in Part III.

Global economy is what it is today because of capital flows occurring on a regular and continual basis. In this set-up, research on the prospects on capital flows to the developing countries, direct investment outflows of selected OECD countries, capital flight from a less developed country into a more developed economy, arguments for increased investment in emerging equity markets, and analysis of capital flows and offshore markets form the final part of this volume.

This work, which started almost two years ago, has come to fruition because of a large number of factors, which include our commitment, perseverance and coordination, on the one hand, and the generous and genuine support of our co-thinkers, many of whom have contributed both with their articles and with active advice at various stages of the project. To them we express our sincere appreciation. Also, we are indebted to Khosrow Fatemi of Texas A & M International University to whom we owe a great deal for his encouragement and intellectual stimulation. We have selected for this publication a number of pieces, which were originally presented at the International Trade and Finance Association Meetings in the University of Reading in the United Kingdom in the summer of 1994, and so we express our gratitude to the Association. We would also like to acknowledge our indebtedness to Shyamasri Ghosh for her editorial comments and professional assistance in the selection and segmentation of various studies. Dee Ghosh and Debbie Ghosh have provided copious assistance in word processing many drafts of several chapters in this book, and for that they deserve our special note of thanks. We recognize that the project would still be in the conceptual state without the active and involved succor from the editorial office of Routledge, and in this context we express our profound gratitude to Alan Jarvis, the then economics editor, who not only took the burden from our shoulders at the right time but treated us with breakfasts and lunches in New York and Washington, DC or wherever and whenever we could meet. We must also thank Ceri McNicol, Joanne Mattingly, Alison Kirk, Geraldine Lyons, Alan Fidler and many other members of Routledge who made all the contacts, communications and corrections to enable the project to run smoothly in bringing the book to its final form.

Dilip K. Ghosh
Cherry Hill

Edgar Ortiz
Mexico City

1

INTRODUCTION

The global structure of financial markets: an overview

Dilip K. Ghosh and Edgar Ortiz

The global structure of financial markets is a major and yet a topical issue because of its practical importance and theoretical significance. The world economy was born with the dawn of international trade, and foreign exchange has had its own role in that economic activity from that time on. The Gold Standard, however, made the world economy effectively a domestic economy in terms of transaction units of money – the so-called *numéraire*. With the collapse of that system in the early 1930s, the blizzard in currency convertibility forced trading nations to invent and accept the Bretton Woods system. Tranquillity replacing turbulence of the 1930s ruled the international markets until the early 1970s. Anarchy and volatility induced by the breakdown of the Bretton Woods system and the Gold Pool that anchored the value of the dollar in the foreign exchange market devastated financial and trade transactions (Baillie and McMahon 1989). The conditions for the free fall of the American dollar, which was significantly realized in this period, finally gave way to financial stability, and the new global structure of financial markets emerged.

What is the global structure of financial markets? There is no unique answer to this question, and yet there are good answers, which we have tried to provide in this chapter. It is hard, maybe impossible, to identify the birth of the global structure of financial markets as we know it today. It almost always existed as it does now. Yet, on a serious note, one has to recognize the period when cross-listing of securities in different markets such as New York, London, Tokyo, Singapore, and so on, and simultaneous trading of those assets, came into being under floating exchange rates. The beginning of this structure can be identified with the visible forces of market integration or the disappearance of market segmentation. The dynamics of arbitrage make it impossible to derive any yield differential across national markets in a truly structured and integrated market set-up. That means a CDE equity traded both in Tokyo and London should and usually will give the same yield in both markets at the same point of time. Interspacial price

1

discrimination on cross-listed securities are thus ruled out by the forces of competition, given the fundamental uniformity in the national laws of different countries in regard to market operations or regulations. In fact, in such an integrated market structure, a dollar will bring the same rate of return regardless of its investment in one national market or in another and whether that dollar is put to use in one line of financial product or another.

The follow-up question then is: how well-integrated are these markets across nations? A series of serious studies (see, for example, Ghosh and Khaksari 1993, Koch and Koch 1993, Stansell 1993, to note a few only) examining the degree of market integration, or absence thereof, are already in existence, and the burgeoning literature on this question is never on the wane. All these studies and research notwithstanding, we do not have convincing evidence that we operate under a uniquely defined global market. Most appropriately perhaps, we should characterize our environment as the global structure of financial markets – a network of many markets – in which individuals and institutions, micro agents, and macro players access to any or almost any market independent of its national jurisdiction on a regular basis.

This global structure stands on the terra firma of several building blocks. In the broad sense, it consists of global capital markets, global foreign exchange markets, and a global banking network of institutions. We use the word *global* to highlight the interconnectedness of these markets and institutions, and here that signifies a distinction from the domestic markets *per se*. Originally, most equity markets traded securities of the domestic corporations, and foreign investors or corporations were barred from participating in such markets by laws and traditions. Several such markets still exist in several regions, but many of the markets are open to trade regardless of the traders' citizenship or residency. Exchange rate convertibility and hedging instruments have created climates of covered arbitrage and, as a result, most markets irrespective of their locations have become truly global. Offshore markets, eurocurrency, eurobonds and the like have tied the world together quite neatly, and virtually free capital flows have colored the landscape of financial markets. Although in many respects eurobonds are the replica of domestic bonds in basic features, differences exist underneath the indentures. Domestic bonds issued by domestic borrowers are issued within the jurisdiction of the domestic currency. A US bond (denominated in US dollars) is traded in the United States as a British bond (denominated in pounds sterling), is traded in the United Kingdom. A foreign bond is a debt instrument denominated in a foreign currency and issued by a foreign borrower in the country which is not the home of the borrower. If a German firm issues bonds in dollar terms in New York, it should be considered as a foreign bond. A eurobond, by contrast, is a bond issued, say, by a French corporation in the United States in the denomination of French francs. Currently, it is estimated that eurobonds are the

2

largest and least-restricted sources of long-term debt capital for public corporations. Still, a large percentage of this market is populated by fixed-rate straight issues that characterize the traditional domestic and foreign bond markets, but the growing number of these assets, approximately 25 percent of the issues, are floating-rate notes, and around 20 percent of the total issues are linked with equity. International equity markets, another component of the global capital market, consist mostly of the world's major stock markets and the emerging stock markets. Table 1.1 and Table 1.2 give the overview of these markets. As already noted at the outset, all these stock markets are primarily national exchanges as most of the turnover stems from intra-country trading. But, in the changing economic environment conditioned by speed of transaction and financial technologies, it has become as simple for an Australian mutual fund to buy and sell AT&T stock in New York as it is for a Chicago investment company. Differrent currencies, time zones, and different national regulations create some barriers in such transaction structures, but overall frictions or impediments are so minor that essentially markets appear closely linked and integrated. The British "Big Bang" of reforms and the introduction of Stock Exchange Automated Quotations (SEAQ) have removed many restrictions on trading rules and facilitated flows of securities exchange in London. Cross-listing of many securities in New York, London, Tokyo, Paris, Singapore, and so on has globalized the equity market significantly. In the academic literature, it has been repeatedly pointed out that global diversification yields better returns and lower risk for a portfolio compared to a domestic portfolio, and investment houses have recognized this academic research result through their regular practices. International capital asset pricing models have become common jargon in the global marketplace.

Along with global capital markets one can easily notice global commodity markets. We find that Chicago, London, New York, Tokyo, Johannesburg, and others markets trade commodities like gold, silver, soybeans, oilseeds, wheats, etc. in spot, forward, futures, and options markets. The cost-of-carry theory attempts to set up the basic relationship between the futures and the spot price as follows:

$$F_t = S_0(1 + r_t + c_t)^t$$

where F_t = futures price of the commodity for delivery at time t from now; S_0 = spot price of the commodity now; r_t = interest rate for the time t; and c_t = non-interest cost of carry, expressed as a percentage rate. In the global market context, arbitrage involving capital issues and commodities is a powerful investment strategy.

A second major building block is the well-linked foreign exchange market, which has most effectively helped the growth of the global financial markets. Foreign exchange markets are the vehicles for currency trade – the

3

Table 1.1 Characteristics of major stock markets

	Exchanges (volume)	Execution	Settlement	Regulation
United States	New York (80%), American (15%), Boston, Cincinnati, Midwest, Pacific, Philadelphia, NASDAQ (over-the-counter, screen-based).	Open outcry on exchanges; telephone for OTC. All share in registered form. Commissions negotiable.	Fifth business day after trade date. NYSE trades clear through National Stock Clearing Corporation. Depository Trust Company holds securities for its members.	SEC
United Kingdom	International Stock Exchange (London: includes Birmingham, Manchester, Liverpool, Glasgow, Dublin); Unlisted Securities Market.	Telephone/screen market (SEAQ). Must be through Stock Exchange member. Commissions negotiable. Most shares in registered form; physical delivery is normal.	2–3 week account period. Central clearing system, Talisman, operated by Stock Exchange.	Dept. of Trade
Japan	Tokyo (83%), Osaka, Nagoya, five others. Exchange has three sections: first is large shares (96% of capitalization); second is new or unlisted shares; third is unlisted shares trading over the counter.	By the Zareba (open outcry) method. Must be through member of Japan Securities Dealers Association. All equity is in registered form. Fixed commissions.	Fourth business day after trade. Clearing through Japan Securities Co., subsidiary of Tokyo Stock Exchange.	Ministry of Finance
Germany	Frankfurt (60%), Düsseldorf (20%), Munich, Hamburg, Stuttgart, Hanover, Berlin, Bremen. Official market supplemented by semi-official market with less stringent listing rules. Also OTC market.	Large stocks trade continuously. Smaller stocks dealt at a price set daily.	Two business days (five days by arrangement). Delivery through German banks. Settlement via regional clearing agencies (Wertpapiersammelbanken) or the Auslandskassenverein for foreign securities.	Stock Exchange Board

France	Paris (95%), Lyons (4%), Bordeaux, Lille, Marseilles, Nancy, Nantes. Three markets: Cote Officielle: large and foreign companies; Second Marche: small and medium-size; Marche Hors-Cote: over-the-counter market.	Forward market, some trades cash. Automated execution system replacing system of placing orders in pigeonholes. Price movement restrictions: 5% cash, 8% forward.	Forward: last working day of month. Cash: immediately after trading session.	COB
Switzerland	Zurich (60%), Geneva (20%), Basle (10%), Bern, St. Gallen, Lausanne, Neuchâtel. Three markets: Official: on floor of exchanges between members; Semi-official: on floor, in unlisted companies; Unofficial: telephone, interbank trading in unlisted companies and new issues. Registered, bearer, and participation certificates exist.	Open outcry for official/semi-official markets. 70% of trades are for spot settlement, but forward trades up to nine months possible.	Spot: within three days. Forward: last day of month. Stocks deposited in SEGA (centralized clearing house) and book-entry transfers made.	Swiss National Bank
Canada	Toronto (75%), Montreal (20%), Vancouver (5%), Alberta, Winnipeg. Over-the-counter market trades unlisted shares.	On the floor of the exchanges, through member firms. Automated execution for certain trades. Negotiable commissions. Equity is in registered form.	Five business days. Canadian Depository for Securities provides automated clearing and custody services.	Provincial Securities Commission
Australia	Australian Stock Exchange (includes Sydney, Melbourne, Adelaide, Brisbane, Hobart, and Perth). Main Board Market handles large and foreign shares; Second Board, small and unlisted companies.	Between brokers at trading posts on exchanges. Automated trading system in Sydney and Melbourne for actively traded shares. Commissions negotiable. Equity is in registered form. Physical delivery.	Five business days, normally. No official settlement period.	AASE

Table 1.2 Overview of emerging stock markets
(Third Quarter, 1990)

	Market capitalization (US$ millions)	Number of listed companies	Average daily value traded for quarter (US$ millions)	Price–earnings ratio
Latin America				
Argentina	3,438	174	3.16	−4.35
Brazil	24,907	584	17.56	7.18
Chile	11,216	216	2.82	6.17
Colombia	1,335	80	0.25	11.06
Mexico	27,998	205	52.65	10.27
Venezuela	5,219	66	2.70	19.33
East Asia				
Korea	93,886	669	233.53	19.12
Philippines	6,634	151	4.59	24.32
Taiwan, China	64,958	193	2,834.79	21.96
South Asia				
India[a]	46,412	2,471	86.36	27.04
Indonesia	7,109	116	17.97	30.48
Malaysia	38,143	266	49.56	19.93
Pakistan	2,832	473	1.03	10.35
Thailand	22,582	204	101.77	12.24
Europe/Mideast/Africa				
Greece	16,475	129	18.08	26.69
Jordan	2,009	105	2.67	7.76
Nigeria	1,400	126	0.04	5.96
Portugal	8,875	181	7.14	15.54
Turkey	26,342	100	21.74	40.10
Zimbabwe	1,853	56	0.19	10.09

[a] Bombay only.

swap of one national money for another money – through informal inter-bank connections or formal exchanges such as the International Monetary Market (IMM) of the Chicago Mercantile Exchange (CME), the London International Financial Futures Exchange (LIFFE), and so on. Like commodities, currencies are traded in spot markets, forward markets, futures markets, options markets, and swap markets. Forward contracts, futures contracts, options contracts, and swap contracts form what is more popularly known as currency derivatives, which have grown enormously over the past quarter of a century. Hedging, arbitrage and speculation have become the regular means to grow in the financial markets.

A spot contract is a contract for undelayed delivery of one currency in exchange for another currency. If $2 are exchanged now for £1, we say that the spot rate of exchange is 2. A forward rate is the price of, say, 1 pound sterling in terms of US dollars agreed upon now for the settlement of the exchange at a later date. If the 30-day forward rate is 2.15, it means that today two traders agree that 30 days from today they will exchange dollars for pounds at the rate of \$2.15 = £1. The futures price is a forward price with some institutional attachments, most significant of which is a daily market-to-market feature that mandates the end-of-the-day cash settlement via a tripartite structure involving the buyer, the seller, and the clearing house each day from the beginning of the contract through its final maturity unless the contract is closed out before the maturity date. Options on a currency are contingent claims, traded in markets for prices (called premiums), which can provide hedge and the means to speculate for the expectation of higher profits. However, options have spread their tentacles in all areas – capital markets, commodity markets, money markets. So options on interest rates, options on futures, options on options, options on swaps (swapsions) are widely available in financial markets. As we have inadvertently mentioned the term 'swap', it should be explained first.

A swap is a deal of exchange for one set of cashflows for another when the flows are denominated in different currencies or the exchange of a fixed rate of interest for a variable interest rate. When cashflows in dollars are exchanged for cashflows in pounds, for instance, it is a case of simple currency swap. When a fixed interest rate is traded for a variable interest rate, it is an interest rate swap, often called 'plain vanilla swap'. A mixture of these swaps is known as 'circus swap'. A more complex circus swap involving several parties, interest structures and currencies creates a 'cocktail swap' that eliminates the risk exposure of the bank or the swap dealer. Most of the swap deals that came into existence in the early 1980s onward are virtually the extensions of back-to-back loans and parallel loans, which became popular in the United Kingdom in the 1970s as a device to circumvent foreign exchange controls to stem the British capital outflows. Swaps are a design to hedge in global markets with different positions.

The current network of banking institutions across nations with vibrant corresponding systems provides another pillar in the edifice of the global structure financial markets. Originally, in a country like the United States, banks were in a unit banking system in which even cross-state border business was not allowed. Now, in the changing financial framework, colored and conditioned by the competition of offshore centers and forces of market integration, major banks are engaged in global business as multinational corporations like IBM, Coca-Cola, and others. Citibank, Barclays, and others are doing almost as much banking business overseas as they are doing in their home economies. Some estimates indicate that Japanese banks had increased their international loan portfolio by 300 percent before even the current decade stated. With Edge Act and Agreement Corporations, International Banking Facilities (IBFs), and the ever-increasing presence and growth of eurocenters, the Single European Act, and other developments have made globalization of the financial services industry a near-perfect entity.

In the worldwide web of international finance all the building blocks have created one unique edifice, and that edifice is the structure of financial markets. Individuals and institutions as borrowers, lenders, and regulators, and some of these participants playing more than one role at the same time, make this structure evolve more and more minute by minute. Let us illustrate one mixed bag of operations undertaken in this global structure of financial markets involving almost all three constituent blocks of the structure. Consider an investor who can borrow M from Citibank in New York at $r = 10$ percent for a year (or for a month). If he finds that international investment may bring him some fortune, he may exchange that borrowed amount of M for, say, pound sterling at the spot rate of exchange, $S = 2.00$, and get £(M/S), which then he will invest in the UK at a British bank at $R^* = 9.5$ percent (or in an immunized bond portfolio or some investment), and thus make £$(M/S)(1 + r^*)$ at the end of the year (or the period chosen), which amount he should sell in the initial period at the forward rate, say, $F = 2.15$, and reconvert his £$(M/S)(1 + r^*)$ into the dollar amount of $(M/S)(1 + r^*)F$. Subtracting the initial amount borrowed and the accrued interest, he now makes the net amount of $M\{(F/S)(1 + r^*) - (1 + r)\}$. If the amount is positive, he will do that, and if the amount turns out to be negative, he will borrow initially from a British bank, convert the pound amount into dollars, invest in the US, reconvert the dollar amount by a forward position, and pay off the borrowed funds and interest. If, however, the amount $M\{(F/S)(1 + r^*) - (1 + r)\}$ is zero, he has no opportunity in risk-free global investment. In the simple illustration, only the risk-free situation has been considered. If the investor does not wish to cover his position that will emerge at the end of the year, he will not take the forward or similar contract. The example is a case of covered interest arbitrage. If the investor wants to sell the amount that will emerge at the end of the year, it will be a case of spot speculation. More complex scenarios involving portfolios of assets with different maturities and variable interest rates or rates of return are usually handled in the global markets, and hedging or speculative devices are complex and numerous. International diversification in a pure form, and in its complex format, is often the project of our financial experts.

In this volume we study various aspects and environments of this network of connected markets. Developed and developing (often called 'emerging') markets are exhibited, and issues as old as diversification, risk assessment, deregulation, correlation and co-movements are the legitimate elements of our investigation. Often the question is asked: why would a market player move out of one market and move into another? Is it to avoid all the player's eggs being in one basket, or must something else be examined? Edgar Ortiz (Chapter 2) has studied the globalization of business in the context of emerging markets and shows why and how this nascent economic ambience is meaningful for a profit-seeking enterprise. Beta has been with us formally as a measure of risk since its debut in the hands of Nobel laureate, William Sharpe. Numerous uses and interpretations of this concept have been noted in the received literature on financial economics. International capital asset pricing models – an obvious extension of CAPM – have enriched our understanding of risk and return in the wider market context. In an earlier and yet quite recent piece, Prakash, Reside, and Smyser (1993) have provided a simple procedure to derive the best linear unbiased estimator of global beta under the wide-sense stationarity of random stochastic error term for the market model. Ghai, deBoyrie, and Prakash (Chapter 3) move further by designing methods to estimate global beta when some of the wide-sense stationarity assumptions are not satisfied. Here they provide an alternative measure of global beta when the rates of return on the security and market index are not measured from their respective means. This work thus modifies the Gauss–Markov measure of Prakash, Reside and Smyser.

It has already been noted that globalization offers more and more benefits with the world becoming a global village. Even though that happens to be the case, there may exist some perverse effects of globalization. The theory of second best is probably the reason for such a perverse effect when some deregulation and economic liberalization occurs. Rollinat outlines those perverse effects in the Latin American financial markets in Chapter 4. Most markets are regulated, and debate has always been touched off on the merits and drawbacks of regulatory constraints. Some regulations are lifted, and others are put in, and that appears to be the common experience in the financial world in particular. Interest Equalization Tax (IET, 18 July 1963), the Foreign Credit Restraint Program (FCRP, first instituted as a voluntary measure in February of 1965), which became legally binding later (on 1 January 1968), and other regulatory conditions were governing the markets and flows of funds. In the early 1980s, winds of deregulation started blowing in the United States. The Depository Institutions Deregulations and Monetary Control Act (31 March 1980), and the creation of International Banking Facilities (3 December 1981) came as two major deregulatory measures in the American financial network, and globalization got a new lease of life. How does deregulation affect market operations and efficiency? Cabello's study of deregulation and the Mexican stock market (Chapter 5) offers an insight on the issue, and, since it is research on a small country which was trapped under many pre-existing constraints, it has a special importance in this evolving new global order.

How much hedging opportunity does one get in less-developed soft-currency countries must also be a question of high importance from both the practical and theoretical points of view. Of significance too is the question as to the merits of diversification and the derived end results.

9

Luc Soenen and Steve Schrepferman deal with both the issues in Chapter 6. The turnaround of Latin American economies has been led by privatization and economic liberalization. Taking the viewpoint of investors in six Latin American countries and the United States, they show that five Latin American equity markets outperformed the US stock market from 1989 through 1993. The results show that diversifying in equities across Latin American markets was beneficial for US investors, but not vice versa. Currency hedging is favorable and thus useful for investors from Latin America, but not vice versa. Meric and Meric contend in Chapter 7 that low correlation among national stock markets is recognized as evidence in support of the benefits of international portfolio diversification. Their findings show that correlation coefficients between stock markets on a global scale (18 such markets being considered) have increased considerably – implying thereupon that benefits from diversification have decreased substantially – in the post-1987 crash period. It is further shown that the co-movement patterns of the world stock markets have changed significantly after the crash. In their Chapter 8 study, Urrutia and Malliaria investigate the relationship between S&P 500 Spot, S&P 500 Futures, Oil Spot and Oil Futures in the wake of the Gulf War – another external shock effect like the 1987 crash. Making use of the event-study methodology and Granger causality tests they confirm two hypotheses: (i) that the impact of the Gulf War was stronger on the oil market than on the equity markets (Standard and Poor's Spot and Futures); (ii) that there was an increase in the causal relationship between stock and oil prices during this war situation. They show that the high degree of diversification of the S&P 500 index lessened the impact of higher oil prices.

Foreign exchange markets are the most important ingredients in the weaving of the global structure of financial markets. These markets exist in organized exchanges such as the International Monetary Market (IMM) in the Chicago Mercantile Exchange, the London International Financial Futures Exchange (LIFFE), the Tokyo International Financial Futures Exchange (TIFFE), the Singapore International Monetary Exchange (SIMEX), in each of the major banks, in each international airport, and in many other cities of the world. Transmission speed, telecommunication technology and information superhighway provide the instant data transfer and real-time on-line data screen, and thus smooth out market misalignments quite significantly. Yet perfect synchronization is a virtual impossibility. The resultant effect is diverse and complex plays in agiotage. Recently, a series of studies have explored the feasibility of currency market arbitrage. Although numerous works on speculation are available in the literature, works on the practical design on speculative strategies are relatively scant. Ghosh fills up the niche in Chapter 9. First, the menu on speculative strategies in the absence of transaction costs and hedging are presented. Then transaction costs are introduced in the way these costs surface to an investor, and finally strategies on covered speculation with currency derivatives, simple and synthetic, are spelled out within the framework of theoretical analysis of a micro agent's rational behavior. Casseli and Cividini (Chapter 10) then move to the macro framework against the backdrop of the puzzling changes of the US current account deficit in response to a large depreciaton of the dollar, and discuss to what extent exchange rate movements are reflected in price level in both the short-run and in the long-run time horizon. They produce empirical evidence on the pass-through phenomenon for the leading European countries by using the OECD data.

Foreign exchange rates are significant catalysts in global markets, and so an understanding of their movements in the marketplace is of major importance. In Chapter 11 Parhizgari and deBoyrie attempt to forecast foreign exchange rates. A further understanding of foreign exchange rates should come from existing and evolving theories on exchange rates. Several approaches to the dertermination of exchange rates are known to date, and in Chapter 12 Koundinya revisits some of those theories – the asset market approach, the monetary approach and so on – and studies the record since the inception of the Bretton Woods system. One must remember that the foreign exchange rate has many types of quotations in the marketplace. Spot rate, forward rates, and currency future are often used and much discussed in both theoretical literature and trading rooms. Forward and futures contracts are often used to hedge and to speculate in currency markets. In what respects are these contracts different? Malliaris (Chapter 13) develops the essential elements of the conceptual differences between forward and futures prices and offers several computational illustrations. The conceptual differences are expressed precisely in mathematical equations which specially demonstrate the similarities and differences in these two concepts.

It has been noted already that risk is a big issue in the global economy. In our illustrative scenario we innocuously mentioned the concept of immunized portfolio without explaining it at that point. Dandapani, Prakash, and Duhlia pick up the issue of immunization in Chapter 14 and relate it to currency risk. By introducing Special Drawing Rights Futures they attempt to deal with currency risk in the field of international trade and financial transactions. In international markets where commodities and currencies are traded side by side, it should, under ideal conditions, establish the law of one price. This law was first stated by Cassel as the 'purchasing power parity'. Simply put, if a troy ounce of fine gold sells for $380 in the US, and 1,140 pesos in Mexico, then, barring transport cost and other trade impediments, one should be able to ascertain that $1 = 3 pesos. In technical expression, $E = P/P^*$, where E is the exchange rate between the US dollar and the Mexican peso, P the price of the international commodity (here, gold) in the United States in dollars, and P^*

the price of the same commodity in Mexico in pesos. Upon the logarithmic differentiation one then finds that $\hat{E} = \hat{P} - \hat{P}^*$, where the hat over the variable represents the percentage change in the variable. This is the relative purchasing power parity. It means that exchange rate appreciation or depreciation is equal to the difference between the rates of change in the price level (that is, inflation rates) in the two countries. If the inflation rate in the US is 4 percent and that in Mexico is 24 percent, then the Mexican peso depreciates by 20 percent. In economies full of many internationally traded goods and many non-traded goods, this relation is not expected to hold in precise terms. Many studies have focused on the validity of the purchasing power parity, and it appears that there is a sense that in the long run this parity holds. Vincent Dropsy examines this parity in the peso/dollar case in Chapter 15. Peso devaluation (and depreciation) has been attributed to several factors, and here Dropsy's study probes into this relationship by applying modified unit root tests and attempts to find out if deviations from the equilibrium relationship can be explained by exogenous shocks.

Banks are the most active financial intermediaries, and through these institutions a flow of funds takes place from the surplus economic units to deficit spending units. The Society for Worldwide International Financial Telecommunication (SWIFT), the Clearing House for Interbank Payments Systems (CHIPS), the Bank for International Settlements (BIS), and many such institutions and facilities, along with banks, their correspondents, affiliates, subsidiaries and offshore banking centers constitute the global banking sector. This sector get involved with and facilitates global transactions in all types of trade and finance. How do these institutions fare in the maze of complex operations occurring all the time? How does a nation's central bank perform in its regulatory role? Edgar Ortiz (Chapter 16) examines contestable markets and the activities of Mexican banks in the wake of the new tri-country trading bloc, popularly known as NAFTA. Mariano Rojas (Chapter 17) then takes up and re-examines the evolutionary structure of another Latin American nation – Costa Rica. Next, in Chapter 18, Chatrath, Ramchander and Song investigate the transmissions and interdependencies in bank lending and borrowing markets across 11 developed countries. Monthly time-series of prime and three-month negotiable CD rates spanning the interval January of 1972 to December 1992 are fitted to a vector autoregressive model. Their empirical results are indicative of significant bilateral interaction among the bank lending and borrowing markets. The German rates are found to have a significant influence on the European bank lending and borrowing markets, but are themselves Granger-caused by the US rates. Interestingly, the Japanese rates are found to be relatively insulated from the changes in the external rates. In the new environment of the European integration process, it is often believed that the Bundesbank serves more or less as the central bank of the European community. In Chapter 19, Etebari and Kaen try to determine if the Bundesbank's announcement on interest rates affected ERM equity markets. They show that German interest rate policy affected not only the German stock market, but the policy had its imprints on the ERM equity markets as well. In this changing environment it is worth examining the evolution of the multinational banking of the leading economy of the world. It has been noted many times in the recent past that the American banks have lost their leading position, their worldwide hegemony, in competition with other foreign banks. In the top ten list US banks once dominated overwhelmingly. But that dominance has disappeared in the 1990s. Hine and Olienyk, in Chapter 20, provide an explanation of the rise and fall of US banks in the global set-up.

Two things have contributed to the growth of globalization. International trade first, and capital flows next, or, more correctly, one feeding the other almost simultaneously has given us the global village we now live in. From the study of international economics, and in the comprehension of the balance of payments account of any nation, one may note that trade surplus (deficit) of a country *vis-à-vis* another dictates a capital account deficit (surplus) as an accommodating adjustment. If Japan has an $80 billion trade surplus with the US, Japan will have about that much capital inflow into the US (capital outflow from Japan). Is this the only scenario for capital flows? How these outflows or inflows work their way through the economy, and how meaningful this issue of capital flows is, should be areas worth investigating. Ramcharran leads the discussion on capital flows in Chapter 21. The rapid increase in private capital flows in recent years to the developing countries, he finds, has been due to market-oriented reform policies, debt reduction and rescheduling strategies, liberalization of capital markets, and privatization. It is argued that if such flows are to continue, then those policies should continue. The developing countries that are not attracting foreign investors should introduce such reform policies. The Zaman and Fahri study (Chapter 22) by contrast examines the determinants of foreign direct investment outflows of selected OECD countries and gives another perspective on capital flows.

Some thoughts have been presented already on how to attract investment funds into the developing countries. In Chapter 23, Avgustinous, Lonie, Power and Sinclair advance the argument for increased investment for a British investor in a portfolio comprising British and emerging market assets, and contend that this cocktail yields an advantage for the investor. Fausto Hernández-Trillo explores financial diversification in the case of Mexico in Chapter 24. Zdanowicz, Welch and Pak look at the issue of capital flight taking place from India to the United States under invoicing impropriety in Chapter 25. Next, Benu Varman-Schneider follows up the issue, and explains capital flows more as capital flight from some Latin American countries into the United States in consideration of economic efficiency and political and social stability by way of data analytic technique that captures the influence of political and social variables through efficiency terms. The book is concluded by a theoretical analysis of capital flows and offshore markets, in which Ghosh discusses the factors that influence capital flows in the macroeconomic structure and ties up the issue in the context of offshore deposits, liquidity, exchange and interest rate changes and the incipient effects on capital flows.

The global structure of financial markets is always in the growth mode, and to capture this evolving set-up is an impossibility. We have tried to present some aspects of this changing structure. Many issues remain underexplored, and many areas even untouched. A number of issues and important facets of the subject are covered in this volume, and it is hoped that this will enable others to pick up the remaining issues and/or to polish the ones discussed. It is in this sense we think our effort is a contribution to the growing literature.

REFERENCES

Baillie, R.T. and P.C. McMahon (1989) *The Foreign Exchange Market: Theory and Econometric Evidence*, Cambridge University Press.

Dwyer, G.P. Jr and R.W. Hafer (1993) "Are National Stock Markets Linked?," in *International Financial Market Integration* (ed. S.R. Stansell), Oxford: Basil Blackwell.

Duffey, G., and I.H. Giddy (1978) *The International Money Market*, Englewood Cliffs, N.J.: Prentice-Hall.

Ghosh, D.K. (1997, forthcoming) "Profit Multiplier in Covered Currency Trading with Leverage," *The Financial Review*.

Ghosh, D.K. and E. Ortiz (1994) *The Changing Environment of International Financial Markets: Issues and Analysis*, London: Macmillan.

Ghosh, D.K. and S. Khaksari (1993) "International Capital Markets: Integrated or Segmented?," in *International Financial Market Integration* (ed. S.R. Stansell), Oxford: Basil Blackwell.

Giddy, I.H. (1991) *Global Financial Markets*, Lexington, Mass.: D.C. Heath & Co.

Grabbe, J.O. (1991) *International Financial Markets*, New York: Elsevier Science Publishing Co.

Klinghoffer, A.J. and D.K. Ghosh (1984) *Problems of International Finance and Prospects for American Policy*, College Park, Md.: World Academy Press.

Koch, P.D. and T.W. Koch (1993) "Dynamic Relationships among the Daily Levels of National stock Indexes," in *International Financial Market Integration* (ed. S.R. Stansell), Oxford: Basil Blackwell.

Niehans, J. (1984) *International Monetary Economics*, Baltimore, Md.: The Johns Hopkins University Press.

Prakash, A.J., M.A. Reside and M.W. Smyser (1993) "A Suggested Simple Procedure to obtain BLUE Estimator of Global Beta," *Journal of Business, Finance and Accounting*, 20(5), September, 755–60.

Solnik, B. (1991) *International Investments*, Reading, Mass.: Addison-Wesley Publishing Company.

Stansell, S.R. (1993) *International Financial Market Integration*, Oxford: Basil Blackwell.

Tapley, M. (ed.) (1986) *International Portfolio Management*, London: Euromoney Publications.

Part I

GLOBAL CAPITAL MARKETS

2

GLOBALIZATION OF BUSINESS AND FINANCE AND EMERGING CAPITAL MARKETS

*Edgar Ortiz**

INTRODUCTION

Growth in trade and investments, important changes in production and technology, meaningful innovations in telecommunications and computer applications, and a generalized trend towards liberalization and deregulation of domestic and international markets have led during the last two decades to a closer and deeper interaction among international markets, e.g. economic and financial globalization. As a result the structure of financial markets has changed significantly and new international business opportunities, operations, networks and challenges have appeared. Correctly, changes at the end of the twentieth century have been identified as an early stage of another "great leap forward." (Tung and Miller, 1990). Financial systems from both developed and developing countries have been subject to change. However, transformations in the developing countries have been deeper because most of them were characterized by some form of "financial repression" and protectionism. Hence, those changes could be characterized as a systemic transition from highly state-intervened to market-oriented and open economies. In addition, financial transformation in the developing countries could be identified as a strategy followed to promote favorable links with international financial markets, and as a transition to higher stages of economic development. Finally, in some cases, this situation could be also identified as an about face from state-led socialism into capitalism. The domestic and international factors that impact the nature of these promising transitions need to be further analyzed.

A key component of recent changes in the financial sector from the developing countries has been the impressive growth and internationalization of their capital markets. These markets have acquired great importance for the mobilization of international resources to support the continuing and expanding needs of those countries to finance their economic activity. However, this role cannot be successful unless some local inefficiencies

17

that reinforce each other are eliminated. High returns and a favorable prospective, involving migrations to competing markets, have fueled a great deal of interest in investing in and studying the characteristics of the most successful "emerging capital markets." Nevertheless, the literature has neglected to examine the relationship and implications that inefficiencies derived from traditional patterns of corporate governance, asymmetrical information and weak links of foreign capital flows with the real sectors of the economy can have on the integration of those markets with the world economy. Possible instabilities due to the integration of the local markets with regional and global markets need to be assessed, too.

This chapter deals with those issues. Its aim is to explain whether globalized business and global finance contribute to eliminate the roots of those problems. The chapter is organized in five sections, in addition to this introduction. The first of these deals with globalization and corporate governance and agency problems in the developing countries; the next focuses its analysis on the problems related to asymmetrical information; this is followed by a section which examines the nature of capital flows to the developing capital markets. In the penultimate section possible impacts of economic and financial integration with trading partners and the liberalized world at large are analyzed. The final section forms the conclusion of the chapter.

CORPORATE GOVERNANCE AND EMERGING CAPITAL MARKETS

In the developing countries family owned businesses are still the preferred form of corporate governance. There is no separation between ownership and management. This is the case even for large firms that play an important role in the economy and for firms registered at the local stock market (Fischer *et al.*, 1994; 1995a). Often, these businesses have evolved into complex but limited size conglomerates, known as "groups," composed of rather small firms in different lines of business, many times without a strong relationship among them. The group is a multi-enterprise corporation that draws its capital and management expertise from the family and a tight circle of friends. In modern times, their presence was favored by protectionism, which led to the formation of natural monopolies. That is, monopoly profits due to protectionism allowed groups to secure and sustain a share of the market.

This form of ownership has brought about several types of inefficiencies that deter market activity. First, it must be mentioned that capital markets remain relatively small because the number of shares released to the market is scanty, because owners-managers do not want to lose control of the corporation. Second, it must be pointed out that firms become inefficient, and because of their protected inward-oriented production and sales, exports are low and group firms are not competitive internationally.

To adjust to changes in world economics, developing countries have liberalized and deregulated their markets and opened their economies to foreign trade and investments. Their inward-oriented development model based on "import substitution" has been replaced by a new market-oriented and outward-oriented development model. Financial liberalization and deregulation has meant an end to financial repression and enabled a profound re-structuring of their financial sectors. Five important changes in the structure of the financial sector can be identified in recently liberalized and deregulated markets from developing countries:

1 Emphasis on private financial intermediation. This has meant strengthening local institutions and orienting them towards market activity. In some cases it has also meant privatization of nationalized institutions, like the commercial banking system in Mexico; it has also meant diminished intermediation through development banking institutions. Following World War II the number and operations of these institutions skyrocketed, partly as a response to the lack of well-developed securities markets. Their growth and goals were often unplanned; rather they resulted from populist practices, and their administration became inefficient. Nevertheless, although their role was in general positive in promoting economic development, their overwhelming presence inhibited the growth of financial markets.
2 A generalized move towards "universal banking." Although specialized banking institutions still are an important part of the financial sector, most developing countries are promoting "multiple services" banking, "all in one counter services." This change has been prompted by the need to promote economies of scales and scope, and better and wider financial services.
3 The creation of new financial institutions, particularly non-banks. Since savings is the key to promote economic development, and for many countries the propensity to save has remained low, the creation of non-bank institutions has been seen as a means to increase local savings and investments, as well as to lower overreliance on foreign debt.
4 Impressive growth and greater importance and internationalization of local securities markets. Moreover, governments began using money and capital markets to fund government needs, to end with traditional inflationary alternatives. Corporations also increased their acquisition of funds from the local securities markets. Although banking institutions also internationalized their operations, and mobilized international savings to the local economy, the securities markets became in the late 1980s and early 1990s the main mechanism to mobilize international

savings to fund the government and local firms (Classens, *et al.*, 1993; Gooptu, 1993).

5 Increased participation of foreign financial intermediaries in local markets. In some countries this marked the end of total closure to foreign entries. Greater participation of foreign financial intermediaries has taken place in varied forms: outright establishment of subsidiaries or branches, acquisitions of local institutions, and joint ventures with local intermediaries.

Liberalization and deregulation, should help to end inefficiencies derived from protectionism. They should also lead to the formation of larger and internationally competitive firms. Nevertheless, global finance and the changing structure of local financial markets does not seem to be altering existing patterns of corporate ownership and control. Indeed, it can be affirmed that the internationalization of corporate financing is rather favoring further forms of capital concentration. This is because firms from developing countries have issued neo-equity titles with limited rights at international capital markets. Corresponding to this type of issue are American Depository Receipts, Global Depository Receipts, "neutral shares," authorized by the authorities and sold exclusively to foreigners, and country funds. Free subscription shares compose only a small part of shares sold to foreigners. The main reason being an overhang of traditional standards which limit foreign investment in local firms to certain levels, commonly 49 percent of total capital.

The limited vote characteristic of securities sold to foreigners has allowed local entrepreneurs to retain the control and ownership of the corporation. It is worth noting that in some cases funds raised at international markets have been used to purchase the interests of other majority shareholders, concentrating ownership and control in fewer hands. An example is the case of Televisa, Mexico's multinational television and entertainment corporation; following the sale of American Depository Receipts (ADRs) in 1992 its property concentrated in one family, displacing two other large family shareholders (Ortiz, 1996).

Furthermore, limited rights has also led to a lack of identification of foreign investors with local firms. Mostly they have been only interested in economic gains – high returns. That is one reason why investments in the emerging markets have been mainly institutional, carried out by mutual funds and pension funds with no interest in the decision-making processes of the corporations themselves. Finally, the permanence of traditional forms of ownership and control also implies that the growth of domestic corporations in the developing countries will be limited. Current owners are not interested in sharing control of the corporation with potential large shareholders from the local and international markets. Neither will investors seek to invest indefinitely in low growth corporations. All this means that the internationalization of financing of firms from developing countries cannot contribute decisively to the formation of viable corporations, large and capable of taking advantage of the opportunities open to them by global business. It also means that local firms will not face agency problems derived from widespread ownership. However, some situations, like unfavorable business conditions and greater needs for funds by local firms, could lead to conflict between limited vote shareholders and common shareholders. Indeed, since neo-equity shares resemble debt instruments, to sustain investment in local firms, conflicts will have to be solved through swap schemes, for instance ADRs for common capital, which would open the doors to foreign shareholders to a full participation in the affairs of the corporation, even as majority holders. Once this takes place, agency problems would appear and firms from emerging markets would enter a learning process to deal with them through market mechanisms.

The need for additional funding to support projects related to exports, as well as to purchase advanced technologies to remain competitive might force some groups to open up a bit to foreign capital. However, the initial stages in this direction would be rather characterized by the formation of joint ventures and strategic alliances. Thus, possible agency conflicts would arise between a domestic group and a foreign multinational firm. Many more years would still have to pass till emerging markets mature, and agency problems and other problems have similar characteristics as those present in the developed markets today.

ASYMMETRICAL INFORMATION AND FOREIGN PORTFOLIO INVESTMENTS

An important extension of closed ownership and management in developing countries is the endurance of asymmetric information. Market participants have unequal access to key financial information about corporate performance, or even to price and volume quotation information associated with securities trade. In addition to releasing to the market a limited amount of capital, owner-managers do not intentionally deliver key information to diminish challenges from potential new shareholders in order to retain control of the corporation.

The problem is magnified by the fact that accounting standards in many developing countries are frail or differ significantly from developed country norms. In addition, underdeveloped publishing and computer information systems, as well as underdeveloped corporate and financial market rating and analysis limits the availability and quality of information. Finally, unreliable macroeconomic data restricts the scope and soundness of country risk analysis and systemic risk determination, i.e. the relationship between local and international variables with market performance from emerging capital markets.

21

Besides local problems that asymmetrical information generates, it is important to recognize that at the international level asymmetrical information leads to extremely high required rates of return by foreign investors and to problems of adverse selection which can lead to important fragilities in domestic financial markets; in turn, this could end in severe financial crisis when international investors adjust their portfolios to overcome undesired risk levels and lower than desired rates of return (Mishkin, 1991).

Although asymmetrical information cannot be associated with all corporations from developing countries participating at international financial markets, it is important to note that difficulties in obtaining high quality information from underperforming borrowers or corporate capital issuers from emerging markets will cause good companies to end up paying high interest rates on their debt instruments and high rates of return on their equity issues, which is known as the lemon effect (Fischer *et al.*, 1995b). Cost of capital for these corporations would be abnormally high and might weaken their competitive edge. If these payments increase significantly because of increased demand for international funding, or because of some crowding-out effect on international resources, portfolio investments in the emerging markets would decline, which in turn would lead to a fall of corporate investments and aggregate economic activity.

Summing up, asymmetrical information at the international level lessens the confidence of investors, reduces the liquidity of secondary markets, thereby increasing costs of capital and transaction costs, which in turn leads to underinvestments by firms. Furthermore, since investors are affected both in relation to the prospects of emerging markets corporations, or else with respect to market and macroeconomic perspectives, financial fragility might ensue.

As a result what can be experienced in developing countries is remarkably large, indeed overgrown, capital markets, dynamic but inefficient and fragile. Weak efficiency might be present, which seems to be a general attribute of the most important emerging markets, but unfair pricing would also be present. Semi-strong and strong efficiency would not be present.

Similarly, inefficiencies and asymmetrical information make it difficult to monitor the market and to manage portfolio holdings rationally. For this reason, international investors, particularly professional managers of institutional funds, endeavor to cash out capital gains from their portfolios and to seek alternative investment opportunities in other markets, which increases market volatility. Finally, asymmetric information can also affect intermediaries such as dealers or specialists, which leads to wider bid-ask spreads, high commissions and floating costs, increasing market inefficiencies and the cost of corporate capital. It should also be pointed out that in some cases portfolio account managers from developed countries might deliberately withhold asymmetrical information problems to their clients to secure for their companies and themselves large profits associated with sales and purchases of emerging market securities.

To overcome these problems it is therefore imperative to improve information systems in the developing countries and to open up further local firms to foreign investors. Widespread ownership, which includes foreign ownership, and reliable and well-distributed financial information are key factors to promote the rise of internationally competitive firms in the developing countries, as well as the consolidation of efficiency in their markets.

REVERSIBILITY OF CAPITAL FLOWS TO THE DEVELOPING CAPITAL MARKETS

The rise of capital markets has been largely determined by massive capital flows from the developed countries, which substituted previous patterns of foreign debt financing. Four stages of foreign funding to the developing countries can be identified in modern times (Ortiz, 1996):

1 moderate borrowing from international official institutions;
2 excessive borrowing from private international banking institutions;
3 restricted credit during the debt crisis;
4 massive mobilizations of international savings for lending to governments and corporations, and equity funding to private corporations through the securities markets.

Following World War II, foreign debt from the developing countries came mostly from official international organizations, mainly the World Bank, the International Monetary Fund, and some regional development banks such as the Interamerican Development Bank, the Asian Development ment Bank, etc., and some binational credits established to promote trade, i.e. exports from the developed countries/imports from the developing countries. Most credits were granted in relation to specific development projects and careful cost–benefit analysis. Under this scheme, foreign debt remained reasonably low and manageable.

A new pattern of development financing appeared as a result of the limited resources of official international organizations, increasing developing needs, and the oil crisis of the early 1970s. Originally, this crisis, along with exchange rate flotation, due to the collapse of the Bretton Woods agreement, increased sharply the needs of developing countries to meet payments due to higher oil imports. Foreign debt was used to cover these needs, but this led to profound imbalances in the current accounts of most developing economies. However, the rise of oil prices also led to a high concentration of foreign exchange revenues among oil exporting countries. Since those revenues exceeded their capacity to absorb capital, they ended as deposits at international private banks – petrodollars. Banks allocated substantial parts of those funds to foreign loans to developing countries. Debt from these countries thereby became debts to private banking institutions.

Imprudent borrowing and lending followed. Countries borrowed beyond their capacity to pay. Bankers lended, omitting formal credit analysis. Loans were given to countries based only on country risk analysis and went to a general fund often used by governments to cover current needs, not to promote specific development projects.

Unfavorable conditions at international markets caused sharp increases in interest rates and a severe decline in oil prices. Although this decline favored oil importing countries, those two shocks severely affected highly indebted countries, particularly oil exporting countries, e.g. Mexico. As a result, highly indebted countries were unable to meet their international obligations. Mexico astonished the world in August 1982 when announcing that it could not meet its international obligations. That announcement marked the beginning of the debt crisis of the 1980s. Consequently, a new stage on development financing came about: restricted international credits. Most loans were destined for the repayment of existing debts. No fresh funds were available for development. Indebted countries restricted imports and increased exports, mainly due to large devaluations of their currencies rather than by productivity gains. But all revenues were directed to servicing foreign debt.

A new stage of foreign financing began by the end of the 1980s. The situation improved as a result of meaningful debt rescheduling, a cut in interest rates and in the amount to be paid, due to arduous negotiations throughout the years, and above all the Baker and Brady plans which favored large indebted countries such as Mexico.

Simultaneously, many developing countries had begun to undertake ambitious economic and financial reforms to adjust their economies, and to respond to the challenges of globalization. Developed countries also adopted some important measures allowing local investors and institutions to invest in foreign securities, as well as allowing the participation of foreign firms in their financial markets using neo-equity instruments, or else allowing private placements. This is the case of Rule 144-A, for instance, which opened up the door of US capital markets to firms from the developing countries through issues of American Depository Receipts and private placements.

In this manner funds began to be mobilized to firms from the developed countries, and their securities markets grew impressively. Financial liberalization and innovations paved the way for similar practices to become extensive in developing money markets. There, government securities were highly demanded by international investors, as in the case of the Mexican Tesobonos, a short term instrument tied to the value of the dollar. In brief, developing financing acquired three new important characteristics which contrasted sharply with previous stages. First, the mobilization of international private savings to the developing countries was made through securities markets, both money and capital markets. Second, the mobilization of international savings was not limited to sovereign debt; funds to support corporate loans or equity issues were also mobilized. Finally, international savings from the developed countries were mainly channeled by institutional investors. All this has led to: (a) the diminished importance of commercial banks in the developing economies, (b) a transformation in the nature of domestic debt, for significant parts of domestic debt have been held by foreigners, and (c) increased international reserves needs; in addition to regular needs for trade, transference, debt servicing, etc., holdings of reserves must also be sufficient to cover flows in the financial markets, which in some circumstance could involve massive withdrawals of funds from local institutions. This raised the question of whether or not private capital flows to emerging markets are sustainable. It also implied that since debt holdings became less important the possibility of another crisis of payments is unlikely.

Most analysts believe that a generalized reversal of flows, leading to a financial crisis, is unlikely. However, a "highly foreign financed" economy could face some problems due to short levels of international reserves. Many countries may experience volatile financial flows (Dadush *et al.*, 1994). One important argument against reversal is that half the flows to developing economies correspond to foreign direct investment. However, further analysis reveals that international portfolio holdings have been superior to foreign direct investments in the last few years. In addition, significant amounts of foreign funds correspond to short term securities from emerging capital markets. Any instability in the emerging capital markets induced by internal or external forces would therefore lead to significant portfolio withdrawals.

On the other hand, equity flows are also subject to reversals. Most portfolio investments at emerging capital markets have been made at the secondary markets. Hence, portfolio investments have not been linked to corporate investments. Partly, this has been the result of tight corporate control and the nature of "neutralized" capital sold to foreigners, previously examined. Economic short term gains has been the guiding motivation for foreign portfolio investors. That gives those investments the character of liquid assets. Moreover, large proportions of those investments have been carried out by institutional investors. Therefore, in case of an unfavorable situation, mutual funds and pension funds would make large withdrawals from their holdings in a faltering emerging capital market. It is also worth noting that equity instruments are priced at the market; the trend has been towards appreciation. Hence, remittances would be based on those amounts. That means increased pressures on international reserves. A

25

developing nation would have to count with higher amounts of dollars than those nations which entered the international capital markets earlier.

Thus, the determining factor as to whether foreign investments are in hot or cool money seems to be the link that those investments establish with the real sectors of the economies of developing countries. If the links are weak, no matter how large or small they are, their holders would be easily tempted to leave an emerging market when unfavorable conditions arise. If the links are weak, foreign exchange revenues from those investments would only temporarily strengthen the nation's international reserves. If they are not "neutralized" inflation could result. However, their use to support the external sector of the economy can also be harmful. In the case of Mexico, for instance, an overvalued peso and high imports of intermediate and consumption goods were largely supported with dollar reserves from foreign portfolio investments. An unsustainable situation (see Cabello, Chapter 5 in this volume).

It is worth noting that an international financial crisis cannot be ignored. The Mexican crisis of December 1994 showed that the expectations of international investors change drastically when one large emerging market fails, which also leads to defensive portfolio withdrawals from some other markets; this was the essence of the "tequila effect" of 1994 and early 1995. Negative impacts could become extensive to developed countries as a result of underperforming and losses in the foreign holdings from key institutions. Moreover, capital markets from the developed countries would also suffer a set-back because trade on emerging capital issues is made through them and their local intermediaries.

At any rate, a financial crisis originating from investments in emerging capital markets, limited to a specific country or a group of countries, would be of a different nature and would be played by different actors than in the debt crisis of the 1980s. Payment difficulties would arise because, as pointed out, large shares of portfolio investments in the emerging securities markets have been made in the money markets. To that should be added possible insolvencies originating in the bonds markets and insolvencies originating from loans made by corporate and financial institutions to foreign private banks. But the main thrust of the crisis would be related to massive withdrawals from the equity markets.

Concerning the actors, private international banks would still be an important interested party with which corporations and governments would have to negotiate a solution. However, the main parties would be institutional investors from the capital exporting countries, and private institutions from the capital importing countries. It is precisely for this reason that solutions will have to be market-oriented, with government support from developed and developing countries being necessary. The most feasible solution would be a new form of swaps, as previously suggested: exchange neutral equity for shares with full rights. To allow this mechanism to work, governments would have to liberalize their foreign investments laws. Since Mutual Funds and Pension Funds do not by their very nature participate directly in corporate management, the solution should also include the establishment of some sort of trusts, associated with the institutional investors, to participate in the management of the emerging market corporations.

ECONOMIC AND FINANCIAL INTEGRATION AND EMERGING CAPITAL MARKETS

The surge in capital flows to the developing countries has made them part of globalized business and globalized finance. Inefficiencies and protectionism still present in both developed and developing countries have prevented the full integration of emerging capital markets with the leading international financial markets. Interest rates and required rates of return between developed and developing countries differ significantly, underlying the existence of segmented international markets. Thus, in the case of the emerging markets, it is internationalization rather than integration which should be acknowledged. They have become valuable mechanisms to overcome financial segmentation. Financial opening has induced firms from the developed countries to acquire capital in foreign markets. Similarly, foreign investors have been induced by high returns to purchase securities from corporations from developing countries.

At any rate, the internationalization of emerging capital markets should lead to further international financial integration. For the developing countries this means that to take full advantage of opportunities offered by international markets to increase local investments, risks associated with integration must be taken into account. One important aspect that must be considered is the impact of financial integration on local business cycles. Integration to the world markets implies higher correlation with their movements, and higher affinity with the factors that influence market activity in the developing countries. In this respect, the business cycles of developing countries will begin to show similar paths and characteristics as those from the developed countries. An important implication of this is that conventional tools to overcome undesirable trends will not be sufficient. Indeed, the success of the policies undertaken to end recessionary conditions, for example, would largely depend on the economic and financial policies of the developed countries. That is, for the developing countries, due to the size of their economies, financial integration will lead to a loss in the effectiveness of conventional economic policy tools, particularly monetary and financial.

Moreover, since economic integration is taking place above all among regional blocs, this means that the small countries in a bloc would depend significantly on the monetary and financial policies of their large partners.

However, since large blocs have been forming as a "second best" response to promote growth, productivity and increased competitiveness of local firms in relation to firms from other blocs, it is important to note that economic and financial policies should therefore begin stressing regional actions. Economic and financial policies should stress the elimination of asymmetries among partners. Indeed, to built up viable corporations, policies for the entire bloc should be sapped. For instance, the North American Free Trade Agreement should be revised to ensure that Mexico participates fully in regional growth. Regional integration is essentially a strategy to promote economic growth. Trade and investments in the real sector need an adequate financial infrastructure. Hence, greater harmonization of financial regulations must be sought among trading partners, and market segmentations should be eliminated. In relation to capital markets this means that various mechanisms should begin to be established to end inefficiencies in the Mexican stock market, the weaker partner. This means, in affinity with the analysis here presented: promoting wider corporate ownership, opening up more local firms to foreign investors, improving corporate and capital market information systems, tying up portfolio investments to real corporate investments, the prevention of reverse flows, and the harmonization of financial regulations.

CONCLUSION

The dramatic changes in world economics and finance which have taken place during the last two decades have restructured the traditional composition of world financial markets. The new international context includes profound changes in the financial systems from the developing countries and the internationalization of their money and capital markets. Those markets still suffer some inefficiencies that prevent developing countries taking full advantage of global business and global finance opportunities. Above all, those inefficiencies prevent the growth and consolidation of internationally competitive firms. Moreover, those inefficiencies could trigger local and international crises, as well as preventing the smooth integration of developing economies with their trade partners and the globalized economy in general.

It is therefore imperative to identify and analyze the importance of these and other inefficiencies that feed each other and prevent greater welfare levels for the developing countries and for the world at large. Further liberalization of their economies is necessary, while at the same time an institutional mechanism should be created to eliminate asymmetries and harmonize regulations.

NOTE

* The author acknowledges support from Programa de Apoyo a Proyectos de Investigacion e Innovacion Tecnologica (PAPIIT) from Direccion General de Asuntos del Personal Academico de la Universidad Nacional. This work is part of Project "Ciclos Economicos en el Bloque de Norteamerica y sus Impactos en la Empresa Mexicana" sponsored by PAPIIT.

REFERENCES

Abkan, P.A. (1993) "Globalization of Stock, Futures and Options Markets," in R.W. Kolb (ed.) *The International Finance Reader*, Miami, Fla.: Kolb Publishing Company, 5–23.

Aburachis, A.T. (1993) "International Financial Markets Integration: An Overview," in S.R. Stansell (ed.) *International Financial Market Integration*, Oxford: Basil Blackwell, 26–41.

Chuppe, T.M., H.R. Haworth and M. Watkins (1989) "Global Finance: Causes, Consequences and Prospects for the Future," *Global Finance Journal*, Vol. 1, No. 1. (Fall): 5–20.

Classens, S., M. Dooley and A. Warner. (1993) "Portfolio Capital Flows: Hot or Cool?," in S. Claessens and S. Gooptu (eds) *Portfolio Investment in Developing Countries*, World Bank Discussion Papers, 228, Washington, DC.

Dadush, U., A. Dhareshwar and R. Johanness (1994) "Are Private Capital Flows to Developing Countries Sustainable?," Policy Research Working Paper 1397, The World Bank.

Dunning, J.H. (1993) *The Globalization of Business*, New York: Routledge.

Eden, L. and E.H. Potter (1993) *Multinational and the Global Political Economy*, New York: St Martin's Press.

Fischer, K.P., E. Ortiz and A.P. Palasvirta (1994) "Risk Management and Corporate Governance in Imperfect Capital Markets," in D.K. Ghosh and E. Ortiz (eds) *The Changing Environment of International Financial Markets. Issues and Analysis*, New York: St Martin's Press, 201–30.

Fischer, K.P., E. Ortiz and A.P. Palasvirta (1995a) "From Banca to Bolsa: Corporate Governance and Equity financing in Latin America," in D.K. Ghosh and S. Khaksar (eds) *Managerial Finance in the Corporate Economy*, London: Routledge, 291–326.

Fischer, K.P., E. Ortiz and A.P. Palasvirta (1995b) "Financiamiento Corporativo e Integracion Financiera: El Papel de las Asimetrías en la Informacion en el Financiamiento Accionario," in A. Giron, E. Ortiz, and E. Correa (comps) *Integracion Financiera y TLC: Retos y Perspectivas*, Mexico, D.F.: Siglo XXI, 371–402.

Gooptu, S. (1993) "Portfolio Investment Flows to Emerging Markets," in S. Claessens and S. Gooptu (eds) *Portfolio Investment in Developing Countries*, World Bank Discussion Papers 228, Washington, DC.

Mintry, P.S. (1987). "Globalization of Financial Markets: Implications for Asian Developing Countries," *International Journal of Development Banking*, Vol. 5, No. 2 (July): 3–20.

Mishkin, F.S. (1991) "Asymmetric Information and Financial Crisis: A Historical Perspective, "in R.G. Hubbard (ed.) *Financial Markets and Financial Crisis*, Chicago: University of Chicago Press, 69–108.

Ohmae, Kenichi (1995) *The Evolving Global Economy. Making Sense of the New World Order*, Cambridge, Mass.: Harvard University Press.

Ortiz, E. (1996) "La Inversion Extranjera de Portafolio en los Mercados de Dinero y Capital de Mexico y su Impacto en la Crisis Mexicana," in I. Manrique (comp.) *Perspectivas Financiera de Mexico*, Mexico, D.F.: UNAM (forthcoming).

Ortiz, E. and V.R. Errunza (1995) "Los Mercados de Capital Emergentes y la Globalización Financiera: Retos para las Finanzas Modernas," in A. Giron, E. Ortiz and E. Correa (comps.) *Integracion Financiera y TLC: Retos y Perspectivas*, Mexico, D.F.: Siglo XXI, 55–86.

Tung, R.L. and E.L. Miller (1990) "Managing in the Twenty-first Century: The Need for Global Orientation," *Management International Review*, Vol. 30, No. 1: 5–18.

3

ON THE ESTIMATION OF GLOBAL BETA

Gauri L. Ghai, Maria E. de Boyrie and Arun J. Prakash

INTRODUCTION

In a recent article Prakash, Reside and Smyser (1993) provided a procedure to estimate the global beta.[1] This was necessitated due to the fact that the beta, the measure of relative systematic risk, in Sharpe's (1963) market model is usually estimated in a single market context (e.g. New York Stock Exchange). The rates of return on an individual and market are respectively computed from the price and index movements in the NYSE. However, many stocks are traded in multiple markets with their own price and index movements. Hence using the data from a single market does not fully utilize all the information. Prakash, Reside and Smyser provide a simple way to overcome this. However, in their derivation they made an assumption that the rates of return on the stock and market are measured from their respective mean rates on return on the stock and the market. This assumption, though mathematically correct, may not be intuitively correct because the global rates of return, though unknown, should be universally the same but may in reality be observed differently in different markets. This chapter corrects this anomaly.

In what follows, to maintain continuity, we provide a brief description of Prakash, Reside, and Smyser's derivation in the following section. Next, the new Gauss–Markov estimator of beta is provided. Finally, in conclusion, future research areas are discussed.

ESTIMATION OF BETA: PRAKASH, RESIDE AND SMYSER'S PROCEDURE

Consider a stock that is being traded in market I and market J. Let there be k markets and

R_{it} = rate of return of the underlying security in market I during time period t ($t = 1, 2, \ldots, n_i$),

R_{It} = rate of return on the Ith market index during time period t (t = 1,2, . . ., n_i),

R_{jt} = rate of return of the same underlying security in market J during time period t (t = 1,2, . . ., n_j)

R_{Jt} = rate of return of the Jth market index during time t (t = 1,2, . . ., n_j). I, J = 1,2, . . ., k.

Let β be the global measure of systematic market risk. Since, globally, beta will be the same, the underlying return generating process for the security in the Ith market is given by:

$$R_{it} = \alpha + \beta R_{It} + \varepsilon_{it} \qquad (t = 1,2, \ldots, n_i) \qquad (1)$$

The number of bivariate observations (R_i, R_I), etc. made in k markets, that is $n_1, n_2, \ldots, n_k$, respectively, may or may not be the same as long as there is reason to believe that beta has not changed. Econometrically, if there is reason to believe that, intertemporally, beta might have changed if $n_i \neq n_j$, then the number of observations will be the same and observations must be made contemporaneously in each market. The properties of the estimator obtained below, however, are unaffected by whether or not $n_i = n_j$.

Since the interest is in finding the best estimator for β, the market risk, there is no loss of generality if we assume that the variables are measured from their respective means. If this is so, the return generating process reduces to

$$r_{it} = \beta r_{It} + \varepsilon_{it} \qquad (t = 1,2, \ldots n_i)$$

where $r_{it} = R_{it} - \bar{R}_i$, etc.

Using the method of least squares, the estimator of beta in k markets with $n_1, n_2, \ldots, n_k$ observations made on the stock, the multimarket BLUE estimator of beta obtained by Prakash, Reside and Smyser is given by

$$\hat{\beta} = \frac{\sum_{\ell=1}^{k} n_\ell Cov(r_\ell, r_{m\ell})}{\sum_{\ell=1}^{k} n_\ell V(r_{m\ell})} \qquad (2)$$

where r_ℓ and $r_{m\ell}$ are, respectively, the rates of return on the stock and the market index in market ℓ (ℓ = 1,2, . . ., k) and n_ℓ is the number of observations of $(r_\ell, r_{m\ell})$ in market ℓ.

A NEW GLOBAL ESTIMATOR OF BETA

We have the market model in the Ith market as

$$R_{it} = \alpha + \beta R_{It} + \varepsilon_{it} \qquad (t = 1,2, \ldots, n_i), (i,I = 1,2, \ldots, k)$$

with the usual wide-sense stationarity assumptions.[2]

32

Minimizing the sum-of-squares

$$Q = \sum_{i,I} \sum_{t} (R_{it} - \alpha - \beta R_{It})^2$$

with respect to α and β we have the normal equations as

$$n_T \alpha + \beta \sum_{i,I} \sum_{t} R_{It} = \sum_{i,I} \sum_{t} R_{it} \tag{3}$$

$$\alpha \sum_{i,I} \sum_{t} R_{It} + \beta \sum_{i,I} \sum_{t} R_{It}^2 = \sum_{i,I} \sum_{t} R_{it} R_{It}$$

where $n_T = n_1 + n_2 + \ldots + n_k$.

Solving the normal equations we have the estimator of α given by

$$\hat{\alpha} = \bar{R} - \beta \bar{R}_m \tag{4}$$

where

$$\bar{R} = \sum_{i} \sum_{t} R_{it} / n_T = \sum_{i} n_i \bar{R}_i / n_T,$$

$$\bar{R}_m = \sum_{I} \sum_{t} R_{It} / n_T = \sum_{I} n_I \bar{R}_I / n_T,$$

$$\bar{R}_i = \sum_{t} R_{it} / n_i \text{ and } \bar{R}_I = \sum_{t} R_{It} / n_I.$$

The estimator of β will be

$$\hat{\beta} = \frac{\sum\sum R_{It} R_{It} - \dfrac{(\sum\sum R_{it})(\sum\sum R_{It})}{n_T}}{\sum\sum R_{It}^2 - \dfrac{(\sum\sum R_{It})^2}{n_T}} \tag{5}$$

Defining:

$$SS_m = \sum_{I} \sum_{t} (R_{It} - \bar{R}_m)^2 = \sum_{I} \sum_{t} R^2{}_{It} - n_T \bar{R}^2{}_m$$

$$SS_{Ri} = \sum_{t} (R_{it} - \bar{R}_i)^2 = \sum_{t} R^2{}_{it} - n_i \bar{R}^2{}_i$$

$$SP_{iI} = \sum_{i,I} R_{it} R_{It} - n_i \bar{R}_i \bar{R}_I$$

$$SP_{g\bar{R}\bar{R}m} = \sum_{i,I} n_i (\bar{R}_i - \bar{R})(\bar{R}_I - \bar{R}_m)$$

33

We have

$$\hat{\beta} = \frac{\sum_{i,I=1}^{k} SP_{iI} + SP_{g\bar{R}\bar{R}_m}}{\sum_{I} SS_{RI} + SS_{g\bar{R}_m}} \tag{6}$$

Denoting the denominator of (6) as SS_m, sum-of-squares for the k-markets, $\underset{\sim}{n} = (n_1, n_2, \ldots, n_k)'$, the column vector of observations, and

$$\hat{\beta}_g(\underset{\sim}{n}) = \Sigma n_i\, (\bar{R}_i - \bar{R})(\bar{R}_I - \bar{R}_m) \,/\, \Sigma\, n_I\, (\bar{R}_I - \bar{R}_m)^2, \text{ and}$$

$$SS_{g\bar{R}_m}(\underset{\sim}{n}) = \Sigma\, n_I\, (\bar{R}_I - \bar{R}_m)^2$$

we have

$$\hat{\beta} = \frac{\sum_{i} \hat{\beta}_i SS_{R_i} + \hat{\beta}_g(\underset{\sim}{n})SS_{g\bar{R}_m}(\underset{\sim}{n})}{SS_m}$$

or

$$\hat{\beta} = \hat{\beta}_1 \frac{SS_{R_1}}{SS_m} + \hat{\beta}_2 \frac{SS_{R_2}}{SS_m} + \ldots + \hat{\beta}_k \frac{SS_{Rk}}{SS_m} + \frac{\hat{\beta}_g(\underset{\sim}{n})SS_{Rg}\bar{R}_m(\underset{\sim}{n})}{SS_m} \tag{7}$$

As one can see expression (7) is quite different in form than (2).

CONCLUSION AND REMARKS

In this chapter we provide an alternative procedure to estimate global beta when the observations on rates of return on the security and market are not measured from their means. The resultant estimator of beta is a weighted average of individual estimators of beta with weights being the ratio of the sum of squares of the securities rates of return in a particular market to the overall (global) market sum of squares. It will be interesting to obtain estimators of beta when the wide-sense stationarity assumptions are not satisfied.

NOTES

1 This chapter provides an alternative measure of global beta when the rates of return on the security and market index are not measured from their respective means. Thus, it modifies the Gauss–Markov estimator of Prakash, Reside and Smyser's (1993) estimator of global beta.
2 Wide-sense stationarity assumptions are:
 (1) $E(\varepsilon_{it}) = 0$
 (2) $V(\varepsilon_{it}) = \sigma^2_{ei}$
 (3) $Cov(\varepsilon_{it}, \varepsilon_{it+s}) = 0 \ \forall \ s = 1,2, \ldots$
 (4) $Cov(\varepsilon_{it}, R_{it}) = 0$

REFERENCES

Prakash, A.J., M.A. Reside and M. W. Smyser (1993) "A Suggested Simple Procedure to Obtain BLUE Estimator of Global Beta," *Journal of Business Finance & Accounting*, 20(5), September, 755–60.

Sharpe, W.F. (1963) "A Simplified Model for Portfolio Analysis, *Management Science*, IX(2), January, 277–93.

4

PERVERSE EFFECTS OF GLOBALIZATION IN TODAY'S LATIN AMERICAN FINANCE

Robert Rollinat

INTRODUCTION

It has now become customary to examine the changing world of banking and finance, the by-product of the worldwide process of liberalization and deregulation of financial activities. This historical mutation has been characterized by the International Monetary Fund (IMF) as a (global) tendency toward banking disintermediation and the development of stock exchange activities.[1]

In Latin America, rapid growth of emerging markets, privatization (or reprivatization) of banks (often implying traditional "development banks"), legalization for the "autonomy" of central banks, accelerated innovation in financial and banking instruments and so on must be considered as specific forms of this process of financial globalization.

Reforms have often been presented as an imperative necessity to improve the efficiency of financial systems. Banks have generally improved their activities in portfolio managing, taken participation in industrial or financial business and offered to their clients new services and instruments with which to invest their money. Since the early 1990s, new foreign capital flows have entered into most Latin American countries. There seems to be a consensus in accepting all these changes as favorable. However, have they globally promoted economic growth or hindered a balanced functioning of financial institutions? This question should also be asked in order to better understand those processes and to formulate stronger alternatives, when needed, to promote a more efficient financing of development.

Considering the present difficulties of banking systems in Latin America, especially since the "Mexican crisis" of December 1994, it is first necessary to recapitulate and analyze the different forms of liberalization during the last period and then discuss their effects on the stability and the credibility of these systems. The "old" regulations of finance have been questioned, but to avoid economic or financial crisis in the future it appears that it would certainly be necessary to establish new forms of control.

LATIN AMERICA'S FINANCIAL LIBERALIZATION

Financial liberalization processes in Latin America have not been the same in the different countries, but some common traits or evolution can be detected. Chile, Colombia, Argentina, Mexico and Venezuela began liberalizing their financial markets in the late 1970s, but those reforms did not endure the debt crisis and bank insolvencies of the early 1980s. In most of these countries, liberalization programs were completely reversed from 1982: the banking system was nationalized in Mexico; the faltering banking system had to be rescued by the state in 1982–3 in Chile. Similarly, in the mid-1980s, Colombia and Venezuela tried to reimpose interest rate controls to face economic difficulties. Peru adopted modest liberalizing policies in the early 1980s, but many banking restrictions were soon reintroduced, culminating with the nationalization of banks in 1987.

It is perhaps in Brazil where financial liberalization has been the most original to the point that it led to a considerable expansion of the market for indexed government bonds.[2] Indexation of financial assets also promoted banking activities and the modernization of their operations, but was detrimental with regard to the development of credit and incurred high costs of intermediation. Nevertheless, in Brazil, liberalization of the banking system remains restricted due to the lack of competition and the existence of barriers to entry in financial services.

A new period began in the late 1980s with the gradual return of international capital flows to Latin America. The most important patterns emerging from these new flows can be summarized as follows:[3]

- development of direct foreign investments due to the privatization policies especially in Argentina, Venezuela, and Mexico;
- increased importance of money and capital market securities issues (commercial papers and certificates on deposits, government short term certificates, corporate and private bonds, and stocks). Portfolio investments in these instruments account for almost 30 percent of the total investment flows to Latin America in 1991;
- reduced role of commercial banks lending to finance these new capital flows (with the exception of Chile).

This international context has had a great impact on the new wave of financial reforms that started in the late 1980s and early 1990s in Latin America. It can be affirmed that deregulation policies on the banking systems in Latin America have been kept in line with the overall world pattern of financial globalization. That is the reason why many analysts think of those processes as irreversible. For its promoters, financial reform was not considered as an end in itself, but as a strategy of articulation of the domestic banking system with other countries and the worldwide economy. However, the concrete forms and application of financial reforms have been appreciably different in the various countries of Latin America.[4]

In Latin America, Chile was the first country concerned with implementing these new patterns of reforms (financial reform of 1986). In Mexico, "legal reforms" undertaken during the 1989–94 period have led to profound changes in the laws regulating most of the financial intermediaries. The new laws on Instituciones de Credito (Credit Institutions) promote the creation of "universal banks," and create or strengthen non-bank intermediaries. Moreover, the banking system was fully reprivatized by the end of 1992. Similarly, the law for Mercado de Valores, the exchange markets, re-regulates investment banks and stock exchange activities. But above all it promotes the internationalization of local intermediaries and corporations at international financial markets, as well as favoring foreign portfolio investments and a restricted participation of foreign financial intermediaries in the local markets. The objective was also to make Stock Exchange transactions more transparent and to allow more competition to enter the market. The law also establishes the new profession of Stock Exchange specialist.[5]

The general tendency of new financial laws in Latin America is to permit banking firms to participate, directly or through subsidiary companies, in all credit and finance operations. However, although these reforms have led to a multiservices form of banking, a partial form of specialization has been maintained in most countries. In Colombia, for instance, "ley 45" of 1990 has preserved, along "universal" banks, traditional *corporaciones financieras* and *cajas de ahorro y vivienda* (respectively, investment banks and saving and housing banks). Similarly, "Ley Marco" 35 of 1993 defines the constitutional role of the state in regulating financial, insurance and banking activities. It maintains the provisional transfer of funds from banks to specific investments determined by the government (*creditos forzosos*).[6] Finally, in Ecuador and Venezuela, financial reforms have maintained, co-existing with the "universal" banking model, specialized institutions.[7]

Nevertheless, beyond their institutional consequences, financial reforms have not only led to a drastic reduction of the goals sought by past regulations (credit restrictions, subsidized interest rates, "forced" investments from private banks), but they have also turned upside down the old forms of property and contributed to the development of new financial structures generally more concentrated, with more complex relations between the different types of banks and institutions. In some countries they have generated oligopolist forms of banking, for instance in the case from the *grupos financieros* in Mexico, Venezuela and Colombia.

Thus, new forms of "financial enterprises" have emerged in most Latin American countries after privatization of banks and the deregulation of financial markets. New financial links have been established, often eliminating old familial systems and leading to conglomerate forms of banking structures with a global strategy for the valorization of assets.

THEORETICAL JUSTIFICATIONS AND THE IMPACT OF BANKING REFORMS

One of the arguments justifying the necessity for financial reforms in Latin America, in accordance with the "old" hypothesis of McKinnon and his followers, was that financial liberalization would end inefficiencies derived from "administrated" rates of interest, preferential credits allocations, mandatory reserve requirements to finance fiscal deficit, and other forms of "financial repression." It was maintained that a rise in interest rates on deposits and liabilities would lead to a significant growth of savings, as well as a more efficient allocation of credits, allowing the appearance of an equilibrium investment rate of return.[8]

In this context, the modernization of financial markets and financial institutions should also be viewed as a response to the debt crisis in a context of increased globalization. Many studies have stressed the role of capital markets and their decisive contribution to economic growth, increasing savings, and linking them with long-term productive activity.[9] The central assumption of this process was that changes would finally lower costs of capital and interest rates. Thus, plagued by the most severe crisis of modern times, the Latin American countries opted for liberating and deregulating their financial markets.

However, Latin America's recent experience does not confirm this analysis. Rather, the liberalization of interest rates has often led, unlike the McKinnon hypothesis sets forth, to further increases in interest rates and to the reduction of credits offered by banks. Liberalization was supposed to be a rational (non-speculative) behavior of economic agents. But in most Latin American countries financial reforms have not led to positive effects on private investment because, in most cases, monetary authorities have been unable to contribute to stabilizing banking deposits or to control successfully risky banking lending practices. And banking managers seem to have been incapable of keeping their institutions in a healthy state.

Some authors have affirmed that if financial markets were sufficiently open (if, for instance, national residents were allowed to hold foreign assets), the effects of credit contraction due to the liberalization of the rates would disappear because those assets could be repatriated and transformed into banking deposits, contributing to an increase of domestic credit supply.[10] It is also said that households could possibly accumulate more bank deposits by decreasing their demand for consumption loans as a result of higher formal sector interest rates, thus increasing global welfare from society.[11] However, this analysis also supposes the existence of efficient financial markets and the rational behavior of money owners, always ready to convert their "unproductive" assets (cash, gold, investments in foreign currencies) into bank deposits. Thus, according to this assumption, a stable and efficient banking organization is also necessary, which is not the case in Latin America.

In fact, during a first phase of liberalization in Latin America, the goals of fiscal adjustment and of confidence in the exchange rate system (generally, fixed exchange rates or tightly managed sliding down systems are used to bring down inflation) have not been purposely achieved, so that interest rate liberalization leads to adjustment through higher inflation and lower economic activity. On the other hand, high interest rates from the formal banking system could also allow the expansion of black or parallel credit markets. In most Latin American countries, informal banking activities (pawnbrokers, shopkeepers, usurers) have remained important, albeit it is difficult to evaluate them. However, in reality, "informal" financial intermediation does not lead to a reduction of transaction costs, the opposite of what some authors had hypothesized. Hence, in a context of rising interest rates and of subsidized credit restriction, credits from informal mechanisms appear as a very costly alternative for potential investors.

Moreover, processes of privatization or important changes in the capital structure of financial institutions have not till now led to a real "rebanking" of Latin American economies. Indeed, in most countries, the ratio banking liabilities/GNP is lower than in the preliberalization period; similarly, only a relatively reduced part of credit is oriented toward production. Private investment processes have generally been hindered and traditional financing of development by specialized institutions has been reduced.[12]

During the 1980s, the expansion of a new model of banking structure ("universal" banking) could have been one of the causes for this problem. This model has been controversial in developed countries. Some bankers remain doubtful about the idea that a single institution could efficiently manage the different functions of banking. For that reason they have proposed a return to some type of specialization.[13] Indeed, "universal" banking, especially in its German model,[14] cannot be considered only as a simple bank *a tout faire* (able to do everything) integrating all types of financial intermediation operations in one institution. Rather, its main activity is to invest in productive firms, especially through capital participation and loans.

But Latin American "universal" banks have generally not extended their activities to new forms of productive investments. With deregulation and increases in interest rates, they have not been able to take the place of the traditional development banks inherited from the Economic Commission for Latin America (ECLA), propositions. In some countries, processes of privatization have significantly reduced the role of these institutions contributing to weaken some well-established circuits of subsidized credit for production or housing.

Discussing the risk of financial instability due to universal banking and applying it mainly to developed countries, G. Benston argues that "both theory and evidence support the expectation that risks are more likely to be reduced than increased should banks be permitted to engage in securities, insurance, and other products and services."[15] However, he recognizes that universal banks would be more difficult to regulate, because their ties to business would be more complex. The advantage of specialized smaller banks with limited functions is that they would be monitored more efficiently by government agents.

In a less developed country's economic and financial environment where the role of state regulation has been only recently reduced, it can be affirmed that specialized providers of financial services still exist. Due to their long experience in their own countries, they can do many things better than universal banks, particularly in handling specific problems of investment banking: long run financing of risky projects, takeovers, leverage buyouts, mergers and all forms of capital restructuring. Thus, they could become a better link between banks and stock markets to induce productive investments and economic growth, and, of course, to eliminate certain distortions such as those previously pointed out.

FINANCIAL LIBERALIZATION AND NEW RISKS OF BANKING SYSTEMS

Concerning the new banking structure of most Latin American countries, four specific causes of systemic risk are generally analyzed in a context of financial liberalization: (1) the increase of risk on bank assets, especially its loans; (2) the difficulty to evaluate the global risk of financial institutions; (3) the increased dependence of banks on liquidity of assets; and (4) a more systematic intervention of monetary authorities due to a greater instability of the system.

It is possible to consider that the liberalization of the external sector has not been neutral: it has hindered the internal capacity of banks and other financial institutions to respond to the financing needs of their economies. It has permitted important entries of capital flows, especially since 1991, but with the inconvenience of often making more difficult the control of monetary aggregates. In fact, it has been demonstrated that these capital flows fluctuate with variations of international interest rates, as well as in response to the evolution of domestic economic variables.[16] The recent experience of bank failures in Venezuela and also the Mexican devaluation of December 1994, illustrate how easily these investments can be taken out to be invested in other markets in case of difficulties. The temporary "bonanza" induced by these flows of capital can also originate in the long-term perverse effects, particularly impacts similar to the so-called syndrome of "Dutch disease," through the balance account.[17]

The difficulty in analyzing the global risk of banking institutions becomes more pronounced, taking into account that banking uncertainty is visible not only through the bank's balance sheets. It is also necessary to consider the "entropy," on the fluctuating measure of risk due to insufficient information.[18] As a global institutional system, banking can have a negative influence on the mechanisms for risk prevention of the so-called "systemic risk."[19] A systemic crisis can involve a transmission effect risk due to an exogenous shock, or else due to a risk of insolvency of the whole system. Universal banks could be more involved in this process than specialized banks because they would be dealing with large financial operations, both in domestic and international markets. Some of their assets have generally more volatile prices because of their dependency on the behavior of foreign investors and on the level of exchange rates. Recent developments, in most Latin American countries, of financial groups, the emergence of structures of financial conglomeration with participation of banking institutions in non-banks (brokers, insurance companies, etc.) and of industrial interests in the banking industry, could have contributed to weaken prudential supervision, facilitating the vulnerability of the whole system.

In that respect, large banking systems would not be a sufficient protection ("too big to fail") and could, on the contrary, stimulate the spreading of systemic shocks, especially when international links add the risk of exchange rates to banking risk. It is generally possible to assert that the confusion between "pure" functions of banking and other finance activities can facilitate the spreading of risk because "market" assets are more sensitive to the price variations of negotiable securities and also to exchange rates.[20]

As a footnote, it must be pointed out that in Latin America, perhaps more than anywhere else, operations of laundering money related with illicit transactions, especially drugs, can also have a negative influence on banking risk. The difficulty to control them must motivate monetary authorities to create specific mechanism of supervision to eliminate this risk.[21] It is difficult to imagine that such controls could be managed in each country through market mechanisms. The need for a supranational authority is emerging.

For a system undergoing liberalization some authors consider that the rise in interest rates leads to an increase in the riskiness of the portfolio of loans from the banking system because safe borrowers are rationed out of the market. Problems of adverse selection and moral hazard in credit markets can accentuate this phenomenon, especially when equity markets are small.[22] The financial system not only becomes more vulnerable to any type of shock such as adverse changes in the terms of trade, but bank managers can also end up taking on more risks if it is known that the government will rescue financial institutions. Moral hazards can also arise because deposit insurance is too extensive.

In Latin America, deposit insurance systems have not been really developed, in spite of some attempts in Brazil, Colombia, Mexico and Argentina. The problem is not confined to the issues of measuring the risk of bank assets and of deriving the fair deposit insurance rate.[23] It is also related to the need of operational microeconomic strategies for individual banks, to perceive global problems tied to interest rates and the "transformation" risks of banking activity. In short, risks of the financial system must be considered as a whole. Deposit insurance systems could be a "private" temporary solution, but the risk is collective and "systemic" risk has to be analyzed. So, to minimize risks and prevent future bank failures, the function of lender of last resort assumed by the Central Bank has to be reinforced.

EMERGING MARKETS AND FINANCIAL INSTABILITY

The spectacular rise of most Latin American securities markets at the beginning of the 1990s can be associated with the processes of globalization initiated in the 1980s, and to the new patterns of "direct" finance that have contributed in most countries to reduce the relative importance of banks in the financing of economic activity. However, in addition to examining this complex evolution,[24] it is necessary to stress some particularities of these markets.

In spite of their exponential development, most of Latin America's stocks markets, as measured by the ratio of capitalization to GDP, have remained small compared with those of developed countries.[25] In the late 1980s, Chile and Mexico can be considered as exceptions. Considering other emerging markets, especially those of Asia, several studies reveal a high correlation between stocks indices and the growth of domestic product. In most countries from Latin America, especially in Argentina and Colombia, the rise of stock market indices, particularly during the period 1987–92 has been much more important than global economic growth. It is also useful to examine the value of new issues as a percentage of GDP or as a percentage of gross fixed investment.[26] In both cases, the size of Latin American primary markets is small and cannot be considered as an important source of investment.

However, this relative weakness of primary stock markets has not prevented, in some countries, the development of dynamic secondary markets as well as of derivative financial products and their markets (stock options, warrants on stocks, options on stock indices or foreign currencies). These products have generally been created by foreign portfolio managers desiring to minimize risks to their investments in the developing countries. In

43

most financial markets of Latin America there are projects to establish or to strengthen derivative markets but until now they have only permitted the application of "defensive" speculative strategies. In recent years, some of these markets have been expanding spectacularly,[27] but they primarily remain dependent upon foreign capital flows and the international conditions of the economy, thus generally remaining poorly connected with the development of local primary and secondary stock markets.

In Latin America, perhaps more than anywhere else, it is possible to affirm that financial markets have never been the ideal markets described by Walras, with their transparent processes of determination of the prices of assets.[28] During the last few years these markets have been reorganized (and in some countries just created), and sometimes they have been subject to very detailed regulations.[29] Investors generally question the excesses of these controls, but paradoxically ask for a more regulated financial environment to protect their investments (demands for contract guarantees, possibilities for legal appeals, transparent tax systems, etc.).[30]

One of the objectives of stock markets is to improve the efficiency and performance of firms through the market for corporate control. This secondary market must be active to have a positive effect on a firm's growth and efficiency. It is not necessary to discuss here the so called agency problem in the corporate structure.[31] It will suffice to recall that in Latin America corporate ownership is highly entrenched and equities markets are not contestable. Many private corporations are often closed with a great majority of voting shares in the hands of a minority of stockholders. These controlling "insiders" can divert resources in a way that might not maximize the value of the firms. Stiglitz has shown that the cost of equity financing could be very high because stock markets are used as a major source of equity capital only by the high risk firms, especially those unable to obtain bank credit.[32]

In a context of macroeconomic uncertainty common to the Latin America region, it would be necessary to make the ownership and the form of control of corporations more transparent. Processes of privatization have generally not led to the release of clear and ample information for small shareholders or new investors. Many examples – in Brazil, Colombia, Argentina and Mexico – indicate that controlling interests still resist opening their capital, and that firms, private and public, resist diluting control.

THE AUTONOMY OF CENTRAL BANKS AND THE STABILITY OF BANKING SYSTEMS

In most Latin American countries during the last decade, financial liberalization has been accompanied with a process granting more autonomy to their central banks.[33] But it must be recognized that the objective of the more independent central banks, especially in Latin American countries, was to permit the control of prices in order to reduce the "inflationary bias" of economic policy. In Latin America, quasi-fiscal activities of central banks[34] had been considered as hindrances to efficient action against inflation.

In the late 1980s and the early 1990s, most Latin American countries have institutionalized, generally by law, the independence or autonomy of their central banks. To establish or reinforce the credibility of these central banks, monetary and inflation targets have been fixed. In some countries (Argentina, Chile, Mexico) local money has been anchored to the dollar with the purpose of stabilizing exchange rates and reducing inflation. Even though that the relation between the degree of "autonomy" of the bank and rates of inflation has not be confirmed[35] (because many other macroeconomic variables can influence inflation, like salaries deflation), this policy is far from neutral regarding the security of domestic banking systems.

In fact, it must be recognized here that one of the traditional functions of central banks is to contain runs of deposits and financial panics by acting as a lender of last resort. They have also to manage the prudential regulation and supervision of banking institutions. The pursuit of price stability is not only a problem of exchange rates; it also depends on monetary and budgetary policies and therefore on the behavior of central banks in relation to the other banks. If this very important function is neglected, financial instability can increase.[36]

Some authors consider that, at least in the long run, the pursuit of price stability will strengthen financial stability because financial disruptions and crises are linked to the instability of inflation and interest rates.[37] But in the short run it is possible to affirm that sharp fluctuations in interest rates induce changes in the asset values of banks which could possibly lead to a crisis. So there may be a short-run trade-off between financial stability and price stability. With increases in the level of interest rates, some banks must raise the rate on deposits in order to prevent a drain of funds. These banks could face liquidity problems and the role of the central bank would be to inject money into the system, neglecting the price stability goal, at least temporarily in order to perform its lender of last resort function.[38]

In Latin America as in other countries, the processes of financial globalization have privileged the equilibrium on the different markets (money, securities, etc.), but to the detriment of the specific relations between monetary regulatory authorities, central banks and the whole banking system. However, it is this complex connection that permits central banks to secure, through the "intermediation" mechanism, the liquidity and the stability of the economy.

Further, in Latin America, the quasi-independence of the central bank has often been criticized, for this bank represents, through its function of lender of last resort, the permanency of the relationship with the government; that is to say, with the political power for decision-making. Because

ROBERT ROLLINAT

the state is necessarily involved in money creation and credit policy, some authors have questioned the perverse effect of the independence of a central bank. What must be the optimal degree of "conservatism" of the public decision-maker to maintain at the same time price stability and an active economic policy? The solution seems to be a form of "policy-mix" with a double choice: inflation vs production and interest rate vs public expenses.[39]

This would be the best way to preserve financial stability. But this policy-mix has not been the choice made in Latin America, because if the autonomy of central banks, formulated and implemented in many countries, has released the central bank from most of its quasi-fiscal obligations, it has at the same time reduced its control on the banking system. Without any doubt, this weakness is one of the roots of the present difficulties of commercial banks in Latin America.

Mexico's recent crisis of December 1994 has revealed serious problems of solvency, not only for banks from Mexico but also concerning banks from other Latin American countries like Argentina and Venezuela. In most of these cases, support or the guaranty of the state has been requested through different rescue mechanisms. In Mexico, for instance, the enormous amount of bad debts from commercial banks (near 13 percent of their lending portfolios), has led to the necessity of recapitalizing most of them to avoid bankruptcies. "Procapte" is a temporary program created to support weakening banks. A substantial improvement is now needed in the banking system to avoid the situation where the government ends up with a substantial amount of subordinated convertible debt. The progressive weakening of the existing shareholders' position could lead to a crawling de facto renationalization of Mexico's banking industry.

One of the perverse effects of the deregulation of the banking system throughout the end of the 1980s has been reducing the traditional protection (tutelage) of central banks on the operations of the other banks. But the paradox is that this "tutelage" is now requested to save institutions from bankruptcy. In this situation it seems difficult to conceive that the legal mechanisms and emerging patterns of organizing the central bank independence should not be questioned in the countries of Latin America where they have been adopted.

CONCLUSION

Since the early 1980s the so-called globalization of the world economy has profoundly modified Latin American financial relations. As a result, financial liberalization and deregulation have been adopted, leading to significant reforms in banking structure and its operations. Significant reforms have also taken place in the real markets and a sharp decrease of intervention of the state in the economy has been present also. As a result important elements of induced globalization in Latin America have also been the privatization of firms from the financial sector and extending autonomy to their central banks.

Conventionally, only the favorable effects of these processes on the expansion of banking and securities market activity have been highlighted. However, the perverse effects of liberalization and deregulation on financial institutions and markets should also be considered. The intensification of capital transfers, and innovations in banks' instruments and finance products cannot be considered, as often hypothesized, as being automatically conducive to a more "productive" activity of banks and markets. In many countries of Latin America financial deregulation processes have led to negative results because financial institutions sometimes seem to have been managed by speculators more interested in short-term monetary benefits rather than by bankers desirous of risking their funds in productive investments.

So new risks have appeared, especially in the banking sector. These risks have been caused or accentuated by international factors such as interest rate increases or sharp exchange rate variations. It is because weakened national regulations have not been able to control these new situations that banking crises have plagued several Latin American countries and have even spread to other nations, as in the case of the Mexican shock of December 1994.

It is now imperative to redefine new forms of regulation in Latin America and to rebuild more institutionalized structures in the financial sector. Financial deregulation or controlled development? To resolve this alternative positively it would be necessary to redefine new forms of public intervention that could contribute to the creation of high-performance financial institutions, able to stabilize a permanent flow of credit toward production. Thus, it must be recognized that in Latin America questioning and replacing the ECLA recommendations system, known by its opponents as "financial repression," has not led until now to a stable financial system able to satisfy this imperative.

NOTES

1 International Monetary Fund, *International Capital Markets*, Washington, DC, 1992.
2 Welch, J.H., *Capital Markets and the Development Process: The Case of Brazil*, London, 1992.
3 Welch, J.H., "The New Face of Latin America: Financial Flows, Markets and Institutions in the 1990s," *Journal of Latin American Studies*, 25, February 1993, pp. 12–13.
4 Rollinat, R., "La finance latino-américaine aujourd'hui: globalisation ou nouvelle intégration-régulation," *Problémes d'Amérique Latine*, No. 12, La Doc. française, Paris, Janvier–Mars 1994.

5 For a full review of financial reforms undertaken in Mexico see the chapter by A. Cabello in this volume.

6 "La ley financiera," *Carta Financiera*, No. 84, Anif., Bogota, 1993.

7 Martinez Neira, N., "Reforma financiera de la poscrisis en América Latina," *Monetaria*, , CEMLA, México, Enero-Marzo 1993.

8 The references listed at the end of this chapter contain key works on financial liberalization and financial repression.

9 Ortiz, E., "Emerging Capital Markets and Economic Development," in K. Fatemi and D. Salvatore (eds), *Foreign Exchange Issues, Capital Markets and International Banking in the 1990s*, Taylor & Francis, Washington, DC, 1993, pp. 170–1.

10 Buffie, E.F., "Financial Repression, the New Structuralists and Stabilization Policy in Semi-Industrialized Economies," *Journal of Development Economics*, Vol. X, No. 14, April 1984, pp. 305–22.

11 Kapur, B.K., "Formal and Informal Financial Markets and the Neo-Structuralist Critique of the Financial Liberalization Strategy in Less Developed Countries," *Journal of Development Economics*, Vol. 30, 1992.

12 Morriset, J., "Does Financial Liberalization Improve Private Investment in Developing Countries?," *Journal of Development Economics*, Vol. 40, February 1993, pp. 133–50.

13 Mayoux, J., "La banque universelle en question,", *Revue Banque*, No. 538, juin 1993, pp. 721–31, Paris.

14 Dupuy, C., and Morin, F., "Le coeur financier allemand," *Revue d'Economie Financiere*, No. 17, 1991, Paris.

15 Benston, G.J., "Universal Banking," *Journal of Economic Perspectives*, Vol. 8, No. 3, summer 1994, p. 126.

16 Calvo, G., Leiderman, N. and Reinhart, N., "Afluencia de capital y apreciación del tipo de cambio real en América Latina: el papel de los factores externos," in J. Garay and J.L. Cardenas (eds) *Macroeconomía de los flujos de capital en Colombia y América Latina*, Bogotá, Tercer Mundo, 1993.

17 Cambiazo, J.E., "Síntomas del mal holandés por la vía de la cuenta de capital," *Monetaria*, Enero–Febrero. 1993, CEMLA, México.

18 Seijas Roman, G., *Políticas y estrategias de la banca múltiple*, El Colegio de México, 1991, ch. 12

19 "Systemic risk can be defined as a major disequilibrium risk resulting from emerging disfunctions in the financial systems when the interactions of individual behavior do not lead to corrective adjustments but, on the contrary, undermine general economic equilibrium." Nouy, D., "Relations interbancaires el risques systémiques," *Revue Banque*, No. 535, Février. 1993, p. 26, Paris.

20 Aglietta, M., "Le risque de système et les moyens de le prévenir dans l'Union économique et monétaire," *Revue d'Economie Financiere*, No. 22, Automne 1992, Paris.

21 "Prevención del uso impropio de la banca," *Carta Financiera*, Octubre 1992, pp. 52–59, Bogota.

22 Cho, Y.J., "Inefficiencies from Financial Liberalization in the Absence of Well-Functioning Equity Markets," *Journal of Money, Credit and Banking*, Vol. 18, No. 2, 1986, May.

23 Jaeger, M., "Application des modèles à d'option à l'analyse de l'activité et du risque bancaires," *Revue d'Economie Politique*, Vol. 104, No. 6, November–December 1994, Paris.

24 See Rollinat, R., "Les marchés financiers latino-américains 'boom' éphémère

ou levier du retour à la croissance?," *Techniques Financières et Développement*, No. 32, September 1993, Paris.

25 Welch, J.H., "The New Face of Latin America," p. 15 and tables on p. 14.

26 Welch, J.H., "The New Face of Latin America," tables on pp. 14 and 16.

27 For example, in 1992 "Bolsa de Mercadorias e Futuros" of São Paulo (Brazil) became the sixth worldwide place for "futures." *Latin American Economy and Business*, March 1993, London.

28 Kregel, J.A., "Some Considerations on the Causes of Structural Change in Financial Markets," *Journal of Economic Issues*, September 1992. See also Christensen, C.

29 As an example, see: "Nuevo estatuto organico del mercado de valores para Colombia," Legis, Bogotá, 1993.

30 Duke, L. and Pappaioannou, M., "L'internationalisation des marchés de valeurs naissants," *Finances et Developpement*, FMI, September 1993.

31 Fischer, K.P., Ortiz, E. and Palasvirta, A.P., "Risk Management and Corporate Governance in Imperfect Capital Markets," in D.K. Ghosh and E. Ortiz (eds) *The Changing Environment of International Financial Markets*, St Martin's Press, New York, 1994.

32 Stiglitz, J.E., "Credit Markets and the Control of Capital," *Journal of Money, Credit and Banking*, Vol. 17, No. 2, May 1985.

33 On the theory concerning the autonomy of central banks see, for instance, Cukierman A., *Central Bank Strategy, Credibility and Independence: Theory and Evidence*, MIT Press, Cambridge, Mass., 1992; and also, by the same author, "Central Bank Independence and Monetary Control," *The Economic Journal*, 104, November, 1994.

34 Ibarra, R., "Nota sobre las actividades cuasifiscales del banco central," *Boletín del CEMLA*, Enero–Febrero. 1991, México.

35 In developing countries, empirical studies seem to indicate that there is no relation between inflation and the legal independence of central banks. See Cukierman, "Central Bank Independence," pp. 1439–40.

36 "Financial stability like price stability is a public good. Central Banks must search for both objectives, they depend on each other." See George, E., "The Pursuit of Financial Stability," *Bank of England Quarterly Bulletin*, Vol. 34, February 1994, p. 66.

37 Baltensperger, E. "Central Bank Policy and Lending of Last Resort," Proceedings of the conference "Prudential Regulation, Supervision and Monetary Policy", Bocconi University, Milan, February 1993 (ed. F. Bruni).

38 Cukierman, A., *Central Bank Strategy*, ch. 7.

39 Villa, P., "Policy-mix et indépendance des banques centrales," *Economie Internationale*, No. 61, 1er trim. 1995, CEPPI, Paris.

5

LIBERALIZATION AND DEREGULATION OF THE MEXICAN STOCK MARKET

*Alejandra Cabello**

INTRODUCTION

"Financial repression" has usually been the dominant characteristic of financial systems from the developing countries. Its high cost was magnified by the debt crisis of the 1980s, and its inadequacy to promote economic development became more evident with increasing world patterns of financial globalization. As a result, to overcome their low savings and investments rates, lower their high dependency on foreign loans, foster a solid link with international markets to attract international flows, and above all to promote higher rates of economic growth, developing countries have enforced important financial liberalization and deregulation processes, which have transformed their financial systems significantly. Although high benefits are expected, the timing and sequencing of financial liberalization and deregulation have been open to debate. Controversy also exists in relation to the conditions that must first be met to implement financial liberalization, and on the degree of participation that securities markets should play in an economy.

Moreover, several financial liberalization processes from developing countries have failed, leading to costly state rescue plans of troubled financial institutions. For this reason it is necessary to identify the nature of financial liberalization and deregulation processes that have been taking place recently in the developing countries.

This chapter is a contribution in this direction. It analyzes the processes of financial liberalization enforced in Mexico during the 1988–94 period. Mexico is an excellent showcase from which many lessons can be drawn for other developing nations, not only because of profound financial liberalization and deregulation policies undertaken during that period but also because it is now undergoing a severe crisis which has often been associated with financial liberalization and deregulation.

The chapter is organized as follows. The section following this introduction briefly reviews the importance of financial liberalization to economic

50

development in a globalized economy. Next, the goals of Mexico's financial liberalization and deregulation, as well as the reforms induced by them in the financial sector during the 1988–94 period, are examined. The institutional and legal changes in the financial sector are then described and analyzed in detail, emphasizing changes promoted in the securities markets. The section which follows analyzes the performance of the securities markets, attempting to determine whether or not financial liberalization and financial deregulation can be associated with the peso crisis that has affected Mexico since December 1994. A short conclusion follows, stressing the macroeconomic conditions necessary to enforce financial liberalization and deregulation policies successfully.

FINANCIAL LIBERALIZATION AND ECONOMIC DEVELOPMENT

The link between financial development and economic development has long been established. Indeed, due to its importance, the financial sector has been identified as the superstructure of a nation's production and real assets, the infrastructure of the economy (Ortiz, 1993). However, in the developing nations over-regulation and the excessive intervention of the state in the economy, known as "financial repression (FR)," have limited the contribution of the financial sector to economic growth. Financial repression has included, among other things, ceilings on savings and lending interest rates, quotes for preferential loans to "priority sectors," excess supervision and regulation of financial markets and institutions, and excess participation of the state on financial intermediation activities through the ownership of commercial banks, developing banks and other financial institutions (McKinnon, 1973).

Financial repression has eventually led to the existence of relatively underdeveloped financial markets and institutions, incapable of promoting adequate levels of savings and investments. Furthermore, it has led to higher costs of credits, inflationary government financing, limited financial innovation, excessive government borrowing – particularly from foreign sources – and an inefficient allocation of resources in the economy. As a result, economic growth has been low and the economy of financially repressed countries has been characterized by regional segmentation and inequities, and sharp income distribution differences (Araya Gomez, 1994).

However, as Edwards and Patrick (1992) correctly point out, we are on the threshold of a new age of global financial markets. A strong market-driven dynamic of international integration of banking, securities, and derivatives markets is bringing about a profound transformation in the structure of local and international financial institutions and markets. Taking into account prevailing trends in world trade and investments, the new era seems to be destined to bring about many opportunities to support

51

business activity. These opportunities will not be available to nations who favor protectionism. Thus, to promote their own savings and investments processes and a more dynamic and efficient international mobilization of international financial flows to finance their economic growth, developing countries need to liberalize and deregulate their financial markets and built up stronger and more efficient financial institutions.[1] Financial repression must be replaced by fully liberalized financial systems.

One important reform that must be taken is the promotion of the securities markets. Particularly, stock markets need to be fostered because they constitute the last stage in financial development, and in today's global economy they might constitute the additional force needed for a take-off into development (Ortiz, 1995). Traditionally, securities markets in the developing nations have remained thin and unimportant, and many developing countries do not even have that sort of market. Besides low economic activity, one important reason for the absence of securities markets in the developing countries has been the high intervention of the state in financial intermediation. Particularly, following World War II, state developing banks burgeoned beyond real needs and became highly bureaucratic and inefficient. This, along with interest rate ceilings, inflationary government financing through reserve requirements to the banking sector, and fixed quotas of loans to "priority" sectors, discouraged savings formation and an efficient allocation of financial resources through market mechanisms. Moreover, because firms enjoyed protected markets they limited their growth to the local market and did not seek significant external financing. Hence they offered small amounts of shares to be traded at the markets. Corporate property and management remained a family affair (Fischer, *et al.*, 1994).

Financial liberalization and deregulation (henceforth FLD) is therefore a challenge that must be undertaken by the developing nations to secure for themselves higher rates of growth and a smooth integration with the international financial markets. But FLD *per se* does not guarantee economic success. Its difficulties and successes can be best illustrated with the Mexican case.

FINANCIAL LIBERALIZATION AND DEREGULATION IN MEXICO

Challenges and strategies

During the last few years, Mexico's financial system has undergone profound transformations, many of these resulting from daring financial liberalization and deregulation policies aimed at adapting it to the emerging patterns of world trade, finance and investments. Reforms to Mexico's financial sector are not new. Indeed, they started as early as the 1970s in an effort to overcome the shortcomings of the model of "stabilizing development" applied since the 1950s. Failures in this inward-oriented model of growth led to fiscal laxness, which made it imperative to make the financial system more flexible in order to prevent capital flight and to avoid the need for inflationary financing.

Recently, Mexico's financial reforms have been aimed mainly at responding to the challenges and opportunities of financial globalization, both from the standpoint of short and medium term macroeconomic stability and the long run promotion mobilization of local and international savings to the local economy. The underlying forces behind these goals have been the deregulation of local markets, financial opening, promotion of financial innovations, and privatization of the banking system, nationalized in 1982.

An important part of this strategy was establishing adequate macroeconomic conditions for financial liberalization, so that no adverse results could take place as a result of its implementation. These conditions can be summed up in stability, i.e. emphasis on inflation control and discipline in public finance, and the development of efficient financial institutions through deregulation. Reforms have also sought to strengthen public financing in a search for non-inflationary sources. In this respect the emerging financial institutions were considered as pillars of economic stability, with the mobilization of local savings and international resources to local public and state enterprises and government agencies.

Three components of the financial liberalization carried out in Mexico are: (1) a new orientation in the role of financial institutions; (2) emphasis on savings formation; and (3) emphasis on investment and on the efficient allocation of resources. Mexican monetary authorities were convinced that changes in the financial sector could affect both the levels of financial intermediation and the overall volume of savings, which would further investment and growth (Aspe, 1993: 72). That is why savings have become the key variable to determine monetary policy. Indeed, in the aftermath of the debt crisis, the main challenge for the Mexican authorities was increasing local savings levels.[2] Consistent with the attainment of this goal were the pursuit of fiscal discipline; the promotion of innovative mechanisms to increase forced savings, among which must be mentioned Sistema de Ahorro para el Retiro (SAR: a retirement savings system),[3] and new regulations concerning financial intermediation supervision. Multiple diagnoses affirm that Mexico's challenge to its immediate future is increasing local savings, for their low level is also leading to low rates of investment. Indeed, compared with the successful economies from South-East Asia, Mexico's savings and investments are relatively low in relation to its GDP. In the Asian countries these variables account for 30 percent of GDP; in Mexico only for 16 percent (Mansell Carstens, 1995).

To understand the nature of the changes needed, it is important to identify four factors that have influenced the behavior of savings in modern Mexico:

1 Voluntary savings were not substituted with new forms of non-inflationary forced savings; the bulk of the population had no access to any mechanism to save for retirement or for the protection against risk.[4]
2 Financial innovations have promoted voluntary savings; but due to the lack of hedging instruments against inflation and exchange rate risks, people have preferred to purchase real estate and durable goods.
3 Income inequities have prevented growth in savings. Furthermore, it is worth mentioning that contrary to the Kaldorian view, increasing the participation of labor in national income has led to increases in voluntary savings.
4 Negative interest rates have diminished the levels of voluntary savings.[5]

In order to overcome the shortcomings inhibiting savings and investments, Mexican authorities have implemented a complex set of financial reforms since 1988. Furthermore, besides overcoming those restrictions to savings and investments, deregulation and liberalization have aimed at modernizing domestic financial intermediaries to make them internationally competitive, capable of pooling resources at international markets, and to channel them efficiently to the local economy.

Financial reforms have been focused on the financial opening and deregulation of financial markets; financial innovation; the strengthening of financial intermediaries; privatization of the commercial banking sector; and financing government deficit without recurring compulsory reserve requirements, but thorough non-inflationary instruments. Privatization and strengthening market activity had high priority because *de facto* nationalization of credit was identified as the main reason for a loss of capacity in the banking sector for credit analysis and its efficient allocation. Similarly, over-regulation was reducing flexibility to financial institutions and leading to the creation of innumerable subsidies which made credits more expensive (Aspe, 1994: 1044).

Financial liberalization and deregulation policies

Post-World War II quantitative controls

Following World War II, Mexico's financial system was characterized by financial repression. During the period between the early 1950s and the early 1980s quantitative measures prevailed to regulate and control financial intermediaries. Among these measures must be mentioned the imposition of reserve requirements, selective credit quotas, borrowing at interest rates predetermined by Banco de México. Nevertheless, departure from this rigid system began in 1976 with the creation of multiservices banking (*banca multiple*). Further, in 1978 Certificates of the Treasury (CETES) were created. This marked the beginning of the development of a domestic money market. Originally, yields for CETES were fixed by the authorities; by the last quarter of 1982 auctions became formalized and participants could bid for both yield and amounts (Aspe, 1993: 74). During that period an effort was also made to enhance the role of the securities markets.

Responses to the debt crisis

However, financial liberalization really started as a response to the debt crisis in the early 1980s. Mexico underwent a drastic adjustment process. The banking system was nationalized at the beginning of the debt crisis, but authorities restructured its oversized and inefficient structure, merging some banks and liquidating the smallest and least efficient ones. The goals were to promote economies of scale and eliminate inefficiencies. Similarly, investment banks and brokerage houses, which were part of the nationalized banks, were soon returned to their owners. These measures, along with reforms in the Mexican Stock Market law, led to a remarkable growth in the capital market during this period. In addition efforts were made to curb the impacts of the crisis, giving high priority to the control of inflation and favoring high real interest rates. These policies helped to prevent capital flight, and above all developed monetary discipline.

End of financial repression

This phase of FLD began in 1988 and ended in 1989. Initially, a gradual elimination of quantitative controls were enforced. First, credit quotas to high priority sectors were eliminated. Beginning October 1988, only a bank's resources coming from checking and savings deposits remained subject to the high priority sectors' credit allocations and reserve requirements. Compulsory reserves were revoked for banking liabilities collected through non-traditional bank instruments. But reserve requirements for these instruments were replaced by a "liquidity coefficient requirement" consistent in the obligation of maintaining 30 percent of the portfolio of assets in interest bearing government paper. Later, this reform was extended to traditional time deposits in April 1989, and to checking accounts in August of the same year (Aspe, 1993: 77). Finally, in 1989 the compulsory liquidity coefficient requirement was eliminated and instead the authorities issued a ten-year variable-rate government note, to be used and traded among banks to meet their voluntary reserve needs. This ended the transition from a repressed financial system to one based on the market.

ALEJANDRA CABELLO

Full fledged financial liberalization

Early reforms[6]

Transition from financial repression to a freer financial system was supported with significant reforms to the monetary law. On December 1989, a set of financial reforms submitted earlier by President Salinas de Gortari were approved by the Congress. Those laws aimed at reforming existing regulation for financial intermediaries. Their main purpose was to advance the institutional development of the Mexican financial system, above all redefining its structure, diminishing excess regulation and improving supervision, regulating possible excesses from financial intermediaries, strengthening their capital, promoting economies of scale and scope, and promoting a wider market coverage, and greater competition.

Among the reforms undertaken must be mentioned the substantial changes to the Law for Credit Institutions, and the Law for the Securities Market. Although changes to the banking laws were more ample than those proposed for the securities exchange, interest for promoting its development was also clear. Other laws reformed included: the Law for Public Service in Banking and Credit; the Law for Insurance Companies; the Law for Bonding Institutions; The General Law for Auxiliary Credit Institutions and Activities, and the Law for Investment Funds. Moreover, it is worth noting that changes to the banking laws were tangled in a sharp debate due to implied changes to the Constitution, modifying its Articles 28 and 123 to allow private ownership of these institutions.[7] One important transitional aspect of these legal changes centered in giving greater autonomy to the management of state-owned banks. The new banking laws sought to strengthen the role of their administrative boards in the decision-making processes of their institutions. These boards were granted the right to name and remove their chief executive, which under the nationalized scheme of bank ownership was a right of the President, through a process carried out by the Ministry of Finance. In the new law it was also established that the Board should approve its own financial programs and investment and expenditure budgets. The Board was also given the right to approve the location or relocation of its institution's branches, agencies and representative offices throughout the country; the acquisition, leasing or sale of equipment; the initiation of expansion facilities, etc. However, these changes did not imply a total loss of control by the state, for it maintained a position of majority participation in the Boards of the banks (Ortiz Martínez, 1994: 59).

These reforms were also set forth in accord with the deregulation about the operations from banking institutions, as well as to promote a more active participation from the private sector in the capital and management of these institutions, privileging majority control by Mexican nationals.

56

The capital of multiple banking institutions was divided in three series of shares: Series A (remaining always at 51 percent) subscribed by the Federal government, development banks, holding companies of financial groups and the Banking Protection Fund; Series B (which could amount up to 49 percent) to be subscribed by Mexican nationals or legal Mexican corporations alone; and Series C (which could represent up to 30 percent of total capital), for any of the above plus foreign nationals, but not foreign governments and their entities.[8] Another important part of this strategy was opening further development banks to private investment through Certificates of Capital Participation, which aimed at strengthening their capital. These shares are composed of Series A, owned by the government (66 percent), and Series B, owned by private individuals (34 percent), with an individual cap of 5 percent (before 1 percent).[9]

Finally, in relation to banking supervision, prudential regulation began to be emphasized, but Mexico's Banking Commission (Comision Nacional Bancaria) was granted attributes to sanction all those institutions which do not fulfill or violate the established norms.[10]

The most important changes concerning the Securities Market Law, which regulates investment banks, brokerage houses, and the management of investment funds, centered on promoting conditions that favor a greater participation of the capital markets intermediaries in foreign markets; redefining the treatment of privileged information (promoting greater information and transparency); the deregulation of capital market operations to promote greater competitiveness and to make operations more flexible; and the legal creation of capital market specialists (*especialista bursátil*). In relation to foreign investments, the law was reformed to allow the participation of foreign investors with up to 30 percent of the capital of a brokerage house, with a cap of 10 percent on individual ownership.[11] Concerning investment funds, the law was modified to deregulate their operations and simplify their administration. Investment societies represent the most important vehicle for accessing the stock market by small and medium size investors. Thus, these reforms aimed at increasing local savings.

The law of the securities markets was also reformed in 1989–90 to allow the integration of financial intermediaries into financial groups. Stipulations were made to allow the creation of holding companies to administer these groups, and the participation of foreign investors in the common capital of a holding company was prohibited. Concretely, the law also mandates that the holding company must be at least conformed by three non-bank financial intermediaries, and the holding company must own at least 51 percent of the capital of each one. Similarly, it was mandated that the holding company maintains full responsibility on the losses of all its member institutions (Ortiz Martínez, 1994: 69).

In 1990 a new Law to Regulate Financial Groups appeared, allowing banking institutions to be part of this form of financial organization, i.e. creating universal banking as an alternative for the financial institution's organization and operation. The main objective of this reform was to allow sharing in costs and infrastructure, as well as offering better services to the clients (Aspe, 1993: 83).

In relation to supervision and monitoring, the role of the Comision Nacional de Valores (CNV), Mexico's Securities Exchange Commission, was also redefined. It was granted the right to impose those sanctions contemplated in the laws and to enforce operating rules without consent from the Ministry of Finance. Similarly, it was granted greater autonomy in the management of its revenues and expenditures, and it was granted the right to approve directly the authorization for functioning, or the order of revocation to investment societies.

The possibility of introducing derivatives into the Mexican stock market was considered early in 1991. The introduction of futures, options, warrants, and swaps was examined as a means to decrease volatility in the underlying market, as well as to increase capital formation and to enable Mexico to compete more favorably for resources in the international markets. Based on a viability study, the project for the introduction of warrants and options was approved. Its norms were set forth in Memorandum 10–157, which identifies the legal nature of these instruments. Later, in January 1993, a Committee of Derivative Products was formed by the Comision Nacional de Valores, the Mexican Stock Market, and the Mexican Association of Brokerage Houses to establish a working plan (Olloqui, 1993). Warrants were finally introduced in the Mexican market in September 1993.

Further institutional reforms

In addition to strengthening the banking system, stock market intermediaries and fostering the creation of universal banking institutions, financial reforms also contemplated the creation or strengthening of other non-bank intermediaries and fostering savings by creating a system of savings for retirement.

Savings banks The new General Law for Auxiliary Credit Organizations and Activities created savings banks (*Cajas de Ahorro*), recognizing them as an important mechanism to induce savings among the popular classes. The new law aims at recognizing, organizing, and giving clear rules for the operations of savings banks, and is expected to give greater security and development possibilities to their operations (Ortiz Martínez, 1994: 103–4). Four important reasons are given for their creation: (1) they ensure greater competition among agents; (2) they create greater economic rationality; (3) they stimulate economic growth and better standards of living for

58

the people; and (4) they are the best mechanism to pool resources from small savers and channel them to productive processes. Specifically, the law sets forth that captured savings be made exclusively among its members, for posterior allocation among themselves; that the authorization of the Ministry of Finance is necessary for its constitution and formation; and that common capital must be integrated by social parts of equal value, conferring the same rights, and must be fully paid when issued. Similarly, the law specifies that savings banks will be based in a new form of organization – the savings and loans societiy – which has legal standing, variable capital, limited responsibility of its members to the amount of their contributions, of indefinite life, and residence in the national territory. Their names are followed by the words "Sociedad de Ahorro y Préstamo (Savings and Loans Society).[12]

Savings for retirement system This system was created as a mechanism of social security and to foresee important impacts on savings and investment. This system is acknowledged in various reforms and additions to the Social Security Law, and in the Internal Revenue Law in a decree passed on 24 February 1992. Furthermore, in relation to state workers, a decree passed on 27 March 1992 created a system of savings for retirement for all those state employees subject to benefits from the Social Security Institute for State Employees (ISSSTE: its Spanish acronym). With all this background, on 4 January 1993 the system for savings for retirement was given legal status, becoming part of ISSSTE. This system makes it obligatory for all state agencies and enterprises to make a contribution of 5 percent for housing, in addition to the 2 percent already supplied (González-Mendez, 1993). This 2 percent is reserved for retirement. For this purpose, this law reformed, and made some additions to, the Law of the Institutions of the National Housing Fund for the Workers.

Reforms to the Law for Credit Institutions and the Law to Regulate Financial Groups The Law for Credit Institutions and the Law to Regulate Financial Groups were also modified on 9 June 1992. The most important changes were those concerning common capital for credit institutions and the capital of holding companies of financial groups. Percentages of participation now allowed are 51 percent for Series A, and up to 51 percent for Series B, the remaining 49 percent to be distributed among shares A, B, or C. Ownership in shares C cannot exceed 30 percent of that amount. Furthermore, paid-in capital can be formed by an additional part, represented by shares Series L issued up to 30 percent of common capital (Ortiz Martínez, 1994: 110). Similarly, in this reform it was specified that shareholders (legal or individual), Mexican or foreigners, have voting rights concerning objectives, mergers, separations, transformation, liquidation, and listing and delisting in any stock market. A stipulation was also made to allow holdings of financial groups to acquire debt to increase their resources.

Further liberalization and deregulation of the securities market

In May 1993, the President sent to the Congress six new important bills to reform the financial system: the Law for Credit Institutions, the Law to Regulate Financial Groups, the Law for the Securities Exchange Market, the General Law for Auxiliary Credit Organizations and Activities, the General Law for Institutions and Mutualist Societies for Insurance, and the Federal Law for Bonding Institutions. The main objective of these reforms was to promote greater competitiveness among financial intermediaries, as well as granting them new powers in their operations, and to deregulate their operations significantly. It was also sought to harmonize the laws applicable to different financial intermediaries, particularly in relation to sanctions, administrative procedures, and a redefinition of transgressions and faults.

The most important changes concern the Law for the Securities Exchange Market. This law was modified in order to adapt the securities market to the growing internationalization of the financial markets. A system of international prices was created to enhance the dealing of local intermediaries in foreign securities, as well as strengthening trade in foreign markets, particularly titles issued by local firms at international markets. Public offerings of foreign issues were also allowed locally, independently of the nationality of the issuer.

To promote efficiency and transparency in the market, the concept of privileged information was redefined.[13] Sanctions were also established to prevent the misuse of this type of information. Concretely, the law stipulates that Board members, top executives, managers who misuse privileged information will face a veto from five to six years long. Other important reforms of this law refer to rating institutions, which originally were approved to operate in 1989. In the reforms proposed in 1993 regulations governing the operation of these institutions were increased. The law indicates that Comision Nacional de Valores can pass any provisions relating to the periodic information that these institutions must provide it with; the Commission can also require them to release certain information to the public, and other aspects relating to the services given to their clients. It is also stipulated that any misleading information can lead to the revoking of their operations.

Concerning foreign securities, the reform also contemplated making use of foreign governmental institutions devoted to the custody of securities, as well as making available the services of the Mexican Institute for the Custody of Securities to foreign financial institutions. It also considered that securities received for deposit be kept at foreign financial institutions, as well as at other centralized deposit institutions, whether national or foreign.

In relation to brokerage houses, the law specifies that their specialized activities can be freely carried out in foreign markets. It also regulates their systems of accounting and the register of their securities operations. Similarly, provisos were introduced authorizing brokerage houses to carry out trust activities in relation to business related to their activities. Reforms to the Law of the Securities Exchange Market also allow the purchase of shares by issuing companies, including brokerage houses, which should be made with charges to their common capital account. In relation to issuing shares with no voting rights, or with restricted voting rights, criteria were unified. Thus, as in the case of banks and financial holding institutions, and taking into account the law of foreign investments, a cap of 25 percent was established in relation to common capital, considering that for this type of share brokerage houses and brokerage specialists can only issue shares of Series L.

Finally, the law also establishes that boards governing the exchange market be composed equally of members representing brokerage houses and brokerage specialists up to 50 percent, and the remaining 50 percent with members of recognized professional achievement and who don't have administrative positions at financial institutions.

Autonomy of the Central Bank

One of the most important reforms of the financial sector was the approval of the law giving autonomy, from the executive power, to the Central Bank, Banco de México. The original bill was presented to the Congress by the President on 17 May 1993 and was finally approved in December of the same year. The initiative also contemplated reforms to Articles 73 and 123 of the Constitution. These Articles needed to be changed to give Congress the right to legislate on matters concerning central banking and the intermediation of financial services, and to reform some stipulations relative to the law applicable to employees from that institution, originally considered under the law for public employees. The constitutional reforms were approved on 20 August 1993 and published in *Diario Oficial*, Mexico's public records gazette. The text of the reformed Articles indicates that the state will have a central bank, which will be autonomous in the execution of its functions and administration. Its main objective is to secure the stability of the purchasing power of the national currency, and in addition to strengthen the states national development. No authority can order the Central Bank to grant finances to the state.

The functions carried out exclusively by the Central Bank in strategic matters concerning coining currencies and issuing bills are not considered to constitute a monopoly. The Central Bank, in the terms established by the law and with the participation of specific finance authorities, regulates the exchange rate, controls financial intermediation and financial services, and with the necessary authority has rights to carry out such regulations and provide for their observance. The bank is administered by a Governor appointed by the President with full approval by the Senate, or else the Permanent Legislative Commission were the Senate not in session.[14] Finally, the reforms to the Law of Banco de México, approved by the Senate on 14 December 1993, underlie the intention of the Mexican government to maintain the stability of the purchasing power of the national currency and to promote a healthy development of the financial and payments system (Banamex-Accival, 1994: 30).

The Law also sets the maximum limit that the Central Bank can lend to the Federal government, which is equivalent to 1.5 percent of expenditures contemplated in the Federal Expenditures Budget. Those resources can only be used to compensate for temporary disequilibria between revenues and expenditures, and the Bank can decide if the government can make use of that credit alternative (Banamex-Accival, 1994: 30). However, this limit can be exceeded in order to service internal debt.

Other important stipulations establish that the Central Bank can set restrictions to assets and liabilities operations, from credit institutions, brokerage houses, foreign exchange houses, and financial groups, which imply exchange rate risks. The Central Bank can compensate for increases in the money supply by acquiring foreign exchange (sterilization of foreign flows), or by placing securities from the federal government in the market. Reserve requirements cannot exceed 20 percent of the liabilities from banking institutions and 50 percent in the case of trust institutions (except those from the Federal government).

In relation to the goal of maintaining a smooth functioning of Mexico's financial system, the Law does not specify any supervision criteria. In relation to the administration of the Central Bank, it is established that this must be carried out by a governing board consisting of five members: the Governor, who presides over it, and four lieutenant governors elected by the Senate by nomination from the Executive. The Governor is designated by the President from the members of the Board, and the choice must be confirmed by the Senate. The mandate periods are six years for the Governor and eight years for Board members. They can be elected for more than one term. The Governor's mandate starts at the beginning of the fourth calendar year of each presidential term.[15]

The law approved by the Senate set 1 April 1994 as the date to start the new regime of the Central Bank. In a transition proviso, the term of office of the first Governor will be just over three years (the term expires 31 December 1997), in order to adapt this new central banking regime to expected changes in presidential terms. Finally, the Central Bank must report to the government and the public at large about its functions. In

January of each year it must send to the executive power and to the Congress its goals concerning the monetary policy to be followed during the year, and each April must give a report about the preceding year (Banamex-Accival, 1994: 30–5).

NAFTA and financial reforms in Mexico

Finally, it is worth noting that FLD was implemented in accord with, and to a great extent was influenced by, Mexico's negotiations for economic integration with its developed northern neighbors. Chapter 14 of the North American Free Trade Agreement (NAFTA), finally approved to start in January 1994, deals with financial services. There each country agreed to grant national treatment to the financial institutions of its trade partners.

However, Mexico's financial opening was programmed as a gradual process and with some restrictions to foreign investors.[16] Basically, Canadian and US financial institutions were granted immediate access to the local market, but with some limits until the year 2000. Banking institutions initially face an individual ceiling of 1.5 percent and on the aggregate of 8 percent of total domestic capital in the sector. The aggregate limit increases to 15 percent by the year 2000. Concerning securities services, the initial limit is 10 percent and increases to 20 percent the same year. Security brokerage firms can have an initial participation of 4 percent of the market. After the year 2000 limits would be relaxed, but Mexico retains the right to impose limits if aggregates of Canadian and US banks move beyond 25 percent of domestic capital.

The individual limit of 1.5 percent should be removed by the year 2000 for banking institutions growing through internal funds, including allocations from the parent. However a 4 percent limit will be in effect. If a subsidiary of a Canadian or US bank has interests of 0.5 percent in a Mexican bank, the foreign institution can buy a local bank whose share of the market is 3.5 percent, which would be within the maximum allowed of 4 percent.

Finally, a 30 percent limit on common stock is fixed for joint investments carried out by Canadian and US investors in the Mexican banking sector. The limit does not apply to investments made in foreign subsidiaries. Similarly, foreign investment in brokerage houses is also limited to 30 percent: individual investment should not exceed 10 percent. Individual Mexican investors, however, can invest up to 15 percent of capital of these institutions, with the authorization of the Ministry of Finance. The above rules do not apply to investments made by foreign subsidiaries.

In short, although financial reforms in Mexico were intense, during the 1988–94 period, financial institutions and financial markets remained somewhat protected in spite of an important agreement on trade and investments with the United States and Canada.

FINANCIAL LIBERALIZATION AND DEREGULATION AND THE PERFORMANCE OF THE MEXICAN SECURITIES MARKET

Trends in foreign direct and portfolio investments in Mexico

Mexico's recent financial crisis has illustrated that the integration of "emerging capital markets" to the world financial markets can be also accompanied by high instability and economic setbacks. Financial liberalization and deregulation have often been identified as important causes for the crisis. Trends in the Mexican securities markets seem to confirm this hypothesis, but the root of Mexico's crisis is essentially related to erroneous policy-making.

In 1980 total capitalization of the stock market amounted to only $12,994 million and traded value to $3,262 million. By the end of 1988 these indicators had increased to $13,784 and $5,732 million, respectively.

During the following years, Mexican Stock Market (MSM) activity grew spectacularly as a result of financial liberalization and deregulation, and in response to favorable investment regulations and laws and the positive economic perspectives, partly due to the North American Free Trade Agreement. By 1994, market capitalization increased to $129,850 million, while trading value amounted to $84,101 million.[17] Furthermore, foreign investments in the MSM became an important part of foreign direct investment flows during the 1988–94 period. Table 5.1 shows that foreign direct investments reached a total of $77,938.4 million by the end of 1994. Thus during the period under consideration, FDI more than tripled the amount of $24,087.4 million accumulated until 1988.

Table 5.1 Direct and stock market investments in Mexico, 1989–94
(million dollars)

Year	Annual			Cumulative balance		
	Total	Direct	Stock market	Total	Direct	Stock market
1971				3,882.4		
1976				5,315.8		
1982				10,876.4		
1988				24,087.4		
1989	2,913.7	2,499.7	414.0	27,001.1	26,587.1	414.0
1990	4,978.4	3,722.4	1,256.0	31,979.5	30,309.5	1,670.0
1991	9,897.0	7,015.2	2,881.8	41,876.5	37,324.7	4,551.8
1992	8,334.8	5,705.1	2,629.7	50,211.3	43,029.8	7,081.5
1993	15,617.0	4,900.7	10,716.3	65,828.3	47,930.5	17,897.8
1994	12,110.1	8,026.2	4,083.9	77,938.4	55,956.7	21,980.9

Source: Secofi, Dirección General de Inversión Extranjera.

Table 5.1 also reveals another important change in foreign investment patterns in Mexico. Until 1988, portfolio investments were negligible in Mexico, to the extent that they were not formally registered. This was the result of restrictive regulations to invest in the local securities markets. Other problems like economic instability, lack of confidence in the peso, and restrictive regulations in the developed countries also contributed to this problem. However, financial liberalization in Mexico made its capital markets accessible to foreign investors. Furthermore, deregulation in the developed countries played a key role in making possible the portfolio investments of its nationals in securities from emerging capital markets. In the US this is the case of regulation 144A. Indeed, 33 Mexican corporations have issued ADRs at the New York exchange markets since 1990.

As a result cumulative portfolio investments during the 1989–94 period were $21,980.9 million, which accounted for 28.2 percent of total foreign investments received.[18] Moreover, portfolio investments increased steadily in importance till 1993. In 1989 these investments accounted for only 14.2 percent of foreign investment flows for that year. In 1993 portfolio investments accounted for two-thirds of foreign investments in Mexico. In 1994, direct investment flows increased sharply, but flows to the stock market showed a sluggish growth, a total of only $4.1 billion for the year.

Foreign flows to the Mexican money markets were also of significance. Table 5.2 reveals that by November 1994 foreign investors held a total of $23,292.8 million of total domestic debt (29.11 percent). These holdings concentrated in *Tesobonos* ($13,552 million in February 1995), an instrument denominated in dollars, created in 1991. Thus, foreign portfolio investments became the Achilles heel of the liberalized Mexican securities markets. Indeed, Table 5.3 shows the market value and composition of portfolio investments in the stock market and the amounts and composition of foreign investments in the money market. The fall in the stock market from November to December was 36.14 percent in dollar terms; the fall in the market value of foreign holdings in the capital market neared $15.9 billion, i.e. 31.6 percent of the total market value reported in November. This suggests that the fall in the market value of foreign holdings reported for December was due to significant withdrawals from foreign investors. The contribution of portfolio disinvestments to the Mexican crisis is confirmed by examining the market value of foreign stock market holdings for the following two months. By February 1995 the stock market had fallen 190 percent from its November level, while the value of foreign holdings plunged to $18.9 billion, a fall of $31,365.45 million – 62.3 percent lower than its November level. In the short term securities market the picture was also dramatic. Foreign holdings of domestic debt decreased by the end of December to $19,576.8 million, that is by $3,716 million. These trends would seem to confirm reports that on the days surrounding the peso

Table 5.2 Holdings on Mexican domestic debt, 1994 (million dollars)

	Total	%	Banking sector	%	Banco de Mexico	%	Foreign nationals	%	Mexican nationals*	%
Cetes	20,230.90	25.3	277.80	32.4	12,270.00	26.5	5,637.57	24.2	2,045.80	21.3
Bondes	3,109.47	3.9	99.72	11.6	1,898.45	4.1	63.57	0.3	1,047.73	10.9
Tesobonos	47,630.47	59.6	132.54	15.5	28,001.77	60.5	16,299.66	70.0	3,196.50	33.4
Ajustabonos	9,049.00	11.3	347.00	40.5	4,116.00	8.9	1,292.00	5.5	3,294.00	34.4
Total	80,019.84	100.0	857.06	100.0	46,286.22	100.0	23,292.80	100.0	9,584.03	100.0
Percent – Nov.	100.0		1.07		57.84		29.11		11.98	
Total	74,660.5		1,348.6		42,407.6		20,632.6		10,271.7	
Percent Dec.	100.0		1.8		56.8		27.6		13.8	

Source: Bolsa Mexicana de Valores, Anuario Bursatil, 1994.
* Corporate and individual holdings – includes stock brokerages firms.

Table 5.3 Market value of foreign portfolio holdings in the Mexican money and stock markets

	Total*	ADR's	Mexico fund	Free subscription*	Neutral fund	Other†
Foreign investments in the capital markets						
Million dollars						
1989	808.00	402.00	264.00	107.00	35.00	
1990	4,079.46	2,086.83	243.85	1,072.74	676.03	
1991	18,542.51	13,733.46	499.33	2,960.96	1,348.76	
1992	28,668.00	21,153.95	619.00‡	5,096.98	1,798.08	
1993	54,484.29	33,959.55	1,238.06	12,906.07	6,380.61	
1994 (Nov.)	50,311.45	29,056.66	1,183.25	12,968.64	7,102.89	
1994 (Dec.)	34,395.00	21,163.00	766.00	8,100.00	4,348.00	19.00
1995 (Jan.)	22,973.00	14,681.00§	562.00	4,791.00	2,913.00	26.00
1995 (Feb.)	18,946.00	12,612.00§	450.00	3,549.00	2,292.00	43.00
Percent						
1989	100.00	49.75	32.67	13.24	4.33	
1990	100.00	51.15	5.98	26.30	16.57	
1991	100.00	74.06	2.69	15.97	7.27	
1992	100.00	73.79	2.16	17.78	6.27	
1993	100.00	62.33	2.27	23.69	11.71	
1994 (Nov.)	100.00	57.75	2.35	25.78	14.12	
1994 (Dec.)	100.00	61.53	2.23	23.55	12.64	0.06
1995 (Jan.)	100.00	63.91	2.45	20.85	12.68	0.11
1995 (Feb.)	100.00	66.57	2.38	18.73	12.10	0.23

	Total	Cetes	Pagafes	Bondes	Tesobonos	Ajustabonos
Foreign investments in the money market						
Million dollars						
1991	5,466.28	2,952.34	21.08	725.84	257.03	1,509.99
1992	14,206.87	9,150.98	0.00	1,236.64	197.37	3,641.12
1993	22,083.16	15,478.45	0.00	836.53	1,241.78	4,526.40
1994 (Nov.)	23,292.80	6,071.20	0.00	187.70	15,654.70	1,379.10
1994 (Dec.)	19,576.80	2,531.70	0.00	28.60	16,491.00	524.70
1995 (Jan.)	19,411.90	2,870.00	0.00	16.10	16,052.60	473.30
1995 (Feb.)	17,424.30	3,393.60	0.00	41.50	13,552.90	436.30
Percent						
1991	100.00	54.01	0.39	13.28	4.70	27.62
1992	100.00	64.41	0.00	8.70	1.39	25.63
1993	100.00	70.09	0.00	3.79	5.62	20.50
1994 (Nov.)	100.00	26.06	0.00	0.81	67.21	5.92
1994 (Dec.)	100.00	12.93	0.00	0.15	84.24	2.68
1995 (Jan.)	100.00	14.78	0.00	0.08	82.69	2.44
1995 (Feb.)	100.00	19.48	0.00	0.24	77.78	2.50

Sources: Developed from Bolsa Mexicana de Valores, Anuario Bursátil, 1993 and 1995, and Bolsa Mexicana de Valores, Indicadores Bursátiles, various issues, 1993–5.
Notes:
* Since 1992 includes Investment Societies and the accounts for third parties from Citibank.
† Includes derivatives and intermediate market shares.
‡ October 1992.
§ Includes ADRs and GDRs.

devaluation of 20 December 1994 capital flight from the Mexican securities markets neared $19 billion.

Nevertheless, the crisis cannot be attributed directly to financial liberalization and deregulation, but rather to bad policy-making. The figures on securities market trends, previously analyzed, show that the liberalized Mexican securities markets have an enormous potential to promote Mexico's economic development. But that potential remained rather unexploited because an effective link between investments in the capital markets and corporate activity was not established. Similarly, foreign investments in the money markets, due to their short term nature, were not tied in to any development plans either. Simply, they were government domestic debt held by foreign nationals. Since large amounts of this debt were denominated in dollars, those holdings drastically changed the character of domestic debt to that of foreign debt. Foreign portfolio investments therefore had a high potential to be withdrawn if negative conditions appeared.

Unfortunately, that situation took place because by 1994 it became obvious that the economic bonanza of the previous years was illusory. Since 1988 the balance of trade of the Mexican economy showed huge annual deficits: $20.7 billion in 1993 alone and an accumulated amount of $82.2 billion for the 1989–93 period.[19] Moreover, in order to control inflation the peso was overvalued. Its overvaluation neared 30 percent by the end of 1994.

Nevertheless adjustments were not made in time, they were postponed on purpose since the end of 1992, when the first symptoms of disequilibria came to the forefront. Thus, instead of adjusting the exchange rate and the balance of payments, foreign portfolio investments were promoted to increase international reserves. Thus, foreign portfolio investment flows, rather than supporting investments, were used to support *consumption*, for deficits were mainly due to imports of intermediate goods for the production of consumption goods, and imports of consumption goods *per se*, too. Less than 20 percent of imports were related to purchases of capital goods or technology (Ortiz, 1994).

The reasons for resisting adjustment seem to be rather political, albeit with an economic slant, and personal. To diminish opposition to the North American Free Trade Agreement in the United States, Mexico needed to show an image of prosperity and to give an assurance that it would not take jobs away from US workers. Economic bonanza, although sustained artificially, coupled with high imports from the United States reinforced that view, giving the image that Mexico would be a sound trade partner whose long run growth would create local and US employment. That image was so well maintained and promoted on a worldwide basis that Mexico even became a member of the OECD in April 1994. Mexico seemed to be in a process of rapidly becoming a "first world country," and its President, Salinas de Gortari, was internationally considered to be a great statesman.

The Indian uprising in the State of Chiapas exacerbated the situation of Mexico. That movement started precisely when the government was ready to celebrate the formal initiation of the North American Free Trade Agreement on 1 January 1994. Although this uprising raised some worries among investors in the Mexican securities markets, it did not lead to massive withdrawals of capital. Thus, adjustment policies could have been implemented early in 1994, but the President continued resisting this because presidential elections were due to take place. A devaluation would have increased popular discontent against Partido Revolucionario Institucional, PRI, the ruling party.

Further, the political environment got more complicated because on 23 March 1994 the PRI candidate was assassinated in Tijuana. Then massive withdrawals took place, estimated at $11 billion, to the extent that President Clinton hastily created a $6 billion rescue package for the Mexican economy. This allowed the Mexican government to sustain its overvalued peso and high imports policies. Elections took place on 22 August 1994. Ernesto Zedillo, the official candidate, was elected President by a narrow margin. Beyond this event, independently of further political instability due to further political assassinations, the decision not to devalue the Mexican peso seems to have been solely determined by President Salinas's ambition to become the first president of the emerging World Trade Organization. Traditionally in Mexico, devaluations have been carried out by the outgoing president, which allows the incoming president to start "without blemishes." But President Salinas refused to assume this role, even though meetings between Zedillo and Salinas and his cabinet to take that decision were reported to have taken place. Thus, when President Zedillo began his term, the problem had become unmanageable. The situation was aggravated by the fact that his own cabinet was also incapable of proposing smooth devaluation policies. As a result the peso devaluated drastically, and irate local and foreign investors defensively withdrew their investments from the local markets, leading to Mexico's most profound crisis of the century.

CONCLUSION: THE MACROECONOMIC CONDITIONS NECESSARY TO ACCOMPANY FINANCIAL LIBERALIZATION

The economic situation leading to the Mexican crisis underlies the fact that legal reforms *per se* are not sufficient to stimulate savings and investment processes and to promote the development of a strong, financial system well linked with the real sector. For FLD to be successful it is also necessary to achieve and maintain certain favorable macroeconomic conditions. Otherwise, financial reform could have negative effects on the economy. Viewed from another angle, economic goals require fast liberalization and deregulation reforms, but these reforms must be consistent with the economic goals. That is, economic and financial plans must move together and complement each other. In this respect, the Mexican FLD experience, before the crisis, has been summed up in ten important principles (Aspe, 1993: 92–4).

1 Before starting financial liberalization economic stabilization must be achieved, above all in public financing.
2 Financial liberalization must go beyond the simple liberalization of interest rates and the elimination of quantitative restrictions on credit.
3 Timing and sequencing of reforms to be enforced is very important.
4 The financial system should not be subject to experiments.
5 Greater financial liberalization and innovation must be accompanied by effective supervision laws and mechanisms.
6 The financial system must be financially sound when liberalization takes place.
7 Financial intermediaries must be kept apart from their industrial and commercial clients.
8 Before opening the financial sector to foreign competition it is advisable to give domestic financial institutions time to become aware of and used to conditions prevailing in international competition.
9 Once the financial liberalization process ends, the next step is to move towards the establishment of universal banking.
10 It is important to bear in mind that financial institutions can and must have strong lasting social impacts.

Undoubtedly, these guidelines derived from the Mexican FLD processes are sound and should be followed by governments from developing nations implementing liberalization and deregulation policies. But paradoxically they were not fully applied in Mexico.

However, to some extent they do reflect the Mexican case before the peso devaluation of 1994. But even then they reveal that FLD in Mexico was not well undertaken. Stabilization was not firmly entrenched when financial liberalization started. Moreover, financial liberalization does not seem to have followed a well-thought-out and timed plan. An examination of Mexico's FLD processes reveals, rather, that they were undertaken in a heuristic manner. Only in that way can it be explained why, for instance, reforms to the banking system required several laws, each one tuning-up previous resolutions. Indeed, contrary to the recommendations outlined above, the financial system does seem to have been subject to experiments, even if they were unintentionally instrumented. Similarly, supervision seems to have faltered because the government was unable to detect and prevent failures in the banking system, and failed to set up mechanisms to prevent panic withdrawals from investments in the local securities markets. The weakening of the banking system, due to excessive overdue loans, also reveal that state-owned banks were not really financially sound before reprivatization and FLD.

In sum, FLD in Mexico was rapid and led to profound changes in its financial institutions and markets. However, it was not actioned via a well-thought-out plan, and above all it was implemented in an unbalanced economy and with insufficient links with the real sector. Thus, although financial intermediaries grew significantly and revealed a high potential to support local investments and economic growth, FLD also led to some "perverse effects,"[20] including massive withdrawals of portfolio investments, which led to the peso crisis now affecting Mexico.

Thus, from the Mexican experience, it can be concluded that in addition to the macroeconomic conditions outlined above FLD requires that economic stabilization and equilibria be firmly achieved, the external sector must be balanced, and the exchange rate must be in equilibrium. Overvaluation and its use as a mechanism to control inflation should be avoided. Also, adjustment and financial liberalization and deregulation policies should not be subordinated to political and personal interests. And most important of all, FLD processes should be enforced in order to promote strong links between financial activity and investments in the real sector.

NOTES

* The author wishes to thank Programa de Apoyo a Proyectos de Investigacion e Innovacion Tecnologica (PAPIIT) from Universidad Nacional Autónoma de México for its support for this research.
1 Deregulation is really part of financial liberalization. That is the meaning taken in this work, although for clarity in the exposition sometimes both concepts are used simultaneously. However, it is worth mentioning that liberalization is often only identified with the elimination of restrictions on monetary policy and with the opening of local markets to foreign markets and foreign investments. Deregulation is often limited to changes in laws and regulations that hinder free market activity, or else promote market-oriented institutions.
2 These three goals, particularly the promotion of local savings, remain in the forefront and are the basis of policies designed to overcome Mexico's current crisis and to set the ground for long run growth.
3 SAR was introduced as part of a bill for social security reforms in 1992. See Mansell Carstens (1992).
4 In this respect it is worth noting that Mexican authorities were open to lessons derived from the Chilean experience. See Cortes-Douglas (1992).
5 These reasons for low savings are stressed by Aspe (1993). For other causes for low savings in Mexico see Garrido (1995).
6 Unless otherwise indicated this section is based on Ortiz Martínez (1994).
7 For a summary on this debate see Ortiz Martínez (1994: 71–87).
8 CNB, *Ley de Instituciones de Crédito, 1990*, Arts 11–15.
9 *Ley de Instituciones de Crédito*, Arts 32–3. These shares were created during

the government of President De la Madrid, 1982–8, right after the nationalization of the banking sector (carried out by the previous president, Lopez
Portillo) to curb down dissatisfaction from the private sector.
10 See Comision Nacional Bancaria, *Ley de Instituciones de Crédito*, Titulo VII,
Capitulo 1.
11 *Ley del Mercado de Valores*, Art. 17, 17 July 1990.
12 *Ley General de Organizaciones y Actividades Auxiliares de Crédito*, Art. 38-
A, 1990. The new law passed in 1993 retains this regulation (Cap. II).
13 It refers to knowledge of actions, wrongdoings, etc. that could lead to influen-
cing securities prices in the stock markets, while such information is not
publicly known. See Ortiz Martínez (1994: 114).
14 *Constitución Política de los Estados Unidos Mexicanos*, 1994, Arts 28, 39.
15 Summarized in Banamex-Accival, *Examen de la Situación Económica de
Mexico*, (Enero 1994), pp. 30–5.
16 For an evaluation of the implications of this issue see Ortiz (1994).
17 International Financial Corporation, *Emerging Markets Fact Book 1995*, Washington, DC: IFC, 1995.
18 Portfolio investments are registered as foreign direct investments because the
above figures basically refer to new issues at the international capital markets,
which therefore should be intended for capital expansion.
19 Excludes subcontracting (*maquila*) activity, which began to be reported in the
trade balance in lieu of services since 1993. Banco de México, *Informe Anual*,
various issues, 1988–94.
20 On this issue, see Chapter 4 by Rollinat in this book.

REFERENCES

Araya Gomez, I. (1994) "De la Repression Financiera a la Liberalizacion Finan-
ciera en una Economia en Desarrollo: Una Revisión de la Literatura," *Inversión
y Finanzas* (Mexico), Vol. 2, No. 1, pp. 5–21.
Aspe, P. (1993) *El Camino Mexicano de la Transformación Económica*, Mexico:
Fondo de Cultura Economica.
Aspe, P. (1994) "La Reforma Financiera en Mexico," *Comercio Exterior*
(Mexico), Vol. 4, No. 12, Diciembre, pp. 1044–8.
Banamex-Accival, (1994) "Autonomia del Banco Central," *Examen de la Situa-
ción Económica de Mexico*, Enero, pp. 29–35.
Comision Nacional Bancaria (1990) *Ley de Instituciones de Crédito*, Mexico:
CNB.
Comision Nacional Bancaria (1993) *Ley General de Organizaciones y Actividades
Auxiliares de Crédito*, julio.
Comision Nacional de Valores (1993) *Ley del Mercado de Valores*, Mexico: CNV.
Constitucion Politica de los Estados Unidos Mexicanos (1994) Mexico: Berbera
Editores.
Cortes-Douglas, H. (1992) "Financial Reform in Chile: Lessons in Regulation and
Deregulation," in D. Vittas, ed., *Financial Regulation. Changing the Rules of
the Game*, Washington DC: The International Bank for Reconstruction and
Development/The World Bank.
Diario Oficial de la Federación (1993) 20 de agosto.
Diario Oficial de la Federación (1993) 23 de diciembre.
Edwards, F.R. and H.T. Patrick (1992) "Introduction," in F.R. Edwards and H.T.
Patrick, eds, *Regulating International Financial Markets: Issues and Policies*,
Boston: Kluwer Academic Publishers, pp. 1–10.

Fischer, K.P., E. Ortiz and A.P. Palasvirta (1994) "Risk Management and Corporate Governance in Imperfect Markets," in D.K. Ghosh and E. Ortiz, eds, *The Changing Environment of International Financial Markets. Issues and Analysis*, New York: St Martin's Press, pp. 201–30.

Garrido, C. (1995) "Ahorro en Mexico: Problemas y Perspectivas," In A. Giron, E. Ortiz and E. Correa eds, *Integracion Financiera y TLC. Retos y Perspectivas*, Mexico: Siglo XXI, pp. 213–33.

González Mendez, H. (1993) "Desregulación Financiera en Mexico," *Monetaria*, Mexico: CEMLA, abril–junio.

Instituto Mexicano del Mercado de Capitales, AC (1992) *Contexto Legal del Mercado de Valores*, junio.

International Financial Corporation (1995) *Emerging Markets Fact Book 1995*, Washington, DC: IFC.

La Jornada (1995) martes febrero 7, p. 1.

McKinnon, R. (1973) *Money and Capital in Economic Development*, Washington, DC: Brookings Institution.

Mansell Carstens, C. (1992) "The Savings for Retirement System: Mexico's Revolutionary Pension Fund Reform," *Business* (Mexico), April.

Mansell Carstens, C. (1995) *Las Finanzas Populares en Mexico*, Mexico: Ed. Milenio/ITAM/CEMLA.

Olloqui, G. (1993) "Los Warrants en el Mercado Mexicano," *El Mercado de Valores*, Mexico: Nacional Financiera, No. 2, Enero 15, pp. 11–14.

Ortiz, E. (1993) "Globalizacion Financiera y Desarrollo: Papel de los Mercados de Capital," *II Congreso Nacional Academico en Administracion, Contaduria e Informatica y VII Simposio Hispanico sobre Negocios y Economia* (Memoria), Mexico: UNAM/FCA.

Ortiz, E. (1994) "NAFTA and Foreign Investment in Mexico," in A.M. Rugman, ed., *Foreign Investment and NAFTA*, Columbia, S.C.: University of South Carolina Press, pp. 155–79.

Ortiz, E. (1995) "Take-off into Development and Emerging Capital Markets: Stages of Financial Development and Equity Financing," in H.P. Gray and S.C. Richard, eds, *International Finance in the New World Order*, New York: Pergamon, pp. 71–88.

Ortiz Martínez, G. (1994) *La Reforma Financiera y la Desincorporación Bancaria*, Mexico: Fondo de Cultura Económica.

Rollinat, R. (1996) "Perverse Effects of Globalization in Today's Latin American Finance," in D.K. Ghosh and E. Ortiz, eds, *The Global Structure of Financial Markets*, London: Routledge.

Vitas, D. ed. (1992) *Financial Regulation. Changing the Rules of the Game*, Washington, DC: The World Bank.

6

LATIN AMERICAN EQUITY MARKETS

Benefits from diversification and currency hedging

Luc Soenen and Steve Schrepferman

The turnaround of Latin American economies has been led by the forces of privatization and economic liberalization. The emergence of equity markets in Latin America is part of a general process of globalization of capital markets in the last decade. This chapter investigates diversification benefits and currency hedging benefits for investments in the equity markets of Latin America. We take the viewpoint of investors from six Latin American countries and of the US. Investing in any of the Latin American equities was more risky than investing in the domestic stock market. Five Latin American equity markets outperformed the US stock market over the 1989–1993 period. However, investors from Brazil, Chile and Mexico were not better off investing in foreign equities than investing in their domestic stock markets. Currency hedging is especially favorable to investors from Latin America investing in the US, but not vice versa. Diversifying equities across Latin American markets was beneficial for US investors but not so for Latin American investors. The results support international diversification for risk reduction purposes but not as a means to increase returns.

In the 1960s and 1970s, when the first attempts at regional economic integration began, most Latin American countries were addicted to state intervention and vigorous protection against the outside world through import substitution. State monopolies and private cartels were created in addition to uncompetitive labor legislation. Overdebtedness at the national and corporate level created a massive debt crisis in the 1980s which led to a decade of stagnation and restructuring. Only in the late 1980s did a major political and economic policy change happen which abandoned the inward looking, state-oriented and undisciplined economic and monetary policies of the past. A turnaround, first in Chile and soon thereafter in Mexico and followed by the other Latin American nations, was created by three major trends pursued all over Latin America, i.e. privatization, deregulation and trade liberalization. The restoration of financial stability has led to a renaissance in economic growth in many Latin American countries. As a result the long-term outlook for growth in most of Latin America has become better than ever before. A prime example of the improved tenor of the times is passage of the North American Free Trade Agreement (NAFTA) at the beginning of 1994 and the "summit of the Americas" held in Miami in December 1994. There is a general improved climate for trade and investment activity in Central and South America. The investors' enthusiasm over the region's trend toward democracy, economic liberalization and increased monetary discipline, is reflected in the creation of several Latin America country funds and the Latin America Investment Fund. The number of US retail and institutional clients interested in Latin America continues to surge[1] as is exemplified by the amount of money in Baring Asset Management's Latin funds which totaled some $300 million in 1993 and $1.3 billion by the end of 1994. Similarly Scudder Stevens & Clark's Scudder Latin America Fund, which had $10 million in 1992, had ballooned to $800 million by 1994. Investors' interest in Latin America's equity markets has already resulted in the emergence of many theme funds focusing on such areas as privatization, infrastructure, telecommunications, construction, etc.

The emergence of equity markets in Latin America and elsewhere is part of a general process of globalization of capital markets in the last decade. The emerging markets, in general, attract international investors because of the high returns typical of high-growth economies and the low correlation coefficients with developed security markets as well as among themselves. This chapter analyzes the risk and return of investing in Latin America's emerging equity markets. In contrast with prior studies on emerging stock markets which have taken the US investor's perspective, using the US dollar as the *numéraire* currency, this chapter looks at the international investment in the Latin American equity markets from the point of view of each of the Latin American countries considered. We analyze diversification benefits and currency hedging benefits not just in a mean/variance framework but also using the geometric mean. We argue in accordance with Jorion (1985) that gains in returns claimed by other studies of international portfolio management are "illusory – but the risk reduction factor is highly significant." The reduction in risk also shows up in the geometric mean return. The geometric mean is the way portfolio performance is most often judged and is of special interest since a reduction in risk by international diversification will result in an increased geometric mean return, even if the arithmetic mean is unaffected.

ANALYSIS OF RISK AND RETURN UNHEDGED LATIN AMERICAN EQUITIES

The asset choices used in this study are the emerging national equity markets for six Latin American countries (Argentina, Brazil, Chile, Colombia,

Mexico and Venezuela) and the US equity market. Monthly returns for the emerging markets were obtained from various editions of the International Finance Corporation (IFC) *Annual Emerging Stock Markets Factbook*. The selection of the six Latin American countries was determined by the availability of stock market data from IFC sources. The stock market data for the US, the foreign exchange rates and interest rates were compiled from the IMF's *International Financial Statistics* publications. Data cover the period from January 1989 through December 1993. Generic information about the Latin American stock markets and exchange rates is summarized in the appendix (see pp. 87, 88). We refer to Park and Van Agtmael (1993) for a discussion of each individual Latin American stock market and a brief profile of their major listed companies.[2]

Figure 6.1 illustrates the relative size and rate of growth for the six Latin American stock markets under study. The average growth rate in market capitalization over the 1988–93 period was 52 percent. The fastest growing stock markets were Argentina with 85 percent and Mexico with 71 percent annual rates of growth. Total market capitalization of all six stock markets at the end of 1993 equaled US$406 billion. About half (49.4 percent) of the total is represented by Mexico, followed by Brazil (24.5 percent), Chile (11 percent) and Argentina (10.8 percent). The tiny stock markets of Venezuela and Colombia can be categorized as "emerging markets" as they represent respectively only 2 percent and 2.3 percent of the total market capitalization for the six countries considered.

We examine the *ex post* risk/return relationship for the seven stock markets from the viewpoint of investors from each of these countries. Table 6.1 summarizes the average return and volatility of the international equities. The returns shown in Table 6.1 are all in terms of the *numéraire*

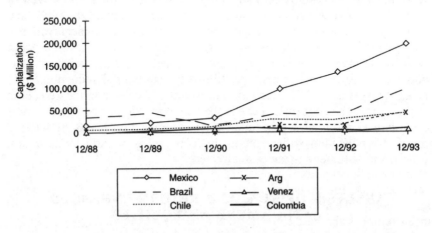

Figure 6.1 Market capitalization of selected Latin American stock markets, December 1988 to December 1993

76

Table 6.1 Performance of unhedged equities

Investor's perspective		Country of investment						
		Argentina	Brazil	Chile	Colombia	Mexico	Venezuela	US
Argentina	AM	0.2278	0.2932	0.2080	0.2057	0.2211	0.1844	0.1819
	GM	0.1531	0.1041	0.1497	0.1513	0.1624	0.1298	0.1312
	SD	0.5504	0.7358	0.4751	0.4493	0.4724	0.4547	0.4284
	CV	2.4159	2.5091	2.2842	2.1836	2.1363	2.4654	2.3551
	SI	0.3298	0.3356	0.3403	0.3548	0.3701	0.3038	0.3165
Brazil	AM	0.3282	0.3518	0.2793	0.2847	0.2938	0.2688	0.2544
	GM	0.2708	0.2168	0.2670	0.2688	0.2810	0.2451	0.2467
	SD	0.4444	0.6511	0.1843	0.2074	0.1814	0.2501	0.1402
	CV	1.3540	1.8508	0.6599	0.7286	0.6174	0.9303	0.5510
	SI	−1.7294	−1.1443	−4.4351	−3.9154	−4.4262	−3.3112	−6.0083
Chile	AM	0.0793	0.1093	0.0375	0.0421	0.0506	0.0287	0.0192
	GM	0.0383	−0.0059	0.0352	0.0366	0.0466	0.0173	0.0186
	SD	0.3338	0.5435	0.0696	0.1124	0.0921	0.1608	0.0364
	CV	4.2093	4.9699	1.8577	2.6657	1.8198	5.6046	1.8909
	SI	0.1872	0.1703	0.2974	0.2256	0.3671	0.0739	0.0669
Colombia	AM	0.0862	0.1122	0.0429	0.0466	0.0560	0.0335	0.0242
	GM	0.0433	−0.0010	0.0402	0.0417	0.0517	0.0222	0.0235
	SD	0.3431	0.5292	0.0755	0.1077	0.0961	0.1599	0.0360
	CV	3.9817	4.7180	1.7584	2.3112	1.7143	4.7775	1.4900
	SI	0.1821	0.1672	0.2546	0.2126	0.3367	0.0611	0.0129
Mexico	AM	0.0751	0.1040	0.0337	0.0374	0.0463	0.0233	0.0151
	GM	0.0341	−0.0099	0.0310	0.0325	0.0424	0.0132	0.0145
	SD	0.3328	0.5331	0.0743	0.1070	0.0903	0.1506	0.0343
	CV	4.4314	5.1263	2.2060	2.8589	1.9495	6.4648	2.2758
	SI	0.1602	0.1542	0.1598	0.1461	0.2716	0.0099	−0.1962
Venezuela	AM	0.0871	0.1186	0.0461	0.0496	0.0589	0.0345	0.0270
	GM	0.0460	0.0016	0.0429	0.0444	0.0544	0.0249	0.0262
	SD	0.3294	0.5486	0.0820	0.1094	0.0975	0.1462	0.0399
	CV	3.7803	4.6258	1.7793	2.2085	1.6556	4.2405	1.4793
	SI	0.1531	0.1493	0.1146	0.1175	0.2275	−0.0152	−0.2437
US	AM	0.0693	0.0977	0.0280	0.0320	0.0406	0.0179	0.0096
	GM	0.0285	−0.0152	0.0255	0.0269	0.0368	0.0077	0.0090
	SD	0.3294	0.5274	0.0730	0.1077	0.0891	0.1505	0.0334
	CV	4.7516	5.4005	3.3704	3.3704	2.1930	8.3984	3.4792
	SI	0.1965	0.1764	0.3205	0.2544	0.4044	0.0885	0.1496

Note: Time period January 1989 to December 1993. Monthly returns.
Key: AM – Arithmetic mean; GM – Geometric mean; SD – Standard deviation; CV – Coefficient of variation; SI – Sharpe index.

currency of the investor, i.e. returns on investments in foreign equities have been adjusted for exchange rate changes.[3] In addition to the arithmetic mean returns, we also calculate the geometric mean returns. The arithmetic mean return is the best estimate of the rate of return we could expect to make if we invested randomly in a month during the 1989–93 period. Although the arithmetic mean return can be considered as the best estimate

77

of a one-period investment, it is not the true average rate of return over multiple periods.[4] Maximum terminal wealth or holding period rate of return is also the performance criterion most often used for portfolio managers.

The widely held view that emerging markets are extremely risky when compared with developed markets (see Divecha *et al.* (1992)) certainly holds for Latin America. Since local stock market returns (diagonal in Table 6.1) are highly influenced by local inflation rates, we cannot make reliable comparisons among the equity markets as such. Using returns expressed in terms of a *numéraire* currency (horizontal in Table 6.1), say the US dollar, corrects for the inflation differential between the foreign country and the investor's home country and provides more comparable estimates of risk and return. To evaluate investment performance properly, we must evaluate performance on a risk-adjusted basis. For this purpose we calculate both the coefficient of variation and Sharpe's (1966) reward-to-variability ratio.[5] Because of extreme inflation the mean interest rate for Brazil was an astronomical 1,316 percent causing a negative Sharpe index for all equity investments from the perspective of the Brazilian investor. A similar phenomenon occurred for the Venezuelan investor investing in the home equity market and in the US. Using the Sharpe measure as a benchmark, if one compared investment in domestic stock markets (diagonal in Table 6.1) against the US stock market, it is clear that Argentina, Chile, Mexico and Columbia showed exceptionally good performances. From the viewpoint of the US investor and according to the coefficient of variation, three Latin American equity markets, i.e. Chile, Colombia and Mexico, showed a more favorable ratio than the US. In terms of the more comprehensive measure of portfolio efficiency, the Sharpe index indicates that only the Venezuelan equity market was inferior in performance than the US stock market from the US perspective.

The conclusion reported first by Perold and Schulman (1988) and then by Arnott and Henriksson (1989) for the period 1973 to mid-1987 that "on a stand-alone, unhedged basis, foreign stock markets are much riskier than the U.S. market" certainly does hold for our data period. The standard deviation of a US investor is much higher from investing in the six Latin American countries than from investing in the US. The question is whether this is a generalizable result due to exchange rate risk having a compounding effect on security risk. However, investing in foreign equities resulted in lower risk for the Argentinian, Brazilian and Venezuelan investor in 15 out of 18 possible cases. We cannot conclude that in general investing in any single equity market is riskier than investing at home. In exactly half of the possible cases (21 out of 42) risk was increased; in the other half of the cases it was reduced. Besides, investing in the US equity market showed a lower standard deviation than investing in the domestic stock market for investors from all six Latin American countries.

Jorion (1989) reports that over the period January 1978 to December 1988, unhedged foreign stocks outperformed US stocks by 710 basis points per year on average. Solnik and Noetzlin (1982) show that foreign stocks outperformed US stocks over the period 1970–80 as well. The total volatility of foreign stocks is hardly greater than that of US stocks. Both studies examine the risk and return characteristics of foreign stocks from a US investor's perspective. Since the Latin American equities of Table 6.1 display a higher standard deviation in monthly returns than the US market does, none of the six foreign stock markets dominates US stocks for US dollar-based investors. That is, they do not offer higher returns at less risk. However, since the returns for the seven equity markets show major differences, the unadjusted standard deviation can be misleading. Using the coefficient of variation as a measure of relative variability to compare alternative equity market investments, the investment by a US person in the stock markets of Chile, Colombia and Mexico were less risky than investing at home over the period 1989–93. According to the Sharpe index, i.e. excess return per unit of total risk, and taking the US perspective, all Latin American equity markets except for Venezuela outperformed the US stock market. Actually, Mexican equities outperformed the six other equities in terms of the Sharpe measure. Foreign equities do not perform better than domestic equity markets in 25 out of 42 possible cases (60 percent) and this is especially true for investors from Brazil, Chile and Mexico, i.e. 17 out of 18 possible cases.

HEDGED LATIN AMERICAN EQUITIES

Investing in international equities adds currency risk but likewise enhances the set of return opportunities. However, Eun and Resnick (1988) pointed out that a fluctuating exchange rate contributes to the risk of foreign investment, not only through its own variance but also through its positive covariances with the local stock market returns. Taking the viewpoint of the US investor using the US dollar as the *numéraire* currency, they found that the exchange rate changes *vis-à-vis* the US dollar are highly correlated across currencies. As a result, a large portion of exchange risk would remain undiversifiable in a multicurrency portfolio. A number of studies (e.g., Eaker and Grant (1985), Eun and Resnick (1988), Lee (1988), Thomas (1989), Hauser and Levy (1991), and Soenen and Lindvall (1992)) conclude that the benefits from diversification in developed stock markets are enhanced by hedging the exchange rate risk. However, recent research by Hauser *et al.* (1994) showed that under certain conditions foreign exchange hedging may not be beneficial. In particular, they conclude that hedging currency risk of high-risk emerging markets can decrease the gains from international diversification.

First, we consider the investment in a single foreign equity market as compared to investment in the domestic stock market from the seven countries' viewpoints. Hedged returns are computed using a one-month rolling hedge for each stock market. Currency risk is hedged through a forward sale of the investment amount at the beginning of each month. That is equivalent to borrowing the foreign currency for one month and swapping this amount into the domestic currency of the investor for simultaneous lending in the local market for the same maturity. Interest rates for the various countries were compiled from the IMF's *International Financial Statistics*.[6] The hedged position in the foreign currency equity has a domestic return equal to the foreign equity return plus the one month interest rate differential (equivalent to the one month forward premium or discount on the foreign currency). The amount hedged is equal to the foreign equity position at the beginning of each month because its magnitude at the end of the month is unknown when the hedging decision is made. This constant hedge policy is necessarily imperfect, as the exact amount to hedge is not known because of fluctuations in the foreign currency equity values. The remaining currency exposure is small considering the short hedging intervals. In addition, to maintain a full hedge the forward contract or swap position would have to be continuously monitored. Frequent rebalancing is expensive and may not outbalance the deviation from the optimal full hedge. Table 6.2 represents the risk and return characteristics of hedged Latin American equities along with the US, ignoring transaction costs.[7]

The difference between unhedged (Table 6.1) and hedged returns (Table 6.2) corresponds to the impact of exchange rates on foreign investment. Foreign exchange hedging supposedly eliminates or at least reduces currency risk. This is true for a one-period hedge but here a foreign exchange hedge is executed for a one-month period and is rolled over for 60 consecutive months. When hedging a long-term exposure by repeated short-term hedges actually implies the unknown change in the future, spot rate at the end of each month is replaced by the one month forward exchange rate or the one month interest rate differential between the investor's domestic interest and foreign interest rates. Volatility is reduced when the variability in the interest rate differential is lower than that of the spot exchange rates over the investment horizon.[8] A hedged foreign investment, therefore, will not necessarily have a lower risk than an unhedged investment will have. Table 6.3 summarizes the difference in performance between hedged and unhedged international equity investments, i.e. the changes between Tables 6.1 and 6.2. A negative number in Table 6.3 indicates a reduction in return or risk as a result of hedging.

Hedged Latin American stocks have lower volatility (i.e. standard deviation) than do domestic stocks from a US viewpoint in four out of the six markets considered. However, the results of Table 6.3 show that currency

Table 6.2 Performance of hedged equities

Investor's perspective		Country of investment						
		Argentina	Brazil	Chile	Colombia	Mexico	Venezuela	US
Argentina	AM	0.2278	−0.7684	−0.1610	0.6094	0.7632	0.8346	2.2517
	GM	0.1531	−0.9604	−0.3526	−0.1418	0.1256	−0.1805	0.9912
	SD	0.5504	0.5842	1.2454	2.0107	1.9314	2.4840	3.8094
	CV	2.4159	−0.7603	−7.7368	3.2995	2.5305	2.9766	1.6918
	SI	0.3298	−1.3946	−0.1665	0.2801	0.3712	0.3174	0.5789
Brazil	AM	75.2508	0.3518	56.8045	40.5354	58.7652	35.0939	95.0505
	GM	29.6622	0.2168	43.3553	30.0945	40.3877	28.5717	68.8753
	SD	87.7054	0.6511	45.0584	31.2959	53.1281	22.3811	74.5366
	CV	1.1655	1.8508	0.7932	0.7721	0.9041	0.6377	0.7842
	SI	0.8455	−1.1443	1.2363	1.2602	1.0855	1.5190	1.2605
Chile	AM	0.3249	−09514	0.0375	−0.2896	0.0676	−0.3748	0.6693
	GM	0.1672	−0.9727	0.0352	−0.2437	0.0255	−0.3389	0.7251
	SD	0.5875	0.0701	0.0696	0.2533	0.2886	0.2111	0.4207
	CV	1.8023	−0.0737	1.8577	−1.0246	4.2679	−0.6228	0.5802
	SI	0.5244	−13.8117	0.2974	−1.2096	0.1760	−1.8550	1.5510
Colombia	AM	2.5399	−0.9164	0.1208	0.0466	0.1159	−0.0110	1.0318
	GM	2.3461	−0.9557	0.0874	0.0417	0.0829	−0.0522	1.0084
	SD	0.8312	0.1098	0.2968	0.1077	0.2650	0.2892	0.1520
	CV	0.3273	−0.1198	2.4556	2.3112	2.2875	−26.2123	0.1473
	SI	3.0272	−8.5642	0.3272	0.2126	0.3477	−0.1201	6.6331
Mexico	AM	−0.1050	−0.9354	−0.2079	−0.1724	0.0463	−0.1356	0.6881
	GM	−0.3642	−0.9674	−0.2341	−0.2090	0.0424	−0.2151	0.6631
	SD	0.5517	0.0892	0.2207	0.2511	0.0903	0.3846	0.3001
	CV	−5.2559	−0.0954	−1.0616	−1.4565	1.9495	−2.8352	0.4361
	SI	−0.2298	−10.7266	−1.0408	−0.7734	0.2716	−0.4094	2.2206
Venezuela	AM	0.7680	−0.9135	0.5155	0.1192	0.3629	0.0345	1.4089
	GM	0.0147	−0.9460	0.4340	0.0927	0.2387	0.0249	1.2975
	SD	1.4002	0.0999	0.5371	0.2434	0.6011	0.1462	0.7558
	CV	1.8231	−0.1093	1.0418	2.0416	1.6564	4.2405	0.5365
	SI	0.5223	−9.5128	0.8915	0.3389	0.5427	−0.0152	1.8155
US	AM	−0.4832	−0.9640	−0.5482	−0.5783	−0.5019	−0.5745	0.0096
	GM	−0.6417	−0.9821	−0.5634	−0.5799	−0.5209	−0.5806	0.0090
	SD	0.3258	0.0499	0.1099	0.0892	0.0830	0.1631	0.0334
	CV	−0.6743	−0.0518	−0.2005	−0.1543	−0.1654	−0.2838	3.4792
	SI	−1.4972	−19.3941	−5.0300	−6.5348	−6.1032	−3.5519	0.1496

Note: Time period January 1989 to December 1993. Monthly returns.
Key: AM – Arithmetic mean; GM – Geometric mean; SD – Standard deviation; CV – Coefficient of variation; SI – Sharpe index.

hedging by an investor from Latin America increased the risk of an investment in any single foreign country compared to an unhedged invest-ment in 33 of 42 possible cases. The only exception is equity investments in Brazil, where currency hedging by investors from all other countries resulted in reduced volatility. These findings are in support of the argument recently made by Hauser *et al.* (1994, p. 76) that "Hedging currency risk is

Table 6.3 Difference in performance between hedged and unhedged equities (hedged–unhedged)

Investor's perspective		Country of investment						
		Argentina	Brazil	Chile	Colombia	Mexico	Venezuela	US
Argentina	AM		−1.0616	−0.3690	0.4037	0.5421	0.6502	2.0698
	GM		−1.0645	−0.5023	−0.2931	−0.0368	−0.3103	0.8600
	SD		−0.1516	0.7703	1.5614	1.4590	2.0293	3.3810
	CV		−3.2694	−10.0210	1.1159	0.3942	0.5112	−0.6633
	SI		−1.7302	−0.5068	−0.0747	0.0011	0.0136	0.2624
Brazil	AM	74.9226		56.5252	40.2507	58.4714	34.8251	94.7961
	GM	29.3914		43.0883	29.8257	40.1067	28.3266	68.6286
	SD	87.2610		44.8741	31.0885	52.9467	22.1310	74.3964
	CV	−0.1885		0.1333	0.0435	0.2867	−0.2926	0.2332
	SI	2.5749		5.6714	5.1756	5.5117	4.8302	7.2688
Chile	AM	0.2456	−1.0607		−0.3317	0.0170	−0.4035	0.6501
	GM	0.1289	−0.9668		−0.2839	−0.0211	−0.3562	0.7065
	SD	0.2537	−0.4734		0.1409	0.1965	0.0503	0.3843
	CV	−2.4070	−5.0436		−3.6903	2.4481	−6.2274	−1.3107
	SI	0.3372	−13.9820		−1.4352	−0.1911	−1.9290	1.4841
Colombia	AM	2.4537	−1.0286	0.0779		0.0598	−0.0445	1.0076
	GM	2.3028	−0.9547	0.0472		0.0312	−0.0744	0.9849
	SD	0.4881	−0.4195	0.2213		0.1690	0.1293	0.1160
	CV	−3.6544	−4.8378	0.6972		0.5732	−30.9899	−1.3427
	SI	2.8451	−8.7313	0.0726		0.0111	−0.1812	6.6202
Mexico	AM	−0.1801	−1.0394	−0.2416	−0.2098		−0.1589	0.6730
	GM	−0.3983	−0.9576	−0.2651	−0.2415		−0.2283	0.6486
	SD	0.2189	−0.4438	0.1464	0.1441		0.2340	0.2658
	CV	−9.6873	−5.2217	−3.2676	−4.3154		−9.3000	−1.8397
	SI	−0.3900	−10.8808	−1.2006	−0.9195		−0.4193	2.4168
Venezuela	AM	0.6809	−1.0321	0.4694	0.0696	0.3040		1.3819
	GM	−0.0313	−0.9476	0.3911	0.0483	0.1843		1.2713
	SD	1.0708	−0.4487	0.4551	0.1340	0.5036		0.7159
	CV	−1.9572	−4.7351	−0.7375	−0.1669	0.0008		−0.9429
	SI	0.3692	−9.6621	0.7768	0.2215	0.3151		2.0592
US	AM	−0.5525	−1.0617	−0.5762	−0.6103	−0.5426	−0.5925	
	GM	−0.6702	−0.9669	−0.5889	−0.6068	−0.5577	−0.5884	
	SD	−0.0036	−0.4775	0.0369	−0.0185	−0.0061	0.0126	
	CV	−5.4259	−5.4523	−3.5709	−3.5247	−2.3584	−8.6822	
	SI	−1.6937	−19.5706	−5.3506	−6.7892	−6.5076	−3.6404	

Note: Time period January 1989 to December 1993. Monthly returns.
Key: AM – Arithmetic mean; GM – Geometric mean; SD – Standard deviation; CV – Coefficient of variation; SI – Sharpe index.

beneficial in developed, but not in emerging stock markets." This is further exemplified by a drop in the Sharpe measure hedged versus unhedged equities for all six Latin American countries from the US perspective, while hedging US equities by investors from the six Latin American countries always resulted in a lower coefficient of variation (with the exception of a Brazilian investing in the US) and more importantly a higher Sharpe index. Since overall hedged foreign equities show an improvement of portfolio efficiency (i.e. a larger value for the Sharpe index) in exactly half of all possible cases, currency hedging is not necessarily advantageous to the international portfolio investor. However, as suggested earlier, hedged equity investments are particularly appealing to investors from Latin America investing in the US stock market but not vice versa.

LATIN AMERICAN EQUITY PORTFOLIOS

In addition to investigating Latin American stock markets from different investors' viewpoints individually, next we examine them collectively in stock portfolios held in conjunction with domestic stocks. The international portfolios are constructed on the basis of the seven equity markets; that is, including the investor's home country's stock market. Three kinds of internationally diversified portfolios are constructed, i.e. equally weighted (that is one-seventh in each stock market at the start of each month), market capitalization weighted (also monthly adjusted to reflect the relative size of the seven stock markets in terms of US dollars) and minimum variance portfolios.[9] The risk/return tradeoff for these unhedged investment portfolios is reported in Table 6.4.

The general conclusion reported by Jorion (1989) that for US investors "international portfolio diversification has offered sizable benefits in terms of higher return and lower risk" is confirmed by our data analysis. There is strong evidence of lower risk (coefficient of variation) and superior performance (Sharpe index) by investing in Latin American equities. For investors from the six Latin American countries, however, internationally diversified portfolios show higher volatility and lower efficiency in terms of risk adjusted return than investing in the domestic equity market. As was concluded earlier by Soenen and Lindvall (1992), depending on the country's viewpoint diversification into foreign equities is, therefore, not always beneficial. Using the Sharpe measure as a benchmark, over the 1989–93 period Latin American investors would have been better off holding a domestically diversified portfolio than investing in any of the three types of internationally diversified portfolios in 14 out of 18 possible cases.

On average (see Table 6.4), international equity diversification across Latin American markets resulted in a risk reduction with 747 basis points for equally weighted portfolios (a 22 percent reduction compared to the average standard deviation of national stock markets) and with 1,417 basis points using minimum variance portfolios (a 60 percent reduction). It also led to an increase of 26 basis points (2.4 percent) in the arithmetic mean return and an increase of 430 basis points (79 percent) in the geometric mean return for equally weighted portfolios; while there was a decrease of

Table 6.4 Performance of unhedged equity portfolios

Investor's perspective	Arithmetic mean				Geometric mean				Standard deviation			
	Own country	Equally weighted portfolio	Market capitalization portfolio	Minimum variance portfolio	Own country	Equally weighted portfolio	Market capitalization portfolio	Minimum variance portfolio	Own country	Equally weighted portfolio	Market capitalization portfolio	Minimum variance portfolio
Argentina	0.2278	0.2175	0.1838	0.1213	0.1531	0.1637	0.1330	0.0718	0.5504	0.4453	0.4292	0.3710
Brazil	0.3518	0.2944	0.2563	0.2454	0.0763	0.2824	0.2486	0.2381	0.6511	0.1805	0.1393	0.1344
Chile	0.0375	0.0524	0.0208	0.0238	0.0352	0.0478	0.0202	0.0233	0.0696	0.1023	0.0364	0.0315
Colombia	0.0466	0.0574	0.0257	0.0271	0.0417	0.0529	0.0251	0.0266	0.1077	0.1003	0.0357	0.0311
Mexico	0.0463	0.0478	0.0166	0.0193	0.0424	0.0436	0.0161	0.0189	0.0903	0.0977	0.0342	0.0276
Venezuela	0.0345	0.0602	0.0286	0.0270	0.0249	0.0556	0.0278	0.0264	0.1462	0.1027	0.0403	0.0339
US	0.0096	0.0422	0.0111	0.0139	0.0090	0.0380	0.0106	0.0135	0.0334	0.0965	0.0331	0.0269
Average	0.1077	0.1103	0.0776	0.0683	0.0547	0.0977	0.0688	0.0598	0.2355	0.1608	0.1069	0.0938

Investor's perspective	Coefficient of variation				Sharpe index			
	Own country	Equally weighted portfolio	Market capitalization portfolio	Minimum variance portfolio	Own country	Equally weighted portfolio	Market capitalization portfolio	Minimum variance portfolio
Argentina	2.4159	2.0476	2.3356	3.0576	0.3298	0.3844	0.3203	0.2023
Brazil	1.8508	0.6129	0.5436	0.5475	−1.1443	−4.4465	−6.0337	−6.3365
Chile	1.8577	1.9516	1.7507	1.3255	0.2970	0.3481	0.1098	0.2213
Colombia	2.3112	1.7485	1.3861	1.1483	0.2127	0.3356	0.0567	0.1090
Mexico	1.9495	2.0430	2.0549	1.4355	0.2716	0.2664	−0.1516	−0.0922
Venezuela	4.2405	1.7054	1.4119	1.2553	−0.0152	0.2292	−0.2017	−0.2863
US	3.4792	2.2890	2.9779	1.9429	0.1496	0.3892	0.1970	0.3440
Average	2.5864	1.7711	1.7801	1.5304	0.0145	−0.3562	−0.8147	−0.8341

Note: Time period is January 1989 to December 1993. Monthly returns.

394 points (37 percent) in the arithmetic mean return and an increase of 51 points (9 percent) in the geometric mean return for minimum variance portfolios. Market capitalization weighted portfolios showed lower risk in combination with lower mean return compared to the average for the national stock markets. The benefits of international equity diversification are higher when measured in terms of the geometric mean return because any reduction in standard deviation (with a constant arithmetic mean return) has a positive impact on the geometric mean return. Obviously, the benefits from diversification across Latin American countries using minimum variance portfolios are superior compared with those for naive portfolios in terms of risk reduction, but not necessarily in terms of mean returns. Comparing optimal with naive investment portfolios (i.e. equally weighted) the average coefficient of variation is reduced by 41 percent versus 31.5 percent, while the average Sharpe index turned negative largely because of the extreme negative Sharpe measure for Brazil due to horrendously high interest rates in that country (especially during the period September 1992 to December 1993).

CONCLUSION

This chapter examines the risk/return characteristics of investments in six Latin American equity markets over the 1989–93 period. Results are obtained for US investors and for investors from the Latin American countries. Investing in any single Latin American stock market was much more risky than investing in the domestic stock market from the US viewpoint. However, foreign stock market investment showed increased risk in only 50 percent of the cases for investors from Latin America. Five Latin American equity markets, the exception is Venezuela, outperformed the US equity market in terms of the Sharpe measure. Investors from Brazil, Chile and Mexico, however, were not better off investing in foreign equities than investing in domestic stocks.

Since overall currency hedging showed an improvement of portfolio efficiency in exactly half of the instances, we conclude that currency hedging may adversely affect foreign equity investments and, therefore, foreign exchange hedging is not necessarily advantageous to the international investor. Although hedged equities are in general favorable to investors from Latin America investing in the US stock market, this is certainly not the case vice versa.

International portfolio investments across the six Latin American equity markets offered superior performance for US investors. Although over the 1989–93 period Latin American investors would have been better off holding a domestically diversified portfolio than investing in an internationally diversified portfolio. The benefits from diversification across Latin American countries using minimum variance portfolios are obviously greater than those for naive portfolios in terms of risk reduction, but not necessarily in terms of mean returns.

APPENDIX: STOCK MARKET INDEX INFORMATION

Argentina

The base date for the Bolsa Indice General is Dec. 29, 1977 = 0.00001.
The base date for the IFCG Argentina Index is Dec. 1984 = 100.
* 1989 – The peso replaced the austral at a rate of 10,000 australes to 1
     peso.

Brazil

The base date for the Bovespa Index is 1968 = 0.000000001.
The base date for the IGCG Brazil Index is Dec. 1984 = 100.
* 1989 – Bovespa Index was divided by 10 in April 1989.
* 1990 – Bovespa Index was divided by 10 in January 1990.
* 1991 – Bovespa Index was divided by 10 in May 1991.
* 1992 – Bovespa Index was divided by 10 in January 1992.
* 1993 – Bovespa Index was divided by 10 on 26 February 1993.
* 1994 – Bovespa Index was divided by 10 on 10 February 1994.

Chile

The base date for the IGPA Index is Dec. 1980 = 100.
The base date for the IFCG Chile Index is Dec. 1984 = 100.
* 1989 – IGPA Index was divided by 10 in April 1989.

Colombia

The base date for the IBB Index is Jan. 1991 = 100.
The base date for the IFCG Colombia Index is Dec. 1984 = 100.
* 1992 – The Bolsa de Bogota ceased the publication of the General Index
     from 31 Dec. 1990.
   – It introduced a new index (IBB) in January 1992.

Mexico

The base date for the BMV Index is Nov. 1978 = 0.7816.
The base date for the IFCG Mexico Index is Dec. 1984 = 100.
* 1991 – BMV Index was divided by 1,000 in May 1991.
* 1993 – Mexico introduced a new currency, the nuevo peso, effective
     1 January 1993.

– The nuevo peso replaces the peso at an exchange rate of 1,000 pesos for 1 nuevo peso.

Venezuela

The base date for the New BVC Index is 1971 = 100.
The base date for the IFCG Venezuela Index is Dec. 1984 = 100.
* 1989 – The Bolsa de Bogota ceased the publication of the General Index from 31 Dec. 1990.
  – It introduced a new index (IBB) in January 1992.

NOTES

1 See Victoria Griffith, "Branching Out," *Latin Finance*, 62, December 1994, p. 18.
2 For a discussion of restrictions on foreign portfolio investment in emerging stock markets see, for example, Park and Van Agtmael (1993), Hartmann and Khambata (1993) and Sollinger (1992).
3 For example, the mean return of an Argentinian investing at home was 22.78 percent per month, but if the Argentinian had invested in Brazil the mean return was 29.32 percent per month in Argentinian pesos. Since the return in Brazil was 35.18 percent per month stated in Brazilian reals, the Argentinian peso appreciated against the real over this period.
4 The arithmetic mean return (AM) is an approximation of the true multi-period rate of return or geometric mean return (GM). As the variance of the one-period returns grows smaller, this approximation becomes better, i.e. AM = $(GM)^2$ + Var(r). Hence, the simpler arithmetic mean return can be used as an approximation of the more complex geometric mean return in cases in which the variability of the one-period rates is slight. For more detail see, for example, Francis (1991, pp. 25–8).
5 More advanced portfolio performance comparison measures such as Jobson and Korkie (1981) and Gibson *et al.* (1989) were not considered here as all these measures have shortcomings of their own. According to Jobson and Korkie (1981, p. 891) the Sharpe measure appears to have a relatively small number of theoretical objections, but has no accompanying significance test. In calculating the Sharpe index we used the Treasury Bill rate when available, i.e. for the US and Mexico. Because of lack of better data, we used the discount rate for Argentina and Venezuela and the bank deposit rate for Brazil, Chile and Colombia. However, because of the unavailability of interest rates the Sharpe index was calculated for the period starting in April 1990 for Argentina and in March 1991 for Chile.
6 The interest rates used are the lending and deposit rates for each country. Because of the "astronomical" level of interest rates they were only compiled as of April 1990 for Argentina and as of June 1990 for Brazil. Interest rates for Chile were not available before March 1991. The hedging was adjusted accordingly to take these factors into account.
7 Transaction costs in the foreign exchange markets (i.e. the spread between bid and ask rates for a foreign currency) are of the order of 0.1 to 0.5 percent for heavily traded currencies and higher for less widely traded currencies.
8 Empirical evidence shows that forward exchange rates (i.e. interest rate differ-

entials) are at least as volatile as spot exchange rates. Especially in the case of the foreign currencies which follow a long-term trend versus the investor's home currency, a strategy based on rolling over short-term hedges becomes useless (see, for example, Soenen and Madura (1991)).
9 We used the model "Effport" as published in Bodie *et al.* (1989) to determine the minimum variance composition of the international investment portfolios. The actual composition of the minimum variance and capitalization weighted portfolios are available from the authors upon request.

REFERENCES

Arnott, R. and R. Henriksson (1989) "A Disciplined Approach to Global Asset Allocation," *Financial Analysts Journal*, March/April, pp. 17–28.

Bodie, Z., A. Kane and A. Marcus (1989) *Investments*, Homewood, Ill.: Irwin.

Divecha, A., J. Drach and D. Stefek (1992) "Emerging Markets: A Quantitative Perspective," *Journal of Portfolio Management*, Fall, pp. 41–50.

Eaker, M. and D. Grant (1985) "Optimal Hedging of Uncertain Long-Term Foreign Exchange Exposure," *Journal of Banking and Finance*, 9, pp. 221–31.

Eun, C. and B. Resnick (1988) "Exchange Rate Uncertainty, Forward Contracts, and International Portfolio Selection," *Journal of Portfolio Management*, March, pp. 197–215.

Francis, J. (1991) *Investments: Analysis and Management*, New York: McGraw-Hill.

Gibbons, M., S. Ross and J. Shanken (1989) "A Test of the Efficiency of a Given Portfolio," *Econometrica*, September, pp. 1121–52.

Hartmann, M. and D. Khambata (1993) "Emerging Stock Markets – Investment Strategies of the Future," *Columbia Journal of World Business*, Summer, pp. 82–104.

Hauser, S. and A. Levy (1991) "The Effect of Exchange Rate and Interest Rate Risk on International Currency and Fixed Income Security Allocation," *Journal of Business and Economics*, 43, pp. 375–88.

Hauser, S., M. Marcus and U. Yaari (1994) "Investing in Emerging Stock Markets: Is It Worthwhile Hedging Foreign Exchange Risk?" *Journal of Portfolio Management*, Spring, pp. 76–81.

Jobson, T. and B. Korkie (1981) "Performance Hypothesis Testing with the Sharpe and Treynor Measures," *Journal of Finance*, September, pp. 889–908.

Jorion, Ph. (1985) "International Portfolio Diversification with Estimation Risk," *Journal of Business*, 58, pp. 259–78.

Jorion, Ph. (1989) "Asset Allocation With Hedged and Unhedged Foreign Stocks and Bonds," *Journal of Portfolio Management*, Summer, pp. 49–54.

Lee, A. (1988) "International Asset Currency Allocation," *Journal of Portfolio Management*, Fall, pp. 41–57.

Park, K. and A. Van Agtmael (1993) *The World's Emerging Stock Markets*, Chicago: Probus Publishing Company.

Perold, A. and E. Schulman (1988) "The Free Lunch in Currency Hedging Implications for Investment Policy and Performance Standards," *Financial Analysts Journal*, May, pp. 45–50.

Sharpe, W. (1966) "Mutual Fund Performance," *Journal of Business*, January, pp. 119–38.

Soenen, L. and J. Madura (1991) "Foreign Exchange Management: A Strategic Approach," *Long Range Planning*, October, pp. 119–24.

Soenen, L. and J. Lindvall (1992) "Benefits from Diversification and Currency

Hedging of International Equity Investments: Different Countries' Viewpoints," *Global Finance Journal*, 3, 2, pp. 145–58.

Sollinger, A. (1992) "The Emerging Markets Morass," *Institutional Investor*, January, pp. 215–16.

Solnik, B. and B. Noetzlin (1982) "Optimal International Asset Allocation," *Journal of Portfolio Management*, Fall, pp. 11–21.

Thomas, L. (1989) "The Performance of Currency Hedged Foreign Bonds," *Financial Analysts Journal*, May–June, pp. 25–31.

7

GLOBAL CO-MOVEMENTS OF STOCK MARKETS BEFORE AND AFTER THE 1987 CRASH

Ilhan Meric and Gulser Meric

INTRODUCTION

The international stock market crash of October 1987 has received considerable attention in finance literature.[1] Roll (1988), Goodhart (1988), King and Wadhwani (1990), Hamao *et al.* (1990), and Malliaris and Urrutia (1992) have studied the transmission of volatility between international stock markets during the crash. Arshanapalli and Doukas (1993), Lau and McInish (1993), and Lee and Kim (1993) have compared the co-movements of national stock markets before and after the crash.

Arshanapalli and Doukas (1993) use the daily data of five major international stock markets and study the January 1980 to May 1990 time period. Lau and McInish (1993) also use daily data for ten national stock markets and study the 13 March 1986 to 20 December 1989 time period. Lee and Kim (1993) use weekly data for twelve national stock markets and compare the three-year period before the crash with the three-year period after the crash. This study attempts to extend the works of Arshanapalli and Doukas (1993), Lau and McInish (1993), and Lee and Kim (1993). However, it differs from these studies in several respects. We use monthly data and a different methodology, cover a longer and more recent time period, and study the co-movements of eighteen national stock markets. Our objective is to examine the long-term changes in the co-movement patterns of national stock markets after the 1987 crash. Therefore, we study a six-year time period before and after the crash, a time period long enough to analyze the long-term changes in the co-movement patterns of the markets. Moreover, unlike the earlier studies, which use daily or weekly data, we use monthly data in our analysis. Monthly data are more suitable for investigating the long-term co-movement patterns because a month is a sufficiently long time period, so that several-day temporary leads or lags cannot obscure the long-term fundamental co-movements of the markets.

The remainder of the chapter is organized as follows. The next section describes our data and methodology, with the following section comparing correlation coefficients between the eighteen national stock markets before and after the 1987 stock market crash. Then, we compare the volatilities of the national stock markets before and after the crash. The section which follows compares the co-movement patterns of the eighteen stock markets before and after the crash by using principal components analysis. Also in this section, Box's M methodology is used to test the hypothesis that the variance–covariance matrices of national stock market returns are significantly different in the pre- and post-crash time periods. Our findings are summarized and conclusions are presented in the final section.

DATA AND METHODOLOGY

Our study covers two North American (US and Canada), twelve European (UK, Germany, France, Switzerland, Italy, Netherlands, Spain, Sweden, Belgium, Denmark, Norway, and Austria), and four Far Eastern (Japan, Australia, Hong Kong, and Singapore) stock markets. National stock market index returns used in this study are taken from Morgan Stanley Capital International Perspective (MSCIP) publications. MSCIP index returns are based on approximately twelve hundred companies listed on the stock exchanges of these countries. The combined market capitalization of these companies represents approximately 60 percent of the total market value of all stocks traded on the stock exchanges of the eighteen countries.

MSCIP country index returns are adjusted for exchange rate changes. MSCIP publishes quarterly and monthly index returns. The analysis in this chapter is based on the monthly returns. Stock prices are very volatile and show rapid responses to international developments. Therefore, monthly data can provide more accurate information about the behavior of stock market indices than can quarterly data. Furthermore, a month is a sufficiently long time period so that several-day temporary leads or lags in international stock market relationships will not obscure the long-term co-movement patterns of the markets.

We first employ correlation analysis to compare the relationships among the eighteen stock markets before and after the crash. Since we use seventy-two monthly observations for the post-crash period (November 1987 to October 1993), the comparison is made with the seventy-two-month period (October 1981 to September 1987) preceding the stock market crash of October 1987. The stock market index returns used in the analysis exclude the crash month of October 1987. The coefficient of variation figures are used to compare the volatilities of the markets during the pre-crash and post-crash periods.

To compare the co-movements of the eighteen stock markets during the pre-crash and post-crash time periods, we first test the hypothesis that the variance–covariance matrix of the post-crash period is significantly different from the variance–covariance matrix of the pre-crash period by using Box's M-test statistics. Principal components analysis is used to study and compare the co-movement patterns of the eighteen national stock markets during the six-year pre-crash and six-year post-crash time periods.

CORRELATION BETWEEN THE STOCK MARKETS BEFORE AND AFTER THE CRASH

The matrices of correlation coefficients between the eighteen stock markets during the six-year period before the crash and the six-year period after the crash are presented in Table 7.1. The lower diagonal-half of the table shows the correlation coefficients before the crash and the upper diagonal-half shows the correlation coefficients after the crash. The figures in the table shows that correlation coefficients are generally higher in the post-crash period than in the pre-crash period. The average correlation coefficient between the 153 pairs of national stock markets is 0.31 in the pre-crash period and 0.43 in the post-crash period. These results show that the average correlation coefficient among the eighteen national stock markets increased by 39 percent from the six-year period before the crash to the six-year period after the crash.

The degree of dependency (independency) of a country's stock market on (from) the stock markets of other countries can be determined by calculating what may be called a dependency (independency) index.[2] This index is an average of the correlation coefficients between a country's stock market index returns and the stock market index returns of other countries. The average correlation coefficients of the eighteen national stock markets in the six-year pre-crash and the six-year post-crash time periods are presented in Table 7.2. The figures in the table show that the average correlation coefficients of all eighteen national stock markets increased considerably from the pre-crash period to the post-crash period. These results indicate that national stock markets have become much more dependent on one another during the post-crash period compared with the pre-crash period.

The average correlation coefficients show that the Far East stock markets, notably the Hong Kong and Singapore stock markets, were quite independent from the world's other stock markets during the pre-crash period. However, the dependency of these markets on the world's other stock markets increased considerably from the pre-crash period to the post-crash period. In North America, the dependency index of the US stock market increased more compared with the dependency index of the Canadian stock market. In Europe, Austria, Sweden, and Spain have the largest increases and France and Switzerland have the smallest increases in their dependency indices.

93

Table 7.1 Correlation matrices in the pre- and post-crash periods*

	US	Can	UK	Ger	Fra	Swit	Ital	Neth	Spai	Swed	Bel	Den	Nor	Aust	Jap	Ausi	Hong	Sing
US		0.63	0.61	0.37	0.44	0.50	0.15	0.57	0.35	0.49	0.44	0.26	0.47	0.13	0.22	0.24	0.41	0.57
Can	0.70		0.48	0.33	0.30	0.38	0.35	0.50	0.28	0.39	0.37	0.27	0.42	0.18	0.28	0.45	0.53	0.53
UK	0.44	0.52		0.55	0.53	0.67	0.32	0.77	0.57	0.63	0.44	0.51	0.61	0.43	0.50	0.46	0.48	0.61
Ger	0.19	0.15	0.33		0.78	0.66	0.53	0.76	0.49	0.52	0.67	0.60	0.51	0.66	0.33	0.19	0.29	0.44
Fra	0.38	0.38	0.49	0.51		0.60	0.37	0.66	0.49	0.42	0.70	0.49	0.43	0.46	0.38	0.21	0.30	0.32
Swit	0.41	0.48	0.51	0.73	0.60		0.39	0.72	0.46	0.55	0.52	0.55	0.43	0.45	0.47	0.20	0.28	0.47
Ital	0.21	0.25	0.25	0.39	0.37	0.40		0.36	0.46	0.38	0.36	0.43	0.31	0.37	0.44	0.06	0.27	0.37
Neth	0.49	0.52	0.54	0.56	0.48	0.62	0.35		0.52	0.55	0.64	0.53	0.60	0.51	0.42	0.31	0.44	0.58
Spai	0.21	0.21	0.35	0.31	0.52	0.32	0.47	0.31		0.63	0.43	0.54	0.39	0.40	0.53	0.27	0.43	0.54
Swed	0.19	0.28	0.38	0.28	0.33	0.43	0.44	0.28	0.25		0.39	0.48	0.57	0.32	0.51	0.33	0.40	0.65
Bel	0.28	0.26	0.47	0.47	0.58	0.51	0.44	0.45	0.35	0.63		0.54	0.42	0.31	0.40	0.10	0.32	0.37
Den	0.38	0.37	0.33	0.37	0.41	0.46	0.25	0.44	0.19	0.32	0.42		0.44	0.34	0.41	0.24	0.23	0.47
Nor	0.39	0.45	0.49	0.30	0.40	0.49	0.16	0.50	0.25	0.19	0.44	0.42		0.42	0.21	0.30	0.43	0.54
Aust	0.02	0.12	0.22	0.51	0.42	0.48	0.29	0.28	0.25	0.42	0.35	0.16	0.15		0.18	0.24	0.32	0.46
Jap	0.24	0.25	0.28	0.32	0.51	0.35	0.40	0.37	0.34	0.22	0.45	0.30	0.22	0.13		0.16	0.32	0.47
Ausi	0.25	0.47	0.37	0.13	0.16	0.29	0.08	0.22	0.20	0.24	0.15	0.19	0.46	-0.03	0.18		0.24	0.35
Hong	0.04	0.11	0.25	0.23	0.20	0.24	0.19	0.32	0.19	0.24	0.13	0.07	0.35	0.16	0.05	0.26		0.58
Sing	0.32	0.28	0.33	-0.04	0.04	0.08	-0.01	0.20	-0.22	0.24	0.16	0.19	0.43	-0.08	0.11	0.30	0.26	

* The lower diagonal-half of the table shows the correlation coefficients before the crash and the upper diagonal-half shows the correlation coefficients after the crash.

Table 7.2 Average correlation coefficients

Stock market	Pre-crash	Post-crash	Change (%)
North America			
USA	0.30	0.40	+33
Canada	0.34	0.39	+15
Average	0.32	0.40	+25
Europe			
UK	0.39	0.54	+38
Germany	0.34	0.51	+50
France	0.41	0.46	+12
Switzerland	0.43	0.49	+14
Italy	0.30	0.35	+17
Netherlands	0.41	0.56	+37
Spain	0.28	0.46	+57
Sweden	0.30	0.48	+60
Belgium	0.37	0.44	+19
Denmark	0.30	0.43	+43
Norway	0.37	0.44	+19
Austria	0.21	0.36	+71
Average	0.34	0.46	+35
Far East			
Japan	0.28	0.37	+32
Australia	0.23	0.26	+13
Hong Kong	0.19	0.37	+95
Singapore	0.16	0.49	+206
Average	0.22	0.37	+68
Overall average	0.31	0.43	+39

VOLATILITIES OF THE STOCK MARKETS BEFORE AND AFTER THE CRASH

In this section of our study we compare the volatilities of the eighteen national stock markets in the pre-crash and post-crash time periods. The coefficient of variation figures are used in this comparison. The coefficient of variation is computed by dividing the standard deviation of the monthly stock market index returns by the mean value of the monthly stock market index returns in each of the six-year pre-crash and post-crash time periods. The results are presented in Table 7.3. The figures show that the volatilities of the national stock markets increased considerably from the pre-crash period to the post-crash period. The average coefficient of variation for all eighteen stock markets increased by 162 percent from 3.84 in the six-year pre-crash period to 10.07 in the six-year post-crash period.

The Hong Kong and Singapore stock markets were the most volatile stock markets during the pre-crash time period. However, the volatilities of

ILHAN MERIC AND GULSER MERIC

Table 7.3 Volatility of the stock markets

Stock market	Pre-crash	Coefficient of variation Post-crash	Change (%)
North America			
USA	2.87	4.66	+62
Canada	5.31	12.38	+133
Average	4.09	8.52	+108
Europe			
UK	2.82	9.85	+249
Germany	3.18	6.94	+118
France	3.05	5.95	+95
Switzerland	2.76	4.93	+79
Italy	3.86	16.22	+320
Netherlands	2.34	4.66	+99
Spain	4.48	24.19	+440
Sweden	2.67	7.37	+176
Belgium	2.42	7.27	+200
Denmark	5.35	4.98	−7
Norway	3.82	12.61	+230
Austria	3.86	6.15	+59
Average	3.38	9.26	+174
Far East			
Japan	2.49	37.05	+1,388
Australia	4.74	9.31	+96
Hong Kong	5.31	3.35	−37
Singapore	7.72	3.48	−55
Average	5.07	13.30	+162
Overall average	3.84	10.07	+162

these two stock markets appear to have somewhat decreased from the pre-crash period to the post-crash period. In Europe, the volatility of the Danish stock market also shows a slight decrease in the post-crash period compared with the pre-crash period. The volatilities of all the other stock markets show a considerable increase from the pre-crash period to the post-crash period.

In North America, the volatility of the Canadian stock market appears to have increased more compared with the US stock market. In Europe, the volatilities of the Spanish and Italian stock markets appear to have increased considerably more compared with the other stock markets. The volatility of the Japanese stock market appears to have increased much more drastically from the pre-crash period to the post-crash period compared with the other seventeen national stock markets.

COMPARISON OF THE CO-MOVEMENT PATTERNS OF THE STOCK MARKETS BEFORE AND AFTER THE CRASH

In this section of the study, we first test the hypothesis that the variance–covariance matrix of the national stock market index returns in the post-crash time period is significantly different from the variance–covariance matrix of the national stock market index returns in the pre-crash time period. The test statistics are presented in Table 7.4. The test statistics show that the variance–covariance matrix of the eighteen national stock market index returns in the six-year post-crash period is significantly different at the conventional 1 percent level from the variance–covariance matrix in the six-year period preceding the crash.

We next examine the changes in the co-movement patterns of the eighteen stock markets from the pre-crash period to the post-crash period by using principal components analysis. Principal components analysis is first applied to the monthly index returns of the six-year period preceding the crash. To eliminate first-order serial correlation which can result in spurious inferences about the causes of national stock market co-movements, principal components analysis is applied to the logarithms of the index returns. The varimax orthogonal rotation is used to obtain the final factor pattern/structure matrix for an easier interpretation of the principal components. Using Kaiser's significance rule, principal components with eigen values greater than one are retained for analysis. There are five statistically significant principal components in the pre-crash period. The factor loadings of these principal components are presented in Table 7.5. The factor loadings of the stock markets making the greatest contribution to each principal component are marked with an asterisk.

In the pre-crash period, the first principal component is dominated by the stock markets of Canada, the US, the Netherlands, the UK, and Denmark. This principal component explains 36.9 percent of the total variation in the stock market index returns during this time period. The stock markets of Austria, Germany, and Switzerland make the greatest contribution to the second principal component. This principal component accounts for 10.5 percent of the total variation in the stock market index returns. The first two principal components together account for 47.3 percent of the total variation in the stock market index returns.

Table 7.4 Multivariate tests for the homogeneity of the variance–covariance matrices of the pre- and post-crash periods

	Test statistics	P level
Box's M	291.53	
F with (171,61893) DF	1.48	0.00
Chi-square with 171 DF	253.66	0.00

97

Table 7.5 Principal components for the pre-crash period

	PC no. 1	PC no. 2	PC no. 3	PC no. 4	PC no. 5
Canada	0.812*	−0.028	0.066	0.339	0.113
USA	0.804*	−0.011	0.153	0.030	0.136
Netherlands	0.639*	0.457	0.220	0.175	0.123
UK	0.521*	0.216	0.050	0.351	0.221
Denmark	0.521*	0.231	0.349	−0.150	0.306
Austria	−0.051	0.767*	0.288	0.107	0.029
Germany	0.309	0.753*	0.263	0.181	−0.047
Switzerland	0.574	0.595*	0.177	0.248	0.069
Japan	0.101	0.200	0.815*	0.201	0.058
Belgium	0.232	0.301	0.663*	0.160	0.271
France	0.312	0.205	0.585*	0.433	0.001
Spain	−0.004	0.173	0.225	0.663*	−0.017
Sweden	0.213	0.161	0.054	0.596*	0.198
Australia	0.265	−0.237	0.103	0.535*	0.394
Italy	0.233	0.274	0.314	0.532*	−0.251
Singapore	0.237	−0.162	0.187	−0.060	0.762*
Norway	0.427	0.207	0.228	0.204	0.592*
Hong Kong	−0.021	0.414	−0.251	0.332	0.582*
Variance explained	36.9%	10.4%	6.4%	6.0%	5.6%
Cumulative variance explained	36.9%	47.3%	53.7%	59.7%	65.3%

* Stock markets with the highest factor loadings are marked with an asterisk.

The third principal component is dominated by the stock markets of Japan, Belgium, and France. This principal component explains only 6.4 percent of the total variation in the stock market index returns. The stock markets making the greatest contribution to the fourth principal component belong to Spain, Sweden, Australia, and Italy. This principal component accounts for only 6 percent of the total variation in the stock market index returns. The Singapore, Norwegian, and Hong Kong stock markets make the greatest contribution to the fifth principal component. However, this principal component accounts for only 5.6 percent of the total variation in the stock market index returns. The five statistically significant principal components together explain 65.3 percent of the total variation in the stock market index returns during the pre-crash period.

The factor loadings of the statistically significant principal components in the post-crash period are presented in Table 7.6. Unlike the pre-crash period, there are only four statistically significant principal components in the post-crash period. This indicates that the movements of the eighteen national stock markets are more closely tied to one another in the post-crash period compared with the pre-crash period. Furthermore, the four principal components in the post-crash period can explain a greater percentage of the total variation in the stock market index returns compared

Table 7.6 Principal components for the post-crash period

	PC no. 1	PC no. 2	PC no. 3	PC no. 4
Germany	0.851*	0.145	0.225	0.027
Netherlands	0.720*	0.460	0.244	0.144
Austria	0.714*	−0.034	0.055	0.306
Switzerland	0.711*	0.307	0.227	0.033
France	0.692*	0.235	0.241	0.131
Belgium	0.617*	0.376	0.360	−0.193
UK	0.477*	0.382	0.448	0.425
USA	0.160	0.837*	0.027	0.130
Canada	0.201	0.787*	0.058	0.173
Hong Kong	0.212	0.639*	0.369	−0.073
Singapore	0.111	0.639*	0.461	0.127
Norway	0.424	0.454*	0.323	0.179
Japan	0.138	0.138	0.772*	0.066
Sweden	0.176	0.339	0.692*	0.301
Spain	0.337	0.107	0.667*	0.321
Denmark	0.496	0.145	0.592*	0.029
Italy	0.452	0.082	0.515*	−0.207
Australia	0.120	0.221	0.179	0.863*
Variance explained	46.2%	8.8%	6.7%	5.8%
Cumulative variance explained	46.2%	54.9%	61.6%	67.4%

* Stock markets with the highest factor loadings are marked with an asterisk.

with the percentage variation explained by the five statistically significant principal components in the pre-crash period (67.4 percent vs 65.3 percent). This also implies closer co-movements for the eighteen national stock markets in the post-crash period than in the pre-crash period.

Unlike in the pre-crash period, in the post-crash period the first principal component is dominated by the European stock markets. The stock markets of Germany, the Netherlands, Austria, Switzerland, France, Belgium, and the UK make the greatest contribution to the first principal component. This principal component explains 46.2 percent of the total variation in the stock market index returns during this period. The stock markets of the US, Canada, Hong Kong, Singapore, and Norway make the greatest contribution to the second principal component. However, this principal component accounts for only 8.8 percent of the total variation in the stock market index returns in the post-crash period.

The stock markets of Japan, Sweden, Spain, Denmark, and Italy are the greatest contributors to the third principal component. However, this principal component explains only 6.7 percent of the total variation in the stock market index returns in the post-crash period. The Australian stock market is the largest contributor to the fourth principal component. In fact, this principal component appears to have come into existence in the post-crash period because of the independent movements of the Australian stock market from the other stock markets.

The comparison of the co-movement patterns of the eighteen national stock markets in the pre- and post-crash periods reveals that some significant changes have occurred. The European countries appear to be more closely tied to one another in the post-crash period than in the pre-crash period. In the post-crash period, most European stock markets have high factor loadings in the first principal component. The Norwegian stock market, which appears to be somewhat closely aligned with the US, and Canadian stock markets in the second principal component, also makes almost an equally high contribution to the first principal component. Although the stock markets of Italy, Spain, and Denmark make higher contributions to the third principal component, they also make considerable contributions to the first principal component. However, the movements of the Swedish stock market appear to be somewhat independent from the movements of the major European stock markets.

Although the UK and Dutch stock markets were more closely aligned with the US and Canadian stock markets in the pre-crash period, they appear to be more closely aligned with the other European stock markets in the post-crash period. However, they also continue to have quite close ties with the US and Canadian stock markets, as indicated by their high factor loadings in the second principal component in the post-crash period.

The UK stock market appears to be the only stock market with high factor loadings in all principal components in the post-crash period. This implies that the UK stock market has had close co-movements with the stock markets in all four principal components during the post-crash period. The high UK correlation coefficients with the other stock markets in the post-crash period shown in Table 7.1 also confirm this conclusion.

The Hong Kong and Singapore stock markets, which were quite independent from the other stock markets in the pre-crash period, appear to be quite closely aligned with the US and Canadian stock markets in the post-crash period.

SUMMARY AND CONCLUSIONS

Low correlation between national stock markets is often presented as evidence in support of the benefits of international portfolio diversification. Our findings in this study show that correlation between the world's eighteen largest stock markets increased considerably; therefore the benefits of international portfolio diversification diminished substantially, from the six-year period preceding the 1987 crash to the six-year period after the crash.

Although the volatility of national stock markets increased considerably from the pre-crash period to the post-crash period, correlation between national stock markets also increased. This implies that national stock markets have become quite responsive to volatilities in other national stock markets after the crash because only volatilities in the same direction would produce high correlation coefficients.

The variance–covariance matrix of national stock market index returns in the post-crash period appears to be significantly different from the variance–covariance matrix of national stock market index returns in the pre-crash period. Principal components analysis also indicates that the co-movement patterns of national stock markets changed considerably from the pre-crash period to the post-crash period. National stock markets appear to be more closely tied to one another after the crash than before the crash. European stock markets appear to be much more closely aligned in the post-crash period than in the pre-crash period. National stock markets which had independent movements in the pre-crash period, such as the Hong Kong and Singapore stock markets, are highly correlated with the world's other major markets in the post-crash period.

NOTES

1 For a detailed discussion of possible causes of the crash, see Miller (1995) and Parhizgari *et al.* (1995).
2 See Meric and Meric (1989).

REFERENCES

Arshanapalli, B. and J. Doukas (1993) "International Stock Market Linkages: Evidence from the Pre- and Post-October 1987 Period," *Journal of Banking and Finance*, January, pp. 193–208.
Goodhart, C.A.E. (1988) "The International Transmission of Asset Price Volatility," *Financial Market Volatility*, Kansas City, Kans.: Federal Reserve Bank of Kansas City, pp. 79–121.
Hamao, Y., R. Masulis and V. Ng (1990) "Correlation in Price Changes and Volatility Across International Stock Markets," *Review of Financial Studies*, Spring, pp. 281–308.
King, M.A. and S. Wadhwani (1990) "Transmission of Volatility Between Stock Markets," *Review of Financial Studies*, Spring, pp. 5–33.
Lau, S.T. and T.H. McInish (1993) "Comovements of International Equity Returns: A Comparison of the Pre- and Post-October 19, 1987, Periods," *Global Finance Journal*, Fall, pp. 1–19.
Lee, S.B. and K.J. Kim (1993) "Does the October 1987 Crash Strengthen the Co-Movements Among National Stock Markets?," *Review of Financial Economics*, Fall, pp. 89–102.
Malliaris, A.G. and J.L. Urrutia (1992) "The International Crash of October 1987: Causality Tests," *Journal of Financial and Quantitative Analysis*, September, pp. 353–64.
Meric, I. and G. Meric (1989) "Potential Gains from International Portfolio Diversification and Inter-Temporal Stability and Seasonality in International

Stock Market Relationships," *Journal of Banking and Finance*, September, pp. 627–40.

Miller, M.M. (1995) "The 1987 Crash Five Years Later: What Have We Learned?," in D.K. Ghosh and S. Shaksari (eds) *New Directions in Finance*, London and New York: Routledge, pp. 13–21.

Parhizgari, A.M., K. Dandapani and A.J. Prakash (1995) "Black Monday: What Burst the Bubble?," in D.K. Ghosh and S. Khaksari (eds) *Managerial Finance in the Corporate Economy*, London and New York: Routledge, pp. 119–34.

Roll, R.W. (1988) "The International Crash of October 1987," *Financial Analysts Journal*, September/October, pp. 19–35. Reprinted in R. Kamphuis, R. Kormendi and J.W. Watson (eds) (1989) *Black Monday and the Future of Financial Markets*, Homewood, Ill.: Mid America Institute.

8

EQUITY AND OIL MARKETS UNDER EXTERNAL SHOCKS

Jorge Urrutia and A.G. Malliaris

The chapter investigates two hypotheses: first, that the impact of the Persian Gulf Crisis was stronger on the oil market than in the equity market; and, second, that there was an increase in the causal relationship between stock and oil prices during the crisis. Event-study and Granger causality tests confirm both hypotheses. The acceptance of the first hypothesis is consistent with the nature of the conflict which primarily affected the oil market due to the embargo of Iraqi oil. Also, the high degree of diversification of the S&P 500 index lessened the impact of higher oil prices. The confirmation of the second hypothesis agrees with efficient markets in the sense that equity and oil markets reacted quickly and simultaneously to the event.

INTRODUCTION

Global events, such as the market crash of October 1987 and the Persian Gulf Crisis of August 1990, have affected the financial markets around the world. The impact of the market crash on national equity markets has been extensively documented (Roll 1988, Malliaris and Urrutia 1992). However, the Persian Gulf War, even though an important crisis highly publicized by the media, has only been a minor topic of academic research (Malliaris and Urrutia 1994).

It is known that the invasion of Kuwait and the successive events had a negative effect on equity prices and a positive effect on oil prices. The purpose of this chapter is to empirically investigate two hypotheses: first, an event-study methodology is used to investigate the hypothesis that the impact of the Gulf Crisis was stronger on the oil market than in the equity markets; and second, Granger causality tests are employed to investigate the hypothesis of a substantial increase in the causal relationship between stock and oil prices during the Persian Gulf Crisis. The rationale for our first hypothesis is twofold: first, the Gulf Crisis was mainly an oil conflict, and second, the equity indexes contain stocks of companies that benefited from the war, while others were adversely affected. Our second hypothesis is motivated by the efficient market hypothesis. That is, if financial and

103

commodity markets are efficient, then both equity and oil prices change daily responding quickly to fundamental political and war news from the Middle East. This simultaneous reaction to the event increased the short-term linkages between the two markets.

DATA

Daily closing prices for the time period 1 October 1989 through 31 January 1991 are collected from the *Wall Street Journal* for the following instruments: S&P 500 spot, S&P 500 nearby futures, Arab lite oil spot, and crude oil (sweet light) nearby futures.

Daily returns for the spot instruments and daily percentage changes for the futures contracts are computed as $R_t = 100(\ln(P_t/P_{t-1}))$ where P_t and P_{t-1} are daily prices for days t and $t-1$, respectively. The data are divided into an "Estimation Period," from 1 October 1989 to 31 May 1990 (observations $t = -206$ to $t = -44$), and an "Event Period," from 1 June 1990 to 31 January 1991 (observations $t = -43$ to $t = +119$). Thus, both the estimation period and the event period contain 163 trading days. The event day, $t = 0$, corresponds to 2 August 1990, the day of the Iraqi invasion of Kuwait. Other important dates on the sample are 16 January 1991, the beginning of the war between the International Coalition and Iraq ($t = +112$), and January 24, 1991 the start of the ground attack (t = +118).

METHODOLOGY

This chapter uses event-study and Granger causality methodologies. A brief description of both methods follows.

Event study methodology

The mean-adjusted return method is used to compute abnormal returns. In this method, the security's excess return is equal to the difference between the observed return during the event period and the average return of the security during the estimation period. Given the nature of the data used in this chapter the mean-adjusted return is the appropriate methodology since it does not require the use of the "market" portfolio (Masulis 1980; Brown and Warner 1980, 1985).

Let $R_{i,t}$ designate the observed return for security i at day t. Define $AR_{i,t}$ as the excess or abnormal return for security i at day t of the event period given by:

$$AR_{i,t} = R_{i,t} - \overline{R}_i \tag{1}$$

where $\overline{R}_i$ is the simple average of security i's daily returns in the $(-206, -44)$ estimation period, computed as

$$\bar{R}_i = \frac{1}{163} \sum_{t = -206}^{-44} R_{i,t}. \tag{2}$$

The daily abnormal returns for security i are standardized using

$$SAR_{i,t} = \frac{AR_{i,t}}{S_i} \tag{3}$$

where $SAR_{i,t}$ denotes standardized abnormal return for security i at day t, and S_i is standard deviation of returns for security i, during the estimation period, computed as:

$$S_i = \sqrt{\frac{1}{162} \sum_{i = -206}^{-44} (AR_{i,t} - \overline{AR})^2}. \tag{4}$$

where $\overline{AR}$ is the mean abnormal returns.

The $SAR_{i,t}$'s can be accumulated over selected multi-day intervals of the event period as follows:

$$CAR_{t_1,t_2} = \sum_{t = t_1}^{t_2} SAR_{i,t} \tag{5}$$

where CAR_{t_1,t_2} denotes standardized cumulative abnormal returns for security i during the (t_1, t_2) interval of the event period.

The null hypotheses to be tested are that the abnormal return for security i at day t of the event period, $AR_{i,t}$, and the cumulative abnormal return for security i during the (t_1, t_2) interval of the event period, CAR_{t_1,t_2} are equal to zero. The z-statistic for $AR_{i,t}$ is the $SAR_{i,t}$ given by formula (3). The z-statistic for CAR_{t_1,t_2} is calculated as (Patell 1976, Dodd and Warner 1983):

$$z_{t_1 t_2} = \frac{CAR_{t_1 t_2}}{\sqrt{t_2 - t_1 + 1}}. \tag{6}$$

Granger causality tests

The lead-lag tests used in this chapter are based on the Granger tests of causality. A description of several testable forms of Granger causality can be found in Pierce and Haugh (1977), Guilkey and Salemi (1982), and Geweke, et al. (1983). The following version of the Granger causal model is used:

$$\ln Y_t = \alpha_o + \sum_{i = 1}^{m} \alpha_i \ln X_{t - i} + \sum_{j = 1}^{m} \beta_j \ln Y_{t - j} + \varepsilon_t \tag{7}$$

105

$$\ln X_t = a_o + \sum_{i=1}^{m} a_i \ln Y_{t-i} + \sum_{j=1}^{m} b_j \ln X_{t-j} + \mu_t. \tag{8}$$

The definition of causality given above implies that X is causing (leading) Y provided some α_i is not zero in equation (7). Similarly, Y is causing (leading) X if some a_i is not zero in equation (8). If both of these events occur, there is feedback. The statistic is calculated by estimating the above expressions in both unconstrained (full model) and constrained (reduced model) forms, and may be written as:

$$F_1 = \frac{(SSE_r - SSE_f)/m}{SSE_f/(T - 2m - 1)} \tag{9}$$

where SSE_r, SSE_f denote the residual sum squares of the reduced and full models, respectively; T is the total number of observations and m is the number of lags.

Test of cointegration

Engle and Granger (1987) show that if two nonstationary variables are cointegrated the Granger causality tests of the forms of equations (7) and (8) are misspecified. Therefore, before testing for causality it is necessary to test for cointegration. This paper uses the Augmented Dickey and Fuller (1981), ADF test of cointegration consisting of running first the cointegration regression

$$\ln X_t = a_0 + a_1 \ln Y_t + \varepsilon_t, \tag{10}$$

and then running the ADF regression on the residuals of (10):

$$\varepsilon_t - \varepsilon_{t-1} = b_0 - b_1 \varepsilon_{t-1} + \sum_{i=1}^{m} b_i(\varepsilon_{t-i} - \varepsilon_{t-i-1}) + \mu_t. \tag{11}$$

The null hypothesis of no cointegration is $H_0: b_1 = 0$ in equation (11). If the null is rejected, variables X_t and Y_t are cointegrated and the Granger regressions (7) and (8) are misspecified and must be corrected with an error correction term, which corresponds to the lagged residuals ε_{t-1} of regression (10).

ANALYSIS OF THE EMPIRICAL RESULTS

This section presents and discusses the results from the event-study and causality tests.

Event-study results

The behavior of spot and futures prices is examined for an event period containing 163 trading days. Thus, the event period extends from day -43

to day +119 relative to the initiation of the Persian Gulf Crisis. The day $t = 0$ corresponds to 2 August 1990: the day Iraq invaded Kuwait.

The standardized cumulative abnormal returns are presented in Table 8.1. As expected the CARs are negative for equity and positive for oil. However, the CARs are negative but insignificant for the spot and futures S&P 500. On the other hand, the spot and futures oil exhibit statistically significant positive CARs from one day after the invasion of Kuwait to one day after the initiation of the war (from $t = +1$ to $t = +113$). Therefore, the cumulative abnormal returns confirm our first hypothesis that the Persian Gulf Crisis had a more significant impact on the oil market than in the stock

Table 8.1 Standardized cumulative abnormal returns (CAR) for the S&P 500 index and oil spot and futures from 43 days before to 119 days after the invasion of Kuwait (day '0' = 2 August 1990)

| Event day | S&P 500 | | | | Oil | | | |
| | Spot | | Futures | | Spot | | Futures | |
	CAR	z-score	CAR	z-score	CAR	z-score	CAR	z-score
−40	1.121	0.560	0.921	0.461	−4.085	−2.042*	−3.827	−1.914
−30	−0.706	−0.189	−0.065	−0.017	−4.248	−1.135	−6.632	−1.772
−20	−0.508	−0.104	−0.117	−0.024	−1.878	−0.383	−2.824	−0.576
−10	0.174	0.030	0.395	0.068	6.007	1.030	2.367	0.406
−5	−1.371	−0.220	−1.220	−0.195	9.193	1.472	7.102	1.137
−4	−1.632	−0.258	−1.526	−0.241	9.249	1.462	6.989	1.105
−3	−2.165	−0.338	−2.117	−0.331	10.141	1.584	6.389	0.998
−2	−1.738	−0.268	−1.553	−0.240	9.782	1.509	6.836	1.055
−1	0.228	0.035	−1.493	−0.228	10.803	1.647	8.021	1.223
0	−1.774	−0.267	−1.747	−0.263	12.727	1.919	10.031	1.512
1	−2.639	−0.393	−2.509	−0.374	18.073	2.694*	13.518	2.015*
2	−4.067	−0.600	−4.075	−0.601	22.333	3.293*	16.399	2.418*
3	−6.365	−0.928	−6.786	−0.990	27.566	4.021*	23.096	3.369*
4	−6.291	−0.908	−6.174	−0.891	27.997	4.041*	23.581	3.404*
5	−5.529	−0.790	−5.667	−0.810	27.867	3.981*	19.359	2.766*
10	−5.230	−0.712	−5.272	−0.717	29.893	4.068*	20.458	2.784*
20	−8.934	−1.117	−9.419	−1.177	29.551	3.694*	19.771	2.471*
40	−14.761	−1.611	−14.752	−1.610	51.733	5.645*	41.159	4.491*
60	−12.825	−1.258	−12.896	−1.265	43.184	4.235*	34.757	3.408*
90	−9.182	−0.793	−9.349	−0.808	34.425	2.974*	23.285	2.011*
110	−12.379	−0.998	−12.422	−1.001	33.059	2.664*	25.230	2.033*
111	−13.044	−1.048	−12.900	−1.036	26.234	2.107*	31.172	2.504*
112	−12.764	−1.022	−12.889	−1.032	39.133	3.133*	30.059	2.407*
113	−12.204	−0.974	−12.002	−0.958	40.259	3.213*	33.146	2.645*
114	−9.495	−0.755	−8.820	−0.702	21.969	1.748	13.514	1.075
115	−8.551	−0.678	−8.405	−0.667	17.510	1.389	8.255	0.655
116	−8.828	−0.698	−8.632	−0.682	17.837	1.410	13.257	1.048

* Significant at the 5 percent level or better.

market. Intuitively, this is because the primary impact of the Iraqi invasion of Kuwait was on oil prices, due to the oil embargo imposed by the allies to Iraq. While the Iraqi invasion was initially interpreted as a local conflict between two Arab oil producing countries, the strong reaction of the US to the Iraqi aggression, along with the UN condemnation and the Iraqi oil embargo, rapidly gave this crisis a global dimension with a significant increase in oil prices. On the other hand, the US equity market experienced a lesser negative impact probably because the S&P 500 index contains only a small number of companies with oil reserves, the stocks of which appreciated because of anticipated higher profits from higher world oil prices. Also, the overall negative impact of an increase in the price of oil in such a broad index is lesser because of the effect of portfolio diversification.

Plots of the CARs are presented in Figures 8.1 to 8.4. As expected, the graphs show the opposite reactions of the equity and oil markets to the Persian Gulf Crisis. Visual inspections of the graphs also suggest that spot and futures returns were highly correlated during the event. This implies

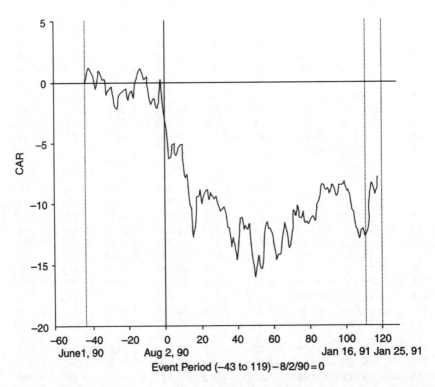

Figure 8.1 Cumulative abnormal returns (S&P 500 spot), mean adjusted returns method

108

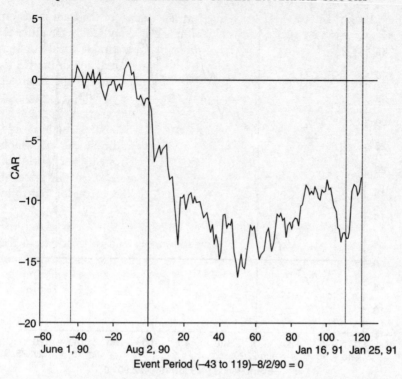

Figure 8.2 Cumulative abnormal returns (S&P 500 futures), mean adjusted returns method

that the price fluctuations were due to news from the Persian Gulf and not the effect of extra trading activities in the futures exchanges. Thus, it does not seem that futures markets contributed to increase price volatility during the Gulf Crisis.

In order to further explore the differential impact of the Persian Gulf Crisis on the oil and markets, mean differences of CARs are computed. In the days immediately following the invasion of Kuwait – that is, in the $(+1,+3)$ and $(+1,+5)$ intervals – the mean differences of CARs between the spot S&P 500 and oil are -19.43 ($z = -7.93$), and -18.90 ($z = -5.98$), respectively. For the interval immediate before the start of the war $(+111, +112)$ and the periods immediate after the start of the war $(+113, +114)$ and $(+113, +116)$, the mean differences of CARs are -6.46 ($z = -3.23$), 20.43 ($z = 10.22$) and 25.23 ($z = 8.92$) respectively. Similar results (not reported here) are obtained for the futures contracts. All these differences of means are significant at the 5 percent level or better, and reinforce our finding that the Persian Gulf Crisis had a bigger impact on the oil market than on the stock market.

109

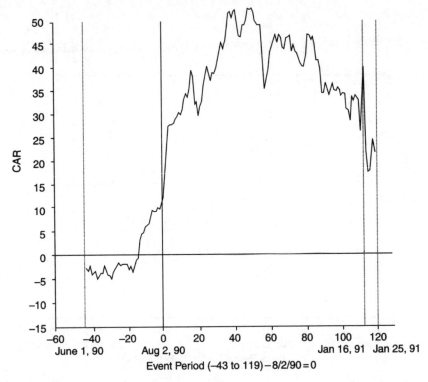

Figure 8.3 Cumulative abnormal returns (oil spot prices), mean adjusted returns method

Causality test results

In order to better capture and contrast the impact of the Gulf Crisis on the relationship between equity and oil markets, the data have been divided in two sets: the pre-Gulf Crisis period, from 1 October 1989 to 31 May 1990; and the Gulf Crisis period from 1 June 1990 to 31 January 1991.

Prior to the implementation of the causality tests we test the time-series for integration and cointegration. The ADF tests of stationarity for the price levels are presented in Table 8.2. The null hypothesis of nonstationarity cannot be rejected for any of the cases; thus, prices are unit roots. The ADF tests of stationarity for returns or percentage price changes, shown in Table 8.3, indicate that the null of nonstationarity is rejected in all cases. Therefore, prices of S&P 500 and oil, spot and futures, are integrated of order one, $I(1)$, and it is necessary to test for cointegration.

Panel A of Table 8.4 shows that cointegration for the pre-Gulf Crisis period is partially rejected. On the other hand, Panel B indicates that all prices are cointegrated during the Gulf Crisis period. Giving that the results of the tests of cointegration are mixed we proceed as follows: when the

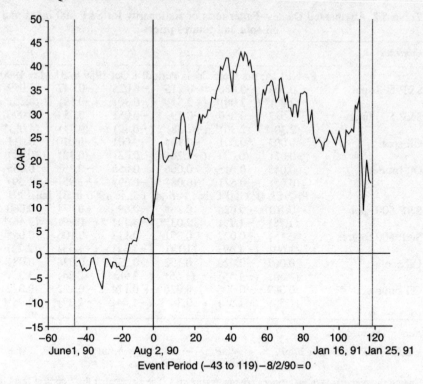

Figure 8.4 Cumulative abnormal returns (oil futures prices), mean adjusted returns
method

prices are not cointegrated, the causality tests are conducted by running regressions (7) and (8). When cointegration is present the error correcting terms are incorporated in the regressions.

The results of the Granger causality tests are presented in Table 8.5. Panel A indicates that no lead-lag relationship is detected for the pre-Gulf Crisis period. On the other hand, Panel B shows a dramatic increase in causality during the period of the Persian Gulf Crisis. In effect, strong contemporaneous causality and feedback are found during the period of the conflict. These results confirm our second hypothesis that equity and oil markets are efficient and stock and oil prices changed quickly responding to fundamental news coming from the Gulf. The efficient price reaction increased the linkages of these markets during the crisis. Our result is consistent with those reported by other studies about equity prices behavior during global shocks. In this respect, Malliaris and Urrutia (1992) show that during the October 1987 Stock Market Crash contemporaneous causality increased among national equity markets.

111

Table 8.2 Augmented Dickey–Fuller tests of stationarity for S&P 500 index and oil spot and futures prices

Contract	b_0	b_1	b_2	b_3	b_4	R^2
	PANEL A: pre-Gulf Crisis Period: 1 Oct 1989 to 31 May 1990					
S&P 500 spot	0.504	−0.086	−0.215	−0.025	−0.047	0.099
	(2.08)*	(−2.08)*	(−2.57)*	(−0.30)	(−0.59)	(4.25)*
S&P 500 futures	0.522	−0.089	−0.197	−0.051	0.057	0.096
	(2.30)*	(2.30)*	(−2.38)*	(−0.49)	(0.71)	(4.09)*
Oil spot	−0.003	0.001	−0.105	−0.001	0.010	0.011
	(−0.05)	(0.01)	(−1.26)	(−0.02)	(0.12)	(0.42)
Oil futures	0.045	−0.015	0.006	−0.056	−0.158	0.035
	(0.65)	(−0.67)	(0.08)	(−0.69)	(−1.95)	(1.39)
	PANEL B: Gulf Crisis Period: 1 June 1990 to 31 Jan 1991					
S&P 500 spot	0.161	−0.028	0.163	−0.090	−0.071	0.060
	(1.78)	(−1.79)	(2.03)*	(−1.11)	(−0.89)	(2.44)*
S&P 500 futures	0.157	−0.027	0.091	−0.113	−0.106	0.055
	(1.69)	(−1.69)	(1.14)	(−1.41)	(−1.33)	(2.22)
Oil spot	0.067	−0.020	0.132	−0.236	0.028	0.081
	(1.60)	(−1.55)	(1.65)	(−2.98)*	(0.34)	(3.35)*
Oil futures	0.089	−0.026	0.026	−0.114	−0.192	0.072
	(1.58)	(−1.55)	(−0.34)	(−1.44)	(−2.37)*	(2.95)*

Notes: The model is

$$\ln P_t - \ln P_{t-1} = b_0 + b_1 \ln P_{t-1} + b_2(\ln P_{t-1} - \ln P_{t-2}) + b_3(\ln P_{t-2} - \ln P_{t-3}) + b_4(\ln P_{t-3} - \ln P_{t-4}) + \varepsilon_t$$

The null hypothesis is $b_1 = 0$ (prices are non-stationary). The *t*-critical at the 5 percent level is −2.88 (from Dickey and Fuller 1981).
An asterisk * indicates that the individual regression coefficient is different from zero at the 5 percent of confidence level.

SUMMARY AND CONCLUSIONS

The chapter has investigated two hypotheses: first, that the impact of the Persian Gulf Crisis was stronger on the oil market than on the equity market; and second, that there was an increase in the causal relationship between stock and oil prices during the Persian Gulf Crisis. We have used data for the spot and futures S&P 500 index and the Arab oil from October 1989 to January 1991. The empirical results have confirmed our hypotheses. In effect, we have found that the impact of the Gulf Crisis was stronger on the oil market than on the equity market. This is consistent with the nature of the conflict, which primarily affected the oil market due to the embargo imposed to Iraqi oil. Also, the lesser impact on the S&P 500 is explained by the high degree of diversification of the index, which includes several stocks that benefited from high oil prices. The Gulf Crisis also produced a dramatic increase in causality between the equity and oil markets. This is consistent with the notion of efficient markets in the sense that both markets reacted quickly and simultaneously to the fundamental

Table 8.3 Augmented Dickey–Fuller tests of stationarity for S&P 500 index and oil spot and futures returns

Contract	b_0	b_1	b_2	b_3	b_4	R^2
	PANEL A: pre-Gulf Crisis Period: 1 Oct 1989 to 31 May 1990					
S&P 500 spot	0.012	−1.524	0.246	0.166	0.065	0.633
	(0.11)	$(-7.60)^a$	(1.46)	(1.29)	(0.81)	(66.30)*
S&P 500 futures	0.003	−1.442	0.187	0.088	0.088	0.625
	(0.03)	$(-7.34)^a$	(1.12)	(0.69)	(1.10)	(64.09)*
Oil spot	−0.163	−1.142	−0.043	0.047	0.063	0.55
	(−0.89)	$(-6.67)^a$	(0.29)	(0.40)	(0.76)	(47.40)*
Oil futures	−0.103	−1.227	0.225	0.161	−0.007	0.508
	(−0.63)	$(-7.10)^a$	(1.58)	(1.41)	(−0.09)	(39.77)*
	PANEL B: Gulf Crisis Period: 1 June 1990 to 31 Jan 1991					
S&P 500 spot	−0.055	0.998	0.157	0.061	−0.023	0.434
	(−0.58)	$(-6.48)^a$	$(1.21)^a$	(0.57)	(−0.28)	(29.36)*
S&P 500 futures	−0.056	−1.046	0.140	0.030	−0.092	0.475
	(−0.56)	$(-6.35)^a$	(1.03)	(0.27)	(−1.14)	(34.54)*
Oil spot	0.247	−1.110	0.239	−0.008	0.019	0.481
	(0.50)	$(-6.74)^a$	(1.71)	(−0.07)	(0.23)	(35.37)*
Oil futures	0.197	−1.202	0.235	0.121	−0.081	0.513
	(0.43)	$(-6.86)^a$	(1.65)	(1.05)	(−0.97)	(40.25)*

Notes: The model is

$$R_t - R_{t-1} = b_0 + b_1 R_{t-1} + b_2(R_{t-1} - R_{t-2}) + b_3(R_{t-2} - R_{t-3}) + b_4(R_{t-3} - R_{t-4}) + \varepsilon_t$$

where

$$R_t = 100\ln(P_t/P_{t-1})$$

The null hypothesis is $b_1 = 0$ (returns or percentage of price changes are non-stationary). The t-critical at the 5 percent level is −2.88 (from Dickey and Fuller 1981).
An "a" indicates rejection of the null at the 5 percent of confidence level.
An asterisk * indicates that the individual regression coefficient is different from zero at the 5 percent of confidence level.

political and war news coming out of the Middle East. Our results agree with the reported increase in causality among financial markets during global events, such as the market crash of October 1989.

Table 8.4 Tests of cointegration between the S&P 500 index and oil spot and futures prices

Dependent variable	Independent variable	b_0	b_1	b_2	b_3	b_4	R^2
		PANEL A: pre-Gulf Crisis Period: 1 Oct 1989 to 31 May 1990					
S&P 500 spot	Oil spot	0.0002	0.1644	−0.3223	−0.1462	−0.1341	0.169
		(0.17)	(4.31)*a	(−4.20)*	(−1.84)	(−1.75)	(7.86)*
Oil spot	S&P 500 spot	−0.0020	0.0544	−0.1067	−0.0592	−0.0355	0.053
		(−1.09)	(2.79)*	(−1.32)	(−0.72)	(−0.43)	(2.15)
S&P 500 futures	Oil futures	0.0001	0.1538	−0.2990	−0.1786	−0.0470	0.148
		(0.06)	(3.99)*a	(−3.84)*	(−2.26)*	(−0.60)	(6.73)*
Oil futures	S&P 500 futures	−0.0011	0.0703	−0.0535	−0.1744	−0.1463	0.083
		(−0.64)	(2.85)*	(−0.67)	(−2.23)*	(−1.85)	(3.49)*
		PANEL B: Gulf Crisis Period: 1 June 1990 to 31 Jan 1991					
S&P 500 spot	Oil spot	−0.0003	0.1829	−0.1580	−0.3067	−0.0769	0.174
		(−0.38)	(4.49)*a	(−1.98)*	(−4.10)*	(−0.99)	(8.07)*
Oil spot	S&P 500 spot	−0.0018	0.1775	−0.1714	−0.3264	−0.0722	0.186
		(−0.36)	(4.50)*a	(−2.15)*	(−4.39)*	(−0.93)	(8.75)*
S&P 500 futures	Oil futures	−0.0003	0.2598	−0.2797	−0.3088	−0.2261	0.247
		(−0.41)	(5.83)*a	(−3.67)*	(−4.28)*	(−3.05)*	(12.54)*
Oil futures	S&P 500 futures	−0.0014	0.2661	−0.2899	−0.3135	−0.2379	0.257
		(−0.39)	(5.98)*a	(−3.82)*	(−4.37)*	(−3.22)*	(13.25)*

Notes: The model used to test for cointegration is the following:

$$\ln P_t = a_0 + a_1 \ln P_{2t} + \varepsilon_t \tag{1}$$

$$\varepsilon_t - \varepsilon_{t-1} = b_0 + b_1 \varepsilon_{t-1} + b_2 (\varepsilon_{t-1} - \varepsilon_{t-2}) + b_3 (\varepsilon_{t-2} - \varepsilon_{t-3}) + b_4 (\varepsilon_{t-3} - \varepsilon_{t-4}) + \mu_t \tag{2}$$

The coefficients in the table are from equation (2).
The null hypothesis is H_0: $b_1 = 0$ (no-cointegration).
The t-critical at the 5 percent level in 3.17 (from Engle and Granger 1987).
An "a" indicates rejection of the null hypothesis of no-cointegration at the 5 percent of significance level.
An asterisk * indicates that the individual regression coefficient is different from zero at the 5 percent level.

Table 8.5 Causality tests between S&P 500 index and oil spot and futures prices

Dependent variable	Independent variable	b_0, β_0	b_1, β_1	b_2, β_2	b_3, β_3	$H_0: \sum_{i=0}^{3} b_i = 0$ $H_0: \sum_{i=0}^{3} \beta_i = 0$
PANEL A: Pre-Gulf Crisis Period: 1 Oct 1989 to 31 May 1990						
S&P 500 spot	Oil spot	−0.9487 (−0.98)	−1.6401 (−0.74)	−1.0082 (−0.73)	−0.1379 (0.14)	1.318
Oil spot	S&P 500 spot	−0.0063 (−0.94)	0.0164 (2.04)*	−0.0058 (−0.71)	−0.0026 (−0.38)	1.468
S&P 500 futures	Oil futures	−0.2243 (−0.27)	−1.3758 (−0.43)	−1.5435 (−1.31)	−0.7819 (0.92)	0.589
Oil futures	S&P 500 futures	−0.0023 (0.29)	0.0084 (0.88)	−0.0141 (−1.48)	0.0092 (1.18)	0.888
PANEL B: Gulf Crisis Period: 1 June 1990 to 31 Jan 1991						
S&P 500 spot	Oil spot	−1.1213 (−5.99)*	1.5224 (4.97)*	−0.4767 (−1.73)	−0.1837 (0.90)	10.258[a]
Oil spot	S&P 500 spot	−0.1721 (−5.79)*	0.0646 (1.18)	0.0211 (0.47)	0.0764 (2.35)*	15.581[a]
S&P 500 futures	Oil futures	−1.3620 (−8.33)*	1.7759 (5.33)*	−0.2790 (−1.10)	0.1661 (0.83)	19.310[a]
Oil futures	S&P 500 futures	−0.2321 (−8.33)*	0.1490 (2.51)*	0.0355 (0.78)	0.0308 (0.92)	20.87[a]

Notes: The causality models are:

$$\ln X_t = a_0 + a_1 \ln X_{t-1} + a_2 \ln X_{t-2} + a_3 \ln X_{t-3} + b_0 \ln Y_t + b_1 \ln Y_{t-1} + b_2 \ln Y_{t-2} + b_3 \ln Y_{t-3} + C_0 \varepsilon_{t-1} + \phi_t \ (Y \rightarrow X)$$

$$\ln Y_t = \alpha_0 + \alpha_1 \ln Y_{t-1} + \alpha_2 \ln Y_{t-2} + \alpha_3 \ln Y_{t-3} + \beta_0 \ln X_t + \beta_1 \ln X_{t-1} + \beta_2 \ln X_{t-2} + \beta_3 \ln X_{t-3} + \delta \varepsilon_{t-1} + \varepsilon_t \ (X \rightarrow Y)$$

The null hypotheses are

$$H_0: \sum_{i=0}^{3} b_i = 0, \quad \sum_{i=0}^{3} \beta_i = 0$$

An "a" indicates the null hypothesis is rejected at the 1 percent of confidence level.
The $F_{critical}$ are $F_{152, 4} = 2.37$ at 5 percent; 3.32 at 1 percent
$\qquad$ $F_{153, 3} = 2.60$ at 5 percent; 3.78 at 1 percent
An asterisk * indicates that the individual regression coefficient is different from zero at the 5 percent confidence level.

REFERENCES

Brown, S.J. and J.B. Warner (1980) "Measuring Security Price Performance," *Journal of Financial Economics*, 8: 205–58.

Brown, S.J. and J.B. Warner (1985) "Using Daily Stock Returns: The Case of Event Studies," *Journal of Financial Economics*, 14: 3–32.

Dickey, D. and W. Fuller (1981) "Likelihood Ratio Statistics for Autoregressive Time Series with a Unit Root," *Econometrica*, 49: 1057–72.

Dodd, P. and J.B. Warner (1983) "On Corporate Governance: A Study of Proxy Contests," *Journal of Financial Economics*, 11: 401–38.

Engle, R.F., and C.W.J. Granger (1987) "Cointegration and Error Correction: Representation, Estimation, and Testing," *Econometrica*, 55: 251–76.

Geweke, J., R. Meese and W. Dent (1983) "Comparing Alternative Tests of Causality in Temporal Systems," *Journal of Econometrics*, 21: 161–94.

Guilkey, D.K., and M.K. Salemi (1982) "Small Sample Properties of Three Tests for Granger Causal Ordering in a Bivariate Stochastic System," *The Review of Economics and Statistics*, 64: 668–80.

Malliaris, A.G. and J.L. Urrutia (1992) "The International Crash of October 1987: Causality Tests," *Journal of Financial and Quantitative Analysis*, 27: 353–64.

Malliaris, A.G. and J.L. Urrutia (1994) "The Impact of the Persian Gulf Crisis on National Equity Markets," *Advances in International Banking and Finance*, 1: 43–65.

Masulis, R.W. (1980) "The Effect of Capital Structure Change on Security Prices: A Study of Exchange Offers," *Journal of Financial Economics*, 8: 139–78.

Patell, J.M. (1976) "Corporate Forecasts of Earnings per Share and Stock Price Behavior: Empirical Tests," *Journal of Accounting Research*, 14: 246–76.

Pierce, D.A., and L.D. Haugh (1977) "Causality in Temporal Systems: Characterizations and a Survey," *Journal of Econometrics*, 5: 265–93.

Roll, R. (1988) "The International Crash of October 1987," *The Financial Analyst Journal*, 44: 19–35.

Part II

GLOBAL FOREIGN EXCHANGE MARKETS

9

NAKED AND COVERED SPECULATION IN FOREIGN EXCHANGE MARKET

Dilip K. Ghosh

INTRODUCTION

Speculation is an assumption of calculated risk by an individual investor or a firm with a view to making profits from future markets condition(s) the investor expects to happen. Sometimes the investor takes a speculative market position without an underlying cover, which is a *naked speculation*. If the expectations on the future unknown(s) materialize, the investor makes the pre-calculated amount(s) of profit. Since expectations may prove incorrect, an investor sometimes or often tries to insure himself against financial fatality by way of holding some fall-back positions. If the investor does speculate with such underlying protection, it becomes a *covered speculation*. In this chapter an attempt is made to demonstrate how speculation yields profits to an investor in the foreign exchange markets – first without and then with protective measures. In the following section we present the analytical structure of naked speculation without, and then with, transaction costs. In the next section we give an exposition of covered speculation with currency options and synthetic combinations thereof. In the final section we make some concluding remarks.

NAKED SPECULATION

Investors are not alike. Some are risk averse, and some are risk lovers. The risk-free investment strategies of a rational individual or institution in currency markets with spot and forward contracts with and without transaction costs are usually discussed under the rubric of arbitrage and hedging (see Ghosh 1994). Here, in this work, an attempt is made to explain the rational behavior of an economic agent who chooses to assume risk in investment strategies. Risk refers to entering or plunging into uncertainty and unknown variables in the decision-making process in the expectation of generating positive rates of return. We confine our discussions here

119

within the scope of operations in spot and forward markets in currency trading.

It is generally believed that in the financial world, the higher the risk one assumes, the higher the return one should expect in exchange. It is this general belief that drives an investor – individual or institution – into the choice of an investment menu with calculated risk. Empirical evidence often shows that an investor does really well on average in terms of returns by risky investment designs. We try to bring out the core of such risky investment, which is called *speculation*. Speculation, as already noted, is the act of assuming a calculated risk in the expectation of higher rates of return on the invested amounts. The existing literature is replete with research pieces on speculation. Various aspects of this economic activity have been examined by the studies of Friedman (1953), Tsiang (1959), Grubel (1966), Kenen (1965), Spraos (1959), Niehans (1984), Feldstein (1968), Kohlhagen (1979), McKinnon (1979) and Wihlborg (1978). Here, in this work, we plan to examine and explore the situations involving speculation for a rational investor in the currency markets. To do so, we first assume that the investor faces no transaction cost in his/her financial operations in the market. Later we relax the assumption of the absence of transaction costs in the calculation of rational speculation and profit measurement.

Investment strategy with risk

Forward speculation and spot speculation without transaction costs

Consider the following data for an investor on the computer screen or what is collected upon a telephone call to a bank or a foreign currency dealer:

current spot rate of exchange (S) = 2.00,
1–year forward rate of exchange (F) = 2.15,
1–year domestic rate of interest (r) = 10 percent, and
1–year foreign rate of interest (r^*) = 9.5 percent.

Assume that the investor believes that spot rate of foreign exchange a year from today $(\tilde{S})$ will be 3 (that is, $3 = £1). This belief may come from a phone call or fax transmittal of the investor's investment adviser or from a forecasting service or simply out of a sixth sense. Now, if the investor acts on this predicted value of the foreign exchange rate, either forward speculation or spot speculation will be entered into.

Forward speculation without transaction costs

Forward speculation involves either the purchase or sale of forward contracts by the investor to enable the earning of profits by taking exactly the opposite position on the maturity date of the forward contract in the foreign exchange market. Spot speculation similarly involves the purchase or sale of foreign exchange in the spot market today with a view to making a profit in future by taking exactly the opposite position. If, as we have already assumed, the *expected* spot rate of exchange one year from now is 3, the investor can make a profit of $0.85 (= $3 − $2.15) *times* the value of the forward contract the investor enters in now. Simply, pound sterling is bought (the foreign currency in the example) at the rate of $2.15 = £1 now in the forward market – that is, the investor agrees to deliver $2.15 for each British pound at the end of one year. On the settlement date on the agreed-upon forward contract, the investor gets a British pound for giving $2.15 to the counter-party, and then sells the just-acquired British pound at $3 = £1. By doing so – that is, by buying pounds at the forward market now and selling these at the future spot market at the then spot rate, a profit is made. If the investor's forward contract size is £10,000,000, a total profit of $8,500,000 is made (= $0.85 × 10,000,000). If the future spot rate is predicted to be 1.20 (which is less than the forward rate of 2.15), the investor makes money in this case by selling a forward contract on pounds. If the investor enters into a forward sale contract of British pounds (that is, a forward purchase of US dollars), he/she gets $2.15 for the sale of each British pound, then buys back pounds in the future spot rate of $1.20 = £1. Effectively, then, the investor makes $0.95 per pound. If the forward contract size is £10,000,000, the investor obviously makes a total profit of $9,500,000. The rules are then as follows:

If $(\tilde{S} > F$, buy foreign currency forward, and total profit is $= (\tilde{S} − F).A_F$; (1a)
If $\tilde{S} = F$, buy or sell foreign currency forward, and total profit is *zero*

$$(= (\tilde{S} − F).A_F);$$ (1b)

If $\tilde{S} < F$, sell foreign currency forward, and total profit is $= (F − \tilde{S}).A_F$. (1c)

Here A_F is the amount of the forward contract (contract size) in foreign currency denomination. Now, the question is: what happens if the prediction on the spot rate a year from now becomes incorrect? From the illustration it is clear that as long as the spot rate one year from today is not less than the one-year forward rate, a forward *buy* contract of the foreign currency will not yield a loss to the investor, and similarly as long as the spot rate one year from today is not more than the one-year forward rate, a forward *sell* contract of the foreign currency will not yield a loss to the investor. The situations beyond the dividing line obviously create a loss for the speculator.

Figure 9.1 illustrates the results graphically. Along the horizontal axis we represent the forward contract maturity (settlement) date; the vertical axis measures the forward rate and the spot rate of exchange on the date of forward contract maturity. The line AKB defines the spot rate on the forward contract maturity date, and DKG represents the forward rate of

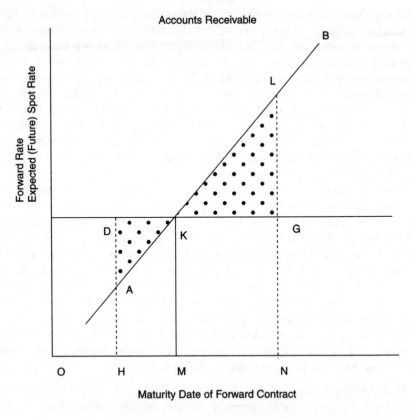

Figure 9.1 Profitable choice: forward buy or sell

exchange. With this diagram, we show the investor with a forward *buy* or *sell* contract of the foreign currency. If the contract maturity date is denoted by any point to the right of M (say, N) that corresponds to the spot rate above the forward rate (NL exceeds NG), the investor makes a profit on the forward *buy* contract (by GL *times* the amount of the contract size). If, on the other hand, the forward contract is a *sell* contract, and the maturity date of the forward contract is denoted by point to the left of M (say, H), he makes a profit to the tune of AD *times* the forward contract size. The opposite happens, that is a loss is incurred by the investor, if at point N the investor holds a forward *sell* contract, and at point H he/she holds the forward *buy* contract. Since the investor does not have a crystal ball, and hence any prediction on the future spot rate may prove significantly wrong, he/she may end up with a big loss for a speculative position with forward contract(s). In the situation of accounts payable one gets the opposite results.

Note that forward speculation involves hardly any money being tied up until the settlement date arrives. It is a commitment (with probably a small percentage of the investor's line of credit attached to the contract). So, if the forward contract brings a fortune to the investor, it is made virtually at the very instant the forward contract is settled and takes the opposite position in that instant spot market is taken. The annual rate of return is more than finite.

Spot speculation without transaction costs

Consider now the other alternative – spot speculation. In this case, the investor may choose to buy (or sell), for instance, pounds at the current spot rate to sell (or buy) the currency in the future spot market, depending on his/her prediction on the spot rate of exchange at a future date. Consider, once again, the same set of data we have presented earlier (this time forward rate is being ignored for the obvious reason):

current spot rate of exchange (S) = 2.00,
1–year domestic rate of interest (r) = 10 percent, and
1–year foreign rate of interest (r^*) = 9.5 percent.

Assume that the investor believes that the rate of exchange one year from today is going to go up, and assume that he/she thinks that it will be 3. Under this assumed scenario, if he/she has one British pound one year from now, it could be sold for \$3.00. Since the present value of £1 a year from now is £1/(1 + r^*) (which is, in this case, equal to £0.9113242 = 1/1.095), the investor needs \$$S$/(1 + r^*) (that is, \$2/1.095) now. The cost of borrowing (or the opportunity cost of) this dollar amount for one year from now being factored into the calculation, the dollar amount at the end of one year becomes equal to $S(1 + r)/(1 + r^*)$ (or, 2(1.1)/1.095). Then one may easily derive the following decision rules:

If $\tilde{S} > S \dfrac{(1 + r)}{(1 + r^*)}$, buy foreign currency spot, and total profit is defined by:

$$= [\tilde{S} - S \frac{(1 + r)}{(1 + r^*)}].A_S \qquad (2a)$$

If $\tilde{S} = S \dfrac{(1 + r)}{(1 + r^*)}$, buy or sell foreign currency spot, and total profit is *zero*

$$= [\tilde{S} - S \frac{(1 + r)}{(1 + r^*)}].A_S \qquad (2b)$$

If $\tilde{S} < S \dfrac{(1 + r)}{(1 + r^*)}$, sell foreign currency spot, and total profit is measured by:

$$= [S \frac{(1 + r)}{(1 + r^*)} - \tilde{S}].A_S \tag{2c}$$

Here A_S is the size of the spot contract in foreign currency denomination. One should recognize now that if the prediction on the one-year spot rate is proved incorrect, the investor may end up with a reduced profit from his original estimate or with a loss, depending upon the actual value of the future spot rate of exchange.

Take a close look at the spot speculation, forward speculation, and arbitrage which is brought out in this context as well. Note the following profit measures out of these three operations in the currency market:

$$P_S \equiv \tilde{S} - S \frac{(1 + r)}{(1 + r^*)} \tag{3a}$$

is the measure of profit if the investor speculates in the spot market;

$$P_F \equiv \tilde{S} - F \tag{3b}$$

is the measure of profit if the investor speculates in the forward market;

$$P_A \equiv F - S \frac{(1 + r)}{(1 + r^*)} \tag{3c}$$

is the measure of (covered interest) arbitrage profit.

Combining these three measures of profit, one can easily rewrite (3a) as follows:

$$P_S \equiv \tilde{S} - S \frac{(1 + r)}{(1 + r^*)} = [\tilde{S} - F] + [F - S \frac{(1 + r)}{(1 + r^*)}] \tag{4}$$

Therefore, we find that

$$P_S = P_F + P_A. \tag{5}$$

One may then conclude that *spot speculation is equivalent to forward speculation and arbitrage together.*

It is quite apparent at this stage that given the predicted value of the future spot rate of exchange, a speculator may engage in both spot and forward speculation. The speculator may find it profitable to engage in either of these speculative strategies. Look at Figure 9.2 in which the horizontal axis measures the predicted value of the future spot rate of exchange ($\tilde{S}$) and the vertical axis measures the forward rate of exchange (F). The distance OA measures the value $S(1 + r)/(1 + r^*)$ (in the illustrative case, it is equal to 2.0091324). The perpendicular ABC (which represents the condition of equality $\tilde{S} = S(1 + r)/(1 + r^*)$) is the dividing line between spot purchase and spot sell positions in the speculative

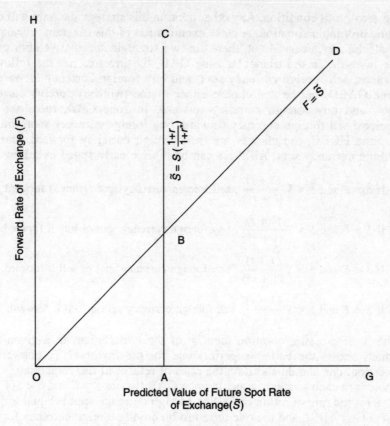

Figure 9.2 Profit (loss) possibilities with naked spot speculation

strategy. The area to the left of this ABC line defines the condition in which $\tilde{S} < S(1 + r)/(1 + r^*)$, which signifies, as already noted, the spot sell of the foreign currency. The zone to the right of the line ABC obviously earmarks the profitable area for speculative spot purchase of foreign currency. On this line the investor is choice-neutral. Next, look at the line OBD, which represents the equality between forward rate and future spot rate of exchange: $F = \tilde{S}$. Along this line, the investor should be indifferent between forward purchase and forward sale. But, in the zone above this line, $\tilde{S} < F$, which means that the profit-seeking speculator will sell foreign currency forward; in the opposite scenario – that is, below this line OBD (which depicts the condition: $\tilde{S} > F$) – the investor will take the speculative position to buy foreign currency at the forward rate. Notice that this diagram has four distinct zones: (a) triangular area OAB, (b) open-ended area GABD, (c) cone-type area CBD, and (d) area HOBC. If the investor locates himself on point B (which is the intersection between OBD and ABC), it will be found that speculation – both spot and forward – results in

125

the zero-profit condition. Any other point in this strategy diagram will offer some profitable situation. A close examination of this diagram reveals that in all the zones carved out, there are two strategic speculative choices for the investor. In the triangular zone OAB, the investor has the following choices: sell foreign currency spot, and buy foreign currency forward. In zone GABD, he/she can choose either of the two: buy foreign currency spot, and buy foreign currency forward. In zone CBD, there are two choices: sell foreign currency forward, buy foreign currency spot. Finally, in zone HOBC, the choices are: sell foreign currency forward, and sell foreign currency spot. All these can be more clearly stated as follows:

If $\tilde{S} > F$ and $\tilde{S} < S \dfrac{(1 + r)}{(1 + r^*)}$, sell foreign currency spot or buy it forward. (6a)

If $\tilde{S} > F$ and $\tilde{S} > S \dfrac{(1 + r)}{(1 + r^*)}$, buy foreign currency spot or buy it forward. (6b)

If $\tilde{S} < F$ and $\tilde{S} > S \dfrac{(1 + r)}{(1 + r^*)}$, buy foreign currency spot or sell it forward. (6c)

If $\tilde{S} < F$ and $\tilde{S} < S \dfrac{(1 + r)}{(1 + r^*)}$, sell foreign currency spot or sell it forward. (6d)

The most pressing question then is: of the two choices in a given zone which one is the better (superior) one for the investor? To answer this question, one should ascertain the rates of returns of the competing pair of choices in each strategic zone. In zone OAB (where $\tilde{S} > F$ and $\tilde{S} < S(1 + r)/(1 + r^*)$) the rate of return on selling foreign currency spot is equal to $[\{S(1 + r)/(1 + r^*)\}/\tilde{S}]$, and the rate of return on buying foreign currency forward is defined by $[\tilde{S}/F]$. So, it appears then that:

if $\dfrac{S \dfrac{(1 + r)}{(1 + r^*)}}{\tilde{S}} > \dfrac{\tilde{S}}{F}$, he should sell foreign currency spot instead of buying it forward; (7)

if $\dfrac{S \dfrac{(1 + r)}{(1 + r^*)}}{\tilde{S}} < \dfrac{\tilde{S}}{F}$, he should buy foreign currency forward instead of selling it spot (8)

From (7) and (8) one can derive that:

if $F > \dfrac{\tilde{S}^2}{S \dfrac{(1 + r)}{(1 + r^*)}}$, he should sell foreign currency spot instead of buying it forward; (7*) if $F < \dfrac{\tilde{S}^2}{S\,\dfrac{(1+r)}{(1+r^*)}}$, he should buy foreign currency forward instead of selling it

spot.   (8*)

Obviously, $F = \dfrac{\tilde{S}^2}{S\,\dfrac{(1+r)}{(1+r^*)}}$ is the dividing curve between the above two

choices.   (9)

In Figure 9.3, the curve OBE is that dividing line which represents the

condition: $F = \dfrac{\tilde{S}^2}{S\,\dfrac{(1+r)}{(1+r^*)}}$. So, above this curve OBE the investor should

engage

only in selling foreign currency spot, and below this curve he should buy
foreign currency forward.

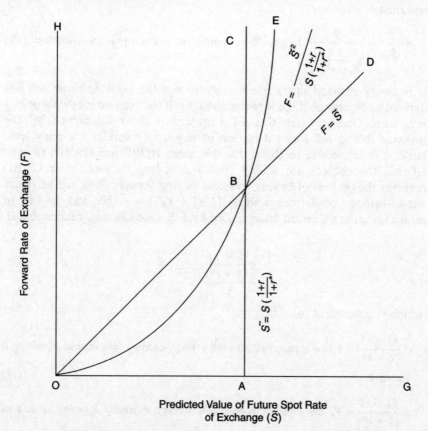

Figure 9.3 Profit menu with single choice under speculation

127

Next, consider the rates of return from speculative forward sale and speculative spot purchase of the foreign currency. The rate of return on the speculative forward sale of the foreign currency is defined by $F/\tilde{S}$, and the rate of return on speculative spot purchase is given by $\dfrac{\tilde{S}}{S\dfrac{(1 + r)}{(1 + r^*)}}$. Then

if $\dfrac{F}{\tilde{S}} > \dfrac{\tilde{S}}{S\dfrac{(1 + r)}{(1 + r^*)}}$, he should sell foreign currency forward instead of

buying it spot; $\hspace{4cm}$ (10)

if $\dfrac{F}{\tilde{S}} < \dfrac{\tilde{S}}{S\dfrac{(1 + r)}{(1 + r^*)}}$, he should buy foreign currency spot instead of selling it

spot; $\hspace{4cm}$ (11)

and then

if $\dfrac{F}{\tilde{S}} = \dfrac{\tilde{S}}{S\dfrac{(1 + r)}{(1 + r^*)}}$, he should be indifferent to these two above choices. (12)

It is easily realized that these conditions are the same as those we just derived to determine if the investor should sell foreign currency spot or buy it forward. One may state that if the investor is above the curve OBE, the investor should sell forward instead of buying the foreign currency spot. Now, it is instructive to check into the zones HOBC and GABD. In zone HOBC, the choices are selling spot and selling forward; zone GABD presents the options of buying spot and buying forward. The rate of return out of selling spot is measured by $[\{S(1 + r)/(1 + r^*)\}]/\tilde{S}$, and the rate of return on selling forward is computed by $F/\tilde{S}$. One can now realize that if:

$$\frac{S\dfrac{(1 + r)}{(1 + r^*)}}{\tilde{S}} > \frac{F}{\tilde{S}},$$

which is equivalent to:

$S\dfrac{(1 + r)}{(1 + r^*)} > F$, the investor should sell foreign curreny spot instead of selling it

forward; $\hspace{4cm}$ (13)

$S\dfrac{(1 + r)}{(1 + r^*)} < F$, the investor should sell foreign currency forward instead of

selling it spot. $\hspace{4cm}$ (14)

Similarly, one can determine that

if $S \dfrac{(1 + r)}{(1 + r^*)} > F$, the investor should buy foreign currency forward instead of

buying it spot; (15)

if $S \dfrac{(1 + r)}{(1 + r^*)} < F$, the investor should sell foreign currency forward instead of

selling it spot (16)

Figure 9.4 presents a new set of strategic zones defined by two curves, OBE (which represents $(\tilde{S}^2/\{S(1 + r)/(1 + r^*) = F)$ and KBJ (for which $S(1 + r)/(1 + r^*) = F$). To the left of the OBE curve and under the KBJ line, the investor should sell foreign currency spot; to the left of the OBE curve and above the KBJ line, the investor should sell foreign currency forward; to the right of the OBE curve and under the KBJ line, the investor should buy foreign currency forward; and to the right of the OBE curve and above the KBJ line, the investor should buy foreign currency spot.

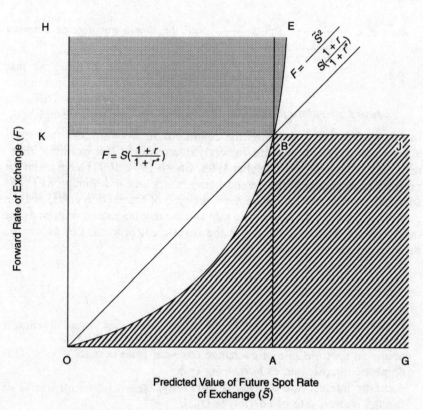

Figure 9.4 Profit zones with single strategy under speculation

129

DILIP K. GHOSH

More clearly,

when $F > \dfrac{\tilde{S}^2}{S\dfrac{(1 + r)}{(1 + r^*)}}$, and $S\dfrac{(1 + r)}{(1 + r^*)} > F$, he should sell foreign currency

spot; (17)

when $F > \dfrac{\tilde{S}^2}{S\dfrac{(1 + r)}{(1 + r^*)}}$, and $S\dfrac{(1 + r)}{(1 + r^*)} < F$, he should sell foreign currency

forward; (18)

when $F < \dfrac{\tilde{S}^2}{S\dfrac{(1 + r)}{(1 + r^*)}}$, and $S\dfrac{(1 + r)}{(1 + r^*)} > F$, he should buy foreign currency

forward; (19)

when $F < \dfrac{\tilde{S}^2}{S\dfrac{(1 + r)}{(1 + r^*)}}$, and $S\dfrac{(1 + r)}{(1 + r^*)} < F$, he should buy foreign currency

spot. (20)

Forward speculation and spot speculation with transaction costs

In this section, we re-examine the conditions for forward and spot speculation with transaction costs. Recently, many works (for example, Blenman 1992; Blenman and Thatcher 1995; Ghosh 1994, 1997) have taken the position of introducing the spread between *ask* and *bid* quotations in the spot and forward markets to capture one type of transaction costs, and the difference between the *borrowing* rate and the *lending* rate of interest as the other type of transaction costs in the investment process. Let us rewrite these quotations as follows:

current spot *ask* rate of exchange (S^a),
current spot *bid* rate of exchange (S^b),
1–year forward *ask* rate of exchange (F^a),
1–year forward *bid* rate of exchange (F^b),
predicted spot *ask* rate of exchange one year from now ($\tilde{S}^a$),
predicted spot *bid* rate of exchange one year from now ($\tilde{S}^b$).
domestic interest rate of *borrowing* (r_B),
domestic interest rate of *lending (investing)* (r_L).
foreign interest rate of *borrowing* (r_B^*),
foreign interest rate of *lending (investing)* (r_L^*).

130

Forward speculation with transaction costs

Following the procedures outlined earlier, we can state the rules of rational investment behavior of a speculator as follows:

if $F^a < \tilde{S}^b$, buy foreign currency forward, and total profit = $(\tilde{S}^b - F^a).A_F$; (21)

if $F^b < \tilde{S}^b$, sell foreign currency forward, and total profit = $(\tilde{S}^b - F^b).A_F$. (22)

Assume, for the sake of simplicity, that S, F, and $\tilde{S}$ are the mid-rates of exchange. That is, S is the mid-rate between S^a and S^b, F is the mid-rate between F^a and F^b, and $\tilde{S}$ the mid-rate between $\tilde{S}^a$ and $\tilde{S}^b$. Under these assumptions then, one can have the following relationships:

$$S^a = S(1 + T_s), \; S^b = \frac{S}{1 + T_s},$$

$$F^a = F(1 + T_f), \; F^b = \frac{F}{1 + T_f},$$

$$\tilde{S}^a = \tilde{S}(1 + T_{\tilde{s}}), \; \tilde{S}^b = \frac{\tilde{S}}{1 + T_{\tilde{s}}},$$

$$r_B = r(1 + \tau), \; r_L = \frac{r}{1 + \tau}, \; r^*_B = r^*(1 + \tau^*) \text{ and } r^*_L = \frac{r^*}{1 + \tau^*}.$$

Here T_s, T_f, and $T_{\tilde{s}}$ are the transaction costs on current spot, forward, and future spot markets. Similarly, τ, and τ^* measure the transaction costs associated with interest rates in the domestic and the foreign markets, respectively. Now, one can rewrite (5.21) as follows:

when $F(1 + T_f)(1 + T_{\tilde{s}}) < \tilde{S}$, buy foreign currency forward; (23)

Similarly, (22) can be re-expressed as follows:

$F > \tilde{S}(1 + T_f)(1 + T_{\tilde{s}})$, sell foreign currency forward; (24)

Figure 9.5 shows the picture of profitable forward speculation. The horizontal and vertical axes measure predicted future mid-spot rate of exchange ($\tilde{S}$) and mid-forward rate of exchange (F), respectively. The line OA depicts the condition: $F = \tilde{S}$. The line OB represents $F = \tilde{S}(1 + T_f)(1 + T_{\tilde{s}})$, and line OC defines the condition: $F = \tilde{S}/(1 + T_f)(1 + T_{\tilde{s}})$. Obviously, in the area above the line OB in this diagram, $F > \tilde{S}(1 + T_f)(1 + T_{\tilde{s}})$, which means that the speculator should sell foreign currency forward. In the area below the line OC where $F < \tilde{S}/(1 + T_f)(1 + T_{\tilde{s}})$, the profit-seeking speculator should buy foreign currency forward. In the cone BOC there is no scope for profitable arbitrage. A close look at the diagram reveals that the greater the transaction costs, the further out will be the

131

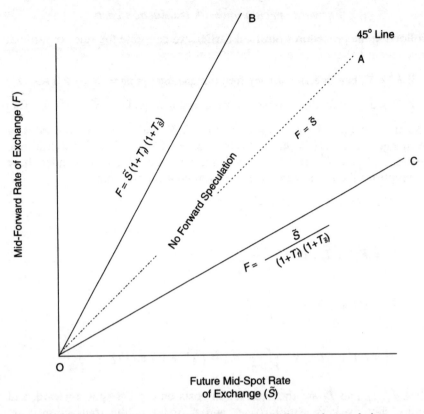

Figure 9.5 Zones of profitable/unprofitable forward speculation

lines OB and OC from the line OA, which in turn would indicate smaller scope for profitable forward speculation.

Spot speculation with transaction costs

Again, the same procedures as before indicate that the speculator should buy foreign currency spot if

$$\tilde{S}^b > S^a \frac{1 + r_B}{1 + r_L},$$

which is equivalent to:

$$\tilde{S} > S \frac{(1 + T_s)(1 + T_{\tilde{s}})(1 + r_B)}{(1 + r_L^*)}. \tag{25}$$

The investor should sell foreign currency spot provided the following holds:

$$S^b > \tilde{S}^a,$$

which means:

$$S > \tilde{S}(1 + T_s)(1 + T_{\tilde{s}}) \tag{26}$$

Figure 9.6 portrays the profitable choices of the speculator in the spot market. Here also the horizontal and the vertical axes represent $\tilde{S}$ and F. The perpendicular KL defines $\tilde{S} = S/(1 + T_s)(1 + T_{\tilde{s}})$, and the perpendicular MN represents $\tilde{S} = S(1 + T_s)(1 + T_{\tilde{s}})(1 + r_B)/(1 + r_L^*)$. The area to the left of the line KL represents the condition that $\tilde{S} < S/(1 + T_s)(1 + T_{\tilde{s}})$. So in this area – that is, for any combination of F and $\tilde{S}$ that lies in this area – the speculator should sell foreign currency spot. It is evident, as it ought to be, that there is no constraint on the forward rate (since it is a spot market strategy alone). The area to the right of the vertical line MN (for which obviously $\tilde{S} > S(1 + T_s)(1 + T_{\tilde{s}})(1 + r_B)/(1 + r_L^*))$ defines the scope for profitable speculation when the investor buys foreign currency spot. The area between these KL and MN lines defines the corridor that offers no

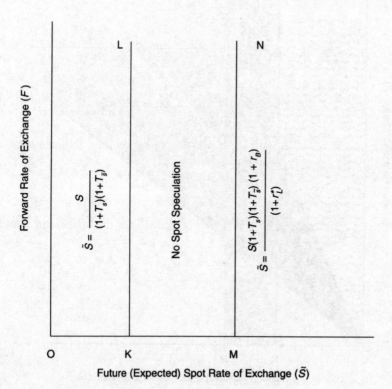

Figure 9.6 Spot speculation

133

scope for profitable spot speculation. It should be pointed out that the higher the transaction costs, the wider the corridor and vice versa. If foreign lending rate r_L^* is very high, then, *ceteris paribus*, it may tend to exert the effect of narrowing the corridor on non-profitable spot speculation. One may recall the interest rate relationships we have outlined earlier: $r_B = r(1 + \tau)$, $r_L^* = r^*/(1 + \tau^*)$, make use of these relationships in (25), and arrive at:

$$\tilde{S} > S \frac{(1 + T_s)\,(1 + T_{\tilde{s}})\,(1 + r)\,(1 + \tau)\,(1 + \tau^*)}{(1 + r)}. \qquad (25)$$

Forward and spot speculation in one framework

Now, put both Figure 9.5 and Figure 9.6 together, and the picture presented in Figure 9.7 is arrived at. Here the cone BOC specifies the zone of no

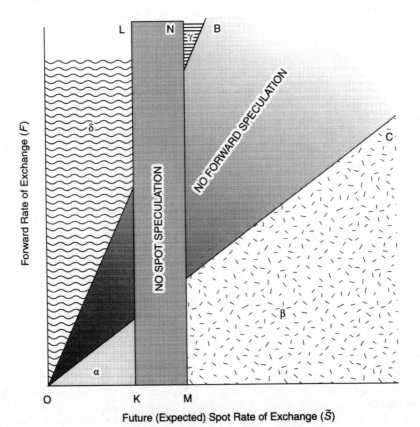

Figure 9.7 Spot and forward speculation

134

forward speculation, and the vertical corridor between the lines KL and MN demarcates the zone of no spot speculation. The overlapping area obviously defines the scope of non-speculative activities, both spot and forward. In this diagram, the triangular area (designated as α) offers the scope for speculative selling of foreign currency in the spot market and purchasing of it in the forward market. The area β defines a buy forward and sell spot strategy. The area denoted by γ is for buying in the spot market and selling in the forward market, and finally, zone δ prescribes the strategies of sell spot and sell forward. Once again we provide the following decision rules for the speculators in the designated zones as follows:

α: sell foreign currency spot, or buy it forward;
β: buy foreign currency spot, or buy it forward;
γ: buy foreign currency spot, or sell it forward;
δ: sell foreign currency spot, or sell it forward.

Once again one has to choose between the two profitable choices in each area of operation. The exact procedures that we have used in the absence of transaction costs will narrow the choice set under different conditions.

COVERED SPECULATION

In this section, we attempt to step out of the zone of unguarded risk by offering some levels of insulation through derivative securities on the currencies under consideration. Here, we present some special currency options – put option and/or call option or synthetic combinations thereof – to protect the speculator who has love for risk in order to set better returns but does not wish to sustain great losses in the lust for money. What can such a speculator do in this situation? In this section we present a number of possibilities that may sterilize the investor from financial catastrophe resulting from speculative zeal.

Consider the earlier data and a put option with the following information on it: put option premium (P_p) = \$0.05, its exercise price (X_p) = \$2.35, and its time to expiration matching the maturity of the forward contract. Under this situation the effective exercise price of the put (X^*_p) is \$2.35 − \$0.05 = \$2.30. In this event, if the speculator expects the future spot rate to be \$3, he should buy pounds forward with the purchase of a put. If the future spot rate proves incorrect, he still has the option of getting out with a profit of \$0.15 (= \$2.30 − \$2.15) per pound upon the exercise of the option. As long as the effective exercise price (X^*_p) is greater than or equal to the forward quote, a speculative position with forward and put purchase of pounds cannot hurt. If the probability of the exercise of the put equals the probability that the investor's expected value of the spot rate will prove true, then speculation is gainful. Technically, $E(\pi) = \{p_1(X^*_p - F) + p_2(\tilde{S}^+ - F)\}A_F$, where π stands for profits, p_1 measures the probability of exercising the option, and p_2 measures the probability of realizing the expected outcome $\tilde{S}^+$. That means, in this illustrative case, that $E(\pi) = \{\frac{1}{2}(\$0.15) + \frac{1}{2}(\$0.85)\}1,000,000 = \$500,000$ (the contract size being £1,000,000). If the put is available for $0.05 with the exercise price of $2.15 (and hence the effective exercise price of $2.10), the expected value of the same speculative strategy will be $\{\frac{1}{2}(\$2.10 - \$2.15) + \frac{1}{2}(\$3.00 - \$2.15)\}1,000,000 = \$400,000$. From these illustrations, one may easily arrive at the conclusion that as long as the effective exercise price of the put option is at most the same as the positive difference between the expected future spot rate and the forward rate, speculation is financially worth while. Figure 9.8 depicts the picture of what sort of speculation the investor should engage in.

So far we have looked at the expectation that the future spot rate will be above the forward rate. If, however, the expected value on the future spot rate is below the currently quoted forward rate – that is, $F = 2.15$, and $\tilde{S}^+ = 2.00$ – the investor should enter into a forward sell contract on the British pound here. By entering into this sell contract, the investor will sell pounds to get $2.15 on each pound sold at the end of the contract maturity, and then buy each pound for $2.00, thus making a profit of $0.15 per pound. Given this scenario, if the expectation is realized, the naked speculative long position on forward contract is all that the investor can achieve. However, when he/she is not so sure that $\tilde{S}^+ = 2.00$, exposure should be hedged by buying a call option at some appropriate cost. If a call is available at an exercise price of $2.05 for a premium of, say, $0.05, the investor's effective exercise price then becomes $2.10, and the profit upon a possible exercise of the option is $2.15 - $2.10 = $0.05 per pound. Expected profit is measured by the following:

$$E(\pi) = \{p_1(F - X^*_c) + p_2(F - \tilde{S}^+)\}A_F$$

In this instance, the profit out of a contract of £1,000,000 is then $\{\frac{1}{2}(\$2.15 - \$2.10) + \frac{1}{2}(\$2.15 - \$2.00)\}1,000,000 = \$100,000$. It is clear from this case that as long as $X^*_c \leq F$, there is no loss in going long on call. More

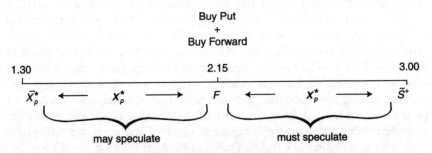

Figure 9.8 Covered speculation with put option

correctly, as long as $\tilde{S}^+ \leq X_c^* \leq F$ holds, there is no loss (profits in strict inequality conditions). Figure 9.9 defines the covered profit opportunities, and further specifies conditions when one must and when one may profitably speculate with mathematical expectation. In our analysis, we have only considered the possible two outcomes, which may be all right if we are with the European options and the expected value of future spot rate $\tilde{S}$ is fixed. However, when the American options are introduced into the picture, any outcome from X_p^* to $\tilde{S}^+$ may occur with equal probability. The probability density for this situation is appropriately defined by the uniform distribution:

$$\int_{-\infty}^{\tilde{S}^+} f_s(S) \, dS, \text{ where } f_s(S) = \frac{1}{\tilde{S}^+ - X_c^*} \, , X_c^* < S < \tilde{S}^+;$$

$$= 0, \text{ otherwise;}$$

$$= 0 \text{ for } \tilde{S}^+ < X_p^*$$

$$= \frac{Z - X_c^*}{\tilde{S}^+ - X_c^*} \text{ for } X_p^* \leq Z \leq \tilde{S}^+$$

$$= 1 \text{ for } Z > \tilde{S}^+.$$

From this probability distribution, the mean $(\mu_S) = E(S)$, and variance (σ^2) are as follows:

$$\mu_S = \frac{\tilde{S}^+ - X_c^*}{2} \, , \qquad \sigma^2 = \frac{(\tilde{S}^+ - X_c^*)^2}{12} \, .$$

Similar results are in order for call options in the American style. These calculations are meaningful only in the event that the investor has expectation that the value of the future spot rate will be either $\tilde{S}_u > F$ or $\tilde{S}_l < F$. In reality, however, the investor may be given the prediction on future S

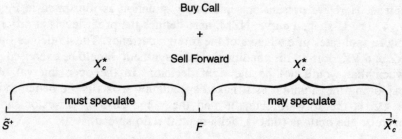

Figure 9.9 Covered speculation with call option

137

within a range such that $\tilde{S}_1 < F < \tilde{S}_u$. In this situation, it appears that the investor should go long on both put and call. Before entering further into this range we should consider the entire range of possible values on the future spot rate of exchange ($\tilde{S}$) in the interval between 0 and infinity. With effective exercise price of, say, put option and the expected value of $\tilde{S}$ lying in the closed interval of 0 and ∞, the probability density function must be a normal distribution of S, and the moment generating function is defined by the following expression:

$$\int_{X_c^*}^{\infty} \frac{1}{\sigma\sqrt{2\pi}} e^{-0.5\frac{(S-\mu)^2}{\sigma^2}} \, dS,$$

whence $\mu_s = \mu$, $\sigma_s^2 = \sigma^2$ are given by some a priori estimates. Now we see that the investor is in a position to create a rich variety of synthetic combinations when the expected value of the future spot rate of exchange is not known. So we attempt to illustrate a few cocktails with put and call options in this context.

Merton (1973), Garman and Kohlhagen (1983), and Grabbe (1983) have discussed options in depth, in ways that fit our specific conditions. With a full comprehension of these works and proper utilization of these models the investor can create a number of straddles, strangles or delta-neutral ratio spreads to create different U-shaped profit (loss) functions. A *straddle* or a *strangle* is a combination of a call and a put, but in the straddle both the exercise price and the expiration date on put and call are the same; in a strangle, put and call options have the same expiration date but a different exercise price. A *spread* is combination of options of different series but of the same class. Figures 9.10, 9.11, 9.12, 9.13, and 9.14 exhibit profit (loss) functions of these three synthetics. It should be noted at this point that the lower the volatility (σ), the higher the loss, and the higher the volatility the lower the loss (or greater the profit) for both straddle and delta-neutral ratio spreads. For a strangle profit is potentially greater with more time remaining and vice versa. If the calculation of the implied volatility exceeds the critical value, it pays to take the covered straddle or delta-neutral ratio spread. Here we present one interesting situation as illustrated in Figure 9.14. The U-shaped curve, NZM, here defines the profit levels at different future spot rates of exchange of the foreign currency. The 45-degree lines, RZ and VZ, portray the conditions where synthetic should be exercised and when that would not be the right decision. In the open interval, AB, exploiting the situation as if naked speculation exists is the better choice if OZ is the forward rate; beyond the range AB, the investor should exercise the options (that is, delta-neutral ratio spread).

138

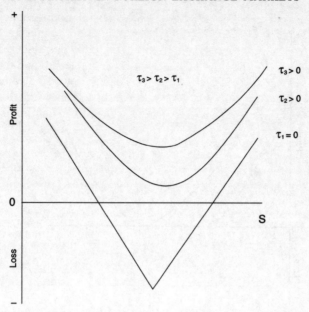

Figure 9.10 Option-based profit profiles, different expiration times

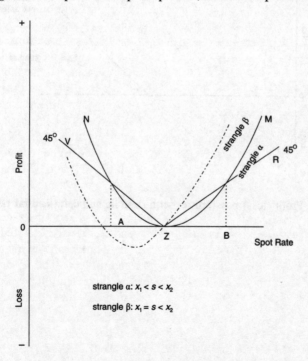

Figure 9.11 Profit (loss) possibilities with strangle

139

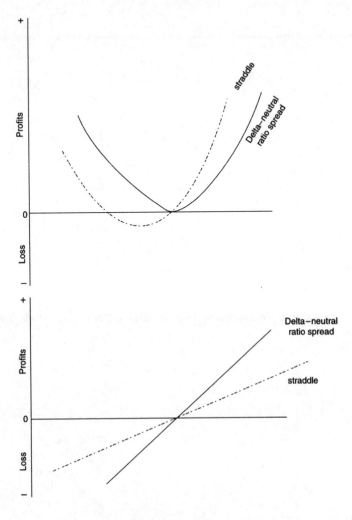

Figure 9.12 Profit (loss) possibilities with straddle and delta-neutral ratio spread

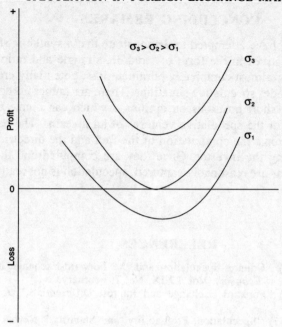

Figure 9.13 Profit (loss) possibilities with different volatilities

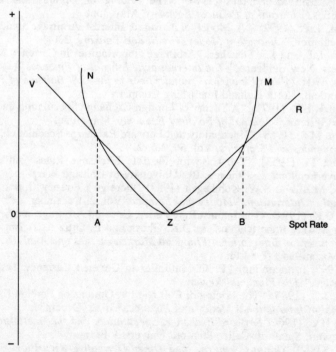

Figure 9.14 Profit possibilities: options *vis-à-vis* forward contracts

CONCLUDING REMARKS

In this chapter we have attempted to demonstrate that a synthetic structure of currency derivatives in the form of straddle, strangle and ratio spread can completely, or almost completely eliminate loss, potentially creating a profit condition under speculative situations. There are numerous combinations – sometime short positions on options – which can create an even better insulation for the speculative ventures of an investor. The parabolic profit (loss) functions, the computation of the foci and the directrices may be problems facing the investor. Once they are computed and the probability distributions are reasonably captured, speculation is not really a leap into the dark.

REFERENCES

Auten, J.H. (1961) "Counter-Speculation and the Forward-Exchange Market," *Journal of Political Economy*, Vol. LXIX, No. 1, February.

Auten, J.H. (1963) "Forward Exchange and Interest Differentials," *Journal of Finance*, March.

Baumol, W.J. (1957) "Speculation, Profitability, and Stability," *Review of Economics and Statistics*, Vol. XXXIX, August.

Black, F., and M. Scholes (1973) "The Pricing of Options and Corporate Liabilities," *Journal of Political Economy*, May–June.

Blenman, L.P. (1992) "A Model of Covered Interest Arbitrage under Market Segmentation," *Journal of Money, Credit and Banking*, 23(4).

Blenman, L.P. and J.S. Thatcher, "Arbitrage Opportunities in Currency and Credit Markets: New Evidence," *The International Journal of Finance*, 7(1).

Branson, W.H. (1968) *Financial Capital Flows in the U.S. Balance of Payments*, Amsterdam: North-Holland Publishing Company.

Canterbury, E.R. (1971) "A Theory of Foreign Exchange Speculation under Alternative Systems," *Journal of Political Economy*, May–June.

Feldstein, M.S. (1968) "Uncertainty and Forward Exchange Speculation," *Review of Economics and Statistics*, Vol. 50, No. 2.

Friedman, M. (1953) "The Case for Flexible Exchange Rates," in *Essays in Positive Economics*, Chicago: Ill.: University of Chicago Press.

Garman, M.B. and S.W. Kohlhagen (1983) "Foreign Currency Option Values," *Journal of International Money and Finance*, Vol. 2, December.

Ghosh, D.K. (1994) "The Interest Rate Parity, Covered Arbitrage and Speculation under Market Imperfection," in D.K. Ghosh and E. Ortiz (eds) *The Changing Environment of International Financial Markets: Issues and Analysis*, London: The Macmillan Press Ltd.

—— (1997, forthcoming) "Profit Multiplier in Covered Currency Trading with Leverage," *The Financial Review*.

Grabbe, J.O. (1983) "The Pricing of Call and Put Options on Foreign Exchange," *Journal of International Money and Finance*, Vol. 2, December.

Grubel, H.G. (1966) *Forward Exchange, Speculation, and the International Flow of Capital*, Stanford: Calif.: Stanford University Press.

Hull, J. (1989) *Options, Futures, and Other Derivative Securities*, Englewood Cliffs: N.J.: Prentice-Hall.

Kemp, M.C. (1963) "Speculation, Profitability, and Price Stability," *Review of Economics and Statistics*, Vol. XLV, May.

Kenen, P.B. (1965) "Trade, Speculation, and The Forward Exchange Rate," Robert E. Baldwin *et al.* (eds) in *Trade, Growth, and the Balance of Payments, Essays in Honor of Gottfried Haberler*, Amsterdam: North-Holland Publishing Company.

Kindleberger, C.P. (1937) "Speculation and Forward Exchange," *Journal of Political Economy*, XLVII, April.

Kohlhagen, S.W. (1979) "The Identification of Destabilizing Foreign Exchange Speculation," *Journal of International Economics*, Vol. 9, No. 3.

Kolb, R.W. (1994) *Options: An Introduction*, Miami, Fl.: Kolb Publishing Company.

McKinnon, R.I. (1979) *Money in International Exchange*, Oxford: Oxford University Press.

Merton, R.C., (1973) "The Theory of Rational Option Pricing," *Bell Journal of Economics and Management Science*, Vol. 5, Spring.

Neihans, J. (1984) *International Monetary Economics,* Baltimore: Md.: Johns Hopkins University Press.

Spraos, J. (1959) "Speculation, Arbitrage and Sterling," *Economic Journal*, Vol. LXIX, No. 1, March.

Telser, L.G. (1959) "A Theory of Speculation Relating Profitability and Stability," *Review of Economics and Statistics*, Vol. XLI, August.

Tsiang, S.C. (1959) "The Theory of Forward Exchange and Effects of Government Intervention on the Forward Exchange Market," *International Monetary Fund Staff Papers*, Vol. 7.

Wihlborg, C. (1978) *Currency Risks in International Financial Markets*, Princeton Studies in International Finance, No. 44.

Williamson, J. (1973) "Another Case of Profitable Destabilizing Speculation," *Journal of International Economics*, Vol. 3, No. 1, February.

Wilmott, P., J. Dewynne and S. Howison (1993) *Option Pricing: Mathematical Models and Computation, Oxford:* Oxford Financial Press.

10

CONSISTENT ESTIMATES OF EXCHANGE-RATE PASS-THROUGH COEFFICIENTS FOR THE LEADING EUROPEAN COUNTRIES

Paola Caselli and Andrea Cividini

We produce empirical evidence on the pass-through phenomenon for the leading European countries on a statistically comparable basis by using the OECD foreign trade data on the basis of the five-digit SITC classification. In order to assess the importance of simultaneity in estimating the pass-through coefficients in a context of monopolistic competition we have implemented the Limited Information Instrumental Variable Efficient (LIVE) method. The comparison of the OLS and LIVE estimates shows that the pass-through coefficients obtained with LIVE tend to be higher in absolute value and more significant than OLS coefficients. Furthermore, the performance of the equation estimated with LIVE is generally more satisfactory.

INTRODUCTION[1]

The revival of interest in the pass-through, that is to say the extent to which exchange rate movements are reflected in the price level in both the short and long run, dates back to the mid-1980s and focuses on attempts to explain the puzzling behaviour of the US current account deficit after the huge depreciation of the dollar (see, among others, Krugman, 1987; Bryant *et al.*, 1988; Baldwin and Krugman, 1989; and Feenstra, 1989). More recently, the pricing strategies of exporters have been indicated as one of the reasons for the non-inflationary impact of the devaluation of several European currencies (namely the Italian lira, British pound, and Spanish peseta) after the turmoil in the European Monetary System in September 1992. According to this interpretation, exporters reacted to the sudden loss in competitiveness caused by the exchange rate fluctuations by drastically reducing their profit margins in these markets.

Whether this behaviour is to be considered exceptional or consistent with previous experience is a question that still has to be answered. Despite its

144

importance, few empirical studies have been devoted to pass-through in European markets, the work of Knetter (1989, 1992 and 1993) being a notable exception. The aim of this chapter is to fill a part of this gap through an empirical test of the model put forward by Kasa (1992), extended to a context of monopolistic competition so that explicit account can be taken of competitors' behaviour in the determination of the pass-through. Accordingly, for each market under consideration we set up a system of simultaneous export price equations; in this context, as opposed to the monopolistic case, the Ordinary Least Squares (OLS) estimates are inconsistent; to overcome this problem we use an instrumental variable method, the so-called Limited Information Instrumental Variable Efficient (LIVE), first proposed by Brundy and Jorgenson (1971), which allows consistent and efficient estimates of the structural coefficients.

Although simultaneous estimation techniques have been very well known in the econometric literature since the early 1960s, they have rarely been used in empirical studies of the pass-through (see, for example, Baldwin, 1988 and Feenstra, 1989). In order to assess the relevance of the simultaneity issue in our specific context, we carry out several tests comparing the performance of the OLS and LIVE estimates.

Following Kasa's and Knetter's approaches, we use fairly disaggregated data. In order to increase the comparability of the results, reference is made to the statistics on foreign trade published by the OECD on the basis of the five-digit Standard International Trade Classification. This makes it possible to construct sufficiently homogeneous series of export unit values for the main European markets; for each market the data refer to six European exporting countries and four products (see the Data Appendix on p. 166).

The chapter is organized as follows: in the following section we briefly recall the issue of simultaneity arising from our model, which is fully described in Appendix A (see pp. 162–5), and we also present the results obtained for the pass-through coefficients with OLS and LIVE estimators; next, we perform some tests aimed at evaluating the degree of simultaneity for the estimated equation and the prediction accuracy of the LIVE estimates compared with OLS; finally, we draw some conclusions.

OLS AND LIVE ESTIMATES OF THE PASS-THROUGH COEFFICIENTS

The standpoint of this chapter is that of a representative exporter who maximizes his/her profits in his/her national currency. In this case pass-through is the extent to which export prices expressed in national currency rise (fall) as a result of a depreciation (appreciation) of this currency.

In order to test empirically the size of the pass-through, we set up a model that emphasizes the following factors: (i) competition with other exporters in the same market; (ii) the adjustment costs that a producer has to bear in order to modify sales in foreign markets from one period to the next.

The model essentially extends the theoretical framework proposed by Kasa (1992) to monopolistic competition for the case of a monopolist.[2] For each producer, j, selling in a given market, i, we thus derive the following export price equation, in log terms:

$$
\begin{aligned}
p^*_{ji, \, t} = a_0 &+ a_1 p^*_{i, \, t} + a_2 p_{i, \, t} \\
&+ a_3 p^*_{ji, \, t-1} + a_4 p^*_{i, \, t-1} + a_5 p_{i, \, t-1} \\
&+ a_6(\hat{e}_{ij, \, t} - \hat{e}_{ij, \, t-1}) + \xi_{i, \, t}
\end{aligned}
\tag{1}
$$

where p^*_{ji} is the price producer j charges in market i, expressed in the national currency of j;

p^*_i is the competitors' average price in market i, expressed in national currencies,[3]

p_i is the competitors' average price in market i, expressed in currency i;

$\hat{e}_{ij}$ is the nominal bilateral exchange rate between currencies i and j minus the nominal effective exchange rate of currency i;

ξ_i is an uncorrelated disturbance (see Appendix A, pp. 162–5).

The coefficient a_6 directly identifies the extent to which, at time t, changes in the nominal bilateral exchange rate (relative to the effective rate) influence the price expressed in the currency of the exporting countries.[4] According to our model, a_6 should be negative, its absolute value being positively related to the size of the adjustment costs.

Each market, i, can thus be characterized by a system of m export price equations like (1), where m is the number of competitors, together with the identity:

$$
p^*_i = \sum_{j=1}^{m} p_{ji} / m \qquad j \neq i
\tag{2}
$$

Because of identity (2) the m price equations are simultaneous and OLS would give inconsistent estimates of the structural coefficients.[5] In order to overcome this problem, in our empirical analysis we use the instrumental variable method LIVE, proposed by Brundy and Jorgenson (1971).

In the LIVE procedure the instruments are obtained through the deterministic solution of the whole model computed by means of a static simulation; more precisely, given an inconsistent initial estimate of the model, for example with OLS, the LIVE estimate of the structural coefficients can be obtained through a two-step procedure using the results of a static simulation over the sample period as instruments. As shown in Brundy and Jorgenson (1971), consistency is achieved in the first step and efficiency in the second.

It is worth noting that under the standard normality assumptions the LIVE estimator is asymptotically equivalent to the two-stage least squares estimator (Mariano, 1983). However, while the latter is often operationally not feasible because the number of predetermined variables is larger than the number of observations, the LIVE estimator can always be computed, provided a simulation package is available. A detailed description of the algorithm used in our work can be found in Cividini (1991) and in Bianchi et al., (1993).

In our empirical analysis we consider four products: polypropylene, car tyres, truck tyres and cars (see the Data Appendix on p. 166).[6] For these four products, the export unit values are analysed for six European countries (Germany, France, Italy, the United Kingdom, the Netherlands and Belgium)[7] with respect to the four largest European markets (Germany, France, Italy and the United Kingdom). We thus estimate, on quarterly data covering the period 1978: 2–1991: 4, 16 systems, each constituted by seven simultaneous equations. To avoid distortions in the estimation of the coefficients due to differentiated trends in cost, the export unit values are related to the unit labour cost of the manufacturing sector (see the Data Appendix). This should result in the dependent variable reflecting the changes in unit profit margins quite accurately.

Tables 10.1a–d report the OLS and LIVE estimates of the impact pass-through (i.e. the parameter a_6 of equation (1)) together with their asymptotic t-statistics. As a general observation, it is worth noting that in both procedures the coefficients exhibit the expected negative sign in about 90 percent of all cases.[8] However, LIVE estimates tend to be more significant and larger in absolute value; this is true for all the markets and products considered. More precisely, LIVE estimates are negative and significant in 51 cases (64 percent of the total), against 43 cases (54 percent) for the OLS estimates; moreover, in around half of these cases their absolute value is greater than one.[9] These empirical findings appear to confirm the importance of the pass-through phenomenon in the European markets even in a period in which exchange rate fluctuations among European currencies are limited by the existence of the EMS.[10]

Let us now focus on the LIVE estimates. As regards the results by product, car tyres have the largest number of significant coefficients (85 percent), followed by polypropylene (75 percent), truck tyres (70 percent) and cars (only 25 percent); for the first three products the coefficients tend to be quite large in absolute value. Pass-through thus occurs more frequently for the less differentiated products, for which markets can plausibly be assumed to be more competitive; moreover, when it does occur, the effects on prices are substantial.

The results for cars are particularly interesting, although they need to be treated with caution because of the heterogeneity of this product group. Pass-through is significant (and large in absolute value) in two cases on the

147

Table 10.1a Results of the estimation of equation (1) for export prices on the Italian market* (estimated pass-through coefficients and related asymptotic t-statistics)

Exporting countries / Products	Germany†		France		United Kingdom		Netherlands		Belgium	
	OLS	LIVE	OLS	LIVE	OLS	LIVE	OLS	LIVE	OLS	LIVE
Polypropylene	-1.27	-1.46	-1.21	-1.52	-0.53	-0.39	-1.64	-1.93	-1.43	-1.68
	(4.09)	(4.23)	(3.92)	(4.06)	(1.43)	(0.87)	(4.33)	(4.57)	(3.58)	(3.49)
Car tyres	-1.22	-1.38	-0.73	-0.71	-0.81	-1.07	-1.14	-1.42	-0.60	-0.64
	(4.42)	(4.57)	(3.18)	(3.02)	(1.73)	(2.05)	(1.93)	(2.26)	(2.18)	(2.19)
Truck tyres	-0.43	-0.73	-0.20	-0.41	-1.24	-1.01	0.08	-0.31	0.03	-0.46
	(1.84)	(2.74)	(0.94)	(1.78)	(2.73)	(2.16)	(0.16)	(0.63)	(0.08)	(0.96)
Cars	-0.07	0.00	-0.59	-0.44	-1.17	-1.21	-1.10	-1.07	-0.21	0.07
	(0.34)	(0.01)	(2.33)	(1.78)	(2.51)	(2.45)	(2.50)	(2.41)	(0.69)	(0.24)

* Quarterly data: 1978: 2–1991: 4.
† Western regions.

Table 10.1b Results of the estimation of equation (1) for export prices on the German market*† (estimated pass-through coefficients and related asymptotic t-statistics)

Exporting countries / Products	France OLS	France LIVE	Italy OLS	Italy LIVE	United Kingdom OLS	United Kingdom LIVE	Netherlands OLS	Netherlands LIVE	Belgium OLS	Belgium LIVE
Polypropylene	-0.41	-1.06	-1.06	-1.46	-1.20	-1.17	-0.05	-1.63	-1.09	-2.34
	(1.09)	(2.51)	(2.01)	(2.51)	(3.78)	(3.56)	(0.14)	(3.31)	(3.37)	(5.21)
Car tyres	-0.69	-0.81	-0.74	-0.86	-0.93	-0.77	-1.06	-1.78	-0.91	-1.32
	(3.39)	(3.52)	(2.43)	(2.74)	(3.42)	(2.36)	(4.26)	(6.45)	(4.10)	(4.84)
Truck tyres	-0.61	-0.73	-0.50	-0.63	-0.84	-0.79	-0.84	-1.48	-0.81	-1.26
	(2.96)	(3.47)	(1.48)	(1.78)	(3.32)	(3.03)	(2.56)	(4.17)	(1.91)	(2.79)
Cars	-0.32	-0.41	-0.20	-0.25	-1.18	-1.26	0.17	-0.93	-0.67	-1.46
	(1.46)	(1.78)	(0.62)	(0.76)	(4.86)	(4.82)	(0.32)	(1.40)	(2.42)	(3.93)

* Quarterly data: 1978: 2–1991: 4.
† Western regions.

Table 10.1c Results of the estimation of equation (1) for export prices on the French market* (estimated pass-through coefficients and related asymptotic t-statistics)

Exporting countries / Products	Germany OLS	Germany LIVE	Italy OLS	Italy LIVE	United Kingdom OLS	United Kingdom LIVE	Netherlands OLS	Netherlands LIVE	Belgium OLS	Belgium LIVE
Polypropylene	−0.96	−1.88	−0.44	−0.74	−0.63	−0.42	−0.55	−1.35	−0.84	−1.78
	(2.75)	(4.09)	(0.99)	(1.64)	(1.44)	(0.96)	(0.95)	(2.07)	(2.30)	(3.79)
Car tyres	−1.07	−1.41	−0.93	−1.06	−1.01	−0.90	−0.64	−0.89	−1.13	−1.44
	(4.12)	(4.87)	(3.01)	(3.25)	(6.18)	(5.35)	(2.27)	(3.26)	(4.45)	(5.17)
Truck tyres	−0.87	−1.61	−0.90	−1.22	−0.92	−0.83	−0.27	−1.19	−1.37	−1.64
	(3.21)	(4.95)	(2.89)	(3.70)	(5.87)	(5.05)	(0.60)	(2.43)	(5.53)	(6.16)
Cars	0.22	−0.35	−0.31	−0.47	−0.88	−0.79	−0.25	−0.52	−0.06	−0.27
	(0.78)	(1.02)	(1.02)	(1.51)	(2.92)	(2.61)	(0.61)	(1.18)	(0.26)	(1.11)

* Quarterly data: 1978: 2–1991: 4.
† Western regions.

Table 10.1d Results of the estimation of equation (1) for export prices on the UK market* (estimated pass-through coefficients and related asymptotic t-statistics)

Exporting countries Products	Germany†		France		Italy		Netherlands		Belgium	
	OLS	LIVE	OLS	LIVE	OLS	LIVE	OLS	LIVE	OLS	LIVE
Polypropylene	-0.53	-0.85	-0.61	-1.13	1.27	1.02	-0.77	-1.28	-1.03	-1.55
	(1.43)	(1.87)	(1.36)	(2.06)	(1.45)	(1.06)	(1.88)	(2.55)	(2.05)	(2.41)
Car tyres	-0.63	-0.93	-0.14	-0.16	-0.54	-0.51	0.06	-0.02	-0.60	-0.61
	(1.99)	(2.60)	(0.70)	(0.77)	(1.56)	(1.42)	(0.25)	(0.10)	(2.43)	(2.23)
Truck tyres	-0.75	-0.81	-0.77	-0.71	-1.69	-1.82	-0.54	-0.71	-1.11	-1.11
	(3.06)	(3.06)	(2.21)	(1.92)	(3.15)	(3.23)	(1.39)	(1.74)	(4.10)	(4.00)
Cars	0.01	-0.12	-0.09	-0.06	-0.33	-0.46	0.03	-0.09	0.12	-0.10
	(0.04)	(0.51)	(0.28)	(0.18)	(0.72)	(0.89)	(0.12)	(0.28)	(0.42)	(0.33)

* Quarterly data: 1978: 2–1991: 4.
† Western regions.

Italian and German markets and in one case on the French market; on the UK market coefficients are never significant.[11] It is also worth noting that in the short run UK car exporters almost fully compensate for the effects of exchange rate fluctuations on their profit margins in all three main European markets.[12] This result indicates that UK producers have less power to set prices than their European competitors.

As to the overall results by market, pass-through is particularly pronounced in the German and French markets, with respectively 80 and 70 percent of negative and significant values in large part exceeding one. It is somewhat smaller in the Italian market (65 percent of negative and significant cases) and especially in the English market (only 40 percent).[13] The tendency to limit price fluctuations in the currency of the importing country is thus greatest in the German and French markets; this indicates that it is more difficult for foreign firms to pursue strategic pricing policies in these two markets with the aim of increasing or defending market shares.

COMPARING THE PERFORMANCE OF OLS
AND LIVE ESTIMATES

In the previous section we have shown that LIVE estimates of the pass-through coefficients are generally higher in absolute value than OLS estimates, and tend to be more significant. This results should suggest that, in empirical analysis, pass-through coefficients might be biased downwards whenever simultaneity among competitors' prices is not correctly accounted for in the estimation procedure.

In order to assess the relevance of the simultaneity bias in our specific context, we have carried out the test proposed by Wu (1973) and Hausman (1978), which is based upon the discrepancy between the LIVE and OLS estimates.[14] High values of the test, associated with low probabilities, indicate the presence of simultaneity; therefore OLS give inconsistent estimates of the structural coefficients.

The results of the Wu–Hausman test are reported in Tables 10.2a–d. In the 80 cases considered, the null hypothesis cannot be rejected except in 21 cases at the critical level of 5 percent.[15] As regards products, simultaneity is crucial for polypropylene, car tyres and truck tyres;[16] on the contrary it does not seem to be particularly important for cars in all markets, except the United Kingdom. The results for cars, compared with those obtained for the other three products, are strikingly different; they suggest that European car producers tend to have a high degree of monopoly, so that the competitors' pricing policies are less relevant in determining the degree of the pass-through.

After having ascertained that simultaneity is relevant in the estimation of the pass-through coefficients, our next step is to compare the overall performance of OLS and LIVE estimates. Since the two estimators have

Table 10.2a Degree of simultaneity for export prices on the Italian market (Wu–Hausman test and RMSE)

Exporting countries / Products	Germany* Prob. Wu–Hausman†	RMSE‡ OLS	RMSE‡ LIVE	France Prob. Wu–Hausman	RMSE OLS	RMSE LIVE	United Kingdom Prob. Wu–Hausman	RMSE OLS	RMSE LIVE	Netherlands Prob. Wu–Hausman	RMSE OLS	RMSE LIVE	Belgium Prob. Wu–Hausman	RMSE OLS	RMSE LIVE
Polypropylene	0.4	0.156	0.139	0.0	0.118	0.114	0.0	0.248	0.215	0.2	0.163	0.130	0.0	0.150	0.140
Car tyres	0.7	0.062	0.054	6.3	0.045	0.045	0.3	0.144	0.126	4.6	0.141	0.117	100.0	0.077	0.076
Truck tyres	2.4	0.050	0.044	0.1	0.043	0.044	0.3	0.120	0.109	10.5	0.104	0.109	0.6	0.133	0.117
Cars	100.0	0.043	0.041	100.0	0.071	0.074	100.0	0.333	0.247	100.0	0.152	0.121	100.0	0.057	0.052

* Western regions.
† Prob. Wu–Hausman is the probability that the equations *are not* simultaneous.
‡ RMSE have been computed on the basis of the results of the dynamic simulation of the model in the period 1978: 2–1991: 4.

Table 10.2b Degree of simultaneity for export prices on the German market* (Wu–Hausman test and RMSE)

Exporting countries / Products	France Prob. Wu–Hausman†	RMSE‡ OLS	RMSE‡ LIVE	Italy Prob. Wu–Hausman	RMSE OLS	RMSE LIVE	United Kingdom Prob. Wu–Hausman	RMSE OLS	RMSE LIVE	Netherlands Prob. Wu–Hausman	RMSE OLS	RMSE LIVE	Belgium Prob. Wu–Hausman	RMSE OLS	RMSE LIVE
Polypropylene	0.7	0.169	0.082	4.2	0.183	0.107	22.9	0.201	0.132	0.1	0.185	0.077	0.1	0.165	0.159
Car tyres	3.3	0.064	0.042	26.1	0.106	0.081	0.8	0.125	0.080	0.2	0.063	0.053	3.1	0.063	0.048
Truck tyres	0.7	0.045	0.045	0.0	0.057	0.061	0.8	0.069	0.065	0.0	0.052	0.055	1.1	0.096	0.100
Cars	47.2	0.045	0.045	65.6	0.078	0.073	10.0	0.116	0.112	3.7	0.131	0.120	0.9	0.058	0.056

* Western regions
† Prob. Wu–Hausman is the probability that the equations *are not* simultaneous.
‡ RMSE have been computed on the basis of the results of the dynamic simulation of the model in the period 1978: 2–1991: 4.

Table 10.2c Degree of simultaneity for export prices on the French market (Wu–Hausman test and RMSE)

Exporting countries / Products	Germany* Prob. Wu–Hausman†	Germany* RMSE‡ OLS	Germany* LIVE	Italy Prob. Wu–Hausman	Italy RMSE OLS	Italy LIVE	United Kingdom Prob. Wu–Hausman	United Kingdom RMSE OLS	United Kingdom LIVE	Netherlands Prob. Wu–Hausman	Netherlands RMSE OLS	Netherlands LIVE	Belgium Prob. Wu–Hausman	Belgium RMSE OLS	Belgium LIVE
Polypropylene	0.2	1.563	0.168	5.2	0.108	0.089	3.5	0.400	0.125	3.2	0.139	0.097	0.2	0.292	0.128
Car tyres	0.0	0.087	0.046	1.5	0.098	0.059	0.5	0.136	0.071	3.3	0.056	0.048	0.1	0.132	0.106
Truck tyres	0.0	0.140	0.087	0.2	0.101	0.058	0.0	0.096	0.060	0.0	0.116	0.070	0.9	0.069	0.049
Cars	0.4	0.062	0.040	13.4	0.070	0.053	38.4	0.121	0.095	38.6	0.094	0.067	12.9	0.060	0.052

* Western regions.
† Prob. Wu–Hausman is the probability that the equations are not simultaneous.
‡ RMSE have been computed on the basis of the results of the dynamic simulation of the model in the period 1978: 2–1991: 4.

Table 10.2d Degree of simultaneity for export prices on the UK market (Wu–Hausman test and RMSE)

Exporting countries / Products	Germany* Prob. Wu–Hausman†	Germany* RMSE‡ OLS	Germany* LIVE	France Prob. Wu–Hausman	France RMSE OLS	France LIVE	Italy Prob. Wu–Hausman	Italy RMSE OLS	Italy LIVE	Netherlands Prob. Wu–Hausman	Netherlands RMSE OLS	Netherlands LIVE	Belgium Prob. Wu–Hausman	Belgium RMSE OLS	Belgium LIVE
Polypropylene	0.1	0.129	0.099	0.0	0.159	0.503	0.8	0.302	0.298	0.0	0.166	0.264	0.0	0.165	2.628
Car tyres	0.2	0.239	0.123	0.8	0.219	0.040	8.2	0.306	0.062	3.5	1.082	0.149	0.5	0.116	0.083
Truck tyres	0.0	0.041	0.038	0.0	0.060	0.057	0.0	0.074	0.067	0.0	0.096	0.090	6.2	0.051	0.049
Cars	1.2	0.058	0.052	6.0	0.065	0.055	0.5	0.067	0.061	0.0	0.082	0.075	1.8	0.076	0.122

* Western regions.
† Prob. Wu–Hausman is the probability that the equations are not simultaneous.
‡ RMSE have been computed on the basis of the results of the dynamic simulation of the model in the period 1978: 2–1991: 4.

fairly different statistical properties, a comparison can be made only by using the results obtained from a simulation of the whole model. For each of the 16 export prices systems we therefore perform a dynamic simulation over the sample period 1978: 2–1991: 4, both with OLS and LIVE estimates; then we compute the Root Mean Square Error (RMSE), which measures the degree of accuracy of simulated values with respect to historical values; the results are shown in Tables 10.2a–d.

To begin with, it will be noted that RMSE improves in most of the cases when the dynamic simulation is performed with LIVE estimates. In many circumstances the improvement is substantial. Consider, for example, the export prices of polypropylene and car tyres in the German and French markets and those of truck tyres in the French market. As expected, given our previous results, the improvement is weaker for cars. Let us point out two extreme cases. The first is that of German polypropylene export prices on the French market; here OLS estimates give rise to particularly large errors, whereas the performance of the equation estimated with LIVE is satisfactory compared with those of the other competitors in the same market. The contrary occurs for Belgian export prices of the same product in the English market: in this case OLS estimates give much more satis-factory results.[17] In order to have a clearer idea of the difference between OLS and LIVE performance, we have plotted the dynamic simulation errors of some equations (Figures 10.1–10.8). These plots confirm that the capability of the price equations to track history over the sample period is systematically higher when the coefficients are estimated with LIVE. It is also interesting to note that LIVE performance appears to be particularly good in the instance of the largest OLS errors.

Finally, to assess the prediction accuracy of our export price equations, we have also computed the Theil's U statistic over the period 1992: 1–1992: 4 (see Tables 10.3a–d). Although the results are not particularly striking, LIVE estimates predict better than OLS in 43 cases (out of 80); in many other cases the differences are almost negligible. Quite surprisingly, here the best LIVE performance is recorded for cars: in 15 cases LIVE coeffi-cients predict better than OLS.

CONCLUSIONS

In this chapter we have presented an empirical analysis of the pass-through coefficients for six European countries with respect to the four main European markets, using OECD disaggregated foreign trade data for four different products. By extending the model proposed by Kasa (1992) to monopolistic competition, we have derived, for each market and each product considered, a system of simultaneous export price equations.

The aims of our analysis have been: (i) to produce empirical evidence on the pass-through phenomenon for the leading European countries on a

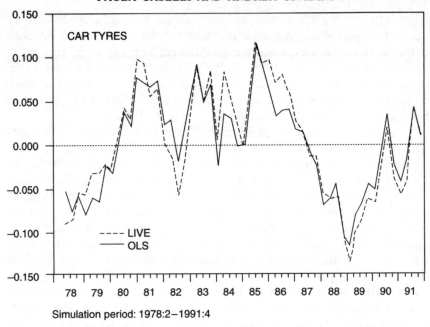

Simulation period: 1978:2–1991:4

Figure 10.1 Dynamic simulation of German export prices on the Italian market
(percentage deviations from actual values)

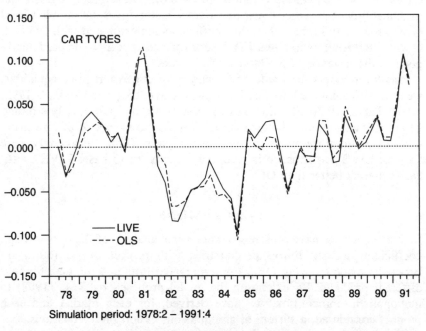

Simulation period: 1978:2 – 1991:4

Figure 10.2 Dynamic simulation of French export prices on the Italian market
(percentage deviations from actual values)

156

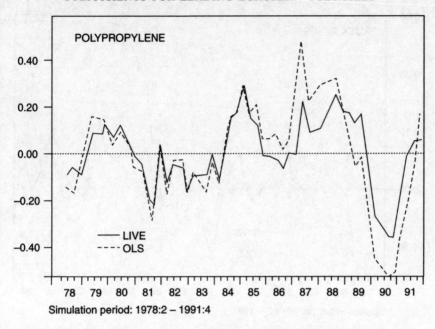

Figure 10.3 Dynamic simulation of UK export prices on the German market
(percentage deviations from actual values)

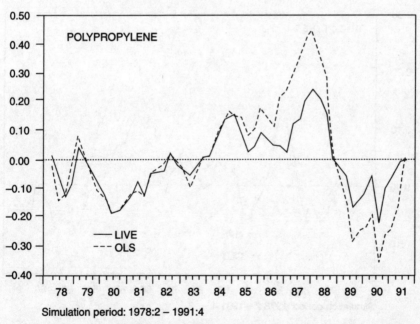

Figure 10.4 Dynamic simulation of Italian export prices on the German market
(percentage deviations from actual values)

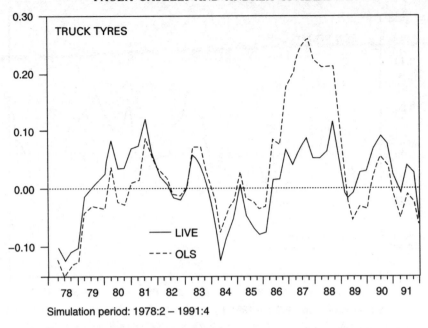

Figure 10.5 Dynamic simulation of UK export prices on the French market
(percentage deviations from actual values)

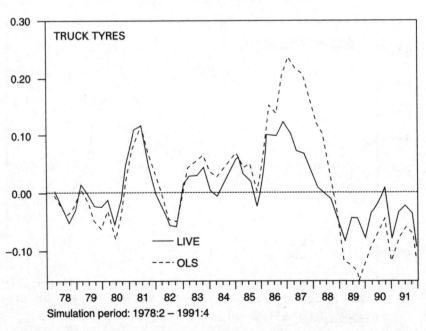

Figure 10.6 Dynamic simulation of Italian export prices on the French market
(percentage deviations from actual values)

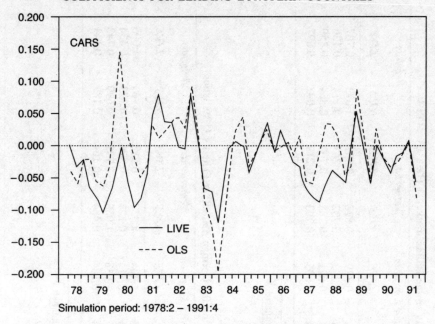

Figure 10.7 Dynamic simulation of German export prices on the UK market
(percentage deviations from actual values)

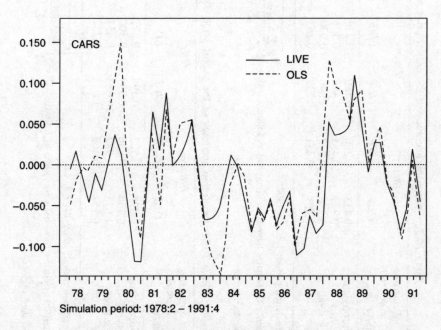

Figure 10.8 Dynamic simulation of French export prices on the UK market
(percentage deviations from actual values)

Table 10.3a Prediction accuracy of the export price equations on the Italian market* (Theil's U statistics†)

Exporting countries Products	Germany‡		France		United Kingdom		Netherlands		Belgium	
	OLS	LIVE	OLS	LIVE	OLS	LIVE	OLS	LIVE	OLS	LIVE
Polypropylene	0.413	0.280	0.460	0.229	0.560	0.389	0.878	0.593	1.073	0.707
Car tyres	0.379	0.451	0.476	0.501	0.403	0.292	0.732	0.267	0.118	0.126
Truck tyres	0.346	0.312	1.046	0.900	0.809	0.671	0.785	0.760	0.364	0.359
Cars	0.431	0.451	0.237	0.253	0.778	0.595	0.293	0.219	0.093	0.097

* Simulation period: 1992: 1–1992: 4.

† Theil's U statistics have been computed as follows: $U = \sqrt{\dfrac{\sum \left(\text{actual} - \text{simulated}\right)^2}{\sum \left(\text{actual}\right)^2}}$

‡ Western regions.

Table 10.3b Prediction accuracy of the export price equations on the German market*‡ (Theil's U statistics†)

Exporting countries Products	France		Italy		United Kingdom		Netherlands		Belgium	
	OLS	LIVE	OLS	LIVE	OLS	LIVE	OLS	LIVE	OLS	LIVE
Polypropylene	0.592	0.522	0.595	0.627	2.465	1.405	2.337	0.512	0.763	1.090
Car tyres	0.730	0.836	0.359	0.300	0.395	0.314	0.227	0.376	0.373	0.434
Truck tyres	1.055	0.982	0.683	0.658	1.925	1.938	1.058	0.772	0.699	0.743
Cars	0.154	0.162	1.012	0.733	0.174	0.184	0.484	0.164	0.187	0.141

* Simulation period: 1992: 1–1992: 4.

† Theil's U statistics have been computed as follows: $U = \sqrt{\dfrac{\sum \left(\text{actual} - \text{simulated}\right)^2}{\sum \left(\text{actual}\right)^2}}$

‡ Western regions.

Table 10.3c Prediction accuracy of the export price equations on the French market* (Theil's U statistics†)

Exporting countries	Germany‡		Italy		United Kingdom		Netherlands		Belgium	
Products	OLS	LIVE	OLS	LIVE	OLS	LIVE	OLS	LIVE	OLS	LIVE
Polypropylene	0.108	0.198	1.317	1.582	0.595	0.434	0.982	1.063	0.400	0.552
Car tyres	0.419	0.603	0.306	0.425	0.353	0.493	0.349	0.339	0.215	0.215
Truck tyres	0.180	0.209	0.567	0.636	0.616	0.699	0.250	0.288	1.593	1.753
Cars	0.537	0.425	0.832	0.785	0.503	0.399	0.347	0.294	0.132	0.122

* Simulation period: 1992: 1–1992: 4.

† Theil's U statistics have been computed as follows: $U = \sqrt{\dfrac{\Sigma \left(\text{actual} - \text{simulated} \right)^2}{\Sigma \left(\text{actual} \right)^2}}$

‡ Western regions.

Table 10.3d Prediction accuracy of the export price equations on the UK market* (Theil's U statistics†)

Exporting countries	Germany‡		France		Italy		Netherlands		Belgium	
Products	OLS	LIVE	OLS	LIVE	OLS	LIVE	OLS	LIVE	OLS	LIVE
Polypropylene	0.303	0.350	0.531	0.519	0.387	0.430	0.337	0.362	0.848	0.769
Car tyres	0.368	0.380	1.122	1.057	0.381	0.491	0.299	0.272	0.236	0.372
Truck tyres	0.244	0.290	0.663	0.815	0.880	0.898	0.707	0.737	0.852	0.919
Cars	0.413	0.270	0.445	0.301	1.213	0.915	0.357	0.212	0.127	0.120

* Simulation period: 1992: 1–1992: 4.

† Theil's U statistics have been computed as follows: $U = \sqrt{\dfrac{\Sigma \left(\text{actual} - \text{simulated} \right)^2}{\Sigma \left(\text{actual} \right)^2}}$

‡ Western regions.

statistically comparable basis; (ii) to assess the importance of simultaneity among competitors' prices in estimating pass-through coefficients. With respect to the first issue, our results show that European exporters in the short run tend to adjust their profit margins fully for the effects of exchange rate fluctuations in order to maintain constant prices in the currency of the importing country; full pass-through occurs quite often, especially for the less differentiated products. This helps to explain why, after the 1992 exchange rate turmoil, import prices of manufacturers of devaluating countries generally increased much less than the amount of depreciation. Our results also suggest that European exporters have somewhat higher pricing-setting power in the English market than in the other largest European markets. With respect to the second issue, our tests indicate that simultaneity among competitors' prices has to be taken into account in the estimation of the pass-through. In order to obtain consistent estimates of the structural coefficients we have proposed an instrumental variable method, LIVE, that is based on the results of the static simulation of the whole model and has the very good property of always being computable if a simulation package is available.

The comparison of the OLS and LIVE estimates shows that the pass-through coefficients obtained with LIVE tend to be higher in absolute value and more significant than OLS coefficients. Furthermore, the performance of the equations estimated with LIVE is generally more satisfactory. We can thus conclude that there is a general improvement when moving from inconsistent to consistent estimates of the pass-through coefficients, especially when the products considered are less differentiated.

APPENDIX A

The model

The model extends that proposed by Kasa (1992) for the case of a monopolist to the context of monopolistic competition. Let there be m identical producers, each operating in a different country and selling his products in n different markets. First, assume that the producer can change the quantities he sells from one period to the next without incurring any costs beyond those associated with production. In each period, t, the total profits of producer j, expressed in national currency and earned on sales in the n markets, are given by:[18]

$$\Pi_j = \sum_{i=1}^{n} Q_{ji} \, P^*_{ji} \left(Q_{ji} \right) - c \left(Q_j \right) \qquad i \neq j \qquad (1a)$$

where Q_{ji} is the quantity exported to foreign market i;

P^*_{ji} is the price producer j charges in market i, expressed in the national currency of j;

$Q_j = \sum_1 Q_{ji}$ is the total quantity produced by j;

$c\left(Q_j\right)$ are the total production costs.

The demand for j's products in market i is given by the following function (Dixit and Stiglitz, 1977; Aizenman, 1989):

$$Q_{ji} = \left(P^*_{ji} E_{ij}/P_i\right)^{-\beta_i} Z_i \qquad \beta_i > 1 \qquad (2a)$$

where E_{ij} is the exchange rate expressed as the number of units of currency i needed to buy one unit of currency j;

P_i is the aggregate price index expressed in currency i, which comprises the prices of all the competitors in market i, including producer j;

Z_i is the total demand, in real terms, in market i.[19]

Producer j determines the quantities to be sold in the n markets so as to maximize, for each period t, the flow of profits constrained by equation (2a), assuming that the quantities produced by competitors are given. In order to keep the analytical structure manageable, marginal production costs are assumed to be constant and for the sake of simplicity are set equal to one. In this case the producer can solve the optimization problem in each of the n markets separately, since the optimal quantities ($\tilde{Q}_{ij}$) do not depend on the total amount produced (Q_j). In the absence of adjustment costs and assuming that all producers have complete information, the problem is reduced to determining the quantities Q_{ji} that maximize equation (1a) under the constraint of equation (2a). It can easily be shown that:

$$\tilde{Q}_{ij} = K^{-1} \frac{E_{ij}^{-\beta_i}}{\prod_{k=1}^{m} E_{ik}^{-\beta_i/m}} A_i \qquad \text{where } K = \beta_i/(\beta_i - 1) \qquad (3a)$$

$\tilde{Q}_{ji}$ is thus perfectly determined once the values of A_i, all the bilateral exchange rates and the parameter β_i are known. In this case, prices in the currency of the exporting country are determined exclusively on the basis of the unit costs (which have been assumed not to depend on the exchange rate) and the price elasticity of demand. Changes in exchange rates are therefore transmitted in full to the prices expressed in the currency of the importing country. The implications are accordingly analogous to those of a monopoly model (Kasa 1992). The only difference concerns the level of

163

the mark-up, which in this case depends on the elasticity of demand with respect to the prices of similar products rather than the average price level.

Consider now the case in which the producer faces quantity adjustment costs, which are assumed to be given, at time t, by:

$$AC_{jt} = \frac{1}{2} \sum_{i=1}^{n} h_i \left(\frac{Q_{ji,t}}{Q_{ji,t-1}} - 1 \right)^2 \qquad h_i > 0, \, i \neq j \qquad (4a)$$

Equation (4a) indicates that the total adjustment costs are the sum of those incurred in changing the quantities sold in each market, for which the specific adjustment costs are summarized by the parameter h_i. In this case the producer determines the quantities sold in order to maximize, under the constraint of equation (2a), the following function:

$$\max_{\{Q_{jt,t}\}} E_0 \sum_{t=0}^{\infty} \delta^t \left(\Pi_{jt} - AC_{jt} \right) \qquad (5a)$$

where E_0 is the "value expected at time 0" and δ the discount factor, which is assumed to be exogenous and constant. The problem can be simplified, without losing its essential features, by considering a linearization of equation (5a) around the equilibrium point on the hypothesis of null adjustment costs. In this way it can be reformulated as follows:

$$\min_{\{q_{it}\}} E_0 \sum_{t=0}^{\infty} (\tfrac{1}{2}) \delta^t \left[\sum_{i=1}^{n} w_i (q_{ji,t} - \tilde{q}_{ji,t})^2 + (q_{ji,t} - q_{ji,t-1})^2 \right] i \neq j \qquad (6a)$$

where $q_{ji,t} = \log(Q_{ji,t})$ and the parameter w_i represents the costs of deviating from the equilibrium quantities $\tilde{q}_{ji}$ relative to those incurred in changing the quantities sold in the various markets. Equation (6a) is a quadratic loss function that allows the model to be reformulated as a partial adjustment model, whose first-order conditions are given by:

$$w_i (q_{ji,t} - \tilde{q}_{ji,t}) + (q_{ji,t} - q_{ji,t-1}) - \delta \cdot E_t (q_{ji,t+1} - q_{ji,t}) = 0 \qquad (7a)$$

$$\forall i \neq j$$

Equation (7a) can be solved for the quantity actually sold in market i at time t:

$$q_{ji,t} = \lambda_i q_{ji,t-1} + (1 - \lambda_i)(1 - \lambda_i \delta) \sum_{s=0}^{\infty} (\lambda_i \delta)^s E_t \tilde{q}_{ji,t+s} \qquad (8a)$$

where λ_i is the stable solution $(\lambda_i < 1)$ of the characteristic equation associated with (7a); the value of λ_i is negatively related to that of w_i. Consequently, high values of λ_i correspond to relatively high adjustment costs. In order to solve equation (8a), it is necessary to go back to equation (3a), which can be rewritten in log form as:

$$\tilde{q}_{ji,t} = -k - \beta_i \hat{e}_{ij,t} + a_{i,t} \tag{3a'}$$
$$\text{where } \hat{e}_{ij,t} = e_{ij,t} - \bar{e}_{i,t}$$

and $e_{ij,t}$ and $\bar{e}_{i,t}$ are respectively the log of the nominal bilateral exchange rate between currencies i and j and that of the nominal effective exchange rate of currency i. At time t, the producer forecasts the future values of $\tilde{q}_{ji}$ on the basis of the known values of a_i and $\hat{e}_{ij}$ and of their expected values, which will depend on the type of stochastic process they follow.

Let's assume that the variable a_i follows a random walk with a drift and that it is independent of the exchange rate. It is also assumed that the demand variables in the various markets are not correlated, i.e. $\text{cov}(a_{i,t}, a_{k,t}) = 0$ $\forall t$, $\forall k \neq i$. The expected sum, discounted to the present, is therefore proportional to the value observed at time t, plus a constant. As regards the variable $\hat{e}_{ij}$, it is assumed that its path can be represented by an AR(1) model on the first differences (Caselli, 1993, 1994).

Substituting the expressions for the expected values of a_i and $\hat{e}_{ij}$ in equation (8a) and using equation (2a), we obtain, after some simple substitutions, the following expression for the variable p_{ji}^* :

$$p_{ji,t}^* = a_0 = a_1 p_{i,t}^* + a_2 p_{i,t} \tag{9a}$$

$$+ a_3 p_{ji,t-1}^* + a_4 p_{i,t-1}^* + a_5 p_{i,t-1}$$

$$+ a_6 (\hat{e}_{ij,t} - \hat{e}_{ij,t-1}) + \xi_{it}$$

where ξ_{it} is an uncorrelated disturbance and $p_i^* = p_i - \bar{e}_i$ is the competitors' average price expressed in national currencies.

Thus, the coefficient a_6 directly identifies the extent to which, at time t, changes in the nominal bilateral exchange rate (relative to the effective rate) influence the price expressed in the currency of the exporting country. The coefficient a_6 depends in a rather complex way on many parameters of the model; in particular, it is expected to be negative and its absolute value is positively related to the size of the adjustment costs (λ_i).

DATA APPENDIX

The series of average export unit values of the four products considered were constructed for all the seven countries considered on the basis of the OECD's annual statistics on *Foreign Trade by Commodities* (Series C) by dividing the exports to each market (expressed in dollars at current prices) by the corresponding quantities (expressed in different units according to the product).

The data for the period 1978–87 were classified on the basis of Revision 2 of the Standard International Trade Classification (SITC) and those for the period 1988–92 on the basis of Revision 3 (except for the US, for which Revision 3 applies from 1989).[20]

The codes referred to are as follows:[21]

	SITC2	SITC3
1 Polypropylene	58321	57511
2 Car tyres	62510	62510
3 Truck tyres	62520	62520
4 Cars	78100	78120

The annual series of export unit values for each exporting country were transformed into quarterly data using the generalized least-squares method proposed by Chow-Lin with the following seasonally adjusted indicators:

(a) exports of goods (in value terms) to the various markets as a ratio to those to the OECD countries as a whole;
(b) the export unit values of manufactures (in dollars).

The series obtained in this way were transformed into indices with 1980 as the base year.

The average prices of competitors were computed as the simple geometric mean of those of each country, including the price of the country under consideration. It should be noted that when the outlet country was one of the exporting countries, the price of the latter was excluded so that, for instance, the price of Italy's competitors in the German market includes that of Italy but not that of Germany.

The data on unit labour costs in the manufacturing sector are based on the annual statistics for each country published by the Bureau of Labor Statistics, except in the case of Italy, for which the Istat quarterly series of unit labour costs in manufacturing was used. The annual series were transformed into quarterly data, using the OECD's series for hourly earnings in manufacturing, and then transformed into indices with 1980 as the base year.

The quarterly data on exchange rates *vis-à-vis* the dollar were based on the IMF's *International Financial Statistics* and used to obtain all the cross rates. The series were subsequently transformed into indices with 1980 as the base year. The effective exchange rates for each outlet market were constructed as the simple geometric mean of the rates *vis-à-vis* all the competitors in that market, in a similar way to the prices of competitors.

166

NOTES

1 We wish to thank Carlo Bianchi, Irene Finel-Honigman and the participants to the IV ITFA International Conference, held in Reading, 13–16 July 1994 for helpful comments and remarks. The responsibility for any errors is of course our own. The views expressed in this chapter are our own and do not necessarily reflect those of the Bank of Italy, where we are employed in research.

2 The model is fully described in Appendix A to which the interested reader may refer (pp. 162–5). See, also, Caselli (1993). A similar approach can be found in Feenstra *et al.* (1993).

3 $p_i^* = \sum_{j=1}^{m} p_{ji}^* / m \qquad j \neq i$

where m is the number of competitors in market i.

4 It is worth noting that because of the existence of several competitors in the same market the pass-through is influenced not only by the bilateral exchange rates, as in the monopolist case, but also by the effective exchange rate.

5 In principle, we cannot rule out the possibility of simultaneity between prices and the exchange rates. However, the results of the Wu–Hausman test do not corroborate this hypothesis, which is usually not considered in empirical works using disaggregated data (see, for example, Knetter, 1989 and 1993, and Kasa, 1992).

6 The selection was determined by the need to avoid product groups whose contents had been modified by the 1988 revision of the SITC. Some problems arise in connection with cars, which include passenger vehicles of all engine types and sizes and therefore constitute a rather heterogeneous aggregate.

7 In addition to these six countries, competitors include Japan and the United States.

8 The total number of cases is 80 – 20 that is, for each market.

9 In eleven cases the value is higher than 1.5. There is only one obviously implausible value: the coefficient of the prices of Belgian exports of polypropylene to Germany, which is equal to 2.34 (see Table 10.1b). Absolute values greater than one can be associated with the existence of increasing marginal costs (see Sundaram and Mishra, 1992).

10 These findings are consistent with those obtained by Sapir and Sekkat (1995).

11 Our results for cars are consistent with those presented in Feenstra *et al.* (1993) who use more disaggregated data.

12 Large pass-through coefficients for UK car exporters are also reported by Knetter (1993).

13 However the percentage is about 53 if cars are excluded.

14 Under the null hypothesis that the endogenous regressors are not asymptotically correlated with the contemporaneous error term, the Wu–Hausman statistic has a chi-squared distribution with degrees of freedom equal to the number of endogenous regressors (Bowden and Turkington, 1984). In our specific case, the number of degrees of freedom is 2, since p_i^* and p_i are the only endogenous regressors in equation (1).

15 At the critical level of 10 percent, the number of cases falls to 15.

16 The null hypothesis is rejected in only 9 cases out of 60 at the critical level of 5 percent.

17 In both cases the high values of RMSE are due to the dynamic instability of the estimated equations arising because the coefficient of the lagged dependent variable is greater than one.

18 For the sake of simplicity the subscript t has been omitted. The model can

PAOLA CASELLI AND ANDREA CIVIDINI

easily be extended to the more general case in which each producer also sells in his domestic market. This possibility is not considered here since the data used refer only to export unit values (see the Data Appendix on p. 165).

19 Z_i can be interpreted as the quantity index associated with P_i and can be written as $Z_i = A_i P_i$, where A_i is the total expenditure in market i in nominal terms.
20 See United Nations (1986).
21 The switch from SITC2 to SITC3 did not involve any change in the content of the codes considered.

REFERENCES

Aizenman, J. (1989) "Monopolistic Competition, Relative Prices and Output Adjustment in the Open Economy", *Journal of International Money and Finance* 1, 5–28.
Baldwin, R. (1988) "Hysteresis in Import Prices: The Beachhead Effect", *American Economic Review*, September, 773–85.
Baldwin, R. and P. Krugman (1989) "Persistent Trade Effects of Large Exchange Rate Shocks", *Quarterly Journal of Economics*, Vol. CIV, November, 635–54.
Bianchi, C., G. Bruno and A. Cividini (1993) "Efficient Instrumental Variables Estimate of Large Scale non Linear Econometrics Models", Paper presented at the 15th Annual Meeting of the Society of Economic Dynamics and Control, June.
Bowden, R.J. and D.A. Turkington (1984) *Instrumental Variables*, New York: Cambridge University Press.
Branson, W.H. and R.C. Marston (1992) "Price and Output Adjustment in Japanese Manufacturing", in B.G. Hickman (ed.) *International Productivity and Competitiveness*, Oxford: Oxford University Press.
Brundy, J.M. and D.W. Jorgenson (1971) "Efficient Estimation of Simultaneous Equations by Instrumental Variables", *Review of Economics and Statistics* 53, 207–24.
Bryant, R., G. Holtman and P. Hooper (1988) *External Deficits and the Dollar: The Pit and the Pendulum*, Washington, DC: The Brookings Institution.
Caselli, P. (1993) *Prezzi all'esportazione e tassi di cambio: una verifica empirica*, Banca d'Italia, *Temi di Discussione*, no. 213.
Caselli, P. (1994) "Pass-Through and Export Prices: An Empirical Test for the Leading European Countries", *International Review of Applied Economics*.
Cividini, A. (1991) "Simultaneous Estimation of Large-scale Econometric Models: Some new Applications of the Solution Algorithm", in M. Bertocchi and L. Stefanini (eds) *Large-scale Economic and Financial Applications: New Tools and Methodologies*, Milano: Franco Angeli.
Dixit, A.K. and J.E. Stiglitz (1977) "Monopolistic Competition and Optimum Product Diversity", *American Economic Review*, June, 297–308.
Feenstra, R.C. (1989) "Symmetric Pass-Through of Tariffs and Exchange Rates Under Imperfect Competition: An Empirical Test", *Journal of International Economics* 27, 25–45.
Feenstra, R.C., J.E. Gagnon and M.M. Knetter (1993) *Market Share and Exchange Rate Pass-through in World Automobile Trade*, National Bureau of Economic Research Working Paper No. 4399 (30 pp.).
Hausman, J.A. (1978) "Specification Tests in Econometrics", *Econometrica*, Vol. 46, November, 2251–71.
Kasa, K. (1992) "Adjustment Cost and Pricing-to-Market. Theory and Evidence", *Journal of International Economics* 32, 1–30.

Knetter, M.M. (1989) "Price Discrimination by U.S. and German Exporters", *American Economic Review*, March, 198–210.

Knetter, M.M. (1992) *Is Price Adjustment Asymmetric?: Evaluating the Market Share and Marketing Bottlenecks Hypotheses*, National Bureau of Economic Research Working Paper No. 4170 (25 pp.).

Knetter, M.M. (1993) "International Comparison of Pricing-to-Market Behavior", *American Economic Review*, June, 473–86.

Krugman, P. (1987) "Pricing to Market When Exchange Rate Changes", in S.W. Arndt and J.D. Richardson (eds) *Real-Financial Linkages among Open Economies*, London: MIT Press.

Mariano, R.S. (1983) "Lecture Notes in Econometrics", Mimeo, University of Pennsylvania, Philadelphia.

Sapir, A. and K. Sekkat (1995) "Exchange Rate Regimes and Trade Prices. Does the EMS Matter?", *Journal of International Economics* 38, 75–94.

Sundaram, A.K. and V. Mishra (1992) "Exchange Rate, Pass Through and Economic Exposure: A Review", *Journal of Foreign Exchange and International Finance*, Vol. VI, No. 1, 38–52.

United Nations (1986) *Standard International Trade Classification. Revision 3*, Statistical Papers Series M No. 34/Rev.3 (130 pp.).

Wu, D. (1973) "Alternative Tests of Independence Between Stochastic Regressors and Disturbances", *Econometrica* 41, 733–50.

11

ON FORECASTING FOREIGN EXCHANGE RATES

Ali M. Parhizgari and Maria E. de Boyrie*

INTRODUCTION

The purpose of this chapter is to provide a synthesis of a select group of foreign exchange forecasting models. This group, which constitutes the bulk of contributions made in this field, is mostly econometric in structure, with models ranging from the single equation type to more complex systems.

The foundation of the majority of econometric models which are designed to forecast foreign exchange rates rests on four major sets of theories – i.e., asset market doctrines, monetary hypotheses, portfolio balance conditions, and parity fundamentals. Though this categorization is not exhaustive and may be somewhat arbitrary, it, however, embodies the bulk of the literature produced on this topic so far.

Further details and sub-sets of these theories of foreign exchange and forecasting models are summarized below:

1 Asset market doctrines:
    (a) flexible price monetary models;
    (b) sticky price monetary models;
    (c) portfolio balance models.
2 Monetary hypotheses.
3 Portfolio balance conditions.
4 Parity fundamentals:
    (a) interest rate parity;
    (b) purchasing power parity;
    (c) International Fisher Effect;
    (d) forward discount bias.

By way of an introduction to these theories (see, for example, Ethier 1979, Turnovsky 1981, Horne 1983, Stulz 1987, Grinols and Turnovsky 1994, and Bougheas 1994), it should be pointed out that the asset market doctrine approach to exchange rate determination may be branched out into three areas: (a) flexible-price monetary models that determine the exchange rate under monetary equilibrium conditions and purchasing power parity (see, for example, Frenkel 1976, Backus 1984, Frenkel 1992, and McDonald and Taylor 1993); (b) sticky price monetary models that maintain monetary neutrality across steady states, but allow money to influence real variables in the short run (see Dornbusch 1976, Buiter and Miller 1981 and MacDonald and Taylor 1993); and (c) portfolio balance models that emphasize the wealth effect on assets demands and the role of the exchange rate in the valuation of foreign assets (see Min and McDonald 1993).

The monetary hypotheses and the portfolio balance conditions models of exchange rate determination relax the assumptions of zero real interest rate differential and zero risk premium in accordance with the purchasing power parity and the uncovered interest rate parity (see, for example, Frenkel 1992).

The fourth set of theories, i.e. the parity fundamentals, are fairly straightforward. Notable in this set are the models based on: (a) interest rate parity (Aliber 1973, Giddy 1976, Isard 1978, Hilley *et al.* 1979, Taylor 1989, and Choie 1993); (b) purchasing power parity (Officer 1976, Officer, *et al.* 1982); (c) international Fisher effect; (d) forward discount bias (Bilson 1978, Frenkel 1978, Meese and Rogoff 1983, Gregory and McCurdy 1984, Fama 1984, Bilson 1985, Hodrick and Srivastava 1986, Froot and Frankel 1989); and (e) one or more combinations of these sub-sets (see, for example, Isard 1978).

On the empirical front, the above theories have led to a diffusion of models and tests that could further be divided into structural and non-structural ones. The structural models, which in turn may be linear or nonlinear, are mostly of econometric nature. The non-structural models range from the design survey/consensus building approaches to more sophisticated ones in the area of artificial intelligence (AI).

To manage this presentation the scope of this chapter is limited to the structural (econometric) models of exchange rate forecasting that are built upon the above four major underlying theories of exchange rate determination.

In the following sections these models are briefly reviewed with the aim of providing a synthesis of the state-of-the-art in foreign exchange rate forecasting.

STRUCTURAL LINEAR MODELS

Both the theoretical and the empirical literature on the asset market view and the other three underlying theories of exchange rates have expanded significantly in the past two decades. The majority of the exchange rate models that have been developed during this period are linear in design and search for the best model among them has been a continuing effort. This search, however, has not been fully successful since the empirical

171

performance of the existing models has not been encouraging. Work by Hacche and Townend (1981), Haynes and Stone (1981), Hooper and Morton (1982), Dornbusch (1983), Frankel (1982, 1984), Backus (1984), Meese and Rogoff (1983, 1984), Woo (1985), Somanath (1986), and Finn (1986), among others, are indicative of the many path-breaking efforts to improve the forecasting performance of these models.

For the purpose of clarity, the structural linear models are subdivided, categorically, into two groups: in-sample and out-of-sample.

In-sample forecasting

A vast amount of literature tests the in-sample forecasting ability of both the monetary approach and the portfolio balance approach models. In the early 1980s, work in this area seemed futile, as studies by Haynes and Stone (1981), Frankel (1984), and Backus (1984) demonstrated that estimates of the real interest rate differential could not explain the in-sample exchange rate changes. In these models, only few of the estimated coefficients had the correct sign and the equations in general had poor explanatory power according to the coefficient of determination.

Rasulo and Wilford (1980) and Haynes and Stone (1981) attribute the poor performance of the monetary approach to the constraints imposed on relative monies, income, and interest rates. Haynes and Stone further find that the constraints used in the monetary approach equations are particularly at fault because they yield biased estimates and reversed signs.

Frankel (1982) provides an alternative explanation for the poor performance of the monetary models. He introduces home and foreign wealth (defined as the sum of government debt and cumulated current account surpluses) into the money demand equations, and ignores any constraints on the domestic and foreign income, wealth, and inflation terms. His results show that his monetary approach equation fits the data well and estimates the signs correctly.

Similar attempts to explain the poor performance of the monetary models and improve upon the results obtained in the previous studies are the work by Driskill and Sheffrin (1981), Boughton (1988), and Hoffman and Schlagenhauf (1983). The results of the studies have not been completely convincing.

Out-of-sample forecasting

To determine how well exchange rate models perform in estimating out-of-sample forecasts, Meese and Rogoff (1983) conducted a seminal study using the dollar–pound sterling, dollar–mark, dollar–yen, and trade-weighted dollar exchange rates for the period of March 1973 to June 1981. The exchange rate models they test are the flexible-price model, the real interest differential model, and the portfolio monetary synthesis of Hooper and Morton (1982). Meese and Rogoff compare the out-of-sample performance of these models to the forecasting performance of four other models, i.e. the random walk model, the forward exchange rate model, a model containing a univariate autoregression of the spot rate, and a vector autoregression model.[1]

Meese and Rogoff models are actually variants of the monetary model of the exchange rate determination.[2] Using a rolling regression approach, they conclude that none of the exchange rate models using the asset approach can really outperform the simple random walk model. In an attempt to improve upon these results, they also examine a reduced-form version of the asset models. These models, which are estimated in first differences, examine several new alternatives. For example, they include unconstrained home and foreign magnitudes, additional explanatory variables, different definitions of variables, and new proxies for inflationary expectations in lieu of long-term interest rates. Their attempt was to no avail.

In a follow-up study and in search of possible explanations for the failure of their reduced-form model to outperform the random walk model, Meese and Rogoff (1984) concluded that the variables in their former reduced-form model were not completely exogenous. Thus, they imposed a set of constraints on the coefficients and re-estimated the models. Once again, their model was not able to outperform the random walk in the short run.

Since Meese and Rogoff's (1983, 1984) work, most of the literature has been devoted to determining whether their specification of the asset reduced-form model, their estimation method, or the models themselves are at fault. Boughton (1987), Woo (1985), Finn (1986), Somanath (1986), and Schinasi and Swamy (1989) have replicated and extended the work of Meese and Rogoff (1984) by estimating different versions of the rational expectations form of the flexible-price model that include a partial adjustment term in money demand. Their work contributes to the literature since they all successfully identify models that at times perform better than a random walk. For example, Finn (1986) concludes that his model forecasts as well as the random walk even though it does not outperform it all the time. Woo's (1985) model, seems to outperform the random walk model for a single currency, i.e. the Deutschmark. Interestingly, Somanath (1986) finds not only that his structural exchange rate models outperform the random walk model but also that the flexible-price, real interest differential, and the hybrid equations of Meese and Rogoff outperform his model for a sample period extending beyond the one employed by the original authors.[3]

Wolf (1987) and Schinasi and Swamy (1989) use a time-varying parameter model to test the real interest differential and the flexible-price equation.[4] Both authors argue that Meese and Rogoff's problem may have stemmed from their lack of attention to the instability of the parameter estimates.

Wolf (1987) uses the Kalman filter methodology to test Messe and Rogoff's reduced-form flexible-price and real interest rate differential models.[5] His conclusion is that both models outperform the random walk model but only for the US dollar–Deutschmark exchange rate. Schinasi and Swamy's (1989) model, which employs a less restrictive time-varying specification, produces better results than the model proposed by Wolf.

STRUCTURAL NON-LINEAR MODELS

Whereas the aforementioned studies have primarily employed linear specifications, research in the late 1980s and early 1990s has concentrated on non-linear foreign exchange models (see, for example, Engel and Hamilton 1990, Chinn 1991, Kuan and Liu 1992, and McGuirk et al. 1993).

Hsieh (1989) finds that changes in exchange rates are actually non-linearly dependent, even though there is some linear dependence in the data. Using daily closing bid prices of five foreign currencies covering the period of January 1974 to December 1983, he tests for non-linear dependence in foreign exchange rates by applying the Brock, Dechert and Scheinkman (BDS) test. Although there is some linear dependence in the data, the BDS test detects strong non-linear dependence, i.e. large and small changes in returns tend to be systematically clustered together when plotted over time. Friedman and Vanderstell (1982), Bollerslev (1986), and Baillie and Bollerslev (1989) confirm the non-linear temporal dependence of exchange rate returns.

Some of the most recent empirical and theoretical results also support non-linearity in the exchange rates (see Engel and Hamilton 1990, Chinn 1991, and McGuirk et al. (1993).[6] Diebold and Nason (1990), however, after estimating the conditional-mean functions of ten major nominal dollar spot rates non-parametrically for the period 1973–87, conclude that non-linearities of exchange rates cannot be exploited to generate improved point predictions relative to linear models.

Forecasting non-linear structural models is complex and cannot normally be accomplished without a base model. There have been several attempts in this area. For example, Diebold and Nason (1990) and Mizrach (1992) use a 'weighted nearest neighbor' technique to forecast exchange rate changes. This technique, which is also known as the locally weighted regression (LWR), was initially proposed by Cleveland (1979) and was later refined by Cleveland and Devlin (1988) and Cleveland, et al. (1988).

Using weekly data on ten currencies, Diebold and Nason examine both the in-sample and the out-of-sample predictive performance of their locally weighted regression (LWR) model.[7] Their results show that: (a) both mean squared and mean absolute prediction errors are smaller than those found

174

using random walk, and (b) the in-sample forecasts are slightly better than the out-of-sample results. Given these findings, Diebold and Nason conclude that it is generally impossible to improve much upon the forecasting performance of the simple random walk model.

Engel and Hamilton (1990) employ a 'segmented trend model', wherein a non-stationary time-series is decomposed into a sequence of stochastic segmented time trends for which the in- and the post-sample forecast errors are calculated. Using arithmetic averages of the bid and ask prices of the exchange rates on the last day of each quarter, beginning with the third quarter of 1973 and ending with the first quarter of 1988, they find that both the in- and the post-sample results favor the segmented trend specification over the random walk model, particularly for short forecasting horizons.

Chinn (1991) uses a technique known as 'alternating conditional expectations' (ACE). This technique transforms all the variables in order to obtain a linearized relationship between the transformed variables.

Using quarterly data on bilateral exchange rates between the US and Germany and Japan for the period of January 1974 through December 1988, Chinn's forecasting results show that both the in-sample and out-of-sample non-linear forecasts contain substantial improvements over the random walk model. Under a rolling regression approach, however, the results indicate that the random walk still dominates, although these results are only marginal and insignificant. In general, these efforts demonstrate that non-linear specifications do somewhat better than most linear models in relatively longer (four-quarter) horizon.

CONCLUSION

The forecasting of foreign exchange rates is a mystery to some and yet a sophisticated form of economic/financial analysis to others. Notwithstanding the many significant contributions that have been made in this area, the outcome has been less than desirable so far. Thus, the search for a new innovative approach to improve the accuracy of foreign exchange forecasts still remains a continuing challenge.

The above brief examination of the literature on forecasting foreign exchange demonstrates that neither the theoretically structured asset market models nor the *ad hoc* non-linear models offer consistent improvement over the forecasting performance of the random walk model, which in turn is viewed unsatisfactory.

Most of the asset market models tested exhibit poor performance in predicting changes in exchange rates. Non-linear models seem to fare better in this regard, though a generalization is still impossible. In some cases, the non-linear models outperform the random walk model for *in-sample* predictions. The results, however, are mixed for the *out-of-sample* prediction.

A major source of the problem, which is often ignored or treated casually, lies in two underlying assumptions which are embedded in most of the foreign currency forecasts. These are: (a) the assumption that a fully floating exchange rate system would prevail during the forecasting horizon of the models, and (b) the presumption that the researchers' expectations about the future economic/financial conditions (variables) are to be materialized. Though the shortcomings of these restrictive assumptions are often acknowledged, the models lack by design the necessary built-in mechanism in terms of the structure or the specific variables included in them to account for this problem. Thus, to the extent that these assumptions are violated after the forecasts are made, inaccuracies in prediction should be expected (see Goldberg 1994, Safizadeh and Fatemi 1991).

This review thus underscores the need for a model, or set of models, that can better explain changes in foreign exchange rates. Considering that today's *major* currencies are "managed float" and that the current modeling efforts to forecast the currencies have so far been mostly "conditional", innovations in modeling that would invoke a built-in mechanism to adjust the forecasts, should the underlying assumptions be violated, are highly desirable.

NOTES

*The authors are, respectively, Professor of Finance and International Business and Assistant Professor of Finance with Florida International University. They are grateful to their colleagues in the Finance Department and to the participants of the Finance Workshop Series for helpful comments and discussions. All remaining errors, of course, are the authors' alone.

1 A popular null hypothesis in the foreign exchange literature is that exchange rate movements are a random walk. In the efficient markets literature, it is argued that prices in speculative markets fully reflect all currently available information as well as all future developments that can be forecasted with any certainty. Furthermore, changes in market price are claimed to reflect new information released to the market, which forces the revision of expectations and therefore, prices. In speculative markets news announcements generate effects that can force large price revisions. Therefore, from an efficient market perspective, this period's price is related to the last period's price in the following manner:

$$s_t = s_{t-1} + e_t$$

where s_t is the log of the exchange rate in period t.

2 They are derived from the equation

$$s = \alpha_0 - \alpha_1 m + \alpha_2 m^* + \alpha_3 y - \alpha_4 y^* - \alpha_5 r + \alpha_6 r^* - \alpha_7 \pi + \alpha_8 \pi^* - \alpha_9 CTB$$

where s is the log of exchange rate, m is the log of money supply, y is the log of income, r is the short-term interest rate, π is the log of the expected inflation rate, and CTB is the cumulated trade balance.

3 Somanath considers five structural models. Four of them are monetary models represented by the general model:

$$s_t = b_0 + b_1(m_{DM} - m_\$)_t + b_2(i_{st,DM} - i_{st,\$})_t + b_3(i_{lt,DM} - i_{lt,\$})_t + b_4(w_{DM} - w_\$)_t$$
$$+ b_5(CTB_{DM} - CTB_\$)_t + b_6(y_{DM} - y_\$)_t + e_t$$

where m = log of money supply, I = short- and long-term interest rate, w=log of real wealth, CTB = cumulated trade balance, and y = log of real income.
The fifth structural model is a portfolio balance model as expressed by:

$$s_t = c_0 + c_1(MB_{DM} - MB_\$)_t + c_2(B_{DM} - B_\$)_t + c_3(FA_{DM} - FA_\$)_t + u_t$$

where s = DM/$ exchange rate, MB = monetary base, B = private holdings of government bonds, and FA = private foreign assets.
Somanath imposes restrictions similar to those of Bilson (1978), Hooper and Morton (1982), and Frankel (1982).
4 The time-varying parameter model presented by Schinasi and Swamy (1989) is derived from the general specification of the monetary model as expressed by:

$$s_t = \beta_0 + \beta_1(m_t - m_t{}^*) + \beta_2(y_t - y_t{}^*) + \beta_3(r_t - r_t{}^*) + \beta_4(\pi_t^e - \pi_t^{e*}) + \beta_5(TB_t - TB_t{}^*) + u_t$$

where m = money supply, y = industrial production, r = short-term interest rate, π^e = expected inflation, and TB = cumulated trade balance. They test the model using the restrictions: $\beta_4 = \beta_5 = 0$, $\beta_5 = 0$, and unequal coefficients for the trade balance. They also lag the dependent variable as an explanatory variable in order to allow for short-run deviations from long-run purchasing power parity. Unlike the Meese and Rogoff (1983) study, Schinasi and Swamy allow for all the coefficients to vary.
5 For the specification of Meese and Rogoff's model, see note 2.
6 Other authors who have researched the non-linearity evidence are Diebold (1988), Hsieh (1992), and Meese and Rose (1991).
7 The ten weekly dollar spot rates Diebold and Nason (1990) use are the Canadian dollar (CD), French franc (FF), German mark (DM), Italian lira (LIR), Japanese yen (Yen), Swiss franc (SF), British pound (BP), Belgian franc (BF), Danish kroner (DK), and Dutch guilder (DG). The sample size is equal to 769, from 3 January 1973 to 23 September 1987.

REFERENCES

Aliber, R.Z. (1973) "The Interest Rate Parity Theorem: A Reinterpretation," *Journal of Political Economy*, 81(6), 1451–9.

Backus, D. (1984) "Empirical Models of the Exchange Rate: Separating the Wheat from the Chaff," *Canadian Journal of Economics*, 17(4), 824–46.

Baillie, R.T. and T. Bollerslev (1989) "The Message in Daily Exchange Rates: A Conditional Variance Tale," *Journal of Business and Economics Statistics*, 7(3), 297–305.

Beckman, S.R. (1994) "A Rational Foundation for Wishful Exchange Rate Forecast," *International Review of Economics and Finance*, 3(4), 393–8.

Bilson, J.F. (1978) "The Rational Expectations and the Exchange Rate," in J.A. Frenkel and H.G. Johnson (eds) *The Economics of Exchange Rates: Selected Studies*, Reading, Mass.: Addison-Wesley.

Bilson, J.F. (1985) "Macroeconomic Stability and Flexible Exchange Rates," *American Economic Review*, 75(2), 62–7.

Bollerslev, T. (1986) "Generalized Autoregressive Conditional Heteroskedasticity," *Journal of Econometrics*, 31(3), 307–28.

Bougheas, S. (1994) "Asset and Currency Prices in an Exchange Economy with Transactions Costs," *Journal of Macroeconomics*, 16(1), 99–107.

Boughton, J.M. (1987) "Tests of the Performance of Reduced-Form Exchange Rate Models," *Journal of International Economics*, 23(1/2), 41–56.

Boughton, J.M. (1988) "Exchange Rates and the Term Structure of Interest Rates," *International Monetary Fund Staff Papers*, 35(1), 36–62.

Buiter, W.H. and M.H. Miller (1981) "Monetary Policy and International Competitiveness: The Problem of Adjustment," in W.A. Eltis and P.J. Sinclair (eds). *The Money Supply and the Exchange Rate*, New York: Oxford University Press.

Chinn, M.D. (1991) "Some Linear and Nonlinear Thoughts on Exchange Rates," *Journal of International Money and Finance*, 10(2), 214–30.

Chinn, M.D. and J. Frankel (1994) "Patterns in Exchange Rate Forecasts for Twenty-Five Currencies," *Journal of Money, Credit and Banking*, 26(4), 759–70.

Choi, K.S. (1993) "Currency Exchange Rate Forecast and Interest Rate Differential," *Journal of Portfolio Management*, 19(2), 58–64.

Cleveland, W.S. (1979) "Robust Locally Weighted Regression and Smoothing Scatterplots," *Journal of the American Statistical Association*, 74(368), 829–36.

Cleveland, W.S. and S.J. Devlin (1988) "Locally Weighted Regression: An Approach to Regression Analysis by Local Fitting," *Journal of the American Statistical Association*, 83, 596–610.

Cleveland, W.S., S. Devlin and E. Grosse (1988) "Regression by Local Fitting: Methods, Properties, and Computational Algorithms," *Journal of Econometrics*, 37(1), 87–114.

Diebold, F.X. (1988) "Serial Correlation and the Combination of Forecasts," *Journal of Business Economics and Statistics* 6(1), 105–12.

Diebold, F.X. and M. Nerlove (1989) "The Dynamics of Exchange Rate Volatility: A Multivariate Latent Factor ARCH Model," *Journal of Applied Econometrics*, 4(1), 1–22.

Diebold, F.X. and J.A. Nason (1990) "Nonparametric Exchange Rate Prediction?," *Journal of International Economics*, 28(3/4), 315–32.

Dornbusch, R. (1976) "Expectations and Exchange Rate Dynamics," *Journal of Political Economy*, 84(6), 1161–76.

Dornbusch, R. (1983) "Flexible Exchange Rates and Interdependence," *International Monetary Fund Staff Papers*, 30(1), 3–38.

Driskill, R.A. and S.M. Sheffrin (1981) "On the Mark: Comment," *American Economic Review*, 71(5), 1068–74.

Engel, C., and J.D. Hamilton (1990) "Long Swings in the Dollar: Are they in the Data and Do Markets Know It?," *The American Economic Review*, 80(4), 689–713.

Engel, C. and J.D. Hamilton (1994) "Can the Markov Switching Model Forecast Exchange Rates?," *Journal of International Economics*, 36(1/2), 151–65.

Ethier, W. (1979) "Expectations and the Asset-Market Approach to the Exchange Rate," *Journal of Monetary Economics*, 5(2), 259–82.

Fama, E. (1984) "Forward and Spot Exchange Rates," *Journal of Monetary Economics*, 14(3), 319–38.

Finn, M.G. (1986) "Forecasting the Exchange Rate: A Monetary or Random Walk Phenomenon?," *Journal of International Money and Finance*, 5(2), 181–93.

Frankel, J.A. (1978) "Purchasing Power Parity: Doctrinal Perspective and Evidence from the 1920s," *Journal of International Economics*, 8(2), 169–91.

Frankel, J.A. (1982) "The Mystery of Multiplying Marks: A Modification of the Monetary Model," *Review of Economics and Statistics*, 64(3), 515–19.

Frankel, J.A. (1984) "Tests of Monetary and Portfolio Balance Models of Exchange Rate Determination," in F.O. Bilson and R.C. Marston (eds) *Exchange Rate Theory and Practice*, Chicago: University of Chicago Press.

Frankel, J.A. (1992) "Monetary and Portfolio-Balance Models of Exchange Rate Determination," in J.M. Letiche (ed.) *International Economic Policies and Their Theoretical Foundations: A Sourcebook*, San Diego, Calif.: Academic Press.

Friedman, J. and S. Vanderstell (1982) "Short-Run Fluctuations in Foreign Exchange Rates: Evidence from the Data 1973–1979," *Journal of International Economics*, 13, 171–86.

Froot, K. and J. Frankel (1989) "Forward Discount Bias: Is it an Exchange Risk Premium?," *Quarterly Journal of Economics*, 104(1), 139–61.

Giddy, I.H. (1976) "Integrated Theory of Exchange Rate Equilibrium," *Journal of Financial and Quantitative Analysis*, 11(5), 883–92.

Goldberg, L.S. (1994) "Predicting Exchange Rate Crises: Mexico Revisited," *Journal of International Economics*, 36(3/4), 413–30.

Gregory, A.W. and T.H. McCurdy (1984) "Testing the Unbiasedness Hypothesis in the Forward Foreign Exchange Market: A Specification Analysis," *Journal of International Money and Finance*, 3(3), 357–68.

Grinols, E.L. and S.T. Turnovsky (1994) "Exchange Rate Determination and Asset Prices in a Stochastic Small Open Economy," *Journal of International Economics*, 36(1/2), 75–97.

Hacche, G. and J. Townend (1981) "Exchange Rates and Monetary Policy: Modeling Sterling's Effective Exchange Rate, 1972–1980," *Oxford Economic Papers*, 33(Supplement), 201–47.

Haynes, S. and J. Stone (1981) "On the Mark: Comment," *American Economic Review*, 71(5), 1060–7.

Hilley, J., C. Beidleman and J. Greenleaf (1979) "Does Covered Interest Arbitrage Dominate in Foreign Exchange Markets?," *Columbia Journal of World Business*, Winter, 99–107.

Hodrick, R. and S. Srivastava (1986) "The Covariation of Risk Premiums and Expected Future Spot Exchange Rates," *Journal of International Money and Finance*, 5(Supplement), S5–S22.

Hoffman, D. and D.E. Schlagenhauf (1983) "Rational Expectations and Monetary Models of Exchange Rate Determination: An Empirical Examination," *Journal of Monetary Economics*, 11(2), March, 247–60.

Hooper, P. and J. Morton (1982) "Fluctuations in the Dollar: A Model of Nominal and Real Exchange Rate Determination," *Journal of International Money and Finance*, 1(1), 39–56.

Hooper, P. and J. Morton (1989) "Testing for Nonlinear Dependence in Daily Foreign Exchange Rates," *Journal of Business*, 62(3), 339–68.

Hoque, A. and A. Latif (1993) "Forecasting Exchange Rate for the Australian Dollar vis-a-vis the US Dollar using Multivariate Time-Series Models," *Applied Economics*, 25(3), 403–7.

Horne, J. (1983) "The Asset Market Model of the Balance of Payments and the Exchange Rate: A Survey of Empirical Evidence," *Journal of International Money and Finance*, 2(2), 89–109.

Howrey, E.P. (1994) "Exchange Rate Forecasts with the Michigan Quarterly

Econometric Model of the US Economy," *Journal of Banking and Finance*, 18(1), 27–41.

Hsieh, D.A. (1989)"Testing for Nonlinear Dependence in Daily Foreign Exchange Rates," *Journal of Business*, 62(3), 339–68.

—— (1992) "A Nonlinear Stochastic Rational Expectations Model of Exchange Rates," *Journal of International Money and Finance*, 11(3), 235–50.

Isard, P. (1978) "Exchange Rate Determination: A Survey of Popular Views and Recent Models," *Princeton Studies in International Finance*, Vol.42.

Liu, F.-R., M.E. Gerlow and S.H. Irwin (1994) "The Performance of Alternative VAR Models in Forecasting Exchange Rates," *International Journal of Forecasting*, 10(3), 419–33.

McDonald, R. and M. Taylor (1989) "Foreign Exchange Market Efficiency and Cointegration: Some Evidence from the Recent Float," *Economic Letters*, 29, 63–8.

McDonald, R. and M. Taylor (1993) "The Monetary Approach to the Exchange Rate: Rational Expectations, Long-Run Equilibrium, and Forecasting," *International Monetary Fund Staff Papers*, 40(1), 89–107.

McGuirk, A., J. Robertson and A. Spanos (1993) "Modeling Exchange Rate Dynamics: Non-Linear Dependence and Thick Tails," *Econometric Reviews*, 12, 33–63.

Meese, R. and K. Rogoff (1983) "Empirical Exchange Rate Models of the Seventies: Do they Fit Out of Sample?," *Journal of International Economics*, 14(1/2), 3–24.

Meese, R. and K. Rogoff (1984) "The Out-of-Sample Failure of Empirical Exchange Rate Models: Sampling Error or Misspecification?," in Jacob Frenkel (ed.) *Exchange Rates and International Macroeconomics*, Chicago: University of Chicago Press.

Meese, R. and A.K. Rose (1991) "Nonlinear, Nonparametric, Nonessential Exchange Rate Estimation," *American Economic Review*, 80(2), 192–6.

Min, H.G. and J. McDonald (1993) "The Portfolio-Balance Model of Exchange Rates: Short-Run Behavior and Forecasting," *International Economic Journal*, 7(4), 75–87.

Mizrach, B. (1992) "Multivariate Nearest-Neighbor Forecasts of EMS Exchange Rates," *Journal of Applied Econometrics*, 7(Supplement), S151–S164.

Officer, L.H. (1976) "The Purchasing Power Parity Theory of Exchange Rates: A Review Article," *International Monetary Fund Staff Papers*, 23(1), 1–60.

Officer, L.H., E. Altman and I. Walters (1982) *Purchasing Power Parity and Exchange Rates: Theory, Evidence, and Relevance*, Greenwich, Conn.: JAI Press.

Rasulo, J.A. and D.S Wilford (1980) "Estimating Monetary Models of the Balance of Payments and Exchange Rates: A Bias," *Southern Economic Journal*, 47(1), 136–46.

Safizadeh, H. and A. Fatemi (1991) "A Logit Methodology for Predicting the Imposition of Exchange Controls," *Journal of Economics and Business*, 43(4), 389–402.

Schinasi, G. and P.A. Swamy (1989) "The Out-of-Sample Forecasting Performance of Exchange Rate Models when Coefficients are Allowed to Change," *Journal of International Money and Finance*, 8, 375–90.

Somanath, V.S. (1986) "Efficient Exchange Rate Forecasts: Lagged Models Better than the Random Walk?," *Journal of International Money and Finance*, 5(2), 195–220.

Stulz, R.M. (1987) "An Equilibrium Model of Exchange Rate Determination and

Asset Pricing with Nontraded Goods and Imperfect Information," *Journal of Political Economy*, 95(5), 1024–40.

Taylor, M.P. (1989) "Covered Interest Arbitrage and Market Turbulence," *Economic Journal*, 90(396), 376–91.

Turnovsky, S.J. (1981) "Asset Market Approach to Exchange Rate Determination: Some Short-Run Stability, and Steady-State Properties," *Journal of Macroeconomics*, 3(1), 1–32.

Wolf, C.P. (1987) "Forward Foreign Exchange Rates, Expected Spot Rates, and Premia: A Signal-Extraction Approach," *Journal of Finance*, 42, 395–406.

Woo, W.T. (1985) "The Monetary Approach to Exchange Rate Determination Under Rational Expectations," *Journal of International Economics*, 18, 1–16.

12

EXCHANGE RATE THEORIES AND THE BEHAVIOR OF EXCHANGE RATES

The record since Bretton Woods

Ramakrishnan S. Koundinya

INTRODUCTION

The recent experience of exchange rate volatility, and the implications to internal economic management, have brought the exchange rate policy issue back to the forefront. Theories of exchange rate economics during the par value exchange rate regime and the post-Bretton Woods flexible rate environment largely failed to provide an understanding of the exchange market pressures in the earlier regime, and the empirical behavior of exchange rates during the post-Bretton Woods period. Theoretical models that come under the rubric of asset market approaches seen as the most promising methodology for understanding the underlying economics of exchange market behavior came far short of the proponents' expectations when the time came to explaining the record of exchange rate movements of the past two decades. The dilemma of living with seemingly rational market forces working with transient expectations (a notion that sounds more and more like the blind man's elephant), and the consequences to viable internal economic policy objectives, has turned the past quarter century of the monetarists' dream world of "freedom to choose" into an era of unique political economics, with the soothsayers of all hues discrediting each other's view of foreign exchange market economics. Exchange rate dynamics since 1973 have confounded even the most ardent exponents of the flexible rate regime, without providing a window for arguing the case for a return to a fixed rate regime. This chapter broadly sketches the key approaches to modeling exchange rates, and the difficulties of understanding recent exchange rate behavior. The consequences of the fuzzy state of knowledge on the efficacy of relying on foreign exchange market forces to resolve the conflicts of internal economic policy objectives among the leading economies, and the challenges

182

to the notion of world market integration through unhindered market forces, are also briefly discussed.

IN THE BEGINNING: BRETTON WOODS AND THE EXCHANGE RATE REGIME

The articles of agreements adopted in Bretton Woods in 1944 attempted to establish a two-pronged approach to exchange rate policy setting by member nations. The articles required that the signatories make a commitment to sustaining a par value or fixed exchange rate system in the short run, but permitted the option to seek realignment of the par value to correct persistent balance of payments problems indicative of "fundamental disequilibrium". The agreement reflected a compromise position between the gold standard system, and a relatively flexible system where exchange rates would be more actively managed. The approach was a result of the desire on the part of leading industrial nations not to be subjected to the extreme pressures for adjustments imposed by the gold standard system. However, it was also clear to the signatories from pre-war experience that leading nations could succumb to an endless sequence of competitive devaluation without a formal commitment to a par value system. It was hoped that so long as appropriate macro policies were followed, and that there was relative flexibility of price levels the automaticity of the adjustment process would ensure the ability of countries to sustain par values. The articles also established the International Monetary Fund (IMF) to ensure compliance to the international monetary system envisaged in its articles. The articles thus reflected to a large extent a relatively conservative view of the need for discipline to ensure adjustments to imbalances, and a recognition that the exchange rate could be a useful and necessary policy variable so long as decisions pertaining to changes in the rates were subjected to scrutiny by the IMF, the agency created by the signatories specifically for this purpose. While such an arrangement seemed to have designed a system with straightforward guidelines for exchange rate policy, both the notion of appropriate macro policies and the notion of fundamental disequilibrium were left undefined and fuzzy. It was for the IMF and the nations with persistent balance of payments problems to work out whether the difficulties were due to macro policy issues or are symptomatic of fundamental disequilibrium. As the postwar period of economic activity progressed the IMF took the role of disciplinarian. Nations with persistent deficits, industrially and politically weak, came under severe pressure for adjustments.

The post-Bretton Woods era was characterized by extreme pressures for reconstruction and growth in the industrial nations and the desire to alleviate poverty in the developing countries through economic growth. This led to the dominance of growth-oriented national policy priorities during this period. For many nations growth policies meant accumulation of persistent trade deficits at the prevailing par values. Deficit nations resorted to financing rather than implementing adjustment policies. The nations that had persistent surpluses maintained the exchange rate at the par to ensure competitive positions in the international markets. Industrial nations with strong labor movements and relative rigidity in the price levels chose to emphasize growth polices even at the cost of significant inflation. Thus, the Bretton Woods system was biased right from the beginning. The need to resort to the option of using external funds to finance desirable internal macro policies of economic growth incurring persistent deficits masked real disequilibrium situations in leading economies that warranted tough adjustment policies. The IMF had neither the power nor a system to ensure automatic adjustment through an enforcement of defined policy alternatives, irrespective of the economic standing of the nations. The leading nations ignored their commitment when it came to following internal policies consistent with the par value system. By 1973 the system envisaged in the Bretton Woods agreement became untenable.

TOWARDS INCREASED FLEXIBILITY: THE DEBATE AND THE OUTCOME

The par value system and the recurring balance of payments problem experienced by a number of countries opened up theoretical investigations on the foundations of the adjustment mechanism under the Bretton Woods regime of pegged rates. The classical emphasis on adjustments solely through prices gave way to the dual emphasis on the role of incomes and prices in the adjustment process. Sidney Alexander's (1959) absorption approach to the balance of payments broke new ground by focusing attention on the importance of policy measures in bringing about balance between aggregate income and expenditures as a method for ensuring external equilibrium. Johnson (1958), in his synthesis of balance of payments problems, extended the absorption approach by incorporating the role of monetary authority as managers of country's reserves. In his view the balance of payments problem is fundamentally a monetary phenomenon. He characterizes the policy options for correcting deficits as falling into two categories: policies of "expenditure reduction" and "policies of expenditure switching." From this analysis it was an easy step for the monetarists to suggest a move towards a freely floating system. It was propounded as the most appropriate vehicle to ensure domestic policy priorities and yet insulate each nation's economy from external disturbances. The underlying premise was that the exchange rate is the relative price of one currency in terms of another. Furthermore it was emphasized that the free market forces of supply and demand in the foreign exchange market would determine the appropriate prices. The market would, in situations of imbalances reflecting excess demand (excess supply) at the going rate, induce rate changes in the direction that in due course would bring about equilibrium in the external sector. The simplicity of the system and the efficacy of the system in continually assisting the adjustment process by timely and relatively small movements in exchange rates were touted as key advantages. The strongest selling point was that the system would provide the most effective means for the pursuit of an independent domestic economic policy agenda. Opponents feared that the absence of a commitment to a disciplined approach to the pursuit of domestic policy objectives might lead to unstable exchange rate variability. They also were concerned that speculation could be potentially destabilizing. However, the opponents could not contest the view expressed by the proponents that there was no a priori reason to assume nations would follow inherently destabilizing domestic policy objectives, nor was there a case for assuming that profit-making speculation could be destabilizing. Even as the debate on the appropriate international monetary system was raging in the academic circles the reality of the imminent collapse of the Bretton Woods system was apparent by the late 1960s and early 1970s. In 1973 the US gave up on its commitment to the gold parity rate set by the Bretton Woods agreement and let the dollar devalue. From then on the monetary system slipped into a loosely managed flexible system with the markets calling the shots, but with the lead country central bankers intervening as demanded by their policy prerogatives. The Reagan era saw the closest form of freely floating rate regime, due mostly to the policy preference of the Reagan presidency for non-intervention in the marketplace. This was also an era of unprecedented growth, budgetary deficits and current account deficits. The movement of exchange rates during this period offered the real test for the monetarists' view of the efficacy of the floating rate regime and their theories of exchange rate determination.

ASSET MARKET APPROACHES TO MODELING OF EXCHANGE RATES

The exchange rate is a price, but a unique and different type of price. It is the price of one country's money in terms of another country's money. It is unique in the sense that change in that price influences all prices in the basket of goods consumed by the communities in the respective countries. A change in the exchange rate reflecting the change in price of one currency in terms of another will have a pervasive effect on all other prices and affect income, wealth, and the welfare of the communities. The exchange rate is thus a critical price, the movement of which is of great importance to the policy-makers. Clearly, understanding the determinants of the exchange rate is of paramount importance in guiding exchange rate policy. This explains the perennial flow of research material on this subject.

Exchange rate models proposed since the early 1970s specifically focus on the determinants of exchange rates as opposed to the post-Bretton Woods literature that focused on balance of payments problems and the causes of "fundamental disequilibrium". The collapse of the Bretton Woods arrangement, and the evolution of a flexible exchange rate system, caused this natural shift of research focus. The variety of modeling approaches presented during this period all come under the rubric of asset market approaches. The early models were largely the counterpart to the monetary approach to balance of payments. The approaches focus on the role of money and other assets on the determination of exchange rates. These models thus extend the notion of equilibrium beyond the goods market and include the asset markets. All the asset market approach models start with the theme that the exchange rate is determined by the demand (supply) of national moneys, the assumption that capital is perfectly mobile, and that the covered interest rate parity relation holds. Beyond this the varieties of models diverge on specific sets of assumptions regarding the substitutability of domestic, and foreign assets. The models grouped under monetary models assume perfect substitutability of foreign and domestic assets. This implies that asset market arbitrage would ensure equality of nominal interest rate differential and expected change in exchange rates. This implies that the assumption of uncovered interest parity will hold. Models that do not assume perfect substitutability of assets in the domestic and foreign markets are classified as portfolio balance models.

Monetary models that assume the validity of purchasing power parity (PPP) are sub-classified as flexible price monetary models. Monetary models that allow systematic deviations from PPP in the short run, but postulate a long-run equilibrium, are classified as sticky price monetary models.

Flexible price monetary models

These models are extensions of the quantity theory of money and are driven by a behavioral money demand equation that specifies demand for money balances in the respective countries as a function of prices, real income and the level of nominal interest rates. Early versions of the model are due to Frenkel (1976), and Bilson (1978a). Given the assumption of the validity of PPP, the exchange rate specification reduces to

$$S(t) = k + a \ (Md(t) - Mf(t)) - q \ (Yd(t) - Yf(t)) + 1 \ (Rd(t) - Rf(t))$$

where $S(t)$ is the spot rate of exchange; k, a and q are the parameters;

$Md(t)$, $Mf(t)$ is the logarithm of domestic and foreign money supplies;

$Yd(t)$, $Yf(t)$ is the logarithm of domestic and foreign real income;

$Rd(t)$, $Rf(t)$ represents the nominal domestic and foreign interest rates.

As can be seen from the reduced form equation a relative increase in domestic money supply will increase $S(t)$, the home currency value of foreign currency, resulting in the depreciation of domestic currency. An increase in relative real income would result in an appreciation of domestic currency. The model's conclusions follow from the dynamics of demand for real money balances holding money supplies constant. Increased real income leads to increased demand for real balances that translates as a reduction in home prices and, consequently, appreciation of the home currency. An increase in interest rate reduces the demand for real money balances and thus results in the depreciation of the home currency. Given the assumption of the validity of uncovered interest arbitrage, and that expectations are rational, the monetary model can be respecified as:

$$S(t) = Z(t) + K1* E(S(t + 1))$$
$$Z(t) = K2* (Md(t) - Mf(t)) - K3* (Yd(t) - Yf(t)) + K4$$

where $E(S(t+1))$ is the exchange rate expected to prevail next period, and
$Z(t)$ is the set of fundamental determinants of exchange rates.

Sticky price monetary models

A critical assumption of the flexible price model is the validity of purchasing power parity. In the absolute form, PPP implies that the real exchange rate is "one," and in the relative version, where exchange rate changes are determined by inflation differences, the real rate is a constant even if different from one. A large body of literature devoted to the testing of PPP relations has conclusively proved that continuous PPP assumption does not hold, thus rejecting flexible price monetary models. Dornbusch (1976) proposed his version of the monetary model that has come to be known as the "sticky price" monetary model. The model allows overshooting of exchange rates from the long-run equilibrium as a consequence of sticky prices in the goods market. The model predicts currency appreciation in the short run as interest rates rise followed by a slow depreciation to validate uncovered interest arbitrage. Frenkel (1979) extended the model to include differential inflation.

Portfolio balance models

A common feature of the portfolio balance models is the rejection of the monetary model's assumption of the perfect substitutability of domestic and foreign assets. Early versions of these models are due to Branson *et al.*

(1977, 1979), and Dooley and Isard (1982). The portfolio balance models hold the view that foreign exchange is a risky asset and that the domestic investors will require a risk premium to hold it. This implies that interest differential equals the expected change in exchange rates and a premium for risk. Portfolio balance models specify exchange rate changes as determined by real income, interest rates, price levels, risk, and wealth. Changes in these variables lead to portfolio reallocations between domestic and foreign assets leading to capital flows, which in turn affect exchange rates. Exchange rate changes in turn affect wealth and other variables that determine portfolio choices. The contribution of the portfolio balance models is the emphasis on the role of wealth and the impact of changes in it on the exchange rates.

THE BEHAVIOR OF EXCHANGE RATES: THE RECORD

After almost a quarter of a century of living with flexible exchange rates, of which the decade and a half since 1980 has provided an environment as close as is feasible to market-determined floating rates, it is common knowledge that the swings in the nominal exchange rates are far more substantial than expected by both the proponents and opponents of the floating exchange rate system. Theories of exchange rate determination simply proved inadequate in explaining the reality of exchange rate movements. Some of the early empirical studies (Bilson 1978b, Dornbusch 1979) seem to support the models in general. However, tests of the models with 1980s data (see for example Frenkel 1984, Backus 1984) raised doubts as to the models' performance even with in-sample observations. Later studies covering a variety of versions of asset market models of both monetary and portfolio versions by Boughton (1988), and Kearney and McDonald (1990) also concluded that the models did not perform with in-sample data of more recent periods.

Meese and Rogoff (1983), in their seminal study on the out-of-sample performance of these models using data on dollar–pound sterling, dollar–mark, dollar–yen, and trade-weighted exchange rates for the period March 1973 to June 1981, showed that a "naive" random walk model performed significantly better than the theoretical model(s) in predicting exchange rate movements. While a number of new approaches to estimating the long-run relations using cointegration techniques are being pursued, the reality is the continuation of a very volatile exchange market contrary to expectations.

The experience of the past decade and a half has revealed a number of recurrent features regarding the short-term behavior of exchange rates of the leading currencies. Month-to-month variations among the key currencies are quite large, spot and forward rates exhibit pronounced positive correlation, and the variations of the rates are much higher than the underlying inflation rates. Movements over longer periods seem to suggest consolidation of short-term fluctuations leading to a seemingly cyclical pattern. A more disturbing aspect is the persistent departure of real exchange rates from their equilibrium rates. The purchasing power parity notion, the key building block of the theoretical models, almost completely falls apart, leading to a significant positive correlation between nominal exchange rate movements and real exchange rate movements. Real exchange rates during the floating period vary to a far greater extent than during the previous regime. The relative variance of the real exchange rates during the floating rate period was around fifteen times higher compared to the prior period (Krugman 1989). The significant variability raises some critical issues regarding the impact on the real economies of the nations and related welfare implications. These real exchange rate movements are reflected in the swings that occur in unit labor costs when measured in common currency units. These variations are highly visible and noteworthy for the United States economy. The strength of the dollar during the 1980–85 period meant a rise of labor costs in the US of around 50 percent over the prior years. This was followed by a sharp drop during the 1985–87 period following a corresponding weakening of the dollar exchange rate. More recently the strengthening of the Japanese yen has pushed their labor costs significantly, opening the issue of overvaluation of the yen and the competitiveness of the Japanese economy. Such changes in labor costs would have meant serious dislocations in large segments of major economies if it were not for the number of ways with which affected industries adapted to the intense competitive disadvantages. Possible misalignment with PPP and wide swings in competitive positions implied by the currency variability pose a problem to promoting policies for global integration of trade and capital flows.

CONCLUSIONS

Post-Bretton Woods experience and the record of currency variability since 1973 bring out a major issue that has remained unsettled for a long time in international finance. The issue is the role of public policy in managing exchange rates rather than letting the asset markets dictate the prices between national moneys. The expectation that market-determined exchange rates would insulate the economies from the transmission of inflation, smoothly adjust towards equilibrium real rates, enable pursuit of independent domestic economic policy goals, inhibit destabilizing speculation, and enable closer integration of world markets through market-driven free trade and capital flows has not been borne out. In contrast, nations have been forced into intermittent international conferences to confront the issues of economic policy coordination. Industries have been forced to accommodate the competitive pressures imposed by inordinate adverse movements in the exchange rates to protect their long-term interests and avoid serious dislocations in their major market segments. The international community has to contend with increasing pressures for trade protection, and capital controls in industrial nations. There is an increasing recognition in academic and policy circles that there is a need to articulate a more coherent approach to dealing with exchange rate policy that is more socially efficient and conducive to global integration. The path towards achieving this goal is yet to evolve however.

REFERENCES

Alexander, S.S. (1959) "Effects of a Devaluation: A Simplified Synthesis of Elasticities and Absorption Approaches," *American Economic Review* (March).

Backus, D. (1984) "Empirical Models of Exchange Rate: Separating the Wheat from the Chaff," *Canadian Journal of Economics* 17 (Nov.): 824–46.

Bilson, J.F.O. (1978a) "The Monetary Approach to the Exchange Rate: Some Empirical Evidence," *IMF Staff Papers* 25: 48–75.

Bilson, J.F.O. (1978b) "Rational Expectations and Exchange Rates," in J.A. Frenkel and H.G. Johnson (eds) *The Economics of Exchange Rates: Selected Studies,* Reading, Mass.: Addison-Wesley.

Boughton, J. (1988) "The Monetary Approach to Exchange Rates: What Now Remains?," *Princeton Essays in International Finance* 171, Princeton, N.J.: Princeton University Press.

Branson, W.H., H. Halttunen and P. Masson (1977) "Exchange Rates in the Short Run: The Dollar Deutschemark Rate," *European Economic Review* 10 (Dec.): 303–24.

Branson, W.H., H. Halttunen and P. Masson (1979) "Exchange Rates in the Short Run: Some Further Results," *European Economic Review* 12 (Oct.): 395–402.

Dooley, M.P. and P. Isard (1982) "A Portfolio Balance Model of the Dollar–Mark Exchange Rate," *Journal of International Economics* 12 (May): 257–76.

Dornbusch, R. (1976) "Expectations and Exchange Rate Dynamics," *Journal of Political Economy* 84 (Dec.): 1161–76.

Dornbusch, R. (1979) "Monetary Policy Under Exchange Rate Flexibility," in *Managed Exchange Rate Flexibility: The Recent Experience*, Federal Reserve Bank of Boston Conference Series, 20, Boston: Federal Reserve Bank of Boston.

Frenkel, J.A. (1976) "A Monetary Approach to the Exchange Rate: Doctrinal Aspects and Empirical Evidence," *Scandinavian Journal of Economics* 78(2): 200–24.

Frenkel, J.A. (1979) "On the Mark: A Theory of Floating Rates Based on Real Interest Differentials," *American Economic Review* 69 (Sept.): 610–22.

Frenkel, J.A. (1984) "Tests of Monetary and Portfolio Balance Models of Exchange Rate Determination," in J.F.O. Bilson and R.C. Marston (eds) *Exchange Rate Theory and Practice*, Chicago: University of Chicago Press.

Johnson, H.G. (1958) "Towards a General Theory of The Balance of Payments," in H.G. Johnson (ed.) *International Trade and Economic Growth,* London: Allen and Unwin.

Kearney, C. and R. McDonald (1990) "Exchange Rate Volatility, News and Bubbles," *Australian Economic Papers* 70 (June.): 1–20.

Krugman P.R. (1989) *Exchange Rate Instability*, The Lionel Robbins Lectures, Cambridge, Mass.: The MIT Press.

Meese, R.A. and K. Rogoff (1983) "Empirical Exchange Rate Models of the Seventies: Do they Fit Out of Sample?," *Journal of International Economics* 14 (Feb.): 3–24.

13

FORWARD AND FUTURES MARKETS

Conceptual differences and computational illustrations

Mary E Malliaris

This chapter develops the essential elements of the conceptual differences between forward and futures prices and offers several computational illustrations. The conceptual differences are expressed precisely in mathematical equations which specially demonstrate the similarities and differences in these two concepts. To study the impact of the independent variables that enter the equations for futures and forward pricing of contracts, several computational examples are presented, which could not be performed easily without computers.

INTRODUCTION

The financial uncertainty of the late 1970s and the 1980s has generated great interest in the futures and forward markets. Both markets can be used by a firm which owns an asset and wishes to protect its value from potential price decline. The firm could hedge the value of its asset by selling a forward or futures contract at the current price of its asset with an agreement to deliver such an asset at a prespecified future date. If, between now and the delivery date, the price of the asset declines, the firm is perfectly protected because of its forward or futures contract which has locked in the current price. However, if the price of the asset increases, by analogy, the firm could not enjoy any windfall profit because the futures or forward contract has prespecified the price.

To the nonspecialist, forward and futures markets are similar. Actually, numerous empirical studies have compared futures and forward prices and have often been unable to confirm always statistically significant differences. For example, Puglisi (1978), Capozza and Cornell (1979), Rendleman and Carabini (1979) and Vignola and Dale (1980) compare the prices for treasury bill futures contracts with the forward prices implied by the interest rates of treasury bills traded in the spot market. These studies do not detect specific and consistent differences between futures and forward prices for the US treasury bill market. Similarly, Cornell and Reinganum (1981) compare futures and forward prices for foreign exchange markets. They find that the foreign data reveal that mean differences between forward and futures prices are insignificantly different from zero in a statistical sense. The mean discrepancy found is less than the mean bid–ask spread in the forward market in 18 of the 20 cases studied, and it barely exceeds it in the remaining two cases. On the other hand, French (1983) claims that there are significant differences between futures and forward prices in the copper and silver markets.

It is the purpose of this chapter to use decision-making and simulation techniques to illustrate numerical differences and similarities between forward and futures prices. Cox *et al.* (1981), Jarrow and Oldfield (1981), French (1983) and others develop detailed theoretical models of forward and futures prices but do not do any simulations. Thus, this chapter demonstrates the positive impact of computing in teaching business students the subtle differences between the two important concepts of forward and futures contracts. Although standard textbooks, such as Kolb (1994), introduce these concepts they do so without any mathematical derivations or any computational illustrations.

The next section develops the analysis of a forward price while the third section presents futures pricing. Using Lotus 1–2–3, several numerical examples simulate forward and futures pricing in the fourth section. Conclusions are presented in the final section.

FORWARD PRICES

A firm which purchases a forward contract agrees to buy a specific asset on a specified future date for an agreed price. This price is called the forward price.

To motivate the pricing of a forward contract consider the simple two-period case. Let t denote today and $t + 1$, $t + 2$ denote the subsequent two periods. The contract will be executed on period $t + 2$. Denote by V_{ij} the price of the asset at period $t + 2$ when the economy is at state i at $t + 1$ and at state j at $t + 2$. Assume that both i = 1,2 and j = 1,2. In other words, we assume that the economy experiences two states in each period. Allowing more states is straightforward.

There are two relevant economic variables: V_{ij}, i.e., the price of the asset, and r_{ij}, i.e., interest rates. Figure 13.1 illustrates that moving from period t, now, to period $t + 1$, tomorrow, the economy's interest rates will go either to r_1, with probability P_1 or to r_2 with probability $P_2 = 1 - P_1$. From period $t + 1$ to $t + 2$, interest rates will go to r_{11} or r_{12}, provided they were at r_1 at $t + 1$ (with probabilities P_{11} and P_{12} respectively) or to r_{21} or r_{22} (with probabilities P_{21} and P_{22} respectively) provided they were at r_2 at $t + 1$.

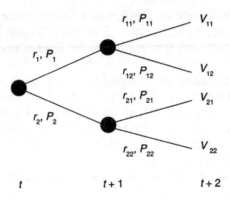

Figure 13.1 Two-state probability tree (1)

The V_{ij} denote expectations about the price of the asset at time j provided that state i of the economy materialized at time $t + 1$.

Since no money changes hands at time t, both the buyer and the seller of the forward contract are willing to transact if the present values of the expected price V_{ij} and the forward price, denoted $G(t)$ are equal. Note that although $G(t)$, the forward price, is agreed upon today (at time t) it is paid at time $t + 2$; this explains why we consider present values. Such present values are given by

$$G(t) \left[\frac{P_1 P_{11}}{(1 + r_1)(1 + r_{11})} + \frac{P_1 P_{12}}{(1 + r_1)(1 + r_{12})} + \frac{P_2 P_{21}}{(1 + r_2)(1 + r_{21})} + \frac{P_2 P_{22}}{(1 + r_2)(1 + r_{22})} \right]$$

$$= \frac{V_{11} P_1 P_{11}}{(1 + r_1)(1 + r_{11})} + \frac{V_{12} P_1 P_{12}}{(1 + r_1)(1 + r_{12})} + \frac{V_{21} P_2 P_{21}}{(1 + r_2)(1 + r_{21})} + \frac{V_{22} P_2 P_{22}}{(1 + r_2)(1 + r_{22})} \quad (1)$$

From (1) we can immediately solve the forward price $G(t)$ given below

$$G(t) = \frac{\dfrac{V_{11} P_1 P_{11}}{(1 + r_1)(1 + r_{11})} + \dfrac{V_{12} P_1 P_{12}}{(1 + r_1)(1 + r_{12})} + \dfrac{V_{21} P_2 P_{21}}{(1 + r_2)(1 + r_{21})} + \dfrac{V_{22} P_2 P_{22}}{(1 + r_2)(1 + r_{22})}}{\dfrac{P_1 P_{11}}{(1 + r_1)(1 + r_{11})} + \dfrac{P_1 P_{12}}{(1 + r_1)(1 + r_{12})} + \dfrac{P_2 P_{21}}{(1 + r_2)(1 + r_{21})} + \dfrac{P_2 P_{22}}{(1 + r_2)(1 + r_{22})}} \quad (2)$$

Having obtained the forward price for the simplified two-state, two-period case we next present the futures price.

FUTURES PRICE

Let $H(t)$ denote the futures price agreed upon today to be executed at period $t + 2$. What makes the computation of the futures price interesting is the institutional procedure called *daily settlement*. According to this procedure,

FORWARD AND FUTURES MARKETS

administered by the Clearing Authorities of Futures Exchanges, the futures contract, both for the buyer and the seller is priced to market daily. Thus, if the futures price at $t + 1$ is H_i with $i = 1,2$ denoting the state of the economy, then unless $H_i = H(t)$, the party in whose favor the price moved by $H_i - H(t)$ must immediately be paid this amount by the losing party. Recall that such settlement does not occur in a forward market. The economic justification of daily settlement is explained by the desire of organized exchanges to reduce risk by allocating potential price changes across the life of the futures contract in lieu of a one-time settlement at the maturity of the contract.

Using the same decision theoretic diagram (Figure 13.1), note that daily settlement means that the H_i, $i = 1,2$ must be adjusted by the amount

$$H_i - H(t) \tag{3}$$

which, if appropriately discounted, should be a fair game with zero present value. In symbols,

$$\sum_i \frac{[H_i - H(t)]P_i}{1 + r_i} = 0 \tag{4}$$

which yields that

$$H(t) = \frac{\dfrac{H_1 P_1}{(1 + r_1)} + \dfrac{H_2 P_2}{(1 + r_2)}}{\dfrac{P_1}{(1 + r_1)} + \dfrac{P_2}{(1 + r_2)}} \tag{5}$$

So far, it appears that $H(t)$ in (5) resembles (2). However, note that H_1 and H_2 in (5) are each discounted values of the asset prices expected to prevail at $t + 2$. For $i = 1,2$, observe that

$$H_i = \frac{\dfrac{V_{i1} P_{i1}}{1 + r_{i1}} + \dfrac{V_{i2} P_{i2}}{1 + r_{i2}}}{\dfrac{P_{i1}}{1 + r_{i1}} + \dfrac{P_{i2}}{1 + r_{i2}}} \tag{6}$$

Put H_i, $i = 1,2$ of (6) in (5) and perform the necessary algebra to conclude that

$$G(t) = \frac{\dfrac{V_{11} P_1 P_{11}}{(1 + r_1)(1 + r_{11})} + \dfrac{V_{12} P_1 P_{12}}{(1 + r_1)(1 + r_{12})} + \dfrac{V_{21} P_2 P_{21}}{(1 + r_2)(1 + r_{21})} + \dfrac{V_{22} P_2 P_{22}}{(1 + r_2)(1 + r_{22})}}{\left[\dfrac{P_1}{1 + r_1} + \dfrac{P_2}{1 + r_2}\right]\left[\dfrac{P_1 P_{11}}{1 + r_{11}} + \dfrac{P_1 P_{12}}{1 + r_{12}} + \dfrac{P_2 P_{21}}{1 + r_{21}} + \dfrac{P_2 P_{22}}{1 + r_{22}}\right]} \tag{7}$$

A simple comparison of (2) and (7) shows that both expressions have the same numerator. Therefore differences or similarities between $G(t)$ and $H(t)$ depend on the denominator. Fisher Black (1976) showed that when

195

interest rates are nonstochastic, i.e. constant, then $G(t) = H(t)$. This is trivial to see from the explicit expressions in (2) and (7). In general, however, forward prices, $G(t)$, need not be equal to futures prices, $H(t)$.

SIMULATIONS

Even in the simple two-period, two-state economy with varying expected prices at $t + 2$ and varying interest rates and probabilities, it is cumbersome to perform calculations according to (2) and (7). Such calculations how-ever, are obtained easily using Lotus 1–2–3.

Example 1

As a first simulation example, consider Figure 13.2. This example illus-trates that short-term interest rates have equal probability 1/2 to drop to 5 percent or rise to 9 percent. If the former happens, then there is probability 2/3 that the rate will only increase to 6 percent and a smaller probability 1/3 that it will increase to 8 percent. If the latter occurs, the rates will decrease to 8 percent with probability 1/3 and will decrease even further to 7 percent with higher probability 2/3. The expected values of the asset, depending on what is anticipated during $t + 1$, are given as 420, 200, 150, and 75. The Lotus 1–2–3 results are:

$$G(t) = \frac{125.7861 + 29.3948 + 21.2368 + 21.4353}{0.2994901 + 0.146972 + 0.141578 + 0.285804} = 226.4168$$

$$H(t) = \frac{125.7861 + 29.3948 + 21.2368 + 21.4353}{0.934906 + 0.934633} = 226.4293$$

with an insignificant difference of 0.006 percent.

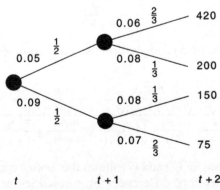

Figure 13.2 Two-state probability tree (2)

Example 2

Figure 13.3 illustrates the effects of changing interest rates. Note that the various probabilities and terminal values of the asset remain the same as in Example 1.

The Lotus 1–2–3 results are:

$$G(t) = \frac{107.0336 + 26.5922 + 23.7959 + 24.0315}{0.254841 + 0.132961 + 0.158639 + 0.320420} = 209.3221$$

$$H(t) = \frac{107.0336 + 26.5922 + 23.7959 + 24.0315}{0.944152 + 0.916137} = 209.7791$$

Note that as a result of changing interest rates, the difference between forward and futures prices has increased by 0.218 percent.

Example 3

In contrast to Examples 1 and 2, we now study again the influence of interest rates by allowing such rates to vary significantly. Specifically consider Figure 13.4.

The Lotus 1–2–3 results are:

$$G(t) = \frac{83.3333 + 21.36752 + 22.89377 + 23.57378}{0.198412 + 0.106837 + 0.152625 + 0.314317} = 195.7655$$

$$H(t) = \frac{83.3333 + 21.36752 + 22.89377 + 23.57378}{0.892857 + 0.856589} = 197.6542$$

with a difference of 0.965 percent.

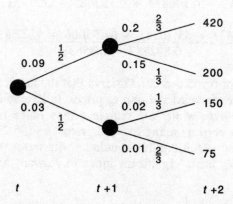

Figure 13.3 Two-state probability tree (3)

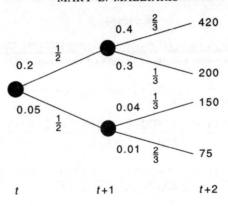

Figure 13.4 Two-state probability tree (4)

It is worth noting that two important results occur as interest rates change. First, the values of futures and forward prices change from around 226 in the first example to around 209 in the second example, and finally to around 195 in the third case. Second, the values of the forward and futures prices deviate because of the magnitude of interest rate changes.

Example 4

The complexity of the derived formulas for $H(t)$ and $G(t)$ does not allow straightforward analysis of the impact of changes in the inputs of the formula to the changes in the dependent forward and futures values. In this example we illustrate the impact on $H(t)$ and $G(t)$ of changes in the terminal values of V_{ij}, i=1,2, j=1,2. The Lotus 1–2–3 results are:

$$G(t) = \frac{83.3333 + 43.80341 + 61.05006 + 122.5836}{0.198412 + 0.106837 + 0.152625 + 0.314317} = 402.4397$$

$$H(t) = \frac{83.3333 + 43.80341 + 61.05006 + 122.5836}{0.892857 + 0.856589} = 406.3356$$

with a difference of 0.965 percent. Observe that the range of expected spot prices V_{ij} influences forward and futures prices. In Example 3 the V_{ij} prices range from 75 to 420, while in Example 4 they range from 390 to 420 (Figure 13.5). The corresponding forward prices are 195.77 and 402.39. In accordance with our intuition, this simulation illustrates that the expected terminal values V_{ij} are a significant input in forward and futures asset pricing.

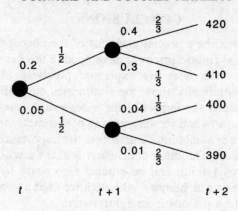

Figure 13.5 Two-state probability tree (5)

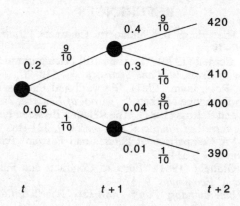

Figure 13.6 Two-state probability tree (6)

Example 5

The role of probability changes on the forward and futures prices is illustrated in this example. Consider Figure 13.6. The Lotus 1–2–3 results are:

$$G(t) = \frac{202.5000 + 23.65384 + 32.96703 + 3.677510}{0.482142 + 0.057692 + 0.082417 + 0.009429} = 416.0309$$

$$H(t) = \frac{202.5000 + 23.65384 + 32.96703 + 3.677510}{0.845238 + 0.744241} = 417.7627$$

with a difference of 0.417 percent. This example clarifies the role of probability distributions. More specifically, higher probabilities for higher terminal values led to higher forward and futures prices as contrasted between Examples 4 and 5.

199

CONCLUSIONS

This chapter presents the essential elements of the conceptual differences between forward and futures prices as developed in the financial literature. These conceptual differences are expressed precisely in mathematical equations which specifically show the similarities and differences in the two concepts. To study the impact of the independent variables that enter the equations for futures and forward pricing of contracts, several Lotus 1–2–3 simulations are presented to demonstrate the importance of computing in business education. The main conclusion is that currently the topic of forward and futures pricing can be studied rigorously by mathematical analysis and computing techniques. Although we used a two-period model, its generalization to n periods is straightforward.

REFERENCES

Black, F. (1976) "The Pricing of Commodity Contracts," *Journal of Financial Economics*, 3, 167–79.

Capozza, D. and B. Cornell (1979) "Treasury Bill Pricing in the Spot and Futures Markets," *Review of Economics and Statistics*, 61, 513–20.

Cornell, B. and M. Reinganum (1981) "Forward and Futures Prices: Evidence From the Foreign Exchange Markets," *Journal of Finance*, 36, 1035–45.

Cox, J., J. Ingersoll and S. Ross (1981) "The Relation Between Forward Prices and Futures Prices," *Journal of Financial Economics*, 9, 321–46.

French, K. (1983) "A Comparison of Futures and Forward Prices," *Journal of Financial Economics*, 12, 311–42.

Jarrow, R. and G. Oldfield (1981) "Forward Contracts and Futures Contracts," *Journal of Financial Economics*, 9, 373–82.

Kolb, R. (1994) *Understanding Futures Markets*, Fourth Edition, Miami, Fla.: Kolb Publishing Company.

Puglisi, D. (1978) "Is the Futures Market for Treasury Bills Efficient?," *Journal of Portfolio Management*, 4, Winter, 64–7.

Rendleman, R. and C. Carabini (1979) "The Efficiency of the Treasury Bill Futures Market," *Journal of Finance*, 39, 895–914.

Vignola, A. and C. Dale (1980) "The Efficiency of the Treasury Bill Futures Market: An Analysis of Alternative Specifications," *Journal of Financial Research*, 3, 169–88.

14

IMMUNIZING CURRENCY RISK IN INTERNATIONAL TRADE AND FINANCE

The development of a SDR futures market

*Krishnan Dandapani, Arun J. Prakash
and Karen Duhala*

In international trade and finance the *numéraire* currency problem is yet to be resolved. The use of Special Drawing Rights is increasing in international transactions. The valuation of Special Drawing Rights (SDRs) has remained an unsettled issue since their inception, and the techniques used for determining the value of SDRs have considerable impact upon developing countries. SDR valuation itself poses problems in international trade. The potential repercussions to the international monetary system of inducing systematic and unanticipated wealth transfers compounds the problem. Consequently, in this chapter, we evaluate the role of SDRs as international money *numéraire* and the implications of their use in international transactions. We further identify the strategies for nations to neutralize the risk of SDRs fluctuating in international financial, currency and trade transactions. This leaves us to recommend the development of a futures-type market in SDRs. Because such a market would have speculative appeal for international currency traders, we believe it would be an economically viable venture for an established futures exchange.

INTRODUCTION

Special Drawing Rights (SDRs) presently perform the two important functions of reserve asset and international money *numéraire* in global financial markets. Essentially, SDRs are international reserve assets created by the International Monetary Fund to be used in settling balance of payment deficits, and are defined as a basket of five leading currencies. The international monetary system, with many different currencies, is increasingly adopting SDRs as the *numéraire*. For example, since April 1987, thirteen countries had their currency value pegged directly to SDRs and many international transactions are increasingly being based on SDRs' value.[1] By mid-1988 more than $19 billion SDRs (US $22 billion) were outstanding, representing about 4 percent of world international reserves other than gold.[2] And with an increasing IMF commitment to aid economic expansion in Eastern Europe, the importance of SDRs can be expected to rise significantly in the near future.

The valuation of SDRs has remained an unsettled issue since their inception, and the techniques used for determining the value of SDRs have considerable impact upon developing countries. SDR valuation poses problems and potential repercussions to the international monetary system by inducing wealth transfers which may be systematic and unanticipated. Consequently, in this chapter, we evaluate the role of SDRs as international money *numéraire* and the implications of their use in international transactions. We further identify the strategies for nations to neutralize the risk of SDRs' fluctuations in international financial, currency and trade transactions. This leaves us to recommend the development of a futures-type market in SDRs. Because such a market would have speculative appeal for international currency traders, we believe it would be an economically viable venture for an established futures exchange.

SDRs VALUATION

The agreement at the annual meeting of the International Monetary Fund in 1967 paved the way for the SDR, the newly created reserve asset to be administered by the fund, and this new reserve asset was issued to each member country in proportion to its quota in the International Monetary Fund.[3] Initially, the price of SDRs was set in terms of gold. Since at that time many currencies of the world, including the US dollar, were linked to gold, the value of SDRs were linked indirectly with the US dollar and other world currencies. At the time of inception, one unit of SDR account was set equal to 0.888671 grams of gold (1/35 troy ounce). However, the increased linkage of international capital markets over the years due to the growth in information technology necessitated a change, and the transmission of shocks induced by the volatility of the gold prices underscored the need to establish the independence of the SDR.

Around this time many countries, including the US, also broke away from the gold standard. Recognizing the continual state of transition in the world monetary system and the need to minimize the effect of cross-market trading influences, it was deemed optimal to base the value of SDRs on a basket of currencies. Among the several alternative methods of valuation including the standard basket, asymmetrical basket, adjustable basket and the par value technique, the standard basket was chosen as the optimal mode of valuation for the SDRs.[4]

The primary advantage of the standard basket technique was that an appreciation or depreciation of any currency in terms of another currency would increase or decrease the value of SDR in terms of every other currency in the basket. As Chrystal points out, under this new system of valuation with the dollar representing 33 percent of the basket, a 10 percent depreciation of the dollar against all other currencies would cause SDRs to depreciate 3.3 percent against all other currencies, and appreciate 6.7 percent against the dollar.[5] This system has the advantage that a change in the value of any currency is reflected to a lesser degree in the SDR thus making SDRs less volatile, more stable, and increasingly desirable to fit the international role. Sixteen major currencies were chosen with weights as shown in Table 14.1. The interest rate, charges and remuneration payable for SDR denominated deposits were also tied to these major currencies.

These sixteen countries were chosen as representatives based on their quantum of world exports of goods and services, during the period 1968–72, and they were assigned proportional weights to reflect their share of international transactions. However, this method of valuation intensified the two major problems of bilateral trade agreements and cross-currency influences. This valuation method adversely affected bilateral trade arrangements between two countries, where the mode of payments were denominated in SDRs and the financial terms of the bilateral trade are affected by factors over which neither country has control.

Similarly when international transactions were specified in SDRs the industrialized countries whose currencies make up the value of SDRs can benefit to a substantial extent since they can export the depreciations of their currencies through the valuation mechanism of SDRs, and hence initiate a wealth transfer from developing countries to the developed nations, which may be unrelated to any particular trade. One noteworthy

Table 14.1 The valuation of the SDR (1 July 1974)

No.	Currency	Weight of currency units to compute SDR value
1	US dollar	0.4000
2	German mark	0.3800
3	Pound sterling	0.0450
4	French franc	0.4400
5	Japanese yen	26.0000
6	Canadian dollar	0.0710
7	Italian lira	47.0000
8	Netherlands guilder	0.1400
9	Belgian franc	1.6000
10	Swedish krona	0.1300
11	Australian dollars	0.0120
12	Danish krone	0.1100
13	Norwegian krone	0.0990
14	Spanish peseta	1.1000
15	Austrian schilling	0.2200
16	South African rand	0.0082

example of this problem is the OPEC-initiated, oil-induced inflation of the 1970s. An increase in the price of oil affected the developed and industrialized nations more than developing countries because of increased dependence on imported oil, which resulted in a greater deterioration of their currencies. However, since the international money *numéraire* was determined by such industrialized countries, they were able to impart a non-neutral wealth transfer. Similarly, when trade agreements between trading partners are denominated in SDRs, any transactions that affect the future value of the SDRs also affect the trade balance between the participating countries. Thus, irrespective of any bilateral factors that may affect trade, the profitability or loss from any trade would be decided, *ex post*, by the value of the select industrialized countries' currencies. Many nations also have their currencies pegged to SDRs, and a fluctuating SDR value affects these countries' trade balances.

One way to reduce the risk of fluctuations in SDRs is by hedging in the forward/futures market for currencies. Unfortunately, since no organized futures markets exist for SDRs, developing countries which anticipated an adverse movement of their currency values were forced to resort to the less than perfect cross-hedging in the foreign currency futures market. However, the information cost of forecasting the value of SDR, due to its sixteen currency basket valuation framework and the cost of cross-currency hedging, was complex and phenomenal. The inter-market trading strategies also become difficult to execute because of incomplete or inefficient markets. With time, the relative importance of the countries in international trade were also changing, necessitating a revision in the currency basket. It was increasingly felt that a smaller, more representative basket would be more advantageous. Therefore the SDRs valuation was changed to a five-currency basket on 1 January 1981. Beginning 1 January 1986 the weights of the basket of currencies are as shown in Table 14.2, broadly reflecting the relative importance of these currencies in international trade and finance.[6]

While this change has the inherent advantage of computational simplicity, it has accentuated the problem of wealth transfer from the developing countries to the developed countries due to the increased dependency of

Table 14.2 Revised SDR valuation (1 January 1986 to present)

No.	Currency	Percentage weight of currency value for SDR computation
1	US dollar	42%
2	UK pound	12%
3	German mark	19%
4	French franc	12%
5	Japanese yen	15%

SDRs on industrialized countries' currencies. The effect of concentration on a few selected nations' currencies on the overall variability of SDRs is unpredictable depending on the co-movement of the underlying currencies.

IMPLICATIONS OF CHANGES IN CURRENCY BASKET FOR SDR VOLATILITY

Table 14.3 displays the results of an IMF study of the average monthly variability of effective exchange rates between 1974 and 1993 and US dollar exchange rates.[7] Variability is defined as the standard deviation of monthly percentage changes over US exchange rates during the same time period.

A casual perusal of the data reveals that the exchange rates of SDR-based currencies fluctuated more than those of other countries, and this is especially pronounced in 1979 relative to earlier periods. The volatility in the SDR basket of currencies in the 1990s also mirrors the volatility of the pre-1980 era. This is shown in Table 14.4.[8] Table 14.5 shows more recent fluctuations in real exchange rates. These tables illustrate that historically, as well as for the recent past, the fluctuations in exchange rates on which SDR valuation is based is significant.

This fluctuation in the real effective exchange rate implies that when trade takes place between two countries, and the transaction is specified in SDRs, the true terms of trade may be decided *ex post*, and may be beyond the control of the trading partners. For illustration, let us assume that today (contract time) an oil producing country sells 10 million barrels of oil to another country at a cost of 200 million SDRs (price of oil: 1 barrel = 20 SDRs), and that the transfer of oil and SDRs is to take place a year from now (transaction time). Let us further assume that the exchange rate today is 1 SDR = 2.0 purchaser's monetary unit and 1 SDR = 1.0 seller's monetary unit. These terms of trade, and the effect on the purchaser's and seller's domestic prices are illustrated in Figure 14.1a. If, within the year, the seller's economy and purchaser's economy were to grow at a constant rate (positive, negative or zero) as the rest of the countries on which SDR valuation is based, then, at transaction time, neither country is affected and the *real* price of oil is unchanged. A uniform depreciation of both currencies against SDRs (1 SDR = 2.2p and 1 SDR = 1.1s) or appreciation (1 SDR = 1.8p and 1 SDR = 0.9s) leaves the trading patterns invariant to the exchange rate and price fluctuations of SDRs. This is portrayed in Figure 14.1b.

However, if the purchaser's economy and the seller's economy were to grow at an identical rate along with that of the rest of the world, while the economies of the developing nations on which SDR valuation were based grows at a different pace with respect to the trading partners, *ceteris paribus*, the effective value of the SDRs' currencies will depreciate or

Table 14.3 Variability in exchange rates, 1974–93

Countries	Period 1974–77		Period 1979		Period 1980–86		Period 1987–93	
	Effective exchange rate	Dollar exchange rate	Effective exchange rate	Dollar exchange rate	Effective exchange rate	Dollar exchange rate	Effective exchange rate	Dollar exchange rate
Industrial nations:								
France	1.34	1.98	0.64	1.40	1.15	1.59	0.30	0.34
Germany, Fed Rep.	1.22	2.11	0.64	1.47	0.22	0.12	0.09	0.05
Japan	1.48	1.62	2.03	2.23	22.29	24.75	11.72	10.95
United Kingdom	1.23	1.80	2.16	2.63	0.23	0.35	0.11	0.10
United States	0.62	–	0.60	–	0.09	–	0.04	–
Other nations	1.41	2.26	0.94	1.44	–	–	–	–
Developing nations:								
Pegged to dollar	1.05	0.49	1.51	0.80	–	–	–	–
Pegged to SDR	1.66	1.52	2.58	2.60	–	–	–	–

Table 14.4 Maximum swings in real effective exchange rates of five major currencies, 1963–92

	1963–72 (%)	1973–82 (%)	1983–92 (%)
German mark	13	22	21
French franc	27	19	8
Japanese yen	14	35	33
British pound	17	60	12
US dollar	14	32	60
Average	17	34	27

appreciate relative to both the purchaser's and seller's currencies, leading to a change in the real value of SDRs and affecting bilateral trade. For example, if, at transaction time, the purchaser's currency appreciates with respect to the SDR basket requiring 1.8p per 1 SDR while the seller's monetary unit value remains unchanged at 1 SDR = 1.0s, the purchaser would gain from this trade. The purchaser can buy the traded quantity of oil by using only 360 million of the budgeted currency units (360/1.8 = 20 million SDRs). This results in an unanticipated gain to the purchaser (shaded area of Figure 14.2) and an unforeseen benefit from the favorable valuation of SDRs.[9] If the reverse were to happen – that is, if the purchaser's monetary unit depreciates with respect to SDRs, *ceteris paribus* – then the purchaser loses. This is illustrated in Figure 14.3. If, at transaction time, 1 SDR = 2.2p and 1 SDR = 1.0s, then the budgeted 400 million currency units at the new price will facilitate purchase of only 9.09 million barrels of oil. This leads to a real loss for the purchaser (shaded area). If the purchaser still needs the budgeted oil of 10 million barrels, its domestic price at transaction time would be higher and, in bilateral trade, SDR fluctuation creates a wealth transfer.[10]

Two important questions that arise from this volatility are: (a) has the switch from the sixteen currency basket to the five currency basket increased or decreased this wealth transfer?, and (b) how can one hedge against this volatility risk of SDRs? The answer to the first issue is not uncontroversial. The benefits of international diversification cannot be conclusively tested because of several international barriers and market segmentation.[11] The Capital Asset Pricing Model (CAPM), which is extensively used both by academicians and practitioners, is based on the premise that mixing of assets tends to mitigate the riskiness of assets because of the interrelationship between them, and the benefits of such diversification have been clearly established. However, in an international context a correct specification of a testable model has been difficult and imprecise.[12] Hence, one cannot hypothesize that the switch in the valuation of SDRs from a sixteen currency basket to a five currency basket would necessarily

Table 14.5 Variability in real exchange rates, June 1973–88 and 1989–92

Country	June 1973–88				1989–92			
	Mean variation (%)	Standard deviation	Maximum	Minimum	Mean variation (%)	Standard deviation	Maximum	Minimum
United Kingdom	-1.6	14.7	37.2	-35.3	1.82	1.81	4.3	0.0
France	10.3	18.2	55.9	-16.9	-1.94	1.68	0.0	-4.2
West Germany	13.2	19.5	61.8	-14.7	-1.02	2.52	1.9	-5.6
Japan	-15.2	17.2	8.6	-57.1	6.34	5.46	12.5	0.0

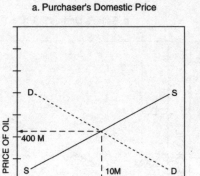
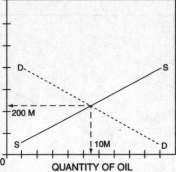

a. Purchaser's Domestic Price

b. Seller's Domestic Price

Figure 14.1a No appreciation on uniform price appreciation or depreciation of SDRs (1)

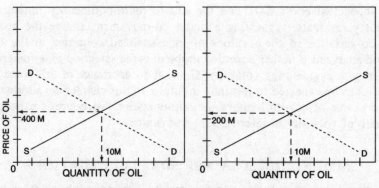

a. Purchaser's Domestic Price

b. Seller's Domestic Price

Figure 14.1b No appreciation or uniform price appreciation or depreciation of SDRs (2)

209

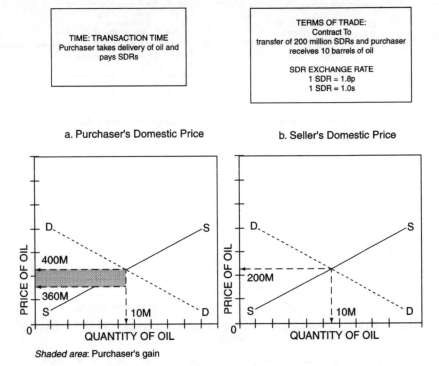

Figure 14.2 Effect when SDRs depreciate with respect to purchaser's monetary unit: world and seller's prices constant

negate the diversification effect. Numerous tests, prior to and after the switch by the international monetary authorities, have sought to determine whether the volatility of SDRs has increased and whether the individual currency weights change has resulted in a minimum variance of the SDRs; but they have not led to any definitive conclusions. One major reason for this inconclusiveness has been the severe multi-collinearity among the currency residuals, suggesting a major co-movement among the growth and co-variation of the fortunes of industrialized countries in the time period analyzed. Another unsettled problem is the selection of a *numéraire* currency to evaluate the volatility. Given the importance of this issue, the debate can be expected to continue in future. In this chapter we address the second issue of how to identify the immunization procedures for hedging the risk of volatility in international transactions.

IMMUNIZING AGAINST SDRs FLUCTUATIONS

One possible method for developing nations to hedge against a fluctuating SDR risk would be through the foreign currency futures market. At present

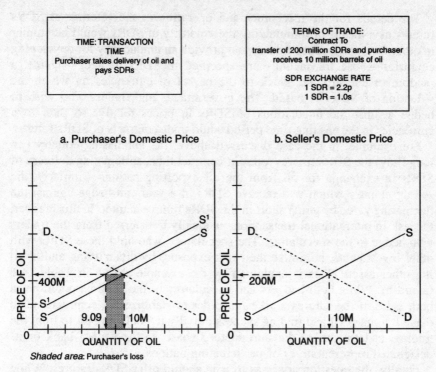

Figure 14.3 Effect when SDRs appreciate with respect to purchaser's monetary unit: world and seller's prices constant

foreign currency futures markets are operational in several major financial centers of the world. In the United States, the International Monetary Market of the Chicago Mercantile Exchange, the Financial Instrument Exchange of the New York Cotton Exchange, and Mid-America Commodity Exchange offer currency futures in the Japanese yen, German mark, Canadian dollar, British pound, Swiss franc and Australian dollar. However, the inter-market trading strategies become difficult to execute because of institutional constraints, high costs and cumbersome procedures. Furthermore, the cross hedging may not be a perfect hedge leading to complete risk neutralization because of the inherent differences in the basis risk of the currencies. Hence the risk in foreign transactions due to the volatility of fluctuations of SDRs cannot be completely nullified. A better method to neutralize this risk would be through the use of an SDRs futures market. Although the financial press has been quoting prices of SDRs along with other currency values for some time, none of the exchanges currently offer any SDR futures. Developing a futures market is a vital and logical step for reducing the volatility of the SDRs and stabilizing the international monetary system.

211

The details for the mechanics and operation of the offering of SDRs futures as a means of immunizing the volatility of SDRs would be similar to other foreign currency futures and provide an unique way for developing countries whose transactions are specified in SDRs to hedge against a random or catastrophic shock to the basket of currencies on which the valuation of SDRs is based. The governments and traders who wish to hedge against the fluctuations of SDRs in prices relative to their own currencies in the ensuing time period could trade contracts of SDRs futures.

For example, in the case discussed above, the purchasing country can long (buy) the SDRs futures today at contract time, anticipating delivery of SDRs in exchange for oil from the oil exporting nations. Similarly, the selling country which will receive SDRs in a year can hedge against the fluctuating value by going short in the SDRs futures market. In this manner, the risk in international transactions is ideally transferred from the traders who hedge to the speculators. The speculators, who hold these SDRs with other investments, minimize their risk exposure by diversifying and holding other assets. This is explained by the example shown in Table 14.6 (a and b). While both hedgers and speculators of the contract could be in both sides of the futures market, in order to stabilize the contract and to make it a financial and trading success initially it would be best to limit the trading, at least during the introductory phase, to the central bank or its designated representatives of participating nations.

Finally, the question arises as to who should offer SDRs futures. While the institutional framework requires detailed planning, an international agency such as the World Bank or the International Monetary Fund could initiate trading on their own behest or provide organizational support and close cooperation for any other institution which wishes to provide these services. The selected institution will also provide adequate market support and market maintenance activities to ensure the constant liquidity and marketability of the new contract, and generate the trading depth and breadth for this new market. An organized and well functioning SDRs market would go far in providing stability to the international market and in promoting international integration, and will further enhance the role of the SDR as an international reserve asset.

CONCLUSIONS

In this chapter we have traced the role of the SDR and its computational framework and analyzed the implications of fluctuations in the value of SDRs for the international monetary system. We have also identified the implications of changing the valuation procedure of SDRs and suggested some ways of neutralizing the riskiness embodied in fluctuations of SDRs for participating nations of the world. The development of the SDRs futures contract appears to be potentially helpful towards the long run

Table 14.6a A long hedge made by the buyer of the product

Cash market	Futures market
Today: contract time	
Contract to buy 1 M barrels of oil. Agree to pay 20 M SDRs one year from now. Today's price: 1 SDR = 2s/1k	Action taken: long SDRs futures each at a price of: 1 SDR = 2s/1k
One year from now: transaction time	
Deliver the SDRs futures at a price of 1 SDR = 2s/1k* (1 + G)	Action taken: reverse trade of today's price of SDRs: 1 SDR = 2s/1k* (1 + G)
Net profit/loss on positions:	
Cash market:	20 M* [(2s/1k) − (2s/1k)* G] (1)
Futures market:	20 M* [(2s/1k)* G − (2s/1k)] (2)
Combined holdings:	Cash + Futures = (1) + (2) = 0.0

Note: G represents the growth rate in the value of the SDR due to its appreciation/depreciation of the five currency basket.

Table 14.6b A short hedge made by the seller of the product

Cash market	Futures market
Today: contract time	
Contract to sell 1 M barrels of oil. Agree to receive 20 M SDRs one year from now. Today's price: 1 SDR = 2s/1k	Action taken: short SDRs futures each at a price of: 1 SDR = 2s/1k
One year from now: transaction time	
Accept the SDRs futures at a price of 1 SDR = 2s/1k* (1 + G)	Action taken: reverse trade of today's price of SDRs: 1 SDR = 2s/1k* (1 + G)
Net profit/loss on positions:	
Cash market:	20 M* [(2s/1k)* G − (2s/1k)] (3)
Futures market:	20 M* [(2s/1k) − (2s/1k)* G] (4)
Combined holdings:	Cash + Futures = (3) + (4) = 0.0

Note: G represents the growth rate in the value of the SDR due to its appreciation/depreciation of the five currency basket.

stability of the international monetary system. The requisite index would be easily constructed, and would provide a variety of quasi-hedging strategies involving holes in the basket, as well as the standard hedging and speculative opportunities.

NOTES

1 International Monetary Fund, *International Financial Statistics*, April 1987.
2 See David K. Eiteman and Arthur I. Stonehill *Multinational Business Finance*, Fifth edition, Massachusetts, Addison-Wesley Publishing Company, 1989, pp 43.
3 See John P. Williamson, "International Liquidity: A Survey," *Economic Journal*, September 1973, for a detailed discussion of the creation of SDRs.
4 See Alec K. Chrystal, "International Money and the Future of the SDR," *Essays in International Finance*, No. 128, June 1978.
5 See Chrystal, International Money.
6 See Bruno H. Solnik, *International Investments*, Massachusetts, Addison-Wesley, 1988, p. 91.
7 See International Monetary Fund *Annual Report*, 1981, p. 42; for later periods the computations were done by the authors.
8 See John Williamson, *The Exchange Rate System*, 2nd edition, Washington, DC, Institute for International Economics, June 1985.
9 Alternatively, we can show that this results in a real loss to the seller and lowers the effective price of oil, as the purchaser can use the 400 million units to buy more SDRs and can obtain more oil.
10 Again this can be analyzed from the seller's perspective and it can be shown this would lead to a *real* increase in the price of oil in bilateral terms, with the seller benefiting as a result.
11 See Bruno H. Solnik, "Testing International Asset Pricing: Some Pessimistic Views," *Journal of Finance*, May 1977, pp. 503–12.
12 See Steven W. Kohlagen, "Overlapping National Investment Portfolios: Evidence and Implications of International Integration of Secondary Markets for Financial Assets," in Donald R. Lessard (ed.) *International Financial Management*, 2nd edition, New York, Wiley, 1985, pp. 97–117.

15

PURCHASING POWER PARITY AND THE PESO/DOLLAR EXCHANGE RATE

Vincent Dropsy

In December 1994, Mexico experienced its fourth balance of payments crisis in twenty years, though for different reasons. Excess government spending and monetary creation have been blamed for the devaluations of the Mexican Peso that had occurred in 1976, 1982 and 1987. However, other significant shocks such as an external debt crisis (1982), a major earthquake (1985) and a deterioration of its terms of trade due to the oil price collapse (1986) could have also contributed to some of the currency problems. This chapter examines whether the Peso has nevertheless obeyed the law of one price in the long run. We apply modified unit root tests to probe long term purchasing power parity and investigate whether deviations from this equilibrium can be explained by exogenous shocks.

INTRODUCTION

The choice of an optimal exchange rate regime in developing countries has been the subject of numerous debates. Exchange rate policies are usually designed to either gain international competitiveness or keep inflation in control.[1] The exchange rate between the Mexican Peso and the US Dollar is a good example of this type of dilemma. The fixed nominal exchange rate was adjusted several times in August 1976, February 1982, December 1987, and recently in December 1994 following a balance of payments crisis. These nominal devaluations made Mexican exports more competitive, but subsequent inflation tended to erase these price advantages in the long run. In other words, the real value of the Peso has often appreciated after a nominal devaluation. In the process, the real exchange rate has been widely fluctuating around its purchasing power parity (henceforth PPP) equilibrium. To stabilize the Mexican currency around its PPP value, various exchange rate regimes (crawling peg, managed float, pure peg, fluctuation bands) have been implemented throughout the 1980s. More recently, the Mexican authorities have adopted a "controlled float within slow-moving bands," with the ultimate objective of nominal exchange rate and price stability. This chapter examines whether the real Peso/Dollar

215

exchange rate has been converging towards a PPP equilibrium. We also investigate whether this equilibrium has been shifted by external shocks between 1957 and 1993.

We conduct various empirical tests of real exchange rate stationarity and stability for the Mexican Peso, using several definitions of real exchange rate. Real exchange rates can be computed on the basis of relative consumer prices to measure deviations from PPP, or on the basis of relative prices of tradables to nontradables as in modern theory. Standard econometrics tests for unit roots are also modified to investigate the permanent or temporary nature of real exchange rate deviations from their equilibrium. In particular, we search for structural breaks that could have generated evidence against PPP. Such shifts in the equilibrium value of the real exchange rate could be explained by either changes in long-run economic fundamentals or inaccurate choices of post-devaluation nominal rates by the authorities. We also estimate the dates of these switches instead of choosing them *ex post*, so that we can better understand the reasons underlying major devaluations. Exchange rate adjustments can then be traced back to inappropriate economic policies or external shocks. Econometric tests are applied to the real Peso/Dollar rate fluctuations over the last 35 years to explore these issues.

In the next section, we briefly retrace the important episodes leading to the Peso devaluations and the various exchange rate regimes to the present date. In section three, we present several econometric tests related to the joint hypothesis of unit roots and structural breaks, which we then apply to the real Peso/Dollar exchange rate in section four. Reflections on the current exchange rate policy in Mexico are offered in conclusion.

NOMINAL DEVALUATIONS AND REAL APPRECIATIONS

In 1976, the Mexican government was forced to devalue the Peso by about 40 percent, ending a 22-year period of a fixed and stable exchange rate relative to the US Dollar. This devaluation was the result of a balance of payments crisis caused by rising fiscal deficits, and the worldwide recession following the first oil shock. After 1976, massive oil discoveries in Mexico induced the government to spend even more and finance its swelling deficits through external borrowing. The unanticipated fall in oil prices and rise in interest rates in 1981 led to several large nominal exchange rate adjustments in 1982 and the beginning of an international debt crisis.

However, the real exchange rate had appreciated over these six years and had almost returned at the end of 1981 to its pre-1976 devaluation level (Figures 15.1 and 15.2). Subsequently, a dual exchange rate was introduced in September 1982, and terminated in November 1991. A crawling peg was adopted for the controlled rate, and the initial large spread between the controlled and the market exchange rate almost disappeared as early as

216

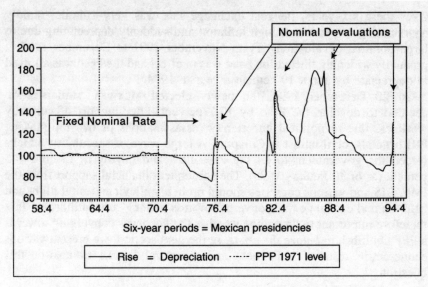

Figure 15.1 Peso/$ real exchange rate (April 1958 to April 1994)

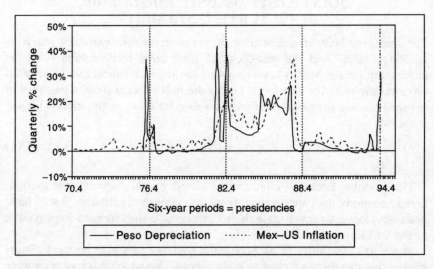

Figure 15.2 Nominal Peso/$ depreciation and inflation differential (April 1970 to April 1994)

1987. However, unexpected events, the Mexico City earthquake of 1985, and the oil price collapse of 1986, as well as volatile inflation also compelled the authorities to change course several times in selecting the slippage rate between the Peso and the Dollar. In 1988, the government maintained a fixed nominal exchange rate before resuming a crawling peg.

Over these six years, the real exchange rate was very volatile, rapidly appreciating in periods of high inflation and suddenly depreciating due to large nominal devaluations. From November 1991 to December 1994, a gradually widening fluctuation band was in effect and the Peso was allowed to depreciate by about 10 percent a year in 1994.

On 20 December 1994, the newly elected Mexican administration decided to devalue the Peso by 12.7 percent, after months of currency weakness due to political uncertainty (assassinations of two top-ranking PRI officials, civil unrest in Chiapas). A large wave of speculative attacks forced the government to let the Peso float and fall by as much as 45 percent (as of 30 January 1995). The subsequent financial support from the IMF, BIS and various countries should probably alleviate capital flight and help the real exchange rate converge towards its long-run equilibrium. It is therefore important to determine whether the Peso was converging towards a PPP equilibrium *before the crisis*. In the next section, we present various econometric tests of unit roots and structural breaks to answer this question.

JOINT TESTS OF UNIT ROOTS AND STRUCTURAL INSTABILITY

The apparent lack of stationarity of many economic variables (such as exchange rates) and the weakness of long term relationships (such as purchasing power parity) have provided an important incentive to develop econometric tests for unit roots. Under the null hypothesis of a unit root in the series y_t, the distribution of the t-statistic for $\alpha_1=1$ in equation (1) is not standard:

$$y_t = \alpha_0 + \alpha_1.y_{t-1} + u_t \tag{1}$$

The popular Dickey–Fuller test is based on this special distribution. Other econometric approaches (e.g., maximum likelihood tests) have been developed to investigate the existence of a unit root, to improve the power of the tests.[2]

Structural instability in an economic system could also produce disturbances that can mimic a random walk process. Standard unit root tests were not designed to differentiate between the true unit root hypothesis and a possible regime shift. Perron (1989) adapted Dickey–Fuller tests to allow for a known shift in the mean or the trend under the null and alternative hypotheses. Following Perron's seminal work, Banerjee, Lumsdaine and Stock (1992) (henceforth BLS) engineered new econometric techniques which simultaneously estimate the unknown date of a possible break and test the null hypothesis of a unit root at that date. Next, we present six tests that we later apply to the real Peso/$ exchange rate.

218

Recursive tests of unit root

The arbitrary choice of the full sample period to test the hypothesis of a unit root makes it difficult to interpret its possible nonrejection. Does the test lack statistical power or has a structural break biased the critical values? A partial solution to this problem is to perform a succession of recursive tests, while increasing the size of the sample from 25 to 100 per cent. The advantage of this procedure is to observe the evolution of the test statistics and interpret a sudden reversal in inference as the corollary of a shock.

We expect the Peso to exhibit such behavior around 1976, after two decades of stable nominal exchange rate. If the null hypothesis of a unit root in the real rate is rejected just before the 1976 devaluation and again several years thereafter, we would be inclined to believe that PPP holds in the long run. For this preliminary investigation of the long-run stationarity of the real exchange rate, we select the Augmented Dickey–Fuller test, whose critical values have been tabulated for various sample sizes by MacKinnon (1990). The null hypothesis is $\Phi_1=(\alpha_1-1) = 0$ in the transformed equation:

$$y_t - y_{t-1} = \Phi_0 + \Phi_1.y_{t-1} + \Sigma_{i=1}^k b_i.(y_{t-i} - y_{t-i-1}) + v_t \qquad (2)$$

Rolling-sample test of unit root

As a variant of the previous method, we keep the size of the sample constant (at eight years, about 25 per cent of the full sample), but proceed to move the sub-sample over time. The test statistics remain identical.

Sequential likelihood ratio test of unit root (BLS)

Banerjee *et al.* (1992) suggested splitting the full sample in two and sequentially estimating equation (3) for each possible breakpoint:

$$y_t = \beta_0 + \beta_1.t + \Gamma_1.y_{t-1} + \Sigma_{i=1}^k c_i.(y_{t-i} - y_{t-i-1}) + w_t \qquad (3)$$

The objective of the test is to compare the maximal value of the Quandt Likelihood Ratio statistics with the corresponding critical values, computed by Monte Carlo simulations. The estimated time of the break is therefore the most probable rupture date and a rejection of the null hypothesis of no break becomes even more reliable.

Sequential test of unit root and shift in mean (BLS)

BLS also allowed the stochastic behavior of y_t (the real exchange rate in our study) to be disturbed by a shift in its mean in both the null and alternative hypotheses. Equation (3) is transformed by a linear combination of the regressors and the addition of a dummy variable identifying the break:

$$y_t = \theta_0 + \theta_1.t + \theta_2.(y_{t-1} - \Omega t) + \Sigma_{i=1}^k \theta_{3,i}.(dy_{t-1} - \Omega) + \theta_{4m}.DM_{b,t} + w'_t \quad (4)$$

where $DM_{b,t} = 1$ if $t > b$, 0 otherwise, $dy_{t-1} = y_{t-1} - y_{t-i-1}$,
$\Omega = \beta_0/(1 - \Sigma_{i=1}^k c_i)$, and the null hypothesis of a unit root is $\theta_2 = 1$.

The breakpoint is selected at the minimum of the t-static $t(\theta_2=1)$ and then compared with the minimal critical value over the sample. The goal of this procedure is to test the unit root hypothesis at the likeliest time of structural break and strengthen the case in favor of stationarity, given the low power of the original ADF test.

Sequential test of unit root and shift in trend (BLS)

A similar method is adopted to permit a break in the trend under both hypotheses. The previous dummy variable in equation (4) is replaced by: $DT_{b,t} = t - b$ if $t > b$, 0 otherwise.

Wright's OLS residual-based CUSUM test

Wright (1993) considered the dual approach to the same problem. He extends the OLS residuals-based CUSUM test of structural stability (initially developed by Ploberger and Kramer, 1992) to nonstationary or integrated variables. The CUSUM statistic is defined as the (adjusted) cumulated sums of the OLS residuals from one of the following regression:

$$y_t = \pi_a + u_{a,t} \quad \text{(stationary variable)} \quad (5a)$$
$$y_t = \pi_b + \beta.t + u_{b,t} \quad \text{(nonstationary trended variable)} \quad (5b)$$
$$y_t = \pi_c + \alpha.y_{t-1} + u_{c,t} \quad \text{(nonstationary integrated variable)} \quad (5c)$$

We apply the first two CUSUM tests to the real Peso exchange rate since a rejection of the null in the model (c) is not informative.

EMPIRICAL RESULTS

We calculate three different versions of the real value of the Mexican Peso relative to the US Dollar, based on the following equation:

$$RX_t = X_t.P_t^{US}/P_t^M \quad (6)$$

where X_t = nominal Peso/$ market average exchange rate, and

(i) for the CPI-based purchasing power parity definition:
P_t^M = Mexican consumer price index, P_t^{US} = US consumer price index.

(ii) for the GDP deflator-based purchasing power parity definition:

P_t^M = Mexican GDP deflator, P_t^{US} = US GDP deflator.

(iii) for the modern theory definition:

P_t^M = Mexican consumer price index (proxy for the price of nontradables),
P_t^{US} = US wholesale price index (proxy for the price of foreign tradables).

We obtain the following key results using quarterly data from the first quarter of 1958 to the last quarter of 1993 (and thus eliminate PPP deviations due to political uncertainties in 1994):

1 Recursive ADF tests (Figure 15.3) provide some initial evidence in favor of a long-run stationary real exchange rate, despite the three major crises of 1976, 1982 and 1987.
2 Rolling-sample ADF tests (Figure 15.4) tend to confirm this first conclusion, although the sizable length of the sub-samples renders these empirical results more difficult to interpret.
3 CUSUM tests (Figures 15.5 and 15.6) distinctively reveal structural instability in the real exchange rate around the 1976 devaluation. Interestingly, signs of instability appear even before the first devaluation, when the model specification is simply a constant real exchange rate. Conversely, the CUSUM test indicates a break in the appreciating trend after 1976 when the model includes a drift.
4 The sequential Quandt likelihood ratio test (Figure 15.7) pinpoints a significant shift in the fundamental real value of the Peso in 1982. We

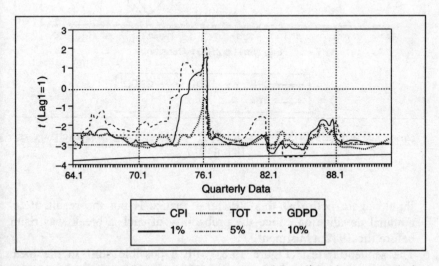

Figure 15.3 Recursive PPP test (1958.1–. . .), real Peso/$ exchange rate (in log)

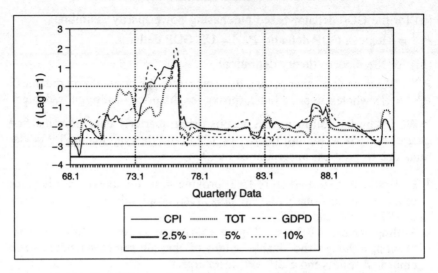

Figure 15.4 Rolling PPP test (10-year sample). real Peso/$ exchange rate (in log)

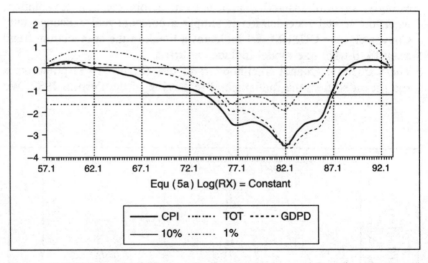

Figure 15.5 Wright's CUSUM test for I (1) variables, real Peso/$ exchange rate (log-quart.)

should again note that this structural change is not the result of the nominal devaluation, since the probability of such a break was rising before the 1982 adjustment.

5 The sequential test (Figure 15.8) with a possible shift in the mean confirms this evidence. However, no significant break in the trend is

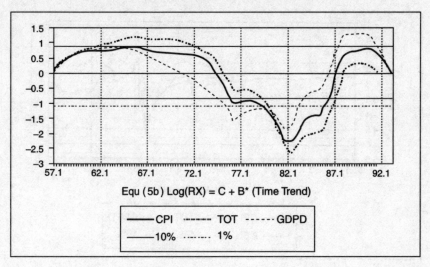

Figure 15.6 Wright's CUSUM test for I (1) variables, real Peso/$ exchange rate (log-quart.)

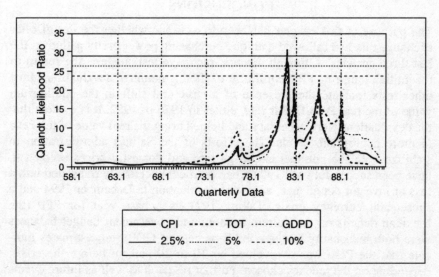

Figure 15.7 Sequential PPP/break rest, real Peso/$ exchange rate (in log)

detected by the alternative sequential test (not shown). Finally, the evidence in favor of a break is stronger for the two PPP-adjusted rates than for the "modern" real exchange rate for most of the previous tests.

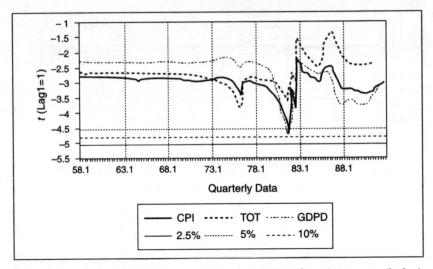

Figure 15.8 Sequential PPP/mean-shift test, real Peso/$ exchange rate (in log)

CONCLUSIONS

The purpose of this chapter has been to examine whether the Peso/Dollar exchange rate had followed a unique purchasing power parity path over the last three decades. Although our first recursive test suggests the return to the initial long-run PPP equilibrium after a nominal devaluation, most other tests indicate the presence of a structural shift in the equilibrium value of the real Peso/Dollar rate, either in 1976 or 1982. It is evident that the devaluations were necessary and helped bring the real value of the Peso to more appropriate levels. The efforts of the Salinas administration to stabilize both the nominal exchange rate and domestic prices seemed to have been successful until 1994 when political uncertainty translated into a loss of investor confidence, an initial devaluation in December 1994 and a subsequent currency crisis. Taking 1971 as a base year for PPP (the Mexican deficits on the current account and government budget balances were both reasonably low, around 2 percent of GDP), our estimates indicate that the Peso was overvalued by 10 to 20 percent before the crisis, depending on the indexes chosen. Further research as well as future events (e.g., inflation trends and capital flows) will provide important clues to determine the new long-run nominal equilibrium value of the Mexican Peso.

NOTES

1 Compare Aghevli *et al.* (1991).
2 Compare Banerjee and Hendry (1992) for a survey.

REFERENCES

Aghevli, B., M. Khan and P. Montiel (1991) "Exchange Rate Policy in Developing Countries," *IMF Occasional Paper*, 78.

Banerjee, A. and D. Hendry (1992) "Testing Integration and Cointegration: An Overview," *Oxford Bulletin of Economics and Statistics*, 54, pp. 225–55.

Banerjee, A., R. Lumsdaine and J. Stock (1992), "Recursive and Sequential Tests of the Unit-Root and Trend-Break Hypotheses: Theory and International Evidence," *Journal of Business and Economic Statistics*, 10, pp. 271–88.

MacKinnon, J. (1990) "Critical Values for Cointegration," Discussion Paper 90–4, University of California, San Diego.

Perron, P. (1989) "The Great Crash, the Oil-Price Shock, and the Unit Root Hypothesis," *Econometrica*, 57, pp. 1361–1401.

Ploberger, W. and W. Kramer (1992) "The CUSUM Test with OLS residuals," *Econometrica*, 60, pp. 271–385.

Wright, J.H. (1993) "The CUSUM Test Based on Least Squares Residuals in Regressions with Integrated Variables," *Economics Letters*, 41, pp. 353–8.

Part III

GLOBAL BANKING ISSUES

16

CONTESTABLE MARKETS AND THE MEXICAN BANKING SECTOR IN THE CONTEXT OF NAFTA

Edgar Ortiz and Alfred Lewis*

INTRODUCTION

Mexico is currently undergoing its most severe crisis of modern times. Following a macro peso devaluation in December 1994, domestic production plunged 6.9 percent in 1995, and an inflation rate of 50 percent reappeared as an important restraining factor to economic recovery. Although the crisis was mainly caused by profound disequilibria in the external sector, the banking and securities markets played an important role too. As a result of financial liberalization and deregulation policies, the recently privatized banking system increased exponentially its bad loans, exposing the economy to severe insolvency problems. Similarly, the money and securities markets became important mechanisms to mobilize international investments to the local markets. However, those funds were not used to support real investments. They were used mainly to solve the government's short term liquidity needs and above all to increase Mexico's international reserves to strengthen massive disequilibria in the current account. That is, foreign exchange obtained through foreign portfolio investments were used to support imports of intermediate and consumption goods. Further, as the crisis ensued, the securities markets became an important mechanism for large capital repatriations that weakened the economy further (Ortiz, 1996).

During the years preceding the current crisis, the Mexican economy experienced a remarkable recovery after the debt crisis of the 1980s. Geared by bold economic policies, the economy showed great dynamism. Policy-making stressed the liberalization and deregulation of the economy to enhance the market and open the economy to foreign trade and investments, financial sector included; the promotion of an export-led industrialized economy; a thorough privatization program of state enterprises, which included reprivatization of the commercial banking system nationalized in 1982 at the break of the debt crisis; and the unprecedented signing with Canada and the United States of a free trade agreement, the North American Free Trade Agreement (NAFTA).

Mexico is now undergoing a harsh adjustment program. Although results still need to be consolidated, it is expected that the economy will begin a steady recovery during 1996. Similarly, NAFTA will continue being an important determinant for Mexico's future economic performance. The NAFTA should help the Mexican economy to accelerate its economic recovery and to promote a high rate of development. Through increased investments from its Northern trade partners, increased trade with them, job creation, and important technology transfers, the economy should perform favorably in the medium and long runs. Thus, in spite of all the current economic problems that now plague the Mexican economy, few doubt that it will achieve a long period of sustained economic growth which eventually will lead it into a definitive take-off into development.

Nevertheless, considering the role that financial markets played in the making of the crisis, one of the many ramifications of Mexico's economic recovery and future economic development is the need for an efficient financial services industry to increase the mobilization of local and international savings to the local firms, as well as enhancing the allocation of resources. The NAFTA enables, although gradually, financial companies from the US and Canada to participate in the Mexican market. Further liberalization policies still under process also make extensive financial openings to institutions from other countries, particularly from Europe and Japan.[1] Success in the application of these policies depends largely on the ability of Mexico's financial institutions to compete with foreign financial intermediaries. A failure to meet this challenge could hinder economic growth as a result of the re-establishment of protectionist policies and regulations to favor local banks and financial institutions, and due to conflicts between foreign intermediaries and the local authorities with regard to the application of certain regulations or financial policies.

Similarly, foreign institutions entering the local financial market can make significant contributions to enhance national development only in a competitive environment, free of collusive forces that restrict their operations. A failure from banking institutions from Canada to enter the Mexican market successfully or to establish operations and economies of scale on a continental, North American basis would not only hinder the development prospects of Mexico, but of all the NAFTA countries, which could lead to severe shortcomings in achieving their integration goals.

In this respect, one aspect that needs to be studied closely, as a step to design appropriate financial and integration policies, is the structure of banking institutions from Mexico in the context of the North American Free Trade Agreement. This chapter addresses that problem, using as a framework of analysis the theory of contestable markets. The chapter is divided into five sections. Following this introduction, the next section sets forth a conceptual framework to examine the strengths and weaknesses of the Mexican banking system based on the theory of contestable markets. In the following section the main stipulations of the NAFTA concerning the banking sector are summarized. The next section examines empirically the structure of the Mexican Banking system. The work ends with a short conclusion, which includes some suggestions for financial policy-making.

ENTRY AND CONTESTABILITY

Traditional theory of competition

Competition in the banking industry can be analyzed by using the same theory which applies to any other industry. However, it is necessary to be aware of the fact that structural regulation, which is a characteristic peculiar to the banking sector, affects its application. This structural regulation does not so much control the efficiency of the production of banking services, but it controls the stability of the system. This supervisory philosophy derives from the banking crises of the 1920s and the depression of the 1930s.

The working of the competitive market forces generally implies both a benefit and a cost for the society as a whole. The benefit derives from the elimination of the less efficient firms and the consequent efficiency gain. The cost is the bankruptcy cost for the society. Usually, the theory assumes that the social cost of bankruptcy is negligible, since it mainly falls unto the shareholders. In the case of a bank, however, there are important externalities to bankruptcy, since it affects a large number of savers and creditors. This is a notable factor both when the bankruptcy is the result of the competitive forces in the financial markets and when it is caused by very close links between banks and industry, like at the beginning of this century. This explains the supervisory policies enforced both in Canada and the United States for the last few decades and their dual goal of separating financial institutions and industry and sheltering banks to prevent bankruptcy. Furthermore, to prevent the spreading of banking failures, governments have also resorted to conjectural government guarantees to ensure the solvency of the banking system. Traditionally, in Mexico financial institutions and firms have maintained strong ties which have given rise to the formation of strong "groups" – sort of family owned conglomerates.[2] Protection from bankruptcy has also been strong both to financial and non-financial firms. Even now, as a result of Mexico's current crisis, the Mexican government has created a rescue package for the banking sector, the costs of which have risen to $83,900 million of new pesos so far, an estimated 5.1 percent of the 1995 domestic product.[3] But the economic panorama should change. Previously, during the 1988–94 period, the

231

government enforced significant financial deregulation and financial liberalization policies. As a response to the crisis, these have been widened. In addition, in spite of Mexico's economic crisis, integration with Canada and the United States should continue to be strong. Thus, as the current crisis subsides, the panorama should also become more competitive. Similarly, separation between financial institutions and industry is just emerging as a result of recent deregulation policies, and the reprivatization of the Mexican banking system is leading to the rise of "universal banking," an institutional framework also present in the Canadian financial system but absent in the United States. Similarly, as in the case of Canada, in Mexico banking institutions operate at a national scale, while in the United States banks operate at the state level, although some breakthroughs are underway.

Bankruptcy is usually the consequence of losses which can be caused either by systematic errors of management or by the competitive interaction of firms in an industry with positive economies of scale, i.e., operating with decreasing average costs. In fact, in this latter case, which has been thought to apply to the banking sector, the theory predicts that an oligopolistic price war could drive some of the competitors out of the market. In this context, financial liberalization and deregulation in Mexico are providing a more competitive environment. However, these policies might trigger a solvency crisis in the banking system due to adverse loan selection and moral hazard. In turn, this would influence the restructuring of the banking system which is occurring in Mexico.

Structural regulations in the banking sector have for a long time avoided the consequence of the competitive mechanism of price wars. Among the developed countries, Italy is an extreme example of this. Since the 1930s, regulations have created rigid barriers to entry and thus the industry has behaved more like a monopoly than an oligopoly (Barina, 1986; Canals, 1993; Strivens, 1992). Without the possibility of new entrants, collusion between banks has become an easy and profitable option. In Mexico, a similar situation prevailed as a result of overnationalistic policies which blocked the entrance of foreign financial institutions to the local market. Now, the NAFTA allows the gradual entrance of financial institutions from Canada and the United States to Mexico, and further liberalization policies will make possible the entry to the local market of institutions from other countries, particularly those in Europe.

Of course, in a situation where institutional regulations do not allow the free working of competitive forces, an efficient equilibrium may never be reached. Then, a natural monopoly arises. This is sustainable if there exists a price and output such that entry by potential competitors is unattractive, while all demand is satisfied and revenues cover total costs of production (Brown-Cruse, 1991).

A natural monopoly with a cost function $C(q)$ and market demand $D(p)$

232

is sustainable if there is a price p and output q such that: (1) $q = D(p)$; (2) $p.q = C(q)$; and $p'.q' < C(q')$ for all $p' < p$; and, (3) all $q' < D(p')$ (Brown-Cruse, 1991). This is a situation which characterizes over-regulated developing economies, or else where banking remains nationalized. Both situations have characterized the Mexican economy. Liberalization and deregulation should end it, but large banks would resist losing their market share.

In a situation of limited entry to the market the measure of performance of the industry is not based on the usual efficiency measures, but is assessed against two types of indicators: (1) indicators relating to the structure, such as the degree of concentration and demand elasticity; and (2) indicators relating to the behavior of firms *vis-à-vis* competitors, such as the strength of a collusive agreement or the speed of adjustment to rivals' moves. However, when there are large economies of scale, this approach can lead to contradictory results, since on the one hand an efficient scale of production is reached when a small number of firms are left in the market and on the other hand high industry concentration tends to lead to an equilibrium far from the competitive equilibrium. Costs thus tend to be higher than the minimum costs and consumer surplus is eroded; that is, an oligopolistic solution is reached.

The theory of perfectly contestable markets has not developed econometric specifications to test its validity for a particular industry. However, Stigler (1968) theorized that the behavior of firms in an industry may be simply derived from the degree of concentration measured by Herfindahl's index:

$$\sum_i^n \left(\frac{X_i}{X_n} \right)^2$$

where X_i = the i market share of the variable measured, and
   X_n = the total market value of the variable.

Results vary between $1/n$ and 1: 1 means total concentration, and $1/n$ an even distribution of the activities tested. Similarly, the inverse of the indexes measure shows the real number of entities participating in the activity being measured. Even distribution or perfect competition is given by n; the lack of it by $1 = 1$ actor. The larger the number of firms in an industry, the nearer the equilibrium is to a Cournot solution and the more difficult collusion becomes. In fact, oligopolistic competitors have unilateral incentives to break collusion agreements, and thus for a collusive behavior to continue successfully over time, some form of control is required (Berger *et al.* 1987; Panzar and Willig, 1977). The cost of applying this control increases with the number of firms and thus collusion becomes less likely as the number of participants increases. Furthermore, as Stigler (1986) has pointed out, with a large number of competitors it is

233

more difficult for a firm to determine whether fluctuations in the demand for its products is due to its competitors' aggressive policies or not. Thus, such a firm is more likely to react to a downward turn of its demand by breaking the agreement.

The structural regulations of the Bank of Italy, for example, have been based on Stigler's theory – not with reference to the national market as a whole, but to local markets. In fact, the Italian national market has been divided into a large number of small local markets and for each of them the authorities have determined the number of banks necessary to stimulate the achievement of a Cournot equilibrium rather than a collusive one. The opening of new outlets has thus been limited in those areas with a high Herfindahl index, causing a reduction of industrial concentration and of the monopoly power of the banks operating in those areas. The Mexican experience might resemble this situation. According to the degree of their coverage the banking system in Mexico has been divided into banks of national coverage, banks with multi-regional coverage, and banks with regional coverage, which should be taken fully into account by newly entering banks.

Contestability and opening of the Mexican banking system

With the opening of the Mexican market, Stigler's oligopoly theory is not really adequate to explain the possible structural changes, since it refers to an oligopolistic market where there is no entry. However, it can be applied to identify the structure of the banking sector before full financial deregulation and liberalization consolidates. This should help to design policies that promote competition and efficiency in the banking sector.

The freedom of entry of foreign banks into national markets makes Baumol et al. (1986) theory of contestable markets particularly relevant. Moreover, this theory is particularly appropriate for the banking industry because it is applicable to multiproduct firms.

The main characteristic of a contestable market is that the behavior of firms does not depend on the number of firms in the industry, but on the conditions of entry and exit. Competition not only refers to market forces inside the industry but also includes potential competition and the transferral of resources from less profitable sectors. For this mechanism to work fully there should be no sunk costs. Contestable markets tend to be efficient, since the freedom of entry has two effects in particular: it causes the exit from the industry of inefficient producers whose production costs are higher than those from potential producers; and the firms in the industry have to produce the quantity at which average costs are at a minimum to avoid the entry of potential competitors. It follows that firms will not earn any economic profits. If this 'hit-and-run' competition is not possible, the contestable solution breaks down and pockets of inefficiency can exist

(Baumol *et al.*, 1986; Brock, 1983; Spence, 1983; Diamond and Dybvig, 1983; Schwartz, 1986).

Since its original formulation, the theory of contestable markets has evolved to consider situations when the costs of exit and entry are not negligible. Although there is not as yet a rigorous formulation, some interesting results have already been achieved by Eaton and Ware (1987), who have developed a model of sequential entry. This formulation is of great relevance for the case of Mexico, for its integration with its Northern neighbors and financial opening to other countries is undoubtedly leading to a sequential entry of foreign competitors, each weighing the advantages and disadvantages of entering a newly opened market. More-over, unrelated but affecting banking structure, it is worth mentioning that the North American Free Trade Agreement contemplates a period of transition which will weigh on the decision to entry of foreign banking institutions to Mexico; albeit, the reforms implemented to overcome the crisis seem to favor a faster and smoother entry of foreign banks to the local scenery.

According to the sequential entry model, the potential entrant in an industry with n firms evaluates the benefits and costs of its entry and enter only if the profit gain is positive. Once part of the industry, all $n + 1$ firms will then have to face the competition of another potential entrant, and so on, until $n + k$ firms constitute an industry where entry becomes unprofi-table. Since profits from collusion are always positive when the number of firms is equal to the efficient number under conditions of competition, positive sunk costs will cause too much entry in the industry. In fact, sunk costs only stop entry when the process of sequential entry is com-pleted.

The main difference between perfect contestability and a model of sequential entry is in the fact that in the latter there is no risk of "hit-and-run" behavior, since the "run" phase is expensive. Thus a firm which enters an industry intends to stay in it and will fight to do so if necessary. The behavior of firms in this case resembles the traditional oligopolistic strategy, with the possibility of a price war. However, the probability of a price war decreases as sunk costs increase.

With high sunk costs, the only reasonable behavior is collusion, and thus potential entrants will expect to be able to gain collusive profits. This leads to the conclusion that the higher the sunk costs, the more likely is collusion and thus the larger is the number of firms in a position to earn positive profits.

According to the theory of contestable markets, when analyzing the structure of an industry with free entry and exit it is important to access the nature of possible sunk costs, since the presence of such costs will affect the behavior of the potential competitor, who needs to decide whether or not to enter the industry. Such costs are not just accounting,

235

but economic costs, and they not only refer to the costs that the bank may have to incur but also to the costs that the public would face if the bank's operations fold. In theory, we would need to extend this analysis to the whole of the productive process, as well as factor markets and product markets, and the structural characteristics of the banking industry.

BANKING AND NORTH AMERICAN ECONOMIC INTEGRATION

NAFTA has brought the possibility of the participation of US and Canadian financial institutions in Mexico. However, there are some limitations. Negotiations in this sector were complex and arduous. Their objective was to promote a flow of freer financial services among the three North American trade partners, which also means freer access of financial institutions of one nation to the markets of the other two nations. However, negotiations were complicated by sharp differences in goals and financial systems and institutions, and differences on their currencies.[4] The most important differences concerning financial institutions and their regulation are derived from the US McFadden and Stell-Glass laws which inhibit banking to state activity and clearly separate investment banking from commercial banking. Canada and Mexico, on the other hand, have national banking systems and are moving towards "universal" banking. On the second issue, the US dollar is the dominant currency in the regions and Canada and Mexico want to retain control on monetary policy-making.[5] In addition to these issues, differences existed because Mexico's financial system is just starting its new conformation, resulting from privatization and deregulation, moving to an industrial structure characterized by the presence of universal banking dominated by large "financial groups." As a result, during the negotiations the Mexican government aimed at obtaining auspicious provisos to ensure the development of domestic financial institutions, as well as to set a cap to the participation of foreign banks in the economy. These problems were solved with an agreement that contemplates national treatment, a programmed period of transition, restricted transborder services, safeguard clauses, and reviewing mechanisms for possible conflicts.

Chapter XIV from the NAFTA provides the principles applicable to financial services in banking, insurance, securities, and "other" financial services. Each country defines its specific liberalization commitments to the other countries, specifications of a transition period, and some safeguard provisions to the principles to be applied. In relation to the banking sector, Mexico's commitments are the following.

Canadian and US financial institutions can enter the Mexican market, but in a limited and gradual way. Most limits will be removed by the year 2000, although this process has been accelerated due to the current crisis, which is examined below. Canadian and US banks can only establish their operations in Mexico through subsidiaries, subject to national laws, as a prudential regulation to allow the local authorities full control on foreign banks, which would not be possible if branching from US headquarters were allowed.

Canadian and US banking institutions initially face an individual ceiling of 1.5 percent and on the aggregate of 8 percent of domestic capital. The aggregate limit will be increased gradually to 15 percent by the year 2000. After the year 2000 most limits will be relaxed, but Mexico reserves the right until 2004 to limit growth for three years if aggregates of Canadian and US banks move above 25 percent of domestic capital.

The individual cap of 1.5 percent must be removed by the year 2000 for banking institutions growing through internal funds, including allocations from the parent. However a 4 percent limit will be put in place. If a Canadian or US bank has interests of 0.5 percent in a Mexican bank, through a subsidiary, the foreign institutions will be allowed to buy a domestic bank that comprises 3.5 percent of the market, which then would total the maximum 4 percent share allowed. Acquisitions made after the transition will be subject to precautionary considerations, and a cap of 4 percent.

In the annexes, a 30 percent limit on common capital is fixed for joint investments carried out by Canadian and US investors in the commercial banking sector. This limit does not apply to investments made in foreign subsidiaries.

Concerning transborder services, the stipulations of the NAFTA give Mexico the right to keep current prohibitions and restrictions to transborder financial services, but Mexico is committed not to introduce any more restrictive rules. In addition, the stipulations in NAFTA allow the free provision of financial services to Mexican residents in transit, as well as for the acquisition of insurance related to tourism and the transport of goods in the host country.

It must also be pointed out that an informal agreement was reached to ensure that Mexico reviews fairly applications to enter Mexico made by Canadians and US parties. No preferences should be given to either party.

Finally, the NAFTA also includes a mechanism to settle disputes, which also applies to the financial sector. Dispute resolution panels will be composed of five members, who will be selected from a trinational roster of financial and legal experts when financial matters are involved. The panel should submit its resolution, confidentially, within 90 days, unless the disputing countries decide otherwise. The disputing parties will have 14 days to provide comments. The final report from the panel should be presented within 30 days of the presentation of the initial report. Countries should then agree to solve the dispute based on the recommendations of the panel. If a panel determines that the responding country has acted inconsistently to NAFTA obligations, and the disputing countries do not reach an agreement within a month (or some other agreed period), the complaining country has the right to suspend the specific benefits to the other country until the dispute is finally solved.

As previously pointed out, the NAFTA places some limits on foreign investments in the local market. However, as a measure to overcome the crisis, foreign participation in financial groups, banks, and brokerage houses has been increased to 49 percent, from the 30 percent cap; the entry of foreign intermediaries and the acquisition of local institutions by foreign institutions has also been promoted and eased. For example, the acquisition of local banks whose share of capital is below 6 percent of the total of the sector is now allowed.[6] Similarly, the aggregate foreign investment limit of 25 percent of domestic capital remains, but is applicable immediately instead of gradually increasing to the year 2004.

In short, the banking sector has remained highly protected in Mexico, in spite of significant liberalization and deregulation policies undertaken during the last few years, and in spite of economic integration with the United States and Canada. The crisis has promoted further liberalization and deregulation. However, as a share of local capital, foreign banks will not be able to grow beyond a 6 percent level on the individual level and 25 percent on the aggregate.

At any rate, concerning Mexico, the need for further real investments and the dynamics of their growth will most likely outgrow the limitations placed on financial investments. Thus, in the context of NAFTA, financial linkages and the participation of foreign banks in the economy should be strengthened to allow a more efficient allocation of financial resources in the region. Restraining financial and financial integration in the area could lead to investment diversions to other areas.

STRUCTURE OF THE MEXICAN BANKING SECTOR

Liberalization and privatization of the banking system

The structure of the Mexican financial system has changed significantly during the last two decades. Three events have influenced its changes: nationalization of the banking system in 1982; strong liberalization and deregulation policies implemented since 1988, which included reprivatization of the banking system; and integration of Mexico's financial markets with the US and Canadian financial markets and institutions.

Recent reforms comprised a complex set of goals meant to develop a stronger financial system capable of competing with international intermediaries and mobilizing international resources to the local economy. These goals can be summarized as follows:[7]

238

1 Financial liberalization; that is, eliminating financial repression and instrumenting money and credit policy through market operations and a central bank autonomous from the executive power.
2 Financial deregulation; that is, the elimination of restrictive supervision and the replacement of it by prudential supervision and rules that promote market activity.
3 Financial innovation which comprises the creation of new instruments for hedging against financial risks, as well as to promote higher levels of savings.
4 Strengthening financial intermediaries to allow them to service larger numbers of customers and offer a wide variety of services.
5 Privatizing commercial banks to end inhibitions to private participation in economic activity, as well as to promote a more efficient allocation of resources.
6 Ending compulsory mechanisms to finance government deficits, as well as promoting an increase in its financing with non-inflationary instruments through credit markets.
7 Internationalizing and integrating local markets, corporations and financial institutions to the international financial markets as a means to mobilize international resources to the local economy.

Privatization of the commercial banking sector started in 1990. The new Act of Financial Institutions established that each Mexican citizen be restricted to a maximum of 5 percent of the voting shares of a financial institution. Foreigners were restricted to the same percentage individually, and no more than 30 percent as a group in any financial institution.

The first step towards the sale of the government's controlling interest in Mexico's eighteen commercial banks began in late September 1990 with the announcement of a registration process for prospective buyers for three banks. According to the General Basis for the Sale of Government Banks, a committee was appointed to manage this issue. This committee had the responsibility of selling the banks to investors of unimpeachable character and high economic capacity, who in turn had to guarantee the distribution of shares among a large number of private investors. The government sold the banks through an auction system. Those people or groups making the highest bids in terms of the bank's net worth were awarded ownership of the bank offered for sale. It is worth noting that in this process, bidders were required to present a specific program for the development of the banking institution they were interested in. During 1991 nine banks were privatized, and nine banks were privatized in 1992. The largest three banks were sold towards the end of 1991 (Banamex and Bancomer) and early 1992 (Serfin). One important aspect that must be mentioned is that competition for the purchase of the banks was high to the point that investors paid high prices, which were reflected in the high price/book value indexes.

The sale of banks was closely linked to the formation of financial groups. In thirteen cases successful buyers were investment banks/brokerage houses; in two cases industrial groups; and in three cases independent entrepreneurs. New legislation passed at the end of 1990, reformed in 1993, contemplates three kind of financial groups: financial groups headed by a holding company; financial groups headed by a bank; and financial groups headed by a stock brokerage house. The financial group headed by a holding company will be the most widely used, since it permits investors to control both a bank and a stock brokerage house. In contrast, financial groups headed by a bank cannot own stock brokerage houses, nor can financial groups headed by a stock brokerage house own a bank.

One of the key changes brought about by state control was the consolidation of banking institutions. At nationalization there were fifty-nine institutions, which were consolidated into eighteen banks, which following privatization are fairly widely held and nationally owned. In addition, before privatization the banking system included one foreign bank, Citibank, and one bank of restricted membership, Banco Obrero. Citibank was limited in its operations to receiving and making foreign loans, although deregulation to widen its operations is moving fast. Similarly, Banco Obrero belongs to the largest workers union, Central de Trabajadores de Mexico.

It is worth noting, that in addition to government-led mergers, the expropriation of the banking sector in 1982 led to a dramatic reshuffling of financial resources and savings which was reflected in the rapid growth on non-banking institutions, especially brokerage houses. Thus, by 1991 when the government began to step back on nationalization, privatization offered brokerage firms a complementary business, and an important part for financial group development. That is why the most important brokerage houses become interested in purchasing banks. Thus, by the end of the privatization programs for banks, thirteen commercial banks were in the hands of groups led by stock brokerage houses, as previously mentioned.

Finally, it must be mentioned that the privatization of commercial banks coincided with the negotiations with Canada and the United States to establish a free trade bloc. This complicated the negotiations, for there was no firmly established banking sector to aid the government in the establishment of guidelines, as was the case in the agriculture, industrial and commercial sectors of the economy. Thus, upon the request of the emerging banking entrepreneurs, gradual opening was negotiated to allow a consolidation of the sector.

Structural trends following liberalization and privatization

The three most striking facts about the Mexican banking system are its high degree of concentration, its changing structure due to the entry of many new small banks, and its high degree of profitability in spite of high bad loans. As shown in Table 16.1, by the end of 1990 the largest bank, Banamex, accounted for nearly 25 percent of total bank assets. Moreover, assets for the three largest banks, Banamex, Bancomer, and Serfin, exceed 60 percent of total banking assets. Assets from the four largest institutions corresponded to almost 70 percent of total banking assets. This pattern of concentration has persisted in Mexico during all its contemporary history. Indeed, in the early 1950s, the four largest commercial banks accounted for 67.5 percent of total bank assets; by the end of the decade the share of assets of the four largest banks had slightly decreased to 66.7 percent (Goldsmith, 1976). Moreover, although from 1961 to 1974 there were ninety-four financial intermediaries, the banking sector behaved as if it was composed of seven to eleven intermediaries, using a Herfindahl's index (Newell, 1978).

This situation did not change significantly with the nationalization of the banking system in 1982. Nevertheless, it is worth mentioning that the government sought to promote economies of scale and greater efficiency by encouraging mergers among banks. Thus, by 1987 the banking system was consolidated into eighteen institutions, with a high degree of concentration. However, it is important to note that from the pre-privatization year of 1990 to the post privatization year of 1994 some important changes have taken place with regard to the participation of several banks in the system as a whole, measured by changes in assets and capital. Table 16.1 shows that Banamex, Bancomer, and Serfin have remained as the three most important commercial banks in Mexico. None the less, their share in total banking assets diminished somewhat, from 62.7 percent to 51.88 percent, a drop of near 11 points. The most important drop was that of Serfin, from 17.79 percent to 12.54 percent. Partly, this change in the importance of the largest banks is related to the entry of two new banks in 1993 and twelve new banks in 1994; however, it must be mentioned that two banks, Union and Cremi, are under government management due to fraudulent use of funds. Unfortunately, no financial information is released about these two institutions now.

The problem of high concentration in the Mexican banking sector is well measured by Herfindahl's index. Table 16.2 summarizes the results concerning assets, capital, profits, and costs. In all cases, the indexes show a high degree of concentration in the Mexican banking system. Indeed, the inverse of the indexes show that by 1990 the Mexican banking system behaved as if it was composed of only seven banks, from the real number of nineteen. This level of concentration is a bit higher once capital and profits are considered. Hence, it can be affirmed that a high concentration in capital favors concentration in profits. Since US and Canadian banks are limited in their size in respect to total capital in the market, many banks from those countries would not find it attractive to open subsidiaries in

Table 16.1 Concentration in the Mexican banking system (millions of new pesos)

Assets:	1990	%	Rank	1991	%	Rank	1992	%	1993	%	1994	%	Rank
Banamex	66,022.00	24.72	1	94,550.48	23.21	1	117,835.09	23.87	133,591.40	21.28	179,925.30	21.35	1
Bancomer	54,526.00	20.41	2	92,334.44	22.67	2	103,294.65	20.93	112,227.70	17.88	151,579.70	17.99	2
Serfin	46,923.00	17.57	3	68,147.34	16.73	3	65,389.95	13.25	66,434.40	10.58	105,698.20	12.54	3
Comermex	17,600.00	6.59	4	24,483.40	6.01	4	30,695.01	6.22	37,869.70	6.03	52,791.10	6.27	5
Internacional	15,376.00	5.76	5	23,698.06	5.82	5	26,926.71	5.45	36,348.10	5.79	42,371.70	5.03	6
Mexicano	11,830.00	4.43	6	13,896.64	3.41	6	25,243.89	5.11	43,388.00	6.91	58,557.60	6.95	4
Mercantil Probursa	7,069.00	2.65	7	10,365.68	2.54	7	13,756.49	2.79	27,131.30	4.32	19,962.60	2.37	13
Atlantico	6,895.00	2.58	8	10,554.14	2.59	8	18,057.14	3.66	24,532.50	3.91	42,103.90	5.00	7
Bancreser	5,811.00	2.18	9	11,661.28	2.86	9	9,527.89	1.93	16,019.70	2.55	20,266.80	2.41	12
Union	5,323.00	1.95	10	6,533.81	1.60	10	12,165.05	2.46	21,556.00	3.43	/*	0.00	
Confia	5,299.00	1.95	11	7,382.78	1.81	11	10,185.02	2.06	12,541.70	2.00	22,032.50	2.61	10
Cremi	4,994.00	1.87	12	8,800.14	2.16	12	13,507.80	2.74	15,465.00	2.46	/*	0.00	
Mercantil del Norte	4,141.00	1.55	13	5,835.31	1.43	13	8,471.71	1.72	12,713.70	2.03	20,405.10	2.42	11
Banpais	3,344.00	1.25	14	3,884.24	0.95	14	12,226.23	2.48	26,712.70	4.26	34,240.90	4.06	8
Promex	3,089.00	1.16	15	4,303.22	1.06	16	4,895.14	0.99	11,918.30	1.90	27,199.60	3.23	9
Centro	2,489.00	0.93	16	3,617.08	0.89	17	4,390.86	0.89	8,003.10	1.27	19,674.20	2.33	14
Banoro	2,187.00	0.82	17	3,689.35	0.91	18	4,286.96	0.87	4,982.80	0.79	10,379.60	1.23	16
Oriente	890.00	0.33	18	1,381.29	0.34	19	2,382.61	0.48	3,521.40	0.56	3,922.70	0.47	18
Obrero	3,324.00	1.24		4,178.00	1.03	15	3,127.00	0.63	3,522.00	0.56	3,861.90	0.46	19
Citibank	N.A.			8,047.20	1.98		7,271.00	1.47	8,691.00	1.38	10,872.50	1.29	15
Interestatal									271.80	0.04	712.60	0.08	24
Interacciones									284.50	0.05	1,843.30	0.22	21
Inbursa											7,031.00	0.83	17
Capital											1,529.10	0.18	22
Industrial											2,021.70	0.24	20

Bank	Value (267,132.00)	%	Rank	Rank	Value (407,343.88)	%	Value (493,636.20)	%	Value (627,726.80)	%	Value (842,597.20)	%	Rank
Promotor del Norte											255.80	0.03	29
Mifel											347.30	0.04	26
Invex											338.40	0.04	28
Del Sureste											1,356.40	0.16	23
Banregio											355.10	0.04	27
Del Bajio											129.00	0.02	32
Quadrum											214.20	0.03	30
Fimsa											158.50	0.02	31
Santander											458.90	0.05	25
Total	267,132.00				407,343.88		493,636.20		627,726.80		842,597.20		
Capital:													
Banamex	4,833.00	29.75	1	1	6,521.31	29.58	8,232.72	27.05	10,408.20	26.33	10,942.70	24.50	1
Bancomer	4,401.00	27.09	2	2	5,939.80	26.94	7,836.27	25.75	9,055.70	22.91	8,734.40	19.55	2
Serfin	1,774.00	10.92	3	3	2,060.56	9.35	2,659.37	8.74	4,020.50	10.17	4,502.80	10.08	3
Comermex	765.00	4.71	4	4	1,089.00	4.94	1,415.25	4.65	1,524.70	3.86	2,086.30	4.67	5
Internacional	621.00	3.82	5	5	842.89	3.82	1,408.35	4.63	1,585.40	4.01	1,854.10	4.15	7
Mexicano	471.00	2.90	7	7	683.78	3.10	1,396.71	4.59	1,723.40	4.36	2,100.10	4.70	4
Mercantil Probursa	268.00	1.65	14	14	377.83	1.71	597.02	1.96	837.20	2.12	735.10	1.65	15
Atlantico	323.00	1.99	10	10	420.01	1.91	864.62	2.84	1,604.30	4.06	1,489.20	3.33	8
Bancreser	139.00	0.86	17	17	272.96	1.24	529.28	1.74	762.50	1.93	857.20	1.92	14
Union	326.00	2.01	9	9	363.01	1.65	1,024.30	3.37	1,282.00	3.24	/*		
Confia	242.00	1.49	15	15	384.51	1.74	560.60	1.84	680.60	1.72	893.80	2.00	13
Cremi	307.00	1.89	12	12	347.81	1.58	606.96	1.99	871.00	2.20	/*		
Mercantil del Norte	474.00	2.92	6	6	694.58	3.15	790.90	2.60	1,044.50	2.64	1,207.30	2.70	10
Banpais	166.00	1.02	16	16	284.33	1.29	664.18	2.18	1,118.30	2.83	1,250.00	2.80	9
Promex	305.00	1.88	13	13	436.33	1.98	487.33	1.60	767.70	1.94	1,022.90	2.29	11
Centro	318.00	1.96	11	11	373.15	1.69	281.18	0.92	469.70	1.19	615.40	1.38	17

Table 16.1 Continued

Capital:	1990	%	Rank	1991	%	Rank	1992	%	1993	%	1994	%	Rank
Banoro	437.00	2.69	8	608.81	2.76	8	556.96	1.83	730.50	1.85	655.50	1.47	16
Oriente	73.00	0.45	18	106.59	0.48	19	127.15	0.42	173.70	0.44	243.40	0.54	21
Obrero	109.00	0.67	18	177.60	0.81	18	285.70	0.94	255.70	0.65	317.00	0.71	18
Citibank				61.40	0.28		108.00	0.35	222.20	0.56	981.30	2.20	12
Interestatal									129.00	0.33	120.00	0.27	32
Interacciones									268.90	0.68	237.90	0.53	22
Inbursa											1,967.00	4.40	6
Capital											274.70	0.62	19
Industrial											123.40	0.28	28
Promotor del Norte											129.20	0.29	27
Mifel											121.30	0.27	30
Invex											153.60	0.34	25
Del Sureste											121.30	0.27	31
Banregio											194.30	0.44	24
Del Bajio											122.70	0.27	29
Quadrum											211.30	0.47	23
Fimsa											149.50	0.33	26
Santander											251.70	0.56	20
Total	16,243.00			22,046.26			30,432.85		39,535.70		44,666.40		

Source: Developed by the authors from information from Comision Nacional Bancaria, *Boletin Estadistico de Banca Multiple*, various issues, 1992–4.
Note: * No information released. Currently under government management (but not nationalized).

Table 16.2 Indexes of banking concentration in Mexico

	1990	1991	1992	1993	1994
Herfindahl's index:					
Assets	0.15	0.15	0.13	0.11	0.11
Capital	0.18	0.18	0.16	0.14	0.12
Profits	0.18	0.24	0.23	0.14	0.14
Costs	0.13	0.13	0.12	0.11	0.11
Inverse:					
Assets	6.8	6.86	7.49	9.13	8.8
Capital	5.46	5.62	6.3	6.95	8.21
Profits	5.51	4.13	4.4	7.32	6.99
Costs	7.61	7.68	8.01	9.23	9.18

Source: Developed from information in Table 16.1.

Mexico, for their activities and profits would be limited. This in turn would have an adverse impact on Mexico's long run growth.

At any rate, liberalization has seemingly led to a positive change towards a more competitive situation. This has allowed some medium and even some small banks to increase their importance markedly. In relation to assets and capital, Banco Mexicano climbed up two positions from sixth to fourth in importance; Banco Atlantico moved up one place to a ranking of seventh in relation to assets. On the contrary Banco Mercantil Probursa dropped from 7th to 13th. Finally, concerning the new entries, it is worth noting that all banks are very small; the only one that stands out is Inbursa, with a ranking of seventeen among the existing thirty-two banks. This situation is well captured by Herfindahl's index. Thanks to financial liberalization, deregulation, and privatization, the banking system now behaves as if it was composed of nine banks. But by 1994 the number of banks had increased to thirty-two, which suggests that both old and new small banks play a modest role in the economy.

Although these changes are important, they do not seem large enough to alter significantly the highly concentrated structure of the Mexican banking system, at least in a short and medium run horizon. However, high concentration is not a characteristic of the Mexican banking sector alone in the North American bloc. In Canada, the five largest banks accounted for 87 percent of total banking assets in the mid-1980s (Shaffer, 1993). Similarly, although in the US there are nearly 9,600 banks, albeit decreasing in number, considerable concentration in assets and capital can be found in the ten largest banks: the four largest account for 56.4 percent of the total capital (Giron, 1995). Indeed, it is important to note that high concentration might not necessarily be an indicator of sustainability if the entry of new institutions is not blocked. Considering the stipulations of the NAFTA, it is worth noting that due to the limits on the size of capital of foreign banks, the three largest banks, Banamex, Bancomer, and Serfin cannot be acquired by foreign banks – their individual size exceeds 6 percent of the market, which according to Mexican authorities ensures that the payments system remains in the hands of Mexican nationals.[8] However, considering that the share of capital from an individual foreign bank has been raised to 6 percent of the total market capital, US and Canadian banks could reach a substantial size, which would allow them to achieve economies of scale and scope. In addition they could be ranked among the ten most important banks, but below the three most important domestic banks. For most foreign banks, however, the situation would be tight and they would remain small, ranking below the ten most important banks. Although, US and Canadian banks can find some special niches in which to open up their subsidiaries in Mexico, this situation stresses the need to continue the strengthening of the domestic banking system and to open the local market further to foreign intermediaries if high goals concerning trade, investments, and international savings mobilization are to be attained.

The performance of Mexican banks was severely affected by the economic "deceleration" and crisis of 1994. From 1990 to 1993 profits increased from $3,006.21 million new pesos to $8,742.20 million new pesos by 1993, a growth rate of 191 percent, well ahead of the 38.7 percent accumulated rate of inflation for the 1991–3 period. Similarly, in the first year (1993) after the privatization process ended, profits increased by 36.17 percent, above the 8 percent rate of inflation for that year. This situation is confirmed by the steady growth in the financial margin of all banks. The mean financial margin in 1990 was 5.66 percent with a standard deviation of 5.11 points. During the process of privatization, mostly during 1991 and 1992, banks improved their profits, reflecting efforts made by the government to strengthen these institutions and to sell them under favorable conditions. After the privatization process ended, profits continued to rise, as is shown by the results obtained in 1993. The financial margin increased to 7.54 percent on average, with a standard deviation of 4.20 points. The extreme cases are very revealing. Although the largest banks obtained higher than average profits, the extremes can be identified with the smallest banks. Banoro's profit margin was 15.56 percent, while Bancentro registered slightly above 0.5 percent as its profit margin for 1993. This situation did not fully reflect in the net margin. It dropped to less than 5 percent during 1991 and 1992. The following year the net margin increased to 6.92 percent, following privatization.

Profits decreased dramatically in 1994. As shown in Table 16.3, profits, in current pesos, dropped from 8,793.5 million new pesos in 1993 to only 3,722.6 million new pesos in 1994, a drop of 57.7 percent (which excludes profits of the two banks taken over by the government, but includes profits from the twelve entries in 1994; the inflation rate was 7.05 percent). For instance, the index of net profits to financial revenues dropped for the

Table 16.3 Key financial trends in Mexican banking (millions of new pesos and ratios)

	Profits (a)					Total costs				
	1990	1991	1992	1993	1994	1990	1991	1992	1993	1994
Banamex	1,004.87	1,406.35	2,260.12	2,307.0	904.6	12,642.95	13,991.0	15,848.0	18,761.9	21,128.6
Bancomer	633.90	1,201.53	1,814.05	1,816.0	866.1	13,259.40	16,941.0	19,895.0	21,425.0	23,707.0
Serfin	349.74	375.29	474.13	885.0	78.0	10,983.26	11,711.0	11,645.0	12,604.0	14,948.0
Comermex	172.54	197.29	160.76	325.0	176.2	4,200.00	4,631.0	4,912.0	5,880.0	6,890.6
Internacional	95.85	−290.09	256.82	391.0	162.7	3,072.49	3,991.0	4,563.0	5,392.0	6,273.5
Mexicano	−67.97	111.77	154.11	475.0	57.1	2,790.93	3,264.0	4,258.0	7,985.0	9,815.2
Mercantil										N.A.
Probursa	54.97	45.98	121.57	310.1	−74.9	2,042.06	1,770.9	2,146.5	3,459.9	3,512.4
Atlantico	58.00	87.81	127.04	326.0	123.2	2,903.34	2,787.3	3,549.2	6,074.5	8,181.6
Bancreser	1.54	38.94	75.50	376.9	233.8	1,003.12	1,601.1	2,151.2	2,444.1	3,508.3
Union	58.50	36.38	110.56	255.1	N.A.	1,294.19	1,686.6	2,257.1	3,494.9	N.A.
Confia	69.99	106.88	70.41	161.6	141.1	1,449.74	1,771.9	2,135.0	2,395.8	3,167.7
Cremi	54.56	62.05	149.06	144.7	N.A.	1,477.43	1,984.5	2,109.3	3,425.1	N.A.
Mercantil del Norte	170.45	184.76	222.31	318.5	338.8	1,114.45	1,148.4	1,551.1	2,081.2	2,656.6
Banpais	41.02	18.92	72.94	210.0	14.0	942.10	852.1	1,884.0	3,552.5	4,989.9
Promex	101.17	95.87	122.39	200.1	253.1	1,027.78	1,106.3	1,276.6	1,843.8	3,167.9
Centro	80.55	100.02	70.04	5.6	50.3	845.51	714.8	847.6	1,071.5	2,175.0
Banoro	111.79	139.06	137.02	191.7	159.9	470.25	641.0	917.8	1,062.4	1,685.9
Oriente	14.74	15.89	22.23	42.9	25.3	308.93	341.3	478.1	717.7	859.0
Obrero	12.75	17.70	−146.50	20.8	−20.2	796.15	643.7	623.0	714.5	717.8
Citibank	N.A.	7.40	−7.30	26.0	110.2	N.A.	1,654.8	1,374.8	1,299.3	1,244.5
Interestatal				3.8	−12.1				92.7	76.3
Interacciones				0.7	11.5				3.5	183.8
Inbursa					151.9					540.1
Capital					22.0					77.7
Industrial					2.1					211.8
Promotor del Notre					7.4					24.7
Mifel					1.3					23.3
Invex					2.9					24.2
Del Sureste					3.4					141.3
Banregio					14.3					19.9
Del Bajio					2.7					8.5
Quadrum					5.1					20.9
Fimsa					−0.9					14.9
Santander					−88.3					60.3
Total	3,018.96	3,959.80	6,266.56	8,793.50	3,722.60	62,624.08	73,233.70	84,222.30	105,781.33	120,057.20
Average										
D. Standard										

Table 16.3 Continued

	Net profit/financial revenue %					Net profit/total revenue %					Profits/Assets %				
	1990	1991	1992	1993	1994	1990	1991	1992	1993	1994	1990	1991	1992	1993	1994
Banamex	7.90	10.08	12.67	10.72	4.18	7.09	8.74	10.73	8.79	3.52	1.52	1.49	1.92	1.73	0.50
Bancomer	4.65	6.92	8.89	7.90	3.86	4.25	6.27	7.81	7.05	3.19	1.16	1.30	1.76	1.62	0.57
Serfin	3.26	3.33	4.05	6.77	0.52	2.99	2.96	3.61	6.13	0.46	0.75	0.55	0.73	1.33	0.07
Comermex	4.11	4.42	3.30	5.33	2.53	3.84	3.89	2.90	4.82	2.22	0.98	0.81	0.52	0.86	0.33
Internacional	3.15	-7.56	5.73	6.77	2.67	2.97	-6.89	4.91	6.02	2.3	0.62	-1.22	0.95	1.08	0.38
Mexicano	-2.54	3.58	3.70	6.04	0.03	-2.34	3.13	3.35	5.49	0.03	-0.57	0.80	0.61	1.09	0.10
Mercantil Probursa	2.74	2.73	5.53	8.63	-2.19	2.59	2.46	5.11	8.03	-1.99	0.78	0.44	0.88	1.14	-0.38
Atlantico	2.12	3.27	3.60	5.20	1.56	1.94	3	3.31	4.83	1.34	0.84	0.83	0.70	1.33	0.29
Bancreser	0.16	2.41	3.38	13.89	5.80	0.15	2.32	3.25	12.74	5.2	0.03	0.33	0.79	2.35	1.15
Union	4.51	2.17	4.96	6.84	N.A.	4.21	2.05	4.55	6.43	N.A.	1.10	0.56	0.91	1.18	N.A.
Confia	5.32	6.78	3.24	6.31	4.15	4.5	5.5	3.00	5.93	3.78	1.32	1.45	0.69	1.29	0.64
Cremi	3.74	3.85	7.48	4.38	N.A.	3.5	3.49	6.74	4.11	N.A.	1.09	0.71	1.10	0.94	N.A.
Mercantil del Norte	14.05	14.83	13.56	13.68	11.00	13.12	13.41	12.28	12.41	9.83	4.12	3.17	2.62	2.51	1.66
Banpais	4.75	2.38	3.79	5.71	0.28	4.12	2.07	3.54	5.28	0.25	1.23	0.49	0.59	0.79	0.04
Promex	9.20	8.20	9.09	10.18	7.25	8.76	7.66	8.34	9.06	6.75	3.28	2.23	2.50	1.68	0.93
Centro	9.17	13.08	7.99	0.52	2.33	8.56	11.78	7.17	0.46	2.08	3.24	2.77	1.60	0.07	0.26
Banoro	20.81	18.89	13.12	15.56	7.66	18.82	17.16	12.05	14.52	7.04	5.11	3.77	3.20	3.85	1.54
Oriente	4.83	4.77	5.04	5.63	2.94	4.37	4.26	4.16	5.24	2.69	1.66	1.15	0.93	1.22	0.64
Obrero				3.38	-3.26	1.57	2.59	-22.10	2.74	-2.82	0.38	0.42	-4.69	0.59	-0.52
Citibank				2.34	9.94	N.A.	0.44	-0.54	1.93	7.58		0.09	-0.10	0.30	1.01
Interestatal				3.38	-6.68				3.17	-6.07				1.40	-1.70
Interacciones				16.67	8.47				17.17	5.82				0.25	0.62
Inbursa					19.74					18.59					2.16
Capital					23.35					22.06					1.44
Industrial					1.03					0.98					0.10
Promotor del Norte					23.13					22.83					2.89
Mifel					5.00					5.4					0.37
Invex					10.74					10.16					0.86
Del Sureste					2.81					2.34					0.25
Banregio					46.56					41.83					4.03
Del Bajio					24.78					24.42					2.09
Quadrum					45.95					18.73					2.38
Fimsa					-9.09					-3.23					-0.57
Santander					N.A.					N.A.					-19.24
Total															
Average	5.66	5.79	6.62	7.54	8.23	5.00	4.81	4.21	6.92	7.01	1.51	1.11	0.91	1.30	0.15
D. Standard	5.11	5.68	3.44	4.20	12.97	4.63	5.01	6.84	4.05	10.16	1.39	1.12	1.51	0.81	3.71

	Employees					Employment change (%)				
	1990	1991	1992	1993	1994	1990	1991	1992	1993	1994
Banamex	31,315	31,964	36,965	33,385	32,609	6.22	2.07	15.65	-9.68	-2.32
Bancomer	37,041	36,414	39,051	35,028	30,706	4.36	-1.69	7.24	-10.30	-12.34
Serfin	22,201	21,919	18,418	18,832	18,319	8.64	-1.27	-15.97	2.25	-2.72
Comermex	12,170	11,411	10,621	11,620	10,338	-0.32	-6.24	-6.92	9.41	-11.03
Internacional	11,337	11,521	10,113	10,094	8,475	-8.10	1.62	-12.22	-0.19	-16.04
Mexicano	7,327	7,265	7,155	7,138	7,435	0.99	-0.85	-1.51	-0.24	4.16
Mercantil Probursa	3,466	3,362	3,690	4,069	3,687	2.03	-3.00	9.76	10.27	-9.39
Atlantico	7,370	7,088	6,326	6,185	5,427	5.81	-3.83	-10.75	-2.23	-12.26
Bancreser	2,389	2,509	2,363	2,529	3,288	2.40	5.02	-5.82	7.02	30.01
Union	4,503	4,734	4,566	5,662	N.A.	4.99	5.13	-3.55	24.00	N.A.
Confia	3,808	4,016	4,197	3,860	4,292	3.85	5.46	4.51	-8.03	11.19
Cremi	4,780	4,464	3,964	3,911	N.A.	-5.92	-6.61	-11.20	-1.34	N.A.
Mercantil del Norte	3,599	3,912	3,871	4,158	4,355	12.01	8.70	-1.05	7.41	4.74
Banpais	3,080	3,094	3,651	4,409	2,950	3.70	0.45	18.00	20.76	-33.09
Promex	4,061	4,088	3,549	3,864	4,065	-1.98	0.66	-13.18	8.88	5.20
Centro	2,884	2,680	2,631	2,655	3,031	4.23	-7.07	-1.83	0.91	14.16
Banoro	2,932	2,993	2,546	2,075	2,466	1.91	2.08	-14.93	-18.50	18.84
Oriente	857	791	817	1,011	1,156	11.30	-7.70	3.29	23.75	14.34
Obrero	1,086	1,350	1,350	1,126	1,036	10.25	24.31	0.00	-16.59	-7.99
Citibank	N.A.	487	564	727	968		N.A.	15.81	28.90	33.15
Interestatal				N.A	396				N.A.	N.A.
Interacciones				N.A	138				N.A.	N.A.
Inbursa					N.A.					N.A.
Capital					N.A.					N.A.
Industrial					242					N.A.
Promotor del Norte					2					N.A.
Mifel					45					N.A.
Invex					6					N.A.
Del Sureste					113					N.A.
Banregio					66					N.A.
Del Bajio					38					N.A.
Quadrum					0					N.A.
Fimsa					89					N.A.
Santander					N.A.					N.A.
Total	166,206.00	166,062.00	166,408.00	162,338.00	145,738.00					
Average						3.44	-0.09	0.2	2.45	-10.22
D. standard										

Table 16.3 Continued

	Profit/employee (b)					Total costs/employee (c)				
	1990	1991	1992	1993	1994	1990	1991	1992	1993	1994
Banamex	3.21	4.40	6.11	6.91	2.77	40.37	43.77	42.87	56.20	64.79
Bancomer	1.71	3.30	4.65	5.18	2.82	35.80	46.52	50.43	61.17	77.21
Serfin	1.58	1.71	2.57	4.70	0.43	49.47	53.43	63.23	66.93	81.60
Comermex	1.42	1.73	1.51	2.80	1.70	34.51	40.58	46.25	50.60	66.65
Internacional	0.85	-2.52	2.54	3.87	1.92	27.10	34.64	45.12	53.42	74.02
Mexicano	-0.93	1.54	2.15	6.65	0.77	38.09	44.93	59.51	111.87	132.01
Mercantil Probursa	1.59	1.37	3.29	7.62	-2.03	58.92	52.67	58.17	85.03	95.28
Atlantico	0.79	1.24	2.01	5.27	2.27	39.39	39.32	56.10	98.21	150.76
Bancreser	0.06	1.55	3.20	14.90	7.11	41.99	63.81	91.04	96.64	106.70
Union	1.30	0.77	2.42	4.51	N.A.	28.74	35.63	49.43	61.73	N.A.
Confia	1.84	2.66	1.68	4.19	3.29	38.07	44.12	50.87	62.07	73.80
Cremi	1.14	1.39	3.76	3.70	N.A.	30.91	44.46	53.21	87.58	N.A.
Mercantil del Norte	4.74	4.72	5.74	7.66	7.78	30.97	29.36	40.07	50.05	61.00
Banpais	1.33	0.61	1.98	4.76	0.47	30.59	27.54	51.60	80.57	169.15
Promex	2.49	2.35	3.45	5.18	6.23	25.31	27.08	35.97	47.72	77.93
Centro	2.79	3.73	2.66	0.21	1.66	29.32	26.67	32.22	40.36	71.76
Banoro	3.81	4.65	5.38	9.24	6.48	16.04	21.42	36.05	51.20	68.37
Oriente	1.72	2.01	2.72	4.24	2.19	36.05	43.15	58.52	70.99	74.31
Obrero	1.17	1.31	-10.85	1.85	-1.95	73.31	47.68	48.15	63.45	69.29
Citibank	N.A.	1.52	-1.29	3.58	11.38	N.A.	339.79	243.76	178.72	128.56
Interestatal				N.A.	-3.06					19.27
Interacciones				N.A.	8.33					133.19
Inbursa					N.A.					N.A.
Capital					N.A.					N.A.
Industrial					0.87					87.52
Promotor del Norte					N.A.					N.A.
Mifel					2.89					51.78
Invex					48.33					403.33
Del Sureste					3.01					125.04
Banregio					21.67					30.15
Del Bajio					7.11					22.37
Quadrum					N.A.					N.A.
Fimsa					-1.01					16.74
Santander					N.A.					N.A.
Total	18,164	23,845	37,658	54,168	25,543	376,786	441,002	506,119	651,612	823,788
Average										
D. standard										

	Bad loans/total loans %					Number of accounts					Number of branches				
	1990	1991	1992	1993	1994	1990	1991	1992	1993	1994	1990	1991	1992	1993	1994
Banamex	2.36	5.60	6.11	7.37	8.37	8,919,607	8,996,447	1,045,566	1,018,600	1,014,565	726	720	630	691	710
Bancomer	3.11	3.45	5.23	7.49	7.26	6,019,018	5,208,155	5,175,274	5,348,000	5,790,786	762	742	765	855	876
Serfin	2.07	4.12	6.43	8.93	8.69	2,479,300	1,857,140	1,952,526	2,301,100	2,134,679	618	608	597	595	561
Comermex	1.46	2.22	5.59	8.66	7.58	1,004,552	999,232	809,780	1,009,400	1,052,053	344	346	349	361	342
Internacional	2.67	2.86	5.88	9.68	10.61	1,136,078	1,058,212	950,918	301,000	374,031	365	363	326	348	450
Mexicano	5.62	6.55	4.49	6.25	5.66	726,925	711,668	636,875	546,700	384,389	316	329	329	237	230
Mercantil Probursa	1.00	1.43	2.02	3.78	6.56	126,010	147,041	159,664	167,584	180,187	92	98	110	125	143
Atlantico	1.95	2.78	4.75	8.23	9.43	444,585	439,562	408,595	306,678	281,263	204	204	207	208	205
Bancreser	2.27	2.85	4.75	4.32	6.08	96,195	93,262	67,835	84,340	116,164	68	70	74	169	341
Union	6.28	6.98	6.33	7.65	N.A.	246,881	230,281	195,378	242,144	N.A.	130	118	125	145	N.A.
Confia	2.26	3.60	4.82	5.43	4.99	315,062	293,699	280,939	280,304	295,903	121	123	137	149	233
Cremi	1.13	1.79	2.67	7.17	N.A.	195,885	204,462	199,531	207,033	N.A.	117	115	114	121	N.A.
Mercantil del Norte	1.72	2.50	2.06	3.84	3.79	200,335	181,442	198,515	211,780	256,817	120	128	130	147	155
Banpais	3.59	3.57	2.34	3.35	6.25	148,707	141,340	162,148	178,354	192,672	100	102	123	149	163
Promex	3.94	5.51	6.99	5.08	5.05	636,931	571,202	533,162	516,200	506,940	154	153	153	162	199
Centro	6.64	6.86	13.55	8.56	5.94	304,078	271,214	225,008	217,633	206,721	104	130	130	127	109
Banoro	1.75	3.27	5.83	9.28	5.76	199,616	125,978	104,019	82,920	113,538	73	74	71	71	203
Oriente	2.60	9.59	9.53	8.02	11.28	43,099	33,786	36,464	37,105	43,734	38	38	47	50	53
Obrero	1.06	12.30	17.47	16.40	15.12	82,169	29,759	31,129	33,371	41,470	25	23	24	23	24
Citibank	N.A.	0.09	0.20	0.10	1.13	N.A.	2,515	3,726	15,432	30,600	N.A.	6	6	6	6
Interestatal				2.77	3.42					9,004				N.A.	22
Interacciones				0.00	3.42					205				N.A.	2
Inbursa					0.02					433					3
Capital					0.00					925					1
Industrial					0.02					4,265					8
Promotor del Norte					0.00					30					8
Mifel					0.00					N.A.					1
Invex				0.54	0.54					1					1
Del Sureste					0.00					3,510					2
Banregio					0.00					754					1
Del Bajio					0.00					106					1
Quadrum					0.00					N.A.					N.A.
Fimsa										3					1
Santander										16					7
Total						23,325,031	21,596,397	13,177,052	13,105,678	13,016,512	4,477	4,490	4,447	4,739	5,061
Average	2.81	4.40	5.85	6.47	4.30										
D. standard	1.65	2.85	3.87	3.50	4.14										

Source: Developed by the authors from information from Comision Nacional Bancaria, *Boletin Estadisco de Banca Multiple*, various issues, 1992–4.
Notes: (a) Monetary amounts in millions of new pesos (b) Individual banks per 10,000 employees (c) Individual banks per 10,000 employees.

largest bank, Banamex, from 10.72 percent in 1994 to 4.18 percent in 1994; similarly, the net margin dropped from 8.79 to 3.52 percent. However, for the banking sector the financial margin increased from 7.54 percent in 1993 to 8.23 percent in 1994, and the net margin increased from 6.92 percent to 7.01 percent, with a sharp increase in the standard deviation to 12.97 revealing a great dispersion in gains and losses. But those results are biased. Using consolidated data for the entire banking system, the financial margin fell from 7.97 percent in 1993 to 3.05 percent in 1994; the net margin also decreased from 7.05 percent to 2.63 percent.[9]

The fall in profits was also reflected in a sharp fall in the productivity of assets. The ratio of profits to assets fell dramatically to 0.15 percent in 1994. At its highest point, this ratio was ten times higher in 1990. Nevertheless, it is important to note that the fall in profits and in the productivity of assets cannot be traced to the crisis alone. Indications of decline have been present since 1991.

Increases in profit margins were accompanied with very high increases in profits per employee. From an average of $18,164 new pesos of profits per employee in 1990, the banking system moved to $54,168 new pesos of profits per employee by 1993 ($39,054 in real terms).[10] Some cost control can be discerned in that change. However, it cannot be attributed to changes in personnel alone. Indeed, as Table 16.3 shows, following privatization, the number of employees decreased only slightly till 1993. Moreover, it can be discerned that during the privatization years significant decreases in employment occurred as a result of the government efforts to strengthen the banks, and in this case sell them free from possible undesirable labor problems. Nevertheless, in addition to the adjustments made by the government during the privatization period, it appears that privatized banks made significant adjustments of their own. Three policies have been implemented. First, increasing the number of employees received from the government as a means to strengthen efficiency and operations, and then introduce selective labor cuts. This seems to have been the strategy followed by some banks such as Banamex and Bancomer, the most important Mexican banks. Second, other banks have preferred to maintain and continue the labor adjustments introduced by the government, although in most cases it has meant modest increases in personnel. Third, surprisingly, some medium and small banks have chosen to increase their personnel significantly, such as in the case of Oriente and Banpais. However, the latter also increased its participation in total banking assets and capital, as examined earlier. Finally, it must be also mentioned that in addition to these adjustments, banks also tried to adjust their personnel by hiring more skilled workers. Thus, it can be concluded that privatization has led to some important shake-outs in employment in the banking sector.

Taking into account the preceding trends, it seems that due to the crisis during 1994 the banking sector made sharp cuts in personnel rather indiscriminately, in an effort to diminish costs and generate profits. Eight out of the sixteen privatized banks (eighteen minus the two intervened in) made substantial cuts in their personnel. The largest cut in relative terms was that of Banpais, −33.09 percent. But Bancreser showed the opposite tendency – an increase of 30.01 percent in the number of employees. Overall employment in the banking sector decreased by 10.22 percent, using consolidated data. Nevertheless, profits per employee plunged to 25,543 new pesos during 1994.

Costs tended to increase significantly, in spite of cuts in the number of employees. On aggregate, costs increased from $62,624.08 million new pesos in 1990 to $105,781.3 million new pesos by 1993, which as in the case of profits was higher than inflation rates. Real growth of costs increased by 21.8 percent for the 1990–3 period. During 1994, total costs for the banking sector decreased dramatically, reflecting lower levels of activity. However, in relative terms this fall was insufficient to improve the situation. Employment decreased by 10.22 percent in 1994. None the less, costs per employee continued its rising trend from 376,786 new pesos per employee in 1990, to $651,611 new pesos by 1993 and 823,788 new pesos in 1994. Thus, cost per employee tended to increase at a faster rate than profits per employee.

Similarly, bad loans have increased sharply following liberalization and privatization. From an average of 2.81 percent of bad loans in 1990, bad loans in 1993 averaged 6.47 percent, with a standard deviation of 3.5 points, tending to increase throughout the years. Furthermore, the non-performing credits from the largest banks reached undesirable levels above 7 percent; for some other banks bad loans accounted for almost 10 percent of their credit portfolio. During 1994 the situation improved because new entries hardly had any bad loans. Taking away their results, for the eighteen privatized banks, plus Banco Obrero, Citibank and the two entries of 1994, which began incurring overdue loans in their second year of operation, bad loans averaged 6.82 percent – a slight increase from 1993.

Credit failures resulted from a high spread between deposits and lending rates (consistently above 10 percent), and particularly high interest rates for credit cards, automobile financing and mortgages. Since 1993 was already a recessive year, this situation led to delays or unfulfillment in the payments of loans. These reached unmanageable and dangerous levels and forced the government to intercede by promoting the renegotiation of bad debts between the banking sector and some sectors of the population – mainly peasants and business from the commercial sector. This situation was worsened by the fact that privatization, liberalization and poor economic conditions led banks to enforce new charges for some services (for example, the payment of utility services at their branches), or else to increase commissions (for example, in credit card collections). These efforts to rationalize costs and revenues should have been more moderate, for they have tarnished the image of banks significantly among large sectors of the population.

Dissatisfaction has not been limited to clients suffering insolvency problems. Clients who fulfill their obligations but feel pressured by high bank rates are perhaps the most dissatisfied. Good clients are also dissatisfied, for they realize that ultimately they are subsidizing insolvent clients, as well as sustaining unjustifiably high bank profits. Finally, it is worth mentioning that the crisis exacerbated these problems during 1995. At the peak of the crisis during February 1995, interest rate charges increased to 150.0 percent on an annual basis! Interest rates on automobile loans and mortgages followed a similar trend, so that defaults increased sharply. These problems led borrowers to consolidate a national organization, El Barzon, to fight against high bank charges and possible takeovers of their properties. As a result, bad loans increased to 13 and even 17 percent of total loans, which forced the government to design the complex rescue plan previously mentioned.

Thus, right now, the banking sector is undergoing a severe crisis, which in turn is preventing a faster recovery of the Mexican economy, for banking activity continues to be the nerve of financial activity in the country. Nevertheless, it is worth noting that the banking system is relatively small in Mexico. As shown in Table 16.3 the number of accounts and the total number of branches is rather small for the size and potential of the economy. By 1994 there were 5,061 for a country of 90 million people, i.e. one branch for ever 17,783 people. Moreover, some branches at key locations have been eliminated, particularly in smaller cities and towns, while apparently redundant branching persists in large cities. Similarly, higher costs in checking services have led some customers to cancel their accounts; low returns in term accounts have also led to the cancellation of some accounts, although many customers find an alternative in the increasing number of fund accounts on fixed and equity instruments offered and managed by banks. Savings accounts have tended to disappear. They were geared to the small saver and, although rates offered have consistently remained below inflation rates, they were an alternative for saving and meeting cash needs for important groups of the population. However, their management absorbed much time and resources and for that reason commercial banks have been steadily moving away, with legal support, from that type of activity. Banamex, for instance, shows a decrease from almost 9 million accounts in 1990 to slightly above 1 million in the following two years. This was mainly due to a sharp cancelling in savings accounts, from 8,996,447 in 1991 to 91,950 in 1992.

Costs and time control considerations somewhat justify this trend. It can also be understood by taking into account that deregulation plans have led the government to promote the operations of credit unions and savings and loans banks once again. However, although the laws to regulate this type of institution have been enacted, a full-fledged sector still doesn't exist. This is therefore an area that the government needs to emphasize during the next few years in order to consolidate the development of the Mexican financial system. It should give banks fiscal incentives to continue small savings operations. Banks themselves must reconsider offering more of these services to the population, not only because currently they are the most fit to carry them out and promote higher levels of savings, but also because such action would strengthen their public image. The public must have great confidence in the banking system in order for it to consolidate its growth and to attain greater benefits from the NAFTA, and for the development of Mexico in general.

CONCLUSION

In spite of current crisis conditions, Mexico's economic prospects are favorable. To reap the benefits that can be obtained from unfettered local markets, the North American Free Trade Agreement, and Mexico's integration to the world economy, will play an important role. However, to achieve those benefits, Mexico needs a strong financial sector. Particular attention must be paid to the development of its banking institutions, not only because this is a sector with severe problems due to overdue loans and overall sagging economic activity, but because its emerging structure still needs to be consolidated with regard to its forms of organization and operations following its privatization and the financial liberalization and deregulation schemes implemented during the last seven years. Also, NAFTA and Mexico's integration to the world's financial markets will bring about competition from foreign banks. Thus, in order to become a leading sector in the development of Mexico, existing banks need to increase their efficiency both for savings mobilization and in the allocation of resources. Recent operations do not seem to point in this direction. Concentration in the banking sector has slightly diminished due to the entry of fourteen new banks. But the banking system, which comprises a total of thirty-two institutions, behaves as if it were composed of only nine. Furthermore, new entries are small. Similarly, some key indicators underlie the fact that the banking system suffers some deficiencies and is still very small. Above all, costs have increased sharply so that in spite of high increases in profits productivity is low, as measured by the ratio net profits over assets.

Moreover, higher profits, higher costs and charges to clients, and decreased quality in some services are tarnishing the image that these institutions have acquired among their customers and the public at large. This could inhibit the growth of savings and investments channeled through these intermediaries, perhaps leading to financial disintermediation and a "disfinancing" of development. In the past, the permissive attitude of banks towards similar problems led to expropriation. The government and banks themselves must join efforts to correct current distortions and lay down the foundations for a strong, efficient and competitive financial sector which is needed to attain a definitive take-off into development. Important steps in this direction are the further opening of local markets to foreign banking institutions beyond the limits set forth in the stipulations of the NAFTA, and the formation of strategic alliances of local banks with foreign intermediaries.

NOTES

* Edgar Ortiz acknowledges the support of Programa de Apoyo a Proyectos de Investigación e Innovación Tecnológic (PAPIIT) from Universidad Nacional Autónoma de México for its support for the ongoing research of "Financial Cycles in the North American Bloc and its Implication of the Mexican Firm." This work is part of that Project. The authors also wish to thank valuable suggestions received from Enrique Arjona, Klaus P. Fischer, Jean-Claude Cosset, and an anonymous referee.
1 For a summary and an evaluation of Mexico's financial liberalization policies see Cabello, Chapter 5 in this book.
2 The theory and implications of this particular form of corporate organization and governance on the growth and financing of the firm from the developing countries is fully analyzed in the works by Fischer *et al.* (1994, 1995).
3 This rescue package includes five programs: funds for restructuring bad loans in real terms units (Unidades de Inversión); funds to support small and medium corporate debtors, credit card holders, and mortgage debt holders; funds to protect depositors strengthening the capital of banks, i.e. through a system of participation of the state in a bank's capital or through shares guarantees; purchases of bad loans; and support to private highway builder's borrowers. See *Criterios Generales de Política Económica*. Secretaría de Hacienda y Credito Público, México, 1995.
4 See Armendariz and Mijangos (1995).
5 It is worth noting that the Mexican central bank lacked autonomy from the Executive power. A new law gives the central bank – Banco de México – full autonomy and defines its tasks more clearly; namely, the promotion of price and exchange rate stability. See Cabello, Chapter 5 in this volume.
6 Reforms to the Law to Regulate Financial Groups, the Law of Credit Institutions, and the Law of the Securities Markets, approved by the Congress on 27 January 1995. See Guillermo Ortiz Martinez, Secretario de Hacienda y Crédito Público, "Programa de Acción para Reforzar el Acuerdo para Superar la Emergencia Económica, " *El Mercado de Valores*, Año LV, 4, abril 1995, pp. 3–24.
7 Five of the seven goals mentioned here are acknowledged by Aspe (1993). Goals 2 and 7 have been added by the authors of this chapter.
8 See "Presentacion," in Comision Nacional Bancaria, *Boletin Estadistico de Banca Multiple*, Tomo XI, Num. 569, Diciembre de 1994.
9 The aggregate average based on the individual margins of each bank is biased because data for 1994 includes new entries which, with one exception, ended with high positive margins mostly because their operations were short and did not involve some of the costs incurred by ongoing banks. For that reason, in

this study some analyses are complemented with ratios derived from aggregate banking data.

10 For this analysis we are also using aggregate date to avoid the bias of averages ratios, as previously explained.

REFERENCES

Armendariz, P. and M. Mijangos (1995) "Problemas de Liberalizacion en el Tratado de Libre Comercio: El Caso de los Servicios Bancarios," in A. Giron, E. Ortiz and E. Correa (eds) *Integracion Financiera y TLC: Retos y Perspectivas*, Mexico: Siglo XXI.

Aspe, P. (1993) *Economic Transformation. The Mexican Way*, Cambridge, Mass.: MIT Press.

Barina, M. (1986) "Changes in the Degree of Concentration of the Italian Banking System: An International Comparison," Working Paper Series, No. 5, Banca Nazionale del Laboro, Rome.

Baumol, W., J. Panzar and R. Willig (1982) *Contestable Markets and the Theory of Industry Structure*, Harcourt Brace Jovanovich.

Baumol, W., J. Panzar and R. Willig (1986) "On The Theory of Perfectly Contestable Markets," in J. Stiglitz and F. Mathewson (eds) *New Developments in the Analysis of Market Structure*, Cambridge, Mass.: MIT Press.

Berger, A.N., G.A. Hanweck and D.B. Humphrey (1987) "Competitive Viability in Banking: Scale, Scope and Product Mix Economies," *Journal of Monetary Economics*, Vol. 20, pp. 501–20.

Brock, W.A. (1983) "Contestable Markets and the Theory of Industry Structure," *Journal of Political Economy*, Vol. 91, No. 6, pp. 1055–66.

Brown-Cruse, J.I. (1991) "Contestability in the Presence of an Alternate Market: An Experimental Examination," *Rand Journal of Economics*, Vol. 22, No. 1, Spring, pp. 136–9.

Cabello, A. (1994) "Deregulation and the Mexican Stock Market," *Proceedings*, International Trade and Finance Association, Fourth International Congress, Reading, England, 13–16 July.

Canals, J. (1993) *Competitive Strategies in European Banking*, Oxford: Clarendon Press.

Diamond, D.W. and P. Dybvig (1983) "Bank Runs, Deposit Insurance and Liquidity, *Journal of Political Economy*, Vol. 91, pp. 401–19.

Eaton, B. and R. Ware (1987) "A Theory of Market Structure with Sequential Entry," *Rand Journal of Economics*, Spring, pp 1–16.

Fischer, K.P., E. Ortiz and A.P. Palasvirta (1994) "Risk Management and Corporate Governance in Imperfect Capital Markets," in D.K. Ghosh and E. Ortiz (eds) *The Changing Environment of International Financial Markets*, New York: St Martin's Press.

Fischer, K.P., E. Ortiz and A.P. Palasvirta (1995) "From Banca to Bolsa: Corporate Governance and Equity Financing in Latin America," in D.K. Ghosh (ed.) *Managerial Finance in the Corporate Economy*, London: Routledge.

Giron, A. (1995) "La Banca Comercial en Canadá, México y Estados Unidos," in A. Giron, E. Ortiz and E. Correa (eds) *Integracion Financiera y TLC: Retos y Perspectivas*, Mexico: Siglo XXI.

Goldsmith, R.W. (1976) *The Financial Development of Mexico*, Paris: OECD.

Newell, R. (1978) "Financial Deepening and Financial Narrowing: The Case of Mexico, 1960–1976," Unpublished doctoral dissertation, University of Texas at Austin.

Ortiz, E. (1995) "Sovereign and Corporate Borrowing and Sustainable Growth: Strategies and a Model for the Design of Payments," in D.K. Ghosh, (ed.) *New Advances in Financial Economics*, New York: Pergamon.

Ortiz, E. (1996) "La Inversion Extranjera de Portafolios en los Mercados de Dinero y Capital de Mexico y su Impacto en la Crisis Mexicana," in I. Manrique, (comp.) *Perspectivas Financieras de Mexico, Mexico*, D.F.: UNAM, 1996 (forthcoming).

Ortiz, E. and A. Lewis (1994) "Financial Integration and Competitiveness of the Mexican Banking Sector: Model and Empirical Tests," Mimeo, UNAM/FCPyS.

Panzar, J.C. and R. D. Willig (1977) "Free Entry and the Sustainability of Natural Monopoly," *Bell Journal of Economics*, Vol. 8, pp. 1–22.

Schwartz, M. (1986) "The Nature and Scope of Contestability Theory," *Oxford Economic Papers*, Vol. 38 (supp.), 37–57.

Shaffer, S. (1993) "A Test of Competition in Canadian Banking," *Journal of Money, Credit and Banking* 25, February, pp. 49–61.

Spence, M. (1983) "Contestable Markets and the Theory of Industry Structure: A Review Article," *Journal of Economic Literature*, Vol. 21, pp 981–90.

Stigler, G.J. (1968) *The Organization of Industry*, Homewood, Ill.: Irwin.

Stigler, G. (1986) *The Theory of Price*, New York: The Mcmillan Company.

Stiglitz, J. and F. Mathewson (eds) (1986) *New Developments in the Analysis of Market Structure*, Boston, Mass.: MIT Press.

Strivens, R. (1992) "The Liberalization of Banking Services in the Community," *Common Market Law Review*, Vol. 29, pp. 283–307.

17

RIVALRY AND EVOLUTION OF AN INDUSTRY'S STRUCTURE

The case of the Costa Rican banking system

Mariano Rojas*

This chapter studies the characteristics of rivalry within an industry. It uses a first-order stochastic Markov process to model the mobility of customers across firms. Transition probabilities matrices are estimated for the Costa Rican banking industry in different periods, and they are used to study rivalry among banks and to explore the evolution of the industry's structure. The Costa Rican banking industry experienced interesting structural changes that make it a useful case study. Following the New Empirical Industrial Organization paradigm, the chapter stresses the importance of intra-industry studies as well as the need of studying rivalry in a way closer to the Austrian approach.

INTRODUCTION

This chapter analyzes the evolution of the Costa Rican banking structure within the general framework of the New Empirical Industrial Organization paradigm (NEIO) and the Austrian approach. Following the NEIO paradigm, it uses longitudinal data to make an intra-industry study of the banking system, and it focuses on the firms as the basic unit of analysis. Besides, the chapter emphasizes the role played by intra-industry rivalry in explaining the evolution of the structure of the industry.[1] From the Austrian School, this chapter borrows the interest for the dynamic aspects of the evolution of an industry's structure and its focus on the equations of motion and the Austrian notion of rivalry.[2]

A dynamic model is used to understand the evolution of the structure of the Costa Rican banking system. The model assumes that banks compete for customers through the implementation of several strategies in multiple dimensions. A first-order stochastic Markov process is assumed to characterize the behavior of the banks' customers. The transition probabilities that describe the mobility of customers become the parameters of the equations of motion that portray the evolution of the industry's structure over time. These transition probabilities can be interpreted as the outcome of a multidimensional rivalry process among banks.

259

The model is employed to study the case of the Costa Rican banking system because it exhibits peculiar and interesting features, which are discussed in the following section.

THE COSTA RICAN BANKING SYSTEM

In 1948, shortly after a two-month civil war, the new provisional government– the *Junta* - dictated a decree nationalizing the three largest private banks in the country. The true reasons behind this nationalization are still matters of controversy. The nationalization decree stated:

> Private banking is nationalized. Only the state will be authorized to mobilize, through its own institutions, the deposits from the public.

This nationalization implied a monopsony for the four government-owned banks in the mobilization of deposits from the public. It did not affect financial intermediation at large.[3] It did not make the operation of private banks illegal, but prevented private bankers from mobilizing deposits from the public. It was still possible for private bankers to participate in the industry with non-deposit funds.

The decree has not been free of criticism and reform initiatives. Some modifications to the related legislation were adopted during the following decades. Nevertheless, the structure of the Costa Rican banking industry remained almost unchanged until the 1980s.

The following are some of the main features of the Costa Rican banking system after the nationalization:

(a) The government-owned banking system consists of four banks: Banco Nacional de Costa Rica, Banco de Costa Rica, Banco Anglo-Costarricense, and Banco Crédito Agrícola de Cartago. Autonomous by law, in practice they became heavily intervened in by the government.

(b) As a result of intense government intervention and the power of the authorities, the prospects for explicit and implicit coordination of the state-owned bank strategies, i.e., tacit collusion, should not be discarded. It is very likely that the Central Bank, as the regulator, became an instrument for the government-owned banks to coordinate their decisions.[4]

(c) The nationalized banks were expected to carry out social objectives. They were forced, for example, to finance specific projects and to help preferred sectors, chosen on the basis of social and political rather than economic criteria. The profit-oriented behavior of the nationalized banks was thus heavily constrained.

(d) The Central Bank implemented strict controls on the allocation of credit and the setting of interest rates, at subsidized levels in many cases.

It is reasonable to hypothesize that the nationalization decree implied collusive tendencies in both the input and the output markets and a behavior of the government-owned banks that contained non-economic considerations. Moreover, lack of competition in the industry may have discouraged the more aggressive pursuit of economic efficiency.

It was not until the 1980s, when a process of deregulation and financial innovation began, that a small number of private banks made their incursion into the banking industry. The emergence of a dynamic private banking sector in the 1980s implies a structural change that goes beyond a simple variation in the concentration index, altering the way in which the nationalized banks behave and their performance in both the input and the output markets. The C_4 index for earning assets(C_4-EA), that was around 99 percent before 1980, went to levels below 70 percent in 1990.

A quick test for the variable C_4-EA using a logistic specification showed that a structural change took place in the banking industry by the beginning of the 1980s. In conclusion, the private banks expanded by taking over the market shares of the large, dominant government-owned banks, whose market shares were changing as well. Therefore, it is interesting to study the characteristics of rivalry among the nationalized banks before and after the incursion of the private banks and to explore the change in the long-run trend of the industry's structure.

THE MODEL

The approach

In order to study the evolution of the Costa Rican banking structure, and to examine the characteristics of the process of rivalry among banks, the investigation uses an eight-step approach.

First, competition is regarded as a dynamic process of rivalry for customers. Banks compete to retain their customers and to attract clients from other banks as well as new customers. The outcome of this process determines changes in the banks' market shares and, in consequence, it determines the evolution of the structure of the banking industry.

Second, the approach assumes that the banks' customers are not homogeneous in their needs and preferences. The competition for clients in this kind of model requires the banks to find their best location in a multidimensional space. The strategies of any bank are oriented towards improving its position in a dynamic environment where the strategies of the other banks, the regulatory and technological framework, and the customers' preferences may change. Some banks may decide not to compete against other banks or to concentrate their efforts on a specific market segment.

Third, rivalry takes place in a dynamic environment with an open area of

261

opportunities. The Costa Rican banks compete through the creation and discovery of new strategies, the modification of past strategies, and the imitation and improvement of the strategies of their rivals. Consequently, the industry is in a state of permanent disequilibrium, with a continuing tendency towards an equilibrium situation that is never reached because of the changing strategic forces that come from within the industry, as well as modifications in the industry's environment.

Fourth, competition for customers takes place in a multidimensional strategic space. The Costa Rican banks can compete in different interconnected markets: the credit market, the demand deposits market, the time deposits market, and in seeking funds from the Central Bank and other sources. They also compete by offering other financial services, such as international transactions.

Fifth, in each of these markets the Costa Rican banks compete in several dimensions. The following are some of the main dimensions in which commercial banks compete: risk involved in the transaction, type of collateral required, kind of insurance/solvency provided, interest rates on deposits and on loans, transaction fees, customer services, speed of the transaction, other services attached to the products, geographical location, portfolio management, economic activities and regions targeted, cost management, administrative efficiency, supporting equipment, speed in the adaptation and generation of innovations, and even non-market activities. This chapter assumes that the banks' financial statements partially reflect the position of the banks in these multidimensional spaces.

Sixth, there is strategic heterogeneity in the Costa Rican banking industry. This heterogeneity is expected to occur for the following reasons:

(a) the strategic space is complex and multidimensional;
(b) the industry experiences numerous changes in the regulatory environment, as well as innovations in the financial sector and transformations in the macroeconomic environment;
(c) the Costa Rican banking industry is for many reasons a new industry, where the rules of the game are not clearly defined and the set of opportunities is not closed. Hence, some banks could try to take advantage of this situation by innovating in many unconventional ways; and
(d) customers are heterogeneous in their needs and preferences.

Different strategic positions lead to disparate degrees of success and failure in the retention and attraction of customers. It is assumed that the Costa Rican banks follow strategic routines and that the propensity to review these strategies is indirectly related to their success.

Seventh, the relative success or failure of the firms in this process of rivalry for customers can be measured in terms of the customers' transition probabilities. Each transition probability indicates the chance that a customer of bank i at time t becomes a customer of bank j at time $t + 1$. If $i = j$ then the transition probability becomes a proxy for the success of bank i in retaining its customers from one period to another. If $i \neq j$ then the transition probability can be interpreted as the relative success of bank j in attracting bank i's customers. A first-order stochastic Markov process is assumed to characterize the mobility of customers among banks. The probability distribution for the customer's purchasing decision is conditional on their previous location. Hence, each transition probability is conditional on the customer's location in the previous period; thus, the following transition probabilities matrix can be formed:

$$
P = \begin{vmatrix}
P_{11} & P_{12} & P_{13} & . & . & . & P_{1n} \\
P_{21} & . & . & . & . & . & . \\
P_{31} & . & . & . & . & . & . \\
. & & & & & & . \\
. & & & & & & . \\
P_{n1} & . & . & . & . & . & P_{nn}
\end{vmatrix} \tag{1}
$$

If there is rivalry fragmentation, or lack of rivalry between banks, it will be reflected in the transition probabilities matrix. The matrix also shows where the process of rivalry is more intense.

Eighth, the transition probabilities describe how the market shares of the banks change over time. In consequence, they become the parameters of the equations of motion of the industry's structure. It is at least theoretically conceivable to find a steady-state situation for the industry's structure, where the banks' market shares do not change and rivalry for customers remains.

The methodology

Therefore, under this approach, the banks become the finite and mutually exclusive states of the first-order stochastic Markov process, and the transition probabilities describe how every one-dollar customer of earning assets, deposits, and the like, moves across these banks over time.[5]

Hence, assuming that there are n banks:

$\theta_j(t)$: expresses the probability that an agent will be in bank j at time t, and
$P_{1j}(t)$: expresses the probability that an agent moves from bank i at time $t - 1$ to bank j at time t.

The following system of n equations relates the probabilities θj over time:

$$\theta_j(t) = \sum_{i=1}^{n} P_{ij}\, \theta_i(t-1) \tag{2}$$

$$j = 1, \ldots, n$$

$$i = 1, \ldots, n$$

It is possible to express the system of equations (2) in matrix form as:

$$
\begin{vmatrix} \theta_1(t) \\ \cdot \\ \cdot \\ \cdot \\ \cdot \\ \theta_n(t) \end{vmatrix}
=
\begin{vmatrix} P_{11} & P_{21} & P_{31} & \cdot & \cdot & \cdot & P_{n1} \\ P_{12} & P_{22} & & & \cdot & \cdot & P_{n2} \\ \cdot & & & & & & \\ \cdot & & & & & & \\ \cdot & & & & & & \\ P_{1n} & P_{2n} & \cdot & \cdot & \cdot & \cdot & P_{nn} \end{vmatrix}
\begin{vmatrix} \theta_1(t-1) \\ \cdot \\ \cdot \\ \cdot \\ \cdot \\ \theta_n(t-1) \end{vmatrix}
\tag{3}
$$

Because the states are mutually exclusive and exhaustive, the following two equations must hold in every period:

$$\sum_{j=1}^{n} \theta_j(t) = 1 \tag{4}$$

and

$$\sum_{j=1}^{n} P_{ij} = 1 \tag{5}$$

$$i = 1, \ldots, n$$

Observe that restrictions (4) and (5) imply that one of the equations in (2) is redundant.

It is common to use micro data to estimate the transition probabilities of a first-order stochastic Markov process. If knowledge about the behavior of individual customers is available, then it is possible to apply econometric techniques to estimate the transition probabilities.[6]

However, for the study of banking industries, information at the customer level is usually unavailable. It is aggregate data, such as the aggregate number of customers in every state, which is at hand. In the case of Costa Rican banks, the information about choices of individual clients is not available. Consequently, this investigation had to rely on aggregate stocks, such as loans and deposits. Fortunately, there are some techniques that permit the estimation of transition probabilities from aggregate data. This chapter follows the technique suggested by MacRae (1977).

MacRae (1977) and Lee et al. (1970) propose the use of a multinomial logit formulation as suggested by Theil (1969). To satisfy the restrictions expressed in equations (4) and (5), the following specification for the transition probabilities is assumed:

$$\ln \left(\frac{P_{ij}}{P_{in}} \right) = \beta_{ij}$$

$$j = 1, \ldots, n - 1$$ \hfill (6)
$$i = 1, \ldots, n$$

Algebraic manipulation of equation (6) leads to:

$$P_{in} \exp (\beta_{ij}) = P_{ij} \tag{7}$$

Adding over j :

$$P_{in} \sum_{j=1}^{n-1} \exp (\beta_{ij}) = \sum_{j=1}^{n-1} P_{ij} \tag{8}$$

$$i = 1, \ldots, n$$

Equation (8), together with equation (5), implies

$$P_{in} \sum_{j=1}^{n-1} \exp (\beta_{ij}) = 1 - P_{in} \tag{9}$$

$$i = 1, \ldots, n$$

Consequently, the transition probabilities can be expressed as:

$$P_{in} = \frac{1}{\left[1 + \sum_{j=1}^{n-1} \exp (\beta_{ij}) \right]} \tag{10}$$

$$i = 1, \ldots, n$$

and using equation (6):

$$P_{ij} = \frac{\exp (\beta_{ij})}{\left[1 + \sum_{j=1}^{n-1} \exp (\beta_{ij}) \right]} \tag{11}$$

$$i = 1, \ldots, n$$
$$j = 1, \ldots, n - 1$$

If the transition probabilities are specified in such a way, the first-order stochastic Markov process can be expressed as:

$$\theta_j(t) = \sum_{i=1}^{n} \frac{\exp(\beta_{ij})}{1 + \sum_{j=1}^{n-1} \exp(\beta_{ij})} * 0(t-) \qquad (12)$$

$$i = 1, \ldots, n$$

$$j = 1, \ldots, n-1$$

Estimation of transition probabilities

Because the variable $\theta(t)$ is not observed, it is necessary to use the vector of market shares of the banks, $m(t)$, as a proxy for $\theta(t)$. It is evident that the expected value of $\theta(t)$ is $m(t)$.[7] Since the vector of observed proportions, $m(t)$, is distributed as a sum of multinomials about $m(t-1)$, the standard regression analysis can be applied to the following system of equations to estimate the transition probabilities:

$$m_j(t) = \sum_{i=1}^{n} \left[\frac{\exp(\beta_{ij})}{1 + \sum_{j=1}^{n-1} \exp(\beta_{ij})} * m_i(t-1) \right] + \varepsilon_j(t) \quad (13)$$

$$i = 1, \ldots, n$$

$$j = 1, \ldots, n-1$$

Because the expected value of $\varepsilon_j(t)$ is zero, nonlinear least squares estimation will produce consistent estimates of the parameters β. Once the estimates of β are obtained, it is possible to indirectly obtain the estimates of the transition probabilities.[8]

Transition probabilities and the evolution of the industry's structure

The first interpretation uses the transition probabilities as the parameters of the equations of motion of the industry's structure. They can be used to appraise how the market shares of the banks change over time as a consequence of the relative success or failure of the banks' strategies.

The equations of motion show that the structure of the industry is not necessarily in equilibrium. The structure follows a trajectory towards an immovable point (steady-state situation), which is not stable and probably will never be reached because of the modifying forces that come both from within and outside the industry. Hence, the industry's structure is in a permanent disequilibrium situation, moving towards an ever-changing long-run equilibrium situation.

Given an original vector of market shares $m(t)$ and the matrix of transition probabilities, it is possible to describe a time path or trajectory for the evolution of the distribution of firm sizes. Furthermore, if it is assumed that the transition probabilities matrix does not change in the future, then it is possible to find at least one immovable point defining the limiting state probability of the process.[9] This immovable point may be interpreted as a long-run equilibrium or steady-state situation for the industry's structure.

Mathematically, given an initial vector of market shares $(m_{1t}, \ldots, m_{nt})$, where m_{jt} represents the proportion of customers in firm j at time t, and given the transition probabilities matrix P, the expected next configuration of market shares can be calculated in the following way:

$$m_{j(t + 1)} = (m_j) * [P] \tag{14}$$

Applying successive substitutions an immovable vector of market shares $E_{j,t + k}$ could be reached, which satisfies the following equation:

$$E_{j(t + k + 1)} = E_{j(t + k)} * [P] \tag{15}$$

Therefore, if there is no change in the transition probabilities matrix, the vector $E_{j,t+k}$ defines the equilibrium situation of the process that explains the evolution of the firms' market shares. It is important to notice that this is in fact a dynamic equilibrium from the firms' perspective and a static equilibrium from the industry's perspective. This notion of equilibrium is stressed by the Austrian School. In the equilibrium situation the firms are in an incessant competition to retain its customers and attract customers from other firms. Hence, there is persistent mobility of customers among firms. But this mobility is such that the vector of market shares (industry's structure) remains stable.

An index of rivalry

An index that summarizes the intensity of rivalry in the industry can be constructed. Several attempts have been made to move from concentration indices, which are based solely on the structure of the industry, to indices incorporating a behavior dimension. Measures such as the Herfindahl index and the C_4 index use market shares, or the size distribution of firms, to calculate concentration ratios. Caves and Porter (1978) recommend a measure based on the instability of market shares, suggesting that a dynamic notion of competition is more useful than a static one. Donsimoni et al. (1984) criticize the structure–conduct–performance paradigm and the concentration measures based on it. They argue for an *appropriate concentration* index that takes into consideration the role played by firms' conduct.

Because the transition probabilities show the outcome of the process of competition, then their values reflect the nature of the firms' conduct, as well as the structural conditions in the industry. This chapter proposes a measure of rivalry in the industry based on the transition probabilities. Therefore, the index is based on changes in market shares rather than on the market shares themselves. This dynamic perspective of the rivalry index is congruous with the intentions of Caves and Porter (1978) and Donsimoni *et al.* (1984). The index that summarizes the intensity of rivalry would be a weighted sum of the off-diagonal transition probabilities, where the weights are given by the average market shares of the firms:

$$R = \sum_{i=1}^{n} \sum_{j=1}^{n} P_{ij} \, \overline{m}_i \qquad (16)$$

$$i \neq j$$

This index shows the average probability for a customer of the industry to switch banks during the period. It may also be interpreted as the proportion of customers in the industry that move across banks. This index could be used as a supplement, and even as a substitute, for the concentration measures based on the size distribution of firms, and its potential use requires further study.[10]

THE RESULTS

Information for total earning assets gathered by the Auditoria General de Entidades Financieras (AGEF, the superintendency of banks) was used to estimate the transition probabilities. The information provided by AGEF allowed for the construction of time-series for the banks' earning assets. This information was available quarterly from June 1974 to December 1990 (65 observations per bank).[11]

Two transition probabilities were estimated using quarterly earning assets information. One for the period from June 1974 to December 1981; and the other for the period from March 1982 to June 1990.[12] These transition probabilities exhibit the outcome of rivalry in the credit market, with a special focus on rivalry among the nationalized banks and the aggregate of the private sector. Hence, it is possible to make time comparisons of the characteristics of rivalry before and after the break point and the change in the trajectory of the industry's structure.

Period June 1974 to December 1981

Table 17.1 shows the estimated transition probabilities matrix for the period from June 1974 to December 1981. During this period, the nationalized banks were practically alone in the industry.

Several null off-diagonal transition probabilities are noticeable.[13] This is an indication of rivalry fragmentation in the industry and of lack of rivalry in general. This result is consistent with the hypothesis of the existence of collusive tendencies in the banking industry.

Even though there seems to be a general lack of rivalry in the industry, it

Table 17.1 Costa Rican banks: transition probabilities matrix, June 1974 to December 1981 (rivalry index: $R = 0.1598$)

Bank	NB1	NB2	NB3	NB4	PB
NB1	0.911	0.000	0.024	0.055	0.011
NB2	0.142	0.791	0.068	0.000	0.000
NB3	0.000	0.176	0.824	0.000	0.000
NB4	0.013	0.278	0.000	0.708	0.000
PB	0.000	0.708	0.000	0.000	0.292

Note: P_{ij}: probability for a one-dollar customer of bank i to become a customer of bank j the next period.
NB$_i$: nationalized bank i.
PB: aggregate of private banks.

is possible to find some spots where rivalry between banks is comparatively intense. For example, bank NB1 seems to be successful in attracting customers from bank NB2; while bank NB2 is successful with respect to customers from banks NB3, NB4, and PB.

The very low retention probability for the private banks shows their nature as banks of passage in the credit market. In this period the private banks faced severe restrictions to gather funds from the public. They were forced to charge higher interest rates on their loans and to specialize in short-term loans. Their main competitive advantage against the nationalized banks was in the speed of their service; thus, long-run credit relationships between the private banks and their customers were difficult to establish.

The rivalry index proposed by this chapter (R) is equal to 0.1598, indicating that the average probability for a customer to switch banks is only 16 percent.[14] This is a relatively low value when compared to the rivalry index for the second period.[15]

The steady-state vector of market shares, constructed with the transition probabilities matrix of this period, is shown in Table 17.2. When the current vector of market shares is compared to the steady-state market

Table 17.2 Costa Rican banks: average and steady-state market share, June 1974 to December 1981

Bank	Average market share	Steady-state market share
NB1	0.451	0.4524
NB2	0.283	0.2777
NB3	0.178	0.1780
NB4	0.082	0.0850
NB5	0.007	0.0069

shares, it is observed that, given the prevailing rivalry in the industry, little structural change is expected.

Thus, the industry's structure was very close to its steady-state situation and no effort from within the industry was apparent to change this structure. This result indicates the existence of conformism by the firms in the industry, and it supports the hypothesis that a cooperative solution existed in the Costa Rican banking industry during this period. The absence of a strong private sector, along with the existence of open mechanisms to coordinate the decisions of the state-owned banks, seems to have been the main factor explaining the easy accommodation of the nationalized banks to the prevailing situation.

Period March 1982 to June 1990, and time comparisons

The second period is characterized by the entry of several private banks and the emergence of a stronger private sector. Table 17.3 shows the estimated transition probabilities.

The number of null off-diagonal transition probabilities is relatively low, showing an increase of rivalry in the industry and, probably, a decline in collusive tendencies.

The private banks, as a group, are now competing against all the nationalized banks, with different degrees of success. Compared to the other state-owned banks, bank NB3 loses a greater proportion of its customers to the private banks.

The ability of the nationalized banks to retain their customers declined significantly. The diagonal elements for the state-owned banks decreased between the two periods. This indicates that there was an increase in rivalry during the second period and that the nationalized banks were unable to retain their customers at the same rate as before. The decline in the diagonal elements of banks NB1 and NB4 was significant; this shows

Table 17.3 Costa Rican banks: transition probabilities matrix, March 1982 to June 1990 (rivalry index: $R = 0.2327$)

Bank	NB1	NB2	NB3	NB4	PB
NB1	0.795	0.112	0.020	0.037	0.036
NB2	0.107	0.728	0.080	0.047	0.028
NB3	0.025	0.000	0.782	0.056	0.138
NB4	0.391	0.167	0.000	0.413	0.030
PB	0.000	0.086	0.000	0.000	0.914

Note: P_{ij}: probability for a one-dollar customer of bank i to become a customer of bank j the next period.
NB$_i$: nationalized bank i.
PB: aggregate of private banks.
Some null values represent, after rounding, very small probabilities.

that the nationalized banks were not symmetrically affected by the expansion of the private banks and by the increase of rivalry in the industry.

It is important to notice that this decline in the diagonal transition probabilities of the nationalized banks is explained not only by the increase in competition from the private banks, but also by the boost in competition among the state-owned banks. If the study is restricted to the nationalized sector of the industry, it is observed that the off-diagonal elements increased for all the banks (except bank NB3). This reflects an increase in the intra-nationalized banks, rivalry between the two periods.

The ability of the private banks to retain their customers increased significantly with respect to the first period, indicating that a change in the nature of these banks took place in the 1980s. The introduction of investment certificates, together with a generalized process of financial innovations, allowed the private banks to circumvent the nationalized banks' monopoly of deposits and to have an easier access to the funds of the public. Additionally, the private banks had access to foreign funds from international organizations. An impressive improvement in managerial techniques should not be neglected.

The rivalry index (R) increased from 0.1598 in the first period to 0.2327 in the second period. The average probability for one customer of the industry to switch banks was almost one and a half times greater than before.

Some spots showing strong bilateral rivalry are evident. For example, banks NB1 and NB2 are attracting each other's customers at significant rates.

The vector of steady-state market shares for this second period is shown in Table 17.4.

When the actual vector of average market shares is compared to the long-run equilibrium vector that dominates the current tendency of structural transformation (steady-state), it is observed that they are different. In other words, if the present rivalry situation were not altered, the industry would experience significant structural change. All the nationalized banks would lose market share, the decline being impressive for NB1 and NB4.

Table 17.4 Costa Rican banks: average and steady-state market share, June 1982 to December 1990

Bank	Average market share	Steady-state market share
NB1	0.385	0.2152
NB2	0.266	0.2290
NB3	0.151	0.1140
NB4	0.061	0.0427
NB5	0.136	0.3624

The private banks would experience a huge increase in their market share in the credit market.

The transition probabilities matrices may be interpreted as the equations of motion that govern the trajectory of the industry's structure towards a steady-state situation. Therefore, it is helpful to compare the two periods in terms of the respective immovable points. A look at the estimated long-run equilibrium situations shows a significant structural change happening in the Costa Rican banking industry.

FINAL CONSIDERATIONS

The methodology used in this chapter permits to move beyond the static notion of competition towards the more dynamic notion of rivalry for customers, which is closer to the Austrian approach to competition.

The use of a first-order stochastic Markov process to model the mobility of customers across firms seems to be very functional. It allows the estimation of transition probabilities, which can be interpreted as both the outcome of the process of rivalry and the parameters of the equations of motion explaining the evolution of the industry's structure.

The application of the methodology to the Costa Rican banking industry shows its potential to study industries within the New Empirical Industrial Organization paradigm. Further research is needed to relate the conduct of the firms to the transition probabilities and to the evolution of the industry's structure.

NOTES

* Universidad de las Americas, Puebla, Mexico. The author thanks Claudio González-Vega for his suggestions, which undoubtedly improved this chapter.
1 See Bresnahan and Schmaleense (1987).
2 See Davies et al. (1988).
3 This nationalization must be understood as a transfer of ownership from private national bankers to the state. Thus, it must not be confused with usual Latin American nationalizations that involve a transfer of ownership from foreigners to nationals.
4 This argument of the regulator as a regulatees' agent was introduced by Stigler (1971).
5 Notice that the definition used refers to the one-dollar customer; the methodology used in the investigation makes it impossible to work with physical customers.
6 See Lee et al. (1970).
7 If the behavior of the customers is characterized by a first-order stochastic Markov process, then the unconditional distribution for $m(t)$ is multinomial about the mean of $\theta(t)$, where $\theta(t)$ is the vector of state probabilities for the underlying Markov process. For an analysis of both the unconditional and the conditional probability see MacRae (1977).
8 Notice that heteroskedasticity exists because $\varepsilon_j(t)$ is not independent of the

predetermined $m(t - 1)$; no attemp was made to correct this problem. Furthermore, the estimates are consistent, but neither unbiased nor efficient because of
the existence of lagged dependent variables in the regression analysis. See
MacRae (1977), and Lee *et al.* (1970).

9 See Howard (1971), p. 33.
10 Notice that the index is sensitive to the way in which the industry is decomposed.
Further research on the relationship between the index of rivalry and some
performance measures is needed to explore criteria for judging its level.
11 Because the figures are provided for high levels of aggregation, it was not
possible to work with the data to adjust the figures for factors such as risk of
loan losses. Therefore, the figures on earning assets must be interpreted as
rough proxies for the concept they were intended to measure; namely, the
participation of the banks in the credit market.
12 The definition of the break point in this case is arbitrary. However, there are
good reasons to believe that the banking situation in the 1970s was different
from the situation in the 1980s.
13 Some null values represent, after rounding, very small probabilities.
14 Notice that in this case the aggregate of the private banks is considered as a
single firm. Therefore, the mobility of customers within the private sector is not
considered in the calculation of the rivalry index.
15 As note 14.

REFERENCES

Bresnahan, T.F. and R. Schmalensee (1987) "The Empirical Renaissance in In-
dustrial Economics: An Overview," *The Journal Of Industrial Economics*, Vol.
XXXV, June.
Caves, R. and M. Porter (1978) "Market Structure, Oligopoly, and Stability of
Market Shares," *The Journal of Industrial Economics*, June, pp. 289–313.
Davies, S. (1988) *Economics of Industrial Organization*, Longman House, New
York.
Donsimoni, M.-P., P. Geroski and A. Jacquemin (1984) "Concentration Indices
and Market Power: Two Views," *The Journal of Industrial Economics*, June, pp.
419–34.
Howard, R.A. (1971) *Dynamic Probabilistic Systems: Markov Processes*, Vol. I
John Wiley & Sons, Inc., New York.
Lee, T.C., G.G. Judge and A. Zellner (1970) *Estimating the Parameters of the
Markov Probability Model from Aggregate Time-Series Data,*. North-Holland
Publishing Company, Amsterdam.
MacRae, E.C. (1977) "Estimation of Time Varying Markov Process with Aggre-
gate Data," *Econometrica* 45, pp. 183–98.
Rojas, M. (1993) "Rivalry and the Evolution of an Industry's Structure: The Case
of The Costa Rican Banking System," Ph.D Dissertation, The Ohio State Uni-
versity, Columbus.
Stigler, G.J. (1971) "The Theory of Economic Regulation," *Bell Journal of
Economic Literature and Management Science*, Spring, pp. 3–21.
Theil, H. (1969) "A Multinomial Extension of the Linear Logit Model," *International Economic Review*, 10, pp. 251–9.

18

INTERNATIONAL INTEREST RATE MECHANISMS IN BANK LENDING AND BORROWING MARKETS

Arjun Chatrath, Sanjay Ramchander and Frank Song

This chapter investigates transmissions and interdependencies in the bank lending and borrowing markets across eleven countries – Belgium, Canada, Denmark, France, Germany, Japan, the Netherlands, Sweden, Switzerland, the USA and the UK. Monthly time-series of Prime and 3-month negotiable certificate of deposits rates spanning the interval January 1972 to December 1992 are fitted to a vector autoregressive model. The empirical results are indicative of significant bilateral interactions among the bank lending and borrowing markets. The German rates are found to have a significant influence on the European bank lending and borrowing markets, but are themselves Granger-influenced by the US rates. The German prominence in the European bank market is further corroborated by the impulse response functions. Interestingly, the Japanese rates are found to be relatively insulated from the changes in the external rates. The results generally suggest that both banks and monetary authorities should be aware of the credit market conditions in the external markets, since their decisions at the micro and macro levels reverberate throughout the global markets.

INTRODUCTION

Financial institutions and markets in industrialized nations have undergone major transformations in the last two decades. Important structural changes in the markets for financial services, new communication and information technology, increasing interdependence of economies, and the interpenetration of national financial systems, have all fostered a competitive environment that is conducive for international banking activity. Moreover, several member countries of the Organization of Economic Development (OECD) have taken deregulatory measures designed to stimulate competition in the intermediation process.[1] There has also been an unprecedented growth in the off-balance-sheet activities of banks, and the rise in financial innovations including interest rate and currency swaps.

In the presence of increasing global competition, the insight into banking

274

specific interest rate relationships across countries is of obvious importance to governments in general and to financial intermediaries and other businesses in particular. First, the strength of intermarket interest rate linkages determines the degree to which intermediaries can successfully pursue independent lending and borrowing policies. In environments in which customers have growing multinational operations, intermediaries that ignore differentials in lending rates may find themselves with a dwindling customer base. Similarly, differences in national deposit rates could lead to significant losses in deposit sources. Second, the presence of international linkages in the market for bank borrowing and lending may put added responsibility on monetary authorities. If banks within a country are able to offer higher deposit rates, they may attract deposits at the expense of banks in other countries. Since financial intermediaries are important conduits through which monetary authorities implement their countries' monetary policies, central banks of countries suffering disintermediation may be pressurized to cut reserve requirements, or be forced to rely on other instruments of monetary policy.[2] In addition, the "lending view" of monetary transmission suggests that there are important linkages between the allocation of bank loans and the performance of the economy (see Bernanke and Blinder 1988, 1992; Romer and Romer 1990; Gestler and Gilchrist 1993). It follows that the effectiveness of a nation's monetary policy is influenced by the extent to which the bank lending rates are dependent on external influences.

The objective of the present study is to investigate the transmissions and interdependencies in the bank lending and borrowing markets across industrialized countries. Although there exists a large body of literature that examines the international linkages in financial markets, the intermarket relationships among financial institutions have yet to be investigated. Since the Prime and CD rates are effectively the barometers of national credit market conditions, we stylize the two rates as representing the lending and borrowing markets respectively. Monthly time-series of these rates spanning the interval January 1972 to December 1992 are fitted to a vector-autoregressive system. The empirical results are indicative of significant bilateral interactions among the bank lending and borrowing markets. While the role of Germany seems to be prominent among the European markets, the German Prime and CD rates in turn are themselves influenced by the US rates. The evidence from the impulse response functions of Belgium, Denmark, France, the Netherlands, Switzerland and the UK indicates that most of the innovations in the German Prime and CD rates are accommodated within three months. Interestingly, the Japanese lending and borrowing markets are found to be relatively isolated from those of other countries.

The rest of the chapter proceeds as follows. The next section reviews the prior evidence on intermarket linkages. The third section discusses the data and the methodology employed in the investigation. The empirical results are presented in the fourth section. A concluding section summarizes the findings of our study.

PRIOR EVIDENCE ON INTERMARKET LINKAGES

There exists a large body of literature on the international interest rate mechanisms. However, several important issues pertaining to the transmissions and interactions in interest rate markets remain unresolved. Early investigations by Hendershott (1967), Argy and Hodjera (1973), and Levin (1974) generally find US interest rates to be insensitive to the influence of foreign markets. The evidence is attributed to the relative isolation of the US interest rate generating processes from external market forces. More recently, Katsimbris and Miller (1993) examined the interest rate linkages within the European Monetary System (EMS) by including the US interest rate as an additional variable. They found Germany to be a dominant player within the EMS. Moreover, the US interest rate is found to play no unique dominant role. While the US interest rate Granger-causes most of the other EMS interest rates, including the German rate, four of the EMS interest rates – Germany, Ireland, Italy and the Netherlands – Granger-cause the US rate.

On the other hand, several studies have suggested that while Germany is an important player in the EMS, the German rates are also affected by innovations in the other EMS countries and the US. For instance, Fratianni and von Hagen (1990) found the interest rate shocks in France and the Netherlands to have had a significant impact on German rates. Artus (1991) allowed for the effects of changes in long-term interest and exchange rates and found strong evidence that German interest rates influenced French rates but were themselves influenced by the rates in the US.

In a recent study, Koedijk and Kool (1992) investigated whether European nations act as a 'Deutschmark zone' by applying a principal components analysis to interest rate differentials within several EMS member nations and the UK for the 1980s. The authors found evidence of independent interest rate differentials originating from the movements in two currency blocks: the first comprising Germany, the Netherlands and the UK, and the second France, Belgium and Italy.

In sum, the hypothesis of complete German or US dominance in interest rate movements is rejected by prior studies, while the weaker notions of US and German leadership are not (also see Schnitzel 1983; Kaen and Hachey 1983; Hartman 1984; Swanson 1988; and Fung and Isberg 1992).[3]

DATA AND METHODOLOGY

The data series employed in this study comprise of monthly observations of Prime and CD rates for eleven industrialized countries for the interval

January 1972 to December 1992. These countries are Belgium, Canada, Denmark, France, Germany, Japan, the Netherlands, Sweden, Switzerland, the USA and the UK.[4] The two sets of interest rates are obtained from the monthly issues of the Morgan Guaranty Trust Company's *World Financial Markets* and from the monthly issues of *International Financial Statistics*.

The Prime and CD rates across all the countries are found to be nonstationary in the levels for the sample period. To enhance the consistency of the VAR estimation procedure, both interest rates are transformed into a stationary series by first differencing.[5]

The study bases its analyses on sample correlations and on the VAR methodology developed by Sims (1980). The VAR specification allows each variable (Prime and CD rates in the present case) to be affected by its own history and the history of the other variables in the system. Within the framework of the current investigation, the methodology allows us to measure the relative importance of each country in generating unexpected variations of interest rates to a particular market. We can thus establish causal ordering among the eleven national markets without a priori restrictions of exogeneity. In addition, the impulse response functions generated from the VAR analysis captures the dynamic interactions of the national Prime and CD rates.

The eleven pairs of interest rate series are fitted to a VAR system:

$$X_t = \sum_{i=1}^{n} \alpha_i L^i X_t + \sum_{i=1}^{n} \beta_i L^i Y_t + \varepsilon_t, \tag{1}$$

$$Y_t = \sum_{i=1}^{n} \gamma_i L^i Y_t + \sum_{i=1}^{n} \delta_i L^i X_t + \eta_t, \tag{2}$$

where X_t and Y_t represent the interest rate series associated with a pair of countries at time t, and L^i represents the lag operator associated with each i. The coefficients to be estimated are α_i, β_i, γ_i, and δ_i, while ε_t and η_t are the random disturbance terms. We employ Akaike's (1973) minimum Final Prediction Error (FPE) criterion in the selection of the optimal distributed lag structure.[6] Defining the vector as

$$V_t = (X_t, Y_t), \tag{3}$$

the system in equations (1) and (2) can be written as a VAR system,

$$V_t = h(V_{t-1}, V_{t-2}, \ldots, V_{t-k}) + z_t. \tag{4}$$

where in equation (3) $h(\bullet)$ is a vector of functions, and z_t is the vector of normally distributed error terms.[7]

In the framework of the Granger causality test, Y causes X if the set of estimated coefficients on the lagged Y in equation (1) is statistically different from zero as a group, and the set of estimated coefficients on the lagged values of X is not statistically different from zero. We follow a similar procedure to test whether X causes Y. A bilateral causality (two-way causality or feedback) between X and Y is suggested when the sets of X and Y coefficients in equations (1) and (2) are simultaneously different from zero. An F-statistic is used to indicate the significance of the causality.

The Granger causality test allows us to analyze the relationship of bank lending and borrowing rates across the eleven countries. However, this test is unable to capture the dynamics and the magnitude of the relationships. Subsequently, we trace out the dynamic responses (impulse response functions) of the markets to innovations in a particular market using the simulated responses of the estimated VAR system.

RESULTS

Tables 18.1a and 18.1b report the Pearson's correlation coefficients among the eleven pairs of countries for the Prime and CD rate series respectively. A temporal examination of the correlation coefficients indicates that almost all the relationships are positive. In the market for bank lending (Table 18.1a), the prime rates of US–Canada and US–Belgium exhibit the highest correlation. We also notice the US Prime rates to be moderately correlated with most of the other European countries, except for Sweden, where the correlation is -0.11. Interestingly, the US Prime rate exhibits no correlation with the corresponding Japanese rate. The patterns are similar in the market for bank borrowing (Table 18.1b), with a few notable exceptions. For instance, we observe that the US–Japan CD rates are more closely correlated in the borrowing market than in the lending market. However, just the opposite is observed in the correlation between Germany–Japan in that the degree of correlation is found to be lower in the borrowing market than in the lending market. Surprisingly, with the exception of Japan–Switzerland, the Japanese Prime and CD rates exhibit little correlation with any of the other countries investigated.

The results from the Granger causality tests for Prime and CD rates are presented in Tables 18.2a and 18.2b respectively. The i,jth entry in the table represents the marginal level of significance associated with the F-statistic from the test of the null hypothesis that the ith country (row) does not Granger-cause the jth country (column). For instance, in Table 18.2a, the Belgium Prime rate is observed to Granger-cause the Canadian rates at the 1 percent level of significance.

An examination of Tables 18.2a and 18.2b reveals that the US, Germany, France and Belgium are the most influential countries in the group in that their Prime and CD rates are found to lead or Granger-cause (at the 5 percent level of significance) the rates of the other countries in the sample. Moreover, while the German rates Granger-cause the French and Belgian

Table 18.1a Sample correlation matrix of Prime rates (January 1972 to December 1992)

Country	BE	CA	DE	FR	GE	JA	NE	SWE	SWI	UK	US
Belgium (BE)	1.00										
Canada (CA)	0.85	1.00									
Denmark (DE)	0.71	0.58	1.00								
France (FR)	0.82	0.67	0.78	1.00							
Germany (GE)	0.62	0.57	0.58	0.74	1.00						
Japan (JA)	0.26	0.04	0.53	0.59	0.53	1.00					
Netherlands (NE)	0.58	0.58	0.64	0.75	0.68	0.53	1.00				
Sweden (SWE)	0.56	0.57	0.17	0.26	0.02	-0.34	0.00	1.00			
Switzerland (SWI)	0.04	-0.03	0.27	0.32	0.41	0.72	0.28	-0.35	1.00		
UK (UK)	0.58	0.59	0.53	0.57	0.48	0.29	0.70	0.01	0.22	1.00	
US (US)	0.83	0.93	0.57	0.72	0.64	0.07	0.63	-0.11	0.50	0.69	1.00

Table 18.1b Sample correlation matrix of CD rates (January 1972 to December 1992)

Country	BE	CA	DE	FR	GE	JA	NE	SWE	SWI	UK	US
Belgium (BE)	1.00										
Canada (CA)	0.59	1.00									
Denmark (DE)	0.72	0.36	1.00								
France (FR)	0.71	0.37	0.76	1.00							
Germany (GE)	0.58	0.29	0.52	0.63	1.00						
Japan (JA)	0.59	0.29	0.34	0.33	0.39	1.00					
Netherlands (NE)	0.77	0.58	0.63	0.69	0.62	0.23	1.00				
Sweden (SWE)	0.31	0.30	-0.07	-0.02	-0.04	0.53	0.06	1.00			
Switzerland (SWI)	0.53	0.32	0.29	0.43	0.69	0.63	0.44	0.45	1.00		
UK (UK)	0.71	0.48	0.55	0.57	0.58	0.36	0.75	0.55	0.25	1.00	
US (US)	0.77	0.68	0.55	0.65	0.66	0.51	0.71	0.60	0.33	0.64	1.00

Table 18.2a Granger causality test of Prime rates: marginal significance levels of the F-test (January 1972 to December 1992)*

Country	BE	CA	DE	FR	GE	JA	NE	SWE	SWI	UK	US
Belgium (BE)		0.001	0.000	0.069	0.953	0.103	0.467	0.067	0.436	0.011	0.036
Canada (CA)	0.116		0.257	0.877	0.015	0.859	0.159	0.185	0.136	0.129	0.571
Denmark (DE)	0.947	0.174		0.611	0.173	0.012	0.172	0.432	0.412	0.250	0.368
France (FR)	0.011	0.030	0.075		0.668	0.047	0.096	0.346	0.342	0.162	0.047
Germany (GE)	0.051	0.163	0.002	0.000		0.143	0.021	0.560	0.005	0.094	0.216
Japan (JA)	0.091	0.939	0.201	0.960	0.874		0.490	0.315	0.359	0.305	0.812
Netherlands (NE)	0.089	0.391	0.000	0.483	0.225	0.413		0.354	0.961	0.004	0.873
Sweden (SWE)	0.527	0.899	0.588	0.468	0.299	0.733	0.285		0.168	0.156	0.011
Switzerland (SWI)	0.049	0.495	0.170	0.433	0.273	0.003	0.254	0.629		0.364	0.846
UK (UK)	0.665	0.875	0.186	0.922	0.655	0.464	0.039	0.016	0.762		0.476
US (US)	0.000	0.000	0.502	0.005	0.003	0.310	0.261	0.173	0.078	0.519	

* The ith,jth entry in this table represents the level of significance associated with the F-statistic from the test of null hypothesis that the ith country (row) does not Granger-cause the jth country (column).

Table 18.2b Granger causality test of CD rates: marginal significance levels of the F-test (January 1972 to December 1992)*

Country	BE	CA	DE	FR	GE	JA	NE	SWE	SWI	UK	US
Belgium (BE)		0.002	0.000	0.049	0.579	0.753	0.706	0.133	0.476	0.012	0.679
Canada (CA)	0.900		0.969	0.925	0.899	0.984	0.784	0.782	0.916	0.594	0.889
Denmark (CE)	0.188	0.954		0.992	0.948	0.029	0.462	0.739	0.349	0.269	0.034
France (FR)	0.125	0.323	0.118		0.766	0.430	0.023	0.079	0.032	0.101	0.017
Germany (GE)	0.002	0.823	0.106	0.034		0.869	0.045	0.387	0.055	0.001	0.214
Japan (JA)	0.630	0.738	0.631	0.192	0.708		0.869	0.558	0.019	0.082	0.047
Netherlands (NE)	0.000	0.000	0.005	0.005	0.632	0.386		0.265	0.166	0.002	0.858
Sweden (SWE)	0.921	0.933	0.163	0.643	0.175	0.837	0.265		0.024	0.437	0.786
Switzerland (SWI)	0.362	0.813	0.467	0.479	0.179	0.949	0.650	0.550		0.783	0.098
UK (UK)	0.235	0.302	0.153	0.586	0.023	0.333	0.476	0.679	0.825		0.048
US (US)	0.377	0.011	0.987	0.646	0.001	0.011	0.063	0.261	0.254	0.766	

* The ith,jth entry in this table represents the level of significance associated with the F-statistic from the test of null hypothesis that the ith country (row)

rates, there are no signs of a feedback effect. However, while Germany plays an important role in the European market, its rates are themselves Granger-caused by the movements in the US interest rate. Notably, Japan is found to play a limited role in the interactions within the interest rate transmission mechanism. While we find the movements in Switzerland's Prime rates to Granger-cause Japan's lending rates, the opposite is true in the borrowing market. The Swedish lending and borrowing markets are found to be relatively insulated from the influence of the other countries. Finally, bi-directional causality is documented between the US–French and US–Belgium Prime rates, and between the US–Japan CD rates.

In sum, the bi-variate causality results provide us with two striking patterns. Firstly, Germany seems to be the prominent nation in the European bank lending and borrowing markets. The movements in the German rates lead to adjustments in the interest rates of Belgium, France, the Netherlands, Switzerland and the UK, in both the lending and borrowing markets. Moreover, only the US rate is seen to influence the German market. This is consistent with the prior evidence on intermarket linkages in interest rates (for instance, see Katsimbris and Miller 1993; Artus 1991). Secondly, the US does not play a unique dominant role in the determination of bank lending and borrowing rates. While the US rate leads most of the European rates, it is also influenced by the movements in the rates of other countries. For instance, Belgium, France and Sweden cause the US Prime rates in the lending market, and Denmark, France, Japan and the UK cause the US CD rates in the borrowing market.

To obtain additional insight into the transmission mechanism of the Prime and CD rate movements, we examine the pattern of dynamic responses of six markets (Belgium, Denmark, France, the Netherlands, Switzerland and the UK) to innovations in the German rates.[8] For this purpose, we employ the simulated response of the estimated VAR system. Tables 18.3a and 18.3b provide the normalized impulse response of the six countries to a typical shock, i.e. positive shocks of one unit deviation, in the German rates. The response to innovations in the German Prime rates and the CD rates are presented in Tables 18.3a and 18.3b respectively. To facilitate the interpretation of both tables, we plot the time-paths of the impulse responses of the six markets to a German shock (see Figure 18.1). It is observed that all of the countries accommodate most of the innovations in the German rates within three months (although, the response to the shock in the lending market is generally found to be relatively sluggish as compared with an equivalent shock in the borrowing market). It may be interesting to note that the UK Prime rates seem to slightly underreact in the month following the German shock. This is corrected, however, by a positive reaction in the subsequent month. Finally, it is observed that while it is the bank lending market that overreacts in Denmark, France and the Netherlands, it is the borrowing rates that are found to overreact in

281

Table 18.3a Impulse response to a unit shock in the German Prime rates (January 1972 to December 1992)

Months after shock	BE	DE	FR	NE	SWI	UK
1	0.25	0.00	0.14	0.23	0.11	−0.07
2	0.21	0.13	0.29	0.33	−0.03	0.21
3	0.22	0.35	0.15	0.33	0.11	0.32
4	0.12	0.11	0.09	0.18	0.03	0.14
5	0.08	0.12	0.10	0.15	0.04	0.09
6	0.05	0.10	0..06	0.09	0.04	0.05
7	0.04	0.06	0.05	0.06	0.02	0.04
8	0.03	0.05	0.04	0.04	0.02	0.04
9	0.02	0.04	0.03	0.03	0.01	0.03

Table 18.3b Impulse response to a unit shock in the German CD rates (January 1972 to December 1992)

Months after shock	BE	DE	FR	NE	SWI	UK
1	0.30	0.00	0.08	0.20	0.16	0.26
2	0.24	0.02	0.16	0.26	0.08	0.29
3	0.05	0.12	0.16	0.21	0.13	0.02
4	0.07	0.02	0.05	0.04	0.02	0.04
5	0.04	−0.01	0.03	0.06	0.02	0.03
6	0.02	0.03	0.03	0.04	0.02	0.00
7	0.02	0.01	0.02	0.01	0.01	0.00
8	0.01	0.00	0.01	0.01	0.00	0.01
9	0.00	0.00	0.01	0.01	0.00	0.00

Belgium, Switzerland and the UK. The results from the impulse response functions generally corroborate the German prominence in the European bank lending and borrowing markets.

CONCLUSION

This chapter provides evidence on the interdependencies in the structure of national bank lending and borrowing rates across eleven industrialized nations. The emphasis has been on investigating the causal patterns and deciphering the mechanism by which innovations in the national Prime and CD rates are transmitted to other markets. The evidence indicates strong interdependencies among the national lending and borrowing markets. The German rates are found to have a significant influence on the European market and are themselves found to be influenced by the US market. Notably, the Japanese rates are found to be relatively insulated from the changes in the external rates. Finally, we analyzed the dynamic responses of Belgium, Denmark, France, the Netherlands, Switzerland and the UK to

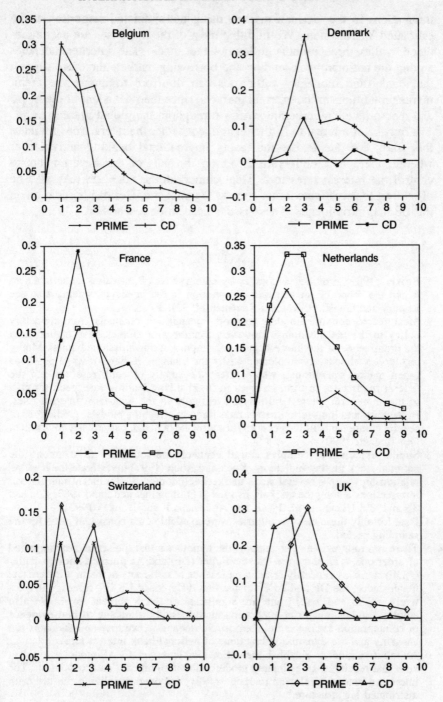

Figure 18.1 Time-paths of impulse responses to German shocks

innovations in the German market, using the simulated responses of the estimated VAR system. We find that most of the responses are accommodated within three months following the shock. The interdependencies among the national bank lending and borrowing markets therefore suggest that banks and monetary authorities can ill-afford to ignore the credit market conditions in the external markets, since their decisions at the micro and macro levels reverberate swiftly throughout the global markets.

It may be of interest to further examine whether the interactions found in this study are due to the increasing international banking activities or whether there is a deliberate effort on the part of the governments to control the interest rates in a 'Deutschmark/dollar zone'. It may also be of interest to investigate issues such as the impact of German unification on the German prominence. These issues need to be researched.

NOTES

1 Broker (1989) provides a country-by-country list of measures undertaken to widen the scope of interest rate competition in the financial system. Also see Khoury and Ghosh (1987) and Kaufman (1992).

2 Most macroeconomic models rely on transmission channels from monetary policy to the real economy. However, a number of studies have documented the prominence of the interest rate as an important transmission channel. Monetary policy shocks are implemented by the changes in bank reserve positions (open market operations), which affect the supply of bank reserves and the federal funds rate. In turn, changes in interbanking lending rates feed through to the short-term interest rates and eventually to the long-term interest rates. Both short- and long-term interest rates directly affect the models' predictions of several components of the economy's aggregate demand, particularly investment (see Bennett 1990).

3 Similar evidence of complex causal channels are found to exist among the national stock market indicators. Koch and Koch (1991) investigate the lead/lag relationships across several stock markets and document significant multilateral intersections among the market (also see Schollhammer and Sand 1987; Eun and Shim 1989; Hamao et al. 1990; and Arshanapalli and Doukas 1993).

4 Data for only these eleven countries were available on a consistent basis for the sampling period.

5 There is strong evidence to support the hypothesis that the series are integrated of order one, I(1), since the Dickey–Fuller (DF) and Augmented Dickey–Fuller (ADF) statistics generally reject the presence of unit roots in the first difference. For instance, the DF and ADF for the first differenced US CD rates are respectively -7.33 and -4.15 and are significant at the 5 percent level. We also employ Engle–Granger cointegration analysis and are unable to find evidence of cointegration for the sample period. Subsequently, we focus on the short-run causality and the dynamic interactions of national bank interest rates.

6 An intuitive guide to establish the optimal lag length in a VAR model is to select an n that results in an estimated model without significant autocorrelation. The interested reader is referred to Hsiao (1981) for operationalizing the test with distributed lag structure.

7 It should be stressed that the VAR model is strictly appropriate only when the

variables are stationary. For nonstationary variables, they are valid only approximately or, in some cases, may not be valid at all (see Charemza and Deadman 1992, p. 194).
8 We concentrate only on the German rates, since Germany alone was found to be the dominant player in both the bank lending and borrowing markets.

REFERENCES

Akaike, H. (1973) "Information Theory and the Extension of the Maximum Likelihood Principle," in B.N. Petrov and F. Caski (eds) *Second International Symposium on Information Theory*, Budapest.
Argy, V. and Z. Hodjera (1973) "Financial Integration and Interest Rate Linkages in Industrial Countries," *International Monetary Fund Staff Papers*.
Arshanapalli, B. and J. Doukas (1993) International Stock Market Linkages: Evidence from the Pre- and Post-October 1987 Period," *Journal of Banking and Finance* 17, 193–208.
Artus, P. (1991) "Transmission of US Monetary Policy to Europe and Asymmetry in the European Monetary System", *European Economic Review* 35, 1369–84.
Bennett, P. (1990) "The Influence of Financial Changes on Interest Rates and Monetary Policy: A Review of Recent Evidence," *Federal Reserve Bank of New York Quarterly Review*.
Bernanke, B.S. and A. Blinder (1988) "Credit, Money, and Aggregate Demand," *American Economic Review* 78, 435–9.
Bernanke, B.S. and A. Blinder (1992) "The Federal Funds Rate and the Channels of Monetary Transmission," *American Economic Review* 82, 901–21.
Broker, G. (1989) "Competition in Banking," in *Trends in Banking Structure and Regulation in OECD Countries*, OECD Catalogue of publications.
Charemza, W.W. and D.F. Deadman (1992) *New Directions in Economic Practice* London: Edward Elgar Publishing Limited.
Eun, C.S. and S. Shim (1989) "International Transmission of Stock Market Movements," *Journal of Financial and Quantitative Analysis* 24, 241–56.
Fratianni, M. and J. von Hagen (1990) "German Dominance in the EMS: The Empirical Evidence," *Open Economic Review* 1, 67–87.
Fung, H.G. and S.C. Isberg (1992) "The International Transmission of Eurodollar and U.S. Interest Rates: A Cointegration Analysis," *Journal of Banking and Finance* 16, 757–69.
Gertler, M. and S. Gelchrist (1993) "The Role of Credit Market Imperfections in the Monetary Transmission Mechanism: Arguments and Evidence," *Finance and Economics Discussion Series (FEDS)* No. 93–5, Board of Governors of the Federal Reserve System.
Hamao, Y., R.W. Masulis and V. Ng (1990) "Correlations in Price Changes and Volatility Across International Stock Markets," *Review of Financial Studies* 3, 281–307.
Hartman, D.G. (1984) "The International Financial Market and U.S. interest rates, *Journal of International Money and Finance* 3, 91–103.
Hendershott, P.H. (1967) "The Structure of International Interest Rates: The U.S. Treasury Bill Rate and the Eurodollar Deposit Rate," *Journal of Finance* 22, 455–65.
Hsiao, C. (1981) "Autoregressive Modelling and Money-Income Causality Detection," *Journal of Monetary Economics* 7, 85–106.
Kaen, F.R. and G.A. Hachey (1983) "Eurocurrency and National Money Market

Interest Rates: An Empirical Investigation of Causality," *Journal of Money, Credit and Banking* 15, 327–38.

Katsimbris, G.M., and S. Miller (1993) "Interest Rate Linkages within the European Monetary System: Further Analysis," *Journal of Money, Credit and Banking* 25, 771–9.

Kaufman, G. (ed.) (1992) *Banking Structures in Major Countries*, Massachusetts: Kluwer Academic Publishers.

Khoury, S.J. and A. Ghosh (1987) *Recent Developments in International Banking and Finance*, Vol. 1, Lexington, Ky.: Lexington Books.

Koch, P.D. and T.W. Koch (1991) "Evolution in Dynamic Linkages Across Daily National Stock Indexes," *Journal of International Money and Finance* 10, 231–51.

Koedijk, K.J. and C.J.M. Kool (1992) "Dominant Interest and Inflation Differentials within the EMS," *European Economic Review* 36, 9253–67.

Levin, J.H. (1974) "The Eurodollar Market and the International Transmission of Interest Rates," *Canadian Journal of Economics* 7, 205–24.

Romer, C.D. and D.H. Romer (1990) "New Evidence on the Monetary Transmission Mechanism," *Brookings Papers on Economic Activity* 1, 149–213.

Schnitzel, P. (1983) "Testing for the Direction of Causation Between the Domestic Monetary Base and the Eurodollar System," *Weltwirtschaftliches Archiv*, 616–29.

Schollhammer, H. and O.C. Sand (1987) "Lead-lag Relationships Among National Equity Markets: An Empirical Investigation," in S. Khoury and A. Ghosh (eds) *Recent Developments in International Banking and Finance*, Vol. 1, Lexington, Ky.: Lexington Books.

Sims, C. (1980) "Macroeconomics and Reality," *Econometrica* 48, 1–48.

Swanson, P.E. (1988) "Interrelationships among Domestic and Eurocurrency Deposit Yields: A Focus on the U.S. Dollar, *The Financial Review* 23, 81–94.

19

EUROPEAN UNION EQUITY MARKET REACTIONS TO THE 1992–93 ERM CRISIS

Ahmad Etebari and Fred R. Kaen

The objective of this chapter is to determine whether Bundesbank interest rate announcements affected ERM equity markets. The purpose for undertaking the research is to evaluate claims that the Bundesbank acts, willingly or unwillingly, as the central bank for all ERM countries. If the Bundesbank is a policy-setting central bank for EU countries, all ERM-country equity markets should be affected by Bundesbank interest rate policy changes. We find that ERM-country equity market returns were affected by the 1992–93 ERM currency crises. Negative returns on ERM-country stock markets were associated with Bundesbank interest rate increases and positive returns on ERM-country stock markets were associated with Bundesbank interest rate decreases. We conclude that Bundesbank interest rate policies affected not only German equity markets but other ERM-country equity markets as well.

INTRODUCTION

European currency markets were in turmoil during much of 1992 and 1993. This turmoil eventually resulted in a major restructuring of the European Exchange Rate Mechanism (ERM), the system by which participating European Community (EC), now the European Union (EU), members maintained fixed-but-adjustable exchange rates among themselves. For many people, the villain responsible for this turmoil was the Deutsche Bundesbank and its anti-inflationary monetary policies; especially its interest rate policies.[1] Popular press accounts of the crisis date its beginning with a supposedly surprise increase in the Bundesbank's discount rate on 16 July 1992 and its end with the decision of European Community finance ministers and central bank governors on 2 August 1993 to substantially widen the range within which bilateral exchange rates could depart from their fixed central rates. Sherman and Kaen (1994) document that Bundesbank interest rate announcements during this period were associated with abnormal exchange rate changes and increased volatility in bilateral German mark/ERM member exchange rates.

The objective of this chapter is to determine whether these Bundesbank interest rate announcements affected ERM equity markets as well as currency markets. The purpose for undertaking the research is to evaluate claims that the Bundesbank acts, willingly or unwillingly, as the central bank for all ERM countries. All ERM-country equity markets should be affected by Bundesbank interest rate policy changes if the Bundesbank is a policy-setting central bank for EU countries. This prediction is based on the findings of many studies which report that central bank discount rate changes are associated with statistically significant abnormal returns on their respective domestic markets (Thornton, 1982; Dueker, 1992; Hakkio and Pearce, 1992; Waud, 1970; Pearce and Roley, 1985; Smirlock and Yawitz, 1985; Born and Moser, 1990; Kaen and Tehranian, 1994). These studies find that central bank interest rate increases are associated with negative equity market abnormal returns, and interest rate decreases with positive equity market abnormal returns.

We find that ERM-country equity market returns were affected by the 1992–93 ERM currency crises. Negative returns on ERM-country stock markets were associated with Bundesbank interest rate increases and positive returns on ERM-country stock markets were associated with Bundesbank interest rate decreases.

Our chapter is organized as follows: The following section contains a brief description of the ERM and a chronology of the 1992–93 ERM crisis with special regard to Bundesbank actions. We describe our research procedures, events and data in the next section. We then report our empirical results, with our conclusions being given in the final section.

THE ERM DURING THE 1992–93 CRISIS

The Exchange Rate Mechanism (ERM) is a system of rules for maintaining fixed-but-adjustable exchange rates among members of the European Community (now European Union) who choose to join the arrangement. ERM member countries define the value of their currencies in terms of the European Currency Unit (ECU) and agree to maintain the market value of their currency within an agreed-upon band around this fixed rate. The process of setting a fixed ECU rate for each currency simultaneously defines the bilateral central exchange rates for the ERM members. Each ERM member is committed to maintaining the market value of its currencies within these bilateral central rate bands (intervention points) through direct intervention in the currency markets and appropriate domestic monetary and fiscal policies. Changes in central rates, called currency realignments, are permitted if the fundamental value of a currency diverges from its ECU and bilateral central rates. However, such changes are undertaken as a last resort measure and are expected to be unnecessary if member countries follow common monetary and fiscal policies.

Prior to the 1992–93 crisis, there had been no ERM exchange rate realignments since early 1987. The Bundesbank describes this period as one of "relative calm" and "free of tensions" as the EC members moved in the direction of a monetary union based on the Treaty of European Unity (the Maastricht Treaty) signed by EC foreign ministers on 7 February 1992 (Deutsche Bundesbank, 1992a).

Then, on 2 June 1992 Denmark held a popular referendum on the Maastricht Treaty and the Treaty was rejected. This rejection, along with concerns about an upcoming French referendum on the Treaty, caused investors and exchange market traders to reevaluate expectations for European Monetary Union (EMU) and question existing ERM central rates. It was against this background of uncertainty about EMU and eventual ratification of the Maastricht Treaty that the Bundesbank raised its discount rate to 8.75 percent from 8.00 percent on 16 July 1992. The Bundesbank said it raised the discount rate "to moderate inflation, monetary growth and the overly rapid expansion of the credit volume, and to strengthen confidence in the maintenance of the stability of the Deutsche Mark even under the currently more difficult conditions in united Germany" (Deutsche Bundesbank, 1992b). The action was widely criticized in the British and French press with the Bundesbank being accused of worsening the existing European recession and pursuing purely domestic policy objectives at the expense of its European neighbors and partners (Marsh, 1992).

Towards the end of August, with the approaching September French referendum on the Maastricht Treaty, a number of ERM currencies and especially the Italian lire began trading near or at their lower German mark intervention points. Under ERM rules, member country central banks were obliged to intervene and support the currencies. This intervention required massive sales of marks by the Bundesbank (DM 44 billion), sales which inflated the domestic German money supply and bank liquidity. According to newspaper reports, Helmut Schlesinger, the Bundesbank president, attended a secret meeting with the German chancellor and other senior German officials on Friday, 11 September 1992 and asked the chancellor to approve negotiations concerning the realignment of ERM currencies. A meeting was held with the outcome being a 7 percent devaluation of the Italian lire on Monday, 14 September 1992, the first exchange rate realignment since 1987. On the same day, the Bundesbank lowered its discount rate from 8.75 percent to 8.25 percent and its Lombard rate from 9.75 percent to 9.50 percent.

These actions were insufficient to calm European currency markets. The British pound came under heavy selling pressure, and both it and the Italian lire withdrew from the ERM a few days later (17 September 1992) amid severe European criticism of Bundesbank and German attitudes. Later in the year, on 23 November 1992, the Spanish peseta and the Portuguese escudo were devalued followed by a devaluation of the Irish punt on 1 February 1993.

Immediately after the Irish punt devaluation, the Bundesbank cut its discount and Lombard rates. This 4 February 1993 rate cut was followed by four subsequent discount and/or Lombard rate reductions during the spring and early summer of 1993. For a brief period, the situation in the ERM appeared calm relative to 1992. During June and early July, 1993 rumors even began circulating in the financial press and among policy economists that the French franc had become the ERM anchor currency.

By the middle of July 1993 turmoil had returned to the ERM. The French franc came under heavy selling pressure, once again necessitating massive ERM intervention by the Bundesbank (DM 60 billion in the latter half of July). This 1993 crisis exploded on 29 July 1993 when the Bundesbank cut its Lombard rate but not the discount rate. Currency market observers and traders interpreted this action as signalling that the Bundesbank was merely making a gesture to placate other ERM countries and was not about to loosen monetary policy and lower domestic interest rates by further cutting the discount rate.

On Sunday, 1 August 1993 a crisis meeting of EC foreign ministers was held – a meeting described in the German press as a French–German duel which the French fought with all the means at her disposal in an effort to force the Bundesbank to cut its interest rates but which the Germans ultimately won. The outcome of the meeting was to widen temporarily the obligatory marginal intervention thresholds of the participants in the ERM from +/−2.5 percent to +/−15 percent around the bilateral central rates.

EVENTS, DATA AND RESEARCH PROCEDURES

We test whether Bundesbank interest rate and related ERM exchange rate announcements during the 1992–93 ERM crisis affected ERM domestic equity market prices and whether these announcements were associated with changes in stock price volatility. We are interested in two types of interest rate announcements: (1) Bundesbank discount and Lombard rate changes and (2) Bundesbank security repurchase agreement announcements.

The Bundesbank's discount rate is the lowest rate at which banks can borrow (rediscount money market paper) from the Bundesbank.[2] The rate is a below-market rate and borrowing quotas are set by the Bundesbank. The "quotas" are considered a permanent source of bank financing, and changes in the quota and rates directly affect the cost and availability of bank credit to German firms.

The Lombard facility is an "emergency" funding facility similar to the US discount window. Lombard rates are always above discount rates and usually serve as a cap on short-term money market rates. Should short-term money market rates rise above the Lombard rate, banks would be motivated to borrow at the Lombard rate rather than in the money market.[3]

Both discount and Lombard rates are set by the Bundesbank at bi-weekly meetings. These meetings are usually held every other Thursday and the meeting dates are known in advance.

Security repurchase agreements (Repos) with German banks are the primary tool used by the Bundesbank for managing the short-term reserve position of German banks. The Bundesbank conducts weekly repurchase agreement tenders with a repurchase rate being established by the Bundesbank. The repurchase rate will seldom exceed the Lombard rate because banks would then elect to use the Lombard facility instead of the repurchase facility for obtaining needed liquidity. In effect, the Bundesbank repurchase rate is capped by the Lombard rate.

However, one strategy the Bundesbank follows for altering monetary policy is to drive up/down market interest rates at its weekly repurchase tenders and subsequently justify an increase/decrease in the discount or Lombard rates on the basis of higher/lower market interest rates. Consequently, financial market participants closely monitor the Bundesbank's security repurchase operations in order to forecast Bundesbank monetary policies.[4]

There were seven discount and/or Lombard rate change announcements during the 1992–93 crisis period. These rate change events are listed in Table 19.1. We also list our Bundesbank related ERM crisis announcements in Table 19.1 because these events were supposedly caused by the Bundesbank's interest rate policies and are identified as major ERM events by the Bundesbank in its publications.

Security repurchase agreement rate changes are listed in Table 19.2. Until the end of September 1992 the Bundesbank used one-month maturity repurchase agreements for controlling interest rate and bank liquidity conditions. On 2 October 1992 the Bundesbank made a major change in its repurchase agreement operating policies by switching to two-week (14-day) maturities. According to the Bundesbank, these 14-day maturities gave it more flexibility to respond to changing financial and economic conditions than did the one-month maturities.

Both variable-rate and fixed-rate repurchase agreement tender offerings occurred during the period. Under a variable-rate offering, banks submit bids for both the quantity of repurchase agreement funds desired and the interest rate they will pay. The Bundesbank arranges the bids in descending interest rate order and then determines how many bids to accept. The average variable interest rate reported in Table 19.2 is the average interest rate on the repurchase agreements entered into by the Bundesbank. Under a fixed-rate offering, the Bundesbank announces the rate it will charge for repurchase agreements and the banks bid only for the quantity of funds

Table 19.1 Bundesbank discount and/or Lombard rate change announcements and major Exchange Rate Mechanism events (1 January 1992 through 2 August 1993)

Date	ERM event
6 April 1992	Portugal joins ERM
16 July 1992	Discount rate raised from 8.00% to 8.75%
14 September 1992	Italian lire devalued
14 September 1992	Discount rate lowered from 8.75% to 8.25%; Lombard rate lowered from 9.75% to 9.50%
14 September 1992	Italian lire devalued
17 September 1992	British pound and Italian lire leave ERM
23 September 1992	France and Germany publish joint statement reaffirming central rates
2 October 1992	Bundesbank moves to 14-day security repurchase agreements to give it flexibility
5 October 1992	Trading day following 14-day security repurchase announcement
23 November 1992	Spanish peseta and Portuguese escudo are devalued
5 January 1993	France and Germany reaffirm central rates
1 February 1993	Irish punt is devalued by 10%
4 February 1993	Discount rate lowered from 8.25% to 8.00%; Lombard rate lowered from 9.50% to 9.00%
18 March 1993	Discount rate lowered from 8.00% to 7.50%
22 April 1993	Discount rate lowered from 7.50% to 7.25%; Lombard rate lowered from 9.00% to 8.50%
1 July 1993	Discount rate lowered from 7.25% to 6.75%; Lombard rate lowered from 8.50% to 8.250%
29 July 1993	Lombard rate lowered from 8.250% to 7.750%
2 August 1993	Wider margins for remaining ERM currencies

Note: The dates are the announcement dates reported in various issues of the *Monthly Report of the Deutsche Bundesbank*.

they want at the fixed rate. The Bundesbank then decides how many bids to accept (quantity of funds to supply) at the fixed rate.

Data and analytical procedures

We collected daily values of stock market indexes for all ERM countries except Portugal from the *Financial Times*. The countries and their respective stock market indexes are listed in Table 19.3. Portugal is not included because no Portuguese index was reported in the *Financial Times*.

We test whether Bundesbank interest rate policy announcements affected domestic equity prices by estimating indicator regression equations and calculating equity index abnormal returns for the individual events. We also test whether there were changes in the volatility of daily equity index returns by dividing the crisis period in intervals based on the ERM events and testing for differences in the variance of daily returns. Finally, we

Table 19.2 Bundesbank security repurchase agreement rate changes

Date	Rate change
3 January 1992	30-day average rate down from 9.550% to 9.425%
8 January 1992	30-day average rate down from 9.401% to 9.400%
26 February 1992	30-day average rate up from 9.400% to 9.450%
25 March 1992	30-day average rate up from 9.450% to 9.550%
8 April 1992	30-day average rate up from 9.550% to 9.600%
6 May 1992	30-day average rate up from 9.600% to 9.650%
22 July 1992	30-day average rate up from 9.650% to 9.700%
16 September 1992	60-day rate down from 9.750% to 9.350%
7 October 1992	14-day rate introduced at fixed 8.900%
21 October 1992	14-day variable marginal rate down from 8.900% to 8.750%
2 December 1992	14-day variable marginal rate up from 8.750% to 8.780%
9 December 1992	14-day variable marginal rate up from 8.780% to 8.800%
16 December 1992	14-day fixed rate down from 8.800% to 8.750%
13 January 1993	14-day fixed rate down from 8.750% to 8.600%
27 January 1993	14-day variable marginal rate down from 8.600% to 8.580%
3 February 1993	14-day variable marginal rate down from 8.580% to 8.570%
10 February 1993	14-day variable marginal rate down from 8.570% to 8.500%
17 February 1993	14-day variable marginal rate down from 8.500% to 8.490%
10 March 1993	14-day fixed rate down from 8.490% to 8.250%
1 April 1993	14-day variable marginal rate down from 8.250% to 8.170%
7 April 1993	14-day variable marginal rate down from 8.170% to 8.130%
14 April 1193	14-day variable marginal rate down from 8.130% to 8.110%
21 April 1993	14-day variable marginal rate down from 8.110% to 8.090%
28 April 1993	14-day variable marginal rate down from 8.090% to 7.750%
5 May 1993	14-day variable marginal rate down from 7.750% to 7.710%
12 May 1993	14-day variable marginal rate down from 7.710% to 7.600%
23 June 1993	14-day variable marginal rate down from 7.600% to 7.590%
1 July 1993	14-day variable marginal rate down from 7.590% to 7.580%
7 July 1993	14-day fixed rate down to 7.300%
14 July 1993	14-day variable marginal rate down from 7.300% to 7.280%
21 July 1993	14-day variable marginal rate down from 7.280% to 7.150%
28 July 1993	14-day variable marginal rate down from 7.150% to 6.950%

Note: The dates are the announcement dates reported in various issues of the *Monthly Report of the Deutsche Bundesbank*.

investigate whether ERM equity markets became more or less "integrated" during the ERM crisis period by examining the bi-lateral correlations of domestic equity market returns denominated in local currency.

EMPIRICAL RESULTS

Indicator regressions for rate change announcements

The effects of Bundesbank discount and/or Lombard interest rate changes on the ERM domestic equity indexes, hereafter equity indexes, were estimated with the following indicator variable regression model:

AHMAD ETEBARI AND FRED R. KAEN

Table 19.3 ERM countries and their respective stock indexes

Country	Stock index	Abreviated name in the study
Belgium	Belgium 20	BELGH-20
Denmark	Copenhagen SE	COPEN-SE
France	CAC General	CAC-GENL
Germany	FAZ Aktien	FAZ-AKT
Ireland	ISEQ Overall	ISEQ
Italy	Banca Com. Ital.	BANC-COM
Netherlands	CBS Ttl. Rtn. Gen.	CBS-TLR
Spain	Madrid SE	MDRD-SE
UK	Ordinary Share	UK-ORDY
ERM countries excluding Germany	Equally Weighted Average of Country Indexes	ERM-G

$$R_{jt} = a + b_1(\text{DLUP})_t + b_2(\text{DLDN})_t + e_t \qquad (1)$$

where R_{jt} = the daily percentage change in equity index j for day t;
$(\text{DLUP})_t$ = 1 if it is the day or day after the discount or Lombard rate was increased, otherwise 0; and
$(\text{DLDN})_t$ = 1 if it is the day or day after the discount or Lombard rate was decreased, otherwise 0.

The regression coefficient on the DLUP variable will be negative if increases in Bundesbank discount and/or Lombard rates "caused" domestic equity prices to fall. Conversely, the regression coefficient on the DLDN variable will be positive if reductions in Bundesbank interest rates were associated with increases in domestic equity prices. The estimated regression equations appear in Table 19.4.

The sign on DLUP is negative for all countries. However, only the Netherlands and the UK indexes have statistically significant negative regression coefficients.

The sign on DLDN is positive for all countries except the UK with the regression coefficients on the French index and the non-German equally weighted index being significant at the 0.05 level. If a one-tail test is used, the coefficients are also significantly positive for Belgium, Ireland and Germany. The evidence is consistent with the hypothesis that Bundesbank interest rate policies affected all ERM domestic equity markets and that market participants associated rate reductions with lower capital costs and/ or improved cash flow prospects for the ERM member country firms. (The UK was not part of the ERM during the period of rate reductions.) As explained in the next section, though, some rate changes contained more information than other rate changes.

The effects of Bundesbank security repurchase agreement rate change

Table 19.4 Indicator variable regressions for Bundesbank discount and/or Lombard rate change announcements during the 1992–3 ERM currency crisis

	Belgium BELG-20	Denmark COPEN-SE	France CAC-GENL	Germany FAZ-AKT	Ireland ISEQ	Italy BANC-COM	Netherlands CBS-TLR	Spain MDRD-SE	UK UK-ORDY	ERM ERM-G
Constant	0.0003	−0.0001	0.0004	0.0002	0.0004	0.0005	0.0007	0.0008	0.0007	0.0008
Std. error of estimate	0.0067	0.0071	0.0097	0.0078	0.0101	0.0168	0.0057	0.0247	0.0094	0.0083
R squared	0.70%	0.21%	1.14%	1.08%	0.88%	0.62%	1.62%	0.35%	0.80%	1.57%
DLUP	−0.0008	−0.0029	−0.0057	−0.0054	−0.0026	−0.0090	−0.0087	−0.0172	*−0.0123*	−0.0077
t-value	−0.1599	−0.5835	−0.8328	−0.9827	−0.3666	−0.7604	−2.1546	−0.9806	*−1.8518*	−1.3179
DLDN	0.0034	0.0015	*0.0058*	0.0038	0.0056	0.0071	0.0025	0.0053	−0.0002	*0.0054*
t-value	1.7294	0.7292	*2.0412*	1.6766	1.9035	1.4388	1.5148	0.7281	−0.0837	*2.2354*
NOBS	429	429	429	429	429	429	429	429	429	429
DF	426	426	426	426	426	426	426	426	426	426

Note: Statistically significant coefficients are shown in italic.

announcements on individual German mark bilateral exchange rates were estimated with the following indicator variable regression model:

$$R_{jt} = a + b_1(REPOUP)_t + b_2(REPODN)_t + e_t \qquad (2)$$

where R_{jt} = the daily percentage change in equity index j for day t;

(REPOUP)$_t$ = 1 if it is a day when the repurchase rate was increased, otherwise 0, and;

(REPODN)$_t$ = 1 if it is the day when the repurchase rate was decreased, otherwise 0.

As with the discount and Lombard rate changes, the expectation would be that reductions in repurchase rates would be associated with increases in equity prices while increases in repurchase rates would be associated with equity price decreases. The estimated regressions are reported in Table 19.5. The results are mixed and none of the regression coefficients are statistically significant at the 0.05 level. These statistical results suggest that, on average, repurchase rate changes were not associated with abnormal equity returns on ERM-country equity markets.

Event-by-event analysis of discount and Lombard rate changes

We estimated the effects of individual discount/Lombard rate changes on domestic equity indexes with an event-style methodology. We calculated abnormal daily percentage price changes for every index and then calculated t-statistics to test whether the abnormal changes were statistically significant.

To calculate the abnormal return we subtracted the expected change from the actual daily percentage change to obtain a mean-adjusted daily abnormal return. The expected change was obtained by averaging the returns over an estimation period which ran from 2 January 1992 through 30 March 1992.

The mean-adjusted abnormal return calculation is:

$$AR_{jt} = R_{jt} - \sum_{t=1}^{n} RE_{jt}/n \qquad (3)$$

where AR_{jt} = mean-adjusted return for index j on event day t;

R_{jt} = daily percentage change in index j for the test period;

RE_{jt} = daily percentage change in index j on day t of the estimation period, and

n = number of days in the estimation period.

The t-statistic was calculated by dividing the mean-adjusted return by the daily standard deviation of the percentage changes. The return standard deviation was calculated over the length of the estimation period. The test statistic, t, is:

Table 19.5 Indicator variable regressions for Bundesbank security repurchase agreement rate change announcements during the 1992–3 ERM currency crisis

	Belgium BELG-20	Denmark OPEN-S	France AC-GEN	Germany FAZ-AKT	Ireland ISEQ	Italy ANC-CO	Netherlands CBS-TLR	Spain MDRD-SE	UK UK-ORDY	ERM-G
Constant	0.0004	−0.0002	0.0008	0.0005	0.0006	0.0008	0.0008	0.0010	0.0006	0.0010
Std. error of estimate	0.0067	0.0071	0.0097	0.0078	0.0102	0.0168	0.0058	0.0248	0.0094	0.0083
R squared	0.54%	0.05%	0.56%	0.87%	0.25%	0.30%	0.23%	0.13%	0.02%	0.43%
REPOUP	−0.0036	0.0007	−0.0036	−0.0015	−0.0039	−0.0072	−0.0021	−0.0064	−0.0011	−0.0043
t-value	−1.3978	0.2439	−0.9794	−0.4939	−1.0122	−1.1269	−0.9494	−0.6741	−0.3054	−1.3487
REPODN	0.0008	0.0006	−0.0025	−0.0031	0.0004	0.0001	0.0003	−0.0016	−0.0002	−0.0001
t-value	0.5487	0.4072	−1.2250	−1.8873	0.1675	0.0309	0.2657	−0.3169	−0.0908	−0.0400
NOBS	429	429	429	429	429	429	429	429	429	429
DF	426	426	426	426	426	426	426	426	426	426

$$t_{AR_j} = \frac{AR_j}{sR_j} \tag{4}$$

where sR_j = standard deviation of daily percentage change for index j during the estimation period of 2 January 1992 through 30 March 1992.

We calculate announcement (event) returns and their associated t-statistics for the announcement day, defined as day 0; for the announcement day plus the day after the announcement (day 0 and day +1); for the day before through the day after the announcement (days −1 to +1); and, for the three days before through the day after the announcement (days −3 to +1). These returns are referred to as the event day returns, two-day cumulative returns, three-day cumulative returns and five-day cumulative returns. The two-day abnormal returns for the indexes are reported in Table 19.6. Table 19.7 contains the cumulative window event-day, two-day, three-day and five-day announcement returns for the six rate reduction announcements and the one rate increase announcement, respectively.

The 16 July 1992 discount rate increase was associated with a negative two-day abnormal return on German equities and negative two-day abnormal returns on every other ERM-country equity index. Statistically significant negative two-day abnormal returns of −1.75 percent appear on the Netherlands index, −3.50 percent on the Spanish index and −2.37 percent on the UK Ordinary Index. The two-day abnormal return on our non-German ERM index was a significant −1.47 percent. This discount rate increase clearly had spillover effects on European equity markets and supports the hypothesis that Bundesbank actions affected other ERM equity markets.

The first Bundesbank rate decrease during the 1992–93 crisis occurs on 14 September 1992. Every ERM-country equity market index has significantly positive abnormal returns on the announcement day. The announcement day abnormal return on the non-German ERM Index is 2.60 percent and is significant beyond the 0.01 level. However, the Italian lire was also devalued within the ERM on the same day; so, it is difficult to disentangle the two events. Further complicating the interpretation of abnormal returns around this first rate reduction announcement is the 17 September 1992 withdrawal of the British pound and Italian lire from the ERM.

The second Bundesbank rate decrease occurs on 4 February 1993, three days after the devaluation of the Irish punt. Once again, all ERM member equity markets show positive abnormal returns on the announcement day. The abnormal return on the non-German ERM Index is a significant 1.47 percent. The two-day abnormal returns are positive for all ERM countries except Denmark. (The UK, which has a negative announcement and two-day abnormal return, had left the ERM.)

Table 19.6 Two-day cumulative returns associated with Bundesbank discount and/or Lombard rate changes during the entire 1992–3 period

Date	Event	Belgium BELG-20	Denmark COPEN-SE	France CAC-GENL	Germany FAZ-AKT	Ireland ISEQ	Italy BANC-COM	Netherlands CBS-TLR	Spain MDRD-SE	UK UK-ORDY	ERM-G
July 16 1992	D up from 8% to 8.75%	-0.0032 -0.3431	-0.0039 -0.7183	-0.0140 -1.2607	-0.0128 -1.5637	-0.0037 -0.4860	-0.0169 -1.4825	-0.0175 -2.6117	-0.0350 -3.7388	-0.0237 -2.2695	-0.0147 -2.6543
Sept 14 1992	D down to 8.25%; L down to 9.50% from 9.75%	*0.0237* *2.5033*	*0.0080* *1.4597*	*0.0280* *2.5166*	*0.0324* *3.9552*	*0.0198* *2.5915*	*0.0172* *1.5159*	*0.0209* *3.1263*	*0.0223* *2.3788*	-0.0020 -0.1955	*0.0172* *3.1044*
Feb 4 1993	D lowered to 8.00%; L lowered to 9.00%	*0.0092* *0.9675*	*-0.0014* *-0.2586*	*0.0299* *2.6871*	*0.0251* *3.0625*	*0.0195* *2.5498*	*0.0270* *2.3745*	*0.0111* *1.6502*	*0.0080* *0.8595*	*-0.0035* *-0.3393*	*0.0125* *2.2448*
Mar 18 1993	D lowered to 7.50%	0.0025 0.2603	-0.0060 -1.0914	-0.0086 -0.7756	-0.0023 -0.2752	0.0387 5.0585	0.0082 0.7223	0.0025 0.3796	-0.0042 -0.4532	0.0084 0.8033	0.0052 0.9329
Apr 22 1993	D lowered to 7.25%; L lowered to 8.50%	*-0.0211* *-2.2295*	0.0092 1.6850	-0.0034 -0.3093	-0.0030 -0.3672	-0.0120 -1.5650	*0.0261* *2.2956*	-0.0099 -1.4713	*0.0166* *1.7795*	-0.0016 -0.1581	0.0005 0.0886
July 1 1993	D lowered to 6.75%; L lowered to 8.25%	-0.0002 -0.0176	-0.0032 -0.5920	-0.0091 -0.8157	0.0003 0.0388	0.0028 0.3712	0.0038 0.3363	-0.0046 -0.6834	-0.0039 -0.4164	-0.0149 -1.4310	-0.0016 -0.2826
July 29 1993	L lowered to 7.750%	0.0166 1.7558	*0.0233* *4.2690*	0.0167 1.5000	*-0.0183* *-2.2361*	0.0081 1.0585	0.0096 0.8470	0.0103 1.5334	*0.0208* *2.2234*	0.0171 1.6415	*0.0153* *2.7592*

Note: The cumulative returns are calculated as the sum of the daily excess returns for the announcement day and the day after the announcement date. t-values are shown below each cumulative return. Statistically significant results at 0.05 are shown in italic.

Table 19.7 Cumulative event-window returns for Bundesbank discount and/or Lombard rate changes

Date	Event window	Belgium BELG-20	Denmark COPEN-SE	France CAC-GENL	Germany FAZ-AKT	Ireland ISEQ	Italy BANC-COM	Netherlands CBS-TLR	Spain MDRD-SE	UK UK-ORDY	ALL-ERM
July 16 1992	Day 0	0.0000	0.0031	−0.0096	0.0000	0.0066	0.0029	−0.0027	−0.0106	−0.0030	−0.0017
		−0.0043	0.0809	−1.2237	−0.0039	1.2267	0.3588	−0.5742	−1.5967	−0.4098	−0.4241
	Days 0, +1	−0.0032	−0.0039	−0.0140	0.0133	−0.0037	−0.0169	−0.0175	−0.0350	−0.0237	−0.0147
		−0.3431	−0.7183	−1.2607	1.6267	−0.4860	−1.4825	−2.6117	−3.7388	−2.2695	−2.6543
	Days −1 to +1	0.0013	−0.0034	−0.0162	0.0134	0.0094	−0.0220	−0.0152	−0.0509	−0.0245	−0.0152
		0.1112	−0.5142	−1.1909	1.3318	1.0009	−1.5771	−1.8521	−4.4387	−1.9161	−2.2330
	Days −3 to +1	−0.0067	−0.0023	−0.0207	0.0002	0.0217	−0.0092	−0.0226	−0.0579	−0.0281	−0.0157
		−0.4450	−0.2605	−1.1727	0.0176	1.7922	−0.5113	−2.1351	−3.9175	−1.7044	−1.7899
Sept 14 1992	Day 0	0.0365	0.0171	0.0268	0.0383	0.0118	0.0327	0.0285	0.0283	0.0261	0.0260
		5.4521	4.4163	3.3975	6.4297	2.1852	4.0651	6.0162	4.2737	3.5441	6.6120
	Days 0, +1	0.0237	0.0080	0.0280	0.0324	0.0198	0.0172	0.0209	0.0223	−0.0020	0.0172
		2.5033	1.4597	2.5166	3.9552	2.5915	1.5159	3.1263	2.3788	−0.1955	3.1044
	Days −1 to +1	0.0284	0.0027	0.0367	0.0362	0.0160	0.0008	0.0302	0.0268	0.0110	0.0191
		2.4534	0.4020	2.6905	3.5989	1.7091	0.0592	3.6785	2.3351	0.8588	2.8040
	Days −3 to +1	0.0303	0.0023	0.0244	0.0133	0.0112	0.0223	0.0273	0.0007	0.0088	0.0159
		2.0271	0.2676	1.3865	1.0254	0.9286	1.2397	2.5802	0.0474	0.5338	1.8137
Feb 4 1993	Day 0	0.0049	0.0150	0.0153	0.0061	0.0138	0.0147	0.0046	0.0049	−0.0032	0.0147
		0.7291	3.8911	1.9390	1.0456	2.5535	1.8269	0.9622	0.7440	−0.4379	3.7515
	Days 0, +1	0.0092	−0.0014	0.0299	0.0251	0.0195	0.0270	0.0111	0.0080	−0.0035	0.0219
		0.9675	−0.2586	2.6871	3.0625	2.5498	2.3745	1.6502	0.8595	−0.3393	3.9411
	Days −1 to +1	0.0115	0.0058	0.0266	0.0317	0.0053	0.0261	0.0150	0.0174	0.0100	0.0225
		0.9929	0.8648	1.9503	3.1530	0.5623	1.8730	1.8252	1.5173	0.7794	3.3149
	Days −3 to +1	0.0262	0.0100	0.0283	0.0377	0.0636	0.0357	0.0212	0.0327	0.0181	0.0427
		1.7539	1.1601	1.6059	2.9101	5.2575	1.9884	2.0046	2.2087	1.0998	4.8627

		(1)	(2)	(3)	(4)	(5)	(6)	(7)	(8)	(9)	(10)
Mar 18 1993	Day 0	0.0007	−0.0003	−0.0042	−0.0009	0.0105	0.0092	0.0014	0.0040	−0.0009	0.0052
		0.0989	*−0.0726*	*−05360*	*−0.1636*	*1.9419*	*1.1463*	*0.3011*	*0.6080*	*−0.1260*	*1.3188*
	Days 0, +1	0.0025	−0.0060	−0.0086	−0.0023	0.0387	0.0082	0.0025	−0.0042	0.0084	0.0071
		0.2603	*−1.0914*	*−0.7756*	*−0.2752*	*5.0585*	*0.7223*	*0.3796*	*−0.4532*	*0.8033*	*1.2707*
	Days −1 to +1	0.0034	−0.0017	−0.0141	−0.0073	0.0492	−0.0109	0.0049	−0.0077	−0.0025	0.0023
		0.2894	*−0.2591*	*−1.0321*	*−0.7295*	*5.2514*	*−0.7854*	*0.5968*	*−0.6686*	*−0.1948*	*0.3358*
	Days −3 to +1	0.0053	−0.0045	−0.0162	−0.0179	0.0549	−0.0338	0.0118	−0.0179	−0.0005	−0.0053
		0.3559	*−0.5257*	*−0.9193*	*−1.3788*	*4.5377*	*−1.8810*	*1.1147*	*−1.2076*	*−0.0302*	*−0.5986*
Apr 22 1993	Day 0	−0.0055	−0.0013	−0.0071	−0.0037	−0.0012	0.0195	0.0017	0.0123	0.0082	0.0064
		−0.8188	*−0.3488*	*−0.8993*	*−0.6297*	*−0.2269*	*2.4233*	*0.3587*	*1.8623*	*1.1071*	*1.6285*
	Days 0, +1	−0.0211	0.0092	−0.0034	−0.0030	−0.0120	0.0261	−0.0099	0.0166	−0.0016	0.0055
		−2.2295	*1.6850*	*−0.3093*	*−0.3672*	*−1.5650*	*2.2956*	*−1.4713*	*1.7795*	*−0.1581*	*0.9826*
	Days −1 to +1	−0.0260	0.0067	−0.0140	−0.0153	−0.0117	0.0175	−0.0118	0.0108	0.0065	−0.0016
		−2.2469	*1.0030*	*−1.0272*	*−1.5241*	*−1.2450*	*1.2579*	*−1.4355*	*0.9391*	*0.5120*	*−0.2304*
	Days −3 to +1	−0.0301	0.0075	−0.0255	−0.0116	−0.0330	0.0363	−0.0144	0.0244	0.0164	0.0007
		−2.0146	*0.8708*	*−1.4495*	*−0.8981*	*−2.7277*	*2.0201*	*−1.3602*	*1.6515*	*0.9940*	*0.0789*
July 1 1993	Day 0	0.0088	0.0009	0.0044	0.0068	0.0036	−0.0024	0.0007	0.0007	−0.0041	0.0025
		1.3208	*0.2222*	*0.5553*	*1.1652*	*0.6746*	*−0.3027*	*0.1516*	*0.1094*	*−0.5551*	*0.6293*
	Days 0, +1	0.0177	0.0017	0.0087	0.0135	0.0073	−0.0049	0.0014	0.0014	−0.0082	0.0049
		−0.0176	*−0.5920*	*−0.8157*	*0.0388*	*0.3712*	*0.3363*	*−0.6834*	*−0.4164*	*−1.4310*	*−0.2826*
	Days −1 to +1	0.0069	0.0004	−0.0187	−0.0034	0.0074	0.0053	−0.0004	0.0020	−0.0116	0.0016
		0.5955	*0.0536*	*−1.3728*	*−0.3352*	*0.7888*	*0.3826*	*−0.0483*	*0.1741*	*−0.9086*	*0.2394*
	Days −3 to +1	0.0073	−0.0218	−0.0051	−0.0014	0.0367	0.0075	0.0022	−0.0023	−0.0126	0.0130
		0.4897	*2.5211*	*−0.2918*	*−0.1066*	*3.0298*	*0.4176*	*0.2120*	*−0.1580*	*−0.7648*	*1.4845*

Table 19.7 Continued

Date	Event window	Belgium BELG-20	Denmark COPEN-SE	France CAC-GENL	Germany FAZ-AKT	Ireland ISEQ	Italy BANC-COM	Netherlands CBS-TLR	Spain MDRD-SE	UK UK-ORDY	ALL-ERM
	Day 0	−0.0025	*0.0132*	−0.0087	−0.0062	*0.0012*	0.0056	0.0052	*0.0152*	0.0130	0.0059
		−0.3683	*3.4248*	−1.1090	−1.0755	*0.2235*	0.6972	1.0879	*2.3051*	1.7690	1.5022
July 29 1993	Days 0, +1	0.0166	0.0233	0.0167	−0.0183	0.0081	0.0096	0.0103	0.0208	0.0171	*0.0194*
		1.7558	4.2690	1.5000	−2.2361	1.0585	0.8470	1.5334	2.2234	1.6415	*3.4861*
(Lombard rate only)	Days −1 to +1	*0.0156*	*0.0260*	*0.0138*	*−0.0231*	*0.0125*	*0.0124*	*0.0143*	*0.0255*	*0.0171*	*0.0224*
		1.3429	*3.8786*	*1.0081*	*−2.2973*	*1.3357*	*0.8939*	*1.7467*	*2.2263*	*1.3405*	*3.2868*
	Days −3 to +1	0.0090	0.0266	0.0246	−0.0169	0.0191	0.0245	0.0242	0.0308	0.0358	0.0310
		0.5985	3.0720	1.3951	−1.3002	1.5772	1.3655	2.2886	2.0832	2.1710	3.5297

Note: Abnormal returns are shown for the announcement day, the announcement day plus the day after, the day before through the day after the announcement, and the three days before through the day after the announcement; *t*-values are shown below corresponding returns, and significant results are shown in italic. For the first event, the 16 July 1992 Bundesbank discount rate increase, the British pound and Italian lire were part of the ERM.

The 4 February 1993 Bundesbank rate reduction action was generally regarded as signalling that the Bundesbank would be following a cautious policy of gradual domestic interest rate reductions in the face of a weakening German economy. Subsequent rate reductions were expected; the timing and the size were unknown. Given this expectational context, market participants could be disappointed about the size of any announced rate reductions, viewing them as insufficient to calm the foreign exchange markets and stimulate economic activity.

We find abnormal returns consistent with this "timing and size" argument for the 18 March, 22 April and 1 July 1993 discount and Lombard rate reductions. Negative two-day abnormal returns appear on four of the seven in-the-ERM country indexes for the 18 March event and five of the seven in-the-ERM country indexes for the 22 April and 1 July events. The abnormal returns on the German FAZ index were among the negative group for the 18 March and 22 April rate reductions. The results suggest that market participants had either fully anticipated the reductions or were disappointed by their size.

The 29 July 1993 reduction in *only* the Lombard rate is associated with sharply contrasting behavior in the German and non-German equity markets. Little market reaction to the rate cut appears on the event day itself. However, for the two-day event period there is a statistically significant −1.83 percent abnormal return on the German FAZ index. In contrast to the FAZ index, every other index has a positive two-day abnormal return and the two-day return on the equally weighted non-German index is 1.53 percent.

The 29 July 1993 Lombard rate reduction produced the culmination of the 1992–93 ERM crises. Crisis meetings were held over the weekend and, on 3 August 1993, government officials announced that the ERM currency fluctuation bands would be widened from 2.5 percent to 15 percent. As developed later (see pp. 305–10), the "unusual" reaction of ERM equity markets to the 29 July Lombard rate reduction may be related to market expectations of how the escalating ERM currency market crisis would be resolved. With a widening of bands, the need for other ERM countries to follow German monetary policy would be reduced, effectively weakening the connection between Bundesbank interest rate policies and the interest rate policies of the other countries.

Repurchase agreement rate changes

We divided our repurchase agreement rate change events into four categories. Category 1 includes all increases in repurchase agreement rates over the entire 1992–93 period; category 2 includes all repurchase agreement rate decreases during this period. These results are reported in Table 19.8 under the headings "All repo up" and "All repo down."

Table 19.8 Cumulative event-day abnormal returns for Bundesbank security repurchase agreement rate changes

Event	Belgium BELG-20	Denmark COPEN-SE	France CAC-GENL	Germany FAZ-AKT	Ireland ISEQ	Italy BANC-COM	Netherlands CBS-TLR	Spain MDRD-SE	UK UK-ORDY	ALL-ERM
All repo up										
Cumulative return	-0.0347	0.0106	-0.0328	-0.0213	-0.0338	-0.0281	-0.0150	-0.0464	-0.0125	-0.0277
t-value	-5.1853	2.7536	-4.1585	-3.6643	-6.2395	-3.4973	-3.1590	-7.0196	-1.7006	-7.0499
All repo down										
Cumulative return	0.0158	0.0336	-0.0741	-0.0807	0.0380	0.0136	0.0098	-0.0650	0.0088	0.0110
t-value	2.3573	8.6798	-9.4122	-13.9079	7.0170	1.6896	2.0642	-9.8284	1.1900	2.8071
14-day repo up										
Cumulative return	-0.0114	0.0100	-0.0066	-0.0031	-0.0174	-0.0178	0.0016	-0.0153	-0.0123	-0.0122
t-value	-1.7049	2.5982	-0.8349	-0.5301	-3.2126	-2.2102	0.3433	-2.3103	-1.6710	-3.1171
14-day repo down										
Cumulative return	0.0139	0.0495	-0.0503	-0.0659	0.0499	0.0623	-0.0005	-0.0516	0.0143	0.0244
t-value	2.0829	12.7926	-6.3824	-11.3563	9.2161	7.7458	-0.1109	-7.8056	1.9445	6.2177

Note: The top entry in each cell is the cumulative percentage change on the announcement day ($t = 0$) over all of the repurchase rate change announcements included in the indicated category. There are five events in the all repo up category and twenty-one events in the all repo down category. On 2 October 1992, the Bundesbank moved to two-week repurchase maturities from two- and one-month maturities to gain control over domestic monetary conditions. The 14-day categories contain only those repo agreement rate change announcements which occurred after the 2 October 1992, policy change. There are two events in the 14-day repo down category. The bottom entry in each cell is the *t*-statistic for the event day abnormal return. Statistically significant results are shown in italic.

On 2 October 1992 the Bundesbank announced that, until further notice, it would offer security repurchase agreements with maturities of two-weeks (14 days), instead of one- and two-months, in order to enable it to respond flexibly to short-term changes in bank liquidity. This change was prompted by "huge foreign exchange inflows in the wake of the turmoil in the EMS" (Deutsche Bundesbank, 1992a: 48). Because of this major policy change, we created categories 3 and 4. Category 3 includes those repurchase rate agreement decreases since the Bundesbank implemented its two-week repurchase strategy; category 4 includes the post-announcement repurchase agreement rate increases.

No clearly identifiable pattern exists among the individual country equity indexes with regard to repurchase agreement rate changes. Both positive and negative abnormal returns are found for up and down changes. However, the abnormal returns on the ERM-G index are significantly negative for increases in the repurchase rate and significantly positive for decreases in the repurchase rates. Thus, from portfolio perspective, ERM country equity market returns behave as expected. Still, the consistently negative signs on French and German equity markets regardless of the direction of the rate change suggest that a more complex political story may lie behind the results.

Interest-rate-related ERM events

Throughout the entire 1992–93 crisis period, the Bundesbank was accused of setting domestic economic priorities above the needs of other European Community countries. Specifically, the Bundesbank was accused of keeping German interest rates "too high," thus impeding the attempts of other European countries to stimulate their economies in the face of high unemployment. The reasoning was as follows. Under the system of fixed ERM exchange rates, all member countries had to have the same interest rate; otherwise, funds would flow from the low-interest rate countries to the high interest rate countries. This fund flow would cause a depreciation of the low interest rate currencies relative to the high interest rate currencies, a depreciation which was not permitted under the rules of the ERM. This situation posed a dilemma for a number of ERM members. They could stay in the ERM and keep their interest rates at German levels or they could lower domestic interest rates and leave the ERM. In the meantime, these countries could blame Germany for the crisis and call on the Germans to lower German interest rates to levels desired by other ERM countries.

From the German perspective, lowering interest rates was thought undesirable because lower interest rates would exacerbate inflationary pressures in Germany. So, while the Germans agreed that lower interest rates for other ERM countries might be good policy; it was not good policy for Germany. It was against this political background that financial markets reacted to news about Bundesbank monetary policies and potential changes in the ERM central rates.

The Bundesbank identifies five important ERM-related events in its 1992 Annual Report. These events are:

1 The departure of the British pound and Italian lire from the ERM on 17 September 1992.
2 A reaffirmation of ERM central rates by German and French monetary authorities on 23 September 1992.
3 The decision by the Bundesbank to move to two-week repurchase agreement maturities on 2 October 1992.
4 The devaluation of the Spanish peseta and Portuguese escudo on 23 November 1992.
5 A second reaffirmation of ERM central rates by German and French monetary authorities on 5 January 1993.

We have added the following two similar 1993 events to the aforementioned five:

1 The devaluation of the Irish punt on 1 February 1993.
2 The widening of ERM bands on 2 August 1993.

The announcement day ($t = 0$) and the two-day event period ($t = 0, +1$) abnormal returns for these events are reported in Table 19.9.

The first event was the departure of the British pound and Italian lire from the ERM on 17 September 1992. The event day abnormal return on the UK Ordinary index was 5.74 percent; on the Italian Banca Index, 3.46 percent. The German FAZ Aktien index event day abnormal return was 1.17 percent. Other country equity indexes with statistically significant event day abnormal returns were Belgium, 1.77 percent and France, 1.63 percent.

The very large positive abnormal returns for the UK and Italy may be related to expectations of lower interest rates and expansionary policies for those countries. In contrast, the German markets might have responded positively because the Bundesbank would no longer need to sell marks (and thereby increase the German money supply) in order to support the pound and the lire. Corroborating evidence for this interpretation is found in the reaction of the German mark bilateral ERM exchange rates to the withdrawal announcement. The mark strengthened against all ERM currencies; an outcome consistent with the cessation of Bundesbank marginal ERM intervention (Kaen and Sherman, 1994).

Complicating the above interpretation, however, is the reaction of equity markets on the day after the withdrawal announcement. On this day all countries except the Netherlands recorded negative abnormal returns. The largest negative abnormal returns were recorded on the Danish index (-1.59 percent), the Spanish index (-1.33 percent) and the German

FAZ Aktien (−1.48 percent). The Danish krone and the Spanish peseta were considered "weak" currencies; they also had the largest fall in their currency values against the German mark on the withdrawal announcement date. Perhaps market participants were reacting to the depreciation of the pound and the lire against the mark and concluding that Danish and Spanish policy-makers would not be able to lower interest rates or pursue expansionary policies without bringing their currencies under pressure within the ERM. As for the German mark, it looked like the Bundesbank would still have to intervene to support some remaining ERM currencies.

This interest rate/intervention story continues to hold for the next major ERM event – the German and French reaffirmation of central rates on 23 September 1992. The two-day abnormal return on the German FAZ Atkien index is a significant 1.89 percent. Significant negative two-day abnormal returns are recorded on the Danish, Irish and Spanish equity indexes, all of whose currencies are considered "weak" within the ERM. Thus, the equity market reactions remain consistent with the hypothesis that a reaffirmation of central rates by Germany means that the Bundesbank will continue to determine interest rate policy for all ERM countries, thereby making it difficult for an ERM country to lower its interest rates for domestic policy reasons. As for Germany, once again the markets may be interpreting the reaffirmation announcement as meaning the Bundesbank will need to engage in marginal ERM intervention to support other ERM currencies. This intervention could limit the Bundesbank's ability to control inflationary pressures at home and/or discourage further interest rate reductions in the face of an expanding money supply caused by the ERM intervention.

Less than two weeks after the central bank reaffirmation announcement, the Bundesbank announced the shortening of its repurchase agreement maturities from two- and one-month to two weeks (14 days). This policy change was motivated by very large capital inflows to German banks caused by Bundesbank marginal ERM intervention. The Bundesbank explained that it was moving to 14-day maturities in order to gain control over bank liquidity and the money supply. The two-day equity market abnormal returns were uniformly negative: −2.89 percent for Germany; −4.41 percent, Belgium; −0.91 percent, Denmark; −3.95 percent, France; −2.75 percent, Ireland; −3.55 percent, the Netherlands; and −3.72 percent, Spain. Simultaneously in the foreign exchange market the German mark strengthened against every EC currency as well as against the US dollar and the Japanese yen (Kaen and Sherman, 1994).

On 23 November 1992, the Spanish peseta and Portuguese escudo were devalued within the ERM. This devaluation is associated with negative abnormal returns for all equity indexes except Ireland, which records a statistically significant 2.07 percent two-day abnormal return. The Spanish equity index records a −1.41 percent two-day abnormal return. The abnormal returns around the peseta devaluation do not conform to the interest

307

Table 19.9 Announcement-day abnormal returns for selected interest-rate-related ERM events.

	Belgium BELG-20	Denmark COPEN-S	France CAC-GENL	Germany FAZ-AKT	Ireland ISEQ	Italy ANC-CO	Netherlands CBS-TLR	Spain MDRD-SE	UK UK-ORDY	ERM-G
Pound & lira Leave ERM										
Day 0	0.0177	−0.0002	0.0163	0.0117	0.0033	0.0346	0.0023	−0.0024	0.0574	0.0178
t-value	2.6427	−0.0415	2.0721	2.0210	0.6144	4.2985	0.4960	−0.3572	7.7843	4.5323
Day 0, + 1	0.0195	−0.0161	−0.0075	−0.0031	−0.0086	−0.0141	0.0127	−0.0157	0.0518	0.0044
t-value	2.0627	−2.9376	−0.6773	−0.3752	−1.1205	−1.2428	1.8888	−1.6829	4.9708	0.7931
France & Germany Reaffirm rates										
Day 0	−0.0032	−0.0194	0.0438	0.0005	−0.0056	−0.0135	0.0017	−0.0124	−0.0045	−0.0036
t-value	−0.4781	−5.0091	5.5667	0.0898	−1.0440	−1.6847	0.3510	−1.8682	−0.6129	−0.9177
Day 0, + 1	0.0040	−0.0170	0.0431	−0.0189	−0.0161	−0.0063	0.0040	−0.0479	0.0137	−0.0069
t-value	0.4217	−3.1167	3.8672	−2.3041	−2.0997	−0.5579	0.5968	−5.1194	1.3101	−1.2473
Bundesbank moves to 14-day repo										
Day 0	−0.0096	0.0091	−0.0157	0.0006	0.0034	0.0061	−0.0052	0.0004	−0.0122	−0.0008
t-value	−1.4389	2.3424	−1.9872	0.1035	0.6258	0.7587	−1.0912	0.0554	−1.6584	−0.2084
Day 0, + 1	−0.0441	−0.0091	−0.0395	−0.0289	−0.0275	−0.0127	−0.0355	−0.0372	−0.0519	−0.0362
t-value	−4.6636	−1.6678	−3.5483	−3.5246	−3.5935	−1.1145	−5.2958	−3.9787	−4.9792	−6.5198
Peseta & escudo are devalued										
Day 0	−0.0061	−0.0131	−0.0012	0.0013	0.0176	0.0050	−0.0028	−0.0044	−0.0010	0.0001
t-value	−0.9087	−3.3993	−0.1570	0.2184	3.2480	0.6168	−0.5919	−0.6685	−0.1301	0.0140

	C1	C2	C3	C4	C5	C6	C7	C8	C9	C10
Day 0, + 1	−0.0126	−0.0295	−0.0211	−0.0155	0.0207	−0.0271	−0.0053	−0.0141	0.0017	−0.0192
t-value	*−1.3295*	*−5.4034*	*−1.8947*	*−1.8925*	*2.7096*	*−2.3831*	*−0.7857*	*−1.5061*	*0.1648*	*−3.4506*
France & Germany reaffirm rates										
Day 0	0.0100	0.0102	−0.0014	0.0112	0.0113	0.0084	0.0050	0.0218	−0.0096	0.0124
t-value	*1.4967*	*2.6380*	*−0.1755*	*1.9241*	*2.0915*	*1.0451*	*1.0626*	*3.2926*	*−1.3002*	*3.1533*
Day 0, + 1	0.0036	0.0206	0.0053	0.0081	0.0277	0.0104	0.0087	0.0198	−0.0072	0.0179
t-value	*0.3811*	*3.7712*	*0.4776*	*0.9872*	*3.6260*	*0.9175*	*1.2970*	*2.1128*	*−0.6863*	*3.2312*
Irish punt is devalued										
Day 0	0.0152	0.0010	−0.0100	0.0059	0.0605	0.0011	0.0086	−0.0021	0.0137	0.0127
t-value	*2.2647*	*0.2605*	*−1.2760*	*1.0096*	*11.1877*	*0.1404*	*1.8212*	*−0.3152*	*1.8579*	*3.2241*
Day 0, + 1	0.0147	0.0042	0.0017	0.0061	0.0583	0.0097	0.0063	0.0153	0.0082	0.0202
t-value	*1.5571*	*0.7751*	*0.1505*	*0.7396*	*7.6242*	*0.8500*	*0.9342*	*1.6340*	*0.7844*	*3.6287*
ERM margins widen										
Day 0	0.0126	0.0330	0.0204	−0.0010	0.0114	0.0168	−0.0032	0.0092	0.0047	0.0196
t-value	*1.8808*	*8.5227*	*2.5901*	*−0.1652*	*2.1077*	*2.0864*	*−0.6759*	*1.3926*	*0.6437*	*4.9838*
Day 0, + 1	0.0098	0.0350	0.0186	0.0114	0.0228	0.0234	0.0036	0.0022	0.0050	0.0233
t-value	*1.0337*	*6.4036*	*1.6740*	*1.3935*	*2.9807*	*2.0543*	*0.5314*	*0.2300*	*0.4797*	*4.1934*

Note: The top entry in each cell is the abnormal return and bottom entry is the corresponding *t*-statistic. Statistically significant results are shown in italic.

rate/intervention story. In particular, we would have expected positive returns on the Spanish index.

On 5 January 1993, the Germans and the French issued another joint statement reaffirming existing ERM central rates. The two-day ERM country equity index abnormal returns for this announcement are uniformly positive.

About a month later, on 1 February 1993, the Irish punt is devalued within the ERM. The two-day abnormal return on the Irish equity index is a statistically significant 5.83 percent. This outcome, unlike the peseta and escudo outcome, remains consistent with the interest rate story. With the devaluation of the Irish punt, Irish policy-makers can follow more expansionary domestic economic policies, including lowering interest rates, with considerably less fear of capital outflows and pressure on the Irish punt within the ERM. The two-day abnormal returns on the other ERM-country equity indexes are also positive but not statistically significant.

As described in earlier sections, the Bundesbank implemented a policy of gradual reductions in its discount and Lombard rates following the devaluation of the Irish punt, with the first rate reduction coming on 4 February 1993. These rate reductions were not sufficient to calm the exchange markets and, on 2 August 1993, wider ERM currency fluctuation bands were announced for all remaining ERM countries except the Netherlands. The Netherlands chose to keep the Dutch guilder within +/−2.1 percent of the German mark.

The 2 August event-day abnormal returns were positive for all indexes except Germany (−0.10 percent) and the Netherlands (−0.32 percent). Statistically significant positive abnormal returns were recorded for Denmark (3.30 percent), France (2.04 percent) and Ireland (1.14 percent) and for the ERM-G index (1.96 percent). These returns continue to be consistent with the story that the Bundesbank was acting as the central bank of the ERM. Once the bands were widened, other ERM countries no longer had to hew to the Bundesbank's interest rate policies and could pursue more expansionary economic policies. In fact, some commentators described the widening of the bands as a face-saving device to avoid admitting that the ERM system of fixed exchange rates had collapsed.

We believe the reactions of ERM-country equity markets to these ERM crises events confirm our hypothesis that the ERM-country financial markets were "tied together" through the German Bundesbank. As long as the countries remained members of the ERM and sought to maintain the agreed upon central rates, equity prices and, therefore, the cost of equity capital, were being determined largely through German interest rate policy and the needs of the domestic German economy.

Equity return volatility

Bundesbank actions, in addition to affecting levels of common stock prices, could affect price volatility. We measure volatility with the standard deviation of daily index returns. We divide the 1992–93 ERM crisis period into intervals based upon Bundesbank discount rate changes and related ERM events, and compare the volatility of the various intervals to a base period and to one another.

Our base period is 1 January 1992 to 15 July 1992, the day before the Bundesbank discount rate increase. The standard deviations for daily percentage price changes are reported in Table 19.10a. Those intervals with standard deviations significantly different from the base period at the 0.05 level are reported in italics. We used a variance ratio F-test to determine statistical significance. The variance ratios are reported in Table 19.10b.

The volatility of ERM member equity markets during the entire 1992–93 crisis period is greater than the base period for all countries. A very noticeable increase in volatility occurs during the period from the July 1992 discount rate increase to the September 1992 discount and Lombard rate decrease for all markets except Ireland. Based on variance ratios, the volatility of the German market during this period is 5.5 times greater than the base period. The volatility of the non-German ERM index is 3.6 times greater than the base period.

The volatility of equity markets following the September 1992 discount and Lombard rate reductions continues to be greater than the base period for all markets; furthermore, the volatility increases relative to the previous period for five of the nine indexes and for the non-German ERM index. Volatility generally decreases in subsequent discount rate reduction periods. The variance ratio for the non-German ERM index falls to 1.1 for the rate reduction period just before the widening of ERM bands. The major exception to this trend is the German FAZ Aktien index which exhibits a variance ratio of 3.4 for this last period.

The statistically significant increase in equity market volatility after the July 1992 Bundesbank rate increase supports the view that Bundesbank actions were directly affecting equity prices. The decline in volatility as the gradualist interest rate reduction policies of the Bundesbank became apparent adds additional support to this view.

Also supportive of this conclusion is the reduction in the volatility of the UK market after the UK leaves the ERM. The variance of UK equity returns after the pound left the ERM was about 71 percent of the variance while it was in the ERM.

Table 19.10a Standard deviation of daily stock index returns during selected 1992–3 ERM crisis intervals

Interval	Belgium BELG-20	Denmark COPEN-S	France CAC-GENL	Germany FAZ-AKT	Ireland ISEQ	Italy ANC-CO	Netherlands CBS-TLR	Spain MDRD-SE	UK UK-ORDY	ERM-G
Base interval: 1 Jan–16 July 1992 increase in D rate	0.0061	0.0055	0.0079	0.0051	0.0060	0.0083	0.0049	0.0072	0.0092	0.0043
16 July 1992 increase in D rate to 30 July 1993	*0.0070*	*0.0075*	*0.0105*	*0.0089*	*0.0119*	*0.0202*	*0.0063*	*0.0240*	*0.0097*	*0.0092*
17 Sep 1992 departure of pound & lire to 30 July 1993	*0.0061*	*0.0072*	*0.0103*	*0.0077*	*0.0126*	*0.0165*	*0.0054*	*0.0257*	*0.0078*	*0.0090*
Discount/Lombard rate change intervals										
16 July 1992 D increase to 14 Sep 1992 D/L reductions	*0.0080*	*0.0073*	*0.0106*	*0.0120*	*0.0056*	*0.0322*	*0.0085*	*0.0118*	*0.0115*	*0.0081*
14 Sep 1992 D/L reductions to 4 Feb 1993 D/L reductions	*0.0070*	*0.0091*	*0.0129*	*0.0088*	*0.0130*	*0.0214*	*0.0055*	*0.0374*	*0.0121*	*0.0118*
4 Feb 1993 D/L reductions to 18 Mar 1993 D reduction	*0.0045*	*0.0057*	*0.0085*	*0.0069*	*0.0110*	*0.0140*	*0.0053*	*0.0092*	*0.0073*	*0.0076*
18 Mar 1993 D reduction to 22 Apr 1993 D/L reductions	*0.0053*	*0.0056*	*0.0076*	*0.0053*	*0.0123*	*0.0132*	*0.0040*	*0.0068*	*0.0052*	*0.0069*
22 Apr 1993 D/L reductions to 1 July 1993 D/L reductions	*0.0062*	*0.0054*	*0.0075*	*0.0054*	*0.0150*	*0.0130*	*0.0061*	*0.0092*	*0.0054*	*0.0059*
1 July 1993 D/L reductions to 22 July D reduction	*0.0060*	*0.0026*	*0.0079*	*0.0095*	*0.0072*	*0.0083*	*0.0055*	*0.0039*	*0.0052*	*0.0045*
Currency devaluation and exit period										
16 July 1992 D increase to 14 Sep 1992 devaluation of lire and 17 Sep departure of lire and pound	*0.0099*	*0.0080*	*0.0116*	*0.0133*	*0.0062*	*0.0324*	*0.0096*	*0.0124*	*0.0125*	*0.0092*
17 Sep departure of lire and pound to 23 Nov 1992 devaluation of peseta and escudo	*0.0077*	*0.0096*	*0.0162*	*0.0104*	*0.0121*	*0.0177*	*0.0068*	*0.0152*	*0.0129*	*0.0108*
23 Nov devaluation of peseta and escudo to 1 Feb 1993 punt devaluation	*0.0056*	*0.0085*	*0.0086*	*0.0071*	*0.0111*	*0.0241*	*0.0035*	*0.0526*	*0.0075*	*0.0129*
1 Feb 1993 punt devaluation to 2 Aug 1993 widening of ERM band	0.0058	0.0055	0.0081	0.0067	*0.0123*	*0.0124*	0.0053	*0.0082*	*0.0059*	*0.0064*
Central rate reaffirmation periods										
23 Sep 1992 German/French reaffirmation of rates to 23 Nov 1992 devaluation of peseta and escudo	*0.0078*	*0.0088*	*0.0119*	*0.0107*	*0.0119*	*0.0173*	*0.0070*	*0.0151*	*0.0122*	*0.0103*
5 Jan 1993 German/French reaffirmation of rates to 1 Feb 1993 punt devaluation	0.0048	0.0086	0.0078	0.0069	0.0123	0.0345	0.0039	0.0858	0.0071	*0.0192*

Note: The cell entries are standard deviations of daily price changes. Each interval runs from the day after the announcement day to the day before the ending date of the interval. Statistically significant results (see Table 19.10b for details) are shown in italic.

Table 19.10b Ratios of variances of daily stock returns during selected 1992–3 ERM crisis intervals relative to variance for the base interval

Interval	Belgium BELG-20	Denmark COPEN-S	France CAC-GENL	Germany FAZ-AKT	Ireland ISEQ	Italy ANC-CO	Netherlands CBS-TLR	Spain MDRD-SE	UK UK-ORDY	ERM-G
Base interval: 1 Jan–16 July 1992 increase in D rate	1.00	1.00	1.00	1.00	1.00	1.00	1.00	1.00	1.00	1.00
16 July 1992 increase in D rate to 30 July 1993	*1.29*	*1.87*	*1.77*	*3.01*	*3.86*	*5.98*	*1.64*	*10.98*	*1.11*	*4.63*
17 Sep 1992 departure of pound & lire to 30 July 1993	*0.99*	*1.71*	*1.69*	*2.23*	*4.37*	*4.02*	*1.21*	*12.63*	*0.72*	*4.44*
Discount/Lombard rate change intervals										
16 July 1992 D increase to 14 Sep 1992 D/L reductions	*1.71*	*1.75*	*1.78*	*5.51*	0.87	*15.26*	*3.04*	*2.65*	*1.55*	*3.62*
14 Sep 1992 D/L reductions to 4 Feb 1993 D/L reductions	*1.31*	*2.75*	*2.66*	*2.96*	*4.65*	*6.70*	*1.26*	*26.71*	*1.72*	*7.58*
4 Feb 1993 D/L reductions to 18 Mar 1993 D reduction	*0.53*	*1.09*	*1.14*	*1.83*	*3.30*	*2.88*	*1.17*	*1.62*	*0.62*	*3.17*
18 Mar 1993 D reduction to 22 Apr 1993 D/L reductions	*0.74*	*1.03*	*0.91*	*1.49*	*4.12*	*2.58*	*0.66*	*0.88*	*0.32*	*2.61*
22 Apr 1993 D/L reductions to 1 July 1993 D/L reductions	*1.02*	*0.97*	*0.90*	*1.08*	*6.14*	*2.47*	*1.56*	*1.60*	*0.34*	*1.91*
1 July 1993 D/L reductions to 22 July D reduction	*0.97*	*0.22*	*0.99*	*3.41*	*1.42*	*1.00*	*1.25*	*0.29*	*0.32*	*1.11*
Currency devaluation and exit period										
16 July 1992 D increase to 14 Sep 1992 devaluation of lire and 17 Sep departure of lire and pound	*2.62*	*2.10*	*2.15*	*6.74*	1.05	*15.38*	*3.88*	*2.95*	*1.85*	*4.60*
17 Sep departure of lire and pound to 23 Nov 1992 devaluation of peseta and escudo	*1.56*	*3.03*	*4.20*	*4.12*	*4.01*	*4.60*	*1.94*	*4.43*	*1.97*	*6.42*
23 Nov devaluation of peseta and escudo to 1 Feb 1993 punt devaluation	0.83	*2.42*	*1.19*	*1.92*	*3.36*	*8.53*	0.50	*52.81*	0.66	*9.11*
1 Feb 1993 punt devaluation to 2 Aug 1993 widening of ERM band	0.88	0.99	1.06	*1.73*	*4.12*	*2.25*	1.18	1.29	0.41	2.23
Central rate reaffirmation periods										
23 Sep 1992 German/French reaffirmation of rates to 23 Nov 1992 devaluation of peseta and escudo	*1.64*	*2.57*	*2.25*	*4.38*	*3.89*	*4.39*	*2.08*	*4.33*	*1.74*	*5.80*
5 Jan 1993 German/French reaffirmation of rates to 1 Feb 1993 punt devaluation	*0.62*	*2.47*	*0.98*	*1.80*	*4.16*	*17.48*	*0.63*	*140.49*	*0.60*	*20.02*

Note: The cell entries are ratios of variances of daily price changes over a given interval relative to the variance of price changes for the base period. Each interval runs from the day after the announcement day to the day before the ending date of the interval. Statistically significant results are shown in italic.

AHMAD ETEBARI AND FRED R. KAEN

Stock return correlations

To further explore the effects of the 1992–93 ERM crisis on ERM-country equity markets, we calculated bilateral equity market return correlations for the period prior to the departure of the pound and lire from the ERM (2 January 1992 through 14 September 1992) and the period after their departure (18 September 1992 through 2 August 1993). We chose this division point because we wanted to test whether the correlation of the UK and Italian equity markets with the German equity market decreased after the pound and the lire left the ERM. The correlation coefficients are reported in Table 19.11.

We found that the correlation of every national equity market with every other national equity market fell in the post-withdrawal period. Clearly, something had affected the degree with which the ERM-country equity markets moved together.

We have no explanation for these results, only a conjecture. Consider the ERM members prior to the withdrawal of the UK and Italy to be akin to economic regions within a larger confederation with a common currency and economic policy. Under these circumstances, the returns of firms within the confederation would be dependent on and tied to this common economic policy. Of course, some regions of the confederation could be experiencing a recession while other regions an expansion, not unlike the situation in the US. Therefore, confederation-wide common economic policies might be "good" for one region and "bad" for another region. Still, there would be common factor – the confederation-wide economic policy – that would be affecting all equity returns. Now, suppose that the confederation "breaks up." No longer is there a common economic policy; instead, individual regions could "go their own way." Under these new circumstances, the correlation among the returns of firms in the various regions may fall, thus producing increased opportunities for reducing systematic risk of owning the securities of the now countries, not regions, as a portfolio of common stock. The result would be not only a reduction in the correlation of returns between the individual countries but also a reduction in the correlation of returns between individual countries and the international market portfolio.

This outcome is precisely what we uncovered. The correlation between individual country equity markets fell and, furthermore, the correlation between the individual equity markets and the ERM-G portfolio also fell for every country except Italy. Our speculation is that with the withdrawal of the UK and Italy from the ERM, investors reassessed the speed as well as the likelihood that European Union countries would move to a common currency and yield control over domestic economic policies to a European central bank and fiscal authority.

314

Table 19.11 Correlation coefficients of stock index returns for ERM countries during the periods before and after the departures of the UK and Italy from the ERM

	Belgium BELG-20	Denmark COPEN-SE	France CAC-GENL	Germany FAZ-AKT	Ireland ISEQ	Italy BANC-COM	Netherlands CBS-TLR	Spain MDRD-SE	UK UK-ORDY	ERM-G
Belgium BELG-20	1.00 / *1.00*									
Denmark COPEN-SE	0.40 / *0.18*	1.00 / *1.00*								
France CAC-GENL	0.52 / *0.30*	0.40 / *0.21*	1.00 / *1.00*							
Germany FAZ-AKT	0.56 / *0.32*	0.40 / *0.09*	0.58 / *0.30*	1.00 / *1.00*						
Ireland ISEQ	0.38 / *0.24*	0.25 / *0.09*	0.37 / *0.09*	0.39 / *0.18*	1.00 / *1.00*					
Italy BANC-COM	0.18 / *0.14*	0.30 / *0.10*	0.21 / *0.20*	0.33 / *0.20*	0.23 / *0.04*	1.00 / *1.00*				
Netherlands CBS-TLR	0.65 / *0.48*	0.29 / *0.17*	0.39 / *0.27*	0.52 / *0.42*	0.40 / *0.31*	0.26 / *0.05*	1.00 / *1.00*			
Spain MDRD-SE	0.47 / *0.02*	0.29 / *−0.09*	0.45 / *0.08*	0.38 / *0.14*	0.33 / *0.07*	0.17 / *0.11*	0.55 / *0.12*	1.00 / *1.00*		
UK UK-ORDY	0.51 / *0.40*	0.28 / *0.07*	0.34 / *0.11*	0.39 / *0.22*	0.47 / *0.25*	0.19 / *0.12*	0.63 / *0.44*	0.59 / *0.07*	1.00 / *1.00*	
ERM ERM-G	0.71 / *0.37*	0.57 / *0.23*	0.66 / *0.44*	0.65 / *0.37*	0.60 / *0.36*	0.62 / ***0.70***	0.74 / *0.37*	0.69 / *0.64*	0.72 / *0.27*	1.00 / *1.00*

Note: The coefficients for the period before the departures of the UK and Italy from ERM are shown in upright type; those for the period after the departure are shown in italic type. The number of observations during these periods are 184 and 254, respectively. With only one exception (see the bold italic coefficient for Italy) plus the ERM-G, the coefficients for the period after the departure are all smaller than those from the period before the departure.

CONCLUSIONS

ERM-country equity market returns were affected by the 1992–93 ERM currency crises and Bundesbank monetary policies which many financial observers believe triggered the crises. The most noticeable effects were the increase in national equity market volatility and the reduction in the correlation of equity market returns, including the correlation of returns with an equally weighted portfolio of ERM-country equity securities.

Bundesbank decisions to increase domestic German interest rates were associated with negative abnormal returns on other ERM-country equity markets, especially the 16 July 1992 discount rate increase which the financial press widely regarded as triggering the exchange rate crisis. Subsequent Bundesbank decisions to lower domestic interest rates initially produced positive abnormal returns on ERM-country equity markets. However, once investors concluded that the Bundesbank would be following a gradualist rate reduction policy, further rate reductions had little effect on the equity markets.

Our overall results are consistent with the hypothesis that the Bundesbank was exerting considerable influence as a *de facto* European central bank. The "tight" money policies it implemented to control domestic inflation and its gradualist, cautionary approach to lowering interest rates during 1992 and 1993 forced other ERM countries to adopt similar interest rate policies or face a run on their currency within the ERM. In order to follow more expansionary domestic policies than the Germans, the countries would have to leave the ERM. The UK and Italy chose to withdraw in September 1992, an event associated with very large positive abnormal returns on their respective equity markets.

Ultimately, the ERM crisis was resolved by widening the ERM currency central rate bands from 2.5 percent to 15 percent. This announcement, which was effectively equivalent to leaving the ERM, was also associated with large positive abnormal returns on the remaining ERM member-country equity markets. The widening of the bands effectively reduced the influence of Bundesbank interest rate policies on European Union equity markets.

NOTES

1 See "Blaming the Bundesbank" by Craig R. Whitney (1993) for a popular account of the ERM crisis. This article is subtitled "The British shout. So do the French. But the stubborn German bank refuses to accommodate Europe by weakening the mark."
2 The explanation of Bundesbank monetary policy, procedures and instruments draws heavily on Bartholomae (1991) and Sherman (1990).

3 At times, banks may borrow heavily from the Bundesbank at the Lombard rate even though it is above the market rate, because the banks anticipate an increase in the offical rates and a related increase in the market rate (Bartholomae, 1991).
4 For example, the following quote comes from a *Wall Street Journal* story about a May 1993 cut in the security repurchase rate: "Analysts said the decline [in the security repurchase rate] was deeper than expected, presaging another small reduction in the central bank's official discount and Lombard rates . . . " "Germany Cuts Refinancing Rate, Setting Stage for Other Drops," *Wall Street Journal*, 13 May 1993, p. A10.

REFERENCES

Bartholomae, A. (1991) "Some Operational and Instrumental Aspects of Monetary Targeting in Germany," Manuscript, Deutsche Bundesbank, Frankfurt am Main, Germany.
Born, J.A. and J.T. Moser (1990) "Bank Equity Returns and Changes in the Discount Rate," *Journal of Financial Services Research* 5, 223–41.
Deutsche Bundesbank (1992a) "The Currency and the Economy," *Deutsche Bundesbank Annual Report 1992*, 12–97.
Deutsche Bundesbank (1992b) "Review of the 1992 Monetary Target and the Raising of the Discount Rate," *Monthly Report of the Deutsche Bundesbank*, August, 15–20.
Dueker, M. (1992) "The Response of Market Interest Rates to Discount Rate Changes," *Federal Reserve Bank of St Louis Review* 74, 78–91.
Hakkio, C. and D. Pearce (1992) "Discount Rate Policy Under Alternative Operating Regimes: An Empirical Investigation," *International Review of Economics and Finance* 1, 55–72.
Kaen, F.R. and H.C. Sherman (1994) "Currency Market Reactions to Bundesbank Interest Rate Policies During the 1992–93 ERM Crisis: What Happened?," Manuscript, University of New Hampshire.
Kaen, F.R. and H. Tehranian (1994) "The Effects of Bundesbank Discount and Lombard Rate Changes on German Bank Stocks," University of New Hampshire, Department of Accounting and Finance, manuscript.
Marsh, D. (1992) "Europeans Impeded by Policies 'Made in Frankfurt'," *Financial Times*, 17, July p.2.
Norman, P. and P. Marsh (1993) "Bundesbank in Firing Line Over Rate Cuts," *Financial Times*, 21 June, p.2.
Pearce, D.K. and V. Vance Roley (1985) "Stock Prices and Economic News," *Journal of Business* 58, 49–67.
Sherman, H.C. (1990) "Central Banking in Germany and the Process of European Monetary Integration," in H.C. Sherman, R. Brown, P. Jacquet and D. Julius (eds) *Monetary Implications of the 1992 Process*, Manchester: Manchester University Press.
Sherman, H.C. and F.R. Kaen (1994) "The Behaviour and Thinking of the Bundesbank," in David Cobham (ed.) *European Monetary Upheavals*, Manchester: Manchester University Press, 82–111.
Smirlock, M. and J. Yawitz (1985) "Asset Returns, Discount Rate Changes, and Market Efficiency," *The Journal of Finance* 4, 1141–58.
Thornton, D.L. (1982) "Discount Rates and Market Interest Rates: What's the connection?," *Federal Reserve Bank of St Louis Review* 64, 3–14.

AHMAD ETEBARI AND FRED R. KAEN

Waud, R.N. (1970) "Public Interpretation of Federal Reserve Discount Rate Changes: Evidence on the 'Announcement Effect,'" *Econometrica* 38, 231–50.
Whitney, C.R. (1993) "Blaming the Bundesbank," *The New York Times Magazine*, 17 October, 19–59 (periodic).

20

THE EVOLUTION OF US MULTINATIONAL BANKING

Susan Hine and John Olienyk

The purpose of this chapter is to offer an explanation for the rise and fall of US banks as dominant world leaders by analyzing the worldwide parametric conditions which have had the most significant impacts upon the banking industry. Four time periods (stages) are delineated, with each characterized by unique economic events which elicited specific types of responses from US banks. The events and responses of one stage lead naturally to those of the next stage in an evolutionary fashion.

INTRODUCTION

The dominance of US multinational banking after World War II was largely a by-product of Pax Americana, which was based on a structural overvaluation of the US dollar under the Bretton Woods system. As a result of its largely accidental dominance of multinational banking, the US was the undisputed world leader in the financial arena well into the 1960s. In terms of asset size, at least six US multinational banks (MNBs) ranked in the top ten worldwide during this period. By 1990, however, this number had dropped to zero with the top rankings passing to the Japanese.

In this chapter the rise and decline in the dominant position of US MNBs are explained by analyzing how events in the real sector influenced behavior in the banking sector. Four time periods (stages) are analyzed with regard to the manner in which events during one time period set the stage for events in the next.

In the first stage, US MNBs are thrust into a leadership role due largely to the fact that US industrial capacity and infrastructure were unscathed and even strengthened during World War II. In the second stage, what turn out to be misguided US reactions to structural problems inherent in the fixed exchange rate system lead to a surge of growth in US multinational banking. Attacks from a variety of sources force the US MNBs into a period of retrenchment and re-evaluation in the third stage. In the fourth and final stage, the focus is on the present-day multinational banking environment and on the evolutionary forces currently at work.

319

HEGEMONIC STAGE (POST-WORLD WAR II
TO EARLY 1960s)

Although the real and financial sector linkages are a fundamental aspect of the changing role of US hegemonic power, this situation is not unique to the US case. Beginning in the late 1870s, the United Kingdom achieved international economic and financial hegemony and maintained it until the beginning of World War II. (Collins, 1988). Great Britain's dominance of world trade was supported by organizationally sound banks run by superior managers which provided the country with the necessary advantages to be the hegemonic world leader (Jones, 1992).

The UKs predominant position was based in part on a free-trade policy, worldwide connections (empire), and a sizable merchant fleet. It was only natural that her MNBs would also develop in the wake of this strong economic growth, since the vast trade networks needed financial support to carry on the business of the empire. However, one effect of the international shift from sterling to dollars which occurred after World War II was to diminish many of the ownership advantages held by British banks. This in turn contributed to the deterioration of her dominance of world trade.

Dramatic and far-reaching changes in the world order ensued following the end of World War II. After the war much of the world's productive capacity lay in ruin, and largely by default the US became the new economic leader of the world. It was, after all, the only industrialized country in a position to assume this responsibility. In the process the seeds of a hegemonic role for US MNBs were planted within the dynamic growth of the real sector.

The first major step toward US dominance was taken with the establishment of the International Monetary Fund (IMF). In an attempt to help restore economic stability in a chaotic world, this resulted in a strong demand for and consequent overvaluation of the dollar. US industrial firms attempted to profit from the higher rate of return inherent in the overvalued dollar by sharply increasing their foreign direct investment (FDI) (Aliber, 1970).

US firms faced little competition in the war-torn countries and pressed their structural advantage. During this period the US multinational enterprises (MNEs) dominated world FDI. Between 1946 and 1960, FDI by US firms grew from $10 billion to $27 billion, while FDI in the US increased from $8 billion to only $10 billion (*Survey of Current Business*, various issues). The US role as hegemonic leader in the industrial sector was taking root.

This rapid growth of FDI brought with it a new problem. The US firms required a good deal of financial support to sustain their overseas expansion, and the financial infrastructure of many host countries was inadequate to meet the needs of these US MNEs. In many cases foreign banks simply did not possess sufficient expertise, nor were they fully equipped to provide the range of support required of them. It was not surprising then that US MNEs depended upon their domestic banks for the unique and vital corporate services they needed (Channon, 1988).

Thus relationship banking, characterized by the development of long-term relationships between banks and nonbank firms, with efficiency being a predominant concern, became the order of the day for US MNBs. The development of relationship banking may best be explained by the presence of barriers to externalization. The MNEs found that they faced barriers to externalization in that they where unable to effectively expand their presence abroad through such means as joint ventures, licensing agreements, and management contracts (Rugman and Kamath, 1987). Likewise, the MNBs found that they were essentially unable to satisfactorily export the financial services required by their customers. The only option, therefore, was for US MNBs to follow their customers to new markets around the world and begin to build global branch networks, thus internalizing their intangible advantages by establishing full-blown banking presence abroad.

Faced with little competition, both the US MNEs and their banks flourished, in spite of the fact that both groups incurred substantial costs of foreignness. Although US multinational banking dominance was becoming well established during this hegemonic stage of development, US banking presence abroad still had not grown dramatically. By the beginning of the 1960s, the number of foreign branches of US banks had increased to only 131, and these branches had assets of only $3.5 billion (see Appendix A on p. 326).

REGULATION-DISTORTED STAGE
(EARLY 1960s–LATE 1970s)

Almost from the very time that it was established, US hegemony was under attack. It is well recognized that the US role under Pax Americana, wherein it accepted the responsibility for nurturing the rebuilding of the world's economies in the post-war period, was highly successful. US banking and industrial hegemony was the driving force behind the rapid growth of the global economy. Ironically, this worldwide economic growth would ultimately be responsible for the decline of that hegemony.

Supported by the strength and size of the US economy, the economies of the other major industrialized countries grew rapidly during the two decades following World War II. "America's industrial hegemony and leadership served as a nursery, as it were, for the quick recovery and miraculous growth of the Japanese economy" (Ozawa, 1991, p. 60). The effect was similar for the other industrialized countries. As these economies continued

321

to expand throughout the 1960s and 1970s, their need for corporate funding grew and the drive to satisfy these funding needs would result in heightened competition among MNBs worldwide.

Although global competition among MNBs was not as yet a major issue, there were other, more immediate problems confronting US hegemony during the 1960s. The most immediate was the worldwide glut of dollars which resulted from the flood of FDI by US firms and the continuing overvaluation of the dollar. The inability of the US to control its balance of payments was causing other industrialized nations to begin to lose confidence in the dollar. There was growing concern that the US would, at some point, be unable to support the dollar with its gold reserves. As a result, currency speculation became destabilizing as foreigners exchanged more and more dollars for other currencies and for gold. The fact that postwar financial markets were becoming more highly developed and integrated greatly facilitated this adjustment process.

In response to the pressure on the dollar, US policy-makers initiated new regulations designed to stem the tide of capital outflow and reduce the current account deficit. These measures, however, had unforeseen consequences which further eroded the hegemonic position of the United States. Three regulatory changes in particular, all enacted in the mid-1960s, strongly stimulated the escape motivation of MNBs. The Interest Equalization Tax made issuance of foreign bonds in the US less attractive by taxing American purchases of those securities. One result was that foreign issuers of dollar-denominated debt were forced to take their business abroad. The Voluntary Foreign Credit Restraint Program made it difficult for banks to make overseas loans directly from their home offices. Since the assets of foreign branches were not included in the guidelines, however, US parent banks could shift foreign credits to their foreign branches and still be in compliance with the law. Finally, the Foreign Direct Investment Program was created for the purpose of limiting the ability of US corporations to transfer funds overseas for direct investment. These programs in concert produced a powerful inducement for US financial institutions to expand their overseas branching networks in order to escape the constraints imposed by the new regulations.

As the US MNBs broadened their presence overseas during the 1970s, they discovered that access to the Eurocurrency market also enabled them to avoid interest-rate ceilings and credit controls in the US. In addition, the absence of reserve requirements, coupled with greater market efficiency and improved communications, resulted in substantial cost savings. Ultimately the Eurocurrency market proved to be a lure for overseas branching operations, not only for the large MNBs but also for the smaller ones as well. Thus a highly competitive, efficient, largely unregulated off-shore banking market was created, and US MNBs used it to escape their onerous regulatory climate at home (Gray and Gray, 1981).

During the regulation-distorted period US MNBs were, in effect, driven abroad to escape ill-conceived but well-intended regulatory changes. They were, however, also drawn abroad by substantial increases in US FDI and by increasingly intense competition from non-US banks which were beginning to threaten their market share. During the period from 1960 to 1978, US FDI increased from $26 billion to $163 billion. In response to this growth in the real sector, the number of foreign branches of US MNBs grew from 131 to 761, with assets of those branches increasing from $3.5 billion to $258 billion during the same period (see Appendix A, p. 326).

DEFENSIVE STAGE (LATE 1970s–LATE 1980s)

By the end of the 1970s, worldwide economic growth had led to increased globalization of MNBs from all industrialized countries. This in turn had created more intense competition among the large MNBs worldwide, with the result that all MNBs found themselves fighting to preserve relationships with their customers. Each US MNB was now in a position in which it faced the possibility of losing customers, not only to a US rival but also to one of a growing number of aggressive and sophisticated foreign competitors. With the global expansion of both MNEs and MNBs, it was now possible for a bank to lose its customers in every location in which the MNE operated. In order to protect their market share, US MNBs were more highly motivated than ever to follow their customers all over the globe (Cho, 1985). Accelerating worldwide economic growth thus fostered increased competition in both the financial and industrial sectors, and the dominant position of the US in both sectors began to wane.

Some of the decline of US multinational banking may be attributed to the "arm's length transactions" way in which US banks conducted business. To be successful with its corporate customers, it is important for a bank to become closely involved with the companies' operations. Foreign banks are able to achieve this intimacy, in part, by engaging in equity financing, a strategy unavailable to US banks because of legal restraints. When banks are part-owners, their vested interest in the success of the business is much greater than if they are merely lenders. Owning an equity stake also provides a great incentive for the bank to determine very quickly how it can best service its customers' needs. The bank will, of course, also do whatever else it can to ensure that its customers prosper.

In the case of Japan, the bank–customer ties are traditionally extremely strong, in part because of the *keiretsu* system. The huge increase in Japanese FDI in the 1980s was, therefore, accompanied by equally dramatic growth in the presence of Japanese banks in foreign markets. In addition to enjoying close ties with their customers, the Japanese banks entered the international arena with other significant advantages over their rivals. The major advantages included a relatively low cost of capital, solid support from the Japanese government, a high domestic savings rate, and staying power which enabled them to implement very competitive pricing practices to capture market share. The result was that both Japanese banks and their customers prospered, while for US MNBs the absence of more intimate relationships with US MNEs made both groups less competitive and more focused on short-term results (Jacobs, 1991). When viewed from the perspective of real-sector and financial-sector linkages this outcome seems quite predictable, yet the ascension of Japanese banking power took many by surprise.

Compounding the difficulties for US banks was a set of new problems at home. These included developing country debt write-offs and rising loan losses due at first to the recession of 1981–2, and later on to the collapse of energy prices and the real estate market. Thus the inability of US MNBs to maintain the necessary strong relationships with important clients, combined with the changing competitive environment and domestic economic conditions of the 1980s, resulted in the loss of US banking hegemony. The decline was rapid and dramatic. In 1983, US MNBs held 28 percent of total international bank assets as compared to Japan's 21.1 percent. By 1991, the US position had shrunk to 10.6 percent while the share held by Japanese banks had grown to 31.4 percent (Ozawa and Hine, 1993). The number of foreign branches of US MNBs peaked at 917 in 1984 and declined to 819 by 1989. Assets of these foreign branches peaked at $390.9 billion in 1981, and had fallen to $305.1 billion by 1989, a decline of almost 22 percent (see Appendix A, p. 326).

COMPETITIVE/STRATEGIC STAGE (LATE 1980s TO PRESENT)

The global economic environment has undergone a series of profound changes in the decade of the 1990s. Primary among these changes have been sharply increased levels of world trade, the emergence of trading blocs in several parts of the world, and marketization, privatization, and strong growth in emerging economies. These factors have resulted in heightened levels of competition in world markets, which in turn has stimulated the drive to increase efficiency in the industrialized world, particularly in the US. Corporate restructuring, deregulation, an expanding domestic economy, and a weak dollar have all contributed to making US firms formidable competitors once again. This re-emergence of US firms has not been confined to the industrial sector. The service sector has continued its rapid growth both at home and abroad and has been responsible for holding down the growth of the current account deficit. Services are less susceptible to competition from the emerging nations, and are an area in which the US has long had a comparative advantage.

Nowhere has the response to the changing conditions been greater than in the banking industry. While the decline in the dominant position of US MNBs during the defensive stage was precipitous, it was not calamitous. US MNBs have not withdrawn from the international scene, nor have they relinquished their leadership role. Rather, it is the form of leadership which has changed. As measured by share of assets or growth of branches, US banking hegemony appears to be permanently lost. In the current global financial arena, however, asset share and growth of branches are less important than profitability, adaptability, creativity, and innovation, and it is in these areas that US MNBs are excelling.

As US banks have faced both an increase in competition from nonbank providers of financial services and a decline in the demand for traditional banking services, they have adapted in several ways. Strategic mergers and increased automation have reduced costs. New technology has allowed banks to offer new types of services to replace business lost in traditional areas. Banks are focusing more on providing products and services which will increase fee income and produce the greatest contribution to the bottom line. These include cash management, investment management, and a wide range of individually tailored derivative products which allow customers to hedge a wide variety of risks. As deregulation continues, banks will inevitably broaden their product lines even further.

In the current environment each bank is being forced to find the special niche which will allow the bank to take advantage of its own particular strengths. Some banks find that strength in merchant banking and related fields, while others focus on the retail or the consumer end of the business. Banks are beginning to rely on purchasing some services from one another as this specialization and consolidation increases. It is important to recognize that a bank's success in the future will not be determined on the basis of its size or the sophistication of its electronic infrastructure. Rather, its success will be determined by whether the bank has a clear understanding of what the needs of its customers are, and whether it has the resourcefulness to find ways to satisfy those needs better than either its bank or its nonbank competitors can.

CONCLUSIONS

As income differentials diminish, both among industrialized nations and between industrialized nations and emerging nations, it is unlikely that any one nation will dominate the world economy like the British, the Americans and, to a lesser extent, the Japanese have done during the past century. It follows that it would be equally unlikely for the type of banking hegemony witnessed in the past to re-emerge.

As barriers to capital movements in general and to FDI in particular continue to fall, industrial firms will continue to become more global. The nationality of the banks which provide services for these MNEs will become less of an issue as continuing deregulation in the financial arena, higher levels of sophistication for all MNBs, and common capital requirements lead to diminished country-specific advantages for all MNBs.

APPENDIX A

Table A20.1 Foreign branches of US banks: total assets in billions of dollars

Year	Number of foreign branches	Gross assets
1955	115	2.0
1960	131	3.5
1965	211	9.1
1966	244	12.4
1967	295	15.7
1968	373	23.0
1969	460	41.1
1970	532	52.6
1971	577	67.1
1972	627	77.4
1973	694	118.0
1974	732	140.5
1975	762	162.7
1976	728	193.9
1977	730	227.9
1978	761	257.9
1979	789	312.9
1980	787	343.5
1981	841	390.9
1982	900	388.5
1983	892	386.1
1984	917	337.4
1985	916	329.2
1986	899	331.5
1987	866	341.7
1988	849	318.4
1989	819	305.1
1990	789	314.6
1991	773	335.4

Source: J.V. Houpt, "International Trends for U.S. Banks and Banking Markets," *Federal Reserve Bulletin*, May 1988 (updated).

REFERENCES

Aliber, R.Z. (1970) "A Theory of Direct Foreign Investment," in C.P. Kindleberger (ed.) *The International Corporation: A Symposium*, Cambridge, Mass.: MIT Press.

Channon, D.F. (1988) *Global Banking Strategy*, New York: John Wiley & Sons.

Cho, Kang Rae (1985) *Multinational Banks Their Identities and Determinants*, Ann Arbor: UMI Research Press.

Collins, Michael (1988) *Money and Banking in the UK: A History*, London and New York: Croom Helm.

Dunning, J.H. (1990) "The Eclectic Paradigm of International Production: a Personal Perspective," *The Nature of the Transnational Firm*, London and New York: Routledge.

Gray, J.M. and H.P. Gray (1981) "The Multinational Bank: A Financial MNC?," *Journal of Banking and Finance*, Vol. 5.

Houpt, J.V. (1988) "International Trends for U.S. Banks and Banking Markets," *Federal Reserve Bulletin*, May.

Jacobs, M.T. (1991) "The Demise of Relationship Banking," *Short-Term America: The Abuses and Cures of our Business Myopia*, Boston, Mass.: Harvard Business School Press.

Jones, G. (1992) "The Legacy of the Past: British Multinational Banking Strategies Since the Nineteenth Century," P.J. Buckley and M. Casson (eds) *Multinational Enterprises in the World Economy: Essays in Honour of John Dunning*, Edward Elgar Publishing.

Ozawa, Terutomo (1991) "Japan in a New Phase of Multinationalism and Industrial Upgrading: Functional Integration of Trade, Growth and FDI," *Journal of World Trade*, Vol. 25, No. 1, February.

Ozawa, Terutomo and S. Hine (1993) "A Strategic Shift from International to Multinational Banking: A 'Macro-Developmental' Paradigm of Japanese Banks qua Multinationals," *Banca Nazionale del Lavoro Quarterly Review*, June.

Rugman, A.M. and S.J. Kamath (1987) "International Diversification and Multinational Banking," in S.J. Khoury and A. Ghosh (eds) *Recent Development in International Banking and Finance*, Vol. 1, Lexington, Mass.: D.C. Heath & Co.

Part IV

CAPITAL FLOWS IN THE GLOBAL STRUCTURE

21

EXTERNAL CAPITAL FLOWS TO DEVELOPING COUNTRIES

Prospects for the 1990s

Harri Ramcharran

The rapid increase in private capital flows in recent years to the developing countries has been due to policies focused on market-oriented reforms, debt reduction and rescheduling strategies, liberalization of capital markets, and privatization. If these flows are to continue then such policies have to be continued. Also developing countries that are not attracted to foreign investors should imitate such reforms. Private capital flows are crucial for the future growth of developing countries since the official (bilateral and multilateral) sources of resource flows exhibited a rapid declining trend in recent years.

INTRODUCTION

One of the consequences of the International Debt Crisis of the 1980s was the decrease in net capital flows to the developing countries. The main source of decrease was in private flows (bank lending, export credits, and foreign direct investment). Official development aid (bilateral and multilateral) remained fairly stable. Since the economic performance of developing countries depends heavily on substantial flow of external resources most of the debt burden countries were affected negatively by capital formation, economic growth, and balance of payments problems. To attract foreign capital most of these countries initiated structural economic reforms (trade liberalization and deregulation), debt reduction strategies (debt buy back, debt for debt swap, and debt for equity swap), and political reforms. By the start of the 1990s, the reforms of a decade ago began to show signs of success as the inflow of external capital began to increase. The recent increase in capital flows has raised questions about their sustainability in the long run. Since external sources of capital are necessary to supplement domestic savings the long run economic growth of the developing countries depends heavily on the continuity of such flows. The purpose of this chapter is to analyze some of the economic factors that

331

influence capital flows to developing countries and discuss their implications on policies that could affect capital flows in the long run.

OVERVIEW OF RECENT CAPITAL FLOWS

As shown on Table 21.1, aggregate net long term resource flows increased from US$121.1 bn in 1991 to US$156.6 bn in 1992, an increase of 29.3 percent, and was increased to US$176.7 bn in 1993. Most of the increase from 1991 to 1992 was from private loans, foreign direct investment, and portfolio equity investments. Private loans increased from US$13.8 bn to US$41.7 bn (by 202 percent), foreign direct investment (FDI) from US$36.9 bn to US$47.3 bn (by 28 percent), and portfolio equity investments from US$7.6 bn to US$13.1 bn (by 72 percent). The category of decrease in resource flows was official development assistance (ODA), a drop from US$62.9 bn to US$54.6 bn (by 13 percent). It is important to note that during the 1980s ODA was the main source of external capital for the developing countries; it represented 69 percent of aggregate flows in 1986 (see Table 21.2). That share decreased drastically over the years to a low of 35 percent in 1992. Because of the Third World Debt Crisis (also in the 1980s) private loans and FDI were not major sources of external capital; they represented 14 percent and 16 percent respectively in 1986. However their importance was enhanced as developing countries implemented drastic economic reforms such as (a) debt reduction and debt

Table 21.1 Aggregate net long-term resource flows to developing countries, 1986–93 ($US bn)

Type of finance	1986	1987	1988	1989	1990	1991	1992	1993
Official development finance	44.0	43.9	40.8	41.1	59.1	62.9	54.6	63.5
Official grants	16.0	16.7	18.3	19.0	28.5	32.9	34.5	35.5
Debt forgiveness (DAC)	0.3	0.2	0.3	0.6	4.3	6.0	2.0	–
Official loans (net)	27.9	27.2	22.5	22.1	30.7	30.0	20.1	27.9
Bilateral	12.8	12.2	11.4	10.4	15.9	15.2	7.9	9.6
Multilateral	15.2	15.0	11.1	11.7	14.8	14.9	12.2	18.3
Private loans (net) and bonds	9.2	8.6	11.0	10.2	12.9	13.8	41.7	43.7
Commercial banks	1.8	1.1	7.9	3.9	−2.5	5.4	18.5	–
Bonds	0.8	1.0	2.9	4.2	2.3	7.4	6.3	–
Suppliers	1.2	0.7	−1.3	0.3	2.1	−2.8	−0.1	–
Other	5.5	5.7	1.5	1.7	11.0	3.7	16.9	–
Foreign direct investment	10.1	14.5	21.2	24.7	26.3	36.9	47.3	56.3
Portfolio equity investment	0.6	0.8	1.1	3.5	3.8	7.6	13.1	13.2
Agg. net L/T resource flows	63.9	67.8	74.0	79.5	102.1	121.1	156.6	176.7

Source: World Debt Tables, 1993–1994, World Bank, Washington, DC, p. 10.

Table 21.2 Percentage distribution of resource flows

	1986	1987	1988	1989	1990	1991	1992	1993
Official development finance	0.69	0.65	0.55	0.52	0.58	0.52	0.35	0.36
Official grants	0.25	0.25	0.25	0.24	0.28	0.27	0.22	0.20
Debt forgiveness (DAC)	0.00	0.00	0.00	0.01	0.04	0.05	0.01	–
Official loans (net)	0.44	0.40	0.30	0.28	0.30	0.25	0.13	0.16
Bilateral	0.20	0.18	0.15	0.13	0.16	0.13	0.05	0.05
Multilateral	0.24	0.22	0.15	0.15	0.14	0.12	0.08	0.10
Private loans (net) and bonds	0.14	0.13	0.15	0.13	0.13	0.11	0.27	0.25
Commercial banks	0.03	0.02	0.11	0.05	−0.02	0.04	0.12	–
Bonds	0.01	0.01	0.04	0.05	0.02	0.06	0.04	–
Suppliers	0.02	0.01	−0.02	0.00	0.02	−0.02	0.00	–
Other	0.09	0.08	0.02	0.02	0.11	0.03	0.11	–
Foreign direct investment	0.16	0.21	0.29	0.31	0.26	0.30	0.30	0.32
Portfolio equity investment	0.01	0.01	0.01	0.04	0.04	0.06	0.08	0.07
Agg. net L/T resource flows	*1.00*	*1.00*	*1.00*	*1.00*	*1.00*	*1.00*	*1.00*	*1.00*

Source: Computed from Table 21.1.

rescheduling strategies, (b) market-oriented reforms, (c) privatization, (d) fiscal consolidation, (e) greater openness to foreign trade, and (f) domestic price liberalization. By 1992 private loans and FDI were 27 percent and 30 percent, respectively, of aggregate external resource. Figure 21.1 graphically presents the percentage distribution of the main categories of capital flows from 1986–93.

ANALYSIS

Official Development Aid includes grants and concessional (low interest) loans for development made either through government (bilateral) or through international agencies (multilateral). Table 21.3 presents data on ODA for OECD countries and for OPEC. The main OECD donors (in terms of dollars) are the USA, France, Japan, and Germany. Interestingly, the USA share (Table 21.4) of OECD's ODA fell from 45.2 percent in 1970 to 20.5 percent in 1991, while Japan's share increased from 6 percent to 19.7 percent. France and Germany's shares were fairly stable during this period. ODA from OPEC countries is relatively small, with the main donors being Saudi Arabia, United Arab Emirates, Kuwait and Iran.

How much ODA the industrialized countries should provide is a crucial question. Root (1994) argued that economic analysis cannot answer this question because it is essentially political in nature. Others contended that ODA will depend on economic conditions in the donor countries (Figure 21.2), for OECD members budget surplus/deficit and economic growth

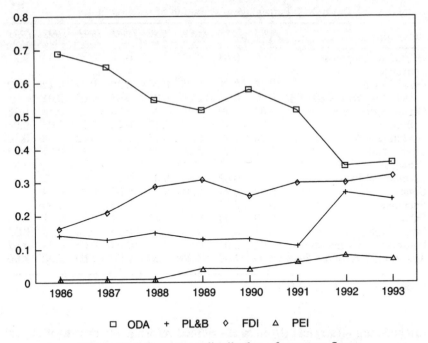

Figure 21.1 Percentage distribution of resource flows

could be the key variables, while for OPEC members the price of oil and current account surplus/deficit are significant. The industrialized countries have agreed to a target of 0.7 percent of their GNP. As presented on Table 21.5, in 1991 only five OECD members (Netherlands, Denmark, Finland, Norway, and Sweden) have reached their target; France, however, during the 1985–90 period, had exceeded this target.

Using time-series data (1975–91) we estimate the impact of economic growth (GR) measured by the annual percentage change in GDP, and budgetary pressure (BUD) measured by the government budget deficit/ surplus as a percentage of GDP on some OECD members' ODA measured by each donor's ODA as a percentage of its GNP. The data are obtained from various issues of *World Development Report* (World Bank), and IMF *International Financial Statistics*. We hypothesize that both independent variables will positively influence ODA/GNP. We also include a trend variable (T). The results, with the t-statistics in parenthesis, are as follows:

USA: ODA/GNP = 10.108 − 0.0136 BUD − 0.0035 GR − 0.0050 T; $R^2 = 0.61$
$\qquad\qquad\qquad$ (−2.78)* $\qquad$ (−1.43) $\qquad$ (−4.26)*

Japan: ODA/GNP = −18.85 − 0.0170 BUD − 0.0035 GR − 0.0096 T; $R^2 = 0.70$
$\qquad\qquad\qquad$ (−1.70) $\qquad$ (−0.544) $\qquad$ (−4.79)*

Table 21.3 Official development assistance from OECD and OPEC members ($US m)

OECD	1970	1975	1980	1985	1987	1988	1989	1990	1991
Ireland	0	8	30	39	51	57	49	57	72
New Zealand	14	66	72	54	87	104	87	95	100
Belgium	120	378	595	440	687	601	703	889	831
United Kingdom	500	904	1,854	1,530	1,871	2,645	2,587	2,638	3,348
Italy	147	182	683	1,098	2,615	3,193	3,613	3,395	3,352
Australia	212	552	667	749	627	1,101	1,020	955	1,050
Netherlands	196	608	1,630	1,136	2,094	2,231	2,094	2,592	2,517
Austria	11	79	178	248	201	301	283	394	548
France	971	2,093	4,162	3,995	6,525	6,865	7,450	9,380	7,484
Canada	337	880	1,075	1,631	1,885	2,347	2,320	2,470	2,604
United States	3,153	4,161	7,138	9,403	9,115	10,141	7,676	11,394	11,362
Denmark	59	205	481	440	859	922	937	1,171	1,300
Germany	599	1,689	3,567	2,942	4,391	4,731	4,949	6,320	6,890
Norway	37	184	486	574	890	985	917	1,205	1,178
Sweden	117	566	962	840	1,375	1,534	1,799	2,012	2,116
Japan	458	1,148	3,353	3,797	7,342	9,134	8,965	9,069	10,952
Finland	7	48	110	211	433	608	706	846	930
Switzerland	30	104	253	302	547	617	558	750	863
Total (OECD)	6,968	13,855	27,296	29,429	41,595	48,114	46,713	55,632	55,519
Total (OPEC)	n/a	5,515	9,636	3,615	3,333	2,369	1,514	6,341	2,680
Total	6,968	19,370	36,932	33,044	44,928	50,483	48,227	61,973	58,199

Source: World Development Report, World Bank, Washington, DC, various issues.

France: ODA/GNP = $-15.14 - 0.0130$ BUD $- 0.0087$ GR $+ 0.0079\ T$; $R^2 = 0.44$
$\qquad\qquad\qquad$ (−0.814) $\qquad$ (−0.805) $\qquad$ (−2.38)*

Germany: ODA/GNP = $-8.75 - 0.0078$ BUD $- 0.0169$ GR $+ 0.0046\ T$; $R^2 = 0.42$
$\qquad\qquad\qquad$ (−0.416) $\qquad$ (−2.69)* $\qquad$ (−1.56)

UK: ODA/GNP = $12.66 - 0.0063$ BUD $- 0.000048$ GR $- 0.0062\ T$; $R^2 = 0.44$
$\qquad\qquad\qquad$ (−0.55) $\qquad$ (−0.007) $\qquad$ (−1.15)

The trend factor as measured by the coefficient of T, is positive and significant in the cases of France and Germany; and is negative and significant for the USA and Japan. This indicates a rising trend in ODA from France and Germany and a declining trend from the USA. Budgetary conditions did not impact ODA in Japan, France, Germany, and the UK, while economic growth did not impact ODA in the USA, Japan, France, and the UK. For the USA the coefficient of BUD, and for Germany the coefficient of GR, did impact ODA but contrary to the way we hypothesized. It must be noted that this is not a rigorous econometric estimate and the results should be interpreted with some caution. Overall our results

335

Table 21.4 Percentage distribution of ODA by countries: OECD

OECD	1970	1975	1980	1985	1987	1988	1989	1990	1991
Ireland	0.000	0.001	0.001	0.001	0.001	0.001	0.001	0.001	0.001
New Zealand	0.002	0.005	0.003	0.002	0.002	0.002	0.002	0.002	0.002
Belgium	0.017	0.027	0.022	0.015	0.017	0.012	0.015	0.016	0.015
United Kingdom	0.072	0.065	0.068	0.052	0.045	0.055	0.055	0.047	0.060
Italy	0.021	0.013	0.025	0.037	0.063	0.066	0.077	0.061	0.060
Australia	0.030	0.040	0.024	0.025	0.015	0.023	0.022	0.017	0.019
Netherlands	0.028	0.044	0.060	0.039	0.050	0.046	0.045	0.047	0.045
Austria	0.002	0.006	0.007	0.008	0.005	0.006	0.006	0.007	0.010
France	0.139	0.151	0.152	0.136	0.157	0.143	0.159	0.169	0.135
Canada	0.048	0.064	0.039	0.055	0.045	0.049	0.050	0.044	0.047
United States	0.452	0.300	0.262	0.320	0.219	0.211	0.164	0.205	0.205
Denmark	0.008	0.015	0.018	0.015	0.021	0.019	0.020	0.021	0.023
Germany	0.086	0.122	0.131	0.100	0.106	0.098	0.106	0.114	0.124
Norway	0.005	0.013	0.018	0.020	0.021	0.020	0.020	0.022	0.021
Sweden	0.017	0.041	0.035	0.029	0.033	0.032	0.039	0.036	0.038
Japan	0.066	0.083	0.123	0.129	0.177	0.190	0.192	0.163	0.197
Finland	0.001	0.003	0.004	0.007	0.010	0.013	0.015	0.015	0.017
Switzerland	0.004	0.008	0.009	0.010	0.013	0.013	0.012	0.013	0.016
Total	1.000	1.000	1.000	1.000	1.000	1.000	1.000	1.000	1.000

Source: Computed from Table 21.3.

Table 21.5 ODA as percentage of donor GNP: OECD

	1970	1975	1980	1985	1987	1988	1989	1990	1991
Ireland	0.00	0.09	0.16	0.24	0.19	0.20	0.17	0.16	0.19
New Zealand	0.23	0.52	0.33	0.25	0.26	0.27	0.22	0.23	0.25
Belgium	0.46	0.59	0.50	0.55	0.48	0.39	0.46	0.45	0.42
United Kingdom	0.41	0.39	0.35	0.33	0.28	0.32	0.31	0.27	0.32
Italy	0.16	0.11	0.15	0.26	0.35	0.39	0.42	0.32	0.30
Australia	0.59	0.65	0.48	0.48	0.34	0.46	0.38	0.34	0.38
Netherlands	0.61	0.75	0.97	0.91	0.98	0.98	0.94	0.94	0.88
Austria	0.07	0.21	0.23	0.38	0.17	0.24	0.23	0.25	0.34
France	0.66	0.62	0.63	0.78	0.74	0.72	0.78	0.79	0.62
Canada	0.41	0.54	0.43	0.49	0.47	0.50	0.44	0.44	0.45
United States	0.32	0.27	0.27	0.24	0.20	0.21	0.15	0.21	0.20
Denmark	0.38	0.58	0.74	0.80	0.88	0.86	0.93	0.93	0.96
Germany	0.32	0.40	0.44	0.47	0.39	0.39	0.41	0.42	0.41
Norway	0.32	0.66	0.87	1.01	1.09	1.13	1.05	1.17	1.14
Sweden	0.38	0.82	0.78	0.86	0.88	0.86	0.96	0.90	0.92
Japan	0.23	0.23	0.32	0.29	0.31	0.32	0.31	0.31	0.32
Finland	0.06	0.18	0.22	0.40	0.49	0.59	0.63	0.64	0.76
Switzerland	0.15	0.19	0.24	0.31	0.31	0.32	0.30	0.31	0.36

Source: World Development Report, World Bank, Washington, DC, various issues.

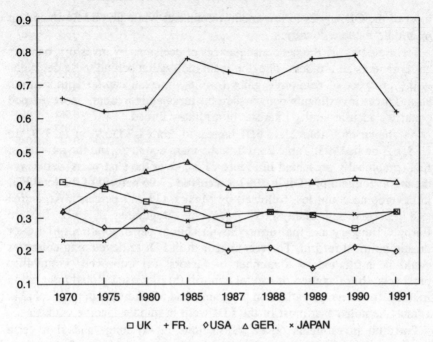

Figure 21.2 ODA as percentage of donor GNP: OECD

show no overwhelming association of budgetary conditions and economic growth with ODA for the main OECD donors.

For the OPEC members, we hypothesize that ODA will be influenced by the price of oil (Poil) and the current account surplus/deficit as a percentage of GDP (CA). The available data permitted us to do estimations for Saudi Arabia, Kuwait, and Iran only. The results are as follows:

Saudi Arabia: ODA/GNP = 539 − 0.0013 CA − 0.049 Poil − 0.270 T; $R^2 = 0.65$
 (−0.06) (−1.50) (−3.15)*

Kuwait: ODA/GNP = 789.77 − 0.0130 CA − 0.033 Poil − 0.390 T; $R^2 = 0.60$
 (−1.80) (−0.728) (−4.30)*

Iran: ODA/GNP = 61.64 − 0.0217 CA − 0.0018 Poil − 0.0308 T; $R^2 = 0.60$
 (−1.50) (−2.61)* (−2.20)*

The trend coefficient is negative and significant for all three members; this indicates an overall declining trend in ODA. Table 21.3 shows that OPEC's ODA decreased from US$9,636 m in 1980 to US$2,680 m in 1991. Neither current account surplus/deficit nor the price of oil (except in the case of Iran where the coefficient has the "wrong" sign) affects OPEC's ODA.

For both OECD and OPEC countries the declining trend in their ODA should be of great concern in terms of growth in developing countries since

337

most of the ODA goes to low-income countries while private flows end up in middle-income countries.

Private flows are the net consequences of decisions by investors, bankers entrepreneurs and traders. The dominant motivation behind these decisions is the prospect of economic gains (profits, interest, capital appreciation, etc.). Direct investments occur when business entrepreneurs in developed countries acquire equity interests in affiliates abroad.

As shown on Table 21.1, FDI increased from US$36.9 bn in 1991 to US$56.3 bn in 1993. Table 21.6 lists the main countries and the amount of FDI (graphically presented in Figure 21.3). Over the past years China was the main recipient of FDI; in 1992 it received 23.96 percent of the total FDI in developing countries, followed by Mexico (11.359 percent), Argentina (8.8 percent), and Malaysia (8.7 percent). Beginning in 1991, Eastern Europe (Hungary and the former Soviet Union) began to attract FDI after drastic political reform. The recent growth in FDI to developing countries could be attributed to a number of factors: (a) improved profitability prospects, (b) relaxation of capital control, (c) increased global integration in trade, (d) active privatization programs, and (e) decrease in political risk. It must be noted that most of the FDI were in middle-income countries.

Portfolio investments cover transactions in (a) long- and short-term bonds, commercial papers, and certificate of deposits (debt portfolio investments), and (b) corporate equities (equity portfolio investment). Portfolio investment flows have continued to increase since 1990. Table 21.7 lists the main recipients and the amounts. East Asia and Pacific and Latin America and the Caribbean were the main areas attracting such flows. Figure 21.4 presents a graphical pattern of the flow over time. Increasing access to the international bond markets and improved formal ratings provided by international rating agencies (Standard and Poor, and Moody's) enable countries, primarily Latin American, to issue a variety of instruments which increase their borrowing. Additionally, due to debt reducing strategies, the secondary market for developing country debt (Brady bond)

Table 21.6 FDI by countries: (US$ m)

	1980	1985	1986	1987	1988	1989	1990	1991	1992
China	0	1,659	1,875	2,314	3,194	3,393	3,487	4,366	11,156
Mexico	2,156	491	1,523	3,246	2,594	3,037	3,632	4,762	5,366
Argentina	678	919	574	(19.00)	1,147	1,028	1,836	2,439	4,179
Malaysia	934	695	489	423	719	1,668	2,333	4,073	4,118
Thailand	190	163	263	352	1,105	1,776	2,444	2,014	2,116
Brazil	1,911	1,348	320	1,225	2,969	1,267	901	972	1,454
Venezuela	55	68	16	21	89	213	451	1,916	629

Source: World Debt Tables, 1993–94, Vol. 2, World Bank, Washington, DC.

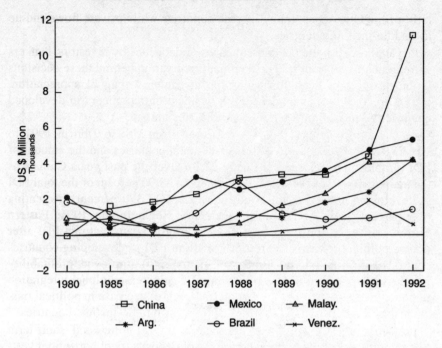

Figure 21.3 FDI by countries (US$ m)

Table 21.7 Portfolio equity flows (US$ m)

	1980	*1985*	*1986*	*1987*	*1988*	*1989*	*1990*	*1991*	*1992*
China	0	0	0	0	0	0	0	653	1,194
Mexico	0	0	0	0	0	0	563	4,404	5,213
Malaysia	0	0	0	87	0	195	293	0	385
Argentina	0	0	0	0	0	8	13	420	392
Thailand	0	44	31	115	487	1,426	449	41	4
Brazil	0	0	0	78	150	0	0	803	1,734
Venezuela	0	0	0	0	0	10	0	100	146

Source: World Debt Tables 1993–94, Vol. 2, World Bank, Washington, DC.

was very successful in providing additional capital. This market was dominated by Mexico, Argentina and Brazil.

An interesting phenomenon was the rapid growth in emerging equity markets (EEM). Gross equity flow during the 1989–93 period was over US$41,075.2 m, with US$14,626.6 m going to the East Asian and Pacific markets, and US$21,674.3 m to the Latin American and Caribbean markets. The spectacular growth in EEM could be attributed to the following factors: (a) higher returns relative to those in the US, (b) capital market

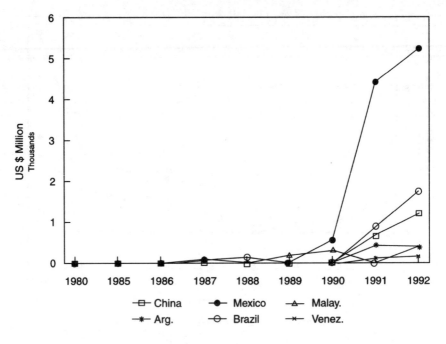

Figure 21.4 Portfolio equity flows

integration, (c) cross-listing, (d) the availability of ADRS, and (e) increase in capitalization

Commercial bank lending resumed in 1990 after years of slowdown due to the international debt crisis. Total credit commitments were US$13.42 bn in 1992 and were expected to reach US$16.8 bn in 1993. In 1992, of a total commitment of US$13.42 bn, East Asia and the Pacific countries (mainly China) received US$9.95 bn, followed by Eastern Europe with US$2.12 bn and Latin America with US$0.94 bn. The main reasons for the increase in bank lending were (a) improved profitability in the developing countries, (b) the reduction of risks due to debt conversion, debt rescheduling, and debt reduction programs, and (c) prospects of economic growth due to market-oriented reforms. Table 21.8 and Table 21.9 indicate the EDT/XGS debt indicator, defined as the ratio of the total external debt to exports of goods and services, and the TDS/XGS debt indicator, defined as the ratio of total debt service to export of goods and services respectively, for some of the main countries. Figure 21.5 and Figure 21.6 show the pattern of these ratios graphically over time. It must be strongly noted that both indicators of external debt decreased over time for these countries. Also we could infer a close association between the increase in FDI, portfolio investment, and bank lending with the decrease in the debt indicators.

Table 21.8 Debt indicator: EDT/XGS (%)

	1980	1985	1986	1987	1988	1989	1990	1991	1992
China	21.2	56.1	76.9	87.6	89.2	90.0	86.8	87.1	76.0
Mexico	259.2	326.0	422.7	363.6	307.0	248.0	243.2	254.0	243.0
Malaysia	44.6	114.0	135.2	108.8	75.9	56.4	46.2	44.5	42.3
Argentina	242.4	493.2	593.3	695.4	517.1	541.1	412.2	443.4	453.5
Thailand	96.8	171.7	152.5	128.8	99.7	87.2	90.2	94.9	–
Brazil	305.0	362.1	452.4	431.0	312.2	286.9	320.5	327.4	310.7
Venezuela	132.0	205.6	305.2	268.3	273.4	207.4	154.5	183.1	219.7

Source: World Debt Tables 1993–94, Vol. 2, World Bank, Washington, DC.

Table 21.9 Debt indicator: TDS/XGS (%)

	1980	1985	1986	1987	1988	1989	1990	1991	1992
China	4.4	8.3	9.6	9.7	9.7	11.4	11.6	12.1	9.6
Mexico	49.1	51.5	54.2	40.1	48.0	41.3	26.3	30.2	44.4
Malaysia	6.3	30.4	21.8	21.2	24.8	15.0	10.3	7.6	6.6
Argentina	37.3	58.9	76.2	74.3	44.2	36.2	40.8	37.6	34.9
Thailand	18.9	31.9	30.1	22.0	20.2	16.3	17.0	13.1	n/a
Brazil	63.1	38.6	47.0	41.9	48.1	39.9	24.2	24.4	24.4
Venezuela	27.2	25.0	45.3	37.8	43.7	24.8	23.2	17.6	19.5

Source: World Debt Tables 1993–94, Vol. 2, World Bank, Washington, DC.

SUMMARY AND CONCLUSION

The rapid increase in private capital flows (FDI, portfolio, and loans) to developing countries in recent years was due to the implementation of policies focused on economic and political reforms. Some of these were debt reduction strategies, liberalization of capital markets, privatization, and expansion of international trade, etc. Our study indicates that the increase in private flows is closely associated with such reforms. Since external capital is crucial for the growth of these countries private flows should be continued. The sustainability of such flows depends on the continuation of such economic and political reforms. Private flows are vital since both bilateral and multilateral aid have been decreasing over the past few years. Other policies to make the markets of developing countries attractive to foreign investors should include (a) financial deepening, (b) infrastructural improvements, (c) inflation control to provide low cost, and (d) more globalization and privatization policies.

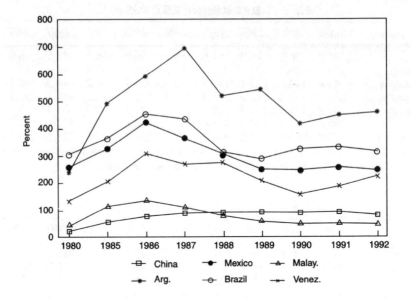

Figure 21.5 Debt indicator: EDT/XGS (percent)

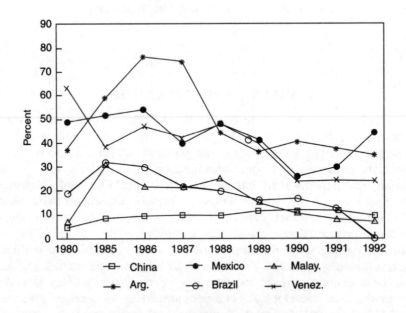

Figure 21.6 Debt indicator: TDS/XGS (percent)

REFERENCES

International Monetary Fund, *International Financial Statistics* (various issues), Washington, DC: IMF.

Root, F. (1994) *International Trade and Investment*, Cincinatti, O.: South West Publishing Co.

World Bank, *World Debt Tables 1993–94*, Washington, DC: World Bank.

World Bank, *World Development Report* (various issues) Washington, DC: World Bank, Oxford University Press.

22

DETERMINANTS OF FOREIGN DIRECT INVESTMENT OUTFLOWS OF SELECTED OECD COUNTRIES

M. Raquibuz Zaman and Fahri M. Unsal

This chapter attempts to identify the determinants of FDI outflows from sixteen developed OECD countries in terms of selected macroeconomic and financial factors. It ascertains the functional relationships between the variables by employing step-wise regression models. Changes in the GNP, the interest rates, the domestic budget deficit, the current account balance, and the exchange rate are found to be the significant explanatory variables. For a clearer understanding of the causes of the FDI outflows from the OECD countries, one needs to assess also the country-specific policy variables that directly or indirectly influence capital flows.

INTRODUCTION

There has been considerable interest among researchers in recent years about the nature, causes and consequences of foreign direct investment (FDI) flows. This interest emanates partly from the rising prominence of Japan as the principal source of FDI outflows in the late 1980s; the enactment of the Single European Act leading to economic integration; and the opening up of new opportunities from the collapse of the socialist economies in Europe and Asia. While the earlier studies tried to evaluate the effectiveness of various incentive packages offered by host countries, including shifts and adjustments in the regulatory practices, some of the recent ones attempted to address the factors that prompt multinational corporations (MNCs) to expand their operations abroad. The latter analyzed FDI flows of specific countries such as Japan, Canada, and the US, into specific countries or regions, e.g., UK, US, and European Union (EU), the successor to the European Economic Community (EEC). However, not much has been done to determine an aggregate function for the outflows of FDIs from a group of countries that provide most of the flows.

This chapter is an attempt to address this void. We have selected sixteen developed countries of the Organization for Economic Cooperation and Development (OECD) and collected data on their FDI outflows between

344

1981 and 1991 to determine whether there exists a functional relationship between FDI outflows and the selected macroeconomic and financial factors. It also points out some of the policy ramifications of this type of macro analysis.

The next section is devoted to a brief literature review, followed by data, specifications, methodology of the study, and the rationale for it. The results of our analysis and the summary and conclusions are given in the final two sections.

LITERATURE REVIEW

The literature on FDI can be classified into two broad categories. The first category consists of those studies that analyze various incentive programs and facilitating policies that attract FDI inflows from the foreign MNCs to host countries. Globerman (1988, pp. 41–9), for example, provides a review of recent government policies of a number of countries towards FDIs. The second category deals with studies that analyze the factors that influence MNCs to expand their operations abroad. Choi (1989, pp. 145–55), Benito and Gripsrud (1992, pp. 461–76), and Rolfe *et al.* (1993, pp. 335–55) provide some examples of this category. Within the second category there are studies that are more relevant for an understanding of the determinants of FDI outflows from specific countries. Some examples of these studies are Mason (1992, pp. 98–115), Balasubramanyam and Greenway (1992, pp. 175–93), and Solocha, *et al.* (1990, pp. 371–86). But the classic studies in this field were done by Dunning (1981, 1988, 1989, and 1993) and Scaperlanda (1967, 1969, and 1983), especially with reference to FDIs in the EC.

Dunning's eclectic paradigm of international production was developed in several works (see Dunning 1981, 1988, 1993a), and was reiterated in his recent book on the globalization of business (1993b). He asserts that the value added activities of the MNCs in foreign countries are due to three factors which are: "O" (ownership specific advantages), "L" (locational advantages), and "I" (internationalization advantages). According to him, the OLI configuration can explain, among other factors, the flows of FDIs into various countries (Dunning 1993b, Ch. 6).

Scaperlanda *et al.* developed statistical models to test the economic integration of the US direct investment flows into the EC since 1951, supporting the tariff discrimination hypothesis regarding locational patterns of FDIs. Yannopoulos (1990) reviewed the empirical results of analyses on the impact of economic integration in Europe on the nature and scope of MNC activities in the early years of the EC and hypothesized the expected shape of FDIs after the completion of the economic union at the beginning of 1993.

These studies, however, do not attempt to ascertain the determinants of

345

aggregate FDI outflows of the major developed economies. One attempt that the authors of this study came across is that by Froot and Stein (1991, pp. 1191–1217) who measured the impact of exchange rate movements on the aggregate FDIs. They found that the exchange rate, through changes in relative wealth, had a systematic effect on FDI, giving credence to the assertion that a depreciated currency can give foreigners some competitive edge on buying controlling interests on corporate productive assets. Incidentally, our study includes changes in foreign exchange rates as one of the explanatory variables. We now turn to the data and the methodology of our study.

DATA AND METHODOLOGY

Data on the outflows of FDIs for the 1981–91 period were collected from the OECD sources (1993, Table II, p. 15). From the International Monetary Fund sources (1992) we collected annual data for Gross National Product (GNP), Current Account Balance (CAB), Consumer Price Index (CPI) as a proxy for the rate of inflation, Foreign Exchange Rate in terms of US dollars (EXC), Domestic Budget Deficit (DBD), and Money Market Rates (MMR) as a proxy for long term risk adjusted cost of capital. The selection of the last variable, MMR, needs some further explanation. For FDI outflows, the relevant rate of interest is the risk adjusted long term cost of capital. However, it is difficult to estimate an aggregate rate for each country with FDI outflows for over a ten year period. For lack of data we used readily available short term money rates as a proxy. In our regression model we used only the changes in the yearly data as explanatory variable to minimize any bias that may exist.

Our data analysis is performed in two stages. First, for each country, we computed correlation coefficients between FDI outflows and the six macro variables. Second, we formulated two regression models, one each for the FDI outflows between 1981 and 1985, and between 1986 and 1991. This was done in order to take into account the importance of a different mix of explanatory variables at these two time periods, marked by such major events as high rates of interest, the Mexican debt crisis, the bank crisis in the US and elsewhere, the collapse of oil prices, the Plaza Accord for currency realignments, and the like. We employed step-wise regression analysis to sort out insignificant variables.

ANALYSIS OF RESULTS

Table 22.1 presents the data on correlations between the FDI outflows and the macro variables for the sixteen OECD countries for the period between 1981 and 1991. The main objective of this analysis was to find out whether or not there was a consistent and distinct pattern of relationship between

Table 22.1 Summary of correlation coefficient FDI outflow versus selected variables

Country	GNP	CAB	CPI	EXC	MMR	DBD
Australia	0.47	−0.11	0.32	−0.03	0.24	0.05
Belgium	0.94*	0.80*	−0.49	−0.69†	−0.40	−0.07
Canada	0.40	−0.46	−0.42	0.33	0.10	0.74†
Denmark	−0.03	0.62†	−0.56	−0.62†	−0.55	0.47
Finland	0.91*	−0.92*	0.28	−0.62†	0.02	0.75†
France	0.98*	−0.53	−0.57	−0.64†	−0.43	−0.09
Germany	0.97*	0.24	0.06	−0.80*	0.12	−0.40
Italy	0.84*	−0.38	−0.23	−0.65†	−0.65†	−0.74*
Japan	0.89*	0.29	0.25	−0.87*	−0.22	n.a.
Netherlands	0.87*	0.81*	−0.03	−0.76*	0.32	0.14
Norway	0.88*	0.01	−0.53	0.12	0.74*	0.07
Spain	0.90*	−0.88*	−0.10	−0.54	−0.17	0.17
Sweden	0.93*	−0.64†	0.61	−0.39	−0.08	0.90*
Switzerland	0.76†	0.78†	0.34	−0.46	0.47	0.19
UK	0.61†	0.79*	0.13	0.24	0.22	0.94*
US	0.89*	−0.45	0.11	0.86*	−0.60†	−0.36

* Coefficients are significant at the 1 percent level.
† Coefficients are significant at the 5 percent level.
Source: Computed by the authors

the FDI outflows and the remaining variables for each of the selected countries. As can be seen from the data, GNP was generally the most highly correlated variable with the FDI outflows, followed by CAB, and EXC. When the level of significance of the correlation coefficients are examined, we see that GNP is significant at the 1 percent level for 11 countries, at the 5 percent level for two (Switzerland and the UK), and not significant for three countries (Australia, Canada, and Denmark). CAB is significant at the 1 percent level for five countries, at the 5 percent level for three, while not significant for eight countries. The correlation coefficients for CPI were not significant for any country. Domestic inflation rates presumably did not affect FDI outflows. EXC is significant at the 1 percent level for four countries, and the 5 percent level for five countries. The coefficient for MMR was significant at the 1 percent level for only Norway, and at the 5 percent level for Italy and the US. DBD was significant at the 1 percent level for Italy, Sweden, and the UK, and at the 5 percent level for Canada and Finland. All the rest were statistically insignificant.

The results were not contrary to our expectations. It should be noted here that the explanatory macro variables with which we are dealing in this study are essentially secondary variables explaining FDI outflows. The primary variables are the incentive packages that are offered by host countries receiving FDI flows. Moreover, the macro variables under study

347

had varied levels of impact on the FDI flows of the diverse OECD countries at different time periods.

Our regression models were based on the hypothesis that the FDI outflows were influenced by the six macro variables outlined in the previous section. Since most such explanatory variables would have lagged effects in the FDI outflows, we used changes in these variables, denoted by "C" before each, for our regression equations. Equation (1) gives the functional relationships between FDI outflows and the explanatory variables for the period between 1981 and 1985. The set of independent variables used are listed below:

$$CFDI_1 = f(CGNP_1, CCAB_1, CCPI_1, CEXC_1, CMMR_1, CDBD_1) \tag{1}$$

A step-wise procedure was used for estimation. Thus, the full model was estimated first, and then the non-significant variables were removed in successive steps. The final equation that includes only the significant variables is reported below with t-scores for slope efficient in parentheses:

$$CFDI_1 = 1005.32 + 5.04\ CGNP_1 + 320.27\ CMMR_1$$
$$(2.90) \qquad\quad (2.11)$$

The t-tests indicated that the $CGNP_1$ variable was significant at the 1 percent and the $CMMR_1$ variable was significant at the 5 percent level. The coefficient of determination (R^2) was equal to 0.42, indicating a moderate fit.

The positive signs of the two coefficients seem to indicate that changes in the GNP and interest rates have direct effects on the FDI outflows. While it is clear that the growth in GNP will provide the MNCs with increased investible funds that they may choose to employ abroad, it is not that clear for the changes in the interest rates. One plausible explanation could be that rising interest rates that spread globally may induce host countries to borrow less funds from commercial sources and procure the needed funds by offering special inducement packages to foreign direct investors.

We have used a different regression model for the 1986–91 period because it represented a global environment that was besieged with economic instability arising out of currency realignments, massive trade deficits for some countries and surpluses for a few, oil price crashes, bank failures, economic recession, etc., etc., that added to the complexity of the decisions for FDI outflows. It is worth pointing out here that 1986 marked the beginning of a sharp upward movement in FDI outflows that continued through 1990. In 1991, there was a 20 percent decline in the overall flows from the peak reached in 1990. Our second regression equation used $CFDI_2$ as the dependent variable and $CDBD_2$, $CCAB_2$, $CGNP_2$, and $CEXC_2$ as independent variables. The resultant Equation 2 is as follows:

$$CDFI_2 = 1768.81 - 193.59\ CDBD_2 - 0.05\ CCAB_2 + 10.37\ CGNP_2 + 43.83\ CEXC_2 \quad (2)$$
$$ (-1.77) \qquad (-1.84) \qquad\quad (4.48) \qquad\quad (2.02)$$

The coefficients for $CDBD_2$ and $CCAB_2$ were significant at the 10 percent and 9 percent levels, while those of $CGNP_2$ and $CEXC_2$ were significant at the 1 percent and 5 percent levels. The R^2 for the equation was 0.70, indicating a relatively good fit. The F-test ($F = 6.56$) showed that the regression in equation (2) was significant at the 1 percent level. The signs of the regression coefficients were as expected from our knowledge about the actual FDI outflows of various countries.

CONCLUSION

Foreign direct investment decisions are complex. Some forms of OLI configuration, as formulated by Dunning, and the various incentive packages that are advanced by host countries, explain more thoroughly the underlying reasons behind investment decisions of MNCs in foreign countries than the macro variables studied here can. Yet this study presents some interesting results that confirm our general understanding of the causes of FDI outflows. It would be worth while to replicate such an exercise in the future with additional data and explanatory variables to reconfirm our findings.

Those who are interested in gauging the magnitude of future FDI flows may like to consider not only the policies of host countries to attract them, but also the variables such as the ones we used to ascertain whether or not such flows would be forthcoming.

REFERENCES

Balasubramanyam, V.N. and D. Greenway (1992) "Economic Integration and Foreign Direct Investment: Japanese Investment in the EC," *Journal of Common Market Studies*, Vol. XXX, No. 2, June, pp. 175–93.

Benito, G.R.G. and G. Gripsrud (1992) "The Expansion of Foreign Direct Investments: Discrete Rational Location Choices or a Cultural Learning Process?," *Journal of International Business Studies*, Vol. 23, No. 3, Third Quarter, pp. 461–76.

Choi, J.J. (1989) "Diversification, Exchange Risk, and Corporate International Investment," *Journal of International Business Studies*, Vol. XX, No. 1 (Spring), pp. 145–55.

Dunning, J.H. (1981) *International Production and the Multinational Enterprise*, London: Allen & Unwin.

Dunning, J.H. (1988) *Multinationals, Technology, and Competitiveness*, London: Unwin Hyman.

Dunning, J.H. (1989) "Foreign Direct Investment in the European Community: A Brief Overview," *Multinational Business*, No. 4 (Winter), pp. 1–9.

Dunning, J.H. (1993a) *Multinational Enterprise and the Global Economy*, Wokingham, Berks: Addison-Wesley.

Dunning, J.H. (1993b) *The Globalization of Business: The Challenge of the 1990s*, London and New York: Routledge.

Froot, K.A. and J.C. Stein (1991) "Exchange Rates and Foreign Direct Investment: An Imperfect Capital Markets Approach," *The Quarterly Journal of Economics*, Vol. 106, No. 4 (November) pp. 1191–1217.

Globerman, S. (1988) "Governmental Policies Toward Foreign Direct Investment: Has a New Era Dawned?," *Columbia Journal of World Business*, Vol. 23, No. 3 (Fall), pp. 41–9.

International Monetary Fund (1992) *International Financial Statistics Yearbook 1992*, Vol. XLV, Washington, DC: IMF.

Mason, M. (1992) "The Origins and Evolution of Japanese Direct Investment in Europe," *California Management Review*, Vol. 35, No. 1 (Fall), pp. 98–115.

OECD (1993) *International Direct Investment Statistics Yearbook 1993*, Paris: OECD.

Rolfe, R.J. *et al.* (1993) "Determinants of FDI Incentive Preferences of MNEs," *Journal of International Business Studies*, Vol. 24, No. 2 (Second Quarter), pp. 335–55.

Scaperlanda, A. (1967) "The EEC and U.S. Foreign Investment: Some Empirical Evidence," *Economic Journal*, Vol. 77, pp. 220–26.

Scaperlanda, A. and L.J. White (1969) "The Determinants of U.S. Direct Investment in the EEC," *American Economic Review*, Vol. 59, pp. 558–68.

Scaperlanda, A. and R.S. Balough (1983) "Determinants of U.S. Direct Investment in the EC," *European Economic Review*, Vol. 21, pp. 381–90.

Solocha, A., M. Soskin, and M. Kasoff (1990) "Determinants of Foreign Direct Investment: A Case of Canadian Direct Investment in the United States," *Management International Review*, Vol. 30, No. 4, pp. 371–86.

Yannopoulos, G.N. (1990) "Foreign Direct Investment and European Integration: The Evidence from the Formative Years of the European Community," *Journal of Common Market Studies*, Vol. 28, No. 3 (March), pp. 235–59.

23

AN EXAMINATION OF THE ARGUMENT FOR INCREASED INVESTMENT IN EMERGING MARKETS

P. Avgoustinos, A.A. Lonie, D.M. Power and C.D. Sinclair

This chapter adopts the perspective of the UK investor and investigates the risk-return advantages of a portfolio combining UK and emerging market securities.

INTRODUCTION

The argument for international portfolio diversification (IPD) has been established with great thoroughness on both theoretical and empirical grounds in the course of the past twenty-five years;[1] it became unremarkable textbook orthodoxy during the 1980s.[2] This chapter addresses a topical question associated with IPD which has been the focus of a number of recently published analyses:[3] are financial institutions forfeiting important portfolio gains by investing too low a proportion of their assets in securities traded in emerging markets?

Our study approaches this issue from a slightly different perspective from that of most other investigations. First, we analyse the gains achieved by adding emerging market securities to a portfolio of UK equities (rather than, as has commonly been the practice, to a portfolio of US stocks). Although it is hard to find an expert who is prepared to recommend that more than one-fifth of portfolio capitalization be allocated to emerging market equities, we examine an equally-weighted portfolio which has up to 90 per cent of funds invested in emerging market securities in an attempt to gauge the possible risk-return benefits of a major commitment to emerging market securities. The gains that ensue are measured in sterling. Second, we apply a procedure that has become commonplace in investigations of the returns on major stock exchanges and test the *stability* of the correlations (a) between nine emerging markets drawn from four different continents and (b) between these markets and the UK over the sixteen-year period 1977–92, as well as across four sub-periods 1977–80, 1981–84, 1985–88, 1989–92. Third, and again quite conventionally, we calculate the mean returns per unit of risk (MRPUR) over the sixteen-year period of the study (a) for separate markets in equities and (b) for different market combinations, in an attempt to determine the *ex post* optimum portfolio selection.

TIME FOR A CHANGE IN PORTFOLIO EMPHASIS?

There are probably few areas in which the gap between theory and practice is quite so marked as in the case for including emerging market equities in institutional portfolios. On the basis of market capitalization an internationally diversified portfolio might be expected to devote roughly 4 per cent of total value to emerging market securities. This proportion is at once well below the percentage recommended by certain recent studies which offer guidance on the composition of a globally diversified optimal portfolio constructed in accordance with Markowitz principles (Speidell and Sappenfield, 1992, suggest 10–15 per cent, and Divecha *et al.*, 1992, advocate that up to 20 per cent be held in emerging market equities), but well above the proportion that many internationally diversified funds currently regard as prudent.

The broad arguments in favour of adopting great circumspection before engaging in direct investment in ESM equities are well known. Emerging markets are believed to be relatively prone to (a) political risk involving military takeovers or simply what the international investor is likely to regard as unwarranted interference with inflows and outflows of capital by government and (b) currency risk, which is often closely linked to the imposition of controls on capital flows which we have classed as a political risk. Their markets are thought to suffer from a greater incidence of thin trading than their developed country counterparts. A further perceived disadvantage of ESMs is the heavy concentration of market capitalization in a fairly small number of securities and the associated problem of the comparatively low liquidity of such markets; Gill and Tropper (1988) suggested that only 3.5 per cent of all securities listed in ESMs fulfilled the minimum liquidity and "visibility" criteria necessary for inclusion in an internationally diversified portfolio. The homogeneity of price movements in equities traded in ESMs, compared with the often markedly different market response of the shares of various industrial sectors in developed stock markets, is seen as a further drawback. The access of overseas investors to emerging markets of high growth potential such as Korea and Taiwan has notoriously been subject to severe restrictions, and many other ESMs like Chile, Greece and Mexico have been characterized as only "relatively free".[4] However by far the most dramatic disadvantage of ESM investment is, superficially at least, the volatility of the returns on equities in individual emerging markets, the proneness of such markets to periods of low or negative growth generating considerable downside risk.

The perceived change in the relative attractiveness of emerging markets is attributable to four principal factors. First, the accessibility of ESMs has recently improved, with further liberalization scheduled. Certain ESMs, such as Argentina, Brazil, Malaysia and Pakistan, have permitted the "free entry" and "free repatriation" of dividends and capital gains since February 1991, and even the closed markets of Korea and Taiwan, which in the past have been accessible only via the device of country funds have announced plans to open up their capital markets by stages. Second, with the passage of years the problems associated with low marketability and thin trading have in general improved, although conditions in certain markets have at times retrogressed; the number of companies listed on their national stock exchanges actually declined between 1981 and 1991 in Argentina, Chile and Mexico. Third, the high median real annualized growth of GDP in ESMs of 4.5 per cent between 1984 and 1992 compared very favourably with the equivalent growth rate of 2.5 per cent in countries with developed markets (Wilcox, 1992) and was reflected in a rise in the annualized compound return of the International Finance Corporation index over the five-year period which ended on 30 June 1991, which was 53 per cent higher than the increase in the US as measured by the S&P index over the same period. Moreover, as various studies have pointed out, the volatility, and consequently the associate downside risk of ESMs *as a whole*, is much lower than that of individual emerging markets.

The fourth factor is perhaps the most significant of all. The stock market crash of October 1987 (and, to a much lesser extent, the Iraqi invasion of Kuwait) has resulted in a sharp increase in the correlations between the returns in the major markets in the world, the growing integration of those markets resulting in a diminution of the rewards to be obtained by IPD which is confined to the securities of developed markets. Speidell and Sappenfield (1992) have further developed Roll's (1988) demonstration of the much greater degree of convergence among developed market returns resulting from the Crash by revealing that the correlation coefficient between the US S&P market index and ESMs rose from 0.07 pre-crash to 0.22 post-crash compared with a corresponding increase from 0.17 to 0.62 in the average correlation between the US S&P index and the returns in developed markets; by contrast an examination of Speidell and Sappenfield's data suggests that the correlations of around a third of ESMs and the US market were virtually unaffected by the Crash.[5]

Although the exploitability of the apparent gains that can be achieved by increased portfolio diversification into ESM has been challenged, the combination of high growth potential and low correlation between ESMs and developed markets represents a phenomenon which is well worth empirical study.

DATA

Datastream was used to obtain monthly price indices for shares traded in nine emerging markets over the period January 1977 to December 1992. In particular the stock market indices for Argentina (ARG), Brazil (BRA), Chile (CHI), Mexico (MEX), India (IND), Korea (KOR), Thailand (THA), Greece (GRE) and Zimbabwe (ZIM) were included in this study. These countries represent the population of emerging markets for which data were available over the 16-year time horizon considered. The sample represents a good geographical spread of countries, including four Latin and Central American countries, three Asian and Far Eastern countries, one European and one African country. The results should therefore not be specific to any one sub-group of emerging markets countries.

In addition, data for the UK stock market are included to provide a comparison between a major developed market and the relatively smaller emerging markets. One might expect that information would be more readily impounded into UK share prices due to the larger number of sophisticated analysts present and the more technologically advanced trading system available in the UK.

All ESM index prices were obtained in US dollars and converted to UK pounds sterling (a) to facilitate comparison between the returns in the different markets, (b) to adjust for the differences in inflation rates according to the Purchasing Power Parity Theory and (c) to adopt the perspective of the UK investor.

Returns for each index were calculated according to the formula:

$$R_{it} = \ln \left[\frac{P_{it}}{P_{it-1}} \right] \left[\frac{X_{t-1}}{X_t} \right] \tag{1}$$

where R_{it} is the return on index i in month t; P_{it} is the price level of the index in month t; X_t is the dollar–pound exchange rate for the period; and ln represents the natural logarithm.

RESULTS

A number of descriptive statistics were calculated for the return series of each emerging stock market (ESM) index and for the UK index over the whole 16-year period; the results shown in Table 23.1; in particular the mean (MEAN), standard deviation (STDEV), minimum (MIN) and maximum (MAX), skewness (SKEW) and beta (BETA) were estimated. There is a wide range of values reported. For example, Chile had the highest return of 2.3 per cent per month for the sample period while Brazil, Greece and Zimbabwe performed badly with average returns of under 0.5 per cent per month for the same period. Surprisingly, the UK stock market performed well, earning an average return of 1.2 per cent per month over the

354

INVESTMENT IN EMERGING MARKETS

Table 23.1 Descriptive statistics for the data

	MEAN	STDEV	MIN	MAX	SKEW	BETA
ARG	0.014	0.246	−1.096	1.020	0.155	0.222
BRA	0.004	0.180	−0.821	0.434	−0.384*	0.361
CHI	0.023	0.109	−0.284	0.492	0.458*	0.267
MEX	0.020	0.149	−0.945	0.400	−2.137*	0.779
IND	0.014	0.082	−0.301	0.320	0.361*	0.024
KOR	0.015	0.096	−0.220	0.381	0.756*	0.398
THA	0.018	0.087	−0.486	0.272	−0.694*	0.487
GRE	0.002	0.099	−0.302	0.455	1.094*	0.147
ZIM	0.004	0.096	−0.326	0.324	−0.334	0.018
UK	0.012	0.055	−0.327	0.125	−1.508*	1.000

Note: Descriptive data are included in the table. The MEAN is the equally weighted average of all observations. STDEV is the standard deviation. MIN and MAX are the minimum and maximum share values respectively. SKEW is the Kendall–Stuart measure of skewness and BETA is the beta of the share relative to the UK index. An * indicates significance at the 5 per cent level.

16-year time span considered. This good performance of the UK stock market was accompanied by a level of risk (as measured by standard deviation) which was small in comparison with the other countries taken individually. By contrast, in the Argentinian stock market a share return of 1.4 per cent per month (only slightly above the UK stock market performance) was achieved with nearly *five* times the level of risk; the Argentinian market was associated with particularly volatile returns since the standard deviation over the 16-year period of the study was 24.6 per cent compared with 5.5 per cent for the UK. This volatility of emerging market returns is confirmed by an examination of the minimum and maximum values, the spread between these figures is much higher for emerging markets than for the UK index.

From the data in Table 23.1, three of the nine emerging market return series exhibit statistically significant negative skewness; the Kendall–Stuart skewness statistics reject the hypothesis of normally distributed returns for Brazil, Mexico and Thailand at the 5 per cent level. The returns for Chile, India, Korea and Greece displayed significant positive skewness. From a risk-averse investor's perspective, investing in these countries possibly represents an attractive option since the positive skewness implies that the return distributions of shares traded on these exchanges have a heavier tail of large positive values and hence a higher possibility of earning positive returns. The fact that the skewness measure of −1.508 for the UK index was greater than the average of the nine emerging markets, taken together, over the 16-year period therefore diminishes the apparent superiority of the UK market performance compared with that of our selection of ESMs. The final column in Table 23.1 shows the beta

355

values which measure the covariability of the returns from converging markets with UK returns standardized by the variance of the returns of UK equities. With the exception of Mexico, all the beta values are relatively small so that casual empiricism suggests that combining shares from ESMs into a portfolio comprised of only UK shares ought to lower the portfolio market risk substantially.

Table 23.2 shows the ratio of mean return/standard deviation of return (the mean return per unit of risk (MRPUR)) for the sample of emerging market indices, and for the UK index, over the whole 16-year period and also in each of the four 4-year sub-periods (1977–80, 1981–84, 1985–88 and 1989–92). A number of points emerge from an examination of the ratios. First, over the whole sample period the UK stock market outperforms all nine of the emerging markets with a MRPUR of 0.218. The range of MRPUR ratios for the emerging markets extends from a low of 0.019 for Brazil and Greece to a high of 0.213 for Chile. These results confirm the findings from Table 23.1 that, for the level of risk involved and given the menu of market indices on offer, the UK stock market appeared to offer international investors an excellent investment opportunity over this 16-year period.

Second, there is a great deal of variability in performance across the four sub-periods. For example, among the emerging markets examined the Chilean stock market was ranked first, ninth, third and first respectively in consecutive sub-periods, with MRPURs of 0.380, −0.259, 0.292 and 0.421. This erratic performance of the Chilean market index typifies the volatile nature of returns in the majority of the nine emerging markets included in this study.

Third, the MRPUR statistics reveal a general decline in the performance

Table 23.2 Mean return per unit of risk (MRPUR) for the sample

	1977–92	1977–80	1981–84	1985–88	1989–92
ARG	0.056 (7)	0.131 (6)	−0.085 (7)	0.032 (3)	0.121 (7)
BRA	0.019 (8)	−0.205 (10)	0.210 (5)	−0.039 (10)	0.041 (8)
CHI	0.213 (2)	0.380 (1)	−0.259 (10)	0.292 (4)	0.421 (1)
MEX	0.133 (6)	0.324 (3)	−0.044 (6)	0.105 (8)	0.388 (2)
IND	0.170 (4)	0.237 (4)	0.346 (2)	0.112 (7)	0.126 (6)
KOR	0.158 (5)	0.079 (8)	0.248 (4)	0.354 (2)	−0.022 (9)
THA	0.204 (3)	0.137 (5)	0.461 (1)	0.156 (5)	0.220 (3)
GRE	0.019 (8)	−0.157 (5)	−0.220 (8)	0.094 (9)	0.149 (4)
ZIM	0.037 (10)	0.131 (6)	−0.221 (9)	0.393 (1)	−0.072 (10)
UK	0.218 (1)	0.346 (2)	0.289 (3)	0.150 (6)	0.132 (5)

Note: The MRPUR of the nine emerging markets and of the UK are shown over the whole sample period and in each sub-period. The mean is the equally weighted average and the risk is the standard deviation. The rankings of the countires are shown in parentheses.

of the UK market throughout the period being considered. The ratio decreases from 0.346 to 0.289 to 0.150 to 0.132 in sub-periods one through four, a reduction in UK performance of 62 per cent over the 16-year period. The overall superiority in performance of the UK equity market between 1977 and 1992 therefore appears to be largely attributable to the exceptional rate of return generated in the years 1977–80 and the good return achieved in the period 1981–84.

Although the UK market outperformed each of its individual emerging market counterparts in terms of MRPUR over the sample period, we proceeded to investigate whether the emerging markets might offer the UK investor high returns for a relatively low level of risk when combined into a portfolio. In particular, equally weighted portfolios of the emerging market indices and the UK index were constructed to examine their MRPUR behaviour as a function of the number, m, of the indices included in the portfolio (out of the total of ten indices available) where m takes values from 1 to 10. More specifically ten MRPUR-optimal portfolios were selected from an array of all possible portfolio combinations for each portfolio size category, and contrasted with the corresponding figures for the portfolio comprised of only UK shares to determine whether any potential benefits from international portfolio diversification exist.

A visual examination of Figure 23.1 reveals that the MRPUR-optimal portfolio curve lies well above the corresponding UK index line from its beginning ($m = 1$) to a portfolio size of five indices. However, increasing

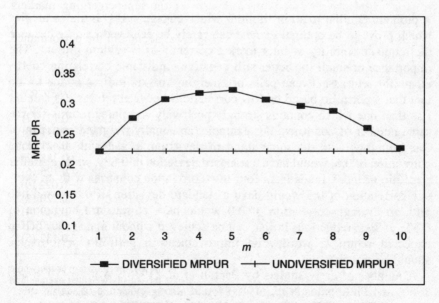

Figure 23.1 MRPUR for diversified and undiversified portfolios

357

the number of indices in the portfolio beyond five reduced the overall benefits from diversifying into shares in emerging markets. In particular, when the market indices of the UK, Chile, India, Thailand and Korea were combined in an equally weighted portfolio the MRPUR increased to 0.3226, 46 per cent higher than the MRPUR achieved by a portfolio containing only UK equities.

The evidence therefore suggests that a portfolio which included emerging market shares held over the period 1977–92 could have offered the British investor a significantly higher MRPUR than a parallel investment strategy in which the choice was limited to UK equities. This finding is hardly novel. Several recent studies have emphasized that the returns in emerging capital markets tend to be uncorrelated with each other and with developed markets (see, for example, Cheung and Ho, 1991; Divecha, *et al.* 1992; and Speidell and Sappenfield, 1992), making international diversification in such markets an attractive investment option. However, this chapter, although similarly emphasizing the gains from diversifying portfolio selection to include the shares of emerging markets, makes two additional points. First, the argument applies even when the proportion of ESM securities is as high as 80 or 90 per cent of portfolio value. Second, the case for emerging market diversification applies to UK investors with at least as much force as it does to the US investors whose perspective is considered in the Divecha *et al.* and the Speidell and Sappenfield studies.

EXPLOITABLE GAINS FROM EMERGING MARKETS

A problem familiar to all institutions which engage in IPD is that strategies which prove to be optimal *ex post* can rarely be achieved *ex ante* because the requisite stability of inter-market correlations is seldom present. The importance of small (or better still negative) and stable correlation coefficients for returns between pairs of emerging market indices is due to the fact that a portfolio based on low correlations between returns has smaller risk than one which contains strongly positively correlated returns for the same number of countries. For example, an equally weighted portfolio of four countries with the same standard deviation, s, and with an average correlation of 0.6, would have a standard deviation of $0.83s$, while a similar portfolio of index funds from four low-correlation countries with an average correlation of 0.3 would have a standard deviation of $0.69s$, and one with an average correlation of 0.0 would have at standard deviation of $0.50s$. If such reductions in risk can be achieved without undue sacrifice in expected return, a worthwhile improvement in portfolio performance should be possible.

A number of early studies by Panton *et al.* (1976), Watson (1978 and 1980) and Philippatos *et al.* (1983) found strong evidence of stable intertemporal relationships among major stock markets. For example, the last of these investigations analysed monthly correlations between US returns and those of fourteen developed countries for a 20-year period and concluded that their results, from a variety of statistical tests, supported the hypothesis of a "stable structure in the inter-temporal relationship among national stock market indices of the industrialised world for intermediate term investment horizons" (p. 67). However, investigations by Grubel (1968), Levy and Sarnat (1970), Makridakis and Wheelwright (1974), Maldonado and Saunders (1981) and Speidell and Sappenfield (1992) revealed substantial instability in correlations between major countries over time.

Makridakis and Wheelwright (1974) found that the correlations between the returns in the US market and the returns in the world's leading exchanges were unstable over a thirty-two month period (1968–1970) for which daily data were examined, a result supported by the earlier findings of Grubel (1968) and Levy and Sarnet (1970) for the same countries over different time periods. Maldonado and Saunders (1981) examined the inter-temporal stability of correlations between monthly returns on a US stock index and the market indices of Japan, Germany, Canada, and the UK over the 22-year period 1957–78. The inter-temporal evidence from their study suggested that annual correlations were "generally random". However, their findings suggested that in the very short term (up to two quarters) a relatively stable relationship existed between inter-country correlations, sufficient for the nimble investor to exploit.

Correlations between each pair of countries, indices were estimated for the whole period and the four 4-year sub-periods. There are 36 inter-country correlations for each sub-period and these correlations are listed in Table 23.3. Substantial benefits from international portfolio diversification among emerging markets appear to exist up to the end of December 1992: for example, for the period as a whole 35 of the 36 correlations reported are less than 0.3. The benefits of international portfolio diversification are even greater in certain of the sub-periods examined: in the first sub-period the correlation between the indices for Korea and Zimbabwe returns was −0.272, while in the second sub-period the correlation between the return indices of Mexico and Greece was an even larger −0.388. However, it is evident that the distribution of the correlations has not been constant over time, and the number of small and negative correlations declined from the period 1977–80 to the period 1981–84, but increased again in the years 1985–92. This relative instability in correlations between returns in emerging stock exchanges is likely to negate any attempt by an investor to generate an *ex ante* optimal international portfolio in spite of the often low correlations which exist in certain periods.

Table 23.4 provides a one-way analysis of variance applied to the correlations in the four separate 4-year sub-periods. The hypothesis that the average correlation in each sub-period is the same is strongly rejected; the p-value is 0.000, which is highly significant. The graphical information

Table 23.3 Correlations of returns for the sample

	1977–92	1977–80	1981–84	1985–88	1989–92
ARG–BRA	0.008	0.274	−0.168	0.269	−0.110
ARG–CHI	0.121	0.135	−0.022	0.109	0.183
ARG–MEX	0.206	0.270	0.117	0.157	0.423
ARG–IND	0.228	0.346	−0.031	0.217	0.307
ARG–KOR	0.003	−0.145	0.097	0.052	0.035
ARG–THA	0.078	−0.123	−0.120	0.138	0.198
ARG–GRE	0.098	0.255	−0.110	0.129	0.099
ARG–ZIM	0.029	0.236	0.054	−0.157	−0.030
BRA–CHI	0.086	0.262	−0.173	0.073	0.291
BRA–MEX	0.042	−0.007	−0.047	0.065	0.158
BRA–IND	0.069	0.213	−0.111	0.037	0.110
BRA–KOR	0.078	0.037	0.113	0.234	−0.020
BRA–THA	0.102	0.069	−0.112	0.180	0.107
BRA–GRE	−0.015	0.146	−0.148	−0.244	0.161
BRA–ZIM	−0.004	0.036	−0.037	−0.058	0.105
CHI–MEX	0.272	0.139	−0.108	0.600	0.381
CHI–IND	0.149	0.188	0.133	0.167	0.234
CHI–KOR	0.168	0.121	0.012	0.405	0.279
CHI–THA	0.243	0.060	−0.159	0.551	0.410
CHI–GRE	0.215	0.235	0.256	0.376	0.066
CHI–ZIM	0.188	0.199	0.132	0.166	0.152
MEX–IND	0.138	0.163	−0.043	0.200	0.244
MEX–KOR	0.229	0.121	0.072	0.371	0.439
MEX–THA	0.373	−0.050	0.187	0.556	0.524
MEX–GRE	0.131	0.129	−0.388	0.373	0.047
MEX–ZIM	0.116	0.028	0.118	0.108	0.193
IND–KOR	0.100	−0.136	0.214	0.198	0.076
IND–THA	0.256	0.200	0.254	0.179	0.349
IND–GRE	0.091	0.270	0.227	0.095	0.038
IND–ZIM	0.058	0.232	0.211	0.242	−0.180
KOR–THA	0.224	0.167	0.071	0.195	0.389
KOR–GRE	−0.017	−0.204	0.174	0.131	−0.145
KOR–ZIM	−0.031	−0.272	0.027	−0.024	0.065
THA–GRE	0.282	0.145	0.126	0.418	0.245
THA–ZIM	0.012	−0.146	−0.051	0.152	0.049
GRE–ZIM	0.100	0.243	0.176	0.104	−0.016
UK–ARG	0.049	0.042	0.031	0.051	0.072
UK–BRA	0.109	0.139	0.097	0.158	0.087
UK–CHI	0.133	−0.129	0.120	0.386	0.220
UK–MEX	0.286	0.088	0.055	0.467	0.371
UK–IND	0.016	0.192	−0.020	−0.010	−0.002
UK–KOR	0.225	0.149	0.104	0.205	0.435
UK–THA	0.306	−0.056	0.064	0.511	0.435
UK–GRE	0.081	0.081	−0.017	0.233	−0.004
UK–ZIM	0.010	−0.192	0.231	−0.099	0.103

Table 23.4 Analysis of variance of emerging markets and of UK and emerging markets

(a) EMERGING MARKETS

Source	DF	SS	MS	F	p
Factor	3	0.5546	0.1849	6.77	0.000
Error	140	3.8249	0.0273		
Total	143	4.3796			

Level	N	Mean	STDEV
B	36	0.1066	0.1545
C	36	0.0262	0.1499
D	36	0.1879	0.1832
E	36	0.1627	0.1714

Pooled STDEV = 0.1653

Individual 95 PCT CI's for mean based on pooled STDEV

```
          +---------+---------+---------+---------
            (----*----)
         (----*----)
                      (----*----)
                    (----*----)
          +---------+---------+---------+---------
        0.000     0.080     0.160     0.240
```

(b) UK AND EMERGING MARKETS

Source	DF	SS	MS	F	p
Factor	3	0.2023	0.0674	2.67	0.064
Error	32	0.8081	0.0253		
Total	35	1.0104			

Level	N	Mean	STDEV
B	9	0.0349	0.1324
C	9	0.0739	0.0772
D	9	0.2113	0.2121
E	9	0.1908	0.1804

Pooled STDEV - 0.1589

Individual 95 PCT CI's for mean based on pooled STDEV

```
       +---------+---------+---------+---------
         (-----*-----)
           (-----*-----)
                        (-----*-----)
                     (-----*-----)
       +---------+---------+---------+---------
      0.00      0.12      0.24
```

in Table 23.4 corroborates the visual impression that there is a significant shift in correlations between the first and second 4-year sub-periods and between the second and the last two 4-year sub-periods. The correlations in the second sub-period were low; the average correlation was approximately 0.03. However, there was a significant rise in correlation over the period 1985–88; in common with several other studies (for example, Roll, 1988; Le, 1991), therefore, we find that correlations increased significantly in the period which included the Crash. In addition, on the strength of the evidence up to December 1991 the effect of the Crash in raising correlations appears to be enduring; the decline in the average correlation from 0.19 in the 1985–88 sub-period to 0.16 in the 1989–93 sub-period is not statistically significant. These results contrast the findings of, for example, Bruce (1989), who found that the risk-return benefits from international portfolio diversification were undiminished in the post-Crash period.

Principal components were used to investigate whether there are some linear combinations of the equity market indices used in this study that can account for much of the variation in the returns. If so, these linear combinations may exhibit more stability over time than was found to exist between individual pairs of markets. Moreover the weights in these linear combinations may be employed to produce a good set of portfolio weightings. A further use of the principal components might be to summarize the way in which returns in emerging markets in general correlate with UK market returns. Table 23.5 shows the mean, standard deviation, return per unit of risk and correlation with the UK market index for each of the principal components. The first and second principal components have a larger mean return, a larger standard deviation of return but a smaller return per unit of risk than the UK, and each is moderately strongly positively correlated with UK market returns. On the other hand the descriptive statistics suggest that the ninth principal component has a larger mean return, a larger standard deviation of return and also a larger return per unit of risk than the UK market, but has very low correlation with the UK market index.

However the weightings associated with the principal components may be negative and consequently a real portfolio could not be based directly on these weights since short selling of shares is rarely permitted in emerging markets. However, in practice this technical problem may be overcome because a feasible portfolio, with non-negative weights, can be constructed from a principal component which has some negative weights by incorporating an appropriate amount of an equally weighted portfolio of all nine emerging markets. Such feasible portfolios appear in the middle panel of Table 23.5 as EMP1 to EMP9. All nine of these portfolios have a larger mean return and a larger standard deviation of return than the UK market index, and with the exception of EMP1, all exhibit larger return per unit of risk than the UK market index. In particular, EMP2, EMP4 and EMP9

Table 23.5 Principal components (PC), corresponding emerging market portfolios (EMP) and selected diversified portfolios with 80:20 UK EMPC MIX (DP)

	Mean	STDEV	RPUR	CORRUK
PC1	0.016	0.110	0.141	0.433
PC2	0.496	4.464	0.111	0.231
PC3	0.006	0.433	0.014	-0.166
PC4	0.014	0.082	0.166	0.069
PC5	0.027	0.091	0.295	-0.199
PC6	0.039	0.219	0.178	-0.035
PC7	0.426	2.244	0.190	0.154
PC8	0.091	0.294	0.308	-0.158
PC9	0.074	0.341	0.216	0.040
UK	0.010	0.067	0.150	1.000
EMP1	0.016	0.109	0.143	0.433
EMP2	0.014	0.082	0.166	0.270
EMP3	0.016	0.075	0.216	0.432
EMP4	0.019	0.109	0.178	0.393
EMP5	0.011	0.130	0.084	0.492
EMP6	0.014	0.088	0.164	0.407
EMP7	0.014	0.076	0.189	0.368
EMP8	0.014	0.078	0.173	0.440
EMP9	0.016	0.076	0.205	0.405
DP2	0.011	0.060	0.179	
DP4	0.011	0.061	0.182	
DP9	0.012	0.065	0.183	

possess attractive combinations of return and correlation with the UK market index.

Prudent British investors might not be comfortable with a portfolio that is completely devoted to emerging markets and may prefer a diversified portfolio that invested, say, 80 per cent in the UK market and 20 per cent in an emerging market portfolio. For three such portfolios the (a) mean (b) standard deviation of the return, and (c) return per unit of risk, are shown in the lower panel of Table 23.5. All three portfolios, DP2, DP4 and DP9, offer improvements in the mean return, in the standard deviation of the returns and in the return per unit of risk compared to investing only in the UK. This improvement is evident, not only over the whole 16-year period of the study, but also over each 4-year sub-period, including even the least promising 4-year period when correlations were at their highest.

CONCLUSION

From a UK investor's viewpoint, substantial gains appear to exist *ex post* from adding emerging market equities to a portfolio composed of only UK shares. In our analysis, these gains reach their optimum when 80 per cent of the portfolio is devoted to shares in four ESMs (Chile, India, Korea and Thailand) and 20 per cent is invested in UK equities. One essential prerequisite for the construction of an *ex ante* optimal portfolio is missing however; correlations between the index returns for the countries considered in this study are unstable from one period to the next. Because the correlations vary unpredictably over time, the capacity of an investor to exploit the gains from IPD must be rather limited.

NOTES

1 Seminal articles justifying IPD were published by Grubel (1968), Levy and Sarnat (1970), Grubel and Fadner (1971), Agmon (1972), Lessard (1974), Solnik (1974a and 1974b), Alder and Dumas (1975) and, with special reference to the UK in the context ot variable exchange rates, Saunders and Woodward (1977). One of the most impressive modern contributions to the theoretical modelling of the gains from international diversification is the sequence of articles by Grauer and Hakansson (1982, 1985, 1986, 1987). The literature on IPD was recently reviewed in Lonie *et al.* (1993).
2 See, for example, Elton and Gruber (1987), Solnik (1991) and Eiteman *et al.* (1992).
3 See, for example, Errunza and Losq (1985), Gill and Tropper (1988), Bailey and Lim (1992), Cheung and Mak (1992), Divecha *et al.* (1992), Speidell and Sappenfield (1992), Wilcox (1992), Cabello (1993), Cheung (1993), Koutmos *et al.* (1993).
4 International Finance Corporation, Emerging Markets Factbook, 1991, pp. 68–70.
5 Gill and Tropper (1988) report that while the US market fell by 23 per cent from October 1987 to March 1988, several ESMs increased in US$ terms over the same period; the Zimbabwean, Korean, Jordanian and Venezuelan markets rose by 32 per cent, 31 per cent, 5 per cent and 4 per cent respectively.

REFERENCES

Adler, M. and B. Dumas (1975) "Optimal International Acquisitions", *Journal of Finance*, 30, pp. 1–20.
Agmon, T. (1972) "The Relations Among Equity Markets in the United States, United Kingdom, Germany and Japan", *Journal of Finance*, 27, pp. 839–56.
Bailey, W. and J. Lim (1992) "Evaluating the Diversification Benefits of the New Country Funds", *Journal of Portfolio Management*, 18, pp. 74–80.
Bruce, B. (1989) "Global Possibilities Abound", *Trusts & Estates*, 128, pp. 30, 32.
Cabello, A. (1993) "Crisis and Performance of the Emerging Latin American Stock Markets", in R. Moncarz and W. Renforth (eds.) *The New World Order and Trade Finance*, Laredo, Texas: Texas A&M International University Press, pp. 571–87.
Cheung, Y.L. (1993) "A Note on the Stability of the Inter-Temporal Relationships Between the Asian-Pacific Equity Markets and the Developed Markets: A Non-Parametric Approach", *Journal of Business Finance and Accounting*, 20, pp. 229–36.
Cheung, Y.L. and Y.K. Ho (1991) "The Inter-Temporal Stability of the Relationships Between the Asian Emerging Equity Markets and the Developed Markets", *Journal of Business Finance and Accounting*, 18, pp. 235–54.

Cheung, Y.L. and S.C. Mak (1992) "The International Transmission of Stock Market Fluctuations Between the Developed and the Asian-Pacific Markets", *Applied Financial Economics*, 2, pp. 43–7.

Divecha, A.B., J. Drach and D. Stefek (1992) "Emerging Markets: A Quantitative Perspective", *Journal of Portfolio Management*, 18, pp. 41–50.

Eiteman, D.K., A.I. Stonehill and M.H. Moffett (1992) *Multinational Business Finance*, 6th Edition, Wokingham: Addison-Wesley.

Elton, E.J. and M.J. Gruber (1987) *Modern Portfolio Theory and Investment Analysis*, 3rd Edition, New York: Wiley.

Errunza, V. and E. Losq (1985) "The Behaviour of Stock Prices on LDC Markets", *Journal of Banking and Finance*, 9, pp. 561–75.

Gill, D. and Tropper, R. (1988) "Emerging Stock Markets in Developing Countries", *Finance & Development*, 15(2), pp. 28–31.

Grauer, R.R. and N.H. Hakansson (1982) "Higher Return, Lower Risk: Historical Returns on Long Run, Actively Managed Portfolios of Stocks, Bonds and Bills: 1936–1978", *Financial Analysts Journal*, 38, pp. 39–53.

Grauer, R.R. and N.H. Hakansson (1985) "1934–1984 Returns on Levered, Actively Managed Long-Run Portfolios of Stocks, Bonds and Bills", *Financial Analysts Journal*, 41, pp. 24–43.

Grauer, R.R. and N.H. Hakansson (1986) "A Half-Century of Returns on Levered and Unlevered Portfolios of Stock, Bonds and Bills, With and Without Small Stocks", *Journal of Business*, 59, pp. 287–318.

Grauer, R.R. and N.H. Hakansson (1987) "Gains from International Diversification: 1968–85 Returns on Portfolios of Stocks and Bonds", *Journal of Finance*, 42, pp. 721–739.

Grubel, H.G. (1968) "Internationally Diversified Portfolios: Welfare Gains and Capital Floss", *American Economic Review*, 58, pp. 1299–314.

Grubel, H.G. and K. Fadner (1971) "The Interdependence of International Equity Markets", *Journal of Finance*, 26, pp. 89–94.

International Finance Corporation (1991) *Emerging Stock Markets Factbook*, Washington, DC: IMF.

Koutmos, G., C. Negakis and N. Theodossiou (1993) "Stochastic Behaviour of the Athens Stock Exchange", *Applied Financial Economics*, 3, pp. 119–26.

Le, S.V. (1991) "International Investment Diversification Before and After the October 19, 1987 Stock Market Crisis", *Journal of Business Research*, 22, pp. 305–10.

Lessard, D.R. (1974) "World National and Industry Failures in Equity Returns", *Journal of Finance*, 29, pp. 379–91.

Levy, H. and M. Sarnat (1970) "International Diversification of Investment Portfolios", *American Economic Review*, 60(1), pp. 668–75.

Lonie, A.A., D.M. Power and C.D. Sinclair (1993) "The Putative Benefits of International Portfolio Diversification: A Review of the Literature", *British Review of Economic Issues*, 15, pp. 1–43.

Maldonado, R. and A. Saunders (1981) "International Portfolio Diversification and the Inter-Temporal Stability of International Stock Market Relationships, 1957–78", *Financial Management*, 10, pp. 54–63.

Makridakis, S.G. and S.C. Wheelwright (1974) "An Analysis of the Interrelationships Among the World's Major Stock Exchanges", *Journal of Business Finance and Accounting*, 1, pp. 195–215.

Panton, D., V. Lesseg and O. Joy (1976) "Comovements of International Equity Markets: A Taxonomic Approach", *Journal of Financial and Quantitative Analysis*, 11, pp. 415–32.

Philippatos, G.C., A. Christofi and P. Christofi (1983) "The Inter-Temporal Stability of International Stock Market Relationships: Another View", *Financial Management*, 12, 63–9.

Roll, R. (1988) "The International Crash of October 1987", in R.W. Kamphuis, R.C. Kormendi and J.W.H. Watson *Black Monday and the Future of Financial Markets*, Chicago: MAI Publication.

Saunders, A. and R.S. Woodward (1977) "Gains from International Portfolio Diversification: UK Evidence 1971–75", *Journal of Business Finance and Accounting*, 4, pp. 299–307.

Solnik, B.H. (1974a) "Why Not Diversify Internationally Rather Than Domestically?", *Financial Analysts Journal*, 30, pp. 48–54.

Solnik, B. (1974b) "An Equilibrium Model of the International Capital Market", *Journal of Economic Theory*, 8, pp. 500–24.

Solnik, B. (1991) *International Investments*, Wokingham: Addison-Wesley.

Speidell, L.S. and R. Sappenfield (1992) "Global Diversification in a Shrinking World", *Journal of Portfolio Management*, 18, pp. 57–67.

Watson, J. (1978) "A Study of Possible Gains from International Investment", *Journal of Business Finance and Accounting*, 5, pp. 195–205.

Watson, J. (1980) "The Stationarity of Intercountry Correlation Co-efficients; A Note", *Journal of Business Finance and Accounting*, 7, pp. 297–303.

Wilcox, J.W. (1992) "Taming Frontier Markets", *Journal of Portfolio Management*, 18, pp. 51–56.

24

RE-EXPLORING FINANCIAL DIVERSIFICATION

The Mexican case

*Fausto Hernández-Trillo**

INTRODUCTION

Investors, when trying to diversify their portfolios, normally look at the correlation coefficient between the returns of two securities, for this is an important component of the variance of a portfolio. When this coefficient is significantly negative, it is said that risk is minimized.

The variance of the portfolio, however, also depends on the volatility of the securities forming the portfolio. In addition, these variances may vary over time; thus, not only do returns need to be diversified but also the volatilities, as some stocks may be related through second moments.

This fact has already been identified by a large number of analysts.[1] However, as Engle and Susmel (1993) point out, most of these works studying volatility are concentrated either on the US market or on national stock markets of developed countries. The purpose of this chapter is to study volatility in the Mexican stock market. In particular, we test for time-varying volatility in stocks of this very concentrated market. Then, we attempt to find portfolios with common volatility. Finally, instead of trying to model the volatility of Mexican financial data, we explore whether it is possible to "diversify" risk through portfolios – if any – formed by stocks in which volatilities move in opposite directions over time.

It is of particular importance for emerging markets to study volatility because this might behave very differently compared to developed markets. The reason for this is that emerging markets are normally more concentrated, reducing the possibilities of diversification within the market. The empirical results confirm that the market is very concentrated.

This chapter is organized as follows. The next section discusses some issues to motivate the empirical part. The third section presents the empirical methodology, while in the fourth section a test for common volatility is performed. The fifth section provides an alternative test for second moments and the results are discussed briefly. Finally, some conclusions are drawn in the closing section.

MOTIVATION

Volatility clustering in stock return series has many theoretical implications, so it is not surprising that researchers have performed numerous empirical applications mainly by making use of the ARCH methodology, developed by Engle (1982), to characterize stock return variances and covariances. For example, Engle and Mustafa (1992) and Engle and Susmel (1993)[2] reported highly significant tests for individual stock returns and international index returns, respectively. However, this line of research has concentrated on the US market and other developed markets.

In effect, there have been a limited number of works studying risk in emerging markets. Among them we find Harvey (1993), where he investigates sources of risk affecting emerging market returns and explains the cross-sectional dispersion in volatility.

However, there is a lack of material dealing with the volatility of the individual stocks of an emerging market. This is the case of Mexican stocks. In the following sections, we test for time-varying volatility of individual stocks in the Mexican market. The following is a brief description of this market.

Evolution of the Mexican financial system

Before 1988, the Mexican financial system was one of the most regulated. There were quantitative restrictions on interest rates, forced lending programs, large barriers to entry, high reserve required ratios, and effective protection against direct foreign competition. As well, trading of fixed-interest instruments on the stock and security exchange was limited because there were no brokerage firms (up to the early 1970s). In 1982, the banking system was nationalized. As a result, non-bank activities started to develop at a high rate, causing a proliferation of brokerage houses. Between 1982 and 1988, assets of non-bank financial institutions rose from 9.1 percent to 32.1 percent of the total financial system assets. However, the surge of government instruments during the 1980s permitted the securities market to grow at a rapid rate.

It was not until the Salinas administration (1988–94), however, that the Mexican financial system began to experience an enormous development. Foreign investors flooded financial markets with huge amounts of capital, this being due to the favorable economic environment that had been created through radical economic reforms. Among these, interest rates were liberalized, target credit was removed, exchange controls were eliminated, universal banking was reinstated, required reserve ratio was eliminated, the Central Bank became autonomous and, most important, the financial sector was opened.[3]

Since then the market has exhibited high expected returns as well as high volatiliy. As of December 1992, the market capitalization was approximately US$135 bn, the number of stocks in the IFC index was 56 and the average correlation of stocks was 0.70. This last figure suggests a high level of concentration.

Although the development of the financial system has been impressive, it is important to point out that this system is highly inefficient. Feliz (1990), Mejiá et al. (1993) and Arellano et al. (1993) provide strong evidence of inefficiency. None of these articles, however, studies volatility. In the following sections we address this issue.

Data analysis

The analysis that follows will be made by using the 14 stocks with the highest level of marketability in the whole market, according to the Mexican stock exchange (Bolsa Mexicana de Valores).[4] We use daily and weekly information (Monday to Monday). The sample period goes from March 1992 to 28 March 1994; the reason is that some of the stocks were only issued recently.

Tables 24.1 and 24.3 present the correlation matrix between the returns of these 14 stocks in a daily and weekly basis, respectively. As these show, all coefficients are positive both daily and weekly; nevertheless, on a daily basis, we see that only 24 out of 105 coefficients are higher than 0.5, while in the second case this is 38 out of 105 coefficients.

In Tables 24.2 and 24.4, the correlation matrix is calculated for the squared returns on a daily and weekly basis, respectively. Surprisingly, we find in both cases that 20 percent of the correlations are negative; furthermore, we also find in many of them high positive correlations (as high as 0.9); in particular, we find that nearly 34 percent of the correlations (35 out of 105 correlation coefficients) are higher than 0.5 on a weekly basis, seven of them reaching coefficients higher than 0.9.

This analysis suggests that the returns on Mexican stocks are also related through their volatilities, implying that these might not be constant over time. In the following section we test for time-varying volatility.

TESTING FOR ARCH EFFECTS

In this section the time-varying volatilities in the returns of the 14 stocks with the highest levels of marketability are tested.

369

Table 24.1 Mexico: correlation matrix for daily returns per share, March 1992 to March 1994

	Apasco	Banacci	Cemex	Cifra	Femsa	Carso	Gfb	Gvideo	Kimberly	Moderna	Serfin	Telmex	Tolmex	Vitro
Apasco	1.000													
Banacci	0.577	1.000												
Cemex	0.630	0.618	1.000											
Cifra	0.651	0.625	0.661	1.000										
Femsa	0.584	0.568	0.605	0.581	1.000									
Carso	0.363	0.367	0.377	0.407	0.431	1.000								
Gfb	0.451	0.557	0.503	0.484	0.488	0.276	1.000							
Gvideo	0.325	0.376	0.355	0.319	0.320	0.191	0.314	1.000						
Kimberly	0.330	0.322	0.345	0.313	0.263	0.228	0.208	0.223	1.000					
Moderna	0.049	0.107	0.103	0.124	0.051	0.055	0.058	0.021	0.057	1.000				
Serfin	0.096	0.111	0.211	0.142	0.200	0.118	0.103	0.092	0.077	0.021	1.000			
Telmex	0.632	0.642	0.660	0.667	0.594	0.451	0.583	0.358	0.343	0.049	0.088	1.000		
Tolmex	0.678	0.640	0.733	0.691	0.624	0.397	0.471	0.416	0.368	0.112	0.213	0.688	1.000	
Vitro	0.234	0.317	0.295	0.297	0.309	0.185	0.316	0.155	0.130	0.002	0.053	0.348	0.329	1.000

Table 24.2 Mexico: correlation matrix for squared daily returns per share, March 1992 to March 1994

	Apasco	Banacci	Cemex	Cifra	Femsa	Carso	Gfb	Gvideo	Kimberly	Moderna	Serfin	Telmex	Tolmex	Vitro
Apasco	1.000													
Banacci	0.329	1.000												
Cemex	0.304	0.312	1.000											
Cifra	0.508	0.399	0.426	1.000										
Femsa	0.427	0.313	0.475	0.440	1.000									
Carso	0.010	0.009	0.002	0.016	0.043	1.000								
Gfb	0.234	0.258	0.270	0.211	0.242	0.031	1.000							
Gvideo	0.038	0.219	0.048	0.029	0.050	-0.021	0.054	1.000						
Kimberly	-0.001	0.009	0.004	0.008	0.017	-0.002	0.079	-0.012	1.000					
Moderna	0.040	-0.018	-0.018	-0.015	0.021	-0.003	0.010	-0.010	-0.003	1.000				
Serfin	0.059	0.075	0.383	0.183	0.396	0.015	0.063	0.056	0.004	-0.002	1.000			
Telmex	0.367	0.437	0.369	0.436	0.298	0.013	0.261	0.085	-0.004	0.021	0.042	1.000		
Tolmex	0.462	0.430	0.596	0.592	0.519	0.007	0.224	0.091	0.001	-0.020	0.471	0.450	1.000	
Vitro	-0.003	-0.001	-0.006	-0.009	0.003	-0.003	0.048	-0.022	-0.003	0.003	0.000	0.023	0.010	1.000

Table 24.3 Mexico: correlation matrix for weekly returns per share, March 1992 to March 1994

	Apasco	Banacci	Cemex	Cifra	Femsa	Carso	Gfb	Gvideo	Kimberly	Moderna	Serfin	Telmex	Tolmex	Vitro
Apasco	1.000													
Banacci	0.642	1.000												
Cemex	0.717	0.757	1.000											
Cifra	0.752	0.735	0.736	1.000										
Femsa	0.665	0.676	0.757	0.650	1.000									
Carso	0.421	0.448	0.474	0.499	0.458	1.000								
Gfb	0.560	0.679	0.571	0.578	0.549	0.447	1.000							
Gvideo	0.419	0.601	0.584	0.501	0.473	0.263	0.465	1.000						
Kimberly	0.389	0.385	0.437	0.275	0.351	0.170	0.221	0.343	1.000					
Moderna	−0.060	0.038	0.150	0.029	0.156	0.099	0.058	0.067	0.053	1.000				
Serfin	0.331	0.556	0.543	0.366	0.468	0.201	0.332	0.362	0.338	0.010	1.000			
Telmex	0.650	0.678	0.676	0.697	0.602	0.520	0.660	0.476	0.336	0.157	0.222	1.000		
Tolmex	0.767	0.783	0.860	0.744	0.766	0.524	0.566	0.584	0.454	0.136	0.553	0.732	1.000	
Vitro	0.297	0.351	0.394	0.413	0.333	0.841	0.324	0.258	0.073	0.089	0.071	0.390	0.392	1.000

Table 24.4 Mexico: correlation matrix for squared weekly returns per share, March 1992 to March 1994

	Apasco	Banacci	Cemex	Cifra	Femsa	Carso	Gfb	Gvideo	Kimberly	Moderna	Serfin	Telmex	Tolmex	Vitro
Apasco	1.000													
Banacci	0.602	1.000												
Cemex	0.640	0.938	1.000											
Cifra	0.703	0.795	0.775	1.000										
Femsa	0.563	0.806	0.819	0.655	1.000									
Carso	0.010	0.037	0.034	0.029	0.037	1.000								
Gfb	0.459	0.647	0.580	0.563	0.517	0.024	1.000							
Gvideo	0.458	0.637	0.647	0.545	0.649	-0.023	0.341	1.000						
Kimberly	0.138	0.182	0.225	0.460	0.173	0.005	0.182	0.097	1.000					
Moderna	0.091	0.020	-0.037	0.029	-0.035	-0.020	0.045	-0.024	-0.022	1.000				
Serfin	0.546	0.919	0.936	0.709	0.792	0.044	0.516	0.643	0.204	-0.014	1.000			
Telmex	0.434	0.421	0.380	0.410	0.298	0.045	0.509	0.213	0.041	-0.064	0.216	1.000		
Tolmex	0.666	0.943	0.958	0.800	0.829	0.062	0.590	0.662	0.192	-0.034	0.946	0.392	1.000	
Vitro	-0.049	-0.014	-0.018	-0.013	-0.015	0.994	-0.018	-0.048	-0.010	-0.019	-0.010	0.023	0.009	1.000

Daily basis

First, we model the returns of each stock on a daily basis. They all adjusted fairly well to an ARCH(1) process[5] as the Box–Pierce test (Q) was satisfactory for all of them. We then applied an ARCH-LM test (à la Engle 1982) to each of these univariate processes. In Table 24.5, the ARCH test is shown. All returns except Carso, Kimberly, Moderna, Serfin and Vitro show evidence of a first-order linear ARCH effect; results are stronger when testing for a fourth-order linear ARCH process (not reported in Table 24.5).

Weekly basis

On a weekly basis, we found that an ARCH(4) process adjusted fairly well to all returns as the Q-Box–Pierce statistic performed satisfactorily for all of them.[6] As in the daily basis test, we applied an ARCH-LM test to each of these univariate processes. Table 24.6 shows the results. Here we observe that all except Carso, Kimberly, Moderna and Serfin show evidence of a fourth-order linear ARCH effect. Basically, these are the same results as those found in the daily basis test.

Table 24.5 Mexico: ARCH test for daily data

Stock	ARCH(1)	Stock	ARCH(1)
Apasco	18.897*	Gvideo	9.95†
Banacci	61.2297*	Kimberly	0.2628
Carso	0.05757	Moderna	0.0062
Cemex	15.3839*	Serfin	0.00642
Cifra	11.8758*	Telmex	13.02*
Femsa	12.1699*	Tolmex	18.47*
Gfb	24.6843*	Vitro	0.00422

* Significant at 5% level
† Marginally significant at 5% level

Table 24.6 Mexico: ARCH test for weekly data

Stock	ARCH(4)	Stock	ARCH(4)
Apasco	10.98051*	Gvideo	9.58357*
Banacci	13.5763*	Kimberly	0.0577
Carso	0.02568	Moderna	0.04182
Cemex	14.1987*	Serfin	0.03233
Cifra	8.4564*	Telmex	9.556*
Femsa	7.72682*	Tolmex	8.62986*
Gfb	9.6390*	Vitro	8.90495*

* Significant at 5% level

These empirical results strongly suggest that the Mexican stocks' returns exhibit time-varying volatility which, together with our previous correlation analysis (especially that with squared returns), implies that these are not independent in second moments. In other words, Mexican stocks' returns are possible related through their volatilities. Therefore, it is necessary to find portfolios that do not display ARCH effects, i.e., to form portfolios that keep their variance constant through time. In the next section, we attempt precisely this.

TESTING FOR COMMON VOLATILITIES

The previous analysis suggested that volatilities of the returns on Mexican stocks are not constant through time. Then, we argued that it was necessary to form portfolios that do not display ARCH effects in order to have their variance stable through time. In this section, we test for common volatilities by using the methodology developed by Engle and Kozicki (1993) and applied to international stock markets by Engle and Susmel (1993).

The test

This test looks for a linear combination (of two series which independently show ARCH effects) that eliminates the ARCH effects. The approach has two steps. First, the series showing ARCH effects need to be found. Then, for those which exhibited them, we proceed to test for common ARCH, trying to find a portfolio of two series that do not display ARCH. We now briefly describe this test as presented in Engle and Susmel (1993).

Suppose we have two series, y_t and x_t, defined as follows:

$$y_t = w_t + e_{yt},$$

$$x_t = \gamma p_t + e_{xt}$$

where

$$e_{yt}|I_{t-1} - D(0, \sigma_y^2), e_{xt}|I_{t-1} - D(0, \sigma_x^2)$$

$$w_t|I_{t-1} - D(0, h_w), h_{wt} = \alpha_{w0} + \alpha_{w1} w_{t-1}^2$$

$$p_t|I_{t-1} - D(0, h_p), h_{pt} = \alpha_{p0} + \alpha_{p1} p_{t-1}^2$$

where σy^2 and σx^2 are constants, h_{wt} and h_{pt} are time-varying and follow a simple ARCH(1) process, I_{t-1} is the information set on which agents condition their decisions at time t, that includes all past information.

Then, variances of y_t and x_t are equal to

$$V(y_t) = h_{wt} + \sigma_y^2,$$

$$V(x_t) = h_{pt} + \sigma_x^2$$

375

respectively, which are clearly time-varying.

The next step is to find any linear combination of y_t and x_t that shows no time-varying volatility. Define $u_t = x_t + \beta y_t$, where the variance of u_t is

$$V(u_t) = \beta^2 h_{wt} + h_{pt} + \beta^2\,\sigma_y^2 + \sigma_x^2$$

If $w_t = p_t$ and $\beta = \gamma$, then $u_t = \gamma y_t + x_t$ which has a constant variance equal to

$$V(u_t) = \gamma^2\sigma_y^2 + \sigma_x^2$$

As indicated, we try to find a portfolio of both series that displays no ARCH; if this exists, it can be expressed as

$$\begin{bmatrix} y_t \\ x_t \end{bmatrix} = \begin{bmatrix} 1 & 0 \\ 0 & \gamma \end{bmatrix} w_t + \begin{bmatrix} e_{yt} \\ e_{xt} \end{bmatrix}$$

where the idiosyncratic noises can be correlated. The test consists of looking for a vector β that minimizes T^*R^2. Engle and Kozicki (1993) show that this T^*R^2 can be obtained from the regression of $y_t - \beta x_t$ on lagged y_t, lagged x_t and the cross product of y_t and x_t. β is obtained by using a grid search.

The application

As Tables 24.5 and 24.6 show, nine out of 14 stocks exhibited ARCH effects. Now, given the results of the squared correlations, there are eight stocks that are suspected of having similar volatility behavior (sharing the same information): Apasco, Banacci, Cemex, Cifra, Tolmex, Femsa, Gfb and Gvideo. Therefore, from these we look for portfolios of each pair of variables that do not display ARCH effects.

In Table 24.7,[7] we present the estimation of the parameter, β, that minimizes the linear combination of both series and its minimum T^*R^2, while in Table 24.8, the results are displayed for all the portfolios that did not exhibit the ARCH effects. Apasco, Banacci, Cemex, Femsa and Tol-

Table 24.7 Mexico: estimation of the parameter, β

Portfolio	Parameter	Minim. test	Portfolio	Parameter	Minim. test
Apa/Ban	−0.212	−5.07	Cem/Cif	−0.3028	−7.04
Apa/Cem	−0.2114	−7.04	Cem/Tol	−0.1013	−3.05
Apa/Cif	−0.0737	−1.76	Cif/Fem	−0.0233	−2.089
Apa/Tol	−0.0779	−3.3862	Cif/Tol	−0.05212	−1.81
Ban/Cem	−1.001	−6.8751	Fem/Gvi	−0.1577	−1.76
Ban/Cif	−0.099	−1.9373	Fem/Tol	−0.4801	−11.46
Ban/Fem	−0.06	−1.561	Gvi/Tol	−0.4783	−7.104
Ban/Tol	−0.1152	−3.208			

Table 24.8 Mexico: ARCH tests for optimal combination

Portfolio	Arch(4)	Portfolio	Arch(4)
Apa/Cem	0.1251	Cem/Tol	4.72
Apa/Cif	0.35465	Cif/Fem	0.03304
Apa/Tol	1.2347	Cif/Tol	0.03233
Ban/Cif	2.0803	Fem/Gvi	0.13543
Ban/Tol	6.516	Fem/Tol	3.37905

mex seem to have similar volatility. As we can observe from the table, ten portfolios exhibit no ARCH effects, i.e., ten portfolios keep variance constant through time, namely, Apasco/Cemex, Apasco/Cifra, Apasco/Tolmex, Banacci/Cifra, Banacci/Tolmex, Cemex/Tolmex, Cifra/Femsa, Cifra/Tolmex, Femsa/Gvideo and Femsa/Tolmex.

The limitation of this test is that we do not have a series large enough to make this more robust. The Mexican market is a relatively new market, in the modern sense, as we pointed out before. Besides, some of the stocks were first issued as recently as 1991.

AN ALTERNATIVE TEST

Motivation of the test

Based on the fact that volatilities of individual series are not constant over time, we argue that it is possible to find portfolios with a stable variance if these are formed with series in which standard deviations move in opposite directions through time.

To see this, we define the variance of a portfolio in the following manner:

$$\sigma_{pt}^2 = \sum_{i=1}^{n} \sum_{j=1}^{m} \theta_i \, \theta_j \, \sigma_{it} \, \sigma_{jt} \, \rho_{ij}$$

where θ is the share of i and j in the portfolio; σ is the standard deviation of series i and j; and ρ_{ij} is the correlation coefficient between i and j. Clearly, σ_{it} and σ_{jt} – and hence σ_{pt}^2 – vary over time. Assuming ρ_{ij} constant, then there may be a combination of series, i and j, in which standard deviations vary in opposite direction through time, thus keeping σ_{pt}^2 more stable over time.

To form a portfolio with securities in which standard deviations of their return vary in opposite directions over time we need, first, to obtain these standard deviations for each point in time. Then, we regress the standard deviations of two securities against each other. If the coefficient obtained from the regression is negatively significant, then they move in opposite directions over time and then it is possible that, through time, the standard deviation of the portfolio could be invariant.

Standard deviations are proxied using Engle's (1982) ARCH methodology. We use the simplest case for the ARCH effect; that is, we obtain the OLS residuals and regress ε_t^2 on ε_{t-1}^2 (with a constant term). These coefficients, jointly with the independent variable, are used to proxy the variance of the series. We do this for the daily basis case since we have already found a first linear ARCH in most of the series. Formally,

$$y_t = \lambda y_{t-1} + \varepsilon_t, \; \varepsilon \sim N(0, h_t)$$

$$h_t = \text{var } \varepsilon_t = \alpha_0 + \alpha_1 \varepsilon_{t-1}^2$$

We use this proxy of the variance to form a portfolio of two series of returns for which variances are negatively correlated; that is, we test $\delta_1 < 0$ in the following equation:

$$\text{var } \varepsilon_{it} = \delta_0 + \delta_1 \text{ var } (\varepsilon_{jt})$$

In the next section, this test is performed for the series of the returns that exhibited an ARCH (1) process for the daily data.

APPLICATION

In Table 24.9, we present the results of the test just outlined. It is important to point out that heteroskedasticity was not detected in these regressions. As can be seen, we reject the null hypothesis of $\delta_1 < 0$ in all possible portfolios. These results contrast with those of common volatility, where we could form ten portfolios with constant volatility. In this alternative test, no portfolio could be formed with stocks in which volatility moved in opposite directions over time.

The results of the alternative test seem more reasonable for the Mexican market. The Mexican market is a very concentrated one, which implies that volatilities follow one of the main stocks. Note that the coefficients of the portfolios formed with Telmex are generally high (as high as 0.8), meaning that Telmex's volatility determines the volatility in the market. This test can also be used to test for concentration.

Surprisingly, in the correlation of squared returns, Telmex does not exhibit high coefficients; this tells us that probably the squared returns are not a good proxy for volatility. It is also important to point out that portfolios formed with Gvideo, though with positive δ_1, are not statistically significant, meaning that this could be a good candidate for portfolios with independent variance.

Note also that the portfolios formed by using the common volatility test are unusual in the sense that, out of ten, seven are formed with cement companies. Furthermore, three of the seven are formed with two cement

Table 24.9 Estimation of the parameter δ_1

Dep. Variable (variance)	Ind. Variable (variance)	Coefficient δ_1	Std. Error
Apasco	Banacci	0.3188	0.03599
Apasco	Cemex	0.165072	0.0256
Apasco	Cifra	0.38541	0.038537
Apasco	Femsa	0.10886	0.013194
Apasco	Gfb	0.22493	0.03691
Apasco	Gvi	0.02085	0.030089
Apasco	Telmex	0.569399	0.058717
Apasco	Tolmex	0.327826	0.029025
Banacci	Cemex	0.33807	0.04629
Banacci	Cifra	0.50051	0.05328
Banacci	Femsa	0.12176	0.01284
Banacci	Gfb	0.209682	0.03641
Banacci	Gvi	0.1407	0.030953
Banacci	Telmex	0.80548	0.062408
Banacci	Tolmex	0.401648	0.042872
Cemex	Cifra	0.26127	0.043422
Cemex	Femsa	0.05599	0.01677
Cemex	Gfb	0.1973	0.0321
Cemex	Gvi	0.03371	0.025924
Cemex	Telmex	0.4723	0.06726
Cemex	Tolmex	0.3699	0.04056
Cifra	Femsa	0.03604	0.0111
Cifra	Gfb	0.1383	0.02595
Cifra	Gvi	0.01722	0.02172
Cifra	Telmex	0.48377	0.05178
Cifra	Tolmex	0.280837	0.02671
Femsa	Gfb	0.24845	0.03841
Femsa	Gvi	0.013022	0.091763
Femsa	Telmex	0.72105	0.18044
Femsa	Tolmex	0.672623	0.0688
Gfb	Gvi	0.06869	0.0399
Gfb	Telmex	0.59309	0.08612
Gfb	Tolmex	0.32623	0.06127
Gvi	Telmex	0.1666	0.0953
Gvi	Tolmex	0.0913	0.0655
Telmex	Tolmex	0.226699	0.02248

companies. These results are a little odd even if different positions are taken. We agree with Quah (1993, p. 390) who argues that "the intellectual success of the common features idea hinges crucially on the researcher's being clear about the implications of the idea in particular applications." In our case common feature analysis was revealed to be not especially informative if we keep in mind that the portfolios found to be optimal did not perform well in the period under study.[8]

One of the main limitations of this alternative test is that we use proxies to perform it. A challenge here for future research is to improve the proxies of variances.

CONCLUSION

This chapter has attempted to study volatility in the Mexican stock market. We have tried to test two alternative ways of finding portfolios with constant volatilities. The first test was based on finding a portfolio that did not display ARCH effects. Here, we found ten portfolios with constant variance. The second alternative test took the volatilities of each stock as variable and tried to find a negative relationship between the volatilities of two stocks so that the variance of the portfolio could be more stable through time. The result here suggests a high concentration of the market because we could not find a portfolio formed with stocks' volatilities behaving in opposite directions.

NOTES

* Professor at Centro de Investigación y Docencia Economicas. Thanks are due to Jose Guedes, Tim Oppler and Alejandro Villagómez. Also to seminar participants at Southern Methodist University, Universidad Nacional Autónoma de México, Centro de Investigación y Docencia Económica and participants of the International Trade & Finance Association Meetings in Reading, England. Errors are my responsibility.
1 For a good review of this, see Bollerslev et al. (1992).
2 An extensive literature review on this can be found in Bollerslev et al. (1992).
3 For a description of the evolution of the Mexican financial system, see Hernández-Trillo (1994). This chapter does not cover the financial crisis of 1995.
4 These are: Apasco, Banacci, Carso, Cemex, Cifra, Femsa, Gfb, Gvideo, Kimberly, Moderna, Serfin, Telmex Tolmex and Vitro.
5 These results are not reported in this work.
6 These results are not reported either.
7 This table only shows the results using daily data. Those using weekly data were quite similar and are not reported.
8 In other comments in the same article, Ericson (1993) points out that cofeatures depend on the choice of lag, while Hansen (1993) and Tsay (1993) generalize the method to multivariate settings with an unknown number of common features. They all stress the necessity of providing a precise definition of the feature specification of interest.

REFERENCES

Arellano, R., G. Castañeda and F. Hernández-Trillo (1993) "El Mercado Accionario Mexicano y sus Implicaciones sobre la Cuenta Corriente," *Economia Mexicana*, II.

Bollerslev, T., R. Chou and K. Kroner (1992) "ARCH Modelling in Finance," *Journal of Econometrics*, 52.

Engle, R.F. (1982) "Autoregressive Conditional Heteroscedasticity with Estimates of the Variance of United Kingdom Inflation," *Econometrica*, 50, No.4.

Engle, R. and Ch. Mustafa (1992) "Implied ARCH Models from Option Prices," *Journal of Econometrics*, 52.

Engle, R. and S. Kozicki (1993) "Testing for Common Features," *Journal of Business & Economic Statistics*, 11 (October).

Engle, R. and R. Susmel (1993) "Common Volatility in International Equity Markets," *Journal of Business & Economic Statistics*, 11 (April).

Ericson, N. (1993) "Comment on Testing for Common Features," *Journal of Business & Economic Statistics*, 11 (October).

Feliz, R.A. (1990) "¿Responde la Bolsa Mexicana a los Fundamentos?," *Estudios Economicos*, el Colegio de Mexico.

Hansen, B. (1993) "Comment on Testing for Common Features," *Journal of Business & Economic Statistics*, 11 (October).

Harvey, C.R. (1993) "Predictable Risk and Returns in Emerging Markets," Mimeo, Duke University, North Carolina.

Hernández-Trillo, F. (1994) "The Evolution of the Financial System in México," Mimeo, Universidad de las Américas-Puebla.

Mejía, J., M. Grados and N. Meunier (1993) "La Eficiencia del Mercado Accionario Mexicano," *El Trimestre Economico*, Mexico.

Quah, D. (1993) "Comment on Testing for Common Features," *Journal of Business & Economic Statistics*, 11 (October).

Tsay R. (1993) "Comment on Testing for Common Features," *Journal of Business & Economic Statistics*, 11 (October).

25

CAPITAL FLIGHT FROM INDIA TO THE UNITED STATES THROUGH ABNORMAL PRICING IN INTERNATIONAL TRADE*

John S. Zdanowicz, William W. Welch and Simon J. Pak

INTRODUCTION

A major problem facing many countries, including India, is capital flight and its resulting economic, political and social impact. Capital flight may also reflect money laundering activities resulting from criminal activities such as drugs and arms smuggling and white collar crimes.

There are many techniques used to expedite capital flight, and a significant amount of research has resulted in detailed explanations of capital flight techniques and in estimates of its magnitude. One technique that can be used to move significant amounts of capital out of a country is the over-invoicing of imports and the under-invoicing of exports.

The focus of our research is on the development of a global price matrix that allows us to analyze every India/United States import and export transaction and determine estimates of the magnitude of capital flight from India to the United States during 1993 due to abnormal pricing.

We compare the prices of India's imports from the United States to the average import prices of similar products imported from the United States by all countries in the world. We also compare India's export prices to the United States to the average export prices of similar products exported to the United States from all countries in the world.

We determine the dollar value of price deviations from average United States/world prices for every India/United States import and export transaction price, for all products. Then we compare the prices of India's imports from the Unites States and exports to the United States to adjusted average United States/world import and export prices to account for different degrees of product heterogeneity that may exist among different countries. This analysis resulted in estimates of capital flight from India to the United States ranging from $4,423 million to $1,622 million during 1993.

We also analyze all of India's import and export transaction prices with the United States and determine the dollar value of price deviations from average India/United States import and export prices. To account for varying degrees of product heterogeneity within India's trade with the United States we also determine the dollar value of price deviations from adjusted average India/United States import and export prices. This analysis resulted in estimates of capital flight from India to the United States ranging from $1,065 million to $370 million during 1993.

We also discuss the use of a global price matrix to detect abnormal transaction prices in India's international trade. The use of statistical price filters can enable India's Customs authorities to establish an efficient audit and inspection process and minimize capital outflows from India to the United States and other countries.

CAPITAL FLIGHT

The analysis of capital flight is a topic that has been discussed at length elsewhere. Walter (1985), Cuddington (1986), and Varman-Schneider (1991) discussed the causes, methods and impact of capital flight on developing countries.

Causes of capital flight

It has been argued that capital flight is a result of economic uncertainty and political instability. Lessard and Williamson (1987) have suggested that international capital flows are caused by deviations in tax rates, inflation, risk of default on government obligations, financial repression, taxes on financial intermediation, political instability and the potential confiscation of wealth. It is also argued that the discriminatory treatment of resident capital, as compared to non-resident capital, contributes to capital flight.

Many other researchers have also focused on factors contributing to capital flight such as fiscal deficits (Dornbusch 1984), devaluation, and the threat of expropriation (Kahn and Ul Haque 1985). It is argued that a major determinant of capital flight is political risk. The analysis of political risk as it relates to the movement of capital is discussed by Dooley and Isard (1980) and Eaton and Turnovsky (1983).

Capital flight methods

The desire to move capital across international borders has resulted in the development of various methods to accomplish this objective such as the following:

383

1 *Smuggling*: This technique requires the purchase of goods, generally precious metals or gems, which are smuggled out of the country and later sold, with the proceeds invested abroad.
2 *Cash movements*: Another form of smuggling is the physical transport of domestic or foreign currency abroad.
3 *Bank transfers*: In countries without exchange controls, bank transfers may be used to facilitate the movement of capital. This technique is not widely used in countries with exchange controls because the transactions are recorded and can be traced.
4 *Abnormal trade pricing*: A common practice used to facilitate capital flight is the falsification of international trade documents. A significant amount of research has focused on the over-invoicing of imports and under-invoicing of exports as a means of shifting capital across borders (see Bhagwati 1964, Bhagwati *et al.*, 1974, De Wulf 1981, and Gulati 1986). Walter (1986) described further the economic impacts of false invoicing of international trade transactions. Abnormal trade pricing may be the least risky technique for shifting capital across borders because government agencies do not have the capability to analyze import and export transactions and determine abnormal pricing.

Impact of capital flight

One approach to analyzing the impact of capital flight is to determine the impact of capital outflows on national utility. Cuddington (1986) discusses the impact of capital flight on social welfare and argues that it causes disutility for many reasons. He argues that capital flight destabilizes domestic financial markets and the efficiency of monetary policy. Capital outflows may lower domestic investment. Capital flight erodes the country's tax base which in turn increases the public sector deficit. The effect of the economic impact of capital flight results in the erosion of the country's political and economic system.

CAPITAL FLIGHT AND INTERNATIONAL TRADE

One of the oldest techniques used to expedite capital flight is the falsification of information on international trade transaction documents. Earlier attempts to determine abnormalities in international trade pricing have compared partner country trade statistics. For more details on this approach see Bhagwati (1964) and Bhagwati *et al.*, (1974). These studies have determined that under-valued exports result in larger capital outflows than do over-valued imports, and the conclusions of our research support this finding. The analysis of aggregate trade between trading partners has been employed as a method to determine capital flight because the methodology to analyze all transactions relating to a country's trade has been too difficult because of data constraints and technological computer limitations. The lack of detailed international trade transaction data and the lack of computing capacity, even when adequate transaction data is available, have made the analysis of international trade pricing a very difficult task. However, international trade pricing is of great interest to both private and public sector organizations as a means of detecting abnormal pricing and measuring capital flight.

International trade pricing

The detection of abnormal pricing in international trade has long been an area of concern to government authorities, international lending agencies, and private sector firms engaged in international trade.

Governments and international lending agencies are interested in the detailed analysis of international trade prices as a means of monitoring and detecting illegal activities and illegal transactions. Abnormal prices in international trade may be due to a lack of knowledge of worldwide prices, but they may also be the consequence of various illegal activities.

Over-invoiced import transactions may be utilized as a means to facilitate capital flight, evade income taxes, and to secretly move money obtained from illegal activities into legitimate investments, i.e., money laundering. Over-invoiced import prices may also serve as a justification for excessively high domestic prices in countries where price controls exist. They may also conceal illegal commissions that are hidden in the inflated prices. Under-invoiced import prices may reflect attempts to avoid or reduce import duties or the dumping of foreign produced goods at below market prices as a means of driving out domestic competition. Under-invoiced export transactions may also be utilized as a means of facilitating capital flight, evading income taxes, and laundering illegally obtained money. Under-invoiced export prices may also be used to avoid or reduce export surcharges in countries where they exist. Over-invoiced export prices might also be used to increase the amount of export subsidies offered by some developing countries. Pak and Zdanowicz (1994a) found significant US tax losses due to over-invoiced imports and under-invoiced exports.

Government authorities and international lending agencies are also interested in detecting abnormal prices as a means of promoting efficiency in their procurement transactions. Economic growth and development are severely hindered when necessary import commodities related to economic development and the welfare of the citizens are purchased at over-invoiced prices. Conversely, the export of domestic goods at below market prices, due to a lack of knowledge of worldwide prices, may result in sub-optimal revenue flows to the country and its industries.

Private sector firms and individuals engaged in international trade are

385

also interested in detecting abnormal import and export prices. The international trade market has been characterized as being highly inefficient due to a lack of detailed global price information. It appears that in many countries prices are determined by "whatever the market will bear." Benchmark prices are unavailable and competitive market pricing is difficult to determine. Domestic importers are concerned that they may be paying too high a price for a commodity, while exporters are concerned that they may be selling for a price below market. In addition, private sector insurers find it difficult to determine the true value of insurable cargo.

The ability to determine the accuracy of international trade pricing should be of great value to market participants in both developed and developing countries. Accurate international trade prices are necessary for the success of economic development programs initiated by international lending agencies. International trade pricing based on well informed market participants is the cornerstone of an efficient and competitive global market structure.

ABNORMAL TRADE PRICING IN
INDIA–UNITED STATES TRADE

The analysis of transactions prices between India and the United States has revealed significant abnormalities in pricing. Over-invoiced imports into India from the United States and under-invoiced exports from India to the United States may be the vehicle by which capital is moved from India to the United States. Our research does not identify the firms engaged in these transactions, but it does reveal significant abnormal transactions prices (see Tables 25.1 and 25.2).

Table 25.1 contains a sample of examples of what appear to be India's under-priced exports to the United States. It lists the average prices of products exported from India to the United States and compares them to the average prices of the same products exported from other countries to the United States during 1993. Similarly, Table 25.2 contains a sample of examples of what appear to be India's over-priced imports from the United States. It lists the average prices of products imported into India from the United States and compares them to the average prices of the same products imported into other countries from the United States. Tables 25.1 and 25.2 contain only a few selected examples of possible abnormal India export and import average prices. The total database, which contains the average import and export price for every product, reveals thousands (and is therefore far too voluminous for this chapter) of similar abnormal average prices.

386

Table 25.1 Underpriced Indian exports to the US, 1993

Product description	World/US average export price	India/US average export price
Exercise cycles	100.39/unit	0.51/unit
Industrial miners diamonds	19.25/car	0.23/car
Diamonds – unworked	617.20/car	5.51/car
Disc harrows	3,821.96/unit	13.89/unit
Insulated electrical conduit	27.51/kg	0.96/kg
Electric cooking stoves, ranges	217.32/unit	5.67/unit
Micrometers and calipers	29.71/unit	1.99/unit
Silk handkerchiefs	61.33/doz	2.66/doz
Granite – roughly trimmed	539.34/cbm	166.30/cbm
Ginseng roots	20.24/kg	1.98/kg
Rubies – cut, not set	31.93/car	2.58/car
Lead acid storage batteries	37.87/unit	0.65/unit
Industrial diamonds – unworked	11.42/car	0.86/car
Radial bearings – >100mm	31.33/unit	16.62/unit
Voltage regulators	121.19/unit	3.39/unit
Facsimile machines	447.54/unit	61.33/unit
Insulated conductors – >1,000V	5.94/kg	0.59/kg
Gloves – seamless	3.01/dpr	0.78/dpr
Sapphires – cut, not set	19.25/car	6.25/car
Coaxial connectors – <1,000V	1.07/unit	0.14/unit
Suspension shock absorbers	17.51/unit	3.87/unit
Glass spectacle lenses – unmounted	10.04/prs	1.28/prs
Bananas – dried	1.36/kg	0.16/kg
Emeralds – cut, not set	69.31/car	13.16/car
Tungsten halogen lamps	4.66/unit	0.57/unit
Tea-kettles – stainless steel	7.45/unit	2.37/unit
Transistors – <30MHz	0.60/unit	0.12/unit

GLOBAL PRICE MATRIX

The objective of our research was to develop a database containing the average prices for all commodities traded between the United States and every country in the world. The development of our global price matrix allows us to estimate capital flight due to abnormal trade pricing. It may also be used as a screening mechanism for countries to monitor and detect abnormal pricing in their international trade transactions.

Database

Our research is based on the data contained in the United States Merchandise Trade Database which is produced by the United States Department of Commerce, Bureau of Census. The 1993 annual database contains transactions data for over 15,000 import harmonized commodity codes and over

387

J.S. ZDANOWICZ, W.W. WELCH AND S.J. PAK

Table 25.2 Overpriced Indian imports from the US, 1993

Product description	US/world average import price	US/India average import price
Tetracyclines	11.74/gm	1,102.50/gm
Videocassette recordings	24.53/unit	1,079.12/unit
Arc welding base metal cored wire	3.16/kg	28.22/kg
Tires – truck/bus, new	154.21/unit	1,604.88/unit
Fans/blowers for motor vehicles	38.45/unit	2,119.13/unit
Plain shaft bearings W/O housing	26.67/unit	148.73/unit
Chlorine	0.98/kg	22.40/kg
Shovel attachments	1,736.21/unit	32,917.10/unit
Thermometers	70.55/unit	281.16/unit
Fixed capacitors – <300V	2.89/unit	46.09/unit
Antihistamines	141.08/kg	1,712.32/kg
Normal – propyl acetate	2.00/kg	9.15/kg
Epoxide resins	4.69/kg	38.31/kg
Dynamite and explosives	5.03/kg	29.31/kg
Starter motors and generators	52.49/unit	394.11/unit
Freezers – <800 liters	425.06/unit	2,869.87/unit
Aluminum oxide	1.09/kg	3.23/kg
Cathode ray display units, mono.	611.15/unit	2,444.94/unit
Radio transmitters – <30MHz	3.084.00/unit	9,105.50/unit
Sheep – live	34.35/unit	133.99/unit
Streptomycins	0.08/gm	0.30/gm
Nickel alloy pipes and tubes	35.11/kg	405.22/kg
Video disks – recorded	180.37/unit	1,072.41/unit
Phthalic anhydride	0.75/kg	3.29/kg
Insulated coaxial cable and conductors	13.02/kg	75.02/kg
Pepper seed for sowing	7.35/kg	33.58/kg
Paints and varnishes	5.04/ltr	11.46/ltr
Carbon black	1.04/kg	3.71/kg

8,000 export harmonized commodity codes, and detail over 18 million import transactions and 13 million export transactions. The harmonized commodity code system assigns specific ten-digit codes to various products imported into and exported from the United States. The classification of commodities by ten-digit harmonized codes was adopted by the United States in 1989. In addition to price and quantity details for all harmonized commodity codes, the database also details the information for approximately 235 countries, each of the 45 United States customs districts, and differentiates between air and sea transportation. The database does not contain the names of the individuals or firms involved in the transactions. Export values are FAS (free alongside ship), and import values are CV (customs value).

388

The price matrix

We combined all records on the 12 monthly United States import databases and 12 monthly United States export databases for the period from 1 January 1993 through 31 December 1993, by harmonized commodity code and by country.

We determined the total United States/world trade for each harmonized commodity code. For each commodity code we determined a frequency distribution of prices for all United States/world transactions during 1993. We have assumed that prices are lognormally distributed to adjust for the skewness of price distributions. We then analyzed total United States/world imports and total United States/world exports and determine the average United States/world import price and average United States/world export price for every commodity.

We recognize that the characteristics of import and export transactions may vary among countries. Therefore we also investigated import and export transactions relative to United States/country trade, for every commodity for all countries. We analyzed total United States/country imports and total United States/country exports and determined the average United States/country import price and average United States/country export price for every commodity traded.

The result of this analysis is a global price matrix. Every country and the world are represented by 236 columns, while every import harmonized code and every export harmonized code are represented by over 23,000 rows. The resulting matrix contains over 5.5 million cells. Each cell contains the average price based on the population of transactions related to the United States import or United States export of a particular commodity from and to a specific country, as well as from and to the world. Some cells are empty if no transactions existed between the United States and a country for a particular commodity.

CAPITAL FLIGHT FROM INDIA

From the global price matrix, we selected the average prices for all commodities traded between the United States and India and the average prices for all commodities traded between the United States and the world. Obviously, United States imports from India are India's exports to the US, and United States exports to India are imports into India from the United States. We analyzed every import and export transaction between India and the United States during 1993.

We first analyzed India's import prices for products purchased from the United States and compared them to the average import prices for identical products purchased from the United States by the world. This allowed us to determine the degree of over-invoicing in India's imports from the United

States based on comparisons to the average import prices from the United States paid by other countries in the world. To allow for the heterogeneity of products being imported by other countries from the United States we analyzed India's import transactions, allowing for various assumptions of country heterogeneity. For every India import transaction we calculated the price deviation when the observed price was greater than the United States/world average import price and greater than the United States/world average import price plus 10, 20, 30, 40 and 50 percent. We estimated the dollar amount over-invoiced for every United States/India import transaction for every commodity and calculated the total dollar amount over-invoiced for each of the above percentage deviation assumptions of country heterogeneity.

We conducted a similar analysis of India/United States export transactions to determine the amount of under-invoicing in India's exports to the United States. For every Indian export transaction we determined the deviation of price when the observed price was less than the world/United States average export price and less than the world/United States average export price less 10, 20, 30, 40 and 50 percent.

We also recognized that there might have been different degrees of heterogeneity of commodities imported into and exported from a particular country in 1993. To account for commodity heterogeneity within a country's trade with the United States we also analyzed transaction prices, assuming different degrees of commodity heterogeneity. We compared transaction prices to historical average United States/India average prices and allowed for deviations of plus 10, 20, 30, 40 and 50 percent for India imports from the United States and − 10, 20, 30, 40 and 50 percent for India exports to the United States.

The results of our analyses are contained in Table 25.3. When comparing India import prices from the United States to average and adjusted world import prices from the United States, the value of over-invoiced India imports ranged from $1,042 million to $788 million. When comparing India export prices to the United States to average and adjusted world export prices to the United States, the value of under-invoiced India export prices ranged from $3,381 million to $834 million.

The results of comparing United States/India import prices to average United States/India import prices and India/United States export prices to average India/United States export prices, assuming different degrees of commodity heterogeneity are contained in the lower part of Table 25.3. When comparing India's import prices from the United States to India's average and adjusted import prices from the United States, the value of over-invoiced Indian imports ranged from $420 million to $251 million. When comparing India's export prices to the United States to India average and adjusted export prices to the United States, the value of under-invoiced Indian export prices range from $645 million to $119 million.

Table 25.3 Income shifted from India to the US through 1993 trades
(US$ millions)

Based on price deviation from	Over-invoiced imports from US	Under-invoiced exports to US	Total trades with US
US/world average:	$1,042	$3,381	$4,423
(+) or (−) 10%	$982	$2,683	$3,665
(+) or (−) 20%	$929	$2,067	$2,996
(+) or (−) 30%	$879	$1,584	$2,464
(+) or (−) 40%	$833	$1,174	$2,006
(+) or (−) 50%	$788	$834	$1,622
US/India average:	$420	$645	$1,065
(+) or (−) 10%	$363	$427	$790
(+) or (−) 20%	$321	$309	$630
(+) or (−) 30%	$288	$230	$518
(+) or (−) 40%	$265	$168	$434
(+) or (−) 50%	$251	$119	$370

The estimates of total capital outflows due to over-invoiced imports and under-invoiced exports are also shown in Table 25.3. Comparing India's import and export prices from and to the United States to the average and adjusted average United States/world import and export prices resulted in estimates of capital outflows ranging from $4,423 million to $1,622 million. Comparing India's import and export prices to and from the United States to average and adjusted average United States/India import and export prices gave us an estimated range of capital outflows from $1,065 million to $370 million.

Table 25.4 shows the dollar value of total imports into India from the United States, the total dollar value of exports from India to the United States, and total trade between India and the United States during 1993.

DETECTING ABNORMAL PRICING: AUDITS AND PHYSICAL INSPECTIONS

Abnormal price transactions in India's international trade may be found by auditing trade documents and by the physical inspection of cargo. Trade documents relating to products imported into and exported from India could be examined to determine if the prices being paid or charged reflect

Table 25.4 India's trades with the US, 1993 (US$ millions)

Directions	Amount
Imports from the US	$2,761
Exports to the US	$4,551
Total trade with the US	$7,312

the market value of the products. With the appropriate computer hardware and software, India's Customs authorities could conduct audits of all of India's import and export transactions, and inspect all abnormally priced products.

In the past it has been difficult for a country's customs service to conduct audits and inspections because of a lack of accurate and detailed price data. Access to a price database that details normal price ranges for all commodities would allow India's customs agency to conduct the necessary audits and inspections. The objective of transaction audits and physical inspection is to determine if reported prices reflect true market prices.

Audits and physical inspections: a cost–benefit approach

The adoption of transaction audits and physical inspections as a means of detecting abnormal prices in international trade is necessary to monitor and minimize capital flight. The issue facing India's government authorities is "what and how much to inspect." This determination of the optimal level of audits and inspections is an economic question that should be evaluated from a benefit vs cost perspective.

The benefits of detecting abnormal international trade prices are many. The minimization of capital flight will provide the additional capital necessary for investment in a country's private and public sector. The minimization of income tax evasion and import duty fraud will add additional revenues to the treasuries of the countries that deter these illegal transactions. The curtailment of the laundering of money attained through illegal activities will generate social benefits, enhance the quality of life of the citizens of the country and may also lead to the seizure of the assets of the criminals engaging in these activities. The detection of illegal dumping by foreign producers will provide protection and foster the development of domestic industry by eliminating unfair competition.

As in all economic activities, the detection of abnormal international trade prices will also require expenditures directly related to the detection process. Countries that choose to engage their own customs agencies to conduct audits and inspections will incur costs related to additional physical space, employees, and other operating expenses. Physical inspections will also generate non-quantifiable costs such as delays in the movement of goods.

Determination of the optimal level of audits and inspections

The determination of the optimal level of audits and physical inspections to detect abnormal pricing is similar to the determination of the optimal level of inspection in a quality control production process. Based on statistical analysis, India can determine the optimal level of audit and inspection by comparing the expected marginal benefit with expected marginal cost at various levels of audit and inspection.

The extreme levels of audit and inspection are 0 percent and 100 percent. With no audits and inspections, no costs will be incurred but no abnormal prices will be detected and no economic gains will be accrued. At the other extreme, the audit of every transaction and the inspection of every commodity will lead to significant benefits, but this level of audit and inspection will also require significant costs. The ratio of net benefits to costs for both of these extreme cases is probably sub-optimal.

Another technique often used in quality control inspections is to conduct random inspections on a subset of the population. This approach implicitly assumes that every item being inspected has an equal probability of being defective. If the random audit and inspection of imports or exports was adopted, the process would also be based on the assumption that all trade transactions have equal probabilities of being abnormal. Random audits and inspections may result in economic losses or gains, depending on the costs of conducting the audits and inspections and the benefits of detecting abnormally priced transactions. However, random audits and inspections are also sub-optimal when compared to statistically based audits and inspections.

Statistical techniques may be employed to determine the optimal level of audits and inspections. These techniques require the analysis of historical price data for every commodity traded and the determination of a price that represents a measure of central tendency and upper-bound and lower-bound prices that represent benchmark prices that indicate abnormality. The objective of using a statistically based audit-inspection program is to select India's international trade transactions that, if audited or inspected, have a high probability of being abnormal, and indicate possible capital flight or mispricing for other purposes. The audit and physical inspection of an international trade transaction would be conducted when the expected marginal benefit of the audit–inspection exceeded the expected marginal cost.

Upper-bound and lower-bound trigger prices could be adjusted over time to reflect historical marginal benefits and costs. Upper- and lower-bound prices could also be adjusted on an *ad hoc* basis by India's government officials based on other factors relating to the pricing of a commodity.

AUDIT AND INSPECTION MODEL

An extension of our research is the development of a computer software technique that allows for statistical analysis of India's international trade transactions for every product as defined by a ten-digit harmonized commodity code. The development of a global price matrix could be utilized by India's government agencies to detect abnormal import and export prices.

We have previously reported our development of such a price matrix for all commodities reported to the US Customs Service (Pak and Zdanowicz 1994b). A global price matrix for India's international trade could be used to monitor and detect historical abnormal transactions prices and to detect abnormal prices in real time as products enter or leave through India's ports.

Two-parameter statistical analysis

This analysis assumes a two-parameter log normal distribution of prices. It proceeds with the following four steps:

1 Determine the average United States/world import price and the average US/world export price for every product.
2 For every product determine the upper- and lower-bound trigger price for United States/world imports and United States/world exports based on mean and standard deviation.
3 For every product, determine the average United States/India import price and the average United States/India export price.
4 For every product determine the upper- and lower-bound trigger price for United States/India imports and United States/India exports based on mean and standard deviation.

Examples

Assume that India is concerned about over-invoiced imports which may result in capital flight. If a shipment of "display units with cathode ray tube (CRT) other than color" (HS Code 8471924075) was being imported into India at a price greater than the predetermined upper-bound trigger price it would signal the need for an audit and possible physical inspection. The following might be the upper- and lower-bound trigger prices for "display units with cathode ray tube (CRT) other than color," based on United States/world and United States/India price filters as of January 1994.

Upper- and lower-bound prices: display units with cathode ray tube

World upper-bound price	$1,281.03/unit
World average price	$611.15/unit
World lower-bound price	$291.57/unit
India upper-bound price	$3,540.42/unit
India average price	$2,444.94/unit
India lower-bound price	$1,688.42/unit

In a similar manner, India's government authorities could detect under-invoiced exports which may also result in capital flight. If a shipment of "suspension shock absorbers for vehicles" (HS Code 8708805000) was being exported from India at a price less than the lower-bound trigger price it would signal the need for an audit and possible physical inspection. The following are the upper- and lower-bound trigger prices for "suspension shock absorbers for vehicles," based on United States/world and United States/India price filters as of January 1994.

Upper and lower-bound prices: suspension shock absorbers

World upper-bound price	$44.87/unit
World average price	$17.51/unit
World lower-bound price	$6.84/unit
India upper-bound price	$5.52/unit
India average price	$3.87/unit
India lower-bound price	$2.72/unit

A sample of detailed examples of other upper- and lower-bound prices contained in the price matrix are contained in Tables 25.5 and 25.6. The total India price matrix contains 521 pages of price data on India exports and 235 pages of price data on India imports.

Table 25.5 Average prices, upper and lower limits for Indian imports from the US, 1993

Commodity code	Description	Unit	Lower limit	US world trade Average price	Upper limit
8469100000	Automatic typewriters and word processing machines	No	$314.1515	$398.3279	$505.0592
8469210000	Electric typewriters, Nesoi, weighing not more than 12 kg, excluding case	No	$111.4734	$217.9036	$425.9492
8469290000	Electric typewriters, Nesoi	No	$124.7798	$193.1815	$299.0797
8469310000	Nonelectric typewriters, weighing not more than 12 kg, excluding case	No	$137.6904	$243.7264	$431.4212
8469390000	Nonelectric typewriters, Nesoi	No	$195.6951	$371.0434	$703.5088
8470100000	Electric calculators capable of operation without an external source of power	No	$44.0598	$103.1265	$241.3784
8470210000	Electronic calculating machines, Nesoi, incorporating a printing device	No	$85.3523	$153.2597	$275.1952
8470290000	Electronic calculating machines, Nesoi, not incorporating a printing device	No	$53.1591	$139.5084	$366.1198
8470300000	Calculating machines except electronic	No	$52.2710	$136.4807	$356.3541
8470400000	Accounting machines	No	$626.3340	$1,557.5289	$3,873.1668
8470500020	Point-of-sale terminal type cash registers	No	$815.7459	$1,434.4912	$2,522.5563
8470500060	Cash registers, except point-of-sale terminals	No	$478.8437	$749.8345	$1,174.1864
8470900010	Postage-franking machines, incorporating a calculating device	No	$891.5734	$1,350.0740	$2,044.3632
8470900090	Ticket-issuing and similar machines, Nesoi, incorporating a calculating device	No	$379.2969	$779.1604	$1,600.5692
8471100000	Analog or hybrid automatic data processing machines	No	$2,506.9212	$5,363.1862	$11,473.7414
8471200030	Digital ADP mach containing in same housing at least a CPU and an input and output unit whether or not combined, with color cathode ray tube (CRT)	No	$2,326.0685	$4,500.3443	$8,707.0085

Code	Description				
8471200060	Digital ADP mach containing in same housing at least a CPU and an input and output unit, whether or not combined, w/cathode ray tube other than color	No	$1,869.2856	$4,408.5104	$10,397.0007
8471200090	Digital ADP mach containing in same housing at least a CPU and an input and output unit whether or not combined, without CRT	No	$1,558.2551	$3,486.0865	$7,798.9792
8471910030	Digital processing unit which may contain in same housing 1 or 2 of the following units: storage, input or output, with color cathode ray tube (CRT)	No	$1,970.0864	$5,741.8598	$16,734.7762
8471910060	Digital processing unit which may contain in same housing 1 or 2 of the following units: storage, input or output, w/cathode ray tube other than color	No	$2,390.1804	$5,575.2496	$13,004.6285
8471910090	Digital processing unit which may contain in same housing 1 or 2 of the following units: storage, input or output, without CRT	No	$801.2733	$2,608.2837	$8,490.4166
8471921030	Combined input/output units, with color cathode ray tube (CRT)	No	$317.6754	$709.4429	$1,584.3505
8471921060	Combined input/output units, with cathode ray tube other than color	No	$496.2936	$1,186.6374	$2,837.2483
8471921090	Combined input/output units, without a cathode ray tube (CRT)	No	$446.7410	$1,076.9708	$2,596.2832
8471922000	Keyboard units	No	$60.9316	$158.5146	$412.3782
8471924025	Display units with color cathode ray tube (CRT)	No	$336.2586	$738.8437	$1,623.4233
8471924075	Display units with cathode ray tube (CRT) other than color	No	$291.5659	$611.1509	$1,281.0327
8471925000	Display units without a cathode ray tube (CRT)	No	$490.0890	$1,103.8993	$2,486.4742
8471927500	Printer units	No	$401.5694	$1,186.8598	$3,507.8278
8471929020	Card key and magnetic media entry devices	No	$581.9249	$1,300.4291	$2,906.0722
8471929040	Optical scanners and magnetic ink recognition devices	No	$474.4097	$996.6331	$2,093.7127
8471929520	Output devices, Nesoi	No	$1,738.0815	$3,517.9783	$7,120.5931

Table 25.5 Continued

Commodity code	Description	Unit	US India trade Lower limit	Average price	Upper limit
8469100000	Automatic typewriters and word processing machines	No			
8469210000	Electric typewriters, Nesoi, weighing not more than 12 kg, excluding case	No			
8469290000	Electric typewriters, Nesoi	No	$539.4837	$547.8249	$556.2949
8469310000	Nonelectric typewriters, weighing not more than 12 kg, excluding case	No			
8469390000	Nonelectric typewriters, Nesoi	No			
8470100000	Electric calculators capable of operation without an external source of power	No	$75.4914	$75.5622	$75.6331
8470210000	Electronic calculating machines, Nesoi, incorporating a printing device	No			
8470290000	Electronic calculating machines, Nesoi, not incorporating a printing device	No			
8470300000	Calculating machines except electronic	No			
8470400000	Accounting machines	No			
8470500020	Point-of-sale terminal type cash registers	No	$769.0114	$974.2834	$1,234.3485
8470500060	Cash registers, except point-of-sale terminals	No			
8470900010	Postage-franking machines, incorporating a calculating device	No			
8470900090	Ticket-issuing and similar machines, Nesoi, incorporating a calculating device	No			
8471100000	Analog or hybrid automatic data processing machines	No	$2,527.6546	$4,638.2132	$8,511.0607
8471200030	Digital ADP mach containing in same housing at least a CPU and an input and output unit whether or not combined, with color cathode ray tube (CRT)	No	$2,174.5550	$4,205.2139	$8,132.1576

Code	Description				
8471200060	Digital ADP mach containing in same housing at least a CPU and an input and output unit, whether or not combined, w/cathode ray tube other than color	No	$2,491.7366	$4,038.5241	$6,545.5062
8471200090	Digital ADP mach containing in same housing at least a CPU and an input and output unit whether or not combined, without CRT	No	$2,374.3571	$4,315.7938	$7,844.6817
8471910030	Digital processing unit which may contain in same housing 1 or 2 of the following units: storage, input or output, with color cathode ray tube (CRT)	No	$4,682.2642	$9,682.6514	$20,023.1628
8471910060	Digital processing unit which may contain in same housing 1 or 2 of the following units: storage, input or output, w/cathode ray tube other than color	No	$5,710.2511	$11,155.1368	$21,791.8747
8471910090	Digital processing unit which may contain in same housing 1 or 2 of the following units: storage, input or output, without CRT	No	$2,180.6660	$4,279.7368	$8,399.3362
8471921030	Combined input/output units, with color cathode ray tube (CRT)	No	$1,897.6289	$2,822.4788	$4,198.0741
8471921060	Combined input/output units, with cathode ray tube other than color	No	$2,586.9048	$6,679.3248	$17,245.8530
8471921090	Combined input/output units, without a cathode ray tube (CRT)	No	$825.5127	$2,577.0812	$8,045.1188
8471922000	Keyboard units	No	$183.9723	$316.6783	$545.1098
8471924025	Display units with color cathode ray tube (CRT)	No	$270.7843	$688.6362	$1,751.2824
8471924075	Display units with cathode ray tube (CRT) other than color	No	$1,688.4227	$2,444.9379	$3,540.4175
8471925000	Display units without a cathode ray tube (CRT)	No	$1,328.7414	$2,086.2299	$3,275.5472
8471927500	Printer units	No	$1,059.8708	$1,849.6978	$3,228.1122
8471929020	Card key and magnetic media entry devices	No	$364.6136	$957.6607	$2,515.3042
8471929040	Optical scanners and magnetic ink recognition devices	No	$1,661.9675	$3,337.0358	$6,700.3765
8471929520	Output devices, Nesoi	No	$1,944.4062	$3,448.7890	$6,117.1092

Table 25.6 Average prices, upper and lower limits for Indian exports to the US, 1993

Commodity code	Description	Unit	Lower limit	US world trade Average price	Upper limit
8708401000	Gear boxes for road tractors, public transport type vehicles, and vehicles for the transport of goods	No	$255.1857	$664.9797	$1,732.8478
8708402000	Gear boxes for passenger motor vehicles	No	$190.3354	$718.3409	$2,711.0758
8708403000	Gear boxes for tractors suitable for agricultural use	No	$110.1211	$403.9242	$1,481.5940
8708405000	Gear boxes for vehicles, Nesoi	No	$170.3962	$553.4032	$1,797.3116
8708501000	Drive axles with differential for tractors suitable for agricultural use	No	$356.1969	$848.4770	$2,021.1103
8708503000	Drive axles with differential for tractors, Nesoi (except road tractors)	No	$2,123.2131	$4,622.6669	$10,064.4862
8708505000	Drive axles with differential for passenger motor vehicles	No	$65.7112	$271.0422	$1,117.9813
8708508000	Drive axles with differential for vehicles, Nesoi	No	$92.4857	$314.3232	$1,068.2639
8708608010	Spindles for non-driving axles for vehicles, Nesoi	No	$2.3128	$25.3072	$276.9166
8708708015	Wheels for vehicles of subheading 8702, 8704 or 8705	No	$17.4426	$46.9485	$126.3667
8708708025	Wheels, of aluminum, for vehicles, Nesoi	No	$20.4895	$40.6111	$80.4929
8708708030	Wheels for vehicles, Nesoi	No	$15.5441	$37.1112	$88.6018
8708708035	Wheels for vehicles, Nesoi	No	$14.3737	$33.5360	$78.2446
8708805000	Suspension shock absorbers for vehicles, Nesoi	No	$6.8352	$17.5123	$44.8682
8708915000	Radiators for vehicles, other than tractors for agricultural use	No	$42.5039	$87.7872	$181.3146
8708992010	Tracklinks for track-laying tractors of headings 8701 to 8705	No	$56.5947	$144.4400	$368.6376
8708993000	Cast iron parts of motor vehicles, Nesoi, of headings 8701 to 8705	Kg	$1.6307	$3.5085	$7.5486
8708995010	Steering shaft assemblies incorporating universal joints for motor vehicles of heading 8701 to 8705	No	$19.7728	$35.5668	$63.9766

Code	Description	Unit			
8708995020	Double flanged wheel hub units, incorporating ball bearings, Nesoi, for motor vehicles of headings 8701 to 8705	No	$16.6062	$27.7385	$46.3337
8708995025	Double flanged wheel hub units, Nesoi, for motor vehicles or heading 8701 to 8705	No	$21.6112	$41.7494	$80.6534
8708995030	Beam hanger brackets, Nesoi, of motor vehicles, Nesoi, other than those designed for the transport of persons or goods	No	$2.2975	$14.3200	$89.2552
8708995045	Slide in campers	No	$3,884.5977	$7,270.3048	$13,606.8997
8708995060	Radiator cores of motor vehicles, Nesoi	No	$27.9145	$50.8145	$92.5007
8708995070	Cable traction devices of motor vehicles, for motor vehicles of heading 8701 to 8705	Kg	$1.8593	$2.3103	$2.8706
8709110030	Works trucks for use in warehouses, factories, etc., electrical, operator riding, not fitted with lifting or handling equipment	No	$13,133.9928	$16,789.5870	$21,462.6454
8709110060	Works trucks for use in warehouses, factories, etc., electrical, except operator riding, not fitted with lifting or handling equipment	No	$944.2675	$2,782.9214	$8,201.7560
8709190030	Works trucks for use in warehouses, factories, etc., other than electrical, operator riding, not fitted with lifting or handling equipment	No	$6,566.0155	$11,335.7080	$19,570.2060
8709190060	Works trucks for use in warehouses, factories, etc., other than electrical, other than operator riding, not fitted with lifting or handling equipment	No	$804.1960	$1,868.0879	$4,339.4305
8710000030	Tracked (including half-tracked) vehicles	No	$21,029.8026	$35,136.2697	$58,705.1371
8710000060	Armored fighting vehicles, motorized whether or not fitted with weapons Nesoi	No	$4,058.7942	$5,727.2705	$8,081.6188
8711100000	Motorcycles (including mopeds) and cycles fitted with an auxiliary motor with reciprocating internal combustion piston engine, cyl not exceeding 50 cc	No	$483.2636	$666.4120	$918.9704

Table 25.6 Continued

Commodity code	Description	Unit	Lower limit	US India trade Average price	Upper limit
8708401000	Gear boxes for road tractors, public transport type vehicles, and vehicles for the transport of goods	No			
8708402000	Gear boxes for passenger motor vehicles	No	$84.9232	$153.3289	$276.8354
8708403000	Gear boxes for tractors suitable for agricultural use	No			
8708405000	Gear boxes for vehicles, Nesoi	No			
8708501000	Drive axles with differential for tractors suitable for agricultural use	No			
8708503000	Drive axles with differential for tractors, Nesoi (except road tractors)	No			
8708505000	Drive axles with differential for passenger motor vehicles	No			
8708508000	Drive axles with differential for vehicles, Nesoi	No	$75.7215	$113.0443	$168.7632
8708608010	Spindles for non-driving axles for vehicles, Nesoi	No			
8708708015	Wheels for vehicles of subheading 8702, 8704 or 8705	No	$73.1336	$93.3119	$119.0576
8708708025	Wheels, of aluminum, for vehicles, Nesoi	No			
8708708030	Wheels for vehicles, Nesoi	No			
8708708035	Wheels for vehicles, Nesoi	No			
8708805000	Suspension shock absorbers for vehicles, Nesoi	No	$2.7175	$3.8724	$5.5180
8708915000	Radiators for vehicles, other than tractors for agricultural use	No	$59.5973	$67.4997	$76.4500
8708992010	Tracklinks for track-laying tractors of headings 8701 to 8705	No		$32.9679	
8708993000	Cast iron parts of motor vehicles, Nesoi, of headings 8701 to 8705	Kg	$3.1894	$3.6930	$4.2760
8708995010	Steering shaft assemblies incorporating universal joints for motor vehicles of heading 8701 to 8705	No	$32.8727	$32.8914	$32.9101

Code	Description	Unit	Value
8708995020	Double flanged wheel hub units, incorporating ball bearings, Nesoi, for motor vehicles of headings 8701 to 8705	No	
8708995025	Double flanged wheel hub units, Nesoi, for motor vehicles or heading 8701 to 8705	No	
8708995030	Beam hanger brackets, Nesoi, of motor vehicles, Nesoi, other than those designed for the transport of persons or goods	No	
8708995045	Slide in campers	No	
8708995060	Radiator cores of motor vehicles, Nesoi	No	
8708995070	Cable traction devices of motor vehicles, for motor vehicles of heading 8701 to 8705	Kg	$269.3318
8709110030	Works trucks for use in warehouses, factories, etc., electrical, operator riding, not fitted with lifting or handling equipment	No	
8709110060	Works trucks for use in warehouses, factories, etc., electrical, except operator riding, not fitted with lifting or handling equipment	No	
8709190030	Works trucks for use in warehouses, factories, etc., other than electrical, operator riding, not fitted with lifting or handling equipment	No	
8709190060	Works trucks for use in warehouses, factories, etc., other than electrical, other than operator riding, not fitted with lifting or handling equipment	No	$346.9564
8710000030	Tracked (including half-tracked) vehicles	No	
8710000060	Armored fighting vehicles, motorized whether or not fitted with weapons Nesoi	No	
8711100000	Motorcycles (including mopeds) and cycles fitted with an auxiliary motor with reciprocating internal combustion piston engine, cyl not exceeding 50 cc	No	$446.9533

J.S. ZDANOWICZ, W.W. WELCH AND S.J. PAK

CONCLUSION: APPLICATION OF THE
GLOBAL PRICE MATRIX

The development of the global price matrix and the analysis of India's trade with the United States has resulted in estimates of significant capital outflows through over-invoiced imports and under-invoiced exports. Our estimates of India's capital flight to the United States during 1993 range from a maximum of $4,423 million to our most conservative estimate of $370 million. Our analysis only considers trade pricing abnormalities in India/United States trade; the analysis of trade pricing between India and other countries may also reveal similar levels of capital outflows. Based on our estimates of capital flight from India to the United States, the economic benefits of detecting and deterring the abnormal transaction prices, related to these capital outflows, appear to be substantial. The application of the global price matrix as a means of determining optimal audits and inspections can facilitate the detection process based on economic benefit–cost criteria.

The actual analysis of international trade prices could be facilitated through workstations located at each of India's ports or on a mainframe computer that is networked to its ports. Data could also be produced in printed format so that smaller and outlying ports that do not currently have a computerized trade data entry system could immediately begin to implement the system manually.

We conclude that having access to this data will allow India the opportunity to adopt a transaction-based audit and inspection program. India will be able to control and determine both the level of physical inspection and the means of inspection that will result in the most cost-effective monitoring of its international trade flows and the detection of capital flight.

NOTE

* This chapter was orginally published in *Finance India*, Vol. IX, No. 3, September 1995, and is reproduced here with permission from the Indian Institute of Finance.

REFERENCES

Bhagwati, J.N. (1964) "On the Underinvoicing of Imports," *Bulletin of the Oxford University, Institute of Economics and Statistics*, Vol. 26, pp. 389–97.
Bhagwati, J.N., A.O. Krueger and C. Wibulswasdi (1974) "Capital Flight from LCDs: A Statistical Analysis," in J.N. Bhagwati (ed.) *Illegal Transactions in International Trade*, Amsterdam: North-Holland Publishing, pp. 148–54.
Cuddington, J.T. (1986) *Capital Flight: Estimates, Issues and Explanations*, Princeton, N. J.: Princeton University Press.

De Wulf, L. (1981) "Statistical Analysis of Under- and Overinvoicing of Imports," *Journal of Development Economics*, Vol. 8, pp. 303–23.

Dooley, M. and P. Isard (1980) "Capital Controls, Political Risk, and Deviations from Interest Rate Parity," *Journal of Political Economy*, Vol. 88, No. 2, pp. 370–84.

Dornbusch, R. (1984) "External Debt, Budget Deficits, and Disequilibrium Exchange Rates," NBER Working Paper 1336, Cambridge, Mass.: National Bureau of Economic Research, April.

Eaton, J. and S. Turnovsky (1983) "Exchange Risk, Political Risk, and Macroeconomic Equilibrium," *American Economic Review*, March, pp. 183–9.

Gulati, S.K. (1986) "A Note on Trade Misinvoicing," Paper presented at conference on Capital Flight and Third World Debt, Institute for International Economics, Washington, DC, October 2–4.

Khan, M. and N. Ul Haque (1985) "Foreign Borrowing and Capital Flight: A Formal Analysis," *Staff Papers*, International Monetary Fund, Vol. 32, No. 4 (December), pp. 606–28.

Lessard, D.R. and Williamson, J. (1987) *Capital Flight and Third World Debt*, Washington, DC: Institute of International Economics.

Pak, S.J. and Zdanowicz, J.S. (1994a) *An Estimate of Lost U.S. Federal Income Tax Revenues Due To Over-Invoiced Imports And Under-Invoiced Exports*, Trade Research Institute Working Paper 9404–01, Miami Fla.: Trade Research Institute, April.

Pak, S.J. and Zdanowicz, J.S. (1994b) "A Statistical Analysis of the U.S. Merchandise Trade Data Base and its Uses in Transfer Pricing Compliance and Enforcement," *Tax Management Transfer Pricing Report*, Vol. 3, No. 1, pp. 50–7, May.

Varman-Schneider, B. (1991) *Capital Flight from Developing Countries*, Oxford: Westview Press.

Walter, I. (1985) *Secret Money: The World of International Financial Secrecy*, Lexington, Mass.: Lexington Books.

Walter, I. (1986) "The Mechanics of Capital Flight," Paper presented at the Conference on Capital Flight and Third World Debt, Institute for International Economics, October 2–4.

26

A FRONTIER FUNCTION ANALYSIS OF CAPITAL FLIGHT FROM SELECTED LATIN AMERICAN COUNTRIES

*Benu Varman-Schneider**

Since the international debt crisis of the 1980s, empirical work on capital flight has grown. In this chapter, two additional explanations are empirically tested to add to the ongoing debate. The first is the role of the United States economy in motivating capital flight from Latin America. The results of this chapter indicate that the United States economy exercises a significant influence on capital outflows. The second addition to the contribution of other studies is that capital flight is related to the efficiency of the domestic economy. Efficiency here is defined as that resulting from the influence of political and social stability as well as the influence of debt negotiations. Frontier functions are used here as a data-analytical technique to capture the influence of political and social variables through the efficiency term. The results are presented for a panel data set of three countries. These are: Chile, Colombia and Venezuela.

INTRODUCTION

In the past decade large-scale capital flight from Latin America and many other developing countries was often considered to be one of the principal factors in precipitating the international debt crisis of the early 1980s. This led to a considerable slow-down in the inflow of foreign capital in many of these countries. The decline in external resources slowed down development and forced the adoption of many adjustment measures. The issue of capital flight gained prominence, especially as an indicator of credibility in obtaining new loans from abroad.

The growing literature on capital flight focused its attention on domestic economic and political factors in explaining capital flight.[1] Although many of these studies focus on interest and inflation rates, the degree of currency overvaluation, growth performance, and regime changes, no attempt has been made to examine the effect of the United States economic performance on Latin America.[2] It is hypothesized that economic and political instability explain capital flight, as also external factors. This study

406

attempts to model both the external set of factors as represented by the performance of the United States and the country-specific factors in explaining capital flight from three Latin American countries, Chile, Colombia and Venezuela.[3] The hypothesis is that if the performance of the United States economy can affect capital inflows, then, for the same set of reasons, a reverse performance can possibly motivate capital flows in the other direction.

The methodology used in this chapter focuses attention on finding the best possible explanation of capital flight. Frontier function analysis is applied to the data set. The analysis is not based on a specific theory of optimizing economic behavior. Rather, it is a new data-analytical application of frontier functions. The influence of economic instability is captured by economic variables, and the capital flight estimates on the frontier are interpreted as economically possible capital flight. This is the maximum outflow of capital. Since the period of analysis is short, the analysis is restricted to an analysis of flows. The objective is to capture the influence of political instability and other qualitative variables such as debt negotiations, during the period under investigation. This is done by a simple function of the deviations from the frontier as a measure of this quantity grouped together as the technical efficiency term.

The chapter is organized as follows. Next we present the capital flight estimation procedure and capital flight estimates for Chile, Colombia and Venezuela. In the same section we present a discussion on the causes of capital flight. In the third section we present some of the important features of a frontier function analysis and its use for the main points of this chapter. In the following section we present the results of our econometric analysis, followed by concluding remarks in the final section.

CALCULATION OF CAPITAL FLIGHT

In this chapter gross capital outflows from developing countries are treated as capital flight. The definition equals measured acquisitions of foreign assets by banks and nonbank private residents plus errors and omissions in the balance of payments. This definition implies a loss in national utility indicated by possible losses in economic returns to the economy in the form of perhaps lower investment, employment, income, and destabilized financial markets.

The gross capital outflows are changes in the stock of private foreign claims. The estimation procedure for gross capital outflows compares the sources of finance (i.e., the increase in gross external debt and net inflow of direct investment capital, both liabilities and assets) on the one hand, with the uses of finance (i.e., changes in official reserves, current account deficits and capital outflows) on the other. Since it is assumed that much of the accumulation of private foreign assets is not recorded, capital outflows are computed in an indirect way as a residual.[4] This residual measure is estimated for Venezuela, Colombia and Chile, and presented in Table 26.1.

Causes of capital flight

Capital flight is a response to economic and political instability. Yet it is problematic to capture these instabilities with a quantitative data series. Varman (1989) and Varman-Schneider and Schneider (1990) try to capture the effect of this instability as leading to jumps in capital flight. Cuddington (1986, 1987) explains capital flight on the basis of a portfolio adjustment model. Dooley (1986, 1988) uses inflation, financial repression and risk premium as the set of explanatory variables in his papers. Pastor (1990) suggests the following variables to estimate capital flight: change in inflation, financial repression, overvaluation, capital availability, country growth rate relative to the United States, labor share and tax increases. Mikkelsen's (1991) set of explanatory variables include lagged dependent variables, changes in the expected relative rate of return, changes in the GDP growth rate and changes in public debt as a percentage of GDP.

The approach in this chapter is as follows. We choose the broad measure of capital flight. This broad measure consists of the assets of the banking sector abroad, portfolio investments, working balances of firms abroad and capital flight. We do not split these up into their respective components because, besides assets of the banking sector, no data series are available. We therefore include explanatory variables that would explain all these

Table 26.1 Gross capital outflows from selected Latin American countries (in millions of US dollars)

	Venezuela (KO)	Colombia (KO)	Chile (KO)
1976	820.75	−311.25	185.30
1977	174.20	349.50	−436.28
1978	1,834.00	33.50	6.25
1979	3,065.09	−361.52	−263.81
1980	5,654.70	−154.10	−651.60
1981	4,978.36	−664.24	−1,356.50
1982	4,570.10	−334.40	2,300.30
1983	9,066.09	189.13	1,649.70
1984	7,815.38	3,240.97	−1,159.41
1985	2,166.38	−1,016.88	581.54
1986	−11,677.70	1,791.77	163.94
1987	−1,003.00	2,821.00	−2,005.00
1988	−237.00	−214.00	−4,352.00
1989	1,666.00	−158.00	−3,403.00

components. We leave out qualitative variables to capture political instability, debt negotiations, debt agreements, social unrest, etc. since the econometric technique adopted enables us to interpret the increase or decrease of their influence.

The specification is based on portfolio theory and adjusted to capture the influence of the United States. The difference between the rate of growth of United States real GDP and that of domestic real GDP in the studied country is included as an explanatory variable, as are also the nominal interest rate in the studied country and the United States interest rate adjusted for the expected rate of exchange rate changes. A measure of overvaluation is included as a proxy for the exchange rate risk for domestic residents. The hypothesis is that an overvalued currency leads to anticipations of a depreciation of the currency and leads to capital flight before the depreciation actually takes place.[5] As a risk measure we also include the domestic budget deficit and the United States budget deficit. The budget deficit is included because of the expected inflation tax and/or the risk of expropriation.[6] The sum of exports and imports was included to capture the working balances component. The variable had to be dropped because of multicollinearity problems.

Estimating equation:

$$\overset{+}{\text{KO/GDP}} = f(\overset{+}{\text{DGDPREALR}}, \overset{+}{\text{USTBAD}}, \overset{-}{\text{TB}}, \overset{+}{\text{LNPR}}, \overset{-}{\text{RAD}}, \overset{+}{\text{USBD}}, \overset{-}{\text{BD}}) \qquad (1)$$

where KO is the measure of capital outflows; DGDPREALR is the difference between the rate of growth of real GDP in the United States and the rate of growth of real domestic GDP; USTBAD is the 30 days treasury bill rate in the United States adjusted for the anticipated depreciation/appreciation of the domestic currency; TB is the domestic interest rate; RAD is the Real Effective Exchange Rate in time period $(t + 1)$ minus the Real Effective Exchange Rate in time period (t), divided by the Real Effective Exchange Rate in time period (t); LNPR is log CPI(t) − log CPI $(t − 1)$; USBD is the United States budget deficit; BD is the domestic budget deficit.

The expected sign is negative for the budget deficit, domestic interest rate and the real expected rate of depreciation. The thesis is that an appreciated currency leads to expectations of a depreciation and thus causes capital flight before the actual depreciation takes place. The expected sign for the remaining variables is positive.

FRONTIER FUNCTION ANALYSIS

Frontier production functions are important for the measurement of technical efficiency of individual firms in an industry. The stochastic frontier production function[7] was individually developed by Aigner et al. (1977)

and Meeusen and van den Broeck (1977). Their main contribution has been to split up the error term into two random components, one associated with the presence of technical inefficiency and the other being a traditional random error. They consider

$$y_i = a_0 + a_1 X_{1i} + a_2 X_{2i} + e_i, \qquad e_i = v_i - u_i,$$

$$u_i \geq 0, i = 1, \ldots, n,$$

where the composed error term consists of the inefficiency term u_i following a one-sided distribution and a symmetric part v_i representing statistical noise. The v_i are assumed to follow a normal distribution and they render stochastic the frontier itself; v_i and u_i are assumed to be independent of each other.

For this chapter we follow the approach set out in Battese and Coelli (1992) who consider a stochastic frontier production function with a simple exponential specification of time-varying effects which incorporates unbalanced panel data. The frontier production function shows the maximum output for a given level of inputs for a given firm. We make a first attempt to extend the application of frontier functions to the field of capital flight. Applications of frontier functions have involved both cross-sectional and panel data. We use balanced panel data for a sample of three countries to illustrate the point. The model can easily be extended to more countries. Our interest is in the factors that maximize capital flight from a given sample of countries. The advantage of this technique is that although we are unable to quantify variables such as political and social instability, debt negotiations and agreements, etc.,[8] we can say something about their influence on capital flight over time. We can also say something about the explanatory power of the independent variables in explaining the frontier.

Model specification

We use a frontier function estimation procedure which provides maximum-likelihood estimates of the stochastic capital flight frontier function. As stated earlier, the specification follows Battese and Coelli (1992):

$$Y_{it} = f(X_{it}; \beta) \cdot e^{(V_{it} - U_{it})}, i = 1, \ldots, N, t = 1, \ldots T,$$

where Y_{it} is the capital flight of the ith country in the tth time period;
$f(\cdot)$ is a suitable function;
X_{it} is the k by 1 vector of explanatory variables of the ith firm in the tth period. In this k by 1 vector one explanatory variable only varies over time and not for individual countries;
β is a k by 1 vector of unknown parameters;

V_{it} is the normal disturbance term $N(0, s_v^2)$;

$U_{it} = (U_i \cdot e^{-\eta(t-T)})$, where η is an unknown parameter and the U_i are positive truncations of the $N(\mu, \sigma^2)$ distribution.

The assumptions are that U_i is a random term and U_i is independent of X_i and V_i.

The U_{it} are the deviations from the frontier. These deviations would represent inefficiency in the production function application, but in our case the higher the deviations the more efficient is the economic system because the capital flight numbers move away from the frontier through the influence of the improvement in the left-out variables. We interpret the deviations from the frontier as efficiency (the same is interpreted as inefficiency in the Cobb–Douglas production function analysis since movements of output numbers away from the frontier mean deterioration in management skill etc.), since capital flight has negative connotations, and reduced capital flight or return of capital flight is being interpreted as a positive phenomenon.

The value of η is important for the interpretation of our model.

$$\eta > 0 \Rightarrow (d/dt)U_{it} < 0$$

$$\eta = 0 \Rightarrow (d/dt)U_{it} = 0$$

$$\eta > 0 \Rightarrow (d/dt)U_{it} > 0$$

If η is greater than zero, we are given to understand that the observed capital flight numbers move closer to the theoretically estimated frontier over time. If η is equal to zero then there is no change over time in the position of the capital flight numbers and the theoretically estimated capital flight. If η is less than zero we are given to understand that the observed capital flight numbers move further away from the theoretically estima'ed frontier over time.

The concept of technical efficiency of firms plays a central role in the development and application of frontier production functions.[9]

For the purpose of this chapter we define technical efficiency as TE_{it} = Actual Capital Flight/Estimated maximum capital flight, where $0 < TE_{it} < 1$.

ECONOMETRIC INVESTIGATION

In this section we first report the results of a pooled regression on a sample of three countries – Venezuela, Chile and Colombia. The results of this regression capture an explanation for the average amount of capital flight.

Pooled regression results

The results (Table 26.2) show that the differences in the rate of growth of real GDP between the United States and the individual country, the United

Table 26.2 Dependent variable KO/GDP: estimation by least squares

Usable observations	33	Degrees of freedom		23
Centered R**2	0.683621	R Bar **2		0.559820
Uncentered R**2	0.704667	$T \times R$**2		23.254
Mean of dependent variable		−0.050963438		
Std error of dependent variable		0.193870829		
Standard error of estimate		0.128625639		
Sum of squared residuals		0.3805247667		
Regression $F(9, 23)$		5.5220		
Significance level of F		0.00044284		
Durbin–Watson statistic		1.909617		

	Variable	Coeff.	Std Error	T-stat.	Signif.
1	Constant	0.933869445	0.163008360	5.72897	0.00000780
2	DGDPREALR	0.007354175	0.002067192	3.55757	0.00167529
3	USTBAD	0.006707117	0.001371595	4.89001	0.00006128
4	TB	−0.007871412	0.003822398	−2.05929	0.05096264
5	LNPR	−2.298645789	0.433780682	−5.29910	0.00002228
6	RAD	−0.012917879	0.003026270	−4.26858	0.00028830
7	USBD	0.005292314	0.000905114	5.84712	0.00000586
8	BD	−0.000043445	0.000018851	−2.30463	0.03055635
9	DCOL	0.155980548	0.086424985	1.80481	0.08421520
10	DCHI	0.086924176	0.089932188	0.96655	0.34382199

Note: KO is the author's own estimate on capital flight based on data from the OECD and the *Balance of Payments Year Book* (IMF, various issues). All other variables are from *International Financial Statistics* (IMF). DCOL and DCHI are the country-specific dummy variables.

States interest rate adjusted for the anticipated rate of depreciation of the domestic currency, the domestic interest rate, overvaluation, the domestic budget and the United States budget deficit, are significant in explaining capital flight. The coefficient for inflation is significant, but does not have the right sign. This would imply that domestic hedges were available to evade the inflation tax as a substitute to investing capital abroad.[10]

We use the computer program Frontier version 2.0 from Coelli (1992). The general model formulation allows us to investigate individual country effects as assumed to be a product of an exponential function of time and a non-negative random variable having truncated normal distribution. The program enables us to calculate asymptotic estimates of standard errors along with individual and mean estimates of technical efficiency.

All the coefficients in the regression shown in Table 26.3 have the expected sign except for inflation. The results indicate the significance of the United States budget deficit and the difference in the rate of growth of real GDP, with the domestic economy and US interest rate adjusted for exchange rate expectations in explaining the flight of capital from Vene-

Table 26.3 Estimates of the Frontier function model

	Coefficients	Standard error	T-ratio
INTERCEPT	0.3770	0.0792	4.7559
DGDPREALR	0.3138	0.0970	3.2340
USTBAD	0.1693	0.0632	2.6766
TB	−0.3942	0.0942	−4.1818
LNPR	−3.9845	0.9705	−3.5015
RAD	−0.4508	0.1783	−2.5284
USBD	0.2228	0.0614	3.6256
BD	−0.3352	0.0897	−3.7337
σ-squared	0.1542	0.0778	1.9822
Mμ	0.3825	0.9585	0.3991
η	−0.5787	0.6944	−0.8334

zuela, Colombia and Chile between 1979 and 1989. Other important influences captured by our model are the influence of the domestic budget deficit, overvaluation, and the nominal interest rate. When we compare these results with the pooled regression analysis we find that the results of the model are almost the same as those of the earlier estimate except that there is a change in the significance of some of the variables in explaining the maximum amount of capital flight. The coefficients of the regressors, the United States treasury bill rate adjusted for exchange rate expectations, overvaluation and the United States budget deficit go down in significance, whereas the coefficients of the domestic interest rate and domestic budget deficit increase in significance.

The results of both the pooled regression and Frontier function estimates highlight the importance of both external and internal factors. The results indicate that the performance of the United States economy is also important in motivating capital outflows.

The η value is negative. The negative value of η would indicate that efficiency has gone down over time. In the example of the Cobb–Douglas production function to which this program was originally applied by Coelli (1992), this would be interpreted as a decline in efficiency because of the influence of the variables not captured by the data such as management skills which are also inputs in producing the maximum output. In our example we interpret the technical efficiency coefficients as inefficiency coefficients to indicate that the Frontier function (maximum capital flight) has a negative connotation. Figures 26.1, 26.2 and 26.3 show the technical efficiency coefficients for the three countries in the sample. (See Table A1.26.1 in Appendix 1, p. 417).

The estimates of technical effiiciency show that up to 1985 the capital flight numbers are closer to the frontier, indicating that political as well as economic instability gave rise to an inefficient environment and were

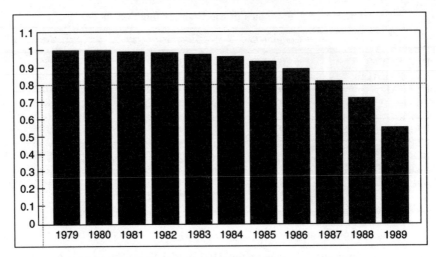

Figure 26.1 Venezuela: technical efficiency estimates

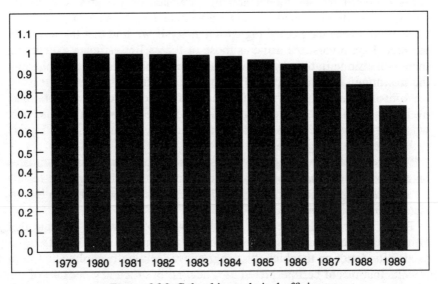

Figure 26.2 Colombia: technical efficiency

responsible along with the economic variables included in the earlier
estimates to explain maximum capital flight. But around 1985–6 the change
in efficiency in the countries studied was underway. The technical efficiency coefficients moved away from the Frontier, indicating a more
efficient economy. However improvements are visible in the 1984–5 period. The improvement in efficiency in 1989 is notable, especially for
Venezuela and Chile. In the case of Colombia and Chile, increase in
efficiency is associated with inflows of capital in the last two years of

414

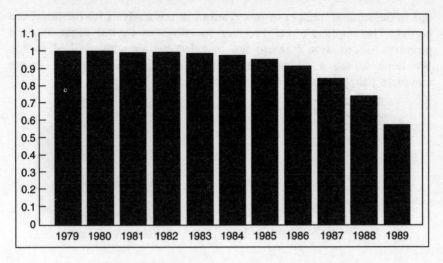

Figure 26.3 Chile: technical efficiency estimates

the sample. In the case of Venezuela, three years of capital repatriation is followed by a reversal. The reversal might be taken as an indication that only economic variables were responsible for the capital flight in 1989. It was not driven by qualitative variables such as political instability.

We cannot make a firm statement in this regard as the T-statistics for η are low.

CONCLUDING REMARKS

This chapter is a first attempt in applying Frontier production functions to the capital flight function and incorporating the influence of the United States economy combined with country-specific factors in motivating capital flight.[11] The results are encouraging. We can say with confidence that the United States economy exerts an important influence on the behavior of the private sector on the three countries. Other important motivating factors are anticipations of depreciation of the real effective exchange rate, the rate of growth of real GDP and nominal interest rates. We can also say with a certain degree of confidence that Frontier functions and the resulting maximum-likelihood estimates are a useful approach in analyzing capital flight estimates. The information that can be interpreted from the results has advantages over OLS. We can say with certainty that the efficiency of our explanatory variables went down after 1985 in explaining the capital flight numbers, since they move further away from the Frontier over time. This, together with the negative value of η, indicates the improvement in the left-out qualitative variables in the model leading to disincentives to maximize capital flight. The T-statistic for η is not significant. This may be due to the limited number of observations in our analysis for the improved period. The application of Frontier functions to capital flight analysis promises information hitherto not revealed by methods applied so far. We hope to see a wider application of Frontier functions to a more complete panel dataset in the years to come.

APPENDIX 1

Table A1.26.1 Technical efficiency estimates

	Venezuela	Colombia	Chile
1979	0.9981410	0.99904954	0.9983042
1980	0.9966863	0.99830518	0.9969770
1981	0.9940967	0.99697879	0.9946139
1982	0.9894941	0.99461727	0.9904126
1983	0.9813372	0.99041911	0.9829627
1984	0.9669549	0.98297592	0.9698138
1985	0.9418256	0.96984247	0.9467987
1986	0.8986255	0.94686545	0.9071072
1987	0.8264709	0.90727259	0.8404376
1988	0.7119686	0.84086210	0.7335733
1989	0.5459789	0.73465492	0.5758838

APPENDIX 2

Table A2.26.1 Venezuela: selected economic indicators

Year	KO1	RAD	RGDPREAL	GDPR	TB	BD	CA
1975	−311.25	n/a	n/a	n/a	16.00	n/a	−171.00
1976	349.50	n/a	−6.62	0.17	20.00	152.78	162.00
1977	33.50	n/a	−1.74	0.27	20.00	122.38	375.00
1978	−361.52	n/a	2.02	0.19	22.00	158.61	258.00
1979	−154.10	3.08	−3.19	0.20	30.00	−216.22	438.00
1980	−664.24	10.37	−6.32	0.20	30.00	−585.87	−205.00
1981	−334.40	6.60	−11.26	0.09	30.00	−1,108.46	−1,961.00
1982	189.13	−0.48	−14.16	0.07	27.00	−1,843.01	−3,053.00
1983	3,240.97	−8.46	−17.46	−0.01	27.00	−1,622.07	−3,003.00
1984	−1,016.88	−12.82	−19.17	−0.01	27.00	−1,651.46	−1,401.00
1985	1,791.77	−25.50	−26.95	−0.09	27.00	−946.53	−1,809.00
1986	2,821.00	−10.87	−22.48	0.00	31.40	−301.66	383.00
1987	−214.00	−3.46	−15.63	0.04	30.80	−251.43	336.00
1988	−158.00	−3.74	−15.61	0.08	33.50	−522.45	−216.00
1989	−16,234.00	−11.67	−19.13	0.01	33.70	−749.41	−201.00
1990	2,969.00	3.12	−20.67	0.02	36.40	0.00	700.00
1991	n/a	9.25	−18.83	0.03	37.20	0.00	2,551.00
1992	n/a	n/a	−100.00	−1.00	26.70	0.00	n/a

Table A2.26.2 Chile: selected economic indicators

Year	KOl	RAD	RGDPREAL	GDPR	TB	BD	CA
1975	185.30	n/a	n/a	n/a	n/a	n/a	−490.00
1976	−436.28	n/a	−61.06	0.37	n/a	134.52	148.00
1977	6.25	n/a	−33.39	0.36	93.77	−148.64	−551.00
1978	−263.81	n/a	−26.40	0.15	62.83	−15.79	−1,088.00
1979	−651.60	16.94	−7.97	0.35	45.06	998.76	−1,189.00
1980	−1,356.50	21.48	2.92	0.33	37.46	1,492.31	−1,971.00
1981	2,300.30	−9.66	5.53	0.18	40.79	846.15	−4,733.00
1982	1,649.70	−18.61	−34.18	−0.25	47.91	−239.64	−2,304.00
1983	−1,159.41	−1.82	−35.90	−0.19	27.95	−518.76	−1,117.00
1984	581.54	−19.42	−15.00	−0.03	27.63	−569.66	−2,111.00
1985	163.94	−15.50	−37.24	−0.17	31.97	−376.83	−1,413.00
1986	−2,005.00	−7.22	−11.84	0.05	18.99	−162.68	−1,192.00
1987	−4,352.00	−6.51	−7.04	0.13	25.22	91.10	−808.00
1988	−3,403.00	2.18	−3.81	0.17	15.10	−49.79	−167.00
1989	−19,395.00	−2.67	0.88	0.15	27.73	0.00	−767.00
1990	−3,166.00	3.02	−10.54	0.10	40.27	0.00	−824.00
1991	n/a	5.86	−7.43	0.13	22.32	0.00	92.00
1992	n/a	n/a	6.40	0.21	18.26	0.00	n/a

Table A2.26.3 Colombia: selected economic indicators

Year	KOl	RAD	RGDPREAL	GDPR	TB	BD	CA
1975	820.75	n/a	n/a	n/a	7.00	n/a	2,171.00
1976	174.02	n/a	8.64	0.14	7.00	−929.37	254.00
1977	1,824.00	n/a	6.65	0.15	7.50	−1,570.46	−3,179.00
1978	3,065.09	n/a	2.14	0.09	7.50	−1,605.40	−5,735.00
1979	5,654.70	9.32	1.34	0.23	11.00	924.06	350.00
1980	4,978.36	13.15	−1.99	0.22	13.00	26.32	4,728.00
1981	4,570.10	8.17	−0.26	0.12	14.00	−908.41	4,000.00
1982	9,066/09	−8.96	0.63	0.02	13.00	−2,951.32	−4,246.00
1983	7,815.38	−15.22	−5.70	−0.00	11.00	−1,019.78	4,427.00
1984	2,116.38	−4.03	−39.60	−0.14	12.29	1,930.45	4,651.00
1985	−11,677.74	−16.50	−5.11	0.04	10.52	3,147.73	3,327.00
1986	−1,003.00	−28.38	−1.33	0.02	8.93	−1,232.83	−2,245.00
1987	−237.00	11.54	−41.74	−0.23	8.94	−2,741.59	−1,390.00
1988	1,666.00	−14.84	6.17	0.29	8.95	−4,667.31	−5,809.00
1989	−23,958.00	−10.21	−61.47	−0.29	28.23	−690.52	2,161.00
1990	766.00	6.86	−20.97	0.13	27.78	537.51	8,279.00
1991	n/a	4.59	−8.89	0.10	31.10	2,359.21	1,663.00
1992	n/a	n/a	−10.83	0.14	35.42	0.00	n/a

Key for Tables A2.26.1–3:
   KO1: Gross capital outflows.
   RAD: Expected rate of depreciation of the real effective exchange rate.
   RGDPREAL: Growth of real GDP.
   GDPR: Gross domestic product's rate of growth.
   TB: 30-day treasury bill rate.
   BD: Budget deficit.
   CA: Current account.
Sources: *International Financial Statistics* (IMF), and own estimates.

NOTES

* The author gratefully acknowledges the financial support of the Volkswagen-Stiftung. This chapter is part of a Volkswagen project titled "Messung von Kapitalflucht als Reaktion auf wirtschaftliche und politische Instabilitäten – eine Fallstudie für ausgewählte lateinamerikanische Länder." She would also like to thank Uwe Jensen for introducing her to Frontier production function estimation, and for his patience in listening to its application to the capital flight problem.

1 See for example, Conesa (1987), Cuddington (1986, 1987), Dooley (1986, 1988), Dornbusch (1984), Mikkelsen (1991), Pastor (1990), and Varman-Schneider (1991a).

2 Researchers emphasize the influence of the United States economy on the resurgence of capital inflows into Latin America in the 1990s. See for example Calvo et al. (1993).

3 The three case studies are used as an illustration to emphasize the main points of this study. The original work was carried out for seven countries, but owing to data problems the results are being presented for a set of three countries where the data was the most reliable.

4 KO = Δdebt + DI + CR + CA, where Δdebt is the change in external debt, DI is net foreign direct investment, CR the change in reserves, and CA the current account surplus. We use the sign convention in the balance of payments here. All the variables in the equation are flow data.

5 See Feenstra (1985) for a formal discussion.

6 See Ize and Ortiz (1987) for a formal discussion of this issue.

7 See Jensen (1993) for a survey of the measurement of individual efficiency with Frontier functions.

8 Varman-Schneider (1991a) made an attempt to model these in an econometric model using vectors of dummy variables.

9 For various definitions of technical efficiency see, e.g., Battese and Coelli (1992).

10 See Cuddington (1986).

11 Varman-Schneider (1994) applies this methodology to a single country, Mexico. The analysis is backed by a description of the Mexican economy and also results estimated by flexible least squares.

REFERENCES

Aigner, D.J., C.A.K. Lovell and P. Schmidt (1977) "Formulation and Estimation of Stochastic Frontier Production Function Models," *Journal of Econometrics*, Vol. 6, pp. 21–37.

Battese, G.E. and T. Coelli (1992) "Frontier Production Functions, Technical Efficiency and Panel Data: With Application to Paddy Farmers in India," *The Journal of Productivity Analysis*, Vol. 3, pp. 153–69.

Calvo G., L. Leiderman and C.M. Reinhart (1993) "Capitol Inflows to Latin America: The Role of External Factors," *IMF Staff Papers*, March.

Coelli, T.J. (1991) "Maximum-Likelihood Estimation of Stochastic Frontier Production Functions with Time-Varying Technical Efficiency using the Computer Program, Frontier version 2.0," *Working Papers in Econometrics and Applied Statistics*, No. 57, Department of Econometrics, University of New England, Australia.

Coelli, T.J. (1992) "A Computer Program for Frontier Function Estimation: Frontier Version 2.0," *Economic Letters*, Vol. 39, pp. 29–32.

Conesa, E.R. (1987) "The Causes of Capital Flight from Latin America," Washington, DC: Inter-American Development Bank.

Cuddington, J.T. (1986) "Capital Flight: Issues, Estimates and Explanations," Princeton Studies in International Finance, No. 58, December.

Cuddington, J.T. (1987) "Macroeconomic Determinants of Capital Flight: An Econometric Investigation," in D.R. Lessard and J. Williamson (eds), *Capital Flight and Third World Debt*, Washington, DC: Institute for International Economics, June, pp. 85–96.

Dooley, M. (1986) *Country Specific Risk Premiums, Capital Flight and Net Investment Income Payments in Selected Developing Countries*, Washington, DC: International Monetary Fund, Research Department, March.

Dooley, M. (1988) "Capital Flight: A Response to Differences in Financial Risks," *IMF Staff Papers*, International Monetary Fund, Vol. 35, No. 3, September, pp. 422–36.

Dooley, M., W. Helkie, R. Tyron and J. Underwood (1983) "The Analysis of External Debt Positions of Eight Developing Countries Through 1990," Federal Reserve Board, *International Finance Discussion Paper 227*, Board of Governors of the Federal Reserve System, Washington, August.

Dornbusch, R. (1984) "External Debt, Budget Deficits and Disequilibrium Exchange Rates," *NBER Working Paper 1336*, Cambridge, Mass.: National Bureau of Economic Research, April.

Dornbusch, R. and J.C. Pablo (1988) "Debt and Macroeconomic Instability in Argentina," in J. Sachs (ed.) *Debt and Policy Issues*, Cambridge, Mass.: National Bureau of Economic Research.

Feenstra R.C. (1985) "Anticipated Devaluations, Currency Flight, and Direct Trade Controls in a Monetary Economy," *American Economic Review*, Vol. 75, June, pp. 386–401.

Gemaehlich, D. (1988) *Kapitalexport und Kapitalflucht aus Entwicklungslaendern – Empirische und Theoretische Analysen vor dem Hintergrund der Verschuldungsproblematik*, IFO – Studien zur Entwicklungsforschung 19, Muenchen: Institut für Wirtschaftsforschung.

Ize, A. and G. Ortiz (1987) "Fiscal Rigidities, Public Debt and Capital Flight," *IMF Staff Papers*, International Monetary Fund, Washington, DC, July.

Jensen, U. (1993) "Measuring Individual Inefficiency with Frontier Functions: Monte Carlo Study," *Discussion Paper No. 68/1993*, Kiel: Institute of Statistics and Econometrics, Christian-Albrechts-Universität Kiel.

Lessard, D.R. and J. Williamson (1987) *Capital Flight and Third World Debt*, Washington, DC: Institute of International Economics.

Meeusen, W. and J. van den Broeck (1977) "Efficiency Estimation from Cobb–Douglas Production Functions with Composed Error," *International Economic Review*, Vol. 18, pp. 435–44.

Mikkelsen, J.G. (1991) "An Econometric Investigation of Capital Flight," *Applied Economics*, Vol. 23, pp. 73–85.

Morgan Guaranty Trust Co. of New York (1986) *World Financial Markets*, February.

Pastor Jr., M. (1990) "Capital Flight from Latin America," *World Development*, Vol. 18, No. 1, pp. 1–18.

Varman, B. (1989) *Capital Flight: A Critique of Concepts and Measures, Including a Case Study of India and the Philippines*, HWWA, Institut fuer Wirtschaftsforschung, Hamburg: Verlag Weltarchiv.

Varman-Schneider, B. (1991a) *Capital Flight from Developing Countries*, Boulder, Colo.: Westview Press.

Varman-Schneider, B. (1991b) "Capital Flight as a Response to economic and Political Instability: A Case Study of Argentina," *Discussion Paper No. 87*, Kiel: Institute of Economic Theory, Christian-Albrechts-Universität Kiel (revised version 1993).

Varman-Schneider, B. (1994) "Economic and Political Instability: Factors in Explaining Episodes of Capital Flight from Mexico (1976–90)," Kiel: Institute of Economic Theory, Christian-Albrechts-Universität Kiel.

Varman-Schneider, B. and W. Schneider (1990). Measuring Capital Flight – A Time Varying Regression Analysis, ASEAN Economic Bulletin, Vol. 7, No. 1, July.

OFFSHORE MARKETS AND CAPITAL FLOWS

A theoretical analysis

Dilip K. Ghosh

INTRODUCTION

In the changing environment surrounding global financial markets, conditioned by American dominance in the middle of rigid regulatory constraints, tax burdens, political suspicion, and many other adscititious factors, offshore banking centers mushroomed from the late 1950s onward. Entrepôt centers and eurocurrency came into existence to satisfy the regulation-choked investors, transnational enterprises, and communist countries such as the then Soviet Union and its satellite countries which wanted to keep dollars, but not under the jurisdiction of the United States. Offshore deposits grew into trillions of dollars in less than half a century. Many estimates are available from the Bank for International Settlements (BIS) and from Morgan Guaranty's regular surveys, and useful analytical as well as empirical studies abound in the existing and ever-growing literature. The early studies by Einzig and Quinn (1977), Duffey and Giddy (1978), McCarthy (1983), followed by more recent research by Park and Essayyard (1990), Roussakis *et al.*, (1994), and many others, have given excellent treatments to various facets of offshore markets, the reasons for their rapid growth, and prospects in this new market morphology.

It is almost unquestionably understood that eurocurrency is a capital outflow of the currency of denomination from the country of jurisdiction. That means, a euro-dollar amount is a capital outflow from the US economy, a euro-franc amount is a capital outflow from France, and so on. Although it is seemingly true, capital outflows may not be an accurate description of reality. In this chapter, we present a theoretical framework to examine if the dollar deposits in the euro-dollar accounts, say, in London (UK), effectively create a drain of capital from the American economy. Interestingly enough, the question refers back to the classic "transfer problem" created by the Treaty of Versailles (1919) whereby Germany was mandated to pay reparations for World War I. Keynes (1929) strongly argued that the recipient countries would lose more than the payments received in the form of reparations from Germany, and this created a serious theoretical debate in the trade literature (see Samuelson 1952, 1954, 1971; Johnson 1955, 1956; Jones 1970, 1975) in an effort to ascertain as to whether the secondary effect of drain would outweigh the primary transfer through reparations. In this case, the issue may be whether the euro-dollars create effective capital outflows. Several efforts have been made to study the liquidity creation by eurocurrency and the effects thereof in the magnitude of change in the money supply in the domestic economy of the currency of denomination. Klopstock (1968), Friedman (1969), Willms (1976), Niehans and Hewson (1976), Grabbe (1991), and Swoboda (1980) have analyzed many aspects relating to this issue, and it would be instructive to bring out some of this development to build the analytical structure for the examination of the impact of offshore funds on capital flows.

OFFSHORE DEPOSITS AND THE MONEY MULTIPLIER

Consider the basic definition of money stock as follows:

$$M = CC + DD^{ON} + TD^{OF} \tag{1}$$

and monetary base (M^B):

$$M^B = CC + RR \tag{2}$$

Let

$$DD^{ON} = \alpha M + \beta \tag{3}$$
$$TD^{OF} = \theta M + \omega \tag{4}$$

Here M stands for money supply in the US economy, CC for coins and currency in circulation in the hands of non-bank public, DD^{ON} for demand deposits onshore (that is, within the legal jurisdiction of the United States), and TD^{OF} the time deposits offshore – that is, outside the legal jurisdiction of the United States). TD^{OF} measure the offshore funds – the euro-dollar deposits – in this analytical paradigm. It is postulated that demand deposits and time deposits are linear functions of stock of money (M), and α, β, θ, and ω are the parameters of the functions defined by equations (3) and (4). Following the traditional route, consider the following behavioral relations:

$$RR_D = r_D(DD^{ON} + r_T TD^{OF}) \tag{5}$$

where RR_D represents the total required reserves for US banks, r_D their required reserve ratio (that is, the ratio of total reserves with the Federal Reserve to total deposits held), and r_T is the ratio of offshore banks' reserves with the US banks (not US Federal Reserve) to their total time deposits ($r_T = R_T/TD^{OF}$, where R_T are the reserves maintained by offshore banks for practical business discipline). One can recognize that any increase (decrease) in euro-dollar deposits must be matched by the equal decrease (increase) in onshore deposits. That means, $d\beta + d\omega = 0$.

Now, after some algebraic manipulations one gets the following expressions upon differentiation:

$$\frac{dTD^{OF}}{d\omega} = \frac{1}{\left[1 + \dfrac{\theta r_D(1 - r_T)}{(\theta + \alpha)(1 - r_D) - 1} \right]} \tag{6}$$

and

$$\frac{dM}{D\omega} = \frac{r_D(1 - r_T)}{1 - (1 - r_D)\alpha - (1 - r_D r_T)\theta} \tag{7}$$

From equation (8), one gets the following expression:

$$\hat{M} = \left[\frac{r_D(1 - r_T)}{1 - (1 - r_D)\alpha - (1 - r_D r_T)\theta} \right] \left(\frac{\hat{\omega}}{M} \right) \tag{8}$$

where a 'cap' over any variable or parameter represents henceforth the percentage change in that variable or parameter. Obviously, from equation (8) one can see that the elasticity of offshore deposits on onshore money supply, defined by, $\hat{M}/\hat{\omega}$, exceeds unity, which means that an increase in offshore deposits results in a higher rate of increase in the money supply in the domestic economy.

The question that follows then is: how are capital flows related to movements of funds to offshore accounts? The link is not immediately visible, but the link is direct via exchange rate change and the impact on interest rates in the domestic economy. Bringing out the Fisherian structure of the economy, we get the celebrated quantity theory, which is expressed as follows:

$$PY = MV \quad \text{for the home economy,} \tag{9}$$

and

$$P^*Y^* = M^*V^* \quad \text{for the foreign economy,} \tag{10}$$

where P stand for the price level, V for the velocity of the circulation of money, Y for the national product (of the domestic economy), and an asterisk connotes the foreign economy. From equations (9) and (10) we obtain:

$$\frac{P}{P^*} = \left(\frac{MV}{M^*V^*} \right) \left(\frac{Y^*}{Y} \right) \tag{11}$$

Now, invoke the purchasing power parity to bring out the rate of exchange of dollars for the British pound (E):

$$E = \frac{P}{P*} \tag{12}$$

and then add equation (12) to equation (13) to derive:

$$E = \frac{P}{P*} = \left(\frac{MV}{M*V*}\right)\left(\frac{Y*}{Y}\right) \tag{13}$$

whence

$$\hat{E} = (\hat{M} - \hat{M}*) + (\hat{V} - \hat{V}*) + (\hat{Y}* - \hat{Y}) \tag{14}$$

It is clear that the percentage change in the exchange rate depends on the differential on the rates of change in the money supply of the two countries, the differential in the rates of change in the velocity of circulation of money, and that of the rates of change in the national products. *Ceteris paribus*, an increase in money supply in the American economy, following an increase in offshore deposits as noted through equation (8), will induce a depreciation in dollars. In the Keynesian–Metzleric framework, we note that a decrease (increase) in domestic interest rate causes a deterioration (an improvement) in current account balance. Since a decrease in interest rate induces an increase in domestic investment, which via the expenditure multiplier increases national income, this in turn stimulates the growth in import expenditure but leaves the export earnings unaffected. This sequence creates through the process an adverse balance on the trade account. It is evident that capital inflows are directly a function of the interest rate, and capital outflows are an inverse function of the interest rate, everything else remaining constant. With these functional identifications, one can produce Figure 27.1 which illustrates the interaction of current account balance (CUAB) and capital account balance (CAAB). The right side of the horizontal axis measures the deficit in current account balance (−CUAB) and the surplus in the capital account balance (+CAAB). The left side of the horizontal axis similarly measures the surplus in the current account balance (+CUAB) and the deficit in the capital account balance (−CAAB). Here we assume that an accommodating adjustment process makes the capital account balance the mirror image of the current account balance or vice versa. The vertical axis measures the US interest rate (or one may measure the interest rate differential, $r - r*$). The intersection of the negatively sloped CUAB curve and the positively sloped CAAB curve defines equilibrium state in the balance of payments, and the magnitudes of current account and capital account balances. At a given exchange rate, say E^0, as Figure 27.1 exhibits,[1] the US economy has OA dollars worth of current account deficits and OA dollars of surplus in the capital account balance. Now, if the offshore deposits cause a depreciation of the dollar via growth in the domestic money supply, the CAAB schedule must shift inward for the favorable impact of depreciation on

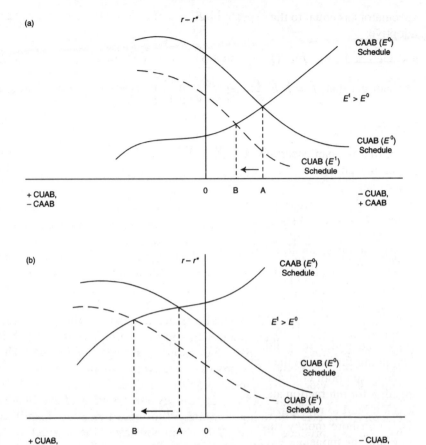

Figure 27.1 Balance of payments equilibrium: current and capital account balances

trade structure, which then will reduce current account deficits (or put current account balance into surplus). The accommodating adjustment in the entire balance of payments will yield a reduction in capital inflow or an increase in capital outflow. Note that we have not considered any shift in the CAAB curve. One may wonder whether the change in money supply will force a shift in capital inflows. In an interesting work, Dornbusch (1976) shows that the change in exchange rate is related to change in money in the following fashion:

$$\hat{E} = (\frac{1}{\sigma})\hat{M} \qquad (15)$$

where σ is the interest elasticity of money, where forward rate of exchange is assumed to be exogenously given, and covered arbitrage is ruled out. If further assumption is made that the forward rate of exchange (F) is set by speculators as equal to the expected future spot rate, where expectations are adoptive:

$$F = \lambda E + (1 - \lambda)E_{-1}, 0 < \lambda < 1 \qquad (16)$$

one can get that, $\hat{F} = \lambda \hat{E}$, and hence:

$$\hat{E} = \frac{1}{(1 - \lambda)\sigma} \hat{M} \qquad (17)$$

From this we can ascertain that the closer the value of λ is to unity, the larger the change in exchange rate corresponding to a given change in money supply. Of course this conclusion is vitiated by the value of σ. With the elasticity of expectation λ less than unity, a depreciation of spot rate brings about a less than proportionate depreciation in the expected future spot rate, or an anticipated appreciation. Furthermore, one can see that if λ is large and σ is small, a large exchange rate change will occur.

The short-run impact of exchange rate change will hardly impact the CAAB schedule, and hence one can conclude that an outflow of funds into an offshore market will lead to a further increase in capital outflows from an onshore market. Primary outflows will be compounded by the incipient secondary outflows. However, the analysis is couched in a short-run framework, and hence its validity in the direction of long-run trend is worth examining further. In the existing literature, it has been pointed out that in the long-run both commodity markets and assets markets must be brought together for interaction and the determination of exchange rate movements. It is not hard to recognize that price level will tend to rise in response to a rise in onshore money supply; as Dornbusch (1976) puts it, "until, in the long run, the monetary expansion is exactly matched by a price increase so that real balances and interest rates are unchanged and the spot and forward rate depreciate in the same proportion as the increase in nominal quantity of money."

Neihans (1984) has presented a significant analytical structure on capital flows, and his analysis has examined three basic factors that may influence capital mobility in and out of a country. Starting off with the basic functional relation that capital outflow (C) is dependent on national income levels, Y, Y^*, interest rates, r, r^*, prices of capital goods, ρ, ρ^*, and exchange rate, E:

$$C = C(Y, Y^*, r, r^*, \rho, \rho^*, E)$$

and, working through the national wealth accounts containing foreign assets in a bilateral framework, he concludes that the effects of interest rates on aggregate capital flows are "fundamentally ambiguous." The effect of a change in exchange rate is also not clear-cut. If the expected exchange rate moves hand in hand with the current rate, and if all bonds are denominated in debtor country currency, one can see that a depreciation increases the domestic currency value of the foreign assets of the depreciating country, and decreases the domestic currency value of the appreciating country. Since the desired assets do not change in such a situation, equilibrium will necessitate a capital inflow into the depreciating country, which signifies that $\partial C/\partial E < 0$. If the creditor currency-denominated bonds are considered, one notices a capital outflow in response to a depreciation, $\partial C/\partial E > 0$. The summary of the results of the wealth effects of exchange rate changes, as presented by Neihans (1984), is shown in Table 27.1.

Now, one may realize that there may be a shift of the CAAB schedule, and it may move bodily upward, or downward, or may stay put. If the original capital account balance curve moves upward, then a depreciation in the exchange rate triggered by original offshore deposits will accentuate capital outflows. But if the curve moves downward, it means that original offshore deposits and the original capital outflow will be at least reversed, and the reversal may extend far enough to cause an overall increase of capital inflow into the inshore economy. In this respect it is a situation reminiscent of the classic "transfer problem," alluded to earlier. Figure 27.2 portrays all these possible scenarios. In Figure 27.2a, CAAB moves upward to the left which in conjunction with the inward shift of the CUAB curve causes additional capital outflows. Figure 27.2b exhibits the shift of the CAAB curve downward to the right, which then creates the reversal of initial capital outflows, and in this specific case an overall increase in capital inflows. Figure 27.2c, the intermediate scenario in which the CAAB schedule does not move at all, shows that initial capital outflows are the net outflows.

In the foregoing section the implicit assumption has been that domestic and foreign assets are not perfect substitutes. So the question now is: what happens to capital outflow (or inflow) if perfect assets substitutions are included. In this scenario, interest rate parity will prevail continuously, and $dE/dt = r - r^*$. The end result of a change in interest rate on capital outflows is not unambiguous. With homogeneous assets across national

Table 27.1 The wealth effects of exchange rate changes

Asset denomination	Depreciating country	Appreciating country	$\partial C/\partial E$
Debtor currency	Gains	Loses	< 0
Creditor currency	Loses	Gains	> 0
Depreciating currency	Unchanged	Gains if debtor	> 0
Appreciating currency	Unchanged	Loses if creditor	< 0
Mixed: creditor depreciates	Gains	Gains	$> = < 0$
Mixed: debtor depreciates	Loses	Loses	$> = < 0$

Source: Neihans (1984).

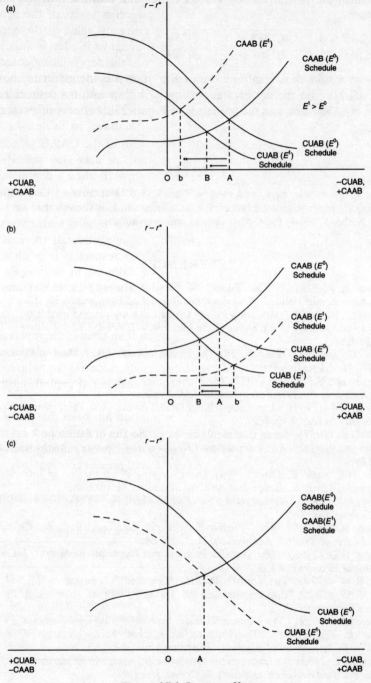

Figure 27.2 Impact effects

economies, the partial derivatives on the capital outflow function are as follows:[2]

$$\partial C/\partial Y > 0 \quad \partial C/\partial Y^* < 0 \quad \partial C/\partial r > = < 0 \quad \partial C/\partial r^* > = < 0$$
$$\partial C/\partial \rho < 0 \quad \partial C/\partial \rho^* > 0 \quad \partial C/\partial E > = < 0$$

All these results thus reinforce the earlier view that the effect of moving funds offshore on the net capital outflow or inflow into the inshore economy is not clear-cut, and the scenarios of Figure 27.2 become relevant once again.

NOTES

1 This diagram was first presented in Ghosh (1987); it appears here with the necessary modifications. Figure 27.2 introduces additional modifications.
2 See Niehans (1984) for further details and derivations.

REFERENCES

Dornbusch, R. (1976) "The Theory of Flexible Exchange Rate Regimes and Macroeconomic Policy," *Scandinavian Journal of Economics*, 78, 2.

Dornbusch, R. (1978) "Monetary Policy Under Exchange-Rate Flexibility," in J.R. Artus (ed.) *Managed Exchange-Rate Flexibility*, Boston: Federal Reserve Bank of Boston.

Duffey, G. and I.H. Giddy (1978) *The International Money Market*, Englewood Cliffs, N.J.: Prentice-Hall.

Einzig, P. and B.S. Quinn (1977) *The Euro-Dollar System: Practice and Theory of International Interest Rates*, London: Macmillan.

Friedman, M. (1969) "The Eurodollar Market: Some First Principles," *Morgan Guaranty Survey*, October.

Ghosh, D.K. (1987) "Some Comments on the Economics of Exchange Rates," in J. Dutta (ed.) *Research in International Business and Finance*, Greenwich, Conn.: JAI Press.

Ghosh, D.K. and E. Ortiz (1994) *The Changing Environment of International Financial Markets: Issues and Analysis*, London: Macmillan.

Grabbe, J.O. (1991) *International Financial Markets*, New York: Elsevier Science Publishing Co., Inc.

Johnson, H.G. (1955) "The Transfer Problem: A Note on Criteria for Changes in the Terms of Trade," *Economica*, N.S., 22, 86.

Johnson, H.G. (1956) "The Transfer Problem and Exchange Stability," *Journal of Political Economy*, 64, 3.

Jones, R.W. (1970) "The Transfer Problem Revisited," *Economica*, N.S., 37, 146.

Jones, R.W. (1975) "Presumption and the Transfer Problem," *Journal of International Economics*, 5, 3.

Keynes, J.M. (1929) "The German Transfer Problem," *Economic Journal*, 39, 153.

Klopstock, F.H. (1968) "The Euro-Dollar Market: Some Unresolved Issues," *Essays in International Finance*, Princeton University, 65.

McCarthy, I. (1983) "Offshore in the Asian Pacific Area," in R. Moxon *et al.*, (eds) *Asia Pacific Dynamics*, Greenwich, Conn.: JAI Press.

Meade, J.E. (1951) *The Balance of Payments*, London: Oxford University Press.

Niehans, J. (1984) *International Monetary Economics*, Baltimore and London: Johns Hopkins University Press.

Niehans, J. and J. Hewson (1976) "The Eurodollar Market and Monetary Theory," *Journal of Money, Credit, and Banking*, 8, 1.

Park, Y.S. and M. Essayyard (1990) *International Banking and Financial Centers*, Boston, Dordrecht, and London: Kluwer Academic Publishers.

Roussakis, E.N., K. Dandapani and A.J. Prakash (1994) "Offshore Banking Centers: Prospects and Issues," in D.K. Ghosh and E. Ortiz (eds) *The Changing Environment of International Financial Markets: Issues and Analysis*, London: Macmillan.

Samuelson, P.A. (1952) "The Transfer Problem and Transport Costs: The Terms of Trade when Impediments are Absent," *Economic Journal*, 62, 246.

Samuelson, P.A. (1954) ""The Transfer Problem and Transport Costs: Analysis of Effects of Trade Impediments," *Economic Journal*, 64, 254.

Samuelson, P.A. (1971) "On the Trail of Conventional Beliefs about the Transfer Problem," in J. Bhagwati *et al.*, (eds) *Trade, Balance of Payments, and Growth: Papers in International Economics in Honor of Charles P. Kindleberger*, Amsterdam: North-Holland.

Swoboda, A.K. (1980) *Credit Creation in the Euromarket: Alternative Theories and Implications for Control*, Group of Thirty, Occasional Papers, No. 2, New York.

Willms, M. (1976) "Money Creation in the Eurocurrency Market," *Weltwirtschaftliches Archiv*, 112.

INDEX

Rogoff, K. 171, 172–4, 188
Roley, V.V. 288
Rolfe, R.J. 345
Roll, R.W. 91, 103, 353, 362
rolling-sample test of unit root 219, 221, 222
rolling regression approach 173, 175
Romer, C.D. 275
Romer, D.H. 275
Root, F. 333
Root Mean Square Error (RMSE) 153–5
Roussakis, E.N. 422
Rugman, A.M. 321
Rule 144-A (USA) 24, 65

Safizadeh, H. 176
Salemi, M.K. 105
Salinas administration 56, 69, 224, 368
Samuelson, P.A. 423
Sappenfield, R. 352, 353, 358–9
Sarnat, M. 359
Saunders, A. 359
savings 53–4, 58–9, 254–5; banks 38
Scaperlanda, A. 345
Schinasi, G. 173–4
Schlagenhauf, D.E. 172
Schlesinger, Helmut 289
Schneider, W. 408
Schnitzel, P. 276
Schulman, E. 78
Schwartz, M. 235
second best theory 9, 28, 36–47, 71
secondary stock markets 43–4
securities market 19, 20, 23–5, 52; deregulation of 55–8, 60–1, 64; in emerging markets 13, 351–64; performance of 64–9
security repurchase agreements 291, 293–4, 296–7, 303–5, 307
segmented trend model 175
sell contract 121–30, 135
sequential entry model 235
sequential likelihood ratio test of unit root 219, 221–2, 223
sequential test of unit root 219–24
Serfin 239, 241–3, 246–51
Shaffer, S. 245
Sharpe, William 9, 31, 77–9, 81–3, 86
Sharpe index 77–9, 81–3, 86
Sheffrin, S.M. 172
Sherman, H.C. 287, 306, 307

short hedge 213
significance rule 97
Sims, C. 277
simultaneity bias 152–62 passim
simultaneous estimation techniques 145
Singapore International Monetary Exchange (SIMEX) 10
Single European Act 7
Sistema de Ahorro para el Retiro 53, 59
Smirlock, M. 288
smuggling 384
Smyser, M.W. 9, 31–2
Social Security Institute for State Employees 59
Social Security Law (Mexico) 59
social welfare (impact of capital flight) 384
Sociedad de Ahorro y Préstamo 59
Society for Worldwide International Financial Telecommunication 12
Soenen, L. 79, 83
Solnik, B. 79
Solocha, A. 345
Somanath, V.S. 172, 173
special drawing rights 11, 201–13
speculation 6; covered speculation 135–43; foreign exchange market 10–11; forward 120–5, 130–2, 134–5; naked speculation 119–35; spot 120, 123–30, 132–5
speculators (currency risk) 212, 213
Speidell, L.S. 352, 353, 358–9
Spence, M. 235
spot contract 6
spot markets 6, 120
spot prices 106–10
spot rate 11, 80, 173, 427
spot speculation: forward and 134–5; with transaction costs 130, 132–4; without transaction costs 120, 123–30
Spraos, J. 120
spreads 138, 139, 141
Srivastava, S. 171
'stabilizing development' 53
standard basket technique 202–3
standard deviation of daily stock index returns (ERM crisis) 311–13
Standard Interntional Trade Classification (SITC) 144–5, 166
Standard and Poor 109, 338, 353; 500 futures 10, 103–4, 107–8, 110,